SUCCESS IN
LAW

FIFTH EDITION

RICHARD **H. BRUCE**, LL.B. F.C.I. ARB

of Gray's Inn, Barrister-at-Law

JOHN MURRAY

Success Studybooks

© Richard H. Bruce 1978, 1988, 1991, 1994, 2001

First published in 1978
by John Murray (Publishers) Ltd
50 Albemarle Street
London W1S 4BD

Second edition 1988
Third edition 1991
Fourth edition 1994
Fifth edition 2001

Cartoons by Michael ffolkes

Typeset in 10.5/12pt Sabon by Wearset, Boldon, Tyne and Wear
Printed and bound in Great Britain by Alden Press, Oxford

A CIP catalogue record for this book is available from the British Library

ISBN 0 7195 7211 8

Contents

Foreword

The study of law was traditionally the preserve of the universities and those entering the legal profession. For the ordinary citizen our law was something to be treated with caution: he felt a sense of suspicion and distrust. Such distrust may well have had its roots in ignorance and misconception, but it was there. Today the picture is a different one. People, as they all so often say, 'know their rights' or, at least, think they do. Television, radio and the press daily bring home to people what our laws are and how they affect us. Quite suddenly 'the law' has become much more accessible to everyone. For this reason, anyone studying law – whether for general interest, at school, or as part of a vocational course – will need a direct and practical book which does not just recite what the law says but clearly explains what the law is. *Success in Law* has been written with this object in mind. It aims to present the general principles of English law in a way that relates theory to everyday experience and in a way which shows its relevance not just to the individual but also to society as a whole.

The examination courses which include a paper on law are too numerous to list but, for all of them, this book will have relevance. It covers the core syllabus requirements of GCSE and A level courses, and students of banking, accountancy, marketing, export, transport and legal executives should find the emphasis on contract of especial use in their courses.

At the outset, I have assumed no prior legal knowledge on the part of the reader. I have tried to avoid footnote-type learning and jurisprudential pettifogging. The aim throughout has been to keep in sight of the practical, everyday application of all topics covered. I hope this approach will remedy the examiner's frequent complaint that students, while able to regurgitate recently memorised rules, are often ill-equipped to apply their knowledge to any practical problem posed.

Examination-style questions are included at the end of each Unit of study. These are valuable for self-assessment and for classwork. When dealing with a problem-style question (is X liable to Y?) the law student should remember that the *reasoning* is as important as the answer. The student should cite the area of law raised by the question, deal with the general points of law, then tie up the law with the given facts. Many problems may deliberately contain scope for argument on both sides, and a carefully argued, but ultimately suspect, answer attracts far greater respect from an examiner than a peremptory, if accurate, reaction of 'Yes. X is liable to Y.'. In dealing with the general law it is very important to include some discussion of the appropriate case-law on the subject.

Like its author, this book has fattened all too noticeably since publication of the first edition in 1978. The introduction of new syllabuses and the unrelenting legislative enthusiasm of government have required continuing revision and expansion. This edition reflects the continuing revelations of human weakness in its treatment of crime and tort. The electoral ambitions and intellectual gyrations of successive political administrations in their often hastily conceived response to perceived public clamour for ever harsher treatment of criminals are exposed as are the same governments' indecision and delay in implementing needed changes to English law with regard to the regulation of both married and unmarried relationships. It is to be regretted that little can be written about any reform of the much derided and unpopular legislation governing financial support for children from these failed relationships. The present edition is the first to take note of the impact upon English law of the recently introduced Human Rights Act 1998. I have endeavoured to state the law as at 1 January 2001.

I have been keenly conscious that few readers will enjoy access to a convenient law library. For that reason I have included numerous extracts from judgments, statutes and other original sources. These not only expound the law, but often show how and why the law has developed in a particular direction. They are, in fact, the law itself.

R.B.

Acknowledgements

I would like to offer thanks to all who have been concerned in writing this book but especially to those mentioned below.

I owe an enormous and fundamental debt to Simon Owen, without whose entrepreneurial enthusiasm the book would never have seen the light of day. Irene Slade, then editor of the Success Studybooks series, sustained me with encouragement from the beginning and her assistant editor, Rosemarie Burston, was always helpful and reassuring. The typescript of this edition has been rescued from my embrace of modern technology by Joyce Lester who, as always, has matched the additional challenges of my concept of calligraphy. My father, John Bruce, read and criticised the drafts of the first edition, bestowing on them his customary care of thought and characteristic clarity of expression.

The need to inhibit my enthusiasm for the latest learning even at page proof stage would challenge any diplomat. In this, as elsewhere, the vigilant editorial skills of Stephanie Richards and Diana Roberts, have also included patience of a high order in their gentle restraint of my attempts to slip in 'just a few lines' of some recent determination or legislation. They and I have all been able to profit greatly from the experience in educational publishing of the present Editor of the *Success* series, Carolyn Burch, for whom a new edition of a general law book then already six years old was a challenge she confidently took in her elegant stride.

Up-to-date statistical information has been most helpfully provided by the Lord Chancellor's Department and, as always, the librarians of Gray's Inn Library have dealt patiently with my many demands upon their time. I am similarly indebted to the Judicial Studies Board for permission to draw upon its Specimen Directions in Unit 3. I have drawn heavily on extracts from the Law Reports and thank both the Incorporated Council of Law Reporting and Butterworth & Co. (Publishers) Ltd for permission to quote from their publications, as well as the Controller of Her Majesty's Stationery Office for allowing me to reproduce parts of various reports. Examination questions are reproduced by courtesy of AQA.

A.D. Peters and Co. kindly allowed me to include the lines of Edmund Blunden, and the musical entreaty to Mrs Worthington is reproduced by courtesy of the Noel Coward Estate and Chappell Music Ltd. I am also grateful to Leon Griffiths and Euston Films for not minding my mention of their ever resourceful character Arthur Daley, and to ACRO for allowing me to make mention of their National Rail Conditions of Carriage. The late Michael ffolkes brought his very individual style to bear upon the text in his inspired cartoons for the first edition.

R.B.

1 The English legal system

1.1 The meaning of law

Many of us spend the greater part of our lives without occasion to consider just what it is that we expect from the legal system of the country in which we live. Nevertheless, we not infrequently express our views of our society in terms that make it clear that our attitudes to the law, even though muddled, are in fact reasonably definite.

On the one hand, we may comment indignantly on what we see as a lack of regulation of others' behaviour, believing that the law should protect not only us and our property but also our own particular sense of what is 'right':

> *'I think it's criminal – they ought to be locked up!'*
> *'Isn't it disgusting? There ought to be a law against it.'*
> *'They shouldn't be allowed to do that, not at their age.'*

On the other hand, we don't always respect it ourselves:

> *'The law is an ass...'*
> *'But I was only parked there for five minutes!'*

Although so much of our everyday life is lived against the background of our laws, few of us have a very clear idea of what 'the law' is, or what it sets out to achieve. If they thought about it, most people would probably agree that law is a system of enforcing both order and a minimum standard of fair play – that it should make the streets safe to walk at nights and see to it that publicans do not cheat their customers by watering down the beer.

No sport or game can be played properly without rules: the more complex the game, the greater the likelihood of disputes between the players and, therefore, the more necessary the rules as a way of settling these disputes. Everyday life is much more complicated than any game: there are more players, a bigger field and almost unlimited activities.

A person living on his own on a desert island can behave exactly as he likes. As soon as a second arrives, however, the two of them must come to some arrangement or agreement as to how they are going to get along together. They acquire rights and duties against each other.

Every society in every age has found it essential to work out a code of rules to which its members must conform for otherwise there would very soon be no society at all – only rival gangs of thieves fighting endless vendettas against one another. In particular, it has been necessary to restrict the complete freedom of each individual member of the society so as to protect all the other members from his or her carelessness, violence or dishonesty. In return, the individual is protected from the carelessness, violence and dishonesty of others.

For example, by regulating the way in which a car owner may drive, the law seeks to protect all the other road users. Motorists must not have the 'freedom' to drive straight past a red light, for, if the lights were not obeyed, many more people would be hurt in road accidents.

As soon as a second arrives, however...

People who disobey the rules laid down by society endanger the lives and the possessions of others.

The rules, of course, are not made by 'society' as a whole, but by the most powerful person or group of people in that society. Karl Marx thought that law was really a means used by one class ('Capital', or the wealthy and powerful land- and factory-owners) to dominate and exploit a weaker class ('Labour', the poor who could only live by their own work). While at certain times in history the law has undoubtedly been used by the rich and powerful to prevent working people from getting a fair deal – for instance, trade unions were for many years declared to be illegal – this was never its only function and, anyway, the present position is very different.

According to constitutional theory, the most powerful group of people in Britain today is the House of Commons, whose members are chosen by elections in which almost every adult has the right to vote. As a result, this most powerful group is representative of all sections in our society and so, again at least in theory, will not attempt to manipulate the law in order to enrich one section of the community at the expense of another – or at least will not take such an attempt to extremes.

We need laws most of all to protect us from the anti-social behaviour of a few bullies, crooks, confidence tricksters and dangerous cranks. If we had no laws and no punishments, how many more harmless people would be robbed, swindled, murdered or raped? In the words of Mr Justice Donaldson, as he then was:

> *Without the rule of law and courts to enforce it, each one of us would be free to push and bully our fellow citizens, and, which may be thought more important, our fellow citizens would be free to push and bully us.*

The law takes away some of our personal freedom but, in return, it gives us most of our protection.

1.2 Law and morality

It was a hot summer's day when Tom parked his car in the High Street. The sun was so warm that the tax disc in its plastic holder fell off the windscreen on to the front seat. Unfortunately, a traffic warden passed by soon afterwards and noticed what had happened. A month later Tom was summonsed to the local magistrates' court, accused of failing to display a valid tax disc.

Dick returned home early one afternoon to discover his wife in bed with Harry, his best friend. Worse still, she told him that Harry was the real father of Samantha, whom Dick had always loved as his daughter. Dick was so distressed that he killed himself by jumping out of the window of the fourteenth-floor flat.

Who do you think is the more immoral, Tom or Harry?

The law will punish Tom but Harry cannot be prosecuted for any crime. The 'moral' of the stories is that law and morality must not be confused. Obviously, the most heinous crimes are also considered by most people to be gravely immoral – for example, murder and rape. In recent years changing moral attitudes have indeed influenced the criminal law: to take one instance, following the Suicide Act 1961, suicide is no longer a crime.

Occasionally, however, the law does still deliberately set out to punish the immoral. To see how this has been done in recent years, some understanding of the law of conspiracy is helpful. The point is well illustrated by consideration of a case which concerned a civil wrong – trespass – rather than an immoral action. Trespass – entering on to another's land without his or her permission – has always been merely a civil wrong against the occupier of land for which he or she could claim compensation from the trespasser and not a crime. This is why an uninvited visitor into the Queen's bedroom in Buckingham Palace could not be prosecuted for his nocturnal wanderings (see Unit 6.6a)). The sign: 'Trespassers will be prosecuted' was long called a 'wooden lie' because a person can only be 'prosecuted' for a crime. However, it now seems that the erectors of such signs were correctly, if fortuitously, anticipating a development in the law.

Kamara v. *Director of Public Prosecutions* 1973 concerned a 'sit-in' staged by some Sierra Leone students at their country's High Commission in London. They were later convicted of the offences of 'conspiracy to trespass'.

Conspiracy is an agreement between two or more persons to commit an unlawful act and is considered later in Unit 3.3b). Four years later, in the Criminal Law Act 1977, Parliament gave statutory effect to this decision by making it a specific criminal offence to trespass on foreign diplomatic or consular premises.

More recently, Parliament legislated in the Criminal Justice and Public Order Act 1994 to limit protest by hunt saboteurs and eco warriors such as 'Swampy' who held up the building of new roads either by taking to the trees or by imitating the actions of moles. The 1994 legislation created a new criminal offence of 'aggravated trespass' which is committed when a civil act of trespass is followed by obstruction or disruption of any lawful activity (such as still, at the time of writing at least, the ritualised disembowelling of foxes in pursuit of the uneatable by the unspeakable).

In *Shaw* v. *Director of Public Prosecutions* 1961, a Mr Shaw had published a *Ladies' Directory*, which was, in fact, a list of prostitutes and their telephone numbers. To publish such a directory was not a criminal offence in itself but Shaw was, nevertheless, convicted of the offence of 'conspiring to corrupt public morals', an offence of wide but uncertain scope.

The conspiracy was found to have taken place between the prostitutes who advertised in the directory and with the people who helped Shaw to distribute it. The controversial decision in this case made it a crime to conspire to do something which before had not even been a civil wrong – it was merely immoral and possibly anti-social. In the House of Lords (see Unit 2.1a)) Lord Reid expressed the view that there was no general offence of conspiracy to corrupt public morals known to law. No one had ever been charged with it before. He went on to say:

> *Notoriously, there are wide differences of opinion today as to how far the law ought to punish immoral acts ... Parliament is the proper place, and I am firmly of the opinion the only proper place, to settle that ... Where Parliament fears to tread it is not for the courts to rush in.*

Viscount Simonds, however, differed in his view of the law. He said:

> *In the sphere of criminal law I entertain no doubt that there remains in the courts of law a residual power to enforce the supreme and fundamental purpose of law, to conserve not only the safety and order but also the moral welfare of the state and that it is their duty to guard it against attacks which may be the more insidious because they are novel and unprepared for.*

His view, and that of the majority in the House of Lords, prevailed.

The same charge of 'conspiracy to corrupt public morals' was levelled in 1971 when the editors of *Oz: the Schoolkids' Edition* were acquitted at the Old Bailey after publishing a magazine which included a depiction of the children's cartoon character 'Rupert Bear' which had become a distinctly more adult 'Rupert Bare'.

In a later case, in December 1985 at Birmingham Crown Court, the publishers of a so-called 'contact magazine' (in which people advertise for sexual partners) were convicted of conspiracy to corrupt public morals.

The respective functions of morality and the criminal law were considered by the Wolfenden Committee which reported in 1957 on homosexual offences and prostitution. The Committee concluded:

> *There appears to be no unquestioned definition of what constitutes or ought to constitute a crime.*

They thought that the function of the criminal law was:

> ...to preserve public order and decency, to protect the citizen from what is offensive or injurious, and to provide sufficient safeguards against the exploitation and corruption of others, particularly those who are specially vulnerable because they are young, weak in body or in mind, inexperienced, or in a state of special physical, official or economic dependence.
>
> It is not, in our view, the function of the law to intervene in the private lives of citizens, or to seek to enforce any particular pattern of behaviour, further than is necessary to carry out the purposes we have outlined.

Quite how far the criminal law ought to intervene in the private lives of citizens came to be considered further in *R* v. *Brown and others* 1993. A number of middle-aged men had formed a group which enjoyed sado-masochistic homosexual practices. Since the Sexual Offences Act 1967 it is no longer unlawful for consenting adults to practise homosexual activities in private. These particular gentlemen involved themselves (and for them unfortunately did so on video recordings which were later to provide the evidence against them) in a number of extraordinary practices of torture, branding and blood-letting which might even have raised the occasional eyebrow at a weekend house party hosted by the Marquis de Sade. These activities undoubtedly caused wounds and actual bodily harm (see Unit 3.5a)) to those on the receiving end of such entertainment. However, when prosecuted for such assaults, the men argued that they had committed no crime where their victims had consented to such unusual practices. The courts, therefore, had to consider not only whether a victim's consent was a defence to a charge of assault but also, in the wider context, the House of Lords had again to consider as a matter of public policy whether such behaviour among consenting adults in the privacy of their own homes should be a matter for the criminal law. In the House of Lords, the judges differed in their views as to the role of the State in regulating such behaviour. The majority view was represented by Lord Templeman who, having referred to the passage already quoted from the Wolfenden Report, said such practices were:

> unpredictably dangerous and degrading to body and mind and were developed with increasing barbarity and taught to persons whose consents were dubious or worthless.

In rejecting the defence raised, Lord Templeman expressed his view as to the rights of the State to punish such behaviour:

> Society is entitled and bound to protect itself against a cult of violence. Pleasure derived from the infliction of pain is an evil thing.

The minority view expressed by Lord Slynn thought that it was not for the courts, in the interests of 'paternalism' or in order to protect people from themselves, to introduce into existing statutory offences concepts which did not properly belong there:

> *It is a matter of policy in an area where social and moral factors are extremely important and where attitudes can change. In my opinion it is a matter of policy for the legislature to decide. If society takes the view that this kind of behaviour, even though sought after and in private, is either so new or so extensive or so undesirable that it should be brought now for the first time within the criminal law, then it is for the legislature to decide.*

In fact, it was not the United Kingdom legislature but, rather, the European Court of Human Rights which was next to consider the issue for in the summer of 2000 that tribunal decided that the United Kingdom's laws discriminated against homosexual men.

More recently, the Court of Appeal was able to distinguish such sado-masochistic practices in *R* v. *Wilson* 1996 when allowing an appeal against conviction for assault occasioning actual bodily harm. The appellant had scarred his initials onto his wife's buttocks but did so with her consent. The judges took the view that this particular expression of matrimonial bonding was more akin to the practice of tattooing which is a lawful activity enjoyed not only by sailors but also by lovers. Some may wonder what constructive purpose the State had perceived in prosecuting matters of such obviously essential personal morality.

1.3 Civil and criminal law

One dark, wet November night, Tom was walking home from his evening-class.

Meanwhile Dick, who had had more than a few drinks with his friends, was driving home in his rusty old car. The road ahead was clear of traffic and Dick was in a hurry. He took a left-hand bend far too fast and then suddenly saw Tom halfway over the zebra crossing. Dick braked harshly but the road was wet, his tyres were bald and his brakes should have been relined weeks earlier. Tom ended up uncomfortably wedged between the road and the front bumper of Dick's car. Both his legs were broken. An ambulance was called and the police also arrived on the scene.

A few days later Dick was charged by the local police with several offences, including driving with excess alcohol in his bloodstream and driving a vehicle with defective brakes. He was convicted of these offences by the local magistrates who disqualified him from driving for twelve months and fined him £750.

As Dick walked home from the court he was hoping that all his troubles were over. However, on the doormat lay a letter from Tom's solicitors. They wrote to say that Tom had been badly injured and would not be able to work for at least another six months. Tom had four children to support and had been earning £700 a week. Accordingly, Tom now expected Dick to pay him **damages** – money compensation for his suffering and for his lost earnings.

In this way Dick came up against the two categories of law. Firstly, in the magistrates' court he saw **public law** – which includes criminal law, constitutional and administrative law – and, secondly, with the letter from Tom's solicitors he discovered **private law** – which includes torts (civil wrongs), contract and family law.

Public law is concerned with the relationship between an individual and the rest of the community as a whole (sometimes referred to as 'the State').

Private law concerns the relationships between individuals in that community insofar as they do not involve or concern the community as a whole.

As Dick found, the same events can make a person liable both in public and in private law. While only Tom had been injured and so only he may claim damages from Dick, it is nevertheless a sobering thought that you or I might be walking across another zebra crossing when Dick comes round another corner. In other words, society as a whole has an interest in making sure that Dick either drives properly or keeps off the roads. This is why society as a whole, represented by the magistrates' court, fined Dick for the way in which he had acted.

In the criminal court Dick was known as the **defendant** or less probably as the **accused**. The local police were the **prosecution**. In the higher courts the prosecution is normally conducted in the name of the Queen or in that of the Director of Public Prosecutions (see Unit 3.7), as in *Kamara*'s and *Shaw*'s cases.

In the civil court – where Tom's claim for damages will be tried – Dick will be called the **defendant** (because he has to defend himself against Tom's claim). The police have no part to play but Tom will come into the picture as the **claimant,** as he is claiming damages. This new term of 'claimant' was introduced in April 1999 and replaced the traditional term of **plaintiff.** 'Plaint' is an old-fashioned word for request and was used as a 'plaintiff' was requesting the court to award damages. This change of terminology was introduced by the new **Civil Procedure Rules 1998** which reflected the massive change in civil procedure throughout England and Wales following the recommendations of Lord Woolf. The word 'plaintiff' is, of course, well enshrined in English law over the centuries and is a term which appears frequently in the various extracts from judgments set out in later Units as well as throughout the main text. The term is deliberately retained throughout the text in respect of litigation before April 1999.

The police and Tom have each to prove to the relevant court that Dick was in the wrong. It is always for the party who brings the defendant to court to prove his case: it is not for the defendant to prove he was not in the wrong.

However, although the burden of proof is always on the prosecution or on the claimant, the standard of proof that is called for in the criminal courts is quite different from that which the civil courts require. In a civil case, the claimant must prove his or her case *on the balance of probabilities,* that is, he or she must show that the defendant is more likely than not to have been at fault. On the other hand, in a criminal case a court must be especially careful before, for example, sending a defendant to prison and so the prosecution must prove its allegations *beyond all reasonable doubt* so that the court is as sure as it is reasonably possible to be.

This need for such cogent evidence was made clear in *Woolmington* v. *Director of Public Prosecutions* 1935, in which a man was accused of murdering his wife. He admitted shooting her but claimed that it had been an accident. In the House of Lords, the Lord Chancellor, Viscount Sankey, emphasised that it was for the prosecution to show that the shooting was not an accident, not for Worthington to show that it was. More generally, and in a phrase famous among lawyers, he stated:

> *Throughout the web of English Criminal Law one golden thread is always to be seen, that it is the duty of the prosecution to prove the prisoner's guilt ... If, at the end of and on the whole of the case, there is a reasonable doubt ... the prosecution has not made out the case and the prisoner is entitled to an acquittal. No matter what the charge or where the trial, the principle that the prosecution must prove the guilt of the prisoner is part of the common law of England and no attempt to whittle it down can be entertained.*

Section 11 of the Civil Evidence Act 1968 allows Tom to tell the civil court about Dick's criminal convictions as evidence of Dick's liability to him. In *Stupple* v. *Royal Insurance Co. Ltd* 1970 Stupple had been convicted of robbing a bank. Money was found at his home. The bank had been insured against robberies and the insurance company which had made good the bank's loss claimed the money found in Stupple's flat.

The Court of Appeal (see Unit 2.1b)) held (that is, it decided) that Stupple's conviction for robbery created a statutory presumption of guilt, so that Stupple would have to prove on the balance of probabilities that his conviction had been wrong and that he had not really robbed the bank at all. In practice, this is a high mountain to climb as it is always very difficult to show that a conviction was wrong. A **presumption** is something which is assumed to be true unless and until the opposite is proved. A **statutory presumption** is simply a presumption which comes about because of an Act of Parliament. Presumptions can nevertheless be rebutted upon other evidence as in *Alan Wibberley Building Limited* v. *Insley* 1999 when the House of Lords regarded as rebuttable an old presumption that the boundary between two pieces of land separated by a hedge and a ditch running alongside one another established that the boundary ran along the edge of the ditch furthest from the hedge. So, too, it has long been presumed that children under the age of ten years are incapable of committing crime. They are said to be *doli incapax* (see Unit 3.4a)). Even after that age a child had been presumed to be *doli incapax* unless the prosecution could prove that the youth knew that what he had done was 'seriously wrong'. Recently, in C v. *Director of Public Prosecutions* 1995, the House of Lords had to consider whether this longstanding presumption was still good law. A twelve-year-old child had damaged a motorcycle and, when seen by the police, ran away. When it was said on the child's behalf that he was *doli incapax* by virtue of his age, the prosecution invited the magistrates to infer that the boy had known that what he had done was seriously wrong because he had run away. The House of Lords recognised that this was a longstanding presumption and still part of English law. It is not to be thought that the judges in the House of Lords were so naïve as to assume that a twelve-year-old boy who steals a high-powered motor car, knocks down a pedestrian and damages other vehicles before running away, is unaware that what he is doing is wrong. However, the House of Lords stepped back from changing this presumption, saying that such a decision was a matter for Parliament and not for the courts. In fact, Parliament did later change the law by the Crime and Disorder Act 1998 (see Unit 3.4a)).

Factors which are relevant in reducing liability for torts – civil wrongs – offer no defence to a criminal charge. So, if Tom had walked out into the road without looking properly he would have been partly to blame for the accident and so the damages payable by Dick would have been reduced in proportion to his share of the blame (see Unit 6.7a)). Tom's own carelessness would not be at all relevant in a criminal court: if the evidence is that the defendant drove 'without due care and attention' it is no defence to say that the damage caused was also someone else's fault.

The respective functions of the civil and criminal law were succinctly explained by Lord Diplock in *Knuller* v. *Director of Public Prosecutions* 1972 when he said:

> *Civil liability is concerned with the relationship of one citizen to another; criminal liability is concerned with the relationship of a citizen to society organized as a state.*

1.4 Sources of law: custom

A custom is a right or duty which has come to exist through popular consent: people thought it right that matters should be ordered in a particular way. Customs are the oldest source of our law and date back to before the Norman Conquest. They could either be 'general' (applicable to the whole country) or 'local'. Any surviving general customs have, in effect, now become part of the common law (see Unit 1.7) and 'custom' today means local custom.

A local custom was in issue in *Mercer* v. *Denne* 1905, where the Court of Appeal affirmed that there was a customary right for fishermen to dry their nets on a particular privately owned beach. The court accordingly ordered the landowner not to build on the beach as to do so would have interfered with the fishermen's rights.

The origins of most customs have been obscured by the passage of time. The courts have long been most reluctant to recognise new customs – 'new' in the sense that no one had claimed their existence in court before – although a later case provides an exception.

In *Egerton* v. *Harding* 1974 both parties owned and occupied land adjoining a common. Some of the defendant's cattle strayed from the common into the garden of the plaintiff who later claimed that Christopher and Eileen Harding should reimburse her for the damage caused by the wandering bovines.

The Hardings' defence was that the plaintiff had been under a duty, arising from a local custom, to fence her land against the common: in other words, that the damage was her own fault for not stopping the cattle from getting in. The trial judge decided that, by custom, a liability existed in owners of land adjoining the common to fence against cattle lawfully on the common and so the plaintiff lost her case.

The Court of Appeal approved the decision of the trial judge when

> ...he recognized that a custom, to be upheld as local law, has to be shown to be of immemorial origin, reasonable, continued without interruption, and certain.

The next year, in *New Windsor Corporation* v. *Mellor* 1975, 81-year-old retired schoolmistress Miss Doris Mellor objected to the Corporation having turned half of a local green (known as 'Bachelors' Acre') into a car park and the other half into a school playground.

The Court of Appeal decided that the green (which in fact was not the preserve of unmarried men and which covered some two acres in all) should not have been put to such use as the local inhabitants had a right to use it for sports and other pastimes. Such right arose not from deeds or statutes but 'by custom from time immemorial'. One of the judges, Lord Denning, lent characteristic colour to his judgment when he quoted the words of the poet Edmund Blunden:

> On the green they watched their sons
> Playing till too dark to see,
> As their fathers watched them once,
> As my father once watched me...

This judgment illustrates how undoubted was the right of the English to play cricket and other games on their village greens. The case is also important for emphasising that a customary right, once established, is not lost because, for some reason, it is not exercised for many years. Miss Mellor's part in the preservation of the rights of the village people was recognised some time later by the award to her of the MBE for services to the community.

The criteria for the validity of a custom, as laid down in *Egerton*'s case, merit consideration one by one:

1. **Immemorial origin** The custom must have existed since 'time immemorial': this elusive point in history is conveniently fixed at 1189, the year King Richard I came to the throne. In practice, however, if the custom can be shown to have existed for a very long time, that passage of time will raise a presumption that it existed in 1189. For example, in *Mercer* v. *Denne* the custom could only be positively proved for seventy years back but was nevertheless recognised as valid.

   This presumption may, of course, be 'rebutted' (shown to be false) as in *Simpson* v. *Wells* 1872, where a custom of running a stall on the highway was shown not to have been authorised before the fourteenth century. The custom had been claimed as a defence to a charge of obstructing the highway.

2. **Reasonableness** The courts will not recognise any custom which is not reasonable. So, in *Bryant* v. *Foot* 1868 a clergyman claimed a customary right to a fee of 13 shillings (now 65 pence) for celebrating a marriage in his particular parish. The court held that such a sum would – in 1189 – have been so extortionate as not to have been reasonable.

3. **Without interruption** The rights granted (or the duty imposed) by the custom must have existed continuously since 1189. The mere fact that for many years no one has chosen to avail himself of his rights is quite irrelevant.

4. **Certainty** In *Wilson* v. *Willes* 1806, certain individuals claimed a customary right to take from the local common as much turf as they needed for their own gardens. Lord Ellenborough held that the alleged right could not be upheld as its extent had not been defined.

5. Lastly, it has long been agreed that there is a fifth criterion, that of **common consent**. This means that everyone concerned must have accepted that the custom did exist and that it was legally binding. The test is that the rights granted by the custom must have been exercised *nec vi, nec clam, nec precario* ('neither by force, nor secretly, nor by special permission'). This was not in point in Egerton's case because that concerned a customary duty.

1.5 Sources of law: common law and precedent

The expression 'common law', mentioned in Unit 1.4, needs a few words of explanation here although the early development of our law will be discussed in greater detail in Unit 1.7.

A thousand years ago the only sources of law were the basic dictates of humanity ('thou shalt not kill'...) and local customs. After the Norman Conquest of 1066, the Royal judges attempted to apply a common law to the whole country. This law was based partly on the Norman law which they had brought with them from France and partly on those English customs which they found to be widespread or 'general'.

The creation of this common law, however, was strictly on an *ad hoc* basis, each problem being settled as it arose. No one actually sat down to compile a list of the laws. How then were people to know what was a crime or, in the event of a dispute between citizens, what were the respective rights of each citizen? Indeed, how are they to know these things now?

The answer is twofold.

Firstly, a small number of very old legal textbooks, compiled from the twelfth century onwards, have survived into the present day.

Secondly, and very much more important, there is the doctrine of **judicial precedent**. Stated simply, this means that, in their work of settling disputes, judges are guided by the decisions of judges in earlier similar cases. So, if a case which is to be tried today is similar to a case tried last week its result is likely to be the same. In this way a body of legal principles has been built up and which may be discovered by examining the judgments in all cases tried to date. For this reason, precedent is often referred to as 'case-law' (the law to be discovered by reading the earlier cases) or as **stare decisis** (because a judge will usually 'stand by the decisions' of his or her colleagues).

Lord Scarman (also the author of the Report into the 1981 Brixton riots) has described the power of the judge as lawmaker in this way in *Duport Steels Ltd* v. *Sirs* 1980:

> *In our society the judges have in some aspects of their work a discretionary power to do justice so wide that they may be regarded as lawmakers. The common law and equity, both of them in essence systems of private law, are fields where, subject to increasing intrusion of statute law, society has been content to allow the judges to formulate and develop the law. The judges, even in this, their very own field of creative endeavour, have accepted, in the interest of certainty, the self-denying ordinance of* stare decisis, *the doctrine of binding precedent, and no doubt this judicially imposed limitation on judicial lawmaking has helped to maintain confidence in the certainty and evenhandedness of the law.*

It is sometimes said that in reaching a decision a judge is merely declaring what the common law has always been. Where, however, a judge has to make a decision on a point of law which has never arisen before in any court (for instance, whether there is such an offence as 'conspiracy to corrupt public morals') this view seems a little unrealistic for the judge appears actually to be creating law – hence the expression 'judge-made law' for judicial precedent.

Lord Denning, in his judgment in the decision of the Court of Appeal in *Gouriet* v. *Union of Post Office Workers* 1977 (when the Post Office Union was ordered by the court not to 'black' letters and other mail to South Africa), had to decide a point with which neither the courts nor Parliament had previously been faced. He emphasised how, in such a situation, it is up to a judge to say what the law is. As Lord Denning put it:

> *Parliament has passed no enactment on it. There is no binding precedent in our books on it. It is a new thing. Whenever a new situation arises which has not been considered before, the judges have to say what the law is. In doing so, we do not change the law. We declare it. We consider it on principle; and then pronounce on it. As the old writers quaintly put it, the law lies 'in the breast of the judges'.*

When a judge simply applies to the facts of one particular case a legal rule previously enunciated in an earlier trial the decision is known as a **declaratory precedent** because it declares existing law. On the other hand, if the case is unlike any previous one, so that it is without precedent, then the judge must make up his or her own mind what the common law is or should be. The judge's decision will then be known as an **original precedent** because a new legal rule originates from it. In this way the common law continues to grow and to consolidate on an *ad hoc* basis. Today, there are so many decided cases on almost every conceivable legal topic that the direct importance of general custom, once the foundation of our law, has been greatly reduced.

Two factors have been especially important in the development of precedent as a source of law. Firstly, the development of printing led to many more reports of decided cases becoming readily available. The growth of precedent as a source of law obviously depended on those decisions becoming widely known for, clearly, the judges could scarcely follow earlier decisions without knowing what they were. Secondly, the hierarchy of the courts became more clearly established. This subject is covered in detail in Unit 2, but Table 1.1 sets out the basic 'pecking order'.

Table 1.1

The hierarchy of the courts			
1	House of Lords	binds	all lower courts (2–5 below)
2 (a)	Court of Appeal (Civil Division)	binds	all lower courts (3–5 below) and usually itself
(b)	Court of Appeal (Criminal Division)	binds	all lower courts (3–5 below)
3	High Court	binds	all lower courts
4	County Court	binds	nobody
5	Magistrates' courts and all others	bind	nobody

To understand Table 1.1 properly it is necessary to realise that there are two kinds of precedent: **binding precedent**, where the judge is bound to apply the legal rule enunciated in the earlier case, and **persuasive precedent**, where the judge will often follow the earlier decision but may refuse to be so persuaded if he or she chooses. For example, the High Court is bound to follow the House of Lords. The decisions of the Privy Council (Unit 2.1) are persuasive precedent as are the decisions of one High Court judge on another.

Problems, however, can and do still arise. In *Colchester Estates* v. *Carlton Industries plc* 1984 a judge of the High Court was faced with a difficult choice. He had to choose between two conflicting decisions of two other High Court judges on much the same point. Mr Justice Nourse expressed the view that since it is desirable that the law, at whatever level it is decided, should generally be certain it followed that when a decision of a judge of the High Court has been fully considered, but not followed, by another judge of the High Court, the second decision should normally be considered as having settled the matter.

The position of the Court of Appeal (Civil Division) merits special mention, principally because of the reforming zeal of Lord Denning and his efforts to escape from the straitjacket of judicial precedent. For example, in *Davis* v. *Johnson* 1978 the Court of Appeal had to consider what protection the courts could give a woman who was beaten up by her lover. Lord Denning, when faced with an inconvenient precedent, held that the Court of Appeal was not bound to follow its own earlier decisions because any such doctrine was not a rule of law but merely a rule of practice. It followed, said Lord Denning, that the doctrine should be modified to allow the Court of Appeal to depart from an earlier decision if, on the later occasion, the judges thought that the earlier decision was wrong. However, when the case went on appeal to the House of Lords these views were rejected. Neither for the first nor last time the House of Lords rebuked Lord Denning and reaffirmed unequivocally that the Court of Appeal is in fact bound by its own earlier decisions.

Lastly, it should be remembered that the doctrine of judicial precedent applies not only to decisions about customs and the common law but also to those about the correct interpretation of Acts of Parliament (see Unit 1.6).

a) The law reports

A law report contains details of the facts of a case, the judge's decision and, most importantly, the reasons for that decision. Reports appear in professional journals such as the *New Law Journal* and *Family Law* and may be bound for ease of future reference. For many years *The Times* has carried law reports which offer prompt, if outline, reports of recent decisions and *The Independent* newspaper also now includes a regular law report. By the nineteenth century law reporting was sufficiently competent for the courts to emphasise the importance of the judges following earlier decisions in similar cases. For example, in *Mirehouse* v. *Rennel* 1833 Baron Parke, a judge, said that precedents must be regarded in subsequent cases and that it was not for the courts 'to reject them and to reject all analogy to them'.

Until about 1870 all law reports were published privately and were identified by the names of the reporters who were barristers. For example, 'Cl. & Fin.' is short for *Clark and Finnelly's Reports*. Unfortunately, not all reports were as accurate as one could have wished and one judge is said to have remarked of one law reporter, a Mr Espinasse, that he did 'not care for Espinasse or any other ass'. One Lord Chief Justice was also recorded as saying that this particular set of Law Reports 'were never quoted without doubt and hesitation'. It was also quipped that Mr Espinasse, who was said to be hard of hearing, 'heard half of a case and reported the other'.

The need for reliable reports was so great that, in 1865, the Incorporated Council for Law Reporting was established, consisting of representatives of the Inns of Court and the Law Society. In 1870 this body began to publish the 'official' law reports which are not official in the sense of being sponsored or published by Her Majesty's Government. Although the courts traditionally like to use the official reports there are also a number of private reports, such as the *All England Reports* (usually abbreviated to *All E.R.*) published by Butterworths. Where such a report is available its reference is given in this book because such a series is more likely to be available in the larger public libraries.

When a case is cited the name of the party bringing the case to court always comes first: he or she will be the claimant in a civil case or the prosecutor in a criminal trial. The prosecutor will often be cited as '*R*', which stands for *Rex* or *Regina* because most important charges before the higher courts are brought in the name of the King or Queen. Alternatively, the first name could be that of the **appellant**, a person appealing against the decision of a lower court. Second place, in the title of the action at least, belongs to the defendant (or in the case of an appeal, the **respondent**). Then, in a detailed reference such as those in the Table of Cases at the end of this book, comes the year of the report, followed by the number of the volume, the abbreviated title of the relevant series of law report and, lastly, the page number.

Quite how this works in practice can be seen conveniently by turning to the reference to the report of a libel case examined in Unit 6.10c). If we want to read about *Broome* v. *Cassell & Co. Ltd* [1971] 2 All E.R. 187 we know that we must look at page 187 in the second volume of the *All England Reports* for 1971.

Broome won his case in the Court of Appeal and Cassells lost. Cassells then appealed to the House of Lords and as the appellants were, of course, the party responsible for bringing the case to court again, in the report of the House of Lords' decision, the order of the names was reversed. The final result is accordingly reported as *Cassell & Co. Ltd* v. *Broome* [1972] 1 All E.R. 801.

Incidentally the 'v.' is pronounced 'and', so that if Mr Black sues Mr White the case sounds more like an old television set than a football match.

Sometimes a reference will include two pages numbers: for instance, [1972] 1 All E.R. 801, 809. This means that the report starts at page 801 but that the relevant quotation is on page 809. In this example, page 809 contains Lord Hailsham's remarks on the duties of the Court of Appeal in the system of the court hierarchy.

Inclusion in the law reports is limited. If you are fined a few pounds in the local magistrates' court for leaving your car where it was less than welcome you are unlikely to achieve any lasting fame by a mention in the law reports. Only those cases which lay down or expand a principle of law are selected for inclusion in the reports, for their purpose is the recording of precedent not the mere chronicling of wrongdoing or litigation.

b) The *ratio decidendi*

We have already seen how, under the doctrine of judicial precedent, a judge trying a case may be obliged to apply a legal principle laid down in an earlier case. This principle is usually known by the Latin phrase *ratio decidendi* (the reason for the decision). Two points must be noted.

Firstly, the *ratio decidendi* must be a legal principle. Suppose, for example, that X kept a cheetah which escaped and chewed off Y's hand and that in the ensuing case the judge held X liable and ordered him to pay Y £100,000 damages for the loss of his hand. The legal principle here is that X should keep his dangerous animal under control and is liable if it escapes and causes damage; this is the *ratio decidendi* of the case. It could be relied on, for instance, in a later case where an escaped leopard bit off a man's foot. That man's damages may be more or less than £100,000 because the specific sum of money was not part of the legal principle: the legal principle is that the leopard's owner will be liable.

Secondly, only that principle of law which was actually applied by the judge in the case can be its *ratio decidendi*. Sometimes in the course of his judgment (the speech made by the judge at the end of the case in which he reviews the facts and gives the reason for his decision) the judge will postulate some hypothetical example: 'But if Mr Smith had done this and Mr Jones had done that, then I would have said...'. Anything said in this way is not part of the *ratio decidendi* but is known by another Latin tag: it is said to be *obiter dictum* (plural, *dicta*) – 'a thing, or things, said by the way'. Also, if three or more judges are sitting together (as happens in the House of Lords or in the Court of Appeal) and one of them takes a different view of the law from that of the others then his dissenting (or minority) judgment is *obiter*, as the view of the law which it expresses was not, in fact, applied in the case.

You should bear in mind these important points:

1. The *ratio decidendi* in an earlier case may be binding or persuasive according to the status of the court which tried the earlier case relative to that of the court trying the present case.

2. *Obiter dicta* can only be persuasive precedent.

3. Both the terms *ratio decidendi* and *obiter dicta* apply only to statements about legal principles and not to matters such as the amount of money to be awarded for a particular injury.

c) Inconvenient precedents

Despite the traditional, pivotal importance of precedent in English law a court will sometimes refuse to follow an earlier decision if it thinks that to apply the old precedent in the circumstances of the new case would be to cause injustice.

A higher court may reverse or over-rule the decision of a lower court. The decision of the lower court is **reversed** if the party who lost because of that decision appeals to a higher court and that higher court finds in his or her favour, saying that the legal basis (the *ratio decidendi*) of the lower court's decision was unsound. A decision is **over-ruled** where the decision of a lower court is said by a higher court trying an entirely different and separate case to have been wrong – for instance, if in *Black* v. *White* decided in 2000 the Court of Appeal should say that *Brown* v. *Green* was wrongly decided back in 1900. Over-ruling does not retrospectively alter the outcome of the earlier case any more than an increase in train fares means that you have to pay extra for last year's journeys; the effect is only upon those who come after.

Any precedent set by a court of equal or lower status may well be only persuasive; if this is so there is clearly no particular difficulty in discarding it. The situation is not as easy, however, where an earlier case laid down a precedent which is binding. For, as Lord Hailsham said in *Cassell & Co. Ltd* v. *Broome* 1972:

> ...*in the hierarchical system of courts which exists in this country it is necessary for each lower tier ... to accept loyally the decisions of the higher tiers.*

In practice, however, a lower court may sometimes be able to avoid applying a binding precedent in one of the following two ways:

1. The court (that is, the judge or judges trying the case) may **distinguish** the precedent. This means that the court may point to some difference between the facts (the events which led to the litigation) in the earlier case and those in the case now being considered. The court may then say that, in view of this difference, the precedent set by the earlier case is not binding (because its *ratio decidendi* was based on different facts). As you read through this book you will see how distinguishing works in practice.

2. The court may say that the earlier decision was made *per incuriam* or through lack of care. This does not mean that the earlier judges were slap-happy but, rather, that something of relevance had not been brought to their attention – for instance, the report of a yet earlier case or an Act of Parliament. It is partly for this reason that the reports include a list of cases cited by counsel (the lawyers arguing the case).

The importance of lawyers keeping up to date with their research by regularly reading the Law Reports which are produced on a weekly or even daily basis was underlined by the Court of Appeal in *Copeland* v. *Smith* 2000. 'After all' said one judge:

> *if this is not done, judges may be getting the answer wrong through the default of the advocates appearing before them. The English system of justice has always been dependent on the quality of the assistance that advocates give to the bench.*

This is one of the reasons why, in contrast to systems of justice in other countries, English judges are almost invariably in a position to give judgment at the end of a straightforward hearing without having to do their own research and without the State having to incur the cost of legal assistance for judges because they cannot rely on the advocates to show them the law they need to apply. . . . It is, of course, the duty of an advocate under the English system of justice to draw the judge's attention to authorities which are in point even if they are adverse to that advocate's case.

It should be noted that a court, by way of *obiter dicta*, may disapprove of an earlier case if its *ratio decidendi*, while not directly in point in the case then being tried, is thought to be unsound.

d) Advantages and disadvantages of precedent

Professor Geldart has suggested that the advantages of this system are:

(i) **Certainty.** Because judges follow earlier decisions one can predict the likely outcome of a case. This means that people can usually find out what their rights and duties are without the expense of going to court. The value of this benefit is not to be underestimated for, as Lord Justice Russell rightly observed in *Gallie* v. *Lee* 1969:

> *Litigation is an activity that does not markedly contribute to the happiness of mankind, though it is sometimes unavoidable. An abandonment of the principle that this court follows its own decisions on the law would I think lead to greater uncertainty and tend to produce more litigation.*

(ii) **Room for growth,** by way of original precedent. For example, in *Packer* v. *Packer* 1953 Lord Justice Denning, as he then was, grasped the nettle boldly, saying:

> *What is the argument on the other side? Only this, that no case has been found in which it has been done before. That argument does not appeal to me in the least. If we never do anything which has not been done before, we shall never get anywhere. The law will stand still whilst the rest of the world goes on: and that will be bad for both . . .*

In *Parker* v. *British Airways Board* 1982 (see Unit 6.6c)) another future Master of the Rolls strove to resolve an apparently simple point which had puzzled academics for many years. Lord Justice Donaldson said:

> *As a matter of legal theory, the common law has a ready-made solution for any problem and it is only for the judges, as legal technicians, to find it. The reality is somewhat different. Take the present case. The conflicting rights of finder and occupier have indeed been considered by various courts in the past. But under the rules of*

> *English jurisprudence, none of their decisions binds this court. We therefore have both the right and the duty to extend and adapt the common law in the light of established principles and the current needs of the community. This is not to say that we start with a clean sheet. In doing so, we should draw from the experience of the past as revealed by the previous decisions of the courts.*

The ability of the common law to develop in line with changed social standards was well exemplified by the decision of the House of Lords in *R* v. *R* 1991 (see also Unit 3.5d)) when the House of Lords turned their backs on the principle set out by Sir Mathew Hale in 1736 to the effect that a husband could not be guilty of rape upon his wife. Lord Keith, many years later, reflected on the changes in society which required a corresponding change in the law:

> *The common law is, however, capable of evolving in the light of changing social, economic and cultural developments. Hale's proposition reflected the state of affairs in these respects at the time it was enunciated. Since then the status of women, and particularly of married women, has changed out of recognition in various ways ... One of the most important changes is that the marriage is in modern times regarded as a partnership with equals and no longer one in which the wife must be the subservient chattel of her husband.*

While judges must adapt to changing social circumstances (and in so adapting may be viewed as making law themselves), they repeatedly remind themselves that it is not the function of the courts to usurp the role of Parliament. In *C* v. *DPP* 1995 one of the judges, Lord Lowry, suggested that judges navigating across an uncertainly chartered sea should bear in mind the following five principles.

Firstly, if a solution is doubtful, the judges should be wary of imposing their own remedy. Secondly, caution should prevail if Parliament had rejected opportunities of clearing up a known difficulty or had legislated while leaving the difficulty untouched. Thirdly, disputed matters of social policy are less suitable areas for judicial intervention than purely legal problems. A fourth guide was that fundamental legal doctrines should not be lightly set aside and, finally, judges should not make a change unless they can achieve finality and certainty.

In setting out these principles, Lord Lowry had also had the benefit of considering the draft judgment of the House of Lords in *R* v. *Clegg* 1995. In this case, which caused considerable political unrest in Northern Ireland, Lee Clegg, then serving with the Parachute Regiment, was on duty in Belfast when a stolen car approached a check-point. The soldier opened fire and killed both the driver and a passenger. Private Clegg, charged with murder, relied on the defence of self-defence but was convicted. The question arose on appeal whether Private Clegg was guilty of murder when, but for the excessive and disproportionate use of force, he would have been entitled to a lesser verdict of manslaughter. The point was far from merely an academic issue because conviction for manslaughter allows the court a wide discretion as to sentence. Those convicted of murder are automatically subject to life imprisonment. Was this decision for the judges or for the politicians? Lord Lloyd trod a cautious path:

> I am not averse to judges developing law, or indeed making new law, when they can see their way clearly, even where questions of social policy are involved. A good recent example would be the affirmation by this House of the decision of the Court of Appeal (Criminal Division) that a man can be guilty of raping his wife ... But in the present case I am in no doubt that your Lordships should abstain from law-making. The reduction of what would otherwise be murder to manslaughter in a particular class of case seems to me essentially a matter for decision by the legislature, and not by this House in its judicial capacity. For the point in issue is, in truth, part of the wider issue whether the mandatory life sentence for murder should still be maintained. That wider issue can only be decided by Parliament.

(iii) **Its practical nature.**
(iv) **Scope for detail.** If there were only a formal legal code there would be great difficulty caused by the almost certain arrival of unforeseen situations, events and disputes.

In a Note of the House of Lords in 1966, Lord Gardiner said:

> Their Lordships regard the use of precedent as an indispensable foundation upon which to decide what is the law and its application to individual cases. It provides at least some degree of certainty upon which individuals can rely in the conduct of their affairs as well as a basis for orderly development of legal rules.

On the other hand, Professor Geldart found the following disadvantages:

(i) **A rigidity** which fetters the judge's discretion in individual cases. So, in *Gallie* v. *Lee* 1969, Lord Justice Salmon, after speculating on the possibility that the Court of Appeal might one day abandon its practice of considering itself bound by its own previous decisions, concluded:

> In the meantime I find myself reluctantly obliged to accept the old authorities, however much I disagree with them.

More recently, in *White* v. *White* 1998 the President of the Family Division, Dame Elizabeth Butler-Sloss warned:

There is a danger that practitioners in the field of family law attempt to apply too rigidly the decisions of this court and of the Family Division, without sufficiently recognising that each case involving a family has to be decided upon broad principles adapted to the facts of the individual case.

(ii) **A sophistry** which allows a judge to magnify the smallest distinction between the facts of two cases so as to be able to distinguish the precedent.

(iii) **A complexity**, which can be seen by visiting a Law Library, where there are tens of yards of shelves holding hundreds of volumes containing reports of many thousands of individual cases. Fortunately for lawyers needing to carry out their research this practical problem has been mitigated by the advent of modern technology enabling reports which had previously occupied many yards of book shelves now to be stored on CD-ROM disk. Computer-aided transcripts can now even be downloaded from the Internet within only a few hours of judgment.

In the 1966 Note mentioned earlier, the House of Lords announced that although in the past it had considered itself bound by its own previous decisions it would not continue to do so because as Lord Gardiner observed:

Their Lordships nevertheless recognize that too rigid adherence to precedent may lead to injustice in a particular case and so unduly restricts the proper development of the law

An application of this refusal to be bound by its own previous decisions can be seen in *R* v. *Shivpuri* 1986 when the House of Lords rejected their then still recent decision in *Anderton* v. *Ryan* 1985. In each case the courts had been required to consider the position where people had been prosecuted for attempted criminal acts. Although the issues involved were very similar the results were very different (see Unit 3.3c)).

A particular difficulty facing a litigant (one who goes to court to have a dispute settled) is that, in theory at least, precedents never wear out. However, although a litigant may reasonably expect a similar result on similar facts heard, say, in 2000 and in 1990, the result may be very different if the precedent relied upon had been established in 1890, for changing social conditions are often reflected in changes in the law (see Unit 1.9).

When the law on a particular topic has become settled it may be **codified** – that is, put into an Act of Parliament. For instance, much of the existing business law and commercial practice was codified in the Sale of Goods Act 1893, now replaced by the Sale of Goods Act 1979. In 1985 the Law Commission published a Report and draft Bill which would codify much of our substantive criminal law in the same way as the Criminal Attempts Act 1981 codified the old common law rules of attempt (see again Unit 3.3c)).

1.6 Sources of law: statutes and delegated legislation

We have seen how custom, the earliest source of law, in time gave way in importance to precedent. Today, statutes (also known as **Acts of Parliament**) are of increasing importance, principally because the swiftest and clearest way to change or add to the law is by statute. Statutes are the supreme source of law; a new Act of Parliament over-rules any existing custom, case-law or earlier Act with which it is in conflict.

a) How statutes are made

Every statute starts out as a Bill – a proposed new Act. Before it becomes a statute it must be approved by both Houses of Parliament (the Commons and the Lords) and by the Queen. In practice, once both Houses of Parliament have passed the Bill, the Queen's approval (known as the **Royal Assent**) is automatic, for in a democracy it is accepted that the Queen should take no actively political part in government.

A Bill may be first introduced in either the Commons or the Lords except that any Bill providing for the spending of public money (a **money bill**) must first be introduced in the Commons. Nowadays, most Bills are **public bills**, that is they are sponsored by the government so as to implement its political policy. For example, by introducing the Trade Union and Labour Relations Bill in 1974 the then Labour Government set out to do away with much of the preceding Conservative Government's Industrial Relations Act 1971. When the Tories regained power in 1979 the new Thatcher Government set about dismantling the previous socialist protection of trade union interests by its Employment Acts of 1980 and 1982.

Less common are **private members' bills** which may be the idea of just one Member of Parliament, often supported by an extra-parliamentary 'pressure group'. Because of the demands on parliamentary time made by the public bills there is little opportunity for private members' bills to be debated and few ever become statutes. Some such bills, nevertheless, have had a great effect on our law. For example, much of our modern divorce law stems from the crusading work of A. P. Herbert and his Matrimonial Causes Act 1937. Since then the finer sensibilities of maiden aunts have been saved from unexpected contact with purveyors of lascivious literature and cinematographic sin by the Indecent Displays (Control) Act 1981, pioneered by Conservative MP Tim Sainsbury. Similarly, the public's 'right to know' how its money is being spent by local councils was recognised by the Local Government (Access to Information) Act 1985 championed through Parliament by the Conservative Member for Hornchurch, Robin Squire. On the other side of the House, an attempt to outlaw the 'page three' type of pin-up in Clare Short's Indecent Displays (Newspapers) Bill failed in 1986 to become law. More recently, in the Spring of 2000 Andrew Dismore, Labour Member for Hendon and a solicitor, introduced the Corporate Homicide Bill which would create a new offence of corporate killing intended to make it easier to convict companies of unlawful killing (see also Unit 3.5c)).

A Bill introduced into the House of Commons will pass through the following stages before it becomes law.

(i) **First reading** An official reads out the title of the Bill and the name of the MP introducing it. The Bill is ordered to be printed.
(ii) **Second reading** The major proposals set out in the Bill are debated and a vote may be taken. If the Bill is approved it will go on to the committee stage.
(iii) **Committee stage** A committee of MPs, known as a 'Standing Committee', and so constituted in their numbers as to reflect the strength of the parties, will now consider the proposals in detail, clause by clause. An especially important Bill may be considered by a 'Committee of the whole House', a committee of which every MP is a member.
(iv) **Report stage** The committee reports back to the House, probably proposing amendments to the Bill.
(v) **Third reading** This is the final debate on the major proposals. Afterwards a vote is taken.

The procedure in the Lords is similar.

Even when a Bill has received the Royal Assent and has become a statute it may well not come into force immediately. For example, the Estate Agents Act 1978 did not come into force until May 1982 and the controversial Police and Criminal Evidence Act 1984 did not become law until 1 January 1986 in order to allow the police sufficient time to receive the extra training they required. Similar needs to train lawyers and judges required a delay in the implementation until October 2000 of the Human Rights Act 1998 and, at the time of writing, it is a mystery when, if ever, the Family Law Act 1996 will be fully brought into force. On the other hand, it is most unusual for a statute to be retrospective in effect (that is to affect people's rights and duties for any period before it was passed) though, by way of exception, the War Damage Act 1964 did absolve the government from liability for events which had taken place during the Second World War. The Human Rights Act 1998 will also apply some retrospective measures, for the new legislation, which at last incorporates the European Convention of Human Rights into domestic law, will apply to proceedings 'whenever the act in question took place'. It is, however, clearly established that a law giving rise to penal sanction should not be retrospective in its effect – otherwise perfectly lawful acts would become criminal offences months or even years later. Indeed, the courts presume that an Act of Parliament was not intended to operate retrospectively unless the contrary intention appeared clearly or by necessary implication. In *L'Office Cherifien* v. *Yamashita Limited* 1993 the Court of Appeal described the rule that a person should not be held liable or punished for conduct not criminal when committed as one which was fundamental and of long standing.

The situation would be different, however, if the acts constituted a violation of the laws and customs of war. The War Crimes Act 1991 specifically applies to offences committed during the Second World War. Under this legislation the English courts may try men such as Anthony Sawoniuk who had come to live in England after the war and who, in 1999, was convicted at the Central Criminal Court of murder committed by him in 1942 when a member of the local police in Belorussia, a town then under German occupation.

b) Delegated legislation

In a factory the works manager has overall control of the way the factory is run. As he cannot do everything himself he authorises the foremen and the charge-hands to make routine decisions about how the work is to be done.

Similarly, because today governments find it necessary to make a vast number of detailed new regulations on almost every subject, from the composition of upholstered furniture in the shops to where you may park your car while you go to buy it, Parliament itself cannot find time to attend to every minor detail. It therefore delegates power and responsibility to make regulations to other bodies, such as local authorities: these regulations are known as **delegated legislation**. In this way Parliament is able in an Act to provide a framework and to leave the local authority or other group to fill in the detail. For example, in London the Westminster City Council has made extensive use of the powers given to it under the GLC (General Powers) Act 1982 to close down large numbers of the more lascivious establishments in Soho by using its powers under the Act to require sex shops, cinemas, peep shows and topless bars to pay for a licence from the Council if the business is to go on trading.

An important example of delegated legislation is the **Order in Council**, which is an order of the Privy Council. Many Acts are brought into force by such an Order, signed by a government minister, often the Home Secretary. The Privy Council, incidentally, is a committee of ministers and other powerful people whose traditional duty is to advise the sovereign.

Other forms of delegated legislation are the **statutory instrument**, normally made by a minister, and **bye-laws** made by local authorities and organisations such as the British Rail Board.

Disadvantages of delegated legislation

Because in practice most delegated legislation is prepared by civil servants and then 'rubber-stamped' by the elected representatives, this system has been called 'the New Despotism' for, in effect, it allows the non-elected civil servants to legislate. Nevertheless, Parliament does retain some control over the making of delegated legislation.

A more everyday problem is the sheer number of statutory instruments made each year. It is obviously very difficult for the person in the street to be aware of all of them and so he or she may unwittingly commit a criminal offence. It is generally no defence for an accused person to protest that he or she did not know the law although the Statutory Instruments Act 1946 does provide that it shall be a defence for a person charged with an offence created by a statutory instrument to prove that the instrument had not been issued by Her Majesty's Stationery Office at the date of the alleged commission of the offence. Even then, however, the defence will fail if it is shown that reasonable steps had been taken to bring the instrument to the notice of the public.

Advantages of delegated legislation

The practice of authorising others to make delegated legislation does, of course, allow Parliament to devote itself to the major and nationally important tasks of government. Moreover, it allows the local authority, board or minister to make detailed regulations very quickly if need be and then to keep those regulations under constant review. For example, in immediate response to terrorist bombings in England in 1974, Parliament passed the Prevention of Terrorism (Temporary Provisions) Act 1974 which allowed the Home Secretary, by Order in Council, to proscribe those political organisations which appeared to him to be promoting or encouraging terrorism. Under this Act, the Home Secretary could, of course, today proscribe an organisation which had not been in existence when the Act was passed. Such a prospect illustrates a further advantage of delegated legislation: that it allows the principles laid down in the Act to be applied in circumstances which were unforeseen at the time of its formulation.

Control over delegated legislation

Control over delegated legislation is exercised by Parliament and by the courts.

- *Parliament's control.* Although there is no general rule that delegated legislation is to be 'laid before' (that is, brought to the notice of) Parliament, the individual Act which grants power to make particular regulations (the **enabling Act**) usually does require that they should be so laid. Moreover, statutory instruments are usually subject either to 'affirmative' or 'negative' resolution. If they are subject to **affirmative resolution** they do not become law unless approved by Parliament; if they are subject to **negative resolution** they are and will remain law unless rejected by Parliament within 40 days.

    There are various other Parliamentary safeguards, the most important being the **Select Committee on Statutory Instruments**. This committee of the House of Commons, commonly called the 'Scrutiny Committee', reviews all statutory instruments and decides whether any of them should be brought to the attention of the full House – for instance, because it appears to make an unexpected use of the powers conferred by the original enabling Act.

- *Control by the courts.* The courts will examine any piece of delegated legislation to make sure that it is within the framework contemplated by the enabling Act. For example, in *R* v. *Wood* 1855 the Public Health Act 1848 empowered local Boards of Health to make bye-laws obliging occupiers of buildings to remove 'dust, ashes, rubbish, filth, manure, dung and soil'. One such board made a bye-law under this Act directing all occupiers to remove all snow from the public footpath adjoining their premises. When this bye-law was challenged in the courts it was held that it was *ultra vires* (beyond the powers) of the board to make such an order – the Act was concerned only with the removal of dirty and unhygienic substances and not with preventing people from slipping on a bit of ice.

    Moreover, it is presumed that in the absence of any express sanction the enabling Act does not give the local authority, board or minister the power to:

    - make unreasonable regulations; or
    - allow sub-delegation (that is, grant a third party power to make regulations); or levy taxes; or
    - interfere with the basic rights of the subject (such as freedom of speech).

So it was that in *Attorney-General* v. *Wilts United Dairies* 1922 there was power under the Defence of the Realm Act 1914 for the Food Controller:

> ...to regulate the supply and consumption of food in such manner as he thinks best for maintaining a proper supply of food, and to take such steps as he thinks fit for encouraging the production of food.

The Food Controller ordered that no one should be allowed to deal in milk without a licence from him. This much he was clearly entitled to do.

Milk was scarce in Yorkshire and so the Controller wished to limit the consumption in that county by raising the price by twopence a gallon. As it would have been unfair for the extra twopence to go straight into the pockets of the milk dealers, the grant of a licence to deal in milk in Yorkshire was made conditional on the payment to the Controller of a fee calculated at twopence a gallon on the amount of milk sold. The House of Lords, however, held that the Controller had no power to impose this fee. Lord Buckmaster pointed out:

> *The result is that the money so raised can only be described as a tax, the levying of which can never be imposed upon subjects of this country by anything except plain and direct statutory means ... The powers given by the Act are no doubt very extensive and very drastic but they do not include the power of levying on any man payment of money.*

In *Congreve* v. *Home Office* 1976 the Home Office had threatened to revoke colour television licences in the case of those farsighted, astute individuals who had taken out new licences in advance in order to beat the £6 increase in the fee which came into force in April 1975. The Wireless Telegraphy Act 1949 provided that:

> a licence ... may be issued subject to such terms, provisions and limitations as the Postmaster-General may think fit ... a wireless telegraphy licence may be revoked, or the terms, provisions or limitation thereof varied, by a notice in writing of the Postmaster-General.

The Act certainly gave the minister a discretion as to the issue and revocation of licences but the Court of Appeal held that the minister's discretion was nevertheless fettered to the extent that the courts would intervene if it were exercised arbitrarily or improperly. Nothing in the Act said that people could not delay paying an increased fee by obtaining and holding overlapping licences. For the minister now to turn round and propose to revoke a licence validly obtained was an improper and unlawful attempt to levy money and one which Parliament had not authorised the Home Office to undertake. The demands for the extra £6 were, said Lord Denning,

> *an attempt to levy money for the use of the Crown, without the authority of Parliament: and that is quite enough to damn them.*

...and that is quite enough to damn them...

The validity of rules made under the Prison Act 1952 (which allowed a prison governor to read prisoners' correspondence) came before the Court of Appeal in R v. *Secretary of State for the Home Department, ex parte Leech* 1993. Mark Leech, then serving six years' imprisonment, was involved in some litigation which required him to enter into correspondence with solicitors. He was conscious that anything he said to his solicitors might be censored and even copied to the Home Office. Of course, as a general rule communications between lawyers and clients are privileged and should, accordingly, remain confidential. Every citizen should have unimpeded access to the courts and to confidential legal advice. On the other hand, the Prison Service sought to justify reading correspondence to and from inmates so as to prevent its use to plan escapes or disturbances. The 1952 Prison Act specifically allowed the Secretary of State to 'make rules for the regulation and management of prisons ... and for the ... discipline and control of persons required to be detained therein'. Under the relevant rules made pursuant to the primary legislation it was specifically provided that 'every letter or communication to or from a prisoner may be read or examined by the Governor or an officer deputed by him...'. Mark Leech, however, contended that the 1952 Act did not authorise interference with the solicitor/client relationship with its attached legal professional privilege. The Court of Appeal agreed that this particular prison rule created a substantial impediment both to a citizen's right to unimpeded access to the courts and to his or her lawyers for their advice. It followed that the relevant rule under the Prison Rules was *ultra vires*.

c) Interpretation of statutes and delegated legislation

The chronicler of Alice's journey *Through the Looking Glass* records Humpty Dumpty as saying: 'when I use a word it means just what I choose it to mean – neither more nor less'.

In a world of moving chess-pieces where Red Queens are really kittens, such a flexible attitude to language might perhaps work well enough. Elsewhere, if people are to plan their affairs satisfactorily a far greater precision is required. For example, if an Act refers to 'a month' does it mean four weeks or a full thirty-one days?

In deciding such questions the courts are aided by the Interpretation Act 1978 which lays down many rules for interpreting (or 'construing') Acts of Parliament. For example, this Act says that 'unless a contrary intention appears male includes female' (that is, that 'he' stands for 'she' and so on), that the singular includes the plural and vice versa, and that 'a month' means a calendar month.

In addition, over the years there has grown up (by precedent) a set of more general rules, the most important of which are examined here.

The Literal Rule
This states that simple words which have an obvious everyday meaning 'say what they mean': the courts should give them that meaning without any gloss. If a statute has been poorly drafted the application of the Literal Rule may lead to a result quite at odds with the intention of the Parliament which made it. It used to be thought that it was then up to Parliament to correct its mistakes by passing another Act. Nowadays, however, the courts adopt a more pragmatic attitude and consider the Literal Rule is in these circumstances both outdated and counterproductive. Such an attitude was echoed by Lord Denning in *Engineering Industry Training Board* v. *Samuel Talbot Ltd* 1969 when he said:

> But we no longer construe Acts of Parliament according to their literal meaning. We construe them according to their object and intent.

The Golden Rule
The guidance offered by this rule is that where words in a statute are ambiguous, that meaning should be given which best expresses the intention of Parliament. This intention, however, can only be gleaned by reading the Act as a whole and by reference to the Mischief Rule (see below).

The Golden Rule is widely applied not only to statutes which are clearly ambiguous but also in any case where its use will avoid an absurdity: the point is illustrated by the following extract from Lord Reid's speech in *Luke* v. *Inland Revenue Commissioners* 1963:

> To apply the words literally is to defeat the obvious intention of the legislation and to produce a wholly unreasonable result. To achieve the obvious intention and produce a reasonable result we must do some violence to the words. This is not a new problem, though our standard of drafting is such that it rarely emerges. The general principle is well settled. It is only where the words are absolutely incapable of a construction which will accord with the apparent intention of the provision and will avoid a wholly unreasonable result, that the words of the enactment must prevail.

In short, if at all possible, the court will use the Golden Rule to achieve a result which is both reasonable and in line with the apparent intention of Parliament.

The Mischief Rule
In practice, this is probably the most important of these rules. Stated simply, the rule encourages the court to answer the question 'what does this statute mean?' by asking in turn 'what was the mischief?' (or unsatisfactory state of affairs) which Parliament meant the new Act to remedy. A selection of decisions will show how the rule works in practice. In *Rogers* v. *Dodd* 1968 it was a condition of a coffee-bar's registration under the Brighton Corporation Act 1966 that it should not

remain open after 1.00 a.m. One morning at 1.40 a.m., although the door had been closed for some time, hot-dogs were being served through an open window. Was the coffee-bar still 'open'? Lord Parker applied the Mischief Rule when he said:

> *It seems to me that the mischief aimed at by the Act of 1966 is the congregation of the public in premises where no doubt they are served with refreshments and where abuses are likely to occur in the sense of undue noise to the neighbourhood, peddling of drugs and other such matters.*

A little earlier, in *Smith* v. *Hughes* 1960, Lord Parker had applied the Mischief Rule to a case where two prostitutes had appealed against their conviction for soliciting in a street or public place – an offence under the Street Offences Act 1959. The girls, who were inside a building adjoining the street, had been tapping on the windows to attract the attention of passers-by and, by gesturing, had invited them to come inside. It was clear enough that the women were soliciting, but were they soliciting 'in a street or public place' when the building in which they were was private property? After considering the 'mischief' aimed at by the Act, Lord Parker said:

> *For my part, I approach the matter by considering what is the mischief aimed at by this Act. Everybody knows that this was an Act intended to clean up the streets to enable people to walk along the streets without being molested or solicited by common prostitutes. Viewed in that way, it can matter little whether the prostitute is soliciting while in the street, or is standing in the doorway or on a balcony, or at a window or whether the window is shut or open or half-open; in each case her solicitation is projected to and addressed to somebody walking in the street.*

Judges were again involved with a prostitute in *Director of Public Prosecutions* v. *Bull* 1994 when the Divisional Court had to consider whether the term 'common prostitute', set out in the same Street Offences Act, was limited to female prostitute or whether a man could be prosecuted for loitering for the purpose of prostitution. The judges looked at the Parliamentary debate which preceded the legislation as was now their right following the decision in *Pepper* v. *Hart* (see below) along with the Wolfenden Committee's Report (see Unit 1.2). Consideration of such reading persuaded the judges that the 'mischief' which the Street Offences Act 1959 had been intended to remedy was only the mischief created by women.

Lastly, the courts must be careful at all times how they construe statutes so that it is the will of Parliament which is applied and not the views of the judges. This point was emphatically underlined by Viscount Simonds in *Magor and St Mellons RDC* v. *Newport Corporation* 1951:

> *The duty of the court is to interpret the words that the legislature has used. Those words may be ambiguous, but, even if they were, the power and duty of the court to travel outside them on a voyage of discovery are strictly limited. If a gap is disclosed the remedy lies in an amending Act.*

Later, in *Duport Steels Ltd* v. *Sirs* 1980, Lord Scarman reminded the court of the limits on a judge's powers:

> *Legal systems differ in the width of the discretionary power granted to judges: but in developed societies limits are invariably set, beyond which the judges may not go. Justice in such societies is not left to the unguided, experienced, sage sitting under the spreading oak tree . . .*
>
> *But in the field of statute law the judge must be obedient to the will of Parliament expressed in its enactments. In this field Parliament makes and unmakes the law. The judge's duty is to interpret and to apply the law, not to change it to meet the judge's idea of what justice requires. Interpretation does, of course, imply in the interpreter a power of choice where differing constructions are possible. But our law requires the judge to choose the construction which in his judgment best suits the legislative purpose of the enactment. If the result be unjust but inevitable, the judge may say so and invite Parliament to reconsider its provision. But he must not deny the statute. Unpalatable statute law may not be disregarded or rejected merely because it is unpalatable.*

It may seem strange that, in their inquiry to resolve what mischief Parliament intended to remedy, the judges in England and Wales were traditionally not allowed to look at the records of Parliamentary debate set out in Hansard (the record of proceedings in Parliament). This restriction was at variance with the practice of European courts and was regretted by Lord Denning MR in *Davis* v. *Johnson* 1978 when he considered words used in the Domestic Violence and Matrimonial Proceedings Act 1976. The Master of the Rolls expressed the view that if judges in an earlier decision had been referred to the Parliamentary debates on the then Domestic Violence Bill they would have better discovered the intention of Parliament. He continued:

> *Some may say, and indeed have said, that judges should not pay any attention to what is said in Parliament. They should grope about in the dark for the meaning of an Act without switching on the light. I do not accede to this view. . . . and it is obvious that there is nothing to prevent a judge looking at those debates himself privately and getting some guidance from them. Although it may shock the purists, I may as well confess that I have sometimes done it. I have done it in this very case. It has thrown a flood of light on the position. The statements made in Committee disposed completely of Counsel for the Respondent's argument before us.*

The approach taken by the Master of the Rolls was disapproved upon further appeal to the House of Lords with Viscount Dilhorne, in particular, expressing the view:

> *It cannot be right that a judicial decision should be affected by matters which a judge has seen but to which counsel could not refer and on which counsel had no opportunity to comment.*

Lord Scarman took a similarly cautious stance:

> There are two good reasons why the courts should refuse to
> have regard to what is said in Parliament or by Ministers as
> aids to the interpretation of a statute. First such material is an
> unreliable guide to the meaning of what is enacted. It pro-
> motes confusion, not clarity. The cut and thrust of debate and
> the pressures of executive responsibility, essential features of
> open and responsible government, are not always conducive
> to a clear and unbiased explanation of the meaning of statu-
> tory language. And the volume of parliamentary and minister-
> ial utterances can confuse by its very size. Secondly, counsel
> are not permitted to refer to Hansard in argument.

Such denial of recourse to Hansard was less strictly followed ten years
later when, in *Pickstone* v. *Freemans plc* 1988, the House of Lords was
prepared to look at Hansard's report of the words of a government
minister as he introduced new regulations on equal pay for women.
Such regulations had only been intended to give effect to an earlier
ruling of the European Court and had not been subject to Parliamentary
debate and amendment.

After their decision in *Pickstone* v. *Freemans plc* 1988 the House of
Lords evinced a further and considerable relaxation in the old approach.
In *Pepper* v. *Hart* 1993, a decision which may have a beneficial effect on
many hard-pressed taxpayers generally, a number of teachers at a school
were able to send their sons to that school for fees which were only one-
fifth of the ordinary fees charged to other parents. All too predictably,
this was a benefit on which the tax gatherers sought to tax the parents
by virtue of provisions in the Finance Act 1976. A dispute arose between
the taxpayers and the Inland Revenue as to the level at which 'benefit'
was to be assessed. Was it the full cost of the school fees which other
parents paid? Was it, on the other hand, only that much smaller additional cost to the school of teaching and feeding a handful of additional
children? In short, how were the courts to construe the relevant section
in the Finance Act 1976? The taxpaying parents argued that it was now
appropriate for the courts to look at Hansard in order to ascertain the
intention of the legislature in 1976. One member of the House of Lords,
the then Lord Chancellor, Lord Mackay, a member of the Conservative
Government at the time of one of its many complaints about financing
the provision of legal help to the citizen, expressed concern about the
cost of allowing such consultation. His speech expressed concern that:

> The parties' legal advisers will require to study Hansard in
> practically every such case to see whether or not there is any
> help to be gained from it. I believe this is an objection of real
> substance. . . . Such an approach appears to me to involve the
> possibility of at least an immense increase in the cost of litiga-
> tion in which statutory construction is involved. . . . and I per-
> sonally would not wish to be a party to changing a
> well-established rule which could have a substantial effect of
> increasing these costs.

More generally, however, the House of Lords took note that the modern approach to statutory construction was the **purposive approach** and, with such approach, the old restraints upon Parliamentary material should now be relaxed so as to allow the judges to look at Hansard. It said that this would now be permissible where the legislation was ambiguous or obscure or, alternatively, where the literal meaning led to an absurdity. Further, such a course would now be permissible where the material relied upon consisted of statements by a minister or other sponsor of a Bill and where, said the judges, the statements relied upon were clear. In this case the House of Lords went on to remark that the relevant wording in the Finance Act 1976 was clearly ambiguous. However, by reading what the then Financial Secretary to the Treasury had said during the committee stage of the Bill, the judges in the House of Lords were able to hold that the parental pedagogues could be taxed only on that lesser sum. The minister had earlier assured the Commons that railway employees, entitled to concessionary travel, would not be taxed on their benefit from their employment. Why then should school-teachers be taxed on benefits from their employment? Lord Griffiths grasped the nettle:

> *I have long thought that the time had come to change the self-imposed judicial rule that forbade any reference to the legislative history of an enactment as an aid to its interpretation. The ever-increasing volume of legislation must inevitably result in ambiguities of statutory language which are not perceived at the time the legislation is enacted. The object of the court in interpreting legislation is to give effect so far as the language permits to the intention of the legislature. If the language proves to be ambiguous I can see no sound reason not to consult Hansard to see if there is a clear statement of the meaning that the words were intended to carry. The days have long passed when the courts adopted a strict construction as to the view of interpretation which required them to adopt the literal meaning of the language. The courts now adopt a purposive approach which seeks to give effect to the true purpose of legislation and are prepared to look at much extraneous material that bears on the background against which the legislation was enacted. Why then cut ourselves off from the one source in which may be found an authoritative statement of the intention with which the legislation is placed before Parliament?*

The influence of European Regulations seen in *Pickstone* v. *Freemans plc* 1988 was swiftly apparent once more when, in *Lister* v. *Forth Dry Dock* 1989, the House of Lords had to construe notoriously abstruse regulations relating to the employment rights of employees of a business whose ownership was transferred. The courts had to decide whether the applicants had been employed in the business 'immediately before the transfer' of the business. In approaching this question the court had specific regard to a relevant European Directive (see Unit 1.8), the object of which was to protect the rights of employees in the event of a change of employer. In *Pickstone* v. *Freemans plc* the House of Lords had already held that in order to achieve the manifest purpose of the regulations and to give effect to the clear, but inadequately expressed, intention of Parliament certain words must be read in by necessary implication. The House of Lords continued to adopt this approach, describing it as a 'purposive construction' and one which should be applied even though it may perhaps involve some departure from the strict and literal application of the words which the legislature had chosen to use.

That the modern approach to statutory interpretation is a purposive one was more recently emphasised in *Three Rivers District Council* v. *Bank of England* 1996, litigation which followed the debacle of the liquidation of the Bank of Credit and Commerce International (BCCI). These plaintiffs were some of thousands of depositors who complained that the Bank of England had failed to supervise properly banking operations in the United Kingdom. Would they be allowed to refer to what had been said in Parliament during the passage of the Bills which were to become the Banking Act 1979 and Banking Act 1987? Part of the 1979 Act was intended to allow the United Kingdom to comply with its obligations under a European Directive on the coordination of laws and regulations relating to various credit institutions. The judge took the view, contrary to the arguments of the Bank of England, that it might be important to know how far the 1977 Directive had been enacted in the 1979 Act, a consideration which, in turn, involved a second consideration of the object and purpose of that and the later Banking Act. The judge, mindful that a statute should be construed purposively, was prepared to adopt a more flexible approach to Parliamentary material where there was a European element also to consider.

One further European influence is the recent incorporation into English law of the European Convention on Human Rights in October 2000 through the Human Rights Act 1998. In time, this Act may reduce the significance of the doctrine of precedent in our national law but has already affected construction of statutes. There is now a rebuttable presumption in favour of interpreting Acts of Parliament so as to make the legislation consistent with rights conferred by the Convention. In this regard, Section 3 of the Human Rights Act 1998 provides:

> So far as it is possible to do so, primary legislation and subordinate legislation must be read and given effect in a way which is compatible with Convention rights.

The continuing practical relevance of how a statute should properly be construed was recently underlined when the House of Lords was again asked to consider a problem of statutory construction in respect of the Rent Act 1977. In *Fitzpatrick* v. *Sterling Housing Association Limited* 1999 the courts had to decide whether a homosexual partner was capable of being a 'spouse' or, alternatively, a member of the original tenant's 'family'. The 1977 Rent Act, as amended, allowed a surviving spouse to take over the tenancy upon the death of an original tenant. John Thompson had rented a West London flat where he lived with Martin Fitzpatrick. Upon Mr Thompson's death, Martin Fitzpatrick sought a declaration that he had succeeded to the tenancy under the Rent Act. He claimed that he was 'a spouse' of the deceased or, alternatively, that he was a member of Mr Thompson's 'family'. It was agreed between the parties that Mr Fitzpatrick and Mr Thompson had been partners in a longstanding, close, loving, faithful, monogamous homosexual relationship. Even so, firstly could a man be held also to be the 'spouse' of another man? Secondly, how widely should the concept of 'family' be construed? The breadth of the possible construction of this concept was highlighted by one of the judges, Lord Nicholls:

> 'Family' is a word with several different meanings. In some contexts family means children ('when shall we start a family?'). In other contexts it means parents and children ('accommodation suitable for families'). It may mean all persons connected, however remotely, by birth, marriage or adoption ('family tree'). The present context is statutory protection of the occupants of a dwelling house which is a family home. On the death of the tenant his family cannot be evicted without further ado.
>
> Herein lies the key to the meaning of family in this context. The key is the statutory juxtaposition of membership of the tenant's family and residence with the tenant. The legislation seeks to provide a measure of protection for members of a family who are sharing their lives together as a single family in one home.

Lord Nicholls emphasised the current purposive approach of the courts to legislation. Having offered various examples of how 'family' might be defined, he continued:

> Having regard to the purpose of the legislation, the width of the meaning borne by the expression 'family' does not stop here. As one might expect, the authorities have not drawn a rigid line at this point. A child who is adopted in fact, although not in law, may be as much a member of the tenant's family as a duly adopted child ... More pertinent for present purposes, a man and woman, unmarried but living together as husband and wife, are capable of constituting family.

It was self-evident that Mr Thompson and Mr Fitzpatrick would not have any children. This, however, was no bar to them being members of a family. Lord Nicholls continued to have regard to the purpose of the Rent Act when he said:

> The legislative purpose of protecting members of the family unit and their occupation of a house requires that a couple living together but without children should be as capable of qualifying for protection as a couple living together with a child.

Although the House of Lords took the view that terms such as spouse were gender specific (and so Mr Fitzpatrick failed on one ground), the appeal was allowed on the basis that Mr Fitzpatrick was still a member of John Thompson's family. Lord Nicholls reached the conclusion:

The question calling for a decision in the present case is a question of statutory interpretation. It is whether a same-sex partner is capable of being a member of the other partner's family for the purposes of the Rent Act legislation. I am in no doubt that this question should be answered affirmatively. A man and woman living together in a stable and permanent sexual relationship are capable of being members of a family for this purpose. Once this is accepted, there can be no rational or other basis on which the like conclusion can be withheld from a similarly stable and permanent sexual relationship between two men or between two women. Where a relationship of this character exists, it cannot make sense to say that, although a heterosexual partnership can give rise to membership of a family for Rent Act purposes, a homosexual partnership cannot. . . . As already emphasised, the concept underlying membership of a family for present purposes is the sharing of lives together in a single family unit living in one house.

It is of note that the decision of the House of Lords reflects a judicial awareness of changes in personal morality and social values since the legislation was first enacted. It was the role of the courts to adapt accordingly. Lord Nicholls once again put the issue well:

This submission raises the question whether the word 'family' as used in the Rent Act may change its meaning as ways of life and social attitudes change. Can the expression 'family' legitimately be interpreted in 1999 as having a different and wider meaning than when it was first enacted in 1920? . . . A statute must necessarily be interpreted having regard to the state of affairs existing when it was enacted. It is a fair presumption that Parliament's intention was directed at that state of affairs. When circumstances change, a court has to consider whether they fall within the Parliamentary intention. They may do so if there can be detected a clear purpose in the legislation which can only be fulfilled if an extension is made. How liberally these principles may be applied must depend upon the nature of the enactment, and the strictness or otherwise of the words in which it was expressed.

In the present case Parliament used an ordinary word of flexible meaning and left it undefined. The underlying legislative purpose was to provide a secure home for those who share their lives together with the original tenant in a manner which characterises a family unit. This purpose would be at risk of being stultified if the courts could not have regard to changes in the way people live together and the changes in the perception of relationships. This approach is supported by the fact that successive Rent Acts have used the same undefined expression despite the far-reaching changes and ways of life and social attitudes meanwhile. It would be unattractive, to the extent of being unacceptable, to interpret the word 'family' in the 1977 Act without regard to these changes.

1.7 Sources of law: common law and equity

The origins of the common law were touched upon at the beginning of Unit 1.5. The Norman Conquest of 1066 led, albeit slowly, to an increasingly centralised system of political administration. It had been the custom of the Saxon kings occasionally to call a 'Witan' or council of the leading noblemen, landowners and bishops. Under the Normans this council came to meet more regularly and became known as the *Curia Regis* (Latin for 'King's Council'). Its functions were both executive and judicial and by the thirteenth century three courts of law had grown out of it. All three courts administered the new common law and for this reason are often called the **common law courts**.

(i) **The Court of Exchequer**   The Exchequer dealt with the collection of taxes and the spending of the Royal reserve – the executive functions of the present-day Treasury. Out of this grew a judicial function to try cases connected (sometimes only very tenuously) with the collection of taxes.

(ii) **The Court of Common Pleas**   The *Curia Regis* sat wherever the King happened to be. This could cause great inconvenience to those who looked to it for justice, especially if the King were in some remote part of the country or even abroad. Magna Carta accordingly laid down in 1215 that suits between private citizens 'shall not follow our Court but be heard in some fixed place'. Such suits were known as **common pleas** – 'common' in the sense that the King had no direct interest in the case. The Court of Common Pleas was then set up at Westminster with four judges sitting permanently ('*in banco*').

. . . sat wherever the King happened to be.

(iii) **The Court of King's Bench** Those cases in which the King was interested still had to be heard *coram rege* ('in the presence of the King'), which meant either by the King himself or by members of his council travelling with him. These hearings included most criminal trials because a crime was considered to be an offence not so much against the victim but rather against the King's peace. Even today prosecutions brought in the name of the Queen may still allege an offence 'against the Queen's peace'.

   In time those members of the council who heard such cases were organised into the Court of King's Bench, so called because of a particularly obvious piece of furniture at court.

In practice, the jurisdiction of each court was not as clear-cut as would appear from this account. In particular, the superior status of the King's Bench, derived from its close association with the monarch, allowed it to exercise some supervisory power over the other courts.

Even before the Norman Conquest there existed in England a system of provincial courts, many of which were operated by the local baron almost on a private enterprise basis – he pocketed the fees and he also provided the strong-arm boys to enforce any judgments. The Norman kings were then faced with this dilemma: on the one hand they had no wish to vex the natives by disturbing established institutions but, on the other hand, they were anxious to set up centralised judicial and administrative systems. For this reason the history of the English legal system during the two hundred years following the Conquest is one of rivalry between the baronial courts and the *Curia Regis* courts.

If you lived in, say, Somerset or Northumberland one great disadvantage in taking your claim to the Royal court at Westminster was that Westminster was a long way away and travel was difficult, time-consuming and dangerous. If the people would not come to the King's justices then the answer was clearly to send the justices to the people.

It is well known that soon after William became King of England he sent out commissioners to compile the Domesday Book, a sort of inventory of the kingdom. It is less well known that a regular practice was established of sending out members of the *Curia Regis* to hold a 'General Eyre' – to review local government in the shires (counties) and to collect taxes. The review of local government, even then an expensive problem, included an inquiry into the administration of justice and the hearing of some cases by the Commissioners of Eyre themselves. The General Eyre was abolished in the reign of Richard III (its tax-collecting function had done little for its popularity) but the practice of sending out members of the *Curia Regis* as Royal judges continued. Their authority came from three Commissions from the King:

(i) **The Commission of Gaol Delivery** This empowered the judges to clear the gaols. In those days prison was not so much a form of punishment as a way of keeping a suspected offender under control until the judges arrived. The judges would then try the case, and, in the event of a conviction, would deal out some then perceived suitable punishment, such as death, mutilation or a fine.

(ii) **The Commission of Oyer and Terminer** This empowered the judges to hear (oyer) and settle (terminer) criminal cases. The differences between this Commission and that of Gaol Delivery were highly technical and need not concern the student.

(iii) **The Commission of Assize** This empowered the judges to try both civil and criminal cases which would otherwise have been heard at Westminster. The barons objected especially to this Commission because it was the civil cases that earned the fees. In theory, a litigant could go either to the local court or to the Royal courts at Westminster. Many litigants, however, were discouraged by the journey to London and so, in 1285, the Statute of Westminster II set up a scheme whereby cases would be set down for hearing at Westminster *nisi prius* ('unless before') the appointed date the Commission of Assize had visited the plaintiff's county. In practice, the court officials made sure that the appointed day was well after the Commissioners were expected to visit the county. In this way the Royal justice became more easily available throughout the country. After touring the country the judges would meet at Westminster to compare notes: this led to a uniformity in decisions and encouraged the genesis of a truly common law.

The barons, however, resenting the competition for litigation from the common-law courts, attempted to clip their wings. They based their attempt upon the process by which any action in the common-law courts was begun: the plaintiff's purchase from the Lord Chancellor (a member of the *Curia Regis* and the King's Secretary) of a **writ** or document by which the King ordered the sheriff of the county in which the defendant resided to ensure that the defendant appeared in court on the day appointed for the trial. It was very important to obtain the correct writ; as an indication of the technicalities involved, a different sort of writ was required in each of the following cases:

1. Tom was aggrieved because Dick had taken his silver chalice and refused to return it;
2. Tom was aggrieved because Dick had deliberately taken his chalice;
3. Tom was aggrieved because Dick, to whom he had lent the chalice, had dishonestly sold it to Harry.

The barons reckoned that if they could limit the number of different sorts of writ which could be served by the Chancellor they could limit the growth of the Royal courts. So, in 1258, the Provisions of Oxford laid down that the Chancellor might only issue existing forms of writ and that he was not to go on inventing new ones.

Thus a litigant could now be faced with any one of three problems:

1. he had applied for the wrong sort of writ and had accordingly lost his case;
2. no writ existed that was suited to his case;
3. if he brought his claim in the local court, the court might be overawed by his powerful adversary.

His natural course, therefore, was to appeal directly to the King who, in the political thinking of the day, was 'the fountain of justice'. The King would ask the Lord Chancellor's opinion on such appeals. The Chancellor was a priest and his standing may be judged by the fact that he was often called 'the Keeper of the King's conscience'. The Chancellor would then examine the merits of the case in an informal way and issue instructions to the parties. He might, for example, order one party not to take proceedings in the common-law courts. Anyone who refused to obey the Chancellor's instructions could be despatched to prison for a period of quiet reflection and contemplation upon the merits of the Chancellor's viewpoint.

As a priest, the Chancellor was concerned only with what was fair and equitable and not with the common law concepts of right and duty. For this reason the kind of justice he dispensed was known as **equity**. In time, the Chancellor's function as a judge outgrew his original function of royal secretary and a regular Court of Chancery was set up. Its purpose was to aid not only the oppressed but also the oppressor – if the latter did as the Chancellor said he would save his guilty soul from hell.

Just as the barons and others had objected when the common-law courts began to 'poach' work from the local courts, the common-law judges and lawyers (who were then a separate profession from the practitioners in the Court of Chancery) now in their turn became jealous of the growing importance of equity and were annoyed that business – and, indeed, their fees – were deserting them in favour of the Chancery Court.

Matters came to a head in the *Earl of Oxford's Case* 1615 where Chief Justice Coke (the senior judge in the Court of King's Bench) and Lord Ellesmere (the Lord Chancellor) differed strongly over the purported conveyance of Covent Garden. Lord Ellesmere explained the function of the Chancery Court and of equity when he said:

> *The cause why there is a Chancery is for that man's actions are so diverse and infinite that it is impossible to make any general law which may aptly meet with every act and not fail in some circumstance ... When a judgment is obtained by oppression, wrong, and a hard conscience, the Chancellor will frustrate and set it aside, not from any error or defect in the judgment, but for the hard conscience of the party.*

In the end the King, James I, told Coke and Ellesmere to submit their dispute to the arbitration of Sir Francis Bacon, the then Attorney-General and the King's legal adviser. Bacon decided in favour of Ellesmere and, on his recommendation, James laid down that in future, whenever there was a conflict between equity and the common law, equity should prevail.

However, because of the very nature of equity – because it was so flexible – it was open to criticism on the ground that litigants and practitioners could never predict the outcome of any particular case, and this, of course, led to increased litigation. The seventeenth-century jurist John Selden summed up this difficulty when he wrote in 1617:

> *Equity is a roguish thing; for law we have a measure to know what to trust to. Equity is according to the conscience of him who is Chancellor: as it is larger or narrower so is equity. 'Tis all one as if they should make the standard for the measure we call a foot to be the Chancellor's foot.*

At about the same time, however, Chancellors were beginning to decide cases not by conscience alone but also by considering their own and their predecessors' earlier decisions as precedents to be followed if at all possible. Additional impetus was given to this trend as it became usual for a lawyer, rather than a priest, to be appointed Lord Chancellor. By the beginning of the nineteenth century equity had been formalised into a system nearly as rigid as the common law itself. Further, in 1873–5 the Judicature Acts established the modern unified arrangements of courts which administer common law and equity side by side. The office of Lord Chancellor still exists and the Lord Chancellor now sits as a judge in the House of Lords (see Unit 2.1a)).

One important distinction does nevertheless remain. While a court must give judgment in favour of a claimant or defendant who shows that he or she has a 'legal' right (that is, a common-law or statutory right), it has a discretion whether or not to give judgment in favour of a claimant or defendant who can demonstrate an 'equitable' right only. The terms on which this discretion is exercised are laid down along with the other rules of equity in the so-called **maxims of equity** which are the distillate of the basic principles of equity.

Some of the most important maxims are:

(i) **Equity follows the law.** If a case is covered by a common-law rule equity will apply that rule unless to do so would be against conscience.

(ii) **He who seeks equity must do equity.** Equity will not aid a litigant unless he is himself prepared to act equitably towards his opponent.

(iii) **He who comes to equity must come with clean hands.** This is really another facet of (ii) above. Equity will not help a litigant if his own past conduct towards his opponent has been unconscionable.

(iv) **Equity is equality.** If property owned jointly is to be divided among rival claimants equity will favour equal shares unless there is strong evidence showing that one should have more than the others.

(v) **Equity looks to the intent rather than the form.** Equity will look to what the parties intended rather than to the precise wording of any document they may have signed.

(vi) **Equity will not suffer a wrong to be without a remedy.** We have already seen how the original function of equity was to fill the gaps in the common law.

1.8 Sources of law: Europe

'*Non*' was the general reaction of Charles de Gaulle, the then President of France, to the Conservative Government's application in 1961 and then also the Labour Government's application in 1967 for British membership of the Common Market. France feared loss of her own influence in the Common Market, felt concern for her agricultural profitability and viewed with distrust the special relationship between Britain and America. Such veto was in some ways ironic as the dream of a united Europe was very much that of Sir Winston Churchill who, in 1946, had spoken in terms of 'a kind of United States in Europe' in which, in the aftermath of the Second World War, past foes would unite for common security, peace and prosperity. In this way the tired and war-damaged nations of Europe could band together to form a trading entity which could compete with the might of the American economy, insulate itself against the blasts of the Cold War and find protection against the threat of attack from the Iron Curtain countries. The idea was seen by Churchill as:

> *one family of nations, banded together from the Atlantic to the Black Sea, for mutual aid and protection.*

However, immediately after the Second World War, Britain preferred to continue in her traditional approach to Europe and, as one of the triumphant nations in the war, continued to display the traditional trappings of a world power. It was only in the aftermath of the Suez debacle and her lessening status in the world that Britain sought entry to the Common Market in 1961.

a) Early days

The first major step towards the setting up of the Common Market had been taken in 1951 when, by the Treaty of Paris, the **European Coal and Steel Community** was set up. The organisation had been conceived by Jean Monnet in order to pool the mineral, coal and steel resources of France, West Germany, Italy, the Netherlands and Luxembourg so that these countries (the signatories of the Treaty) would be better equipped to compete against the American economy and, incidentally, less able also to build new tanks or battleships to use against each other.

In 1957 two further organisations were set up by treaty. These were:

1. the European Atomic Energy Community;
2. the European Economic Community.

The first, known for short as EURATOM, was intended to promote the peaceful use of atomic energy and the second is what we now call the European Community (EC), which was brought into being by the Treaty of Rome 1957 when it was known as the European Economic Community (EEC). This title was dropped after the signing of the Maastricht Treaty (and the promise of a single currency to replace the pound) in 1992. Nevertheless, the founding economic aims can be detected in the preamble to the 1957 Treaty when the signatories recognised that:

> *. . . the removal of existing obstacles calls for concerted action in order to guarantee steady expansion, balanced trade and fair competition.*

b) The workings

In order to carry out the work necessary to bring this happy state about, the Treaty established four institutions:

1. the Council of Ministers (since 1992 known as the Council of the European Union);
2. the Commission (after 1992 renamed the European Commission);
3. the Assembly (now referred to as the European Parliament);
4. the Court of Justice.

Each merits individual attention.

The Council

This is a group of ministers from each of the Member States and their representative is usually the Foreign Minister. Ministers with special areas of responsibility, such as agriculture or transport, may also meet their counterparts from other Member States in efforts to resolve differences.

At such meetings, usually held in Brussels, ministers will decide matters of great importance with the aim of ensuring 'co-ordination of the general economic policies of the Member States'. The Council is led by a President who holds office for a six-month term so that, as in the best children's games, everyone gets a go. Less flippantly, the Council issues regulations and directives as a means of implementing policy as examined below.

The Commission

Based in Brussels, this is a policy-making body which also carries out the decisions of the Council as the Commission's political master. The Commission also has a policing role as it is charged by the Treaty with the duty of ensuring:

> ...that the provisions of the Treaty and the measures taken by the Institutions by virtue of the Treaty are carried out...

In discharging this duty, the Commission has had to deal with a wide range of trading irregularities among the Member States such as price-fixing agreements for vitamins, the frustrations experienced by Britons anxious to save money by personal imports of cars from the continent and, as the lorries got stuck on the other side of the Channel Tunnel, France's barriers against British lamb. Figures published in the summer of 2000 suggested that France is the most persistent offender in breaching EU Directives and other rulings but the United Kingdom has not escaped scrutiny and adverse criticism, often for sex discrimination.

The Commission ensures that Member States carry into effect the decisions made in the Common Market by three means:

1. regulations;
2. directives;
3. decisions.

Regulations enjoy a general force and are automatically binding on Member States. **Directives** are also binding on the individual Member States but, unlike regulations, have to be brought into force (for example by statutory instrument, see Unit 1.6). For example, the Road Traffic Act 1988 introduced a requirement for minimum third-party property damage insurance cover of £250,000 in order to give effect to the second EC Directive on Insurance against civil liability in respect of motor vehicles in 1984. **Decisions** may be addressed either to a Member State or a person (either an individual or a company) and are binding on that State or that person.

Each Member State, therefore, has to take steps to make its own national law comply with European Community law. The United Kingdom is no exception and our national law is now necessarily subordinate to European law. The practical effect of this is examined later in Unit 1.8c).

The Assembly

This organisation is now more commonly known as the **Parliament**. The title, however, is a little misleading because the body does not fulfil the legislative function of the Houses of Lords and Commons at Westminster, with the keen party political spin and struggle where the protagonists are urged on by the party 'whips'. The European Parliament, rather, discharges a more advisory and supervisory function and carries out its work in a number of special committees, such as those on agriculture and transport.

Attempts have been made to increase the power of this Parliament and its function as representative of the political views of each Member State's citizens was strengthened in the summer of 1979 when the first direct elections were held. The United Kingdom is now divided into 87 different constituencies and a corresponding number of Members are sent to the Parliament. They are called MEPs to distinguish them from the Members of Parliament (MPs) elected to Westminster. In the mid-1980s Sir Geoffrey Howe QC, as Foreign Secretary, put forward British proposals which would increase the European Parliament's role in creating legislation, so that it could do more to influence the legislative process and would be more likely to be consulted before the Council of Ministers had the last word. Certainly, if the European Parliament does achieve all its plans for us we shall, in Europe, have a common driving licence, which would be sent through the post with a Euro stamp affixed to the envelope. We shall also be able to watch the victorious members of the European sports team celebrate their wins with a hearty rendering of a European anthem and watch it all on a European television channel – as one sceptic was recorded as saying: 'Can you imagine European television? . . . The Eurovision Song Contest every day.'

The Court of Justice

This court, created by the Treaty of Rome, sits at Luxembourg in a building now too small for its expanded work-load. The number of judges has also risen in line with the expanding European Community so that there are now fifteen. Each is drawn from one of the Member States and obviously they have different backgrounds with different training and languages. Each, however, shares the essential qualification required by the Treaty which requires that judges

shall be chosen from persons whose independence is beyond doubt and who possess the qualifications required for appointment to the highest judicial offices in their respective countries.

In this way, lawyers with a lifetime of practical experience in the every-day hurly-burly of courts in the United Kingdom will sit alongside other lawyers who come from an academic background. This is one of a number of differences between the European Court and our national courts where judges are traditionally appointed from the ranks of the practising profession and principally still the Bar (see Unit 2.5). The first judge to be sent to Europe from the United Kingdom was Lord Mackenzie Stuart from the Scottish Court of Session in 1973.

Judges of the European Court are appointed for an initial term of six years and are then eligible for reappointment. This again is in contrast to the English system where, once appointed, judges may sit until they reach the mandatory age of retirement.

A second difference is that a judge of the European Court can only be removed by the unanimous decision of his fellow judges and the Advocates General. In contrast, in England and Wales judges of the High Court may only be removed from office by petition from both Houses of Parliament, and circuit judges may be removed from office by the Lord Chancellor only on grounds of incapacity or misbehaviour.

The judges of the European Court are assisted by other lawyers, also of great distinction, who are known as **Advocates General**. It is the job of these lawyers to help the judges reach their decision by supplementing the arguments of the lawyers appearing before the Court to present their clients' cases. In this way the Advocates General fulfil the role sometimes seen in the English courts carried out by a lawyer who, in the more difficult cases, is asked to assist the judge by researching and arguing less clear points of law. This lawyer is known by the Latin tag of *Amicus Curiae,* which means 'Friend of the Court' and indicates that he or she is not there as counsel for any particular litigant but is in court to help ensure that the right decision is reached. The Advocates General are required to have the same eminent legal qualifications as required of the judges. It is then the job of the Advocates General, under Article 222:

> to present publicly, with complete impartiality and independence, reasoned conclusions on cases submitted to the Court of Justice, with a view to assisting the latter in the performance of its duties . . .

The first English lawyer to carry out such a role was Advocate General Jean-Pierre Warner who in 1981 was appointed a Judge of the Chancery Division of the High Court of Justice and, therefore, became known as Mr Justice Warner.

The importance of the role of the Advocates General is reflected by the inclusion of their arguments in the Law Reports of the European Court's proceedings which appear, for example, in the official reports known as the European Court Reports and the unofficial Common Market Law Reports where reports appear not only in English but also in Dutch, German, Danish and French.

The way in which the Reports record the proceedings before the Court affords some indication of the difference between the approach of the European Court and the English High Court. For example, the judges of the European Court simply put their names to one judgment only. This is in striking contrast to the way all our judges may give their own judgment, for example in the Court of Appeal. The English court's judgment is, therefore, reached by a simple majority which is revealed. The principle of allowing dissenting judgments can be seen all the more vividly in the House of Lords where three judges may decide to allow an appeal which the other two would have dismissed. Although it does not follow that in fact every judge in the European Court is in complete agreement with all of his or her colleagues, such divergence of opinion is not revealed in the final decision, for the judges sitting in their crimson robes appear to speak with one voice. The final judgment may often seem the product of a committee and invariably lacks the expression of dissent and the idiosyncratic style of some English judges whose approach often appears far less formal and much more spontaneous. This was traditionally the engaging style of Lord Denning who began his judgment in the last case he heard in the Court of Appeal (a case involving a contract for the sale of seeds) by quoting from Lewis Carroll's *Through the Looking Glass*:

> *'The time has come', the Walrus said,*
> *'To talk of many things:*
> *Of shoes – and ships – and sealing wax –*
> *Of cabbages – and kings...'*

The way the lawyers go about their work in the European Court is also quite different from England and Wales. Our system, often involving lay jurors, has traditionally attached great importance to the oral presentation of cases where the cut and thrust of argument by counsel plays more part than has ever been the case on the main continent of Europe. Although French has traditionally been the working language of the Court, the lawyers and litigants obviously speak a wide range of different tongues which is obviously a handicap to the English system of oral presentation. Instead, lawyers at the European Court are required to present their arguments on paper and may then only briefly supplement those written submissions by oral argument. Flowery styles of presentation and even the occasional mild histrionics are replaced by a more sober, more clinical – and probably duller – presentation of cases. One of the Commission's directives now allows lawyers of any Member State to appear before the European Court so that our bewigged barristers may now sit among the uncovered heads but grander titles of the *maitres* from France and the *doktors* from Germany. It would be possible for litigants to appear before the European Court without a lawyer but this would be a very rare event. A form of legal aid does exist although it, too, is rare. Although orders for costs are not always made, the Court does have power, as in England and Wales, to order the losing party to pay the costs of the winner. The first case to come before the European Court from the House of Lords was a case involving obscene films and magazines imported into England from the Netherlands. The case (but not the films) is looked at later on in this Unit.

Flowery styles of presentation...

c) The effect on English law

The United Kingdom's entry into the European Community was marked by the signing of the Treaty of Accession in Brussels in January 1972.

As a matter of law, treaties do not automatically become part of our national law (for they are signed not by judges but by politicians) and it was necessary for Parliament to pass the European Communities Act 1972 in order to give effect to our duties under the Treaty. The Act makes general provision for the implementation in the United Kingdom of EC law which is now supreme. Such supremacy is recognised by section 2 of the European Communities Act 1972 which provides:

> ... all such rights, powers, liabilities, delegations, and restrictions created or arising by or under the Treaties ... are without further enactment to be given legal effect ... in the United Kingdom.

No longer then does Westminster have the last word, although in constitutional theory at least it is open to a future government to take the United Kingdom out of the EC. It is a long-established principle of constitutional law that Parliament cannot bind its successors as each Parliament (each sitting of the House of Lords and the House of Commons) is said to be sovereign.

One immediately obvious effect of entry into the EC was recognised at the outset by the European Communities Act 1972 which had to deal with a fundamental principle of **company law**. When a company is formed, the activities which the company may carry on by way of trade are set out in a document known as the **Memorandum of Incorporation**. This document sets out the 'objects' of that company which in turn set out what the company may or may not do. If the company carries out some act which it is not authorised to do, such act has traditionally been said by the English courts to be **outside its powers** or, in the Latin phrase, *ultra vires*. Any act which was *ultra vires* was traditionally held to be void so that people dealing with a company had to be on their guard that the company was authorised to enter into that particular contract. If the company had not been so authorised, the other party (such as a supplier of goods) could not get payment.

Since entry into the EC, however, a company is now normally held liable for any action of its board of directors even if that act was, in fact, *ultra vires*.

Under the European Communities Act 1972 a person dealing with that company in good faith had new protection because section 9 provided that:

> ...any transaction decided on by the directors shall be deemed to be one which it is within the capacity of the company to enter into, and the power of the directors to bind the company shall be deemed to be free of any limitation under the memorandum or articles of association; and a party to a transaction so decided on shall not be bound to enquire as to the capacity of the company to enter into it or as to any such limitation on the powers of the directors...

This provision has since been re-enacted in the Companies Act 1985.

In February 1986 English law on sex discrimination came before the European Court. Helen Marshall, previously a dietician with an English health authority, had been dismissed from her work at the age of 62 years. Any man of that age would have been allowed to continue working if he had wanted to do so but Miss Marshall was dismissed on grounds of her age. The European Court found that this action by her employers had been in breach of a directive issued in 1976 on the equal treatment of men and women.

Sex equality was again the subject of complaint against the United Kingdom in the decision of *Drake* v. *Chief Adjudication Officer* 1986. Mrs Jacqueline Drake complained that the Social Security Act 1975 discriminated against her. She had been turned down for 'invalid care allowance' because she was a married woman living with her husband. Under the 1975 Act, this prevented her from receiving such state benefit even though the allowance would have been paid to a married man who was living with his wife. The matter was referred to Europe under Article 177 (since then renumbered) of the Treaty. The European Court was later to hold that the 1975 Act was contrary to the relevant EC directive on equal treatment of men and women and the United Kingdom government immediately set about amending the national social security regulations.

Generally, however, and in more routine matters, our entry into the EC has had a less immediately obvious effect on our domestic law. As might be expected from an organisation concerned substantially with trade and commerce, the first effects were seen in areas of law which affected commerce, trade and business. Slowly, the EC has been working towards harmonisation on laws affecting trade competition and taxation, including the European-conceived Value Added Tax (VAT) which since 1973 has been imposed on a growing range of goods and services, including lawyers' fees (condemned as a tax on justice) and fuel bills but excluding babies' nappies and, fortunately, law textbooks.

For the person in the street, the effect on English law of our entry into the Community long passed largely unnoticed because much of our domestic law remains untouched. For example, criminal law and family law were substantially unaffected because these laws stem from Parliament at Westminster and the English High Court. The incorporation into our domestic law of the European Convention of Human Rights is, however, likely to have an increasing impact upon even these domestic areas.

In contrast, in commercial disputes the impact was seen immediately. For example, in *Bulmer* v. *Bollinger* 1974 the courts had to consider a dispute over an EC regulation concerning the labelling of wine. The French wine producer, Bollinger, sought an order preventing the English cider makers, Bulmer, from using the word 'champagne' on their products 'champagne cider' and 'champagne perry' on the ground that the apple extract in question came from Herefordshire and Somerset and not, like true champagne, from east of Paris.

Lord Denning, sitting in the Court of Appeal, had to consider what effect the Treaty of Rome and the regulations made under it had on English law. He said:

> *The first and fundamental point is that the Treaty concerns only those matters which have a European element, that is to say, matters which affect people or property in the nine countries of the Common Market besides ourselves. The Treaty does not touch any of the matters which concern solely the mainland of England and the people in it. These are still governed by English law. They are not affected by the Treaty. But when we come to matters with a European element, the Treaty is like an incoming tide. It flows into the estuaries and up the rivers. It cannot be held back. Parliament has decreed that the Treaty is henceforward to be part of our law. It is equal in force to any statute.*

Lord Denning then considered section 2 of the European Communities Act 1972 (the Act that had taken the United Kingdom into the EC) and continued:

> *The statute is expressed in forthright terms, which are absolute and all embracing. Any rights or obligations created by the Treaty are to be given legal effect in England without more ado. Any remedies or procedures provided by the Treaty are to be made available here without being open to question. In future, in transactions which cross the frontiers, we must no longer speak or think of English law as something on its own. We must speak and think of Community law, of Community rights and obligations, and we must give effect to them. This means a great effort for the lawyers. We have to learn a new system. The Treaty, with the regulations and directives, covers many volumes. The case law is contained in hundreds of reported cases both in the European Court of Justice and in the national courts of the Member States. Many must be studied before the right result can be reached. We must get down to it.*

In certain cases the individual Member State may apply its own national law even though, at first blush, it may seem inconsistent with the Treaty of Rome. For example, Article 30 of the 1957 Treaty abolished so-called 'quantitative restrictions' on imports between Member States. The point was taken on appeal in *R* v. *Henn* 1980. Maurice Henn and another man had been convicted at Ipswich Crown Court of customs offences after they had imported obscene films and magazines from the Netherlands. This was contrary to an old nineteenth-century English Act of Parliament which forbade the importation of 'indecent or obscene articles'. This case eventually reached the European Court from the House of Lords but, when first under appeal in the Court of Appeal, it had been argued that since the United Kingdom was now in the Common Market this old 1876 statute was in conflict with Article 30 and was consequently of no force. Such argument found no favour with the Lord Chief Justice who had regard to the provision in Article 36 of the Treaty which allowed each Member State to retain prohibitions or restrictions on imports on grounds of 'public morality, public policing or public security'.

However, an attempt by Customs at Heathrow Airport to prohibit the import into Britain of what was described on the sales invoices as 'window display models' (but which the European Court's judgment described as 'inflatable dolls which were clearly of a sexual nature') was defeated. In *Conegate Ltd* v. *Customs and Excise* 1986 the European Court held that Member States of the EC could not rely on the Treaty unless those States had already legislated to prohibit the manufacture or marketing of those goods in their own countries.

In both *Bulmer* v. *Bollinger* 1974 and *R* v. *Henn* 1980 the court was asked to refer the case to the European Court at Luxembourg for a preliminary ruling on the relevant law. The court had power to take such a course under what was then Article 177 of the Treaty of Rome (now inconveniently renumbered as Article 234) which also empowers the European Court to give a preliminary ruling in matters of law concerning:

(a) the interpretation of the Treaty;
(b) the validity and interpretation of acts of the institutions of the Community; and
(c) the interpretation of the statutes of bodies established by an act of the Council, where those statutes so provide.

In fact, any court at any level in England and Wales has power to refer matters of law to the court at Luxembourg. Even magistrates took such a course in *R* v. *Plymouth Justices, ex parte Rogers* 1982 where the skipper of a French boat was prosecuted for using a fishing net which contravened EC regulations. The defendant asked the local magistrates to refer the case to Luxembourg for a preliminary ruling on the effect of the regulations. The magistrates agreed but the prosecution asked the Divisional Court (see Unit 2.1c)) to review this decision. Although on the facts of this particular case the High Court declined to interfere with the magistrates' decision, the Lord Chief Justice did express the view that this power of referral was rather to be used by the higher courts and that courts of this lower level should exercise considerable caution before themselves referring such a question to the European Court.

How the higher courts should approach a request of this nature had previously been considered by Lord Denning in *Bulmer* v. *Bollinger* 1974 when the French company had made such a request.

Lord Denning held that only the House of Lords (see Unit 2.1a)) as the highest national court was bound to refer such questions to the European Court. A judge has a complete discretion whether or not to do so but should only refer the matter if it is actually necessary to enable him or her to reach a proper decision. If such a referral is actually necessary the judge still retains a discretion whether or not he or she will, in fact, do so and should consider certain guidelines in deciding how to exercise such discretion. In particular:

1. A judge should ask himself how long a time may elapse before a ruling can be obtained from the European Court. That delay may do injustice in any urgent case coming before the judge if the parties have to wait many months in, say, injunction proceedings (see Units 4.19c) and 6.5b)).
2. The judges of the European Court should not have too much work thrust upon them if they are to get through their existing work properly.
3. The matter must only relate to a question of interpretation of the Treaty. It must not be mixed up with the facts. It is the task of the English courts to decide the facts. Any question of interpretation must, therefore, be clearly formulated.
4. The English judge should decide the matter himself unless the point is really difficult and important.
5. It should be remembered that the European court does not itself decide the question of costs (see Unit 2.7). How could it when it does not actually decide the case as a whole?
6. The judges should give proper weight to the wishes of the parties and should hesitate before sending a case to Luxembourg unless both parties agree.

For example, in *Church of Scientology* v. *Customs and Excise Commissioners* 1981 the Court of Appeal declined to send to Luxembourg a case involving the assessment for VAT on books sold by the Church of Scientology (referred to by the judge as the 'taxpayer') because it first had to be decided as a matter of fact whether the taxpayer was genuinely a non-profit-making religious or philosophical body (in which case it need not charge VAT) before the law could be considered further.

The Court of Appeal applied Community law directly to a claim for equal pay brought by a packer who worked for the Freemans mail order company. In *Pickstone* v. *Freemans plc* 1988 Mrs Irene Pickstone would have had no claim under national law as set out in the Equal Pay Act 1970 but she did have a good claim under Article 119 of the EC Treaty. Prior to the hearing, Mrs Pickstone and four other women working at a Peterborough warehouse were paid about £4 per week less than male workers doing what Mrs Pickstone claimed was work of equal value. Her employers had argued that Article 119 of the EEC Treaty was not directly enforceable in the courts of the United Kingdom and that, for that reason, Mrs Pickstone would have to take her case to Europe. The House of Lords, however, thought that the Community law was clear enough for the English courts to apply the European law directly in our national courts.

d) The European Court of Human Rights

It will be recalled that the dream of a United Europe grew in the minds of those who had lived through the Second World War. Across a continent ravaged by the slaughter of millions, a determination rose up to prevent any repetition and to ensure certain essential freedoms for the people of Europe. This resolve led to the signing in Rome of the European Convention on Human Rights in 1950. The United Kingdom moved swiftly to ratify the Convention and it is, therefore, somewhat ironic that the United Kingdom has so often been found to be in breach. By the Human Rights Act 1998, the Convention was finally embodied into national law and sent the legal profession back to school in order to learn about a new regime which will have a profound influence over domestic law, much of which may need substantial revision.

The 1950 Convention, which followed the earlier Universal Declaration of Human Rights proclaimed by the General Assembly of the United Nations in 1948, seeks to give all citizens in Europe certain inalienable rights and fundamental freedoms. The Human Rights Act 1998 now imposes on English law a 'duty to act in a way which is compatible with Convention rights'. For instance, everyone's right to life is to be protected by law as is the right to liberty (which is not to be taken away save in ways prescribed by law – such as imprisonment after conviction by a competent court). Even after conviction, the offender is to be spared torture or any inhuman or degrading punishment, such as the birch. The position of those who are merely suspected of crime is similarly protected by the requirement of a fair trial before an independent and impartial tribunal and with adequate time and facilities to prepare the defence. Individual freedom is further recognised so that everyone has the right to freedom of thought, conscience and religion, along with the right to join a trade union. Men and women of suitable age have the right to marry and to have children and also, within their families, to have their lives, home and correspondence respected. These issues are examined in detail in Unit 3.10.

In order to ensure that the parties to the Convention honour its terms properly, a new court, the European Court of Human Rights, sitting at Strasbourg, was established along with the European Commission on Human Rights. The Commission used to consider references for admissibility. Such a filtering system for complaints helped weed out the frivolous and the futile. For example, a complainant must first have exhausted all his or her national remedies and further must bring any complaint within six months. Since November 1998, however, all functions are discharged by the now full-time European Court of Human Rights. This court sits in four divisions. Plainly inadmissible complaints will be rejected by the committee. The plenary court will determine general procedure while a smaller court, the chamber, will deal with most claims. A small number of the most trying issues will come before the Grand Chamber.

While the State will always be the respondent, any person claiming to be a victim of violation may apply to the court. Decisions may lead to a change in a country's national law as was, indeed, the case with the trade-union legislation passed by the Labour Government between 1974 and 1979.

In *Young, James and Webster* v. *The United Kingdom* 1981 three sacked British Rail employees complained about their dismissal for refusing to join a trade union. The British Railways Board had agreed to a closed-shop agreement so that all its employees had to join a union, such as the National Union of Railwaymen (NUR) or the Associated Society of Locomotive Engineers and Firemen (ASLEF). These three employees objected to being compelled to join. Ian Young, for instance, did not approve of union policy on the nationalisation of industry, objected to being obliged to take part in strikes and was of a different political persuasion from those who generally allied themselves to the Labour Party. Previous freedoms about whether or not to join a trade union had been abolished by the Trade Union and Labour Relations (Amendment) Act 1976. When the three men refused to join a trade union they lost their jobs. It was perfectly plain that Article 11 gave each of them the right to join a trade union but did it also give them the right *not* to join one? The judges at Strasbourg held that the United Kingdom was in breach of the Convention because the stark alternative to these men joining a trade union was that they would all lose their jobs. Such compulsion, it was said, struck at the very substance of the particular freedom guaranteed by Article 11. This decision led to the passing of the Employment Acts of 1980 and 1982 by the Thatcher Conservative Government after its election in 1979. The first statute modified the previous government's legislation so as to allow greater freedom of choice about joining a trade union. The 1982 Act empowered the Secretary of State to compensate people who had lost their jobs for failure to join unions. For example, Ian Young and his colleagues were awarded £146,000 for having been deprived of rights and freedoms guaranteed by the Convention.

The need for English national law to match European requirements was further exemplified in the summer of 1987 when the United Kingdom's latest violation of the European Convention on Human Rights coincided with an outburst of national concern about the ease with which the Social Services on Teesside had been able to take children away from their families. Under our national legislation, the parents of any child so involved had no right to be heard or represented at the hearing or even to be notified of such proposed application. Once the order was made the parental rights were removed and entrusted to the local authority itself. In O v. *United Kingdom* 1987 the European Court of Human Rights held that procedures followed in cases where parental access had been restricted or even terminated had violated the European Convention. Not only had Article 8 been violated by the local authority's failure to respect family life but under Article 6 even the right to a fair trial had been breached. These and other aspects of the Convention are examined in Unit 3.10.

1.9 *Law reform*

Any viable system of law has to combine stability with aptitude for growth and certainty with a degree of flexibility. A set of laws has to adapt itself to changing social trends and to society's varying needs; moreover, since January 1973, English law has had to be brought into harmony with EC legislation (see Unit 1.8). A vigilant eye must accordingly be kept on our laws to see which are still relevant to contemporary life and which are ripe for reform. Such reform may be effected by a higher court over-ruling a decision of a lower court, by 'distinguishing' precedent (see Unit 1.5) or by statute. As we have seen, before 1875 equity was also an important agency of law reform.

Today, however, statute law is the principal agency by which the law is changed, either through public Bills (Bills sponsored by the government) or through private members' Bills, as we saw in Unit 1.6a. Reference was also made there to the extra-parliamentary **pressure groups** of which there are many. Both the General Council of the Bar and the Law Society, as the respective professional bodies for barristers and solicitors, will have an authoritative voice. 'Liberty' (formerly known as the 'National Council for Civil Liberties') is actively concerned with the rights of the individual as against the ever-increasing demands of the State and has made various stands against the growth of bureaucracy, increasing police powers and the trend to a general reduction in personal freedom. The police represent a powerful influence on legislation and the Police Federation has its Parliamentary spokesman to put forward its views. Such views are of great importance in forming Acts such as the Police and Criminal Evidence Act 1984 – it is less clear, however, whether the wishes of the criminal classes were similarly articulated during the passage of the Bill. The Freedom of Information Campaign achieved a measure of success in their resolve to cut down on secrecy in government when the Local Government (Access to Information) Act 1985 came into force on April Fools' Day 1986. 'Justice' (the British branch of the International Commission of Jurists) is concerned with respect for the rule of law and for personal freedom, both in this country and throughout the world. Other groups, whose primary activities may be less closely concerned with politics or the law, also try to bring the pressure of public opinion to bear upon Parliament when they believe that law reform is in the interests of their members. The main work of the Consumer Council, for instance, is the protection of the shopper against shoddy goods or services. The motoring organisations obviously are interested in all aspects of the law affecting motorists who remain both an easy target for the police and an open wallet for the Treasury.

Any government should be anxious to ensure that the law remains relevant to contemporary life but will need advice in deciding what reforms are required. There are now two principal sources from which such advice may be obtained, but some additional consideration of the historic perspective remains appropriate.

a) The Criminal Law Revision Committee

Now abolished, this standing committee had been set up by the Home Secretary in 1959. Whereas each Royal Commission (see below) is appointed to consider a particular topic and is disbanded after it has presented its report, the Criminal Law Revision Committee was a permanent body periodically issuing reports on a variety of subjects; for instance, its eighth report, *Theft and Related Offences*, led to the Theft Act 1968 and its thirteenth report led to the Theft Act 1978 (see Unit 3.6g)). In its seventeenth report, published in 1985, the Committee put forward proposals for the further reform of the law relating to sexual offences, not only rejecting the idea of licensed brothels but also creating new offences punishable by very high fines. An earlier working paper on *Offences Relating to Prostitution* had led to the Criminal Justice Act 1982 which, among other provisions, abolished imprisonment for women convicted of soliciting. The lamentable quality of some recent legislation in the arena of criminal law has prompted calls for the re-establishment of this distinguished body.

b) Royal Commissions

The government may appoint a Royal Commission to look into some particular topic. The membership of a Royal Commission usually includes both lawyers and experts in the topic under review and the Commission is generally referred to by the name of its chairman. For example, the Beeching Commission on Assizes and Quarter Sessions, chaired by Lord Beeching, led to the Courts Act 1971 and the creation of the Crown Court (see Unit 2.2b)). The report in 1981 of the Royal Commission on Criminal Procedure led to the Prosecution of Offences Act 1985 which, in 1986, introduced the Crown Prosecution Service. In the aftermath of the so-called Birmingham Six case (when in March 1991 the Court of Appeal quashed the convictions recorded against six men wrongly convicted of terrorist bombings and mass murder in 1974) the government sought to restore public confidence in the criminal justice system and announced a new Royal Commission on criminal justice under Lord Runciman of Doxford (see Unit 3.8). In retrospect, it may seem ironic that a body set up to limit the scope for further wrongful convictions was to see such a major recommendation as the retention of the citizen's right of silence dismissed by the Home Secretary of the day.

c) The Law Commission

The Law Commissions Act 1965 ('An Act to provide for the constitution of Commissions for the reform of the law') established the Law Commission. As had been the Criminal Law Revision Committee, this is a permanent body. Its members are to be 'suitably qualified by the holding of judicial office or by experience as a barrister or solicitor or as a teacher of law in a university'. They are appointed by the Lord Chancellor and their wide role is set out clearly in section 3 of the Act:

> It shall be the duty of each of the Commissions [there is also a Scottish Law Commission] to take and keep under review all the law with which they are respectively concerned with a view to its systematic development and reform including in particular the codification of such law, the elimination of anomalies, the repeal of obsolete and unnecessary enactments ... and generally the simplification and modernization of the law.

As with the Royal Commissions, the function of the Law Commission is advisory only and its recommendations become law only if they are adopted by Parliament to form the basis of an Act.

When considering a particular topic, the Law Commission first drafts a working paper setting out the aspects of the topic which it believes are of special concern and also setting out its provisional conclusions and proposals. Interested organisations and individuals are then invited to put their views before the final report is drawn up. For example, the Criminal Law Act 1977 was the result of the Law Commission's report, *Conspiracy and Criminal Law Reform*, published in March 1976. This Act imposed a statutory maximum sentence for conspiracy offences whereas the old common law had permitted unlimited punishment (see Unit 3.3b)). The Law Commission published its working paper (No. 82), *Offences Against Public Order*, in 1982, a year after scenes of mob violence and rampage as rioters took to the streets of Britain's cities, reviving memories of war-time *blitzkrieg* for some inhabitants of south London's Brixton. The Law Commission paper was, therefore, all the more urgent and its production was hastened, following as it did the call by Lord Scarman (who also produced his own report), for a restatement of the laws on public order. The working paper proposed a new statutory crime of riot which would carry a maximum sentence of fourteen years' imprisonment. These proposals were incorporated into the Public Order Act 1986 (see Unit 3.10).

In 1985 the Law Commission's report *Rights of Access to Neighbouring Land* proposed a right of householders to apply to the court for access to adjoining land if such access were required for essential repairs to that householder's property. Such recommendations were the subject of legislation in the Access to Neighbouring Land Act 1992.

In 1990 the Law Commission published its working paper (No. 116), *Rape Within Marriage*, and invited comment upon its proposal to abolish the immunity of husbands from prosecution for raping their wives. In the realm of contract law, the Law Commission Report on privity of contract led to the passing of the Contracts (Rights of Third Parties) Act 1999 further considered in Unit 4.14.

Following the Report of the Inquiry into the death of Stephen Lawrence the Home Secretary referred to the Law Commission one of the recommendations advanced by Sir William Macpherson who had chaired such Inquiry. The Inquiry had recommended that further thought be given to permitting acquitted defendants to be re-tried where fresh evidence was presented. In Consultation Paper No. 156, *Double Jeopardy*, the Law Commission further considered this issue and suggested that, as with convictions, acquittals should be open to review on the grounds of new evidence.

Further consideration to strengthening the hand of the prosecution in criminal trials is being given, at the time of writing, for the Law Commission's Consultation No. 158 *Prosecution Appeals against Judges' Rulings* which would allow the prosecution to appeal against rulings made prior to or during the prosecution case on matters such as admissibility of evidence or abuse of process, for example, by pre-trial publicity.

It is by means of such commissions and a healthy public concern and vigilance that, through the medium of Parliament, effect can be given to the dictum of the American poet and academic, Ezra Pound, that:

law must be stable yet it cannot stand still.

1.10 *Questions*

1. Identify the basic rules which a society will lay down to guide the conduct of its members. In what circumstances, and for what reasons, might individuals and groups feel justified in breaking the law?

2. a) State the operation of judicial precedent within the hierarchy of the civil courts.
   b) In respect of three of the following, explain the position where a previous decision by a court is:
      (i) reversed;
      (ii) over-ruled;
      (iii) disapproved;
      (iv) distinguished.

3. 'These are courts of law not of morals.' Is this a cynical abdication of the residual purpose of English law or a proper acceptance of the limits of the modern legal system in the lives of ordinary citizens?

4. a) Name three different forms of delegated legislation.
   b) Name three groups of persons or organisations who usually have the power to make delegated legislation.
   c) Explain how delegated legislation is controlled by:
      (i) Parliament;
      (ii) the courts.
   d) Explain why delegated legislation is necessary and discuss the disadvantages of this method of law-making.

5. With regard to European Community law explain the terms:
   a) regulations;
   b) decisions;
   c) directives.

6. Examine the extent to which membership of the EC has affected the sovereignty of Parliament.

7. What methods exist for changing English law?

8. How far do you consider that the needs of a changing society can be met by any existing mechanism(s) of law reform?

9. Last week Edward was convicted by the local magistrates of an assault occasioning actual bodily harm upon Timothy, who now wants to obtain compensation from Edward for those injuries through the civil courts. Which party will have to persuade the judge that his version of the facts is correct? How can Timothy's position be made easier?

2.1 *The civil courts today*

a) The House of Lords and Privy Council

We have already examined the role of the *Curia Regis* (see Unit 1.7) which fulfilled both legislative and judicial functions. As Parliament developed, the House of Lords – which had maintained a close relationship with the *Curia Regis* – took over the judicial role. By the fifteenth century it was established that the Commons generally did not interfere in the exercise of the judicial function. Later on, appeals from the King's Bench were sent to the House of Lords. Although the Judicature Acts 1873–5 had been intended to create a Supreme Court, political pressure caused the retention of the House of Lords as the ultimate appellate tribunal and, by the Appellate Judicature Act 1876, it was confirmed as the supreme civil appeal court.

The House of Lords is presided over by the **Lord Chancellor** who is a member of the government and usually also a former Member of Parliament. In debates in the Lords he has a function similar to that of the Speaker of the House of Commons. He is also responsible for the administration of justice and for the appointment of judges and of Queen's Counsel. In the law reports he is identified by the initials 'LC' after his name – for example, Lord Irvine of Lairg LC. It is this combination of judicial authority and political power in cabinet which has caused increasing comment recently to the effect that future holders of this great office of State may find it more difficult any longer to sit comfortably on a woolsack stuffed with so many different (and possible conflicting) responsibilities to discharge.

Appeals were originally heard by all members of the House of Lords who were advised by judges specially called in. Since the second half of the nineteenth century, however, lay peers have played no part in the judicial business of the House. When a lay peer last tried to vote, the solution adopted was as effective as it was diplomatic: his vote was just not included in the count. At the same time, legally qualified peers have by convention traditionally spoken in debates only on matters concerning the administration of justice. Recent speeches by some senior judges in such debates have often been trenchantly critical of the grasp (or lack thereof) of legal issues demonstrated by successive political administrations. In the summer of 2000, Lord Bingham of Cornhill noted that, mindful of their judicial role, such judges would not participate in debates where there was a strong element of party political controversy. The difficulty with this self denial is created by the way in which politicians have increasingly turned issues of justice, particularly in the criminal law, and the limitations upon public funding of the courts and those seeking access to them into matters of hot political contention.

Appeals in the House of Lords are now heard by the **Lords of Appeal in Ordinary**, the so-called 'Law Lords'. These judges must have been judges for at least two years or have a ten-year High Court qualification as defined in the Courts and Legal Services Act 1990. In practice, they are promoted from the Court of Appeal. Usually five judges sit together to hear the appeal and their opinions on the case under consideration are delivered in the form of speeches either for allowing or for dismissing the appeal. This, of course, means that an appellant's success or failure may be determined by a 3:2 vote. For example in *R* v. *Bow Street Magistrates, ex parte Pinochet Ugarte* 1998 the House of Lords had to consider whether, as a former Head of State in Chile, the General should be extradited to Spain to face trial for torture. Three judges rejected the claim for immunity while two judges had supported it.

Occasionally, the importance of a matter may justify a greater number of such judges as was the case in the decision in later proceedings against General Pinochet in 1999 when no fewer than seven judges considered whether a former head of state enjoyed immunity from prosecution. Issues of this nature may require considerable research and in the spring of 2000 the government sensibly decided at last to offer these judges some assistance from Legal Assistants who, in practice, are likely to be made up of some of the intellectually most able young lawyers qualifying each year.

The Administration of Justice Act 1969 introduced a new route of appeal designed to save both time and money and known as the 'leap-frogging' procedure. If the point of the appeal turns in part at least on the proper construction of an Act of Parliament the appellant may now by-pass (or 'leap-frog') the Court of Appeal, where a further appeal from that court would have been necessary in any event. This procedure may be used with the consent of both parties where the Appeal Committee of the House of Lords grants leave.

The same 'Law Lords' may also sit in a similar capacity as members of the **Judicial Committee of the Privy Council**. This tribunal hears appeals from Commonwealth countries (although with the passing of empire the number of such appeals is very much on the decline) and appeals from disciplinary tribunals of certain professional bodies (discussed further in Unit 2.4a)), such as the General Medical Council. The advice of the Privy Council is not binding on other courts but it is, of course, very strongly persuasive.

As appeals from Commonwealth countries have waned, issues arising from the devolution of the constituent parts of the United Kingdom have been entrusted to the Judicial Committee which now determines issues relating to the legislative competence of bodies such as the Scottish Parliament under the Scotland Act 1998.

b) The Court of Appeal

This court was set up by the Judicature Acts 1873–5 and now sits in two divisions, civil and criminal. Its constitution is now governed by the Supreme Court Act 1981 which provides generally for its administration. The Supreme Court Act is, however, a misleading title. Originally, under the proposed terms of the reforms carried out by the Judicature Acts 1873–5, the Court of Appeal was intended to be the one and only court to hear appeals. On that basis, it would indeed have been the Supreme Court. However, political pressures at the time decreed otherwise and led to the retention of the House of Lords as, in fact, the supreme court of appeal. Nevertheless, the title of 'Supreme Court' has been retained and is now taken as reference to the Court of Appeal, the High Court of Justice and the Crown Court.

Under the terms of the Supreme Court Act 1981, the Court of Appeal consists of ex-officio judges (such as the Lord Chancellor as head of the Judiciary, the Lord Chief Justice and the Master of the Rolls) and a number of other former High Court judges whose numbers are changed from time to time but who presently fill 36 other seats.

In practice, the court is staffed mainly by **Lords Justices of Appeal** who are not the same as the 'Law Lords' although the press so readily confuses them. A Lord Justice of Appeal is identified in the law report by the initials 'LJ' appearing immediately after the surname as with, for example 'Auld LJ' who, in private life, is not a Lord but is known as Sir Robin Auld and who, at the time of writing, is heading an inquiry into criminal procedure in England and Wales. The advent in April 1999 of the new civil justice system led to the recommendations of the Bowman Report which advocated many routine appeals being heard by just one Lord Justice.

The civil division of the Court of Appeal is presided over by the **Master of the Rolls**, who is not the keeper of a very large and expensive motor car, but is so called because he superintends the admission of properly qualified people to the 'Roll of Solicitors' (see Unit 2.5a)).

The civil division may hear appeals from the High Court, County Courts and some tribunals (such as the Employment Appeal Tribunal). It may also decide appeals on certain 'interlocutory' (preliminary) matters. An appeal may be brought on a point of either law or fact but, in practice, an appellate court is understandably very slow to interfere with a judge's finding of fact: after all, the judge who saw and heard the witnesses give their evidence is pre-eminently best able to decide whom and what to believe or reject. It is for this reason that, in practice, appeals are almost invariably based on points of law not fact. Further, the Court of Appeal is not readily inclined to allow fresh evidence to be introduced on appeal if such evidence could have been called at the first hearing. Further appeal may lie, with leave, to the House of Lords where there is a point of law of general public importance. A successful appellant would normally expect to recover the costs both of the appeal and also of the original trial.

The criminal division is headed by the **Lord Chief Justice**, currently Lord Woolf, and hears appeals from the Crown Court against both conviction and sentence under the provisions of the Criminal Appeal Act 1995 (see Unit 2.2c)).

c) The High Court

The High Court, created by the Judicature Acts 1873–5, is now regulated by the Supreme Court Act 1981. It consists of the Lord Chancellor, the Lord Chief Justice, the President of the Family Division and the Vice-Chancellor. The vast majority of the judges of the High Court (approximately 100 in number) are known as **puisne judges**. This term, which implies no adverse reflection on their physical stamina, is pronounced 'puny'. The judge is given the title of 'Justice', for example Mrs Justice Rafferty who is recognised in the law reports as 'Rafferty J' (where the capital J stands for 'Justice'). Such judges are now appointed from the ranks of all lawyers (and no longer exclusively barristers) who have held the relevant 'High Court qualifications' for ten years. The Courts and Legal Services Act 1990 paved the way for solicitors to appear in the higher courts and in February 2000 the first solicitor, now

Mr Justice Collins, formerly a partner in a large City firm, was appointed to the High Court bench. The basis on which judges hold their office is considered in Unit 2.5f).

The High Court sits in three divisions (the Queen's Bench Division, the Chancery Division and the Family Division), each of which has an unlimited jurisdiction and so may hear cases involving any degree of complexity or any sum of money. Each division requires separate study.

Queen's Bench Division   This is the largest division of the High Court and is the successor to the old common-law courts. It is staffed by the **Lord Chief Justice** (referred to in the law reports as Lord Woolf CJ) and about 86 puisne judges. A large number of judges is required because the division also staffs the Crown Courts (discussed in Unit 2.2) where the judges exercise a mainly criminal jurisdiction. The division enjoys three aspects to its jurisdiction.

1. *First instance.*   The principal jurisdiction of the Queen's Bench Division is in matters such as the larger claims in contract and in tort. Since the Administration of Justice Act 1970 the admiralty jurisdiction of the old Probate, Divorce and Admiralty Division (dealing, it was said, with 'wills, wives and wrecks') has been vested in the Queen's Bench Division. The case is almost invariably tried by a judge sitting without a jury.

2. *Appellate.*   Judges of the Queen's Bench Division also sit as judges of the Divisional Court to hear appeals on matters of law mainly from magistrates' courts. Appeals against decisions made by magistrates which are based on fact are dealt with by a rehearing in the Crown Court.

3. *Supervisory.*   The Queen's Bench Division may control inferior courts and tribunals by prerogative orders such as **certiorari** (literally, 'to be made more certain of'), which is an order used to remove a case from an inferior court for investigation. For example, in *R* v. *Farnham Justices, ex parte Gibson* 1991 the Divisional Court roundly condemned the unjust practice of country magistrates who had required defendants to give their evidence from the dock, instead of allowing them to give evidence from the witness box, as had the police witnesses. By the order of **prohibition** the court may restrain an inferior court from pursuing a particular course of action. Similarly, anybody arrested by the police or anyone else and held for an excessive period may apply to the Queen's Bench Division for an order of **habeas corpus**, which requires the police (or other gaoler) to produce that person at court so that the legality of his or her detention can be considered.

In these ways the judges show the continuing validity of the well-known dictum of Atkin LJ in *R* v. *Electricity Commissioners, ex parte London Electricity Joint Committee Company 1920 Limited* 1924 when he said:

> *Whenever any body of persons having legal authority to determine questions affecting the rights of subjects, and having the duty to act judicially, act in excess of their legal authority, they are subject to the controlling jurisdiction of the King's Bench Division exercised in these writs.*

These individual components are now part of the overall armoury today known as **judicial review** by which the courts can review the legality of actions taken by government, local councils and a wide range of other organisations such as unions and clubs. The procedure is regulated by the Supreme Court Act 1981 and follows the recommendations of the Law Commission's Report on Remedies in Administrative Law (see Unit 1.9). Such applications for review are heard by a special court consisting of two judges who sit as a **Divisional Court**. Applications for judicial review may be made on grounds such as:

1. want or excess of jurisdiction (as when an inferior court, tribunal or public authority exceeds its jurisdiction); or
2. where there is an error of law on the face of the record (as when a judge made a mistake as to law in the course of judgment); or
3. failure to comply with the rules of natural justice (as in cases such as *Ridge* v. *Baldwin* 1963 considered in Unit 2.4a)).

The roots of the court's approach in judicial review are to be found in a cinema in the West Midlands. In *Associated Provincial Picture Houses Limited* v. *Wednesbury Corporation* 1947 the local authority, acting under the Sunday Entertainments Act 1932, imposed a condition that children under the age of fifteen were not to be allowed into the cinema on Sundays. The relevant statute had allowed the licence to be granted upon 'such conditions as the authority thinks fit'. The cinema (or, as it was known in those days, 'picture house') contended that this provision was unreasonable and therefore *ultra vires* of the statute. In a judgment which was to form the basis for judging the reasonableness of all such subsequent decisions Lord Greene MR took a restrictive view of the power of the courts to declare decisions unreasonable and, accordingly, *ultra vires*. For such a decision to have been unreasonable the decision would have to be viewed as one where the authority or other decision-maker had 'taken into account matters which it ought not to take into account, or, conversely, has refused to take into account or neglected to take into account matters which it ought to take into account'.

This remains a strictly limited approach to decisions made by the State or a local authority as was underlined by the House of Lords in *Council of Civil Service Unions* v. *Minister for the Civil Service* 1984. The then government of Margaret Thatcher announced that those working at GCHQ upon intelligence work would no longer be permitted to be members of a national trade union. A number of those then employed at this government listening post sought to challenge the ban, complaining that the correct procedure had not been used and further contending that the employees ought to have been consulted. It could never be for the courts to decide whether the government decision had been a correct one: that was a matter of policy or of operational concern and not for the judges. Their job, rather, was to decide whether the correct procedures had been applied. As had been already said in an earlier case:

> *Judicial review is concerned, not with the decision, but with the decision-making process.*

In rejecting the complaints by the trade union, the judges went on to confine judicial review to three specified heads:

1. illegality, where the decision-making authority had been guilty of an error of law;
2. irrationality (a term now used instead of 'unreasonable'), where the decision-making authority had acted so unreasonably that no reasonable authority would have made that decision;
3. procedural impropriety, where the decision-making authority had failed in its duty to act fairly.

It is clear from the recent refusal of judicial review in *R* v. *Chief Constable of the North Wales Police, ex parte AB* 1998 (where the police had disclosed details about paedophiles living in the area) that the courts will not lightly detect irrationality in operational police matters.

In recent years the work of the courts in hearing applications for judicial review has received considerable public attention as, for example, at Easter 1986 when the Court of Appeal had to review the legality of the so-called 'political will' of the Greater London Council (GLC) when, in the weeks before its abolition, the GLC, under Mr 'Red Ken' Livingstone (later to be elected as Mayor of London in 2000) allocated millions of pounds of ratepayers' money to certain causes by way of grants which would benefit the recipients even after the abolition of the GLC.

Government ministers had also been on the receiving end of writs seeking judicial review as when the board-and-lodging regulations introduced by the then Conservative Government's Social Services Secretary, Norman Fowler, were challenged in the courts. Indeed, the importance of judicial review as a constraint on arbitrary, oppressive or unlawful government action is exemplified in the civil servants' booklet *The Judge over your Shoulder* which offers government departments advice on avoiding such judicial control.

In the *Council of Civil Service Unions* claim the unions were especially unhappy because it had long been standard practice for the employers to discuss with them any proposed alteration to working conditions. In these circumstances the unions had reasonably expected that such discussions would be held. The House of Lords held that the unions had had a 'legitimate expectation' of being able to discuss the proposed alterations. The House of Lords said that an aggrieved person was entitled to seek judicial review if he (or she) could show that a public authority had deprived him of some benefit or advantage which he had been allowed to enjoy in the past and which he would reasonably expect would continue at least long enough for him to discuss its withdrawal: in those circumstances it was proper for the courts to review the government's decision. The further denial by the same government of another 'legitimate expectation' in 1986 was also challenged in the courts. In *R* v. *Lord Chancellor, ex parte Alexander* 1986, barristers complained that the Lord Chancellor had wrongly broken off discussions about the low level of legal aid fees after the General Council of the Bar had submitted a detailed study prepared by accountants and when they had a 'legitimate expectation' that the then Lord Chancellor would consider the report and continue discussions about its conclusions.

Another decision of another Lord Chancellor came to be judicially reviewed in *R* v. *Lord Chancellor, ex parte Witham* 1997 after Lord Mackay, a member of the Conservative Government, had increased the fees payable by litigants upon issues of proceedings. John Witham, refused legal aid and still on income support, could not afford to pay the increased fee. He might have reflected on the provisions of Magna Carta:

To none will we sell, to none deny right or justice.

Mr Witham complained that the way in which the then Lord Chancellor had increased these fees deprived him, as a citizen, of his constitutional right of access to the courts. The Divisional Court held that the relevant Supreme Court Act 1981 had not conferred such powers on the Lord Chancellor to prescribe fees so as totally to preclude citizens from access to the courts. Lord Mackay's actions had, therefore, been *ultra vires* and unlawful. Laws J underlined the gravity of the step taken by the then government:

Access to the courts is a constitutional right; it can only be denied by the government if it persuades Parliament to pass legislation which specifically – in effect by express provision – permits the executive to turn people away from the court door.

On the other hand, shortly after Witham's case, the court rejected a similar protest against the cost of court fees in *R* v. *Lord Chancellor, ex parte Lightfoot* 1998. This time the Lord Chancellor (and, in effect, the government) had made Orders requiring debtors to pay a deposit of £250 upon presentation of a debtor's petition for bankruptcy. For Cleo Lightfoot, deeply in debt, the prospect of bankruptcy was to give her a fresh start but, ironically, in order to be rid of her debts she had to have some money. In a case supported by the Citizens Advice Bureau and others it was argued that as access to the courts is a constitutional right at common law such access could only be abrogated by specific statutory provision in an Act of Parliament. Whether by chance or not (and probably not) Mrs Lightfoot's complaint was heard by the same judge who had tried Mr Witham's complaint. Laws J concluded that his earlier decision in *ex parte Witham* had no application to the present case and was, therefore, able to distinguish the two cases on their facts. In Lightfoot's case there was a specific statutory bankruptcy scheme established under the Insolvency Act 1986. Such scheme was not concerned with the resolution of general disputes but offered only an administrative system to the problem of people, culpably or not, unable to pay their debts. Parliament was taken to have provided specific terms that a debtor should contribute to the costs of administering his own bankruptcy.

The decline of the Major Conservative Government saw a number of government ministers become the subject of much publicised judicial review applications. For instance, in *R* v. *Secretary of State for the Home Department, ex parte Bentley* 1993 the Divisional Court had to consider the refusal of the then Home Secretary, Kenneth Clarke, to grant a free pardon to Derek Bentley, hanged for murder 40 years earlier (see Unit 3.2). At that trial, the jury had made a recommendation for mercy but the Home Secretary at the time, Sir David Maxwell Fyfe, had decided, in the classic phrase, that 'the law must take its course'. The Divisional Court held that the Home Secretary had failed to recognise that the prerogative of mercy should be exercised in many different circumstances and, therefore, that the minister's failure could be reviewed by the courts. It was the view of the judges that the decision of the old Home Secretary in 1953 had been clearly wrong. Later that same month the new Home Secretary granted a partial posthumous pardon upon Derek Bentley whose conviction was later to be quashed in any event even if all too long after the event.

Chancery Division   As the name suggests, the principal judge of this division is theoretically the Lord Chancellor himself. In practice, however, it is headed by the **Vice-Chancellor** (whose name is written in the form 'Sir Andrew Morritt, V-C' where V-C indicates not heroism in the field of battle but the abbreviated title of Vice-Chancellor). The division is the smallest of the three and consists, in the year 2000, of only some seventeen puisne judges. No jury is present and the court sits in London. Its jurisdiction includes trusts, mortgages, the sale of land and company matters. The division has a limited appellate capacity from hearings of the Inland Revenue Commissioners, a body tasked with the determination of disputes between tax inspectors and payers.

Family Division   This is the most recently established division, having been created by the Administration of Justice Act 1970. There are about seventeen puisne judges headed by the **President** (where the new President, appointed in October 1999, was Dame Elizabeth Butler-Sloss, identified in the law reports as 'Butler-Sloss P'). Its original jurisdiction is a wide one covering, as it does, a field of human activity where so much can and does go wrong – divorce, nullity, disputes over the living arrangements for children and the financial disputes which can be the most bitterly contested part of a broken marriage.

There is also a limited appellate jurisdiction over decisions of magistrates' courts when these are sitting as 'family proceedings courts' to deal with matters over children and money where the issues are essentially very simple.

d) The County Courts

County Courts, which have nothing to do with any particular county border, were set up in 1846 to deal with small claims so that such disputes could be settled locally and cheaply. There are now over 200 such courts throughout England and Wales staffed by **circuit judges** who are appointed from lawyers, still mainly barristers, of at least ten years' standing. **Recorders** also sit as part-time judges to hear the very wide range of cases coming before the County Court. Usually, as in the High Court, the judge sits alone to determine issues both of fact and law. Very occasionally, however, a jury will be brought in to determine the facts, of cases involving complaints such as malicious prosecution, false imprisonment and libel. In such cases, the jury will be made up of only eight members and not, as in the Crown Court, the full dozen. The lawyers' speeches, however, are not shortened by one-third as well.

Since the Matrimonial Causes Act 1967, certain designated County Courts have had jurisdiction to hear undefended divorce petitions. This jurisdiction was extended in 1986 to allow the County Courts to try the few remaining defended divorce petitions. A great deal of a County Court's time is now given over to this family work, which includes not only the divorce itself but the wider and usually far more difficult range of ancillary applications covering children and their continuing contact with the other parent and the redistribution of the matrimonial assets by way of property transfer and periodical payments (known more commonly as 'maintenance'). Disputes involving children are heard at a smaller number of hearing centres where specially nominated judges are sitting.

Much of the litigation coming before the County Court is heard by the **District Judge**. Such judges cover a very wide area of work from most matrimonial financial litigation to disputes involving less than £5,000 and tried under the so-called 'small claims track', examined in Unit 2.6a).

Appeal against the decision of the District Judge lies – that is to say, there is a right of appeal – to the Circuit Judge. Such appeals are no longer the subject of a rehearing and are argued only upon submissions as to legal principles. From the Circuit Judge an appeal also lies to the Court of Appeal (Civil Division) but any such appeal is confined to arguments of law.

e) Magistrates' courts

These courts do not exercise any general civil jurisdiction as such, but rather fulfil certain minor functions of an administrative rather than judicial nature. For example, local licensing magistrates had long been regulating the grant of licences to publicans when, in the spring of 2000, the government announced a White Paper which proposed removing this function and leaving such matters to the relevant local authorities. Magistrates also enforce payment of the council tax imposed by local councils when hard-pressed house-holders prove unable or unwilling to meet such impost.

Magistrates also sit as a 'Family Proceedings Court' to hear simple domestic disputes between husbands and wives or other cohabitants over each other's conduct, their children or modest levels of financial provision. Magistrates also have power to make Orders by way of domestic violence injunctions under Part 4, Family Law Act 1996. However, although the Legal Services Commission (which replaced the Legal Aid Board) favours issuing proceedings before magistrates on the basis that their expenditure may be less, the reality is that solicitors generally prefer to issue applications of this kind in the County Court where these matters are determined by professional judges whose jurisdiction and experience are in each case greater. Applications by the local authority for Orders such as Care Orders or Supervision Orders may be heard by magistrates exercising their powers under the Children Act 1989 but guidelines exist for cases of this sort to be transferred upwards either to the County Court or to the High Court if such a hearing may involve length or complexity. For example, a conflict of expert evidence between doctors as to causation of injury may well justify transfer to a superior forum.

2.2 *The criminal courts today*

It should assist the student to consider both the hierarchy of the criminal courts and the procedure in the same sequence which would be followed by way of any prosecution. Almost all such proceedings would be started before a magistrates' court and sent, at least in some cases, to the Crown Court from where any appeal would be heard in the Court of Appeal (Criminal Division).

a) Magistrates' courts

The magistrates' court is the lowest criminal court. Formerly known as the **police court**, it handles far and away the bulk of the criminal charges. Prosecutions start in the magistrates' court and amply over 90 per cent finish there as well, very often upon an early plea of Guilty. In 1998 for example, 1,951,900 people were prosecuted before magistrates while in that year only some 77,794 stood trial in the Crown Court. There are hundreds of such courts throughout England and Wales although the current political will is to concentrate such sittings in fewer but larger court buildings. Critics of this philosophy that bigger is necessarily better have expressed disappointment that justice is less likely to be administered in the local community. Such philosophy is also to be seen in the recent reduction in the numbers of Magistrates' Courts Committees which cover the administrative arrangements for these courts. Further recent changes to the structure of these courts' administration are now consolidated in the Justices of the Peace Act 1997, which makes provision for the appointment and removal both of magistrates and of the clerks who must advise them. Each is now exempted from civil liability for acts done in the execution of their work.

Each court deals with a vast range of different charges in its local area, ranging from murder (which is before magistrates only in the initial stages) to being drunk and disorderly (which may only be dealt with by magistrates).

There is no jury in these courts and all questions of fact and ultimately of guilt or innocence are decided either by a number of lay magistrates (sometimes known as **justices of the peace** – a relic of fourteenth-century English high society and since then, at least historically if much less so today, a post filled by the local landowners and others of standing in the community) or by a lawyer sitting on his or her own and formerly known as a **stipendiary magistrate** (because he was paid a 'stipend') but now granted the grander if less fluent title of **District Judge (magistrates' courts)**. Lay magistrates need have no legal, academic or other qualifications at all although today some basic training is given to instruct them how to behave in court. Critics of this lack of expertise also point to the appearance of many benches as being middle-aged and middle-class, contending that such attributes fail to instill confidence in many of those upon whom they sit in judgment. The point is made with particular emphasis in the suggestion that ethnic minorities especially distrust such tribunals, perceiving lay magistrates as being insufficiently analytical in their treatment of evidence of the police (see also Unit 3.8). On the other hand, the District Judge (magistrates' courts) is a lawyer, appointed from barristers and solicitors of seven years' standing. The legally qualified magistrate sits full-time while the lay magistrate, in contrast, sits only part-time, and is unpaid other than by way of an allowance for expenses such as travel and subsistence. In London and other large cities, legally qualified magistrates sit in the busiest courts where the volume of work is greater and its nature more complex than in country courts, including, for example, extradition proceedings where another country seeks the return of an alleged criminal for trial in that land such as when Spain sought the removal to that country of General Pinochet. Proceedings of this sort of complexity and responsibility are not thought suitable for lay magistrates.

Those appearing before a judge will know the name of the tribunal who is to decide the matter. Traditionally, lay magistrates have presented a wall of anonymity. The High Court, however, has ruled that magistrates may not normally refuse to disclose their names. In *R* v. *Felixstowe Justices, ex parte Leigh* 1987 magistrates had refused to give their names to the press. Mr Leigh, a reporter with *The Observer* newspaper, complained and, in the Divisional Court, the judges (who were, as usual, identified) stressed the importance of open justice. It was said that for magistrates to shelter behind secrecy was inimical to the proper administration of justice. Further, said the court, it was an unwarranted and unlawful obstruction to the right to know who sits in judgment. In the words of Watkins LJ:

> There is, in my view, no such person known to the law as the anonymous J.P.

Whichever type of magistrate is sitting there is also a **clerk to the court** who may be either a barrister or solicitor. In practice, those clerks actually sitting in court to conduct hearings often have only a lesser qualification even though it is their responsibility to advise their benches of magistrates on all matters. At the time of writing in the autumn of 2000, the future role of the clerk is only one of many aspects of procedure being considered by Sir Robin Auld's Inquiry which is expected to introduce some of the most profound changes in the structure of the criminal courts since the Courts Act 1971. Early if only provisional indications are that recommendations may be made which would increase the jurisdiction and sentencing powers of these courts by increasing sentencing powers of district judges to two years. The corollary of such proposals would be that the role of the lay magistrate is likely to be correspondingly reduced and, indeed, much of the minor work presently undertaken by such magistrates, such as unpaid television licences and car tax prosecutions, would be removed entirely from the arena of the courts. So too, there has been speculation that the role of the clerk would be strengthened to something approaching that of a 'mini-judge' who would not only tender the sort of advice presently given, but would be encouraged to lay down firmer guidance on those hearings in which lay magistrates may continue to be involved.

In order to understand the procedure (most easily appreciated by a visit to a busy court) it is helpful to know something about the way offences are classified. In essence there are two kinds of criminal offence: indictable offences – the more serious – and summary offences, which are relatively minor:

- **Indictable offences** are so called because they may only be tried 'on indictment', which means in the Crown Court with a judge and jury. Murder, robbery and rape are all such offences.
- **Summary offences** may only be dealt with in the lower courts – common assault and drunkenness are such matters.

Not all offences are easily classified, however. Obviously charges such as murder are very serious while convivial intoxication is trivial. But what of theft? Shoplifting a packet of mints, while dishonest and certainly criminal, is hardly the sort of heinous offence which would merit the maximum penalty of seven years' imprisonment. In contrast, of course, the same degree of light-fingeredness in a jeweller's shop might net many thousands of pounds and an order of probation is less than likely. Offences such as these, which come before all criminal courts in their tens of thousands every year, have traditionally been open to trial in either the Crown Court or in the magistrates' court. They are known as **hybrid offences**. Such charges, said to be triable **either way**, have traditionally been tried by magistrates only when the defendant has given his or her consent to a summary hearing. Obviously, almost all those pleading Guilty would choose to have their cases swiftly heard by the magistrates and thus know their fate as soon as possible. Further, an early plea of Guilty at the first opportunity has long been seen as some of the best mitigation. This long-standing practice has now been placed on a statutory basis under section 152 of the Powers of Criminal Courts (Sentencing) Act 2000, which specifically requires the court to take account not only of the plea itself but also specifically the stage in the proceedings at which the offender indicated his or her intention to plead guilty. Such a plea is construed as indicating remorse, but, as ever these days, the saving of public money is further reflected in the discount which is traditionally around one-third of whatever sentence would have been imposed upon a conviction after a contested hearing.

On the other hand, those pleading Not Guilty have usually taken the view that their prospects of acquittal by magistrates are generally less and that trial in the Crown Court is a more professional and fairer determination. This matter is considered in greater detail in Unit 3.8.

Proceedings are often begun in the magistrates' court by a **summons**, which is an order of a magistrate inviting someone to attend court 'to answer the said information' – the allegation made in the wording of the summons.

Once the trial has begun the prosecutor will open his or her case dealing, if necessary, with any matters of law raised, and will then call witnesses, who may be questioned (cross-examined) by the defendant or any lawyer acting on his or her behalf. A defendant may choose to give evidence but cannot be compelled to do so. This is not always an easy decision to make for reasons examined in detail in Unit 3.7.

The court then gives its findings (after a retirement where lay magistrates are sitting) but only very exceptionally have lay magistrates given any reasons for that finding, perhaps on the basis, as has been somewhat cynically observed, that even if the finding is correct the reasons may be wrong. The procedure is described in more detail in Unit 3.8, but one effect of the Human Rights Act 1998 is likely to be an end to such unreasoned and sometimes apparently peremptory convictions without the giving of reasons.

As we saw in Unit 2.1, the appeal procedure depends whether the appeal is based on fact or on law. Appeals on fact are heard by the Crown Court where the case is reheard before a judge sitting with lay magistrates who play a full part in the decision whether to allow or dismiss the appeal. Where the appeal is dependent upon the view to be correctly taken of a matter of law (for example, whether a man can be properly convicted of stealing electricity when a fast-moving stream of electrons is obviously not the sort of stuff one can pocket) it is heard in the Divisional Court of the Queen's Bench Division by way of a procedure known as 'case stated'.

. . . whether a man can be properly convicted of stealing electricity.

Historically, a magistrates' court has also had another function: its members would sit as 'examining justices' to operate a filtering process for cases going to the Crown Court. A case could not go straight to the Crown Court. Almost all the cases heard at the Crown Court were sent there after a **committal** in the magistrates' court if the lower court was satisfied that there was a 'case to answer', that is, that the evidence justified a defendant being put to the anxiety and public or private expense of trial on indictment.

This function had, however, already been eroded over recent years before the new provisions set out in section 51 of the Crime and Disorder Act 1998 abolished such committal proceedings in indictable-only cases (charges so serious that only the Crown Court could try). Adults charged with such offences are now sent to the Crown Court forthwith and it is only at that court that the defendant can seek to argue that there was never sufficient evidence to justify such a course and the judge will then have to examine the evidence traditionally rehearsed before magistrates.

At this still early stage, the magistrates will also have to decide whether the defendant should await trial in the peace and quiet of his or her own home (**on bail**) or in the security, if not also the comfort, of Her Majesty's Prison (**in custody**); this, too, is discussed further in Unit 3.8. Appeal against the refusal of bail lies to a High Court judge or, under newer regulations, to the Crown Court which, since the Bail (Amendment) Act 1993, also has power to revoke the grant of bail by magistrates.

b) The Crown Court

The system of sending royal judges out into the country on 'general gaol delivery' (see Unit 1.7) and the holding of the **assizes** (sittings of the court) lasted many hundreds of years. For many years there were two different courts where defendants in criminal charges could be tried: the more serious charges were heard at the **Assizes** while the less grave allegations were tried at **Quarter Sessions** (so called because the court sat at least once every quarter).

It became clear, however, that the system had become outdated – for example, shifting populations had distorted the patterns of work. The report of the Beeching Commission led to the Courts Act 1971 and the creation of a criminal court of first-instance jurisdiction, known as the **Crown Court**. This forum is part of the Supreme Court and sits with a judge and jury. The composition of the Crown Court is also governed by the Supreme Court Act 1981 and by the Crown Court Rules made under that statute.

The court tries all serious criminal charges and sits throughout England and Wales. For administrative convenience, the country is divided into six circuits: Northern, North Eastern, Midland and Oxford, South Eastern, Western, and Wales and Chester. Each circuit is under the supervision of a presiding judge who is responsible for the smooth working of all courts in that circuit. The Crown Court sits at various towns and cities throughout each circuit, for example, on the Western Circuit from Bristol and Exeter to Bournemouth and Winchester, and these are further ranked in three tiers. The first-tier courts, for example those in Bristol and Winchester, hear the most serious charges, while a third-tier court, such as Bournemouth, hears more minor charges. This distinction is further reflected in the judges who sit in those courts:

- The **High Court Judge**, known popularly as the 'Red Judge', from the colour of his or her robes, is drawn from the Queen's Bench Division. Such a judge is addressed in court as 'My Lord' or 'My Lady'.
- A **circuit judge** also sits in the County Court and is addressed as 'Your Honour' regardless of sex. In practice, most Crown Court cases are heard by circuit judges.
- A **recorder**, who will be a practising barrister or solicitor of standing in the profession, sits as a judge on a part-time basis. Such a practitioner is also addressed as 'Your Honour'. Such posts are the first rung on the judicial ladder and have often been seen as essential appointments not only to train the next generation of judges but also simply to cope with the workload of the Crown Court.

For the purposes of trial at the Crown Court offences are classified into four groups:

1. offences which may be tried only by a High Court judge, for instance, murder or treason;
2. offences which are usually tried by a High Court judge, for example, manslaughter or rape;
3. other offences not falling within 4. which may be tried by a High Court judge, circuit judge or recorder, such as robbery;
4. hybrid offences which may be tried by any judge but which are usually tried by a circuit judge or recorder, for example, theft.

As already explained, a defendant does not come direct to the Crown Court but is sent there by the magistrates' court. Normally he (or she) will be sent to the nearest appropriate Crown Court but he can be tried elsewhere if there is such local outrage that jurors drawn from the neighbourhood might be prejudiced against the defendant. For example, the trial of those accused of the terrorist public house bombings in Birmingham in 1974 was held in Lancaster. Similarly, the trial of the so-called Black Panther on four counts of murder was held not in Yorkshire, where the dreadful offences were committed, but in Oxford. The family doctor, Harold Shipman, was convicted at Preston Crown Court of the mass murders of his patients which he had committed in Manchester.

The rules may appear a little complex but a straightforward example should help. Suppose that Tom is charged with murder. This is a 'category one' offence and must be tried in a first-tier Crown Court by a High Court judge or a circuit judge specially licensed to try such a case. Dick, on the other hand, is alleged to have been out shoplifting. Theft may be tried in a third-tier Crown Court by a recorder and so he will be committed to such a court, for example the Crown Court sitting at Croydon.

The judge also sits with a **jury** who will decide whether a defendant is guilty or not guilty. They must, however, follow the judge's rulings as to the law. It is his or her duty to deal with all points of law, to decide questions of the admissibility of evidence and generally to ensure a fair trial.

Jurors are now selected at random from among local residents who are old enough to vote in elections. After the abolition of the rule that only property owners would be eligible to sit on a jury the right to vote is now equated with the duty to serve on a jury. Some people are not eligible to sit on a jury – for example, judges, lawyers and the police. Others, including certain criminals, are disqualified and random police checks are now made to exclude such people from sitting as jurors. Others still may be excused jury service, for example Members of Parliament and members of certain professions, such as dentists and doctors.

When all the evidence has been heard the judge will sum up. The jury must then retire and consider their verdict. At one time the verdict had to be unanimous. Ideally this is still the most satisfactory verdict but, nowadays, if certain conditions have been satisfied, the court may accept a majority verdict where the majority is not generally less than 10:2. Instead of returning a verdict of guilty of the crime charged the jury may convict on a lesser charge; for example, in a murder trial they may convict the defendant of manslaughter. The process of trial in the Crown Court is examined in Unit 3.8.

Appeal, whether in respect of conviction or sentence, lies with leave to the Criminal Division of the Court of Appeal.

The Old Bailey   The Central Criminal Court was set up by an Act of 1834. It is better known as the Old Bailey, from the name of the street in which it stands. In fact, the building stands on the site of the infamous Newgate Prison, one of the less worthy monuments to British justice, or, at least, English law.

The Central Criminal Court is now a Crown Court exercising a solely criminal jurisdiction over the Greater London area and over offences allegedly committed on the high seas. The court sits almost continuously and is staffed by judges of the Queen's Bench Division. In theory, they may be joined by the Lord Mayor and Aldermen of the City of London and by the Lord Chancellor: in practice they are joined by a number of circuit judges, as in any other Crown Court. The only practical difference from other Crown Courts is that the circuit judges are addressed as 'My Lord' or 'My Lady' instead of 'Your Honour' and will generally try more weighty matters. There are many other Crown Courts sitting in London but the most serious charges, such as murder, treason and major robberies, are tried at the Old Bailey.

Topping the older part of the building is the famous statue, *Justitia*, the 'Lady of Justice'. In her right hand she holds a sword, symbolic of the authority of the law, and in her left hand are the Scales of Justice. Above the old doors are the powerful words now selectively adopted in modern legislation: 'Defend the children of the Poor and punish the Wrong-doer'.

c) Court of Appeal: Criminal Division

The existence of a criminal appeal court is of surprisingly recent origin and was, in part at least, the result of grave disquiet arising out of the trial of Adolph Beck. In 1896 Adolph Beck was tried at the Old Bailey for fraud. At his trial, no fewer than ten different witnesses identified him as the culprit. Beck was convicted and sentenced to seven years' imprisonment. It subsequently became evident, if only rather late in the day, that the witnesses had all been mistaken and that Beck was clearly innocent. He was subsequently granted a free pardon.

In 1907 the Court of Criminal Appeal was set up by statute and in 1966 this became the Criminal Division of the Court of Appeal. The court is staffed by Lords Justices of Appeal who often sit with puisne judges of the Queen's Bench Division. The Act distinguishes between appeals based on points of law and those based on fact. Appeals *on law* may be brought as of right. In contrast, anyone basing his (or her) appeal *on fact* (even only in part) must receive leave of either the Court of Appeal or a High Court judge before he may bring his appeal.

While an appeal is pending the court may release the appellant on bail. There is now power for the Court of Appeal to hear fresh evidence where it is expedient in the interests of justice for it to do so, always provided that the evidence is 'capable of belief' (and, therefore, a test no longer as high as the old requirement of being 'likely to be credible') and further provided that there is a reasonable explanation why it was not put before the jury at the Crown Court. In practice, most appeals are based on a misdirection or even non-direction by the trial judge – for example, by omitting to mention in the summing-up the ingredients which have to be proved (such as dishonesty in a case of alleged theft), by insufficient mention of either the burden or standard of proof, or perhaps by the introduction of some improper judicial comment either in the summing-up or at some other stage in the trial. It is, however, very difficult both in criminal and civil cases to appeal on the ground that the judge erred in the exercise of his discretion for, as Asquith LJ noted in *Bellenden* v. *Satterthwaite* 1948:

> *We are here concerned with a judicial discretion, and it is of the essence of such a discretion that on the same evidence two different minds might reach widely different decisions without either being appealable. It is only where the decision exceeds the generous ambit within which reasonable disagreement is possible, and is, in fact, plainly wrong, that an appellate body is entitled to interfere.*

The power of the Court of Appeal to allow an appeal *against conviction* is set out in section 2 of the Criminal Appeal Act 1995. The new test differs from those provisions contained in the old 1968 Act. Today, the Court of Appeal is enjoined to allow an appeal against conviction if it is thought that the conviction is 'unsafe'.

The expression 'unsafe' is not defined in statute. Its meaning, therefore, fell to be considered by Lord Bingham CJ in *R* v. *Criminal Cases Review Commission, ex parte Pearson* 1999 when the then Lord Chief Justice described the approach of the Court of Appeal in this way:

> *In some cases unsafety will be obvious, as (for example) where it appears that someone other than the appellant committed the crime and the appellant did not, or where the appellant has been convicted of an act that was not in law a crime, or where a conviction is shown to be vitiated by serious unfairness in the conduct of the trial or significant legal misdirection, or where the jury verdict, in the context of other verdicts, defies any rational explanation. Cases, however, arise in which unsafety is much less obvious: cases in which the court, although by no means persuaded of an appellant's innocence, is subject to some lurking doubt or uneasiness whether an injustice has been done ... If, on consideration of all the facts and circumstances of the case before it, the court entertains real doubts whether the appellant was guilty of the offence of which he has been convicted, the court will consider the conviction unsafe.*

It is of fundamental importance, however, constantly to bear in mind that the judges in the Court of Appeal do not try the facts of the case – that was done by the jury in the Crown Court. It is not the function of the judges in the Court of Appeal to overturn that verdict of the jury merely because they would not have convicted the appellant. This limitation on the powers of the Court of Appeal has been under sharp public focus in recent years as miscarriages of justice have been more widely publicised. One disturbing reminder of the risks of error is the case of Stefan Kiszko who, in 1992, was cleared of murder after spending sixteen years in jail. Fresh scientific evidence showed that he simply could not have committed the crime in 1975, however strong the evidence then available may have appeared. Also in 1992 the Court of Appeal took an unusual course, when freeing men convicted of the dreadful murder of a police officer in the 1985 Broadwater Farm riots, of expressing the judges' 'profound regret that the appellants had suffered as a result of the short-comings of the criminal process'. It was partly in response to worries such as these, together with limitations set out in the old Criminal Appeal Act 1968, that the **Criminal Cases Review Commission** was set up by the Criminal Appeal Act 1995. The need for such a further avenue of hope for those wrongly convicted and incarcerated had been underlined when the Court of Appeal recognised the constitutional primacy of the jury in *R* v. *McIlkenny* in 1991 when the so-called Birmingham Six again appealed against their convictions in 1975 for the IRA terrorist bombings in Birmingham in 1974 in which 21 people died and many more were seriously injured. Firstly, by 1991 there was fresh evidence which pointed to serious ill-treatment of the appellants by the police and which, therefore, affected the reliability of the various confessions obtained. Secondly, the police evidence as to when notes of interview had been written had been shown to have been false as a result of a new technique of electrostatic document analysis (ESDA). Thirdly, the once seemingly impressive scientific evidence had been discredited. It could not be established that the tests used by the forensic scientist had not been affected by all sorts of materials, even including soap. Such tests did not necessarily detect only nitroglycerine from bombs. For years there had been concern in the press about the validity of these convictions and previous appeals had been dismissed. Conscious of the widespread public concern which was to play a significant part in setting up the Runciman Commission (see Unit 3.8) the Court of Appeal took the opportunity of emphasising the limits of the court's role.

The judges emphasised that trial by jury is the foundation of our criminal justice system. The then relevant Criminal Appeal Act 1968 did not entitle the judges to say whether they thought a person was wrongly convicted. Their job was limited by Parliament to dismissing all appeals unless they thought either that the conviction was 'unsafe or unsatisfactory' or there had been a wrong decision on a question of law or where there had been a material irregularity during the trial. In that particular appeal, of course, the judges regarded the new evidence as discrediting the original scientific evidence and as showing that the police evidence at trial had been so unreliable that the convictions were indeed 'unsafe and unsatisfactory' (a test now watered down).

If the court allows the appeal it may also quash (*not* as some people say 'squash'!) the conviction, with the result that the appellant will go free with no stain on his character. Alternatively, the court may substitute a conviction for a lesser offence or order a retrial in cases where it is in the interest of justice for the appellant to stand trial again so that he or she is not acquitted on some singularly unmeritorious technical defect. On occasion, even though the point raised in the appeal has been decided in favour of the appellant, the court may nevertheless dismiss the appeal 'if they consider that no miscarriage of justice has actually occurred' – for example, where a person is so manifestly guilty that the jury would have convicted anyway.

A person sentenced by a judge of the Crown Court may also appeal *against the sentence* passed upon him if the Court of Appeal grants leave to do so. A convicted person may appeal against the sentence on the ground that the judge passed a sentence not justified by law (for example, sentencing a boy of thirteen years to a term of imprisonment), or where the judge has sentenced on the wrong factual basis or where, and most importantly, the sentence was either 'wrong in principle' or 'manifestly excessive'. It would be wrong in principle for a judge to send a little old lady to Holloway prison for her very first conviction for theft of a tin of baked beans. Even if she had been in trouble before it would still be manifestly excessive for that elderly shoplifter to be sentenced to the maximum of seven years' imprisonment for theft of that same tomato-flavoured carbohydrate.

. . . a conviction for theft of a tin of baked beans.

Within these principles, however, a trial judge rightly has considerable discretion. It follows that even if a sentence is at the top end of the range for a particular offence the Court of Appeal will not intervene unless the sentence was 'manifestly' excessive. If the Court of Appeal decides that the original sentence was so excessive the judges may

(a) quash any sentence or order which is the subject of appeal; and

(b) in place of it pass such sentence or make such order as they think appropriate for the case and as the court below had power to pass or make when dealing with . . . that offence.

A further appeal by either the prosecution or defence lies to the House of Lords but only if a point of law of such general importance is involved that either the Court of Appeal or House of Lords is of the opinion that it ought to be considered by the Lords. Although it is still the general rule that the prosecution at the Crown Court cannot appeal against a jury's acquittal there is power under the Criminal Justice Act 1972 for the Attorney-General (see Unit 2.5d)) to refer a point of law to the Court of Appeal for its consideration. Section 36 of this Act provides:

> Where a person tried on indictment has been acquitted (whether in respect of the whole or part of the indictment) the Attorney-General may, if he desires the opinion of the Court of Appeal on a point of law which has arisen in the case, refer that point to the court, and the court shall, in accordance with this section, consider the point and give their opinion on it.

This then novel proposition topic was discussed by Lord Widgery CJ in *Re Attorney-General Reference* 1974 where he said:

> *Again one observes that for the first time the prosecution is given a limited right of appeal on a point of law following an acquittal on indictment, a right which the prosecution has enjoyed in magistrates' courts for many years but it is a novelty in the Crown Court. The Act and the rules made under it go to great length to ensure that the accused in the court below, who on this hypothesis has been acquitted, shall not be prejudiced by the fact that the Attorney-General seeks the opinion of this court on a point of law.*

The prosecution also now has the right to argue that a particular sentence was 'unduly lenient'. Such power was conferred by section 36 of the Criminal Justice Act 1988 which empowers the Court of Appeal to quash the original sentences and substitute 'such sentence as they think appropriate for the case and as the court below had power to pass'. The power was first used to double to six years' imprisonment the sentence upon a father who had abused his two daughters. As is now common, the Court of Appeal took that opportunity to lay down 'sentencing guidelines' for the assistance of other judges who will have to deal with such men. Shortly thereafter, the Court of Appeal imposed prison sentences on two drivers who, having caused death by reckless driving, had earlier been able to leave the Crown Court free men. Upon reference to the Court of Appeal by the Attorney-General, the court may then pass any sentence which had previously been open to the judge in the Crown Court.

2.3 Special courts

There are still a few courts which perform special functions and which do not form part of the regular court hierarchy.

a) Coroners' courts

The office of **coroner** probably dates back to the twelfth century. Originally, coroners were members of the King's local administrative and judicial team and the word is itself derived from the medieval word *coronne* – a crown. Paradoxically, however, a coroner was elected to this office by the then equivalent of the county council; so, too, today, he (or she) is appointed by the county council although no one may dismiss him except the Lord Chancellor and then only for inability or misbehaviour. He may be a barrister, a solicitor or a doctor but in any case he must be of not less than five years' standing in his profession. His appointment is often on a part-time basis.

The coroner's principal duty nowadays is to inquire into the circumstances and cause of death of corpses found in the area for which he is responsible. In this sense it has humorously been said that the coroner is the person responsible for all the unnatural deaths in the area. He may hold an **inquest** (inquiry) into the circumstances of any death and he must do so where it appears that the death was violent or unnatural or that it occurred in prison. Usually the coroner will summon a jury consisting of between seven and eleven 'good and lawful men' who must return a verdict as to the cause of death – such as death by natural causes, misadventure (accident), suicide or murder. The verdict may be by a majority vote providing that there are not more than two dissidents. In practice, the jury is most strongly influenced in its deliberations by the coroner's summing up of the evidence.

Until some years ago the coroner's court had power, like that traditionally given to magistrates, to commit a person for trial in the Crown Court on a charge of homicide. The last occasion when this power was exercised was in June 1975 when Lord Lucan was committed (albeit in his absence) for trial on a charge of murdering his children's nanny at the end of 1974. This old power was removed by section 56 of the Criminal Law Act 1977 which now provides:

> At a coroner's inquest touching the death of a person who came by his death by murder, manslaughter or infanticide, the purpose of the proceedings shall not include the finding of any person guilty of murder, manslaughter or infanticide; and accordingly a coroner's inquisition shall in no case charge a person with any of those offences.

It is important to remember that a coroner's court conducts an inquest and not a trial. The aim of the court is not to decide guilt or innocence or civil liability but to answer the questions: 'Whose body is this?' and 'How, when and where did he die?' Accordingly, the approach is less formal than in other courts and, in particular, the rules of evidence are relaxed. Even so, interested parties (for example, the deceased's widow or former employer) may be legally represented.

The work of a coroner's court usually attracts little public interest. Consideration of death on the road may be followed by an investigation into fatal accidents on the factory floor. In recent years, however, the role of the coroner has become better known to the public because of the publicity given to various controversial inquests such as that in 1980 of Blair Peach who died when allegedly struck by a police officer at a demonstration against the National Front or that in 1983 of James Kelly who died in police custody in Liverpool. In each case the jury returned verdicts of 'misadventure'. The loss of the Townsend Thoresen ferry, *Herald of Free Enterprise*, which capsized at Zeebrugge in March 1987, led in October 1987 to individual verdicts of 'unlawful killing' of nearly 200 people who died in the tragedy. By their verdict the jury were clearly very critical of the safety standards in a ship which had sailed out of harbour with her bow doors still open. In the spring of 1991 the jury at the inquest into the Hillsborough Stadium disaster (when, in April 1989, 95 Liverpool football fans were crushed to death after the police ordered a perimeter gate to be opened) returned a verdict of accidental death. Disasters on this scale and as also seen in the Thames collision between the *M.V. Bowbell* and the *M.V. Marchioness* in August 1989 when 51 young partygoers drowned, have underlined that coroner's inquests are intended to fulfil neither the role of a criminal court nor of the public inquiry demanded by the relatives of those who died that dreadful summer evening on London's river.

When, on all the evidence, the cause of death is still not clear, the jury may return an **open verdict**, which is one making no particular finding. Such a verdict was returned at the inquest into the deaths of thirteen young people at New Cross, London, in January 1981 when the house, at which they were enjoying an all-night party, caught fire.

Such a verdict was finally returned by the jury in the controversial and much publicised inquest that was held in Leeds in 1982 into the mysterious death in 1979 of a young nurse, Helen Smith, who died after attending an illegal drinks party at a doctor's flat in Jeddah, Saudi Arabia. There had long been widespread rumours of a cover-up into the true background to her death with suggestions of rape and murder.

Initially, the coroner had refused to hold any inquest. He had said that, as the death had occurred in Saudi Arabia, it was outside his jurisdiction. Eventually, the Court of Appeal rejected this restrictive view of a coroner's duty. In *R* v. *West Yorkshire Coroner, ex parte Smith* 1982 the Court of Appeal held that the coroner had no choice in the matter – rather, it was his duty to hold an inquest whether the cause of death had arisen within his jurisdiction or not. The role of the coroner's court was described by Donaldson LJ:

> ...*the presence of a dead human body in this country is a factor of significance. It creates a very real and legitimate interest in holding an inquiry and this interest is in no way extra-terrestrial. In the absence of a death certificate by an appropriate authority in this country it may well be considered essential at the very least to ascertain where the body came from, whether the deceased died in this country and, if*

so, how. The public interest centres on the body which is in this country, on the cause of the death of that body and only incidentally on where that cause or the death itself occurred.

Although it is an inferior court of record, there is still the power to punish contempt in the face of the court. Outbursts in court can, therefore, lead to the coroner imposing a fine, as when Helen Smith's father, a former police officer, was fined for contempt as, sitting in court one day, he accused one of the witnesses at the inquest of murdering his daughter.

The search for the truth was made less speedy or certain by the lack of witnesses who might reasonably have been expected to be in a position to throw some light on the relevant events that night in the spring of 1979. More recently, the public unease at the sight of a number of youths walking away from the inquest into the murder of Stephen Lawrence without giving evidence underlined the limitations on powers as well as the role of a coroner's court. Some would now advocate that high-profile cases such as these might be better investigated by a judge.

Until recently, the coroner had also been responsible for inquiring into the ownership of goods or valuables found in his area. If the true owner of the goods could not be identified the coroner would hold an inquest to determine whether the item in question was **treasure trove** (*trove* is a low-French word meaning 'found' so the phrase simply meant 'treasure that has been found'). Traditionally, a somewhat curious rule would have been applied. If it were the case that the original owner had simply lost the valuables they could then be taken by the finder ('finders keepers'). On the other hand, if the original owner was found to have hidden the valuables deliberately and then, perhaps, died of plague or lost his head on the scaffold before he was able to collect them, the valuables would be taken by the Crown as treasure trove. The old concept of treasure trove came to be abolished by the Treasure Act 1996 which substituted a statutory definition of treasure which is uncommonly complex and unhelpful. Under the new legislation, treasure is:

any object which is 300 years old when found which –

(i) is not a coin but has metallic content of which at least 10% by weight is precious metal;
(ii) when found, is one of at least two coins in the same find which are at least 300 years old at that time and have that percentage of precious metal; or
(iii) when found, is one of at least ten coins in the same find which are at least 300 years old at that time; . . .

The rest of this definition is not spelt out in this text but it is perhaps worth noting that it may certainly be taken to include everything that was formerly treasure trove. Under the Act, a person who finds an object which is treasure must notify the coroner of the find. The coroner will then hold an inquest which, under the new legislation, is to be held without a jury unless the coroner orders otherwise. Once again, one sees the abolition of juries in this jurisdiction as in increasing areas of the criminal law.

There is no appeal from the verdict of the coroner's court. After all, how could there be when the proceedings are by way of inquiry and not of trial? Even so, the conduct of the inquest may be called into question in the High Court by means of an application for an order of certiorari (see Unit 2.1).

Collectors of useless information will be interested to know that the Lord Chief Justice and judges of the High Court are also entitled to sit as coroners.

b) Youth courts

It has long been thought that although a sixteen-year-old youth may not be too young to go shoplifting, to hit old ladies over the head with iron bars, or to throw stones through the windows of shopkeepers so short-sighted as to establish their businesses near football stadia, he is certainly too young to stand trial in the ordinary courts.

For this reason, anyone under the age of eighteen years who is charged with any offence (except homicide) will in general appear in the local youth court (formerly called a **juvenile court**). This is staffed from the same panel who sit in the magistrates' courts but the following special rules apply:

1. A youth court may not sit within one hour of an ordinary magistrates' court having been held in the same building. Ideally, the youth court should sit in a separate building.
2. The magistrates who sit in the youth court, appointed because of their experience of and interest in children, receive extra training.
3. There must be at least one member of each sex on the bench.
4. The press is severely limited in reporting and the public is not allowed into court.
5. To make things more homely, policemen attending may be told not to come in full uniform.
6. The child's parents must also attend unless the court is satisfied that it would be unreasonable to require such attendance.

If the magistrates are satisfied that the 'young person' did commit the offence they do not 'convict' him or her but instead record a **finding of guilt**. People who play with words do get up to some antics! The court is limited in the action it may take but after considering the available reports, including the school report which is usually before it, it may order a fine (possibly to be paid by the parents), probation or a period of community service or any form of discharge. It does not have power to send a miscreant to prison, although it may commit him or her to the Crown Court for the judge to use his greater powers of punishment.

As mentioned earlier, the youth court does not have jurisdiction to try cases of homicide (murder and manslaughter). At the time of writing the appropriateness of trying young people in the Crown Court has recently been called into question by the European Court of Human Rights. In *T* v. *United Kingdom* 2000 the court found that Article 6 of the Convention for the Protection of Human Rights and Fundamental Freedoms had been breached when two boys, aged 10 at the time of the offence and 11 at the date of trial, were tried in the Crown Court for murder. In 1993, a two-year-old toddler, James Bulger, was abducted from a Liverpool shopping centre. Jon Venables and Robert Thompson carried out a brutal murder which revulsed the nation. Special measures had been put in place during the trial to take account of the ages of these two young murderers. Each was only just over the minimum age of criminal responsibility of ten years. After conviction of the murders each boy complained to the European Court on a number of grounds and with varying success before the seventeen judges who heard the complaint. The court ruled that the trial of these children in an adult court room, against the background of national publicity, had amounted to a breach of Article 6 so that the boys had been denied a fair trial. The court said that it considered it essential that a child charged with an offence should be dealt with in a manner which took full account of his age, level of maturity and intellectual and emotional capacities. Steps had to be taken to promote the young defendant's ability to understand and participate in the proceedings. This might, said the court, mean that it would be necessary to conduct the hearing in private so as to reduce as far as possible any feelings of intimidation or inhibition on the part of the child. The three-week trial in the Crown Court with its attendant blaze of publicity was criticised by the court with the observation that the formality and rituals of the Crown Court must have seemed incomprehensible and intimidating for a child of eleven years. The first steps towards reform were taken in February 2000 when the Lord Chief Justice issued a Practice Direction for children and young persons being tried in the Crown Court which was intended to ensure child-friendly hearings so that, for example, the defendant should be allowed to sit with his family and the lawyers should not be robed.

c) Courts martial

These courts deal with offences allegedly committed by members of the armed forces. Their jurisdiction extends to offences under the general law applicable to all citizens and not only to those under the regulations as to military discipline applicable only to servicemen or women. However, if a serious offence under the general law is charged, the trial will be conducted in the Crown Court in the usual way. At the other end of the scale, minor transgressions of service regulations may be dealt with summarily by a senior officer. The position of the individual serviceman or woman has recently been improved by the Armed Forces Discipline Act 2000 which has introduced an appeal from such summary determination to a new body, the 'summary appeal court', which sits to hear appeals against finding or sentence and is staffed both by serving officers and a Judge Advocate.

There is no jury in a court martial. Instead the defendant appears before a tribunal composed of between three and nine officers. They are assisted by a **judge advocate**, a lawyer whose duty it is to advise the officers on law and procedure. His or her role is, therefore, similar to that of a judge in the Crown Court. In practice, a number will have held commissions with the legal departments of the services such as the Army Legal Service. Officers from these services will conduct the prosecution against the defendant who may be represented by civilian lawyers.

Soldiers and airforce personnel facing trial before a court martial will be tried either before a General Court Martial (at least four military members plus the judge advocate) or a District Court Martial, which need have only two military members and has lesser powers of sentence. The fact, however, that the Armed Forces prosecute and try their members led to a recent complaint to the European Court that such court martial was not an 'impartial tribunal' for the purposes of Article 6 of the European Convention on Human Rights. In *Findlay* v. *United Kingdom* 1997 concern was expressed that a court martial was insufficiently separated from the military chain of command properly to be viewed as an impartial tribunal. For example, the Convening Officer (a high-ranking officer) was responsible for the decision to prosecute, for selecting the charges, for the conduct of the prosecution and even for the selection of the members of the court (who might well be junior officers under his command). Findings and sentence were also subject to confirmation by the same military hierarchy. It is important to note, in fairness, that the findings did not indicate actual bias or any lack of impartiality. The criticisms centred upon a system conceived many years earlier and designed to operate in field conditions where lawyers may not readily be found. The response was to introduce the Armed Forces Act 1996 which, in creating new bodies, has clarified the separate functions involved in military justice.

Soldiers convicted of military offences may be subject to a range of punishments such as reduction in rank (a penalty reducing the offender not only in status but substantially in income), fine, reprimand or stoppage of pay.

It is less widely known that courts martial may also try the civilian dependants of members of the Armed Forces and in *R* v. *Martin* 1998 the House of Lords rejected an appeal where it was said on behalf of a nineteen-year-old civilian that he should have been tried not before a General Court Martial but rather in the Crown Court upon the allegation of murder.

A conviction in a court martial may be upset in three ways:

1. No finding of guilt, and no sentence, becomes effective until it is confirmed by the defendant's commanding officer.
2. If the court martial exceeds its jurisdiction the High Court may intervene by way of certiorari, prohibition or habeas corpus (see Unit 2.1).
3. The defendant may appeal (against conviction but not against sentence) to the Courts Martial Appeal Court, which is of equal status with the Court of Appeal. Further appeal lies to the House of Lords, subject to the usual conditions.

2.4 *Tribunals and arbitration*

a) Tribunals

In the twentieth century there was an increasing amount of interference by governments into the life of the citizen. Such interference leads inexorably to the risk of dispute. The existing court structure was already overloaded. What was required was a quick, cheap and convenient system of settlement, staffed by people who knew about the complex questions raised in those disputes which stemmed from such State control. The solution adopted was the **tribunal**. Throughout the country there are scores of different tribunals specialising in various fields, ranging from taxation to the purchase of land and the renting of flats or houses.

The complexity of the procedure varies with the nature of the dispute but as a general rule tribunals aim to do their work with relative informality. The men and women who make up the tribunal are not necessarily lawyers, although many tribunals are headed by barristers or solicitors: indeed, they may be appointed by the ministry which regulates the particular area of governance in dispute. The members may also be qualified in their own particular capacity so that, for example, surveyors sit on Rent Tribunals.

The way in which these tribunals fit into the court structure is a matter on which not everyone is agreed. The Franks Committee concluded in 1957 that they are:

> not ordinary courts but neither are they appendages of government departments.

At the time of writing a further inquiry into the workings of tribunals (which currently determine about half a million applications each year) is being held under the chairmanship of retired High Court judge, Sir Andrew Leggatt.

One difficulty which this new inquiry may have to consider is that such tribunals do not constitute any part of the regular court system by way, for example, of hierarchy or precedent but they are nevertheless subject to control by the courts.

The Lands Tribunal

This is one of the more specialised tribunals. It deals with disputes over the amount of compensation to be paid when a person's land has been subjected to compulsory acquisition – for example, where someone's house has been bulldozed away to make way for a motorway. The importance of this tribunal is reflected, in part at least, by having a judge as its president.

The same tribunal sits in an appellate capacity to hear appeals from Valuation Tribunals where there has been a dispute as to the value of commercial property and against determinations by Leasehold Valuation Tribunals in matters such as service charges.

Mental Health Review Tribunal

Psychiatric patients detained in hospitals in England and Wales are entitled to apply for review of their detention. Applications may be made either by the patient personally or by the patient's nearest relative, or even by the Home Secretary. Such review is carried out by the Mental Health Review Tribunal. Proceedings, which are governed principally by the Mental Health Act 1983, must take place as soon as possible in order to give effect to the European Convention on Human Rights (see Units 1.8 and 3.10) which requires that everyone who is deprived of his or her liberty by arrest or detention shall be entitled to have the lawfulness of such detention speedily decided. The tribunal comprises both lawyers and doctors along with lay members. It is important that the tribunal observes the rules of natural justice and this is best achieved by having a lawyer as president. The patient may be legally represented and the Law Society maintains a list of solicitors with special experience of such work.

After the hearing, the tribunal is empowered to refuse an application for release or to reclassify the patient's stated disorder. Appeal, which is rare in practice, lies on points of law only to the Divisional Court of the Queen's Bench Division.

The Employment Tribunal

The mass volume of legislation on industrial practice and employees' rights over the last three decades added greatly to the importance of the original Industrial Tribunal, first set up by the Industrial Training Act 1964. The then Conservative Government's controversial Industrial Relations Act 1971 extended the role of the tribunal to allow it to hear complaints from former employees who believed that they had been unfairly dismissed from their jobs. Subsequent legislation empowered the tribunal to hear complaints of sexual and racial discrimination as well as claims for redundancy payments and maternity leave. Proceedings are now governed by the Employment Rights Act 1996. The hierarchy is headed by the **President**, who is to be appointed by the Lord Chancellor from barristers and solicitors of not less than seven years' standing. The President must determine where and when the tribunal shall sit. He also selects the three members who are required to make up the composition of the tribunal. One of them, a lawyer, acts as chairman and the two other members, not lawyers, are drawn from panels to represent the employer's side of industry and the trade union viewpoint. Each member plays an active role and all have an equal vote. The decision is reached by a simple majority.

The tribunal is administered by the Central Office and various Regional Offices. A dismissed employee (known as **the applicant**) must bring this complaint within three months of his (or her) dismissal by issuing an **originating application**. This document outlines the nature and terms of his past employment, states his complaint about his old boss and sets out the remedy sought; this can be either compensation or reinstatement. The employer (known as **the respondent**) must then answer the complaint by entering a **notice of appearance**. This document outlines the reasons for dismissal and generally gives the employer's account.

Exceptionally, the burden is on the employer to prove that the dismissal was fair. It is not the job of the applicant to prove that he has been unfairly dismissed for the scales are weighted in favour of the applicant. In an attempt to avoid a full hearing a Conciliation Officer from the Advisory Conciliation and Arbitration Service (ACAS) will endeavour to reach a compromise between the parties. If such an attempt is unsuccessful, however, the case must proceed to a hearing.

On the day, the respondent's case is heard first, as the burden of proof is on him. The employer opens his or her case (by explaining the background) and then calls witnesses to justify the dismissal. This may be on grounds of gross misconduct (such as theft of company money or assault on the managing director), or capacity (which in practice means that the sacked employee was quite useless) or some other ground. The applicant then cross-examines those witnesses and may later give evidence and call other witnesses to support his case. Evidence is given on oath but the strict rules of evidence traditionally applied in courts have long been relaxed so that witnesses may give evidence of what other people not called as witnesses have said.

Each side may be legally represented at the hearing by lawyers or by others such as trade union officials. It is a long-standing criticism of the legal aid scheme that public funding is not available for representation before the Employment Tribunal even though a person's entire future career prospects may be at stake. To help avoid the risk of injustice some lawyers assisted by some law students operate the **Free Representation Unit** (FRU) and advise applicants by writing letters for them and also by representing them at the hearing, all such help being free of charge. Although much of its work is concentrated on employment tribunals, the FRU extends its free service to other tribunals such as Social Security Tribunals, Medical Appeal Tribunals and, of course, the Employment Appeal Tribunal in appeals from the Employment Tribunal.

Once all the evidence has been presented and the arguments of each side concluded, the tribunal may hold the dismissal to have been fair (and therefore dismiss the application) or find it to have been unfair. If the dismissal is found to have been unfair the tribunal may make an award of money to the successful applicant. This award is in two parts. Firstly, the **basic award** takes account of the applicant's age, the length of service prior to dismissal and the income from the employment. Secondly, there is the **compensatory award** which takes account of other factors such as the chances of finding other comparable employment and the cost of looking for such work. In the autumn of 1999 the maximum compensatory award was increased to £50,000, an increase which followed upon the reduction of the qualifying period to just one year of employment. The tribunal also has power to reduce an award because of the applicant's own conduct (even to the extent of 100 per cent contribution in really bad cases) and also has the power, but does not often exercise it, to award costs against the losing party. Appeal lies on points of law only to the Employment Appeal Tribunal.

Employment Appeal Tribunal Proceedings before the Employment Appeal Tribunal (the EAT) used to be conducted amidst the splendour, even if somewhat decayed, of the old ballroom of what had been the Astor family's London town house in St James's Square; the accommodation has now moved to less fashionable premises south of the river. The composition of the EAT, in its conception of balancing employer and employee experience from industry, is similar to that of the Employment Tribunal itself. There is a lawyer chairman (this time a High Court judge) who sits informally and without robes. He is addressed no longer as 'My Lord' but merely called

'Sir'. As before, there are two, but sometimes as many as four, representatives drawn from both sides of industry who have special knowledge or experience of industrial relations. Appeals may only be brought upon points of law and fresh evidence would not normally be allowed in the absence of good reason why such evidence had not been placed before the tribunal in the first place. Appeal lies with leave to the Civil Division of the Court of Appeal.

Immigration Appeal Tribunal

Appeals against the decision of the **Home Office adjudicator** may be taken to the Immigration Appeal Tribunal. The adjudicator, who often sits only part-time, is a barrister or solicitor who hears appeals from the immigration authorities. In the spring of 2000 the government announced that the number of such lawyers was to be doubled in an effort to cope with the mass of applications by asylum-seekers. Appeals against the adjudicator's refusal to allow entry into the United Kingdom or refusal to extend leave lie either on law or fact to the Immigration Appeal Tribunal, which is headed by a High Court judge. The tribunal has power to remit the case to a different adjudicator but must give sufficient and adequate reasons for its determination. Appeal lies on points of law to the Queen's Bench Division.

Other tribunals

Traders dissatisfied with their VAT assessments may now appeal to the **Combined Tax Tribunal** which has recently brought together the work of the old VAT and Duties Tribunal and that of the Special Commissioners of Income Tax. Veterans in dispute with the Department of Social Security over war disablement pensions may take their dissatisfaction to the **Pensions Appeal Tribunal**. Parents dissatisfied with the Child Support Agency's implementation of notoriously complex legislation may refer the dispute to the **Social Security and Child Support Tribunal**.

Control by the courts

The regular courts are able to interfere whenever the legality of the tribunal's action has been called into question.

Firstly, an appeal on a point of law almost always lies to the High Court.

Secondly, the High Court may control the actions of the tribunal by use of prerogative orders such as certiorari (see Unit 2.1) to ensure, for example, that the tribunal applies the rules of natural justice. There are two special rules which must be obeyed:

1. *Audi alteram partem* ('hear the other side'). This is the duty to hear both sides of the case before making up one's mind. This was illustrated in *Ridge* v. *Baldwin* 1963, when a police chief constable who had been suspended from duty pending his trial on corruption charges applied for that suspension to be lifted after his acquittal. The committee never heard him but nevertheless turned down this request. The House of Lords held that Mr Ridge ought to have been given 'a fair opportunity of being heard in his own defence'. Similarly, in *R* v. *Hull Prison Board of Visitors* 1979 the Court of Appeal accepted that the procedure and findings of the prison visitors (in reality, local magistrates) who had to deal with a number of prisoners who had caused a riot in prison were susceptible to certiorari.

The prisoners had complained about the self-evident unfairness in a procedure which had allowed the case to be proved against one prisoner without even allowing him to examine evidence relied upon, or to learn the names of the prison officers who had apparently seen him on the roof let alone to test the quality of their observations or, it seems, even to be given the opportunity to comment on what the prison governor had to say. As Lane LJ rightly observed: 'The prisoner was not told what evidence had been given or what statements had been made affecting him, nor was he given a fair opportunity to correct or contradict them.'

2. *Nemo iudex in causa sua* ('no one should be a judge in his own cause'). The very nature of the judicial process demands that the decision should be reached after impartial and independent consideration of the evidence. In *Dimes* v. *Grand Junction Canal* 1852 a judge who tried the case held some shares in the canal company concerned. Although no allegation of bias was made, the House of Lords expressed the opinion that the judge, as a shareholder, was disqualified from trying such a case.

More recently, a similar point was considered by the Divisional Court in *R* v. *Altrincham Justices, ex parte Pennington* 1975. Two men were prosecuted in the magistrates' court for supplying a lesser weight of vegetables to local schools than they had been paid for. The chairman of the lay bench was an alderman who had been co-opted on to the education committee of the local council and was also a governor of two other schools. The defendants were convicted and applied for certiorari to quash the conviction on the grounds of the magistrate's interest in the subject-matter of the prosecution and the likelihood of bias. The Divisional Court granted the order and quashed the conviction. Lord Widgery CJ explained why this had to be done when he said:

> There is no better rule of natural justice than the one that a man shall not be a judge in his own cause. In its simplest form this means that a man shall not judge an issue in which he has a direct pecuniary interest, but the rule has been extended far beyond such crude examples and now covers cases in which the judge has such an interest in the parties or the matters in dispute as to make it difficult for him to approach the trial with the impartiality and detachment which the judicial function requires.

By requiring tribunals to comply with these rules the superior courts try to ensure that, as Lord Hewart CJ famously said in *R* v. *Sussex Justices, ex parte McCarthy* 1924:

> justice should not only be done but should manifestly and undoubtedly be seen to be done.

Such a case involved a local solicitor who, as was not uncommon earlier in the last century, also acted as part-time clerk to the local magistrates. The position of a judge in the House of Lords came under close scrutiny most recently in *R* v. *Bow Street Metropolitan Stipendiary Magistrate, ex parte Pinochet Ugarte (No. 2)* 1999 when the House of Lords considered the position of one of its own distinguished members. By a narrow majority, the House of Lords had ruled that the former Head of Chile could not claim immunity from prosecution as a former Head of State. The Spanish Government sought his extradition so that he could be tried for various crimes against humanity. In the course of the principal proceedings Amnesty International had been granted leave to intervene. Amnesty International is a worthy charity committed to the observance of the Universal Declaration of Human Rights in regard to prisoners of conscience. Among the volunteers was Lady Hoffman whose husband, Lord Hoffmann, was also a director of Amnesty International Charitable Trust. When General Pinochet's solicitors discovered this they asked for the earlier order to be set aside, contending that Lord Hoffmann's links with Amnesty International were such as to give the appearance of possible bias. No allegation of actual bias was ever put forward; rather, the argument was based on the old requirement that justice should be seen to be done as well as actually being done. In this unusual case the House of Lords took the view that, as Amnesty International had become a party to the appeal and the judge was a director of a charity closely allied to Amnesty International, Lord Hoffman was automatically disqualified from hearing the appeal. The earlier order was accordingly set aside and re-heard by a differently constituted court.

In *R* v. *Gough* 1993 the House of Lords had already considered two rival alternative tests for bias. Was it necessary to show that there was a real likelihood of bias or merely to ask whether a reasonable and fair-minded person sitting in the court and knowing all the relevant facts would have had a 'reasonable suspicion' that a fair trial by the defendant was not possible? It had turned out, when Robert Gough was convicted of conspiracy to rob, that one of the jury at the Crown Court at Liverpool was a neighbour of Gough's brother who had also been arrested but not tried. The House of Lords took a restrictive view and required a real danger of bias on the part of anyone involved in judicial proceedings except where there was a direct pecuniary interest in the outcome of the proceedings (when bias would be assumed).

Tribunals such as the Lands Tribunal exist to resolve disputes between the State and the individual: they are known as **administrative tribunals**. Their composition and procedure are governed by the Tribunals and Inquiries Act 1992 which, for example, requires reasons to be given for the decisions that are made.

In contrast, within various groups and associations there has been set up a machinery for resolving disputes, allowing the organisation to keep some control over its members without always doing its dirty washing in public. The power which such tribunals – called **domestic tribunals** – can exert is very considerable: indeed, they can literally put an end to a person's livelihood. In fairly recent times the approach of some trade unions has been questioned and allegations made about the conduct of hearings which would be an insult to the judicial capacity of a kangaroo as the proceedings moved inexorably towards their pre-arranged decision. The willingness of the courts to prevent such abuse is examined in this unit.

The range of tribunals is a wide one. For example, doctors who peddle drugs under the guise of prescribing medicines may be struck off by the General Medical Council, which itself is regulated by the Medical Act 1983; dentists who fondle their anaesthetised patients may be in trouble with the General Dental Council; solicitors who confuse their clients' money with their own holiday funds will be struck off the Roll of Solicitors by the Solicitors' Disciplinary Tribunal; barristers who fail to maintain the high standards required of them are similarly subject to the control of the General Council of the Bar. Other trades and professions subject their members to similar scrutiny so that, for example, opticians who do not read carefully their own codes of conduct may be looked into by the General Optical Council.

Where the tribunal has been created by statute an appeal will usually lie. For example, the Solicitors Act 1974 allows a disciplinary committee set up by the Law Society to strike a name off the Roll of Solicitors and the solicitor concerned may appeal. Otherwise, the aggrieved person has to rely on the willingness of the courts to become involved in such proceedings.

How far the courts will so interfere was discussed by Denning LJ in *Lee* v. *Showmen's Guild of Great Britain* 1952. Two members of the defendant guild applied to a local authority for a site on a fairground. Frank Lee was granted the site but another man, William Thaw, who had been allocated that site in the past, reckoned that he should have had it. The rules of the guild allowed the guild to fine a member who indulged in 'unfair competition'. Lee was fined and when the fine still had not been paid after one month, the guild, as further provided by the rules, resolved that he cease to be a member. Mr Lee then applied to the court for a declaration that the decision of the guild committee was *ultra vires* ('beyond the powers' of the guild) and void.

The Court of Appeal held that the court had jurisdiction to examine any decision of the guild committee which involved a question of law, including one of the interpretation of the rules. On the facts the committee had misconstrued the rule in question in finding that the plaintiff had been guilty of 'unfair competition' within the meaning of the rule. The committee had acted *ultra vires* and so it followed that their decision to expel Mr Lee had been void. Denning LJ was well aware of the implications of a hearing by such a tribunal:

> *Although the jurisdiction of a domestic tribunal is founded on contract, express or implied, nevertheless the parties are not free to make any contract they like. There are important limitations imposed by public policy. The tribunal must, for instance, observe the principles of natural justice. They must give the man notice of the charge and a reasonable opportunity of meeting it...*
>
> *They [domestic tribunals] wield power as great, if not greater, than any exercised by the courts of law. They can deprive a man of his livelihood. They can ban him from the trade in which he has spent his life and which is the only trade he knows ... A man's right to work is just as important, if not more important, to him than his rights of property.*

These courts intervene every day to protect rights of property. They must also intervene to protect the right to work.

But the question still remains: To what extent will the courts intervene? They will, I think, always be prepared to examine the decision to see that the tribunal have observed the law. This includes the correct interpretation of the rules.

b) Arbitration

We have already seen that the courts exist to settle differences between the parties before them. For many people this system works perfectly well but in some circumstances the courts are not the best-suited forum: they can, for example, be both slow and expensive. Further, it can be a disadvantage that they are open to the public. Suppose that a company is in dispute with its production engineer and that the dispute concerns the company's new process that will enable it to undercut the price in the international market for mobile telephones. Through a hearing in open court, details of the novel integrated circuitry could well reach a rival supplier, which might then be able to market the technology both earlier and more cheaply. Moreover, despite the diversity of judicial talent, the judge may not be able immediately to appreciate the finer points of, say, the intricacies of GSM digital transmission.

It is for these reasons that parties to a contract may wish to provide their own way of settling any future disagreements. Such agreements may provide that a third party should be brought in to decide such dispute. This process is known as **arbitration** and the third party as **arbitrator**. There may be more than one arbitrator so that if the two arbitrators cannot decide the dispute, it may be referred once again, this time to an **umpire**.

This system of resolving disputes has proved attractive to those trading in commodities and to the construction industry. In such arbitrations the arbitrator will be chosen for his special expertise in such fields. For example, parties arguing over the quality of some commodity such as cocoa may prefer to have their differences settled swiftly by an outside expert conducting what is appropriately known as a 'look-sniff' arbitration where the arbitrator will quite literally look at and perhaps even sniff the subject-matter of the dispute. Various trade organisations such as the Association of British Travel Agents (ABTA) run their own schemes for resolving disagreements between their members and disgruntled holidaymakers.

Lord Donaldson MR once put the matter neatly when he said that:

Arbitrators and judges are partners in the business of dispensing justice, the judge in the public sector and the arbitrator in the private sector.

Arbitrators, therefore, need to display qualities similar to those of judges and, in particular, must comply with the principles of natural justice so that an arbitrator must always be (and be seen to be) both disinterested in the subject-matter and outcome of the dispute and unbiased in his dealings between the parties before him.

Arbitration is becoming increasingly controlled by statute. The first Act was passed in the late seventeenth century but the present statutory framework is to be found in the Arbitration Act 1996.

Proceedings normally follow the pattern of civil proceedings in the courts with witnesses giving their evidence on oath and then being cross-examined. After hearing all the evidence and arguments the arbitrator will then 'make his award', that is to say, give his judgment. This award is then final and binding on the parties to that arbitration subject to very limited grounds of appeal on a question of law as limited by section 69 of the Act. The Arbitration Act 1996 also allows an award to be challenged on the basis that a 'serious irregularity' had occurred within the proceedings such as a failure to comply with the general duty upon the arbitrator to act fairly. Section 33 of the Act sets out the guiding principle of good practice for anyone charged with judicial decisions:

> The tribunal shall –
> (a) act fairly and impartially as between the parties, giving each party a reasonable opportunity of putting his case and dealing with that of his opponent, and
> (b) adopt procedures suitable to the circumstances of the particular case, avoiding unnecessary delay or expense, so as to provide a fair means for the resolution of the matters falling to be determined.

Other less formal means also exist for the resolution of disputes. These alternatives to proceedings through the courts have given rise to the general term of Alternative Dispute Resolution, known commonly just as **ADR**.

Many trade associations operate their own schemes, especially in the travel industry for holidaymakers for whom the sun did not seem to shine or who, more reasonably, objected to sharing their hotel bathrooms with another family, especially of cockroaches. The couple whose holiday has served only to underline the problems within their marriage may be helped to avoid divorce (or at least some of the heartache of protracted wrangling over children and money) with the involvement of mediation (see also Unit 5.3).

These forms of ADR have become noticeably more sophisticated in recent years and even to the point now where a number of most distinguished retired judges (including even those once sitting in the House of Lords) are now offering their experience to clients. These services cover two different forms of mediation. 'Facilitative mediation' involves attempts by the mediator to propel the parties in dispute to a binding settlement but does not permit the mediator to offer his or her own views as to the merits of either position. Such ventilation of opinion as to merit is, however, permitted if the parties instead opt for 'evaluative mediation' when legal knowledge and past judicial experience may reveal weakness in one side's previously entrenched position. Obvious advantages of either form of mediation will include the speed and privacy with which differences can be settled.

2.5 *The legal profession*

When, in a fit of pique, a man threatens another that he will 'get my lawyers on to you!' – as if lawyers were some breed of semi-tame mastiffs – he is failing to differentiate between the two parts of the legal profession: the solicitor and the barrister. Each has traditionally had a separate role to play.

a) Solicitors

The first, and usually only, lawyer whom people meet is the **solicitor**. Such lawyers deal directly with the public, advising and assisting on a very wide range of problems and transactions. There are approximately 80,000 solicitors in England and Wales, of whom many work in small firms with perhaps half a dozen or fewer partners. Most such high-street practices deal with a very wide range of work.

For example, one partner may deal almost exclusively with **conveyancing** – that is, with the buying and selling of houses and of land generally. Although the once profitable monopoly enjoyed in this field of work was lost some years ago solicitors still do a good deal of this work despite the advent of the new 'licensed conveyancer' (see Unit 2.5c)). Solicitors also draw up wills and, after a death, administer the deceased's estate. This is known as **probate** (see Unit 5.9b)). Other solicitors will deal with **litigation** – the process of suing through the courts. They will advise, for example, people injured at work or on the road and will strive to get them compensation. Another solicitor may deal with criminal work, some of which he or she will deal with in the local magistrates' court.

Until very recently other work had to be passed to a barrister. In any event, the solicitor will have to advise his or her client on the law and perhaps take statements (known as 'proof of evidence') from any witness who can help. Yet another solicitor in the same firm may deal principally with family work and all the sad repercussions of the current high level of matrimonial breakdown. Increasingly, solicitors are tending to specialise. Such a trend has led also to the creation of specialist associations such as the Solicitors' Family Law Association, a body of solicitors committed to securing amicable resolution of matrimonial breakdown. So, too, steps have been taken to ensure that solicitors who deal with care proceedings (where so-called battered babies and children generally at risk from violence or other forms of abuse may be removed from parental care and placed elsewhere for safety) are specially trained for this socially responsible work. Those solicitors who have received such training have their names added to the Children Panel.

Solicitors who act in this sort of work for clients in conflict with the police, local authorities and other organs of the State require not only legal knowledge but strong personal qualities to deal with people who are frightened, vulnerable and at risk of losing their children or their own liberty. The willingness to take on any client who walks through the door has long been seen as an important aspect of ensuring that everyone may enjoy certain fundamental freedoms and rights. In fulfilling this role lawyers, and probably solicitors in particular, may come into conflict with the State and other sectors of the community. The inability of certain sectors of the community to distinguish between the lawyer and the client has led all too tragically to the murders of solicitors engaged in criminal work during the troubles in Northern Ireland.

As firms get bigger there tends to be an even greater degree of specialisation. Some of the very large London firms, with perhaps 50 or more partners and many other solicitors and assistants, are often highly specialised in fields such as company and commercial work. Their clients will not include the injured workman or the battered wife but rather the banks, the insurance companies and other companies with multi-million-pound businesses. Partners in a small number of such firms can enjoy very substantial incomes wholly unrepresentative of those of solicitors as a whole.

Contrary to long-standing populist but erroneous belief, the incomes of solicitors in these high street practices are often poor these days and have fallen badly behind those of comparable professionals such as accountants, dentists, doctors and veterinary surgeons. Indeed, unlike the fees of these other worthies, the fees of solicitors are subject to scrutiny both by the Law Society and by the courts themselves. At the conclusion of litigation, the solicitor's bill of costs will be assessed (formerly said to be 'taxed') by the court and every aspect of it, from the cost of photocopying documents to sums spent on travel, will be closely scrutinised. The losing party then has to pay only the sum so assessed.

The solicitor's full and rather grandiose title is 'Solicitor of the Supreme Court' and he (or she) remains an officer of the court who owes the court itself a duty in addition to that duty which he owes to his individual clients. A solicitor's training and conduct are overseen by the Law Society, which, situated near the Royal Courts of Justice in London, maintains a 'Roll of Solicitors' – that is, a list of men and women entitled to practise as solicitors in England and Wales. On **admission** (that is, qualification), the new entrant receives a certificate signed by the Master of the Rolls (see Unit 2.1b)).

Conduct and discipline are controlled by the Solicitors Act 1974 (which incidentally provides that a solicitor may not practise if in prison!) and by the Courts and Legal Services Act 1990. From time to time, as with any walk of life, solicitors do get themselves into trouble and are then liable to be 'struck off' the Roll. Lawyers remain easy targets for people's frustrations as they experience the trauma of litigation, and a large number of less serious complaints had swamped the Solicitors' Complaints Bureau which, in 1996, was replaced by the new **Office for the Supervision of Solicitors**. Concerns as to the reasonableness of fees charged, for example, can be allayed or confirmed by the procedure of obtaining a 'Remuneration Certificate', for the calculation of any solicitor's charges must take account not only of the time actually and reasonably spent upon any client's affairs but also other factors such as the value of the property, if any, involved, complexity and, therefore, also the degree of skill and specialist knowledge required.

A solicitor's training is long and arduous. It calls for both a good education and considerable stamina. After a law degree, the student must go on to pass the Law Society's Legal Practice Course. Graduates of other disciplines must first pursue the Common Professional Examination (CPE). The student must then serve a form of white-collar apprenticeship, formerly known as **articles** and now termed a **training contract**, for a period of two years. During this time the candidate is known as a 'trainee solicitor' – this new title replacing the old term 'articled clerk' – and will work under an experienced colleague to acquire the practical skills required in a solicitor's work. During this time the trainee solicitor will receive something less than the often exaggerated income of a 'fat-cat' lawyer which, as from August 2000, is subject to a recommended minimum annual income of £13,000 outside London and £14,600 in the capital, still quite some way below the male manual worker's average income in 2000.

Since 1984 solicitors have been allowed to advertise their services in the press or on radio but until the arrival of the Conditional Fee structure in 2000 very few had done so. Even in today's overtly commercial environment the sight of a high-kicking troupe of trainee solicitors recommending the excellence of their firms has yet to be seen. After all, any publicity is required to comply with the Law Society's own rules about good taste and the advertisement not bringing the profession into disrepute. Claiming superiority over other solicitors or criticism of the firm down the road is similarly forbidden by the Law Society, whose members should, in any event, comply with the Code of Advertising Practice in lending a new meaning to the maxim that advertisements are 'legal, decent, honest and truthful'!

...trainee solicitors recommending the excellence of their firms...

These and other high standards are required of solicitors in all their dealings and they must never do anything to mislead the courts. They enjoy one important privilege, which is that they cannot be forced to disclose – even to the courts themselves – confidential dealings with their clients. Barristers also enjoy such a privilege, which is intended to protect the public when seeking advice. No one else enjoys such a privilege and people such as journalists have even been sent to prison for refusing to reveal the source of their information.

The importance of legal professional privilege is very considerable. It has been the subject of some erosion in recent years but its purpose was clearly expressed by the late Lord Chief Justice, Lord Taylor of Gosforth, in *R* v. *Derby Magistrates Court, ex parte B* 1995:

> *The principle which runs through all these cases, and the many others which were cited, is that a man must be able to consult his lawyers in confidence, since otherwise he might hold back half the truth. The client must be sure that what he tells his lawyer in confidence will never be revealed without his consent. Legal professional privilege is thus much more than an ordinary rule of evidence, limited in its application to the facts of a particular case. It is a fundamental condition on which the administration of justice as a whole rests...*

It goes without saying that any communication in furtherance of a criminal purpose could not give rise to any such privilege and any duty of confidence is always subject to – and indeed overridden by – the duty of any party to comply with the law. In recent years there have been some further inroads into this privilege, for example, in connection with suspected laundering of drugs money. Similarly, so important is the welfare of children that the Family Law Act 1986 empowers the court to order any person to disclose relevant information as to the whereabouts of a missing child.

Most recently in *Paragon Finance plc* v. *Freshfields* 1999 the Lord Chief Justice himself said of legal professional privilege:

> *At its root, lies the obligation of confidence which a legal adviser owes to his client in relation to any confidential professional communication passing between them. For readily intelligible reasons of public policy the law had, however, accorded to such communications a degree of protection denied to communications, however confidential, between clients and other professional advisers. Save where client and legal adviser have abused their confidential relationship to facilitate crime or fraud, the protection is absolute unless the client (whose privilege it is) waives it, whether expressly or impliedly.*

Obviously not every bit of tittle-tattle mentioned over a drink to someone who, by chance, happens to be a solicitor, is privileged. Privilege will attach only to communications between client and lawyer in connection with the obtaining of advice. Even when privilege can be claimed, it remains at all times the privilege of the client and not that of the lawyer. It follows that the client may decide to waive that privilege either personally or through the lawyer acting within the scope of his or her authority on behalf of the client.

One recent and somewhat disquieting example of waiver of such privilege is to be seen in the decision of the Court of Appeal in *R* v. *Bowden* 1999, an appeal arising out of the recent change of law allowing adverse inferences to be drawn in criminal proceedings from the exercise of any residual right to silence. A solicitor who had been called to a police station explained to the police why he had advised his client not to answer any of their questions. In order to prevent any adverse inference being drawn from the defendant's silence when charged with robbery, evidence was called to show to the jury that the defendant had remained silent upon the advice of his solicitor. Once this had happened the prosecution sought to cross-examine the defendant on what, in fact, he had told his solicitor. Having been convicted and sentenced to eight years' detention, the defendant appealed, contending that there had been no waiver of legal professional privilege and that the prosecution should not, therefore, have been permitted to ask questions about the instructions he had given his own lawyer. However, in the Court of Appeal, the Lord Chief Justice went on to say:

> *if when being questioned by the police, a suspect goes beyond saying that he declines to answer on legal advice and goes on then to explain the basis on which such advice has been given, a waiver of legal professional privilege has taken place.*

There is one solicitor with a particularly grand title who takes no private clients at all, but since 1875 his office has been helping many people who would otherwise not be able properly to put their own views or needs before a court. The **Official Solicitor** is appointed by the Lord Chancellor from experienced solicitors. Based in London and assisted by other lawyers, the Official Solicitor involves himself, when invited by the court to do so, in representing those under a disability – for example, the mentally handicapped or children caught up in their parents' wrangling over their young lives. In this latter respect, the Official Solicitor assists a parent whose child has been wrongly removed to another country to obtain that child's speedy return in compliance with this country's obligations under the Hague and European Conventions on Child Abduction. The Official Solicitor may also agree to act on behalf of a child in complex cases under the Children Act 1989 if asked to do so, to protect and promote the child's own interests. It is important to remember that the Official Solicitor does not simply rubber stamp his view on that of another but carries out his own investigation. In some cases the Official Solicitor may, for example, call for expert help from other sources such as doctors and child psychiatrists in particular. The Official Solicitor has also protected the interest of persons remanded in custody on criminal charges and may represent people committed for contempt of court.

While, because of its very nature, the work of the Official Solicitor normally receives little press attention, the role was brought sharply before the public gaze in 1993 when the House of Lords considered the appeal brought by the Official Solicitor who was then representing Tony Bland, one of those severely injured in the Hillsborough Stadium disaster in April 1989 (see Unit 2.3) at a time when the doctors at the hospital wanted permission to withhold treatment which would prolong life for a patient who had no hope of recovery or improvement. More recently, in *Re: A (Children) Conjoined Twins: (Surgical Separation)* 2000, the Official Solicitor acted in poignant proceedings before the Court of Appeal on behalf of a Siamese twin, whose prospects of survival were poor and whose own life imperilled that of her sister.

b) Legal executives

Many solicitors are helped in their practices by **legal executives** who do much of the day-to-day work which requires specialised legal knowledge and experience. Litigation, probate and conveyancing all receive the attention of legal executives, whose training and conduct are controlled by their own professional body, the Institute of Legal Executives. The student must pass a wide range of examinations and after at least five years' experience may be admitted as a Fellow of the Institute. Legal executives do not enjoy the same rights of audience as a solicitor but often appear in the County Court before the district judge on a wide range of matters.

c) Licensed conveyancers

The legal aspects of buying and selling flats and houses, known as **conveyancing**, have long been an important part of many solicitors' practices. Once it was often a profitable aspect of such practices but the Administration of Justice Act 1985 removed solicitors' monopoly in this work by establishing a new Council of Licensed Conveyancers.

Successful candidates in their examinations may now qualify not as solicitors but as **licensed conveyancers**. This new qualification has attracted interest from legal executives who have worked in solicitors' offices and even from some solicitors who have been keen to throw off some of the constraints imposed upon them by the Law Society. Such persons will then be able to enter into a partnership with others such as surveyors and estate agents.

d) Barristers

Traditionally, the relationship between solicitors and barristers was often said to have been analogous to the general practitioner family doctor and the hospital consultant to whom the sick are referred for more specialised investigation and treatment. This analogy has proved ever-increasingly simplistic as many solicitors have developed highly specialised practices themselves. Nevertheless, it is still of some help in understanding why solicitors involve barristers in their clients' problems.

When complex points of law or procedure are raised and **counsel's opinion** (a barrister's advice on a particular problem) is required or when representation in the higher courts is called for, a solicitor will still often instruct a barrister (**brief counsel**) to represent his or her client. As they are an essentially referral profession, barristers are generally forbidden by professional rules from dealing directly with the public. However, even this old convention is subject to qualification these days. In response to the growing intrusion into their world by solicitors, the Bar has recently established the so-called **Bar DIRECT** scheme under which selected occupations, such as the police and chartered accountants, may by-pass the instructing solicitor and instruct counsel direct.

Each barrister in private practice is treated as a self-employed person and may not enter into partnership with any other barrister. Nevertheless, a group of barristers, while working independently of each other and receiving their work (**briefs**) and sometimes even their fees through solicitors, do share accommodation (known as **chambers**), clerical staff (with the old clerk now being replaced by an equally expensive 'practice manager') and facilities such as a library and other more technological equipment which increasingly replace the solitary dusty old Remington typewriter in the clerks' room which, only years ago, would have been regarded as sufficient. In London, most barristers still have their chambers in one of the four Inns of Court where, despite the overcrowding in the old buildings, barristers have lived and worked for hundreds of years, although there is also a modern trend towards a corporate ownership of office accommodation outside the elegant walks of the inns.

Recent pressure to be seen to be offering the highest of standards has led to the creation of the so-called 'Barmark', which is the legal equivalent of the British Standard kitemark. There are also sets of barristers' chambers in other large towns such as Birmingham, Bristol, Exeter, Leeds, Liverpool, Manchester and Taunton. The rapid expansion of the Bar over the last 30 years has led to the opening of a large number of new sets of chambers, and the recent relaxation of professional rules now permits established barristers (and in practice those with an individual following of solicitor clients or largely advisory practices) to practise from their own homes as **sole practitioners**.

A sense of increasing concern as to their future security in an increasingly competitive environment has led many individual barristers to move to different chambers in the last couple of years in particular as they perceive greener grass elsewhere. On the macro-economic scale, too, various sets of chambers have been merging with other sets so as to create so-called super sets of perhaps 70 barristers as the costs of maintaining modern facilities grow at a pace unmatched by fee income, especially that paid from public funds as at the criminal and family Bar.

The student who wishes to qualify as a barrister (that is be **called to the Bar**) must first obtain a good class honours degree. Thereafter, the student must pass further professional examinations in a wide range of subjects. At about this time he or she will eat the regulation number of dinners in his Inn of Court, which is one of the less demanding parts of a Bar student's life. Against the background of often fairly indifferent sustenance, the student has, in this way, been introduced to those with whom he must live and work and from whom, almost by a gentle process of osmosis, he will acquire at least an outline of the ethical and professional standards to be met in practice. The procedure has in recent years been criticised as archaic and irrelevant, criticisms which have been met by allowing students to attend residential weekend courses instead of dining in hall.

The choice by a student of a particular Inn does not determine either the sort of work to be done in future practice or the place where such work will be done. There are four Inns of Court: Gray's Inn, Lincoln's Inn, Inner Temple and Middle Temple. A student who joins, say, Gray's Inn, may well find that he later joins a set of chambers based in, say, the Inner Temple. The inns, with their collegiate atmosphere, provide excellent library facilities for their members and also run training courses intended particularly for their student members. At the time of writing, the Bar, through the medium of the Council of the Inns of Court, is considering whether to allow solicitors who, as a consequence of the Access to Justice Act 1999, have acquired rights of audience in the higher courts to join an Inn of Court.

If successful in the final examination, the student must then spend a further year in **pupillage**. This is a form of white-collar apprenticeship similar to the training contract of potential solicitors. As a pupil he or she will be attached to an experienced practitioner from whom he will learn the practical aspects and professional obligations and courtesies of a barrister's life. Traditionally, the pupil would pay 100 guineas (£105) for the privilege of such tuition but the wish to recruit the cream of each year's newly qualified has led chambers to offer payment for this period of training in the shape of awards. In *Edmonds* v. *Lawson* 2000 the Court of Appeal rejected the argument that a pupil barrister was entitled to payment from chambers of the £3.60 per hour minimum wage. Once fully qualified the new barrister will have to look around for a vacancy in a set of chambers. Competition for places in chambers, even after this long period of training, is exceedingly intense and puts in a new light the words of St Matthew's Gospel that 'many are called but few are chosen'.

During the first three years of practice, the newly called barrister is required to continue with his or her academic education and must attend the New Practitioners' Programme. During this period the new practitioner receives continuing education in terms of procedure, ethics and substantive law. In sharp contrast with the MOT test for old cars, this particular programme of continuing education has, until recently, been confined to those under three years' call. The Bar Council has recently proposed to extend such continuing professional development to all practising barristers throughout their careers.

Like solicitors, many of the 9,932 barristers in independent practice in England and Wales in 1999 covered a wide range of work. Over recent years there has been a growing tendency among barristers to specialise and it is becoming increasingly rare, as was the case not many years ago, to encounter barristers who would deal with, say, crime on Monday, divorce on Tuesday and landlord and tenant for the rest of the week. This trend has been mirrored in the growth of specialist associations such as the Criminal Bar Association, Family Law Bar Association and Personal Injuries Bar Association.

A number specialise in fairly narrow fields such as libel, patent work, taxation and shipping law. The type of work done dramatically affects the level of earnings and those who practise principally in the fields of crime and divorce suffer from earnings which are largely dependent upon public funding and which, for that reason, fall a long way behind the earnings of comparable professions and occupations. Indeed, the level of discontent that this aroused led the Bar to bring legal proceedings against the then Lord Chancellor himself in 1986, claiming that he was in breach of his statutory duty to provide 'fair and reasonable' remuneration.

The **Attorney-General**, himself a barrister, and presently Lord Williams of Mostyn, is regarded as the leader of the Bar. He is legal adviser both to the Crown and to Parliament, of which he is a member. He is appointed to his post by the Prime Minister and is not allowed to practise while in office.

It is the Attorney-General's duty to represent the Crown in both civil and criminal proceedings. In civil proceedings he is under a duty to act whenever the public interest is threatened – as in 1977, when the Post

Office Union threatened to boycott all letters to South Africa. More recently in *Attorney-General* v. *Blake* 2000, the Attorney-General, described as acting as the guardian of the public interest and as an officer of the Crown responsible for assisting in upholding the criminal law, sought to deprive the self-confessed traitor, George Blake, of his royalties from his book, brazenly entitled *No Other Choice*. Blake had earlier been sentenced to 42 years' imprisonment for breaches of the Official Secrets Act 1911. Quite apart from breaches of the criminal law, the Russian spy had breached his own undertaking arising from his employment with the British Security Services. He had also managed to breach the security of Wandsworth Prison as he escaped to Russia. Should such a man earn his profit by doing the very thing he had promised not to do? Lord Nicholls recognised the right of the Attorney-General to take action:

> *In making this claim the Attorney-General asserted not a private right on behalf of the Crown but a claim for relief in his capacity as guardian of the public interest. In this latter capacity the Attorney-General may, exceptionally, invoke the assistance of the civil law in aid of the criminal law. Typically this occurs where an offence is frequently repeated in disregard of an inadequate penalty: see* Gouriet *v.* Union of Post Office Workers.

The Attorney-General may also prosecute in serious offences such as murder or spying, and some charges (such as those brought under the Official Secrets Acts) require his consent before prosecution may be started. He also has power to put an end to prosecutions by forbidding the prosecutor to go on with his case – a process known by the Latin tag *nolle prosequi* (a refusal to pursue) – as he did in March 1982 when Mary Whitehouse, a keen campaigner against (her perceptions of) moral laxity, prosecuted a director of the National Theatre (see Unit 3.7). The role of the Attorney-General was summarised in *Gouriet* v. *Union of Post Office Workers* 1977 by Viscount Dilhorne:

> *The Attorney General has many powers and duties. He may stop any prosecution on indictment by entering a* nolle prosequi. *He merely has to sign a piece of paper saying that he does not wish the prosecution to continue. He need not give any reasons. He can direct the institution of a prosecution and direct the Director of Public Prosecutions to take over the conduct of any criminal proceedings and he may tell him to offer no evidence. In the exercise of these powers he is not subject to direction by his ministerial colleagues or to the control and supervision of the courts.*

Barristers have long enjoyed rights of audience in all courts. In contrast, until very recently solicitors had only a limited right and were excluded from the High Court and Crown Court where barristers would appear robed in wig and gown when appearing in 'open court' as opposed to appearing in ordinary apparel 'in chambers' as when the court is dealing with family work involving injunctions, children or financial ancillary relief.

Most barristers, quite regardless of age, are known as **juniors**. After a number of years of successful practice a junior may apply to the Lord Chancellor to 'take silk', that is to be appointed to the ranks of **Queen's Counsel,** when the barrister is able to place the initials 'QC' after his or her name. Such a barrister is now commonly known as a 'silk', on account of the silk gown now worn, or as a 'leader' because he or she would traditionally not appear in court on his own but, until recent changes, would be accompanied by a junior whom he would lead. In practice, these once strict rules have been relaxed since 1977 so that Queen's Counsel may, if thought proper, appear on their own in court without the assistance of a junior barrister. The unrelenting attack on the scope of public funding has recently caused the present government to announce fresh restrictions on instructing leading counsel under such a certificate.

At the time of writing, there have been renewed calls for the abolition of this status with one Labour MP asking why the Queen should need any Counsel when she does not apparently need so to dignify a Queen's Dentist. The annual round of barristers enjoying their newfound status every Maundy Thursday has recently now been joined by a small band of eminent solicitors.

Unlike solicitors, a barrister may meet his or her client only at a very advanced stage in the steps to trial. Indeed, it is all too often a source of quite understandable distress to the client to discover just short of the door of the court that a substitute barrister has been sent along at the last minute because the original counsel has been delayed in another court. Often this is not the personal fault of the barrister but is, rather, an inevitable and direct consequence of the lack of consultation by those who list cases for trial especially in the Crown Court as well as the difficulty in estimating the duration of any particular case.

Again, unlike the solicitor, a barrister has traditionally never had any contractual relationship with his or her client and has, therefore, not been able to sue for his fee (which, in theory at least, is nothing more than a mere *honorarium*). However, by section 61 of the Courts and Legal Services Act 1990, this longstanding tradition may be approaching some commercial burial. The Act allowed barristers to enter into contracts with their clients. Further, barristers dealing with clients through the Bar DIRECT scheme will be obliged to work against such a contractual background. In practice, however, almost all barristers continue to accept work from solicitors in the absence of any contractual relationship.

Although now only of academic interest since 2000 that same Act also extended to solicitors one special privilege then long enjoyed by barristers as the statute confirmed their immunity for negligence in court. This privilege had been established in *Rondel* v. *Worsley* 1967. A rent-collector employed by the slum landlord Peter Rachman had been convicted of causing grievous bodily harm. He tried to sue his counsel for failing to present his case effectively and to call certain witnesses. Of course, one way in which the guilty can be tempted to challenge their convictions as they while away their time inside is to complain about the lawyers who could not prevent such incarceration. Of the claim's merits (or lack thereof) Lord Hoffman some 33 years later was to say that it represented 'the very paradigm of a hopeless claim by a disgruntled criminal defendant'. At first instance, Lawton J discussed the duties of counsel when he said:

> *He may not provide or devise a line of defence for a client. He may not assert that which he knows to be a lie. He may not connive at, much less attempt to substantiate, a fraud. He may not set up an affirmative case inconsistent with any confession or admission made to him by his client. He must not be a party to any deception of the court.*

In the Court of Appeal, Lord Denning MR dealt further with the duty of a barrister and explained why it would be impracticable to allow claims for negligence for work carried out in court. He said:

> *A barrister cannot pick or choose his clients. He is bound to accept a brief for any man who comes before the court. No matter how great a rascal the man may be. No matter how given to complaining. No matter how undeserving or unpopular his cause ... He has a duty to the court which is paramount. It is a mistake to suppose that he is the mouthpiece of his client to say what he wants or his tool to do what he directs. He is none of these things. He owes allegiance to a higher cause. It is the cause of truth and justice.*

This decision was concerned with the way in which a barrister presented a case in court – in the role of an advocate. It was still not clear whether such immunity extended to other forms of a barrister's work, such as advising in conference, drafting documents or otherwise doing advisory work. That particular matter came to be decided by the House of Lords in *Saif Ali* v. *Sydney Mitchell & Co.* 1978. Many years earlier the plaintiff had been injured in a road accident. His counsel had not advised him properly in the early stages of the consequent litigation. By a narrow vote the House of Lords held that a barrister's immunity should not be wider than was reasonably necessary. Accordingly, a barrister's immunity from suit extended only to those matters of pre-trial work intimately connected with the conduct of the case and not to general advice given months or even years earlier. Of course, no barrister would ever be liable to his or her client just because the case was lost: for a barrister to be found to have been negligent he would have had to have acted quite incompetently. There is, after all, a world of difference between negligence and a mere error of judgment (see Unit 6.3).

Since the high point of *Rondel* v. *Worsley* (and in a world where this sort of immunity is not viewed as consistent with the best interest of the consumer), there have been repeated attempts to erode this special protection. A recent attempt by a former client to sue her barrister came before the Court of Appeal in *Kelley* v. *Corston* 1997 after the client decided that she could not manage on the money she had agreed to accept in proceedings against her former husband. It is extremely difficult for a litigant to appeal against his or her own consent especially where, as here, the consent order had been expressly approved (as is required by the procedure) by the judge who was to try the case. It is a common experience of lawyers that their clients take an unduly optimistic view of the merits of their claims. Some clients also suffer a form of post-settlement remorse in which they persuade themselves that they would have done far better not to have settled. In practice, parties and their advisers are always under pressure to settle, such pressure coming from the judges on occasions and at other times from the continuing need, where relevant, to justify the continuance of a legal aid (now 'public funding') certificate. As Judge LJ remarked in *Kelley* v. *Corston*:

> *Every lawyer in practice and every judge knows that there is no such thing as the case which is bound to succeed. Experience shows that cases with the brightest prospects of success somehow fail and it is difficult to under-estimate the value of the certainty provided by a settlement as opposed to the continuing risks of litigation through to judgment. This factor alone should militate against successful proceedings based on the criticism of advice leading to a settlement.*

Nevertheless, the client complained that she was unable to afford the mortgage on her home and blamed her barrister. At the outset the claim was struck out on the basis that it disclosed no reasonable cause of action but the client appealed. Once again, the Court of Appeal had to consider the extent of an advocate's immunity. In the Court of Appeal Judge LJ recognised the developments in this area over the previous thirty years:

> *Perhaps it should not be necessary to begin consideration of these issues by emphasising that the immunity of the advocate from liability is not founded on some special protection granted by the court to the legal profession to enable lawyers to avoid justifying a complaint by dissatisfied clients. The legal adviser may be held liable for negligent advice to his client in the same way as his medical practitioner or accountant. The immunity arises in very limited circumstances when the general public interest prevails against even a meritorious claim. The trend has been increasingly to limit the circumstances in which immunity may be established and the concept of a blanket immunity is completely out-of-date.*

Of course, in this particular claim, firstly, the plaintiff had expressly agreed to what she got. Secondly, the judge had approved that consent order as being fair in all the circumstances. The background was relevant to the approach of the Court of Appeal to the effect that there should not be collateral attacks on the correctness of a court's judgment upon a contested issue by retrying the same issue in an action against the lawyer who argued the case. Moreover, not only lawyers but judges and witnesses were traditionally free from these claims so as to ensure that trials were conducted without avoidable stress and fear in those who have a part to play in them. The words of one Australian judge remained appropriate:

> *The law protects witnesses and others, not for their benefit, but for a higher interest, namely, the advancement of public justice.*

Because the plaintiff had consented to the judge making the relevant order (who is by no means bound to approve the order) the Court of Appeal could see another difficulty:

> *Litigation which raises the question whether the advocate was negligent in the advice leading to any settlement requiring the approval of the judge is liable to circumvent the principle that the judge may not be asked to explain what he has said or done in court. If such litigation were permitted it is difficult to see how it would be fair to prevent the defendant advocate from seeking to call the judge to demonstrate that the settlement was reasonable.*

The Court of Appeal went on to confirm that an advocate's conduct at the door of the court (the last-minute settlement) was still protected by the immunity because negotiations and the settlements which followed had formed an integral part of the conduct of the case.

This longstanding immunity on grounds of public policy was likely to require some reconsideration in the light of the recent decision of the European Court of Human Rights in *Osman* v. *UK* 1999 (Unit 6.3). The opportunity came before the House of Lords in *Arthur J.S. Hall* v. *Simons* 2000 when a seven-judge tribunal decided by a narrow vote of four to three that this longstanding immunity was no longer appropriate and was an anomalous exception to the principle that there should always be a remedy for a wrong (the legal equivalent of the demand by the clientele of the National Health Service for a pill for every ill).

The original claims had been brought by disgruntled clients against their former solicitors but the issues raised would also intimately affect both branches of the profession. Moreover, the arguments advanced by the solicitors as they sought to argue immunity so as to rid themselves of the claim without a trial on the merits also impinged on the traditional immunity much longer enjoyed by the Bar. The claim was, therefore, to afford the House of Lords an opportunity fully to review the historical development of the immunity and also to consider the changed and increased expectations of the client in a modern society where the consumer is king. Lord Steyn took note of these changes in his speech:

> *The world has changed since 1967. The practice of law has become more commercialized: barristers may now advertise. They may now enter into contracts for legal services with their professional clients. They are now obliged to carry insurance. On the other hand, today we live in a consumerist society in which people have a much greater awareness of their rights.*

The public interest, it was said, was no longer best served by continuing with the immunity, as Lord Hutton put it, 'in the light of modern conditions and having regard to modern perceptions'. Lord Millet, in his speech, was also to note that the protection for the profession against unmeritorious claims now lay in part in the withdrawal of legal aid.

In contrast to solicitors, who retain complete freedom over which clients they will accept and which they will not, the barrister is under a professional duty to accept any brief in a court in which he practises.

This duty is now embodied both in the Bar Code of Conduct and the Courts and Legal Services Act 1990. It is colloquially known as the **cab-rank rule**. This term likens barristers waiting for any client who may need them to licensed taxi-drivers who are forbidden by the Carriage Office to refuse a fare and who are obliged to take that fare where he wants to go.

This duty of counsel to accept 'any brief from the courts in which he professes to practise' is long established. The nature of a case, however gruesome or however politically hostile, is irrelevant. Erskine, deprived of his office of Attorney-General for representing the eighteenth-century politician and author of *The Rights of Man*, Tom Paine, put it dramatically:

> *From the moment that any advocate can be permitted to say that he will or will not stand between the Crown and the subject arraigned in the court where he daily sits to practise, from that moment the liberties of England are at an end.*

e) Fusion

The merger of barristers and solicitors into one single body of lawyers has long been the subject of debate both within and outside the legal profession. The loss of their once lucrative monopoly of conveyancing prompted solicitors to demand rights of audience beyond the County Court and magistrates' courts.

Traditionally, those who have advocated unification or fusion have argued that there would be a reduction in the cost to the client. The need for one lawyer rather than both solicitor and counsel must, at least runs the argument, be cheaper. Those opposed to such a merger would, on the other hand, point to the experience of the American system where, even in a unified profession, a specialist role has nevertheless developed with the emergence of the 'trial lawyer' and the absence of any obvious economy. Experience in other countries of a fused profession has also led to the barbed suggestion that as different lawyers try to do the same job neither does it properly. On the other hand, solicitors seeking wider rights of audience have also been able to point out that the range of lawyers from whom the next generation of judges would be drawn might be enlarged to the benefit of both the country as a whole and the Bench itself.

Those in favour of preserving the traditional distinction between the two branches of a split profession have argued that the Bar's specialisation is the principal attraction of retaining the split profession. They would say that as long as the Bar remains a referral branch of the profession ordinary people all over the country will be able to obtain specific and expert advice from knowledgeable practitioners in any field of law. No small firm of high-street solicitors could possibly offer such specialist skill. In this way, it is said, the ordinary citizen with nothing more than a public funding certificate (the new name for the old legal aid certificate) should, if necessary, be able to consult Queen's Counsel in the same way as the big battalions of international conglomerates and the major insurance companies with whom the citizen is in dispute. Further, so the argument runs, the barrister who works in the higher courts on a daily basis is far better equipped to deal with such demanding work than, say, a sole-practitioner solicitor making only the occasional appearance before a bench of country lay magistrates in between con-veying a couple of semi-detached houses. Moreover, say the opponents of such wider rights of audience, the Bar is a small profession where trust and probity are important and one in which any lapse from high standards will be swiftly detected. This point was underlined by Lord Donaldson MR (himself concerned with the Roll of Solicitors) when the Court of Appeal had to consider an application by a solicitor to appear in the High Court. In 1985 the Liberal Member of Parliament for Rochdale, Cyril Smith, had thrown his weight behind a claim by his solicitor to be allowed to appear in the High Court in order to read out a statement which would settle a libel action brought against the MP by various other Hon. Members in respect of certain comments made about voting habits during the Falklands War. This solicitor (whose main employment with the newspaper *The Times* would have spared him the colossal overheads of private practice) had not wanted to instruct counsel. He claimed that his fees would be lower than those of any of the barristers he had approached, whose fees he castigated as ranging from 'ridiculously expensive' to an almost bargain level of being merely 'unnecessarily expensive'. Rather than simply read the statement himself, the Hon. Member for Rochdale then appealed to the Court of Appeal, which dismissed the appeal. Lord Donaldson MR explained the need to restrict any attempt at open-house advocacy and to maintain high standards:

> *The conduct of litigation in terms of presenting the contentions of the parties in a concise and logical form, deploying and testing the evidence and examining the relevant law demands professional skills of a high order. Failure to display these skills will inevitably extend the time needed to reach a decision, thereby adversely affecting other members of the public who need to have their disputes resolved by the court and adding to the cost of the litigation concerned. It may also, in an extreme case, lead to the court reaching a wrong decision.*
>
> *We are fortunate in this country in having a legal profes-sion, both of whose branches aspire to, and usually attain, equally high standards of professional skill. However, partly as a result of the existing practices of the courts in relation to rights of audience and partly as a result of the Bar's rules of conduct which prevent barristers from doing solicitors' work, their skills and experience are undoubtedly different.*

Lord Donaldson MR went on to discuss the importance of absolute integrity among lawyers themselves. High standards of skill and probity, he said, are not capable of being maintained without peer leadership and pressures and appropriate disciplinary systems, and the difficulty of main-taining them increases with any increase in the size of the group who are permitted to practise advocacy before the courts. The duty of the advo-cate to the litigant must never blind him to his other duty of probity and integrity towards the court itself. Lord Donaldson continued:

> *But quite apart from the public interest in ensuring that advo-cates appearing in the courts have the requisite standard of skill, there is another and even more important requirement.*

> *Here there is no difference between what is expected of the members of each branch of the profession. This is the requirement of absolute probity. The public interest requires that the courts shall be able to have absolute trust in the advocates who appear before them.*

Such an approach by the Court of Appeal was then in tune with the recommendation of the Royal Commission on Legal Services set up in 1976 under Sir Henry Benson. The Commission's wide terms of reference allowed it to examine the structures of the profession, the training of its entrants, the quality of its service to the public and its remuneration. It was the first such Commission since 1851 and reported in 1979. The Commission was unanimously against proposals for the fusion of the profession. It further rejected calls for any general relaxation on the then rights of audience and clearly upheld the Bar's exclusive rights of audience in the higher courts. This Royal Commission was followed by a further Report by Lady Marre on Legal Education and Training. Nevertheless, a government widely perceived by lawyers as hostile to the profession and unsympathetic to the State's role in the provision of legal aid or other assistance to the citizen with problems reneged on its earlier declared acceptance of such advice and, fresh from imposing its massive political will on the teaching and then medical professions, turned its attention to the legal profession. As previously with the teachers and the doctors, the politicians caused great resentment by their proposals, involving government licensing of legal practitioners, which first saw the light of day in a Green Paper described by no less than the then Lord Chief Justice himself as 'one of the most sinister documents ever to emanate from government'. Lord Lane was later to warn of the need for the courts to be able to control the way in which government departments treated the individual citizen. The judges themselves were appalled at the prospect of political control of the courts and of those who would be licensed by the government to practise in those courts. The proposals represented a threat to judicial independence as the executive sought to encroach on the judiciary and, in doing so, to strike at the fundamental concept of the separation of powers – an important feature in the unwritten British constitution. The Master of the Rolls was also to warn in a Parliamentary debate in the House of Lords of the temptations to which governments were subject to ride roughshod over the rights of minorities who disagreed with them, and he recalled the words of one past Prime Minister: 'Get your tanks off my lawn.' Throughout the country, then as now, many lawyers detected the ever-present hand of the Treasury behind the Department of Trade and Industry jargon of 'cost effective services' and 'the discipline of competition' at a time when the government had already taken steps to reduce very significantly eligibility for public funding.

Albeit in much more muted form the Green Paper passed into legislation as the Courts and Legal Services Act 1990. The Act had important consequences for rights of audience, in that solicitors were entitled to appear in the higher courts once they had obtained the necessary qualifications and experience in stages.

f) Judges

To many people, lawyers and laymen alike, the visible mark of success in a lawyer's career is to be made a judge – 'appointed to the Bench'. This system contrasts with, for example, the French system where lawyers must decide early on whether they wish to practise or to be judges. Since the Courts Act 1971 solicitors had been eligible for appointment as recorders (part-time judges) and, therefore, became eligible also for full-time appointment in time. The method of their appointment is one of the distinguishing features of the English judiciary: although judges are appointed by the Crown, they retain their independence from the Executive (that is, the government and other political pressures). This English system of promotion from the ranks of the practising profession was neatly explained by one clergyman turned writer who remarked:

> *Lawyers are the only civil delinquents whose judges must of necessity be chosen from themselves.*

Both prior to and throughout a judge's appointment he or she will attend regular sessions of instructions at seminars held by the **Judicial Studies Board**. Set up in 1979 'to convey in a condensed form the lessons which experienced judges have acquired', this body now has as its Director of Studies a judge who superintends various lectures, training sessions and publications. The Board has been particularly active in the last couple of years in teaching the country's judges the new civil procedure brought about by the changes introduced by Lord Woolf. Judicial students also attend courses in computing provided by the Board, which also publishes specimen directions for use in the Crown Court and guidelines for the assessment of damages for personal injury awards.

There has long been a shortage of judges at all levels of the courts' structure. Delays are ever present and the system copes only because of the large number of deputy judges, such as recorders. The dangers of the then government's failure to provide a satisfactory judicial system were underlined in 1992 by the Lord Chief Justice, Lord Taylor of Gosforth, who, in an unusual public appearance on television giving the Richard Dimbleby Lecture, warned that inadequate provision for the administration of justice could endanger the framework of society and lead to unrest as, for example, in criminal matters where prisoners have served their sentences for imprisonment before their appeals are even heard. In commercial matters, too, businesses which have traditionally contracted to have any future disagreements tried by the courts in England and Wales may well prefer to take their litigation (and many millions of pounds in invisible earnings for the country) to other jurisdictions if their choice is between speedy justice in a foreign court or a three-year wait to get into a London court room. As the Lord Chief Justice himself warned:

> *If the rule of law and citizens' rights are not safeguarded, the result may not only be injustice but even unrest, especially during high unemployment.*

The titles of judges denote their position in the hierarchy. So if John Blank, a lawyer of some years' standing, is appointed a circuit judge, he is known as 'His Honour Judge Blank' and is addressed in court as 'Your Honour'. If, instead, he is appointed as a judge of the High Court, he will be known as 'Mr Justice Blank' and will be addressed in court as 'My Lord'. The latter appointment also carries with it a knighthood. Further promotion to the Court of Appeal is reflected in a change of title to Lord Justice Blank, although in private life the judge remains a knight. Ultimately, there may be appointment to the House of Lords, and this time there is another change in name, to Lord Blank, and with it a seat in the House of Lords.

The role of the judge is complex but amounts to control of the trial, deciding all questions of law and admissibility of evidence and, where he is not also a judge of fact, assisting the jury over the salient points of the evidence and thus ensuring a fair trial. In this way a judge will endeavour to acquit himself of the oath taken upon appointment:

> ...to do right to all manner of people after the laws and usages of this Realm, without fear or favour, affection or ill will.

Judges, once appointed, cannot easily be removed from office. The tenure of their office was governed initially by the Act of Settlement of 1701, which provided that judges held office *quam diu se bene gesserint* which really means as long as they behave themselves. The Supreme Court of Judicature (Consolidation) Act 1925 now provides:

> All the judges of the High Court and the Court of Appeal, with the exception of the Lord Chancellor, shall hold their offices during good behaviour subject to a power of removal by [Her] Majesty on an address presented to [Her] Majesty by both Houses of Parliament.

The Courts Act 1971 provides that circuit judges may be removed by the Lord Chancellor for incapacity or misbehaviour.

Judges have long enjoyed a common-law immunity from any legal proceedings arising from what they say or do while acting in their official capacity. For instance, in *Sirros* v. *Moore* 1974 the plaintiff attempted to sue a judge for false imprisonment. The action failed, for, as Lord Denning MR pointed out in discussing the position of the judge:

> *The words which he speaks are protected by absolute privilege. The orders which he gives, and the sentences which he imposes, cannot be made the subject of civil proceedings against him. No matter that the judge was under some gross error or ignorance, or was actuated by envy, hatred or malice and all uncharitableness, he is not liable to an action ... The reason is not because the judge has any privilege to make mistakes or to do wrong. It is so that he should be able to do his duty with complete independence and free from fear.*

This exemption from liability for damages has been placed on a statutory basis by section 69 of the Courts and Legal Services Act 1990.

In addition to their normal judicial duties judges are sometimes called upon by the government to hold inquiries. For example, in 1994 Sir Richard Scott, the Vice-Chancellor of the Chancery Division, could be seen almost daily on television for some weeks as he cycled his way to conduct his inquiry into the 'Arms to Iraq' scandal. Another high-profile inquiry was that set up under the Police Act 1997 when the retired judge, Sir William Macpherson, chaired the inquiry into the murder of Stephen Lawrence. The latter Report made scathing criticism of the 'institutionalised racism' of the Metropolitan Police and of the incompetence of many of the individual police officers. In October 2000, similar judicial reproof was vented upon incompetent civil servants in the Ministry of Agriculture, Fisheries and Food together with a number of complacent Conservative then ministers when Lord Phillips of Worth Matravers, the present Master of the Rolls, submitted his report into BSE (bovine spongiform encephalopathy or the so-called 'mad cow disease') which so badly affected animals and later humans after the mid 1980s. At the time of writing a second inquiry, chaired by Lord Saville, is being held into the events of 'Bloody Sunday' when in January 1972 a number of protestors and others were killed in Northern Ireland.

A judge also has power to punish people who are in contempt of court, as in *Balogh* v. *Crown Court at St Albans* 1974. A solicitor's clerk was attending a pornography trial at a Crown Court. Whether despite or because of the subject-matter he became increasingly bored. In an attempt to enliven counsel's speeches, he stole a cylinder of nitrous oxide from a hospital and planned to introduce this 'laughing gas' into the air-conditioning plant of the court building. He was stopped before his scheme achieved its intended aim and was brought before a judge. The clerk's next comment served only to add personal offence when he told the senior judge of that new court: 'You are a humourless automaton. Why don't you self-destruct?' The clerk later appealed against the sentence of six months' imprisonment. The Court of Appeal considered the history of a judge's power to punish contempt in the courts. As Stephenson LJ explained:

> ...*the power which the judge exercised is both salutary and dangerous: salutary because it gives those who administer justice the protection necessary to secure justice for the public, dangerous because it deprives a citizen of the protection of safeguards considered generally necessary to prevent justice being obstructed or undermined – even by a practical joker. That is not because judges, jurors, witnesses and officers of the court take themselves seriously in a civilized society: it is because justice, whose servants they are, must be taken seriously in a civilized society if the rule of law is to be maintained.*

The Court of Appeal nevertheless allowed Mr Balogh's appeal and released him from gaol. The solicitor's clerk had reason to be glad that times had changed since 1631 when, in a mixture of English, French and Latin, the law report records how a prisoner:

> *ject un Brickbat a le dit Justice que narrowly mist, & pur ceo immediately fuit Indictment drawn per Noy envers le prisoner, & son dexter manus amputee & fix al Gibbet sur que luy mesme immediatement hange in presence de Court.*

2.6 *To sue or not to sue*

Going to law, say the cynics and the losers, is a lottery. Put less emotively, it may be said that litigation (the process of suing and being sued), like marriage, is not something 'to be taken in hand inadvisedly, lightly or wantonly'.

To sue and then to lose is not only annoying – it is expensive and may be doubly so for you could end up paying not only your own costs but the other party's as well. Even if you win, the other side may not have the cash to pay you and the result, in short, would be a Pyrrhic victory.

There are, therefore, a number of questions which any prospective claimant must consider:

(i) **Have I a course of action?**   This is obvious enough. Check that your grievance is one for which the law provides a remedy: for example, mere vulgar abuse is not slander (see Unit 6.10).

(ii) **Under which head do I claim?**   You take your car to a garage to have the brakes relined but the mechanic makes such a mess of the job that on the return journey it is not your brakes which stop the car but the back of a double-decker bus. Do you sue the garage in contract (for breach of the implied term that a workmanlike job would be done on the brakes) or in tort (for the mechanic's negligent work)? One factor on which the answer may depend is the wording of any exemption clause you may have signed.

(iii) **Whom do I make the defendant?**   This is not such a silly question as it may well look at first sight. For instance, if while you are waiting at the traffic lights a large van on its way to deliver bread-rolls to the local supermarket parks itself up your exhaust-pipe, to whom do you look for compensation? Do you sue the van-driver, Mr Brown? Of course he was at fault and is, therefore, liable but has he the money to pay? He may be what lawyers call a 'man of straw' – one without means. Employers are, however, vicariously liable for the negligent acts of their employees (Unit 6.8b)) and, anyway, are usually insured. So don't just sue Brown: sue the bread company as well – they have the cash to pay up.

. . . a 'man of straw' . . .

Litigation can be a heart-breaking and complex business and few people undertake it without the help of a solicitor. Indeed, there is a wise saying that a man who is his own lawyer has a fool for a client. For that reason, the rest of this Unit is intended for the student and not the litigant in person. It is, in short, a description of 'how it is done' and not 'how to do it'. A further warning is appropriate as it was from 26 April 1999 that, as a result of the overhaul of civil litigation brought about by the report of Lord Woolf and the subsequent Civil Procedure Rules, many textbooks suddenly became seriously out of date.

a) Steps of the trial

Letter before action

Before dashing round to the court office, a prospective claimant should write a 'letter before action' to the intended defendant. This letter sets out the complaint and what the would-be claimant wants the defendant to do about it. With luck or good judgment, this may by itself persuade the recipient to mend his or her ways, thus avoiding the need for litigation altogether.

Which court?

Until a few years ago every case tried in a County Court had to have some geographical link with the court itself. For example, if a driver pursued a motorised blitz down the M4 and hit a Skoda near Slough, a Rover at Reading and a Bentley upon arrival at Bristol, the owners of the damaged vehicles would bring their respective claims in the Slough, Reading and Bristol County Courts. The Courts and Legal Services Act 1990 permitted a claimant to issue such proceedings in any County Court, although the case may be transferred to the defendant's County Court once a Defence has been filed.

Statement of Case

Obviously if somebody is suing you you will want to know what it is all about. For this reason, a claimant must serve on the defendant a claim form which has, under the new rules, also to be accompanied by a statement confirming the truth of the Particulars of Claim. Those claimants who are untruthful in these statements run the risk of punishment for contempt of court. This document will provide a concise statement of the facts relied upon by the claimant and will specify the nature of the remedy sought. While more information is now provided at this early stage than was the case before April 1999 the art of pleading, which once took up so much study by Bar students and then practitioners' time in drafting, has far less importance under the new regime of civil justice which followed upon the Civil Procedure Rules (CPR). An example of essentially simple Particulars of Claim in a run of the mill 'running down' action appears at Figure 2.1. The claim form must be served within four months of issue; the Particulars of Claim may also be served at the same time or, alternatively, within fourteen days. It is important for any claimant seeking money to set out a statement of value. This must be assessed within financial brackets which affect the particular 'track' to which the claim is allotted.

Fig. 2.1 Particulars of Claim

IN THE SOUTH LONDON COUNTY COURT   CASE NO: SL 99 1234

BETWEEN:

OLIVER TWIST   Claimant

and

NICHOLAS NICKLEBY   Defendant

PARTICULARS OF CLAIM

1. On or about 1st January 1999 the Claimant was driving his Ford Mondeo motor car, registration number ABC 123, along the A23 road from Croydon to Brighton when the said motor car was struck and damaged by a motor-cycle, registration number DEF 456, driven by the Defendant.

2. The said collision was occasioned by the negligence of the Defendant.

PARTICULARS OF NEGLIGENCE

  (i)   Driving at an excessive speed.
  (ii) Failing to keep any or any proper look-out.
  (iii) Failing to heed the presence of the Claimant.
  (iv) Failing to brake, steer, swerve or otherwise avoid the Claimant.
  (v) Overtaking when it was not safe to do so.

3. By reason of the matters aforesaid, the Claimant suffered pain, injury, loss and damage.

PARTICULARS OF INJURIES

The Claimant, who was born on 1st January 1980, sustained an undisplaced nasal fracture. The Claimant continues to suffer from a blocked nose and intermittent headaches, shock, pain and suffering. At trial herein the Claimant will rely, inter alia, upon the report of Mr. Black F.R.C.S. dated 1st June 1999 and served herewith.

PARTICULARS OF SPECIAL DAMAGE

Repairs to motor car	£ 1,975.00
Medical fees	£ 700.00
Taxis to hospital	£ 65.00
Damage to clothing	£ 125.50
	£ 2,865.50

AND the Claimant claims:

(1) Damages;

(2) Interest thereon pursuant to Section 69 County Courts Act 1984 from date hereof until judgment herein or sooner payment.

JUSTIN FORTHEMONEY

STATEMENT OF TRUTH
I believe that the facts stated in these particulars of claim are true.
Signed   *Oliver Twist*
Name   Oliver Twist
DATED the 22nd day of June, 1999
To the District Judge and to the Defendant
Wright, Shambles & Crooks
1 Counsel's Row, London, SW27
Solicitors for the Claimant who will accept service of
all proceedings at the above address.

The **case number** is the reference number which the County Court office gives to the case and which must be quoted in all further **pleadings** (the name lawyers give to the preliminary documents such as the Particulars of Claim).

Special damages are those over and above the damage which the law presumes to have occurred and which are easily quantified in money terms – loss of wages, damage to property and so on; they must be specified, item by item, in the claim.

General damages, on the other hand, are those which are not easily quantifiable in money terms – for example, the damage occasioned to a face when flying through a car windscreen. They are not specified in the claim; instead, the judge decides how much the injured person deserves in compensation for the pain and suffering which the court assumes the claimant sustained.

The name at the end is that of the barrister who pleaded (drafted) the document, and below his or her name is the firm of solicitors who are acting for the particular litigant.

Proceedings must be served on the defendant. This may be done by handing, posting, faxing or now, with the defendant's consent, even e-mailing the papers to him or her. Where there are solicitors acting for the defendant, it may be sent to them and they will accept service on their client's behalf.

Defence   It may be that the defendant now decides to pay up. Alternatively, further discussions may take place with a view to settling out of court. This may well mean some give and take on both sides; nevertheless many disputes are settled by negotiation, usually by the respective solicitors in correspondence, or, where that fails, often literally at the court door. The phenomenon of parties suddenly settling bitterly contested cases at the latest possible moment is one inadequately researched by psychologists but well known to lawyers.

If an early settlement out of court proves impossible to achieve, the defendant must file a **Defence**. This document must state which of the allegations in the Particulars of Claim are denied. Under the new regime a bland denial is no longer permitted; the defendant must now set out his or her own version of the matters not admitted. Moreover, if he feels that the claimant has caused him some loss or damage, he may also **Counterclaim**, which means to sue the very person who is now suing him. Such a document might take the form shown in Figure 2.2. Once a Defence has been filed the parties have to complete an allocation questionnaire which will further influence the track along which the litigation is to proceed. Apart from the sum of money at stake regard will be had to factors such as its complexity.

The defendant may accept that he or she is liable but may think that the amount of the claimant's claim is excessive. He may then, if he wishes, lodge with an officer of the court (**pay into court**) a sum of money which he regards as a reasonable estimate of the damages actually sustained. The new Civil Procedure Rules (CPR) in particular merit consideration for the innovative approach to this issue set out in **CPR Part 36** which has formalised the approach of a defendant making a without prejudice offer even before proceedings have been issued. The impact of this approach upon costs is examined in Unit 2.7a).

Fig. 2.2 Defence and Counterclaim

IN THE SOUTH LONDON COUNTY COURT   Case No. SL 99 1234

BETWEEN:

OLIVER TWIST   Claimant

and

NICHOLAS NICKLEBY   Defendant

DEFENCE AND COUNTERCLAIM

1. Save that a motor-car driven by the Claimant and a motor-cycle driven by the Defendant herein were in collision on or about 1st January 1999, no admission is made as to Paragraph 1 of the Particulars of Claim herein.

2. The Defendant denies that the said collision was occasioned by his negligence as alleged in the Particulars of Claim or at all.

3. If, which is not admitted, the Claimant has suffered pain, injury, loss or damage as alleged or at all, the Defendant will contend that such pain, injury, loss or damage was caused solely by or contributed to by the negligence of the Claimant.

PARTICULARS OF NEGLIGENCE

(i)   Failing to keep to the correct side of the road.
(ii) Overtaking when it was not safe to do so.
(iii) Driving at an excessive speed.
(iv) Failing to keep any or any proper look-out.
(v)   Failing to heed the presence of the Defendant.
(vi) Failing to brake, steer, swerve or otherwise avoid the Defendant.
(vii) Failing to wear a seat belt.

COUNTERCLAIM

4. The Defendant repeats Paragraphs 1 to 3 of the Defence herein.

5. By reason of the matters aforesaid, the Defendant suffered pain, injury, loss and damage.

PARTICULARS OF INJURY

The Defendant sustained a broken wrist on his right arm, shock, pain and suffering. At trial herein the Defendant will rely, inter alia, upon the report of Mr. White F.R.C.S. dated 30th June 1999 and served herewith.

PARTICULARS OF SPECIAL DAMAGE

Repairs to motor cycle	£1,245
Loss of wages from 1st January, 1999 to 1st February, 1999 at £2,200 per month, less tax and national insurance	£2,200

AND the Defendant Counterclaims:
(1) Damages;
(2) Interest thereon pursuant to Section 69 County Courts Act 1984 from date hereof until judgment given or sooner payment.

IVAN EDAKE

The Defendant believes that the facts stated in this Defence are true.
I am duly authorized by the Defendant to sign this statement.
Signed: *A. Shyster*
Position held: Solicitor
Solicitor for the Defendant
DATED the 1st day of July, 1999

To the Claimant and to the District Judge of the South London County Court
Stinking, Filthy & Rich
2 Counsel's Row
London, SW27
Solicitors for the Defendant who will accept service of
all proceedings on his behalf at the said address.

Whether or not the claims can be settled without a hearing (and there is ever-increasing pressure upon litigants these days kindly not to trouble the courts) the new procedure is far more likely than before to involve an increasingly interventionist role by the judges. All litigation nowadays has to be viewed against the so-called 'over-riding objective' set out in Part 1 of the Civil Procedure Rules, which replace the old Rules that applied separately to the High Court and County Court. This objective, or what elsewhere might be called a 'mission statement', is, in reassuring and wholly commendable terms, to enable 'the court to deal with cases justly'. Moreover, 'the parties are required to help the court to further the overriding objective'. No one could even contemplate disagreement upon such laudable objectives. The unrelenting commercial drive to reduce cost is, however, potentially at least not without a downside in terms of the quality of justice which may be delivered once the concept of dealing with a case justly is further defined. The detail as to how a court should now act is set out in Part 1 as:

(i) ensuring that the parties are on an equal footing;
(ii) saving expense;
(iii) dealing with the case in ways which are proportionate –
   a) to the amount of money involved;
   b) to the importance of the case;
   c) to the complexity of the issues; and
   d) to the financial position of each party;
(iv) ensuring that it is dealt with expeditiously and fairly; and
(v) allotting to it an appropriate share of the court's resources, while taking into account the need to allot resources to other cases.

Concepts such as 'proportionality' now influence procedure more and more. Claims which may matter very greatly to all the people involved may still not be thought worthy of much court time. Judges now may impose guillotines upon evidence both in terms of oral presentation and severe constraints in respect of disclosure of documents before the hearing. This is especially true of those smaller claims which are unlikely to be allowed to take up more than an hour of court time. These smaller claims will be heard on the so-called 'small claims track'. There are three different tracks:

1. Small claims;
2. Fast;
3. Multi-track.

Claims of up to £5,000, or where the claim for damages for personal injury is under £1,000, will be dealt with as small claims. These are the claims which under the old procedure would have been dealt with by way of arbitration. While the district judge will not be seated under a palm tree it is well known that the procedure adopted is informal and the judge has a very wide discretion how to conduct proceedings. Disclosure is severely limited and experts may be called as witnesses only with leave. Appeals are difficult to bring for they lie only where there has been a serious irregularity in the proceedings or where the district judge is said to have made a mistake of law.

Where the claim is limited to £15,000 and the case will not last more than a day the case will be allocated to the 'fast track'. All other claims will be assigned to the 'multi-track procedure'.

Often at trial it will be necessary for the judge to consider correspondence between the parties or their solicitors. In order to encourage the parties to settle their differences without recourse to the courts the law allows genuine offers of settlement to be protected from judicial eyes by the application to such letters of the label **without prejudice**. Letters so marked may not be shown to the judge in contrast to other letters which, as lawyers say, form the **open correspondence**. Some ignorance nevertheless surrounds the use of the term 'without prejudice'. Only letters aimed at settlement outside the courts may properly be so labelled. If the letter does not deal with the prospect of settlement ('without prejudice' to carrying on with the claim if the offer is not accepted) it cannot be protected from disclosure. It is, by way of example, not possible for a blackmailer to say at his trial that his threatening letter (now the principal exhibit for the prosecution) should not be shown to the jury simply because he had marked his unwarranted demand at the top with the words 'without prejudice'. The true effect of such wording was emphasised in *Dixon Stores Group Ltd* v. *Thames Television plc* 1993:

> The mere fact of heading a letter 'Without Prejudice' is not in the least decisive as to whether or not the letter is in fact privileged but privilege exists in order to encourage such a bona fide attempt to negotiate a settlement of an action and if the letter is not written to initiate or continue such a bona fide attempt to effect a settlement it will not be protected by privilege.

The rationale of this privilege was said by Oliver LJ in *Cutts* v. *Head* 1984 to rest on the following public policy:

> It is that parties should be encouraged so far as possible to settle their disputes without resort to litigation and should not be discouraged by the knowledge that anything that is said in the course of such negotiations (and that includes, of course, as much the failure to reply to an offer as an actual reply) may be used to their prejudice in the course of the proceedings.... The public policy justification, in truth, essentially rests on the desirability of preventing statements or offers made in the course of negotiations for settlement being brought before the court of trial as admissions on the question of liability.

Summary judgment

It had long been recognised that unmeritorious defences (known colloquially as 'holding defences') would be put forward where there was no real defence. The old Rules of the Supreme Court allowed for the procedure of summary judgment (one given in favour of the plaintiff without hearing evidence) where it could be demonstrated that there was no arguable defence. By **Part 24** of the CPR a claimant is now in an even stronger position because of a significant change of wording which allows summary judgment where the other side has no real prospect of defending. Defendants may also use this procedure where it can be shown that the claimant has 'failed to show a case which, if unanswered, would entitle him to judgment or the defendant has shown that the claim would be bound to be dismissed at trial'.

The hearing

Procedures in the County Court and High Court are similar to that of any other court. The claimant's counsel or solicitor opens the case, explains to the judge what the issues are, and then calls witnesses, who may be cross-examined by the defendant's lawyer and then re-examined by the claimant's counsel or solicitor. After the claimant's witnesses have all been examined, the defendant usually calls his or her witnesses and the same round of examination-in-chief, cross-examination and re-examination follows (these terms are explained in detail in Unit 3.8). It is no longer thought appropriate for a witness to tell his own story from the witness box. The new time-saving procedure requires such witnesses to set out their case on paper and such statements will stand as their evidence-in-chief although some general updating or modest amplification may still be permitted. The defendant's counsel or solicitor may then address the judge in argument (known as 'submissions') and, finally, the claimant either in person or through his or her lawyers has the last word. The judge then delivers his judgment, dealing with both the facts as he finds them and the law as he views it.

Costs

While this sensitive topic is specifically considered in Unit 2.7 it is convenient now to note that the old rule remains. Costs are still said to 'follow the event' (in effect, the loser pays the winner's costs), although the new ethos does require a rather more precise examination of the way in which the parties have conducted their litigation so that only partial success or belligerent conduct within the litigation would reduce the amount awarded against the losing party. In simple cases it will be appropriate for the judge to deal with the amount of costs to be paid by way of a 'summary assessment'. It is for this reason that costs estimates have to be prepared and exchanged ahead of hearings. Alternatively, in more complex disputes, the amount to be paid by the paying party must await another day and a 'detailed assessment' as to quantum.

b) Enforcement of judgments

Belief in the 'Majesty of the Law', however popular, is not by itself always enough to persuade the losing side to pay up. If it proves insufficient, the winner must seek to have his or her judgment enforced. Although a court will only take steps to enforce its own judgment when specifically asked to do so, there are a number of ways of persuading or compelling the other side to comply with the judgment.

Execution

This is not as drastic as it sounds because it refers to the loser's property rather than to his or her person. On an application by the successful, but unpaid party, the court may issue a warrant which allows the bailiffs to seize so much of the debtor's property as is needed to satisfy the **Judgment debt** – the amount originally awarded by the judge. The compact-disc-player and microwave oven are obviously likely prey. The Courts and Legal Services Act 1990 prevents the bailiff from seizing tools, books, vehicles and other items of equipment needed by the debtor for use in his or her job. Bailiffs have a discretion over household items but should not seize clothing, bedding, furniture or other such items considered necessary to satisfy the basic domestic needs of the home. This form of enforcement, however, is not much use if the debtor has acquired all his little luxuries on hire-purchase, because in that case they belong not to him but to some finance company; goods obtained on hire-purchase are in fact hired from a finance company until they have effectively been paid for and are only then purchased for a nominal sum.

Whatever is carted away by the bailiffs is later sold by auction and the proceeds are handed over to the creditor (the successful party).

Attachment of earnings order Where a debtor is in employment, the Attachment of Earnings Act 1971 can require his or her employer to deduct a certain sum each week from his wages: that amount is then handed over to the creditor. Protection for the debtor and any family is provided by the concept of a 'protected earnings rate' which is the bottom line required for his own maintenance in the style of a recipient of Income Support.

Garnishee order It may be that Tom has obtained a judgment against Dick for £750, and that Dick has not paid but he, in turn, is owed £750 by Harry. Tom may then obtain a 'garnishee order' from the court ordering Harry to pay him the £750 direct.

Bankruptcy A more drastic option is to make the debtor bankrupt. In effect, this process takes the management of his or her financial affairs out of his hands and places it in those of the court and then the debtor's Trustee in Bankruptcy. The drawback here is not only that the repercussions for the debtor may be far more serious than the small debt really warrants, but also that the creditors are unlikely to recover more than a few pence in the pound. Moreover, those who are owed only small sums will not find this remedy of assistance available to them as the Insolvency Act 1986 raised the minimum to warrant the commencement of bankruptcy proceedings to £750. The pension provision of a bankrupt is likely now to be protected upon implementation of the Welfare Reform and Pensions Act 1999.

Receiver Where the debtor is a person of some substance and has dividends or rents coming in, some trustworthy person such as a solicitor or accountant may be appointed by the court to act as a receiver. He will, as the name implies, receive the dividends or rents on behalf of the debtor and, on his or her behalf, pay the money over to the creditor.

Charging order If the debtor is a land-owner, the creditor may register a charge against the land (as a building society does when it lends money on a mortgage) so that he or she will be entitled to share in the proceeds of any sale. Moreover, the creditor may even insist on the land being sold, so that there will be money out of which he can be paid. Since the Charging Orders Act 1979 it has been possible to obtain a charging order over land jointly owned by the debtor and a third party (such as the debtor's spouse).

2.7 Who pays for it all?

At the conclusion of a big case which has received considerable publicity, newspapers and television will all too often quote some seemingly outrageous figure almost plucked out of the air as being the costs of the action and which may even rise by thousands of pounds between the early and late news bulletins. In this unreliable way the press all too often tends to convey the impression to a public ever ready to believe it that, between them, a couple of barristers have managed to carve up literally tens of thousands of pounds for only a few days' light work, stamping their cards at 10.30 a.m. and going home for tea at 4 p.m. Unfortunately for the pockets of the counsel concerned, such an impression is thoroughly misleading if not also mischievous. Nevertheless, no one, lawyer or layman, would deny that the cost of going to law can be substantial.

The reaction 'That's life!' would indeed have been a stoic one as the British Broadcasting Corporation emerged from the High Court in 1985 after the most costly libel action in English legal history. On the eighty-seventh day of the action the Corporation settled a claim brought by a Harley Street slimming expert, Sidney Gee, after Esther Rantzen's *That's Life* series carried a programme highly critical of the plaintiff. Whatever doubts had unwisely been raised about the plaintiff's practice, there could be no doubting that the British Broadcasting Corporation itself shed very many pounds as it picked up the costs of the action, unofficially estimated at £1,000,000. Fortunately, such cases are wholly unrepresentative of the costs involved.

Anyone who has been to court may well have seen a parade of witnesses for each side. Few witnesses are happy to lose a day's earnings in order to attend court and most keenly seek reimbursement. Some, moreover, may be expert witnesses, professional people like accountants and doctors who have prepared reports and who come particularly expensive. On top of that, counsel and solicitors will probably be engaged. The level of fees charged by the court also rose steeply in 1998 as the government, with its private monopoly control of such matters while talking publicly about competition, pursued its course of making the courts self-financing. It can now cost literally five times as much in court fees just to issue proceedings as was the case only a couple of years ago. All these items involve expense and someone, somewhere, will have to foot the bill. As a general rule that person has traditionally been the loser. Such an approach, however hallowed, is now to be considered in the light of the post-Woolf world where the court should also look more critically at the degree of success enjoyed as well as the conduct of the parties in the litigation. The rules, moreover, have to differ in civil and criminal matters.

a) Civil costs

As already seen, the starting point is that the loser pays the winner's costs. This practice is subject to the court's discretion so that a winning party may not necessarily be awarded his or her costs. For example, in *Dering* v. *Uris* 1964 the plaintiff sued the defendant in respect of libel in the book *Exodus*. The jury, who were obviously not sympathetic to the plaintiff, awarded him contemptuous damages of one halfpenny (see

Unit 6.10c)). The trial judge did not award the plaintiff (claimant) his costs, even though they would have run into thousands of pounds. The defendant had earlier paid £2 into court as his estimate of the plaintiff's damages. It has long been the rule that a claimant who fails to recover more than has already been paid into court by the defendant will be unable to recover any costs incurred after the date of such payment.

Even before the new landscape of the Civil Procedure Rules the courts had increasingly had regard to written proposals for settlement of actions. A party faced with a claim may write a **without prejudice** letter, often known as a **Calderbank** letter after the case of the same name. In such a letter he or she may put forward his proposals for settlement. If the other side fails to match the terms put forward, the court, on learning of the terms of any offer only after judgment, may order the other side to pay the costs incurred after receipt of such a letter. This procedure has proved to be of special relevance in matrimonial property disputes where former spouses will argue about the division of the home and where, obviously, neither spouse can pay into court half the value of their former matrimonial home.

After the new regime of civil litigation introduced in April 1999, parties to litigation must be ever vigilant about the potential impact of any order as to costs. Part 36 of the Rules, although not applicable in small claims, allows a party ('the offeror') to make an offer of settlement any time. The sting in the tail is that a claimant who does not improve on such offer is likely to end up paying the other side's costs after the latest date when the offer could have been accepted within the rules. A claimant may also specifically improve his or her prospects of recovering his costs by making his own Part 36 offer at the outset by indicating the sort of sum he would accept in satisfaction of the claim. These new rules as to costs are obviously intended to discourage people from litigating their disputes because the court even has power to order interest upon its award from the latest date when such proposal could have been accepted by the defendant. Such without prejudice proposals must be kept open for 21 days.

In matrimonial disputes over assets owned by one or both former spouses, the impact of an order as to costs might significantly interfere with the ability of one party to provide a home for the children (such consideration always being uppermost in the court's concerns). Where that party is in receipt of public funding (still more commonly recognised as legal aid), the Regulations allow payment of any costs due to the Legal Services Commission (which, it must always be remembered, *lends* not pays the cost of the lawyers' services) to be postponed until the house is sold. This debt then operates as a second mortgage at a rate of interest which has been significantly higher than that at which building societies were lending money and which provides a good rate of return to the Treasury.

A party who has been awarded costs is nevertheless primarily liable to meet his own solicitor's fees. He will, however, submit it to the other party and seek to recover from him. If the costs are disputed by the other side that party may apply to have the bill assessed by the court so that costs of an unreasonable amount or any which have been unreasonably incurred are reduced or disallowed.

It used to be the case that a party who had not been legally represented could not be reimbursed for the time he had spent in preparing his case but the Litigants in Person (Costs and Expenses) Act 1975 allowed a successful party to recover 'sums in respect of any work done and any expenses and losses incurred by the litigant in or in connection with the proceedings to which the order relates'.

On some occasions, unfortunately, the court also has to consider whether, because of some negligence or other failure, an order for costs should be made also against one party's own lawyers. The Courts and Legal Services Act 1990 empowers the court to order those referred to as 'legal or other representatives' to meet wasted costs, a phrase meaning costs incurred as a result of any improper, unreasonable or negligent act or omission. Care needs to be taken with this wording so as to prevent this device being used to recover through the back door costs which would not otherwise be recoverable against a litigant who was either without funds or publicly funded.

In *Ridehalgh* v. *Horsefield* 1994 the Court of Appeal had to consider this aspect along with the traditional immunity of lawyers from claims for negligence in connection with their court work. As examined already in Unit 2.5d) barristers are as a matter of professional conduct required by the so-called cab-rank rule to accept any brief to appear before a court in which they profess to practise and also to act for any person irrespective of the nature of the case and any belief or opinion which the barrister may have formed. A strict construction of the statute was, therefore, appropriate and it was said that lawyers would not be held to have acted improperly, unreasonably or negligently simply in acting for a client who had pursued a claim or defence which was doomed to failure.

b) Criminal costs

Different considerations must apply in a criminal case. The police may spend literally years in preparing a prosecution. Thousands of hours' overtime will have to be paid for, much travel (seemingly, often to Spain or South America) may have been involved and elaborate security cover may be provided for the trial itself. A man sentenced to a long term of imprisonment would have some difficulty in paying the costs of the winning side. Normally, therefore, the costs of bringing a prosecution and enforcing the criminal law are met out of the public purse at both national and local level.

The Prosecution of Offences Act 1985 provides that a court may order payment of the prosecution costs out of central funds (money provided by Parliament) or may order the convicted defendant to pay the whole or any part of the costs involved. If a defendant is acquitted, the Act seeks to compensate him for expenses properly incurred and the court may order those costs to be paid either out of central funds or by the prosecution.

Moreover, in a Practice Direction for the Crown Court issued in 1999 the Lord Chief Justice indicated that defendants who are acquitted should normally have their costs paid (known as a 'defendant's costs order'). However, such an order need not be made where there are positive reasons for not doing so as where, for example, the defendant's own conduct has brought suspicion on himself.

2.8 *Funding*

The inclusion of this topic by examination boards in the relevant syllabi and the growing unwillingness of successive governments properly to fund this important social service render treatment of this topic increasingly only academic in different common uses of that word.

Litigation, while always to be avoided if at all possible, may prove to be the only way in which a dispute can be resolved or an individual's clear entitlement properly assured. The complexity of some such issues and the need to marshal cogent evidence in support of legitimate needs and entitlements has over the years served to emphasise the corresponding need for expert help to be provided for the poorer members of the community. Sadly, this concern for such people dwindled markedly during the Conservatives' tenure of office during the 1980s when one government minister let the cat out of the bag by describing people such as the worker crippled in the factory or the passenger maimed in a road traffic accident as being only 'state-aided Rotweillers'.

It had been the lawyers themselves who had taken the first steps towards ensuring that deserving cases were not to be defeated by lack of professional representation. Some would act for no fee at all, others for greatly reduced and totally uneconomic fees. Indeed, as this social service withers on the vine these days, lawyers are once again being called to carry out work on a *pro bono* (free) basis.

In the criminal arena there had grown up the tradition of the 'dock brief'. Under this scheme a defendant in a criminal trial could point out any barrister who was present in court but not actually engaged in a case. On payment of the princely sum of £2.4s.6d. (approximately £2.22) the barrister so selected was duty-bound to represent him.

The need for a less haphazard arrangement was met in part, and for criminal trials only, by the Poor Prisoners' Defence Act 1903 which allowed the defence counsel's fees to be paid out of public funds. At first this scheme applied only to trials in the superior courts but was extended to the lower courts by the Poor Prisoners' Defence Act 1930.

Social attitudes underwent a sea change after the Second World War and the post-war Labour Government created both the Legal Aid Scheme and the National Health Service in 1948. Ironically, while the former has been further attacked by that Labour government's successors, the latter remains a sacred cow for politicians who perceive far greater electoral glamour in the provision of cheap dentistry than in the administration of justice. Indeed, those in the campaign for votes in May 1997, who relied on assurances by the present government as they solicited the electorate's support to the strains of the song *Things can only get better*, were soon to realise that this musical assurance was not one which would apply to the provision of help to the citizen in need of legal advice or assistance.

The present statutory scheme is regulated by the somewhat ironically known Access to Justice Act 1999 which, under the umbrella of the Legal Services Commission, has created the Community Legal Service (CLS) for civil work and the Criminal Defence Service for clients needing advice and representation in the criminal courts. The new Commission replaces the old Legal Aid Board which itself had taken over the management of legal aid from the Law Society.

A citizen's legal costs will only be paid out of public funds if he (or she) is so poor that he cannot reasonably be expected to pay for them himself and provided that the claim further satisfies the relevant criteria as to merit. Every applicant must, therefore, complete a form with details of his or her dependants, disposable income and disposable capital. Roughly speaking, 'disposable income' means actual income less income tax, National Insurance contributions and housing costs. 'Disposable capital' includes savings and, at the time of writing, the government has mooted proposals to include equity within a house above £3,000 at a time when the average house price in the United Kingdom was a little above £80,000 with average levels of equity said to be around £20,000. In other words, the latest proposal is to treat the equity in a person's home in the same way that capital in savings had previously been viewed where a limit of £3,000 had been applied along with a weekly disposable income of £52 in order to qualify for free legal aid. Quite how these cuts would promote the declared aim of successive governments of improving the citizen's access to justice is a question that could only ever be answered by a politician.

a) Civil cases

The arrival in April 2000 of the Legal Services Commission was very soon the subject of scrutiny in the High Court because of complaints that the new arrangements would significantly restrict the number of solicitors able to provide clients with help in this way and would, therefore, substantially restrict the traditional freedom of the client to select his own lawyer. Many firms of solicitors will no longer be able to accept such instructions because only those firms which have a legal aid **franchise** are now authorised to provide such a service. Anyone who has a legal problem may now go to any solicitors' offices which display the flowing swirls of the new CLS logo which has replaced the traditionally better known sign of two emaciated pin-men apparently engaged in earnest discussion over a flimsy table.

The prospective new client will then fill in an even more detailed application form than before in support of a request for public funding.

Fig. 2.3 The Community Legal Service logo

In this document, the prospective client must not only provide full details of his or her financial circumstances but must set out detail as to the nature of the problem which requires advice. In particular, the prospective litigant must demonstrate how his or her needs meet the criteria under the so-called 'Funding Code' which contains certain priorities so that special Children Act proceedings, as defined in the Code, receive high priority and other problems experienced by the ordinary citizen receive correspondingly less concern. Some prospective claimants need not even go this far, for one major consequence of the Access to Justice Act 1999 was at a stroke to exclude almost all claims for personal injury from the scope of public funding. The workers injured or the motorist crippled will no longer receive any public assistance with their personal tragedies. Such men and women must now seek other assistance from solicitors in the form of **conditional fee agreements**. Such arrangements would strike horror in the hearts and minds of earlier generations of practitioners and, indeed, until the winds of change blew in from America, the notion of a lawyer having a financial interest in the outcome of his client's case was a particular anathema known as **champetry**. A conditional fee agreement is now defined in section 27 of the Access to Justice Act 1999 as 'an agreement with a person providing advocacy or litigation services' (which in DTI English means a solicitor or barrister) 'which provides for his fees and expenses, or any part of them, to be payable only in specified circumstances' (in other words, upon success in the litigation). Quite what 'success' will mean is very much more difficult to gauge. This warning applies topically these days to those watching advertisements on television for so-called 'No Win, No Fee' litigation. While damages of, say, £50,000 may seem enormous to some armchair viewer, it has to be remembered that damages at that level are only awarded for serious injuries and losses. One major reservation of those uneasy in allowing lawyers to have a direct pecuniary interest in the outcome of litigation is that, in order to avoid many hours of work going unrewarded, some lawyers, inadequately committed to the client's best interests, might be induced to recommend too low a settlement. While it is to be both hoped and indeed expected that generally high standards will reassure the public on this concern, another inadequacy of the system must be that potential claimants with, say, crippling injuries but unclear prospects of success, may experience difficulty in finding solicitors prepared to take on such work. Moreover, such litigation would require other expert input, for example, medical reports, and most experts such as these are unwilling to carry out any such work without the certainty of their own fees being paid, if only by the solicitor or client personally. The extent of this problem can be mitigated by the prospective claimant taking out an insurance policy but, once again, insurance companies do not issue policies without charging sometimes very high premiums and even then on cases where they judge the risk to be commercially prudent for them. Family work, however, is excluded from the concept of conditional fees and public funding remains available for help in disputes over divorce, children and financial matters. As before, special limitations continue to exclude other categories of litigation so that, for example, libel has never merited the grant of legal aid however strong the applicant's case.

Where a **public funding certificate** (the new name for a legal aid certificate) has been obtained against the criteria of financial means both as to capital and income and the merits of the case, such certificate will probably these days still be further limited so as to impose a ceiling upon the costs to be incurred and/or further reference to an outside lawyer for the second opinion to assess further the merits of the case continuing, especially if any offer of settlement has been made. Lawyers providing this service remain under a duty to the Legal Services Commission to report upon any offers and are required to justify continuation of any litigation in such circumstances. Opponents in litigation against legally aided parties may also make their own representations to the Legal Services Commission in an attempt to ensure that the certification is withdrawn. It will, therefore, be seen that, contrary to the mischievous pictures painted by some politicians and certain tabloid publications, the provision of public funding these days is greatly restricted and, arguably, is increasingly failing to cover the people for whose help it had been established half a century earlier.

In recent years the scheme has increasingly come under threat because of the growing sense of despair among lawyers at the way in which the state has regarded their services. At the time of writing, there is rapidly increasing evidence that many firms of solicitors have decided that they can no longer go on subsidising the government or the litigant through the solicitors' own bank overdrafts as the rates eventually paid to them – often after inordinate delay running literally to years – have lamentably failed to keep pace with the cost of providing such a service. Many solicitors have simply pulled the shutters down, as the public are discovering as they trudge from solicitor to solicitor seeking help. Even among those firms of solicitors still willing to undertake such work, there is evidence that the publicly funded client is assigned to the more junior and less experienced members of the firm.

What is so often not understood by the public is that public funding does not provide free help. Such assistance merely lends money to the client who, in the event that he or she 'recovers' or 'preserves' money or property, will become the subject of a charge in favour of the Legal Services Commission so as to ensure that the money is repaid to the state. This claw back is known commonly as the **statutory charge** and can be of great significance in matrimonial proceedings in particular where battling ex-spouses fight over who gets what out of the matrimonial home. Recent regulations allow the costs incurred in pursuing such litigation to attach to any property preserved or to any new property bought with an award of money so that the debt attaches to the property like a second mortgage and the state is able to charge interest upon this money at a presently not unattractive rate of 8 per cent which is returned to the Treasury, a fact which, like the Value Added Tax which is further returned to the Treasury, somehow receives scant acknowledgment by politicians ever ready to complain about the cost of continuing to fund what has long been dubbed 'the Cinderella of the Social Services'.

b) Criminal cases

Criminal legal aid (or public funding) has traditionally been more straightforward. After all, its grant may often be required urgently – since January 1986 it has been available even in the middle of the night as part of the 24-hour Duty Solicitor Scheme set up to balance the increased powers given to the police under the Police and Criminal Evidence Act 1984. Moreover, since October 2000 the state has a duty to comply with the provisions of the European Convention on Human Rights which in Article 6 provides certain minimum rights for everyone charged with a criminal offence. This concept includes the provision of free legal assistance when the interests of justice so require.

Someone arrested in the early hours on a serious charge may well appear the following morning before the local magistrates. The next step may well be to apply to the court for help in preparing his or her defence or otherwise taking advice as to the plea. The court must, therefore, consider not only the defendant's means, but must also look at the nature of the charge itself. The more serious the charge, the more likely it is that the court will grant financial assistance. The corollary is that public funding will not be granted in minor cases. Indeed, it had long been no secret among practising lawyers that some magistrates' courts were very much less willing to grant legal aid than other courts in the country. Against this background the late Lord Widgery, the Lord Chief Justice, had laid down guidelines (known conveniently as the 'Widgery criteria') for magistrates to bear in mind. This guidance was placed on a statutory footing by section 22 of the Legal Aid Act 1988 so that the grant or refusal of legal aid in criminal proceedings included a consideration of the following obvious matters:

(a) the offence is such that if proved it is likely that a court would impose a sentence which would deprive the accused of his or her liberty or lead to loss of livelihood or serious damage to his or her reputation;

(b) the determination of the case may involve consideration of a substantial question of law;

(c) the accused may be unable to understand the proceedings or to state his or her own case because of inadequate knowledge of English, mental illness or other mental physical disability;

(d) the nature of the defence is such as to involve the tracing and interviewing of witnesses or expert cross-examination of a witness for the prosecution; or

(e) it is in the interests of someone other than the accused that the accused be represented.

While many if not all the above criteria always seemed to feature prominently in virtually every application for legal aid, it is of note that the fifth consideration ties in conveniently with the newly introduced restrictions on the right of an accused person to cross-examine witnesses in person where the allegation involves offences of a sexual nature or where children are called as witnesses (Unit 3.8).

Against that criteria the magistrates had to consider also the defendant's financial means – that is to say once again his or her 'disposable' income and capital. These figures were fixed at £3,000 in disposable capital and £52 per week – figures somewhat removed from the misleading picture sometimes painted and suggesting that in this country unlimited legal aid has been freely available to the rich.

With the coming into force of the Human Rights Act 1998 in October 2000, new criteria had to be introduced which are now based more upon merit than means although the capital position of an applicant with free capital above £3,000 will be considered when the extent of any contribution to costs is calculated. Those charged at a police station with 'either way' offences or facing trial in a Youth Court would be eligible for public funding without consideration of their incomes. On the other hand, those accused of indictable only offences or charged by prosecutors other than the police (for example, HM Customs), will still face scrutiny of their incomes. If convicted the defendant then faces substantial costs consequences for the court is likely to have power to make a **Recovery of Defence Costs Order** up to the full amount of the defence costs. Quite how much these would amount to in any event is also unclear at the time of writing for the government has recently put forward more proposals further and substantially to reduce the level of fees allowed to lawyers acting for legally aided clients in the criminal and family courts. At the time of writing, there is all too clear evidence that the practitioners in these fields feel badly treated under these arrangements. Such disillusionment may in time expose the ordinary citizen in need of legal help to the same sort of difficulty which those with toothache have had in recent years trying to find a new dentist prepared to treat them under the National Health Service. The old jibe that the portals of justice, like the Ritz, are open to all, is now no longer even amusing.

c) Other sources of help

Various sources of help may be available to people who, for one reason or another, are not eligible for public funding under the statutory scheme. A number of organisations will help those of their members who become involved in court proceedings and other disputes. The motoring organisations, for example, will instruct lawyers for a member involved either in prosecution for an alleged traffic infringement or in civil litigation relating to the driving or ownership of a horseless carriage. Motor insurance policies may also provide cover against solicitors' costs along with the free windscreen. Trade unions, too, will help their members in litigation concerning their employment.

As the old Legal Aid Scheme falls ever-increasingly short of its original laudable aims, there is an expanding market for legal-expenses insurance. In conception, such policies are similar in aim to the private medical insurance policies taken out by those unimpressed with the state's provision of medical services. The premiums on the legal-expenses policies tend to be really very modest and some schemes even provide for round-the-clock access to legal advice. The government is enthusiastic about this form of insurance compensating for the limitations of the state's scheme. As ever with contracts, however, scrutiny of what is and what is not covered is essential. For example, the high level of matrimonial breakdown in England and Wales means that, on present figures, just over 40 per cent of marriages now celebrated will end in divorce and most policies exclude the cost of family litigation.

Moreover, when assessing the sufficiency of cover, allowance should be built in for an award against the assured for the other side's own costs. Recent regulations, brought about by the European influence on English law, specifically provide that the insured shall be free to choose the lawyer, an important protection against insurers seeking to propel their insured to a narrow range of the insurers' own tame solicitors.

Those unable to afford even modest premiums, those too short-sighted to have taken out any such policy and those who believe that any private enterprise insurance, be it legal or medical, is immoral may instead seek help at a neighbourhood law centre or branch of the Citizens Advice Bureau from where the individual in need can obtain advice or, in more complex matters, be referred to a sympathetic solicitor on the bureau's panel. People with housing difficulties may find help from the staff at a local Housing Centre, while the staff at the local Consumer Advice Centre can help with disputes over shoddy goods. Men and women who have lost their jobs are as ineligible for public funding as they were in the old days of 'legal aid' but, if they wish to institute proceedings before the Employment Tribunal, they may obtain both advice and representation from the lawyers who voluntarily give help at the Free Representation Unit (see Unit 2.4a)). Although hardly a bespoke service for those in need of individual advice, a general perspective of some of the issues and choices may now be gleaned online as various web-sites have opened up offering access to statutes and even law reports, such services being provided both by the government on a free but general basis and by companies such as publishers on a subscription basis. As successive governments have continued to dismantle and emasculate the legal aid scheme, lawyers have responded by giving freely of their time and expertise in cases where legal aid has been denied deserving causes. Help from barristers is available free of charge through the Bar's Pro Bono Unit and from other professional bodies set up on a circuit basis which will provide both advice and representation in court or before a tribunal throughout England and Wales. The extent of such service to the community is not always well known and is certainly less publicly recognised.

2.9 *Questions*

1. a) Describe the relationship between a solicitor and a barrister in bringing a case to trial.
   b) How far does the legal system meet the needs of the citizen for legal advice and assistance?

2. Outline the procedure which would be followed in the trial of a motorist charged with causing death by dangerous driving. Do you think that the ordinary criminal courts are suitable for the hearing of such cases? Give reasons for your answer.

3. During the Christmas period the Chief Constable of Newville decides to concentrate his officers on road traffic duties to discourage drunken drivers. However, he also decides on a policy of cautioning rather than prosecution of people who commit road traffic offences. This concentrated deployment of officers results in the depletion of the mobile vice squad, and therefore he decides not to enforce the legislation concerning street prostitution during the Christmas period. Sutton, a private citizen, is concerned about these decisions taken by the Chief Constable and wishes to challenge them. Advise Sutton.

4. Consider critically the education and training of professional lawyers.

5. To what extent is recourse to the law available to both rich and poor alike?

6. a) Choose one type of administrative tribunal and explain its functions.
   b) Why may parties prefer to refer disputes under commercial contracts to arbitration rather than to the ordinary courts?

7. a) Examine the ways in which a person wishing to pursue a claim in **civil** law may obtain and finance legal advice and representation.
   b) How far does this provision achieve a satisfactory service?

   (AQA)

8. a) Outline the process by which a case is dealt with in a county court.
   b) Why is mediation an attractive alternative to using the courts as means of dispute resolution?

   (AQA)

9. a) Explain the system by which judges are selected, and how they may be dismissed.
   b) How far do these processes give an 'independent' judiciary?

   (AQA)

10. a) Describe the role and powers of magistrates in **criminal** cases.
    b) Consider whether lay magistrates are adequately trained for their work.

    (AQA)

3 | Crime and the criminal

3.1 *Guilty or not guilty?*

'Excuse me, I'm a store detective. Would you mind coming with me to the manager's office?'

A request like this is often the preliminary step towards charging a person with that form of theft popularly known as shoplifting. It can be a particularly difficult charge to resolve because a court must decide whether a defendant was, as is so often said, 'just not thinking' (which can certainly be the case) or whether he or she deliberately intended to avoid payment. Frequently there is no dispute that something was taken from the shop: the defence is rather that the person so accused did not mean to take it without payment. The offence of theft, like many other offences, has two ingredients: the act (in this instance walking out of the shop without paying) and the mental intent (doing it deliberately and dishonestly). Before a person may be convicted, then, the prosecution must prove not only that he took the article in question without paying but also that he actually intended to take it without paying. A lawyer might say that the prosecution has to prove a guilty act (known by the Latin tag as the *actus reus*) and a guilty mind (the *mens rea*), and he might go on to say: '*actus non facit reum nisi mens sit rea*' ('an act is not unlawful unless the mind be guilty').

The principle was reviewed in *Chisholm* v. *Doulton* 1889 by Cave J, who said:

> *It is a general principle of our criminal law that there must be as an essential ingredient in a criminal offence some blame-worthy condition of mind. Sometimes it is negligence, sometimes malice, sometimes guilty knowledge, but as a general rule there must be something of that kind which is designated by the expression* mens rea.

a) Actus reus The *actus reus* is usually a positive act, for example taking something or hitting someone. Occasionally, however, the *actus reus* will take the form of a failure to do something, such as failing to stop after an accident or not paying for a television licence. Such an omission led to a conviction for manslaughter in *R* v. *Pittwood* 1902. Pittwood was a railwayman whose duty it was to keep a gate shut whenever a train was passing along the line. One day he went off to lunch and forgot to shut the gate. The tragic result was that a man crossing the line was struck and killed by a train. Similarly, in *R* v. *Bonnyman* 1942 a doctor was convicted of manslaughter when he failed to look after his sick wife. More recently, the driver of the train involved in the 1989 Purley train crash was sent to prison for manslaughter.

In *R* v. *Stone and Dobinson* 1977 the Court of Appeal had to consider the criminal liability of an elderly and disabled man and his inadequate and ineffectual housekeeper when they failed to look after the man's eccentric sister, Fanny, who was herself far from well. All three had lived in the same house since 1972 but in 1974 the sister died in nauseating circumstances of what one judge described as 'dreadful degradation'. Had Fanny received proper medical treatment three weeks earlier it was likely that she would have lived. Both defendants were charged with manslaughter and, at their trial, the prosecution argued that in the circumstances of Fanny coming to live in their house the defendants had undertaken the duty of caring for her, as she could not look after herself properly, and that they had, with gross negligence, failed in the duty. There was evidence that both defendants had left Fanny to look after herself and had taken no adequate steps to call in a doctor. Each defendant was convicted of manslaughter and their appeals against conviction were dismissed. This case, since then described by the House of Lords as 'troubling', does perhaps now need to be considered in the light of the decision in *Airedale NHS Trust* v. *Bland* 1993 (see Unit 3.5c)).

To discover whether the necessary *actus reus* was present the court must have regard to all the surrounding circumstances; at this stage the intent or belief is not important. For example, in *R* v. *Prince* 1875 Henry Prince was convicted of having taken Annie Phillips, an unmarried girl under the age of 16, out of the possession and against the will of her father. The wording of the 1861 Offences against the Person Act was perhaps quaint in the creation of this offence but the world was then a different place. At that time a girl might marry with her father's consent at the age of only 12 years (the then age of consent). Between the ages of 12 and 21 years the father had a right to possession, a right which mattered more than the girl's own wishes. In the event that a girl was taken out of her father's possession without his consent while she was under 16 he could, by applying for a writ of habeas corpus (see Unit 2.1c)), obtain an order that she be returned to his own possession. The jury found that, although Annie was in fact only 14 years old, she had indeed told Henry Prince that she was all of 18 years. While the jury accepted that Henry held an honest and reasonable belief that this was Annie's correct age, they still convicted Prince, who was then sentenced to three months' imprisonment with hard labour. Once he took the girl away from her parents the *actus reus* was complete. The irrelevance of what Prince had believed was underlined by Blackburn J when he said:

> *It seems impossible to suppose that the intention of the legislature in these two sections could have been to make the crime depend upon the knowledge of the prisoner of the girl's actual age.*

This decision may seem to have been harsh and may readily be seen as inconsistent with the general principle that *mens rea* is a requisite ingredient of criminality. One perception of the judgment is that the offence was then viewed as one of strict liability so far as age was concerned in a Victorian Act of Parliament intended to protect young girls against predatory men. In any event, this decision will now need to be seen in the light of the recent decision of the House of Lords in *B* v. *Director of Public Prosecutions* 2000 considered in Unit 3.4b) in which this old decision was described by one judge as 'a relic from an age dead and gone'.

The reverse situation is illustrated by *R* v. *Deller* 1952, in which Mr Deller was charged with obtaining money by false pretences. He claimed that a car was 'free from all encumbrances' when, in fact, he thought that it was still on hire-purchase. Fortuitously, and for him fortunately, there was a technical defect in the hire-purchase agreement which rendered it void. So, without knowing it, he was actually speaking the truth when he said that the car was free from all encumbrances. In law, therefore, although the *mens rea* was clearly present there could not be said to have been any *actus reus*.

b) Mens rea

As a general rule, by requiring an intent as part of the offence the law seeks to avoid making criminals out of people who are in no way morally at fault. A person, said Cave J 'cannot be convicted and punished in a proceeding of a criminal nature unless it can be shown that he had a guilty mind'. For example, before anyone may be convicted of theft the prosecution must prove (beyond all reasonable doubt) not only that the defendant took something (*actus reus*) but that he was acting dishonestly and that he intended to keep the goods (*mens rea*).

Very often the statute regulating or creating the offence will specify what *mens rea* is required, for example, by using words such as 'fraudulently', 'negligently', 'knowingly' or 'maliciously'. One instance is the Theft Act 1968 which provides that to be guilty of handling stolen goods a man must be proved to have received the goods (*actus reus*) and also to have done so 'knowing or believing them to be stolen goods'. Even when the statute does not indicate a specific intent or, indeed any intent, the courts will presume that Parliament intended that *mens rea* should be required. Lord Reid emphasised the need for such a presumption in *Sweet* v. *Parsley* 1969 when he said:

> *In the absence of a clear indication in the Act that an offence is intended to be an absolute offence, it is necessary to go outside the Act and examine all relevant circumstances in order to establish that this must have been the intention of Parliament ... there has for centuries been a presumption that Parliament did not intend to make criminals of persons who were in no way blameworthy in what they did. That means that, whenever a section is silent as to* mens rea, *there is a presumption that, in order to give effect to the will of Parliament, we must read in words appropriate to require* mens rea ... *It is firmly established by a host of authorities that* mens rea *is an essential ingredient of every offence unless some reason be found for holding that it is not necessary.*

At first blush the law on rape seemed simple enough for the words of the Sexual Offences Act 1956 had been drafted with simple clarity when in section 1 the Act provides that 'it is an offence for a man to rape a woman.'

There were banner headlines in the *Sun* as well as questions in Parliament when the House of Lords affirmed the need for *mens rea* in rape in *Director of Public Prosecutions* v. *Morgan* 1975.

Morgan, an NCO in the Royal Air Force, invited three men to go home with him and have sexual intercourse with his wife. He warned them not to be deterred in the event of her struggling. Indeed, said her husband, she would in fact consent but was rather 'kinky'. In the event, she did struggle and did so most energetically. Nevertheless, and against the background as earlier explained to them, the defendants ignored her protests and assumed it was all part of her pleasure. Failure by the prosecution to prove lack of consent would, of course, lead to an acquittal (that is a verdict of Not Guilty) but what if, as happened in this case, there had been a misunderstanding as to consent? In short, was such a genuine misunderstanding as to consent a defence or did that mistake also have to be a reasonable one?

Lord Cross summarised the question before the House when he said:

> No one suggests that rape is an absolute offence to the commission of which the woman's consent is wholly irrelevant. The point in dispute is as to the quality of belief which entitles the defendant to be acquitted and as to the evidential burden with regard to it.

In short, then, the House of Lords had to decide whether, in rape, the defendant can properly be convicted notwithstanding that he in fact believed that the woman consented if such belief was not based on reasonable grounds.

Lord Hailsham discussed *mens rea* and its implications when he said:

> I believe that mens rea means 'guilty or criminal mind', and if it be the case, as seems to be acceptable here, that mental element in rape is not knowledge but intent, to insist that a belief must be reasonable to excuse it is to insist that either the accused is to be found guilty of intending to do that which in truth he did not intend to do, or that his state of mind, though innocent of evil intent, can convict him if it be honest but not rational.

A majority of the House of Lords took the view that the crime of rape consisted in having sexual intercourse with a woman with intent to do so without her consent or with indifference as to whether or not she consented. It could not have been committed if that essential *mens rea* were absent. It followed that if a man really did believe that the woman was consenting – whether or not his belief was based on reasonable grounds – he could not be guilty of rape.

This situation was altered by the passing of the Sexual Offences (Amendment) Act 1976, which amends the 1956 Act so that a man was held to commit the offence of rape if:

(a) he has unlawful sexual intercourse with a woman who at the time of the intercourse does not consent to it; and

(b) at that time he knows that she does not consent to the intercourse or is reckless as to whether she consents to it.

So today if a man pleads not guilty and says, as in *Morgan*, that he believed, however erroneously, that the woman did consent the jury is, under section 1(2) of the Act, to have regard to 'the presence or absence of reasonable grounds for such belief'.

In effect, therefore, the man's belief must now not only be genuine but must also be seen as having been a reasonable belief if such line of defence is to succeed.

Additional problems have been caused when what has happened has been far beyond anything that was intended to happen. One decision which gave rise to much disquiet was *Director of Public Prosecutions* v. *Smith* 1960.

Smith was driving a car which had stolen goods in the back. A police officer approached and told him to pull into the side of the road. Smith suddenly accelerated away and the officer grabbed on to the car. Smith drove in such a way that he managed to do what he intended – to throw the constable off. Unfortunately, the police officer was thrown into the path of another car which ran over him and caused his death. Smith had not intended actually to kill the constable; he said:

> ...*I only wanted to shake him off.... I didn't mean to kill him but I didn't want him to find the gear.*

Nevertheless, Smith was convicted of murder and the House of Lords said that if (on an objective test) a reasonable man would have contemplated that serious injury was likely to result from certain behaviour and that such injury did in fact result, then a man behaving in this way must be guilty of murder, where the *mens rea* is known almost classically as 'malice aforethought'.

The concern felt at that decision led to Parliament altering the law by section 8 of the Criminal Justice Act 1967 which provides:

> A court or jury, in determining whether a person has committed an offence –
> (a) shall not be bound in law to infer that he intended or foresaw a result of his actions by reason only of its being a natural and probable consequence of those actions; but
> (b) shall decide whether he did intend or foresee that result by reference to all the evidence, drawing such inferences from the evidence as appear proper in the circumstances.

Even then the issue was not beyond dispute and the further views of the House of Lords were sought in *Hyam* v. *Director of Public Prosecutions* 1974.

A discarded mistress wanted revenge on her successor. One night she drove to Mrs B's house where she and her three children were asleep. She poured petrol through the letter-box and set fire to it, taking no steps to give any warning. All she intended to do was to frighten Mrs B into leaving the neighbourhood but two of the children were killed in the ensuing blaze. Pearl Hyam was charged with murder. The House of Lords said that in order to establish the *mens rea* of murder all the prosecution had to do was prove that when the defendant did what she did she knew that it was probable that those acts would result in 'grievous bodily harm' (which means really serious injury) to somebody, even though she did not desire to bring that result about. Those acts, moreover, had to have been deliberate, unlawful and intended to expose a potential victim to the risk of that harm.

The Court of Appeal looked at a far less specific intent in *R* v. *Venna* 1975. Venna had been involved in a struggle with police officers who were trying to arrest him. He lashed out wildly with his legs and in doing so kicked a constable's hand and fractured a bone. He was charged with assault occasioning actual bodily harm and maintained in his defence that all he was trying to do was to get up off the ground. The Court of Appeal upheld his conviction and said that it was not necessary for the prosecution to prove that he had kicked the police officer intentionally. The necessary *mens rea* was established once it had been proved that he had lashed out with his feet (as the learned trial judge said) 'reckless as to who was there, not caring one iota as to whether he kicked somebody'.

Recklessness was also considered by the Divisional Court in *Fagan* v. *Metropolitan Police Commissioner* 1968 where the question arose whether the *actus reus* and the *mens rea* had to be present at one and the same time. A police constable told Fagan where to park his car and insisted that he park nearer to the kerb. In complying, Fagan accidentally drove on to the constable's foot, thereby committing the *actus reus* of assault. The officer's doubtless earnest requests that Fagan should remove the car from his foot met with only an abusive reply; the engine was stopped and the car stayed where it was for some time.

. . . that Fagan should remove the car from his foot . . .

At Fagan's trial for assault his counsel argued, in effect, that the *actus reus* and the *mens rea* had not coincided. Mere failure to remove the car could not, he submitted, in law amount to an assault nor could it provide the necessary *mens rea* to convert the original act of mounting the constable's foot into an assault. However, the Divisional Court upheld the conviction, declining to separate the two ingredients in any sophistical way and James J, as he then was, said:

> *It is not necessary that* mens rea *should be present at the inception of the* actus reus; *it can be superimposed on an existing act.*

This decision came to be considered more recently in *Haystead* v. *Chief Constable of Derbyshire* 2000 when a man appealed against his conviction for assault upon a young child. John Haystead had punched the child's mother as she held the infant in her arms. There could be no defence to a charge of assault upon the mother but should he also be convicted of assaulting the child who fell from the mother's arms as a result of the first blow and then hit his head on the ground? His lawyers argued that he should only be convicted of assault where there had been a direct application of physical contact either with a weapon or by a punch or other blow. Some might well detect policy considerations in the approach of the court for, as Laws LJ noted:

> *In a case such as the present, it seems to me plain that it is right that the offence of assault by beating should be available for the criminal condemnation of the defendant's conduct.*

The Divisional Court dismissed the appeal against the conviction for assault on the child which, said the judge:

> *... was entirely and immediately the result of the appellant's action in punching her. There is no difference in logic or good sense between the facts of this case and one where the defendant might have used a weapon to fell the child to the floor, save only that this is a case of reckless and not intentional battery.*

This case raised a point of law of general public importance and, at the time of writing, it remains to be seen whether a further appeal will be pursued.

A related argument arose in *R* v. *Le Brun* 1991 when a man knocked his wife unconscious during a row. That blow (intended neither to kill nor to cause serious harm) did not kill her. However, the husband then tried to move his unconscious wife and, as he did so, her head hit the pavement with tragic consequences but without any necessary *mens rea* on the husband's part for either murder or manslaughter. The Court of Appeal nevertheless held that even though the *mens rea* in the initial assault and the *actus reus* which caused the death had not coincided, the interval between them did not exonerate the defendant from his conviction for manslaughter.

'Intent' may, in practice, readily be expressed by words such as 'I'm going to get you' in the assault trial or may be inferred by conduct such as the shoplifter looking around and then swiftly pocketing the goods in a case of alleged theft. What, though, if the intent is not so expressed in terms and is not capable of such ready inference? The problem arose in *R* v. *Court* 1988 when Robert Court was in court. The defendant was a shop assistant who had grabbed a twelve-year-old girl when she visited his mother's gift shop. Court struck her about twelve times across her bottom. When asked by the police why he did it, Court told them that he had a 'buttock fetish'. When prosecuted for indecent assault, Court admitted that he was guilty of an assault (by striking her) but denied that the assault had been indecent. He contended that his statement to the police about his 'buttock fetish' should be excluded from the evidence. It was said for him that this particular motive had not been communicated to the girl. In those circumstances, the argument ran, such secret motive could not make indecent an act which was not, by itself, overtly indecent. After all, the application of force to young people's bottoms had long been recognised as legitimate chastisement in the best of families and most expensive of schools. The House of Lords approved the judge's decision that the evidence was both relevant and admissible. The House of Lords, viewing any contrary view as one flying in the face of common sense, held that any evidence explaining a defendant's conduct, whether an admission by him or otherwise, was admissible.

Strict liability Clearly, as a general rule, without *mens rea* there can be no offence. Notoriously, however, there are certain exceptional offences where *mens rea* is not necessarily an ingredient and through which honest citizens have been made, on paper at least, into criminals because their conduct has in some way failed to satisfy Parliament's requirements, especially in matters such as road traffic, food, drink, and tobacco. Such offences may be committed without any deliberate or even reckless intent. Liability, then, is said to be *strict*. The inherent conflict between morality and expediency was summarised by Lord Reid in *Warner* v. *Metropolitan Police Commissioner* 1968 when he had this to say:

> On the other hand there is a long line of cases in which it has been held with regard to less serious offences that absence of mens rea *was no defence. Typical examples are offences under public health, licensing and industrial legislation. If a person sets up as, say, a butcher, a publican or a manufacturer and exposes unsound meat for sale, or sells drink to a drunk man or certain parts of his factory are unsafe, it is no defence that he could not by the exercise of reasonable care have known or discovered that the meat was unsound, or that the man was drunk or that his premises were unsafe. He must take the risk and when it is found that the statutory prohibition or requirement has been infringed he must pay the penalty. This may well seem unjust, but it is a comparatively minor injustice, and there is good reason for it as affording some protection to his customers or servants or to the public at large. These are only quasi-criminal offences and it does not really offend the ordinary man's sense of justice that moral guilt is not of the essence of the offence.*

That guilt will nevertheless attach to a man who morally was not culpable is clear from many nineteenth-century cases, one of which was *Cundy* v. *Le Cocq* 1884 where the defendant victualler sold alcohol to a drunken customer. He did not realise that the man was intoxicated but he was nevertheless convicted of an offence under the Licensing Act 1872. Stephen J explained the conviction in this way:

> I am of the opinion that the words of the section amount to an absolute prohibition of the sale of liquor to a drunken person, and that the existence of a bona fide mistake as to the condition of the person served is not an answer to the charge.

A few years later in *Sherras* v. *De Rutzen* 1895 Wright J resolved the conflict between the presumption of *mens rea* and Parliamentary prohibition in this way:

> There is a presumption that mens rea *is an essential ingredient in every offence but that presumption is liable to be displaced either by the words of the statute creating the offence or by the subject-matter with which it deals, and both must be considered.*

Such an approach was urged upon the House of Lords when a chemist had been prosecuted by his own professional body for an offence under the Medicines Act 1968. This Act restricts the supply of drugs and makes it a specific offence to supply drugs 'except in accordance with a prescription given by an appropriate practitioner' (such as a doctor). In *Pharmaceutical Society of Great Britain* v. *Storkwain Ltd* 1986 a chemist had dispensed controlled drugs in the perfectly honest belief that he had been handed a legitimate prescription signed by a doctor. In fact, unknown to the chemist, the customer who came in had forged the prescription in order to obtain drugs such as Physeptone (a heroin substitute). Was this chemist, duped as he had been, automatically guilty of an offence under the Medicines Act? Alternatively, did the prosecution have to show some improper motive on the chemist's part which amounted to *mens rea*? The House of Lords saw no reason to imply the need for *mens rea* when Parliament itself had made no mention of it. One of the judges explained the policy behind the decision:

> ...it is perfectly obvious that pharmacists are in a position to put illicit drugs and perhaps other medicines on the market. Happily, this rarely happens but it does from time to time. It can therefore be readily understood that Parliament would find it necessary to impose a heavier liability on those who are in such a position, and make them more strictly accountable for any breaches of the Act.

The strict liability nature of current road traffic legislation can be gauged by the large number of convictions recorded by magistrates on motorists who have been breathalysed and found to have been over the limit. Under section 5 of the Road Traffic Act 1988 it is an offence for a person to drive a motor vehicle with such a level of alcohol (whether measured by specimens of breath, blood or urine) as exceeds the prescribed limits. As many otherwise decent, honest people have found all too literally to their cost, it is just no defence to say, 'I did not know. I had no idea. I still can't believe it. I only had two glasses.' The fact is that if the analysis shows a level above the legal maximum (80 milligrams of alcohol in 100 millilitres of blood or its equivalent of 35 milligrams of alcohol in 100 millilitres of breath) the driver will be disqualified from driving for at least a year. This is an example of a mandatory sentence, where Parliament lays down a minimum sentence which will be imposed even if it will cause complete loss of livelihood and myriad other miseries. Other examples of mandatory sentences are considered in Unit 3.9.

The continuing existence of strict liability legislation was confirmed in *Customs and Excise* v. *Air Canada* 1991. One of the airline's Tristar jets had landed at Heathrow with one part of its cargo containing cannabis. No one suggested that the pilot or crew were drug-running but Customs seized the entire aircraft on the statutory ground that the jet had been 'used for the carriage ... of a thing ... liable to forfeiture'. The judge who tried the case echoed the words of Lord Reid in *Warner*'s case in refusing to believe that Parliament could ever have intended such an oppressive result. The judge held that the words in the Act imported an element of knowledge or motive before the plane could be forfeited. Nevertheless, the Court of Appeal held that the liability to forfeiture was absolute and not dependent upon proof of *mens rea* on the part of either the owner or user of the aircraft.

Similarly stern measures have been taken against lorry-drivers who enter the country with illegal immigrants in their lorry or any trailer. Under section 32 of the Immigration and Asylum Act 1999 it is expressly said to be 'immaterial' whether or not the driver knew or even suspected that such an immigrant had been concealed: he or she is nevertheless responsible. Regardless whether the driver is knowingly helping the 'clandestine immigrant' or whether the person has just sneaked on to the back of the vehicle as it moved off the dock on to a ferry the driver will be soon brought to see a different dock to face a fine of around £2,000 per hidden passenger.

While, therefore, Lord Reid had been able to say in *Warner*'s case that convicting people of strict liability offences 'is a comparatively minor injustice', the consequences may still be substantial.

Certainly, the penalties imposed for breach of building regulations applying to a site in Hong Kong were severe, involving both imprisonment and the substantial fine, when in *Gammon (Hong Kong) Limited* v. *Attorney General of Hong Kong* 1984 contractors deviated from an approved plan and part of the building collapsed. Did the prosecution have to prove that the defendant knowingly or intentionally deviated in a material way from the plan? Alternatively, was the offence made out immediately upon proof of any material deviation from the original plans? The House of Lords concluded that the offences were those of strict liability. Lord Scarman, having reviewed earlier authorities, put forward the following propositions:

1. there is a presumption of law that *mens rea* is required before a person can be held guilty of a criminal offence;
2. the presumption is particularly strong with the offences 'truly criminal' in character;
3. the presumption applies to statutory offences and can be displaced only if this is clearly or by necessary implication the effect of the statute;
4. the only situation in which the presumption can be displaced is where the statutes concerned were an issue of social concern; public safety is such an issue;
5. even where a statute is concerned with such an issue, the presumption of *mens rea* stands unless it can also be shown that the creation of strict liability will be effective to promote the objects of the statute by encouraging greater vigilance to prevent the commission of the prohibited act.

'It could be you!' proved to be an unfortunate reminder of the application of strict liability when, in *Harrow London Borough Council* v. *Shah* 1999, local newsagents were prosecuted for selling a national lottery ticket to a person under the age of 16 years. One of the regulations made under the inelegantly entitled National Lottery etc. Act 1993 provided in terms:

> No National Lottery ticket shall be sold by or to a person
> who has not attained the age of 16 years.

Neither proprietor had been in the shop when an employee sold a lottery ticket to a boy of 13 years whom he (as was found) reasonably but mistakenly believed to be at least 16 years old. The question, accordingly, arose whether the prosecution had to prove that the newsagents (or their employees) were aware of the buyer's age or were reckless as to the 13-year-old customer's true age. Put another way, did the regulations create an offence of strict liability? The Divisional Court was to hold that the prosecution did not need to prove either knowledge of the buyer's true age or recklessness as to such age. The judges expressed the view that the offence was plainly not truly criminal in character and that the legislation dealt with an issue of social concern. Young people, it was said, should not have lawful access to a gambling facility where many outlets were daily frequented by children. These arguments clearly weighed with one judge:

> The legislation under consideration is, in my judgment, an excellent example of the sort of legislation contemplated by this proposition. That strict liability attaches to this offence will unquestionably encourage greater vigilance in preventing the commission of the prohibited act. The existence of this quasi-criminal offence obviously imposes a very considerable burden upon honest, decent and law abiding shopkeepers such as Mr & Mrs Shah. No sort of stigma attaches to their offence, having regard to the circumstances, but there is a price to pay if their vigilance, or that of anyone selling these tickets on their behalf, slips even to the extent that mistakenly and in good faith, a lottery ticket is sold to a youngster under 16.

Historians with a knowledge of the eighteenth-century conflicts between England and France will recall how, against a background of the military reverses at Minorca for the English Navy, it was its then Commander, Admiral Byng, who was shot because, as was acerbically noted by the French writer Voltaire, the English found it necessary to shoot an Admiral from time to time 'pour encourager les autres'. The wise Frenchman's descendants, reviewing the philosophy behind these offences of absolute or strict liability, might well now remark 'plus ça change plus c'est le même chose'.

Fortunately, it is still rare for the courts to punish so severely those who never intended to commit an offence. The protection of the ordinary, decent citizen rightly requests proper obedience by the courts to the warning of Lord Goddard CJ in *Brend* v. *Wood* 1946 when the Lord Chief Justice said:

> It is of the utmost importance for the protection of the liberty of the subject that a Court should always bear in mind that, unless a statute, either clearly or by necessary implication, rules out mens rea as a constituent part of a crime, the Court should not find a man Guilty of an offence against the criminal law unless he has a guilty mind.

Nevertheless, Parliament's will is supreme and its aim was well explained by Dean Roscoe Pound when he said:

> Such statutes are not meant to punish the vicious will but to put pressure upon the thoughtless and inefficient to do their whole duty in the interest of public health or safety or morals.

3.2 *Who are all these criminals?*

Tom, Dick and Harry go to the Local Eastminster Bank to make a with-drawal. Unfortunately, none of them has an account at that branch, but, undaunted, Tom reinforces his request by waving a sawn-off shotgun under the cashier's nose and Dick uses similar means to dissuade other customers from jumping the queue. Meanwhile, Harry, with a singularly lawless disregard for the no-waiting restrictions, sits outside in their car revving the engine. All three are subsequently charged with robbery (see Unit 3.6b)). Now Tom and Dick were actually in the bank; but can Harry be convicted of anything more serious than a parking offence?

In law, Harry is every bit as guilty of robbery as the other two. That Harry could be sent to prison for as long as his friends is clear from section 8 of the Accessories and Abettors Act 1861 which provides:

> Whosoever shall aid, abet, counsel or procure the Commis-
> sion of any Misdemeanour ... at Common Law or by virtue
> of any Act passed or to be passed shall be liable to be tried
> indicted and punished as a principal Offender.

'Misdemeanour' was the name used at that time for less serious crimes but since the Criminal Law Act 1967 the word has no special signifi-cance and means simply an offence.

The classic definition of an **abettor** is 'one who is present or encour-ages the principal at the time of the commission of the offence'. It is necessary for the alleged abettor actually to be involved in the crime – the mere fact that Peter and Paul are in the bank on their ordinary busi-ness at the time of the robbery, perhaps already held up in a different sense in a long lunchtime queue, does not, of course, make them abet-tors. The point arose in *R* v. *Coney* 1882, when some spectators at a prize-fight were convicted of assault as what was called 'principals in the second degree' (that is, as abettors). In quashing their conviction, the court held that mere voluntary presence did not make the spectators guilty of any assault; deeper involvement was required.

The Court of Appeal confirmed that approach in *R* v. *Searle* 1971 when some drugs were found in a car which Searle and others were using for a touring holiday. The Court of Appeal held that, if the drugs were the property of and under the exclusive control of only one of the group, the fact that the others were present was not sufficient to make them guilty of aiding and abetting.

A similarly classic definition of a **counsellor** is 'one who, before the commission of the crime, conspires to commit it, advises its commission or knowingly gives assistance to one or more of the principals.'

Obviously, to be guilty of counselling an offence a person must have some idea of what is being planned: for example, if on his way to the Local Eastminster Bank Harry was given directions by a police officer on point-duty this could hardly be said to amount to police corruption. That principle was applied by the Court of Appeal in *R* v. *Robert Millar (Contractors) Ltd and Robert Millar* 1970, when a lorry driver had been convicted of causing death by dangerous driving. The accident was caused by a defective tyre which both the lorry driver and his company's managing director had known to have been faulty. The Court of Appeal held that the managing director's conviction for counselling and procuring the offence was justified by his knowledge of the serious risk of harm to other road users.

Unit 3.1b) illustrated how unintended and unfortunate consequences can, for example, raise what started out as criminal damage to a charge of murder. How then would Harry be affected if Tom shot and killed the cashier? The principle is clear: where people go out on a joint enterprise which they know to be unlawful, they are all equally guilty of what one of their number does. It follows, then, that all three of them would be guilty not only of robbery but also of murder.

The point arose before the Court of Criminal Appeal in *R* v. *Betts and Ridley* 1930, in which the court held that where there was a common design to commit robbery, and during that robbery someone was killed, all the participants in the robbery are guilty of murder even though the others had not specifically consented to such a degree of violence being used. What had happened was that Betts and Ridley had gone out on a 'bag-snatch'. Betts assaulted the carrier who later died. Ridley was only waiting in the getaway car. Both defendants, however, were convicted of murder, and Avory J was emphatic:

> It is clear law that it is not necessary that the party, to constitute him a principal in the second degree, should be actually present, an eye-witness or ear-witness of the transaction. He is, in construction of law, present aiding and abetting if with the intention of giving assistance, he is near enough to afford it should occasion arise.

Would the position be different, however, if Harry had not known that Tom and Dick were carrying guns, or alternatively, had not known that the guns were loaded? In other words, how far is a secondary party liable for the acts of the principal offender when those acts go beyond what had been agreed?

The question had to be considered by the House of Lords in *Davies* v. *Director of Public Prosecutions* 1954, after a gang-fight on Clapham Common. One of the gang had been carrying a knife which he used, with fatal effect, on another combatant. The prosecution were not able to prove that Davies, a member of the gang, had known that any knife was being carried and for that reason he was found Not Guilty of murder – the carrying of the knife had gone beyond anything he had expected.

Questions of public policy and the practical need to control crime committed in the course of joint enterprises were factors which carried weight when in *R* v. *Powell* and *R* v. *English* 1997 the House of Lords once again had to consider what knowledge had to be established on the part of a secondary party to a killing in the course of joint enterprise. In these appeals, the courts had to consider what intention or what foresight was required on the part of a secondary party where the killing occurred in the course of a joint enterprise. Powell and a man called Daniels, together with a third man, went to the house of a drugs dealer. While it was not clear who had pulled the trigger, it was beyond doubt that the drug dealer was shot dead at the door. Both Powell and Daniels were convicted of murder on the basis that, even if they had not themselves fired the gun, they knew that the third man had such a weapon and realised that he might use it to kill or cause really serious injury. Such knowledge and intention were sufficient to make both Powell and Daniels guilty of that murder. In the related appeal Philip English and another man took part in a joint attack on a police officer who was assaulted and struck with wooden posts. Worse still, the other man pulled out a knife and stabbed the officer to death. On the evidence heard at trial it was, at least, a reasonable possibility that English had not known that the other man was carrying the knife. Had the officer died as a result of blows from the wooden posts (or even, say, from fists or kicks) English would clearly have been guilty also of the murder. On these facts, however, the use of the knife was fundamentally different to the use of a wooden post so that English's appeal against his conviction was allowed.

So far, all the examples of abetting an offence have been concerned with what was done either before or at the same time as the commission of the offence itself. What, if any, is the liability of Harry's wife who hides the gang in her house, thus allowing them to lie low until the heat is off? Her position is governed by the Criminal Law Act 1967. Section 4 creates a statutory offence in providing:

> Where a person has committed an arrestable offence, any other person who, knowing or believing him to be guilty of the offence or of some other arrestable offence, does without lawful authority or reasonable excuse any act with intent to impede his apprehension or prosecution shall be guilty of an offence.

The concept of the **arrestable offence** was introduced at the time of the substantial revision of English criminal jurisprudence in 1967, which included the abandonment of old concepts of felonies and misdemeanours. It is defined by the Criminal Law Act 1967, section 2, as one

> for which the sentence is fixed by law or for which a person (not previously convicted) may under or by virtue of any enactment be sentenced to imprisonment for a term of five years.

This Act thus replaces the old common-law offence, long beloved by thriller-writers, of being 'an accessory after the fact'. It seems wide enough to cover even remote assistance given to offenders but some safeguard is provided by the unusual requirement that prosecutions may only be brought with the consent of the Director of Public Prosecutions.

The practical application of this important area of law is well illustrated by the much-publicised case of *Craig and Bentley*. In 1952 two teenagers were charged with murder of a police officer who was trying to arrest them for breaking into a warehouse in Croydon. Bentley, the older but not the leader and a man of limited intellect, was grabbed by the police and was alleged to have yelled to Craig the ambiguous but all-important words: 'Let him have it, Chris.' Craig had a gun which he fired with fatal consequences to a very brave police officer. Bentley never fired any shots and at the trial denied that he had known that Craig had a gun. He was, however, alleged to have told the police: 'I knew he had a gun, but I didn't think he'd use it.'

Both accused were convicted of murder. Craig, who was only sixteen and, therefore, too young to be executed, was, in the time-honoured phrase, 'detained during Her Majesty's pleasure'. Bentley was hanged.

3.3 Inchoate offences

Obviously it is not practicable in a book of this nature to deal with all offences, any more than in a similarly planned medical textbook it would be possible to list all illnesses known to humankind. There are, however, three so-called **inchoate offences**, applicable to almost all more specific offences, which require brief attention: incitement, conspiracy and attempt.

a) Incitement

'See what you can pick up at the shops, love' may in certain households be taken literally and amount to encouragement to pick up goods without paying for them. Such a suggestion would, in those circumstances, amount to the separate offence of incitement, even though the untimely proximity of a store detective may deter the commission of the full offence. Incitement can relate to both indictable and summary offences, but incitement to commit a summary offence (for example, a passenger's suggestion 'never mind the speed limit, we're late enough already') is itself only a summary offence.

Traditionally, some forms of incitement have been regarded as so serious that they merit specific statutory provision, as in the Incitement to Mutiny Act 1797, or the Offences Against the Person Act 1861 which provides for life imprisonment for anyone convicted of soliciting a person to murder any other person.

b) Conspiracy

The very mention of the offence of 'conspiracy' may arouse a particular dread in many people accused of it because of the association with cloaked criminals patiently plotting deadly deeds. However, in English law the concept of such offence is really far more straightforward. It is, in part, still a common-law offence and is, in part, now also a statutory offence. Prior to the Criminal Law Act 1977 the offence was traditionally viewed as an agreement between two or more persons to bring about an unlawful purpose or to bring about a lawful purpose by unlawful means. Its wide-ranging adaptability (and some would say abuse) was to be seen in decisions such as *Shaw* v. *Director of Public Prosecutions* 1961 (the 'Ladies Directory' case) and *Kamara* v. *Director of Public Prosecutions* 1973, where the House of Lords upheld the offence of 'conspiracy to trespass' (since abolished by statute) when some students from Sierra Leone occupied their country's High Commission in London (see Unit 1.2). Following the recommendations of the Law Commission (see Unit 1.9), Parliament introduced the Criminal Law Act 1977. This Act largely abolished the old common-law offence of conspiracy and created a new statutory offence which is committed:

> ...if a person agrees with any other person or persons that a course of conduct shall be pursued which will necessarily amount to or involve the commission of any offence or offences by one or more of the parties to the agreement if the agreement is carried out in accordance with their intentions, he is guilty of conspiracy to commit the offence or offences in question.

The Act, therefore, abolished the old offence of conspiracy at common law but did so subject to its retention in cases of conspiracy to defraud, conspiracy to corrupt public morals and conspiracy to outrage public decency.

As the offence is complete when the agreement is made it does not help any accused person to argue that he or she did not actually carry out the contemplated crime. After all, as Lord Hailsham the then Lord Chancellor emphasised in *Kamara* v. *Director of Public Prosecutions* 1973.

> *The* actus reus *in a conspiracy is the agreement to execute the illegal conduct and not the execution of it. The crime is complete when the agreement is made.*

Even second thoughts and cold feet about completing the agreement constitute no defence.

For example, in *R* v. *Anderson* 1985 a man was charged with conspiracy to effect the escape of a prisoner. At trial the defendant admitted that he had intended to smuggle escape equipment into the prison but maintained that he had never intended to take part in the prisoner's eventual escape. In the Court of Appeal it was held that it would be contrary to public policy and to the intentions of Parliament that a person who entered into an agreement with others who genuinely intended the full offence to be carried out should manage to escape conviction by some privately held rule only to go along with it so far.

Obviously, communication of the unlawful aspect of the conduct contemplated is of the essence of the offence of conspiracy. It makes no difference, however, whether all the conspirators gather together like the Knights of King Arthur's Round Table (known as a 'wheel' conspiracy), or whether Tom tells Dick and Dick, in turn, passes the idea on to Harry (a 'chain' conspiracy). Indeed, in the latter example it may be that the group is so secure against being found out (as is common with terrorist 'cells') that Tom and Harry do not meet each other or know each other's identity. Some conspirators may join in late and others may leave early. Just like members of a large club or motoring organisation, where not every member knows every other member, they are all still involved in the same conspiracy. Even if the conspiracy is made outside the jurisdiction of the English courts the case will be tried in England if the agreement was performed wholly or in part in England, as some Americans found in *Director of Public Prosecutions* v. *Doot* 1973 when they stopped off in England with some hashish hidden in their vans as they attempted to make their way to the United States. Their plan to take the drugs had been hatched many miles away from Winchester Crown Court, or even England, but they were later convicted of conspiracy to import proscribed drugs into the United Kingdom.

Protection for the individual, however, is afforded by restrictions to the effect that a man and wife cannot conspire with each other alone (for they are one in the eyes of the criminal law) and no one can conspire with a child under the age of criminal responsibility.

Prosecutions often involve the bringing both of charges of conspiracy and substantive offences. For example, a gang of shoplifters accused of wholesale theft in Oxford Street, where they were stealing as part of an organised group and doing so to meet orders placed with them by others, might be charged with a long list of individual thefts (such as shoes from Selfridges, dresses from Debenhams, and macs and suspenders from Marks & Spencer's). Alternatively, all those offences might be wrapped up in a general conspiracy charge to steal from shops. At trial, the prosecution will normally be required to select which charge they intend to proceed upon – either the general conspiracy charge or the substantive thefts.

One of the criticisms of the old law was that there was no maximum penalty for the offence of conspiracy. The so-called 'Great Train Robbers' (who astonished the country in 1963 by stealing over £2 million from a mail train) were later convicted of conspiracy and some were sentenced to as much as 30 years' imprisonment. The irony that conspiracy to commit a crime could attract heavier punishment than the full offence has now been remedied so that the maximum sentence for conspiracy to commit an offence is the same as that prescribed for the completed offence.

c) Attempt

Since the criminal law seeks to punish the incompetent offender as well as the more successful villain, an attempt to commit a crime is itself a crime. The concept of attempt is now defined by the Criminal Attempts Act 1981 which by section 1 provides clearly enough:

> If, with intent to commit an offence to which this section applies, a person does an act which is more than merely preparatory to the commission of the offence, he is guilty of attempting to commit the offence.

An attempt is as far as one can go without committing a complete offence. Once again both *mens rea* and *actus reus* are required. The *mens rea* is substantially the same as that required for the completed offence – intent to steal, for example, or to deceive or to cause grave injury. The question which has caused more serious trouble has concerned the nature of the acts required to constitute the *actus reus*. Suppose, for example, that a man sees an umbrella in a stand, believing it to belong to someone else; he takes it away intending to steal it but it turns out that it is his own umbrella. Could he be convicted of attempting to steal?

In *R* v. *Eagleton* 1855 Baron Parke approached the problem in this way:

> *The mere intention to commit a misdemeanour is not criminal. Some act is required, and we do not think that all acts towards committing a misdemeanour are indictable. Acts remotely leading towards the commission of the offence are not to be considered as attempts to commit it, but acts immediately connected with it are.*

The state of the defendant's mind had to be considered in *R* v. *Brown* 1984. Raymond Brown, trying to act as a part-time pimp, had gone up to a woman standing in a road in Sheffield. He offered to fix the lady up with a flat so that she would not have to stand on streets getting cold and promised that he could get her some good clients or, in the vernacular, 'punters'. He thought that the lady in question was a prostitute but, in fact, she was a woman police constable on 'plain clothes' duty. Two of her male colleagues arrested Brown who was charged with attempting to procure a woman to become a common prostitute, an offence under the Sexual Offences Act 1956.

In the Court of Appeal the point was accepted that, in order to attempt to procure a woman to become a common prostitute, the man must, in the first place, believe that she is not a prostitute: after all, if she were already a prostitute she could not now become one. It followed that if Brown had believed that she was already 'on the game' when he first saw her he could not later be trying to persuade her to start up in business as a prostitute.

For many years two alternative tests have been current: the 'equivocality test' and the 'proximity test'. The **equivocality test** invites a jury to look at what the accused did and to ask themselves whether those acts are consistent with an intent to commit a crime, on the basis that a criminal attempt is said to 'bear criminal intent upon its face'. The **proximity test**, on the other hand, requires a jury to look at what the defendant did and see how close he or she came to the completed offence. For example, there are many steps towards the commission of the offence of blackmail (discussed in Unit 3.6h)) such as conducting the research into the victim's dubious past, buying paper and envelopes, writing the letter, saving up for a stamp, posting the letter and so on. At what stage, if at all, was the offence of attempted blackmail committed?

The problem came before the Divisional Court in *Davey* v. *Lee* 1967 when a police officer had seen two men by the edge of a perimeter fence around an electricity load compound in which there was some metal. One of those men had on him a pair of wire-cutters. Both men were charged with an attempt to steal a quantity of metal. The court held that the *actus reus* of attempt is complete if the defendant does an act which is a step towards the commission of the specific crime, which is immediately and not merely remotely connected with its commission, and the doing of which cannot reasonably be regarded as having any legitimate purpose. Diplock LJ rejoiced that this was a matter more of common sense than of jurisprudential nicety when he said:

> *There are some branches of the criminal law in which it is permitted for justices and juries to use their common sense. I am glad to find that I am not constrained by the authorities to say that the law of attempt is excluded from those branches.*

The wording and effect of the Criminal Attempts Act 1981 fell to be considered by the Court of Appeal in *R* v. *Rowley* 1991. The appellant had been convicted of attempting to incite a child to commit an act of gross indecency. The appellant had left notes in various public places to lure boys for immoral purposes. The notes promised to pay pocket money. In quashing the conviction, the Court of Appeal held that the man's notes went no further than seeking to meet the boy or boys in question. Even assuming, said the judges, that the ultimate intention was the commission of gross indecency the leaving of such notes by themselves could not be regarded as more than a preparatory act.

Once of the most arcane areas of dispute in the law of attempt has long been the problem of people attempting to do what is simply not possible. The classic and time-honoured example has long been the man who attempts to steal by pick-pocketing, but chooses to stick his hand in a pocket which is completely empty.

An attempt to clarify this old problem was made in the Criminal Attempts Act 1981 which specifically provided:

> A person may be guilty of attempting to commit an offence to which this section applies even though the facts are such that the commission of the offence is impossible.

This provision has now been considered twice by the House of Lords with different results.

In *R* v. *Shivpuri* 1986 the House of Lords took the unprecedented step of rejecting a decision reached only a year earlier. In *Anderton* v. *Ryan* 1985 the House of Lords had decided that no offence had been committed by Bernadette Ryan when she bought a video recorder believing it to be stolen property. In fact, there was no evidence that the video recorder was actually stolen property and so Bernadette Ryan was charged with dishonestly attempting to handle stolen goods. The House of Lords went on to hold that where a person dishonestly handled goods in the belief that they were stolen when, in fact, they were not stolen he was not guilty of attempting dishonestly to handle stolen goods.

The correctness of such a decision had to be considered again by the House of Lords in 1986 when Pyare Shivpuri appealed against his conviction for attempting to smuggle and harbour controlled drugs. Shivpuri, a journalist, dealt with a package which he thought contained either heroin or cannabis. In fact, the substances were merely snuff or some similarly harmless vegetable matter. When Shivpuri was convicted and sentenced to three years' gaol he must have been fairly hopeful of winning his appeal provided, of course, the House of Lords' decision the year before was still good law. After all, if the substances were not actually controlled drugs how could he be guilty of attempting to deal in or harbour prohibited drugs? Could his case be distinguished from that of Bernadette Ryan? If the cases were indistinguishable the application of the strict doctrine of precedent would require Shivpuri's appeal to be allowed. Alternatively, could the House of Lords depart from such earlier precedent in accordance with the Practice Direction of 1966 (Unit 1.5) despite the obvious need for certainty in the criminal law?

The House of Lords, further abandoning pretensions to infallibility, faced up to the error of their earlier decision, recognising, in the words of Lord Bridge, that Ryan's case was 'incapable of sensible application in relation to the law of criminal attempts'. Lord Bridge grasped the nettle:

> *If a serious error embodied in a decision of this House has distorted the law, the sooner it is corrected the better.*

Accordingly, as Shivpuri had intended to commit the offences of dealing with and harbouring prohibited drugs and had further done acts more than (in the words of the Criminal Attempts Act 1981) 'merely preparatory to the commission of the offence' the House of Lords held that Shivpuri had been rightly convicted.

That a man did not succeed in committing the full offence is possibly a matter for mitigating a sentence. Morally, he is in no superior position, as Lord Reid emphasised:

> *The theory is really an attempt to punish people for their guilty intention. The man who stabs the corpse may be as deserving of punishment as a man who attempts to murder a living person. The accused in the present case may be as deserving of punishment as he would have been if the goods had still been stolen goods.*

3.4 Defences

'It wasn't me.'
'I wasn't there.'
'I didn't do it.'
'Anyway, it was an accident.'

To a greater or lesser extent, each of these phrases indicates a possible line of defence. However, we need to examine the more substantive defences which may be available to a defendant in criminal proceedings.

a) Infancy

In London during the early 1970s, enterprising young children were augmenting their weekly allowances by decapitating parking meters and pocketing their contents. The local constabulary's earnest inquiries would be answered by a chorus of 'Can't touch me, mister, I'm only nine,' and quite correct the little vandals were. The law presumes that children under ten are *doli incapax* ('incapable of wrong'), however wicked the little horrors may be. That principle even availed a child's parents in *Walters* v. *Lunt* 1951 when they were charged with receiving stolen goods. The property in question was a tricycle taken by their seven-year-old son. As he was too young to have stolen the tricycle it was, of course, impossible for the parents to have received stolen goods. (Since the Theft Act 1968, however, the parents would themselves be guilty of theft since their actions would amount to an act of appropriation; see Unit 3.6a)).

. . . and quite correct the little vandals were . . .

Until recently, children between the ages of ten and fourteen still enjoyed very substantial immunity. In addition to the ordinary burden of proof, the prosecution had also to prove that the child had known that what he was doing was really wrong. The prosecution had to go on to show what was known as a 'mischievous discretion'. Until recently it was also presumed that a boy under the age of fourteen years could not commit the offence of rape. Such an irrebuttable presumption has been abolished by the passage of the Sexual Offences Act 1993.

A suggestion that this additional protection for children under the age of fourteen years was outdated and no longer good law was rejected by the House of Lords in *C* v. *DPP* 1995. Accordingly, there had been insufficient evidence to justify a finding that this twelve-year-old child knew that what he had done was 'seriously wrong'. He and another boy had run away when the police approached them as they tampered with a motorcycle. Although the courts recognised that there had long been compulsory education and that children now grow up more quickly than when the 'age of discretion' was fixed at fourteen years in the seventeenth century, it remained a matter for Parliament and not for the courts to change this presumption. Parliament was swift to act and, by section 34 of the Crime and Disorder Act 1998, abolished the rebuttable presumption that a child over the age of ten years was incapable of committing an offence. It remains to be tested whether it is still open to a child under fourteen to argue as a defence that he did not know that what he was doing was seriously wrong.

b) Mistake

We saw in *Director of Public Prosecutions* v. *Morgan* 1975 how defendants on charges of rape said that they were mistaken as to the issue of the woman's consent. Mistake will operate as a defence insofar as it can be said to have prevented the defendant from having the *mens rea* required for that offence.

In the leading case (the term is used for a case which lays down a principle of law) of *R* v. *Tolson* 1889 a court of no fewer than fourteen judges was called upon to decide whether mistake would afford a defence to a woman charged with bigamy. The defendant genuinely and reasonably believed that her husband had been drowned at sea. Obviously had she been correct no offence would have been committed. The Court for Crown Cases Reserved held that a *bona fide* belief held on reasonable grounds in the death of her husband at the time of the second ceremony was a good defence to the indictment. Cave J had no doubt when he said:

> ... *at common law an honest and reasonable belief in the existence of circumstances which if true would make the act for which a prisoner is indicted an innocent act has always been held to be a good defence. This doctrine is embodied in the somewhat uncouth maxim 'Actus non facit reum, nisi mens sit rea'.*

The decision in *Tolson* was recently revisited by the House of Lords in *B* v. *Director of Public Prosecutions* 2000 when it was held that a mistaken belief which would prevent the defendant from forming the necessary mental intent, did not have to be one based upon reasonable grounds. Neither the exposition of the facts nor the analysis of the pivotal issue could be better expressed than in the opening lines of the earlier judgment of Rougier J:

> *At the time of the relevant events the appellant was aged fifteen. On 19 August 1997 he was sitting next to a thirteen-year-old girl on a bus and requested her to give him what he*

described as 'a shiner'. This, in the language of today's gilded youth, apparently means, not a black eye, but an act of oral sex. Despite the girl's refusal, he persisted in his request, although without success. As a result, an information was laid that he had committed an offence by virtue of section 1(1) of the Indecency with Children Act 1960 in inciting a girl under the age of fourteen to commit an act of gross indecency with him. He appeared before the Harrow Youth Court on 27 January 1998 when the justices were asked to determine a preliminary point of law advanced on his behalf, namely whether, assuming for the sake of argument that the appellant genuinely believed the girl to be over fourteen, this would afford him a defence. The justices ruled that the terms of section 1(1) imposed strict liability and a mistaken belief as to the age of the victim could not amount to a defence. The sole question for the consideration of this court is whether that decision was correct.

Looking again at the decisions in *Tolson, Prince* and *Sweet* v. *Parsley*, the House of Lords declined to infer that Parliament had intended to make this offence one of strict liability so that an honest belief as to the age of the child could not constitute a defence. While such a view would obviously make it more difficult to convict people who behaved inappropriately towards vulnerable children, the fault lay with Parliament which so often failed, when enacting legislation creating or restating criminal offences, to state in clear terms whether or not *mens rea* was required. For the immediate purposes of this youthful appellant, however, his own perception of the girl's age afforded a defence. As Lord Steyn concluded:

> *There has been a general shift from objectivism to subjectivism in this branch of the law. It is now settled as a matter of general principle that mistake, whether reasonable or not, is a defence where it prevents the defendant from having the* mens rea *which the law requires for the crime with which he is charged. It would be in disharmony with this development now to rule that in respect of a defence under section 1(1) of the 1960 Act the belief must be based on reasonable grounds. Moreover, if such a special solution were to be adopted, it would almost certainly create uncertainty in other parts of the criminal law. . . . There is no legally sound basis on which it would be possible to rule that the burden is on the defendant to prove an honest belief that the victim was over fourteen years.*

c) Necessity

The gun-slinging cowboys of the Wild West are often credited by their scriptwriters with the dutiful argument that a 'man's gotta do what a man's gotta do'. English jurisprudence, on the other hand, has adopted a more cautious approach.

The most poignant attempt to establish such a defence came before the courts in *R* v. *Dudley and Stephens* 1884. The two defendants had been cast adrift in a boat with a boy called Richard Parker. They drifted for more than eighteen days and were some thousand miles from land.

There was no food or water and all three were in a grossly debilitated state. So desperate was their plight that the two men killed the boy and ate his flesh. Dudley and Stephens were eventually rescued but both were charged with Parker's murder. In their defence they argued necessity. However, in upholding their conviction, the court held that a man is guilty of murder if, in order to escape death from hunger, he kills another for the purpose of eating his flesh, even though he believed that such an act was his only chance of preserving his own life. Lord Coleridge CJ dealt at length with the awful conflict but was understandably cautious when he said:

> *But the temptation to the act which existed here was not what the law has ever called necessity. Nor is this to be regretted. Though law and morality are not the same and many things may be immoral which are not necessarily illegal yet the absolute divorce of law from morality would be of fatal consequence and such divorce would follow if the temptation to murder in this case were to be held by law an absolute defence to it. To preserve one's life is generally speaking a duty but it may be the plainer and the higher duty to sacrifice it.*

The ghastly background to this case, while not a defence, was obviously unique mitigation and the death penalty was commuted by the Home Secretary of the day to a term of six months' imprisonment.

Neither has the concept of necessity met with much greater success in more recent years. For example, in *Buckoke* v. *Greater London Council* 1971, Lord Denning MR discussed the possibility of the driver of a fire engine on its way to rescue a man trapped in a blazing house raising the defence of necessity to a prosecution for driving through a red light. Lord Denning MR, while obliged in the end to reject such a defence, indicated that the solution to the problem was the generous exercise of discretion in deciding whether or not to prosecute: 'Such a man should not be prosecuted. He should be congratulated.'

Recently (although in a civil court), such claim did succeed in *Rigby* v. *Chief Constable of Northamptonshire* 1985 when the police were sued by a man whose gunsmith shop had been set alight and burnt out by a canister of CS gas fired by the police as they tried to flush out a dangerous psychopath who had broken into the shop and armed himself. The police laid siege and eventually fired a gas canister into the shop premises. While the intruder was indeed persuaded to leave, problems arose when the shop was set alight and destroyed by fire. The shopkeeper, Michael Rigby, sued the police alleging trespass and nuisance and also relying on the rule in *Rylands* v. *Fletcher* (see Unit 6.8d)). The police, on the other hand, relied on a defence of necessity which the trial judge accepted as absolving them from liability.

d) Duress

A related defence is that of duress, where the criminal law recognises that human infirmity, and the natural instinct for self-preservation, may override a person's sense of morality. Threats to break the legs of a witness likely to become involved in court proceedings may exercise some influence not only on the nature of evidence given but even on whether the witness comes at all. The Court of Appeal had to consider the dilemma of intimidated witnesses in *R* v. *Hudson and Taylor* 1971, where two teenage girls raised the defence of duress, when they were charged with perjury. This offence consists of deliberately giving false and material evidence on oath. The girls had been witnesses in another case and they explained that in this earlier trial they had been approached by a man who had a reputation for violence. This man had warned the girls, who were principal prosecution witnesses, that if they gave evidence against the defendant they would be 'cut up'. Was this threat of violence sufficient to form the basis of a defence to a charge of perjury? The court expressed the view that duress can provide a defence to all offences except possibly treason and murder. What had to be shown was that the defendant's will had been so overborne by threats of death or serious personal injury that the act had no longer been a voluntary one. Relevant factors to be considered at trial would obviously include not only the imminence of the threat but also whether or not the defendant would have been able to get protection, say, from the police.

Only recently have the courts finally resolved how far the defence of duress may be invoked in cases of murder where the accused was not the principal but rather aided and abetted the actual killer (for example, by driving the killer to the scene of the crime). In rejecting such a defence for either category of crime the House of Lords overruled a case called *Lynch v. DPP for Northern Ireland* 1975 twelve years after the House of Lords had ruled that a man who, in fear of a ruthless IRA gunman, had driven armed men to and from the place where a police officer was killed was not guilty of murder because he had been acting under duress. In the case of *R v. Howe* 1987 the House of Lords held that the defence of duress is not available to a person charged with murder. The difficulty of the decision was well reflected in the words of Lord Hailsham:

> ...while there can never be a direct correspondence between law and morality, an attempt to divorce the two entirely is and has always proved to be doomed to failure and, in the present case, the overriding objects of the criminal law must be to protect innocent lives and to set a standard of conduct which ordinary men and women are expected to observe if they are to avoid criminal responsibility.

The principle was recently held to exclude duress as a defence to attempted murder. In *R v. Gotts* 1992, a teenage boy was told by his father to kill his mother, who was then living apart from the father in a women's aid refuge. The son was told that he would be shot if he did not do what his father ordered. The teenager therefore stabbed his unfortunate mother and caused her serious injury but did not kill her. The House of Lords held that a defence of duress was not available in a case of attempted murder any more than in murder itself. However dreadful the circumstances, anyone contemplating taking the life of another should reflect on the words of Lord Griffiths in *R v. Howe*:

> We face a rising tide of violence and terrorism against which the law must stand firm recognizing that its highest duty is to protect the freedom and lives of those that live under it. The sanctity of human life lies at the root of this ideal and I would do nothing to undermine it, be it ever so slight.

In *R* v. *Graham* 1982, the Court of Appeal emphasised that it is important not only to ask whether the defendant actually believed that he was in real danger but also to consider how a person of reasonable firmness would have acted in those particular circumstances. When, in *R* v. *Willer* 1986, a gang of youths threatened Mark Willer with shouts of 'We'll kill you', and one of their number got into his car, he drove off to the police station. Ironically, Mr Willer was himself prosecuted for reckless driving because he had mounted the pavement in his eagerness to get away from the youths. The Court of Appeal held that in those circumstances the defence of duress had been open to Mr Willer for, as Watkins LJ viewed the position:

> . . . *whether or not upon the outward or the return journey, or both, the appellant was wholly driven by force of circumstance into doing what he did and did not drive the car otherwise than under that form of compulsion.*

The case was different from the traditional concept of duress because Mr Willer was trying to get away from the threat rather than to comply with it. What was clear was that this concept of 'duress of circumstances' was very closely allied with the concept of necessity as a defence. The intimate connection was further underlined in *R* v. *Conway* 1988 when, in another case involving the bad driving of a car, the defendant was to say that he feared for his life and that of his passenger. In the Court of Appeal, Woolf LJ, as he then was, viewed the principles in this way:

> *It appears that it is still not clear whether there is a general defence of necessity or, if there is, what are the circumstances in which it is available. We conclude that necessity can only be a defence to a charge of reckless driving where the facts establish 'duress of circumstances' as in* R *v.* Willer, *i.e. where the defendant was constrained by circumstances to drive as he did to avoid death or serious bodily harm to himself or some other person . . . to admit a defence of 'duress of circumstances' is a logical consequence of the existence of the defence of duress as that term is ordinarily understood, i.e., 'do this or else'. Whether 'duress of circumstances' is called 'duress' or 'necessity' does not matter.*

Each of these early decisions had centred upon bad driving. Could the proposition be taken further, bearing in mind the indications in *Howe* that duress could afford a defence to all cases of murder or, since *Gotts*, attempted murder? An answer came from the Court of Appeal in *R* v. *Pommell* 1995 when the defence of necessity was accepted as being open to a man charged with possession of firearms.

Even where a person's perception of a threat is later shown to have been exaggerated such line of defence will remain open. So it was in *R* v. *Martin* 2000, where the defendant was schizoid (and was on account of his medical condition more likely to take words as serious threats) that the Court of Appeal confirmed that such mistaken belief did not also have to have been reasonable. Of course, in this approach, the judges were also recognising a more general principle of law in mistake as a defence and as seen in *Morgan* 1975 (Unit 3.1b)) and *B* v. *DPP* 2000 already considered in this Unit.

c) Drunkenness

'Well, you see, Sir, I had had a few drinks that night.'

Words such as these are often heard in magistrates' courts up and down the country. At very best they might afford some mitigation and perhaps knock a few pounds off a fine. It is not, as a general rule, a defence to a criminal charge for a man to say that he was drunk at the time. The reason lies in great part in public policy. Were the law otherwise, and you or I were mugged and knocked senseless into the gutter, our assailant, when prosecuted, could turn round, explain in tones of injured innocence that it wasn't his fault and blame it on that one too many. To prevent this abuse the courts have followed the principle expounded by Lord Birkenhead in *Director of Public Prosecutions* v. *Beard* 1920 that

> *a man who by his own voluntary act debauches and destroys his willpower shall be no better situated in regard to criminal acts than a sober man.*

Indeed, in some cases, the law sets out to punish drunkenness itself. For instance, if one day the local constabulary were to inquire solicitously after your eyesight after you have driven through a red traffic light it would, at the very least, be perhaps somewhat injudicious to stagger from the car, fix your accuser with a glazed look and, in slurred speech, excuse your error on the basis that you were too drunk to notice. Moreover, since 1967 the law has even gone some way further. Not only is it an offence to drive while unfit through drink or drugs, but under the so-called breathalyser law, now set out in section 5 of the Road Traffic Act 1988, it is also an offence to drive a motor vehicle with a blood-alcohol level in excess of the permitted limit even though (and this is often misunderstood) the driver is not in fact medically unfit: the aim of the legislation was to stop people driving *before* they became unfit. Such an offence is one of strict liability; indeed, whether one is about to commit such an offence is often just guesswork.

Drink or drugs (for they may be treated in the same way) may, however, in exceptional circumstances afford a defence in offences which require a certain state of mind, and where the drunkenness is of such a degree that the person affected is quite unable to form the specific intent – the *mens rea*. The number of such offences is restricted, however: they include theft, robbery and burglary. Others, such as assault and rape, do not require such a 'specific intent' but only what is sometimes now known as 'basic intent'; thus, as we saw in *R* v. *Venna* 1975, recklessness is sufficient *mens rea* for assault. Similarly in *R* v. *Lipman* 1969, the defendant was found guilty of manslaughter when he killed a friend while on an LSD-induced 'trip', thinking that he was, in fact, fighting snakes.

In other words, drink and drugs can only be a defence where their effect is to prevent the formation of a necessary ingredient of the offence, such as the element of dishonesty in theft. Such a principle reflects only the basis of much of our criminal law, for as Lord Birkenhead remarked in *Director of Public Prosecutions* v. *Beard* 1920:

> *It is true that in such cases the specific intent must be proved to constitute the particular crime, but this is, on ultimate analysis, only in accordance with the ordinary law applicable*

*to crime, for speaking generally (and apart from certain spe-
cific offences), a person cannot be convicted of a crime unless
the mens was rea.*

After many years of being a topic for erudite and academic discussion,
the whole topic of drunkenness was definitively explored by the House
of Lords, when, in *Director of Public Prosecutions* v. *Majewski* 1976,
Robert Majewski was convicted on six counts of various forms of
assault after a fracas in a public house. At his trial, Majewski had given
evidence that during the preceding 48 hours he had been tanked up on
both drink and drugs ('barbs') and, as was said at the trial, had 'completely blanked out'. On appeal, his convictions were upheld. The House
of Lords held that unless the offence was one which required proof of a
specific intent it was no defence to a criminal charge that, by reason of
self-induced intoxication, the defendant did not intend to do the act in
question. It followed that Majewski had been rightly convicted by the
jury and that the limited defence of drunkenness would not be extended.
Lord Simon pointed out that to do otherwise

*would leave the citizen legally unprotected from unprovoked
violence, where such violence was the consequence of drink
or drugs having obliterated the capacity of the perpetrator to
know what he was doing or what were its consequences.*

Such policy was sensible enough for the public's protection where a
person had voluntarily taken excessive drink. What, though, of the
person whose drink had been laced? Was involuntary intoxication to be
accepted as a defence? Such a consideration came before the Court of
Appeal in *R* v. *Kingston* 1994. The appellant had been charged with
indecent assault upon a boy. There could be no doubt that the *actus reus*
of the indecent assault had been carried out because Barry Kingston had
been photographed at the time. Indeed, Kingston had been set up for
blackmail by another man who administered drink and drugs to the
boy. At trial Kingston contended that his drink had been laced and he
knew nothing of the events until he woke up the next day. Could such
involuntary intoxication negative the requisite *mens rea*? The Court of
Appeal, quashing the conviction, held that if drink or drugs, surrepti-
tiously administered, made a person lose self-control and then form an
intent which would otherwise not have been formed, such intent was
not criminal because the involuntary intoxication had negatived any
mens rea.

f) Self-defence

'He was coming for me – so I got in there first' is another of the classic
phrases (along, incidentally, with witnesses swearing on their babies'
lives) often heard in the criminal courts. By these words a defendant
accused of some form of assault is raising the defence of self-defence,
where common sense and the criminal law blend easily together. A
person who is attacked, or who fears that he or she is about to be
attacked, is allowed to take reasonable steps to protect himself, or even
to take reasonable steps to protect another person. In this way the
public-spirited citizen is entitled to use violence on some street thug who
uses violence on his prey.

Ideally, of course, the person who is threatened with violence would retreat if at all possible in order to avoid actual violence. Today, such a course is no longer strictly required. If this ideal course is not open to the citizen he is nevertheless entitled to do what is reasonable in order to defend himself properly. In other words, the force used in self-defence must bear some reasonable relationship to the threat itself. Taking an axe to someone who has slapped your face in a moment of emotional anguish would be in excess of what was reasonable at the time. Similarly, repeatedly kicking a man as he lay helpless on the ground once his attack had been defeated would change the response from one of self-defence to one of revenge. The competing issues were considered by the Privy Council in *Palmer* v. *R* 1971, where Lord Morris summed the matter up when he said:

> *It is both good law and good sense that a man who is attacked may defend himself. It is both good law and common sense that he may do, but may only do, what is reasonably necessary. But everything will depend upon the particular facts and circumstances. Of these a jury can decide. It may in some cases be only sensible and clearly possible to take some simple avoiding action. Some attacks may be serious and dangerous. Others may not be. If there is some relatively minor attack, it would not be common sense to permit some act of retaliation which was wholly out of proportion to the necessities of the situation ... If the attack is all over and no sort of peril remains then the employment of force may be by way of revenge or punishment or by way of paying off an old score or may be pure aggression. There may be no longer any link with a necessity of defence.*

Moreover, as the Court of Appeal emphasised in *R* v. *Rivolta* 1994, it is important for the jury or magistrates to look at the issue of self-defence from the position as it appeared to be to the defendant at the relevant time. For example, a defendant could honestly, but mistakenly, believe that he was about to be attacked. His reaction must, therefore, be judged in the light of the circumstances as they appeared or may have appeared to him at the time. A jury should be directed that, in those circumstances, a person cannot be expected to weigh to a nicety the exact measure of force necessary. The jury should then go on to ask whether, in the light of the assumed circumstances, the defendant used more force than was considered to be reasonable. It follows that if a jury find that a defendant did only what he honestly and instinctively thought necessary, such finding would be potent evidence that the force was indeed reasonable. It is a fundamental point that once the issue of self-defence has been raised it becomes the responsibility of the prosecution to prove that self-defence has no application to the case. If the prosecution cannot do this then the defendant remains entitled to an acquittal.

g) Insanity

A person is presumed to be sane until the contrary is proved. There are two ways in which a defendant's sanity may be called into question at his or her trial. Firstly, the court may have to decide whether or not the defendant is **fit to plead**, that is, whether he is capable of understanding what is going on, of following the trial, instructing his lawyers, or himself examining witnesses. If the jury (and a different one is brought in specially to decide this preliminary point) does decide that the defendant is unfit to plead he will not stand his trial. However, the fly in this otherwise attractive ointment is that the defendant may not go free: he may be detained in hospital until such time as he is fit to stand trial.

If the trial does proceed, the jury may have to decide whether or not the defendant was sane or insane *at the time the offence is alleged to have been committed*. If the defendant is found to have been insane the jury must return a verdict of Not Guilty.

The test which the jury must apply was laid down by the House of Lords in 1843 following the case of a man called Daniel M'Naghten who tried to murder Sir Robert Peel, but instead accidentally killed Peel's secretary. The judges laid down, in what are called the **M'Naghten Rules**, that every man is presumed to be sane until the jury is satisfied that

> at the time of committing the act, the party accused was labouring under such a defect of reason, from disease of the mind, as not to know the nature and quality of the act he was doing, or if he did know it, that he did not know he was doing what was wrong.

Such a test requires some comment. What constituted a 'disease of the mind' was considered by Devlin J in *R* v. *Kemp* 1956 when a man seriously injured his wife by hitting her with a hammer. Both the prosecution and the defence agreed that, at the time he hit her, Kemp had been suffering from arteriosclerosis (a thickening of the arteries which may lead to a stroke) and that he did not know what he was doing. The question, therefore, arose whether this disease was of a mental or a physical nature, and Devlin J, one of the century's most respected judges, said:

> *The distinction between the two categories is irrelevant for the purposes of the law, which is not concerned with the origin of the disease or the cause of it, but simply with the mental condition which has brought about the act. It does not matter, for the purposes of the law, whether the defect of reasoning is due to a degeneration of the brain or to some other form of mental derangement. That may be a matter of importance medically, but it is of no importance to the law, which merely has to consider the state of mind in which the accused is, not how he got there.*

It is also now clear that, to succeed in the defence, a defendant must have lost the power of reasoning. This was not so in *R* v. *Clarke* 1972, when a woman was charged with theft by shoplifting. She had undoubtedly experienced many difficulties in life and had become both depressed and forgetful, so much so that on one occasion she put the sweeping brush in the dustbin and the dirt in the broom-cupboard. In her own words at her trial for putting supermarket groceries directly into her shopping-bag, 'everything seemed to get on top of me'.

She said, in effect, that she had no *mens rea* and had simply been absentminded. The Court of Appeal disapproved the trial judge's direction that her defence would have to be one of insanity and said that the evidence did not show that the woman had lost her power of reasoning (as the M'Naghten Rules require) or that she did not know the nature and quality of her acts.

Of course, if someone walks round a supermarket picking up tins of food thinking that he or she is walking round his back garden pruning roses, then, as the Rules require, he will not know the nature and quality of the act and may raise a defence of insanity.

We have already seen that law and morality are not necessarily the same (see Unit 1.2). In the context of the M'Naghten Rules, however, 'wrong' means simply 'legally wrong'. Upon such definition, it is irrelevant that the reason why a person deliberately takes tins of food from a supermarket without payment is that he or she objects to the shop having so much spare food while half the world is starving. The action is legally wrong: it is still called theft.

Although they will, of course, wish to be guided by the judge and by any medical evidence which is offered, the issue whether or not the accused is sane is a matter only for the jury. The Court of Appeal will not lightly interfere with such a verdict for, said Lord Goddard CJ in *R* v. *Rivett* 1950,

> it is for the jury and not for medical men of whatever eminence to determine the issue.

Another important point is that, contrary to the usual position of any other defendant, it is up to an accused person who pleads insanity to show that he (or she) was insane at the relevant times. He need do so, however, not beyond all reasonable doubt but only to the lesser civil standard; that is, he must prove that it was more likely than not that he was insane at the time of the alleged offence.

Until the late nineteenth century, defendants who were proved insane were found not guilty on that ground. In 1883, however, a man fired a pistol at Queen Victoria, who, it appears, was not amused when the man was found not guilty. The verdict was then changed to one of 'guilty of the act charged but so insane at the time as not to be responsible in law for it'. The pendulum has now swung back, helped on its way by the Criminal Procedure (Insanity) Act 1964, so that today the verdict is 'not guilty by reason of insanity'. In practice, the defendant who had been found not guilty on such grounds would then be detained in hospital.

The position of those found insane or unfit to plead has recently been eased by the Criminal Procedure (Insanity and Unfitness to Plead) Act 1991. The question of whether a defendant is fit to be tried can now be postponed to the start of the defence case. In this way the issue may be avoided completely were the jury to acquit at the close of the prosecution case where the evidence had been shown to be so weak that there was no case to answer (see Unit 3.8). The court retains the power to send a defendant found not guilty by reason of insanity or found unfit to plead (so the trial does not even go ahead) to hospital by means of the 'Admission Order'. The new Act, however, now allows the courts wider and more humane powers. Today, the court may make other orders such as an order for treatment or may even now impose an absolute discharge (see Unit 3.9).

3.5 Offences against the person

a) Assault
Like the geographical disposition of ancient Gaul as described by Julius Caesar, the law of assault may be divided into three parts. The infliction by one person of unlawful force on another may result in three varying degrees of injury. A quick slap round the cheeks from someone rebuffing an unwelcome pass may be no more than **common assault**. The Saturday night inebriate who blacks the eye of the publican who invites his customers to drink up and let him get to his bed would be guilty of an assault occasioning **actual bodily harm**. The mindless thug who uses a flick-knife to slash the face of any football spectator whose loyalties lie with the rival team would be convicted of assault occasioning **grievous bodily harm**. Each type of assault was put on a statutory basis by the Offences Against the Person Act 1861 as now amended.

Firstly, however, it is important to understand what an assault is. Strictly speaking, the offence of **assault** occurs when one person causes another to apprehend immediate unlawful personal violence. In this way, raising one's fist to another person, as in the classic boxer's pose, may, strictly, amount to an assault. It is when the raised fist actually comes into contact with the soft fleshy tip of the other person's nose, or some other part of his body, that the hostile act becomes not just assault but also a **battery**. A battery may be defined as the actual application of unlawful force. In day-to-day practical terms, this distinction has become blurred and an assault may be conveniently defined as any act by which a person intentionally or recklessly causes another to apprehend immediate and unlawful violence. In *R* v. *Mansfield Justices, ex parte Sharkey* 1985 Lord Lane CJ underlined the distinction in this way:

> *An assault is any act by which the defendant intentionally, or recklessly, causes the victim to apprehend immediate unlawful violence. There is no need for it to proceed to physical contact. If it does, it is an assault and a battery. Assault is a crime independent of battery and it is important to remember that fact.*

Unlike other offences, such as those involving dishonesty under the Theft Acts 1968 and 1978, no specific mental intent is required for an assault to take place. In *R* v. *Venna* 1975 (see Unit 3.1b)) it was held to be sufficient that the defendant had lashed out at the police officers with his feet 'reckless as to who was there, not caring one iota as to whether he kicked somebody'.

The least serious case of assault, which may only be tried by magistrates, is the offence of **common assault**. A shove or slap which caused no injury would fall into this minor category. When the blow is more forceful and some injury is caused to the victim, the culprit has committed the offence of assault occasioning **actual bodily harm** contrary to section 47 of the 1861 Act of Parliament. The phrase 'actual bodily harm' means exactly what it says – there must be some actual bodily injury even though the injury need be neither serious nor long-lasting. Where the injury is really serious the assailant will be charged with assault occasioning **grievous bodily harm**. In cases involving personal violence it is often not clear whether the injuries suffered by the victim were really intended by the assailant. Anyone who causes grievous bodily harm 'with intent' commits a very serious offence, often close to attempted murder. Under section 18 of the 1861 statute the offence carries a maximum sentence of life imprisonment. The wicked use of the jagged edge of a broken beer bottle in a public house 'glassing' is an obvious example of grievous bodily harm with intent.

To the surprise of many lawyers, more than a century after the legislation was enacted, the courts were called upon to decide whether unforeseen consequences of a wrongful act should be punished according to the intent or to the consequences. In *R* v. *Parmenter* 1991 the House of Lords had to consider the appeal of a father who had caused injury to his three-month-old son. The father had admitted causing the injuries but contended that they had been inflicted unintentionally because he had no previous experience with babies and had not realised that he had been handling his son so roughly that the child might suffer injury. However, the House of Lords held that for assault occasioning actual bodily harm it was sufficient for the prosecution to prove that the defendant committed the assault and that actual bodily harm resulted. It would not be necessary, said their Lordships, to prove that the defendant intended to cause some actual bodily harm or was reckless as to whether such actual bodily harm would be caused.

Whether actual bodily harm could be caused in the absence of any physical contact came to be considered by the Court of Appeal in *R* v. *Ireland* 1997. The defendant had made a number of telephone calls to women. When the women answered the telephone there was silence. The women complained that they suffered significant psychological symptoms such as anxiety and inability to sleep. The defendant argued that such evidence did not amount to an apprehension on the part of the victim of immediate unlawful violence and that psychological harm did not amount to violence. The argument was rejected by the Court of Appeal, which expressed the view that the fact that violence is inflicted indirectly, causing psychological harm, does not make the act any less an act of violence.

Under section 20 of the 1861 Act it is an offence, though a less grave one, if a person 'shall unlawfully and maliciously wound or inflict any grievous bodily harm upon any other person'. It will be seen that the defendant does not need to have had the intent of causing grievous bodily harm. Nevertheless, if that is the outcome of his unlawful action the offence is proved.

Of course, in either case the prosecution still needs to prove that there was actually a 'wound' – that is to say that the continuity of the skin was broken; a mere bruise would not be sufficient. Otherwise, the words 'unlawfully and maliciously' do not add much of significance. Offences under section 20 carry a maximum sentence of five years' imprisonment – the same maximum penalty as for assaults occasioning actual bodily harm.

When a person causes injury to another and, as the result of such injury the other person dies, he or she may be guilty of **homicide**. Whether that homicide, which really means killing someone, is murder or manslaughter depends on the *mens rea* of the defendant.

b) Murder

In order to secure a conviction for murder the prosecution must prove that the defendant unlawfully injured a living person and did so with the requisite *mens rea* either of murder or of causing really serious harm. Until recently it was also part of the requirement that death should occur within a year and a day. This rule, dating from the thirteenth century, was no longer thought appropriate with advances in medical care and where persons injured may survive on life support machines for at least a year and a day. Upon advice from the Law Commission (see Unit 1.9) Parliament enacted the specifically named Law Reform (Year and a Day Rule) Act 1996, which removed this limitation period for death by murder. The impact was first seen in the case of a father who injured his baby son in February 1997. Craig Coleman was convicted of causing grievous bodily harm but after that conviction his child died and seventeen months after the injuries had been inflicted Coleman pleaded guilty to murder.

Obviously the victim must have been alive at the time of the *actus reus* – the only offence committed by a man stabbing a corpse is one of attempted murder (see Unit 3.3c)). Less academic a problem is that of the unborn baby: the law requires the child to have an existence independent of its mother. Since the Abortion Act 1967, abortion is now legal where the pregnancy is ended after two doctors have certified that the continuance of the pregnancy could cause greater mental or physical injury to the woman than if it were terminated, or where there is a substantial risk of the child being deformed.

The grave words 'malice aforethought' are used to describe the *mens rea* of murder and, as a Royal Commission on Capital Punishment commented, are 'simply a comprehensive name for a number of different mental attitudes'. The words do not imply any special ill-will or careful preparation beforehand.

The prosecution must prove that what the defendant did was a *sine qua non* – that is, that had the defendant not done what he or she did the victim would not have died. So, if after a fracas in a public house a man sees his doctor for a bloody nose and then receives such hopelessly negligent treatment that he dies, the court must decide whether it was the initial injury to the nose or the doctor's incompetence which led to his death. Such a situation arose in *R* v. *Jordan* 1956. The defendant stabbed a man in a café. That man later died and James Jordan was charged with his murder. However, fresh medical evidence came before the Court of Appeal that death had not in fact been caused by the stab wound but rather by the treatment of terramycin, an antibiotic drug to which the deceased was intolerant, and by the intravenous introduction of abnormal quantities of liquid, so that death in fact resulted from broncho-pneumonia. In quashing the conviction Hallett J said:

> *It is sufficient to point out here that this was not normal treatment. Not only one feature, but two separate and independent features, of treatment were, in the opinion of the doctors, palpably wrong and these produced the symptoms discovered at the post-mortem examination which were the direct and immediate cause of death, namely, the pneumonia resulting from the condition of oedema which was found.*

However, this does not mean that because the ambulance was held up in traffic a person can escape conviction for murder if it was his act which put the victim in urgent need of that ambulance as in *R* v. *Smith* 1959, when a soldier stabbed another man in a fight at their barracks. The man's lung was pierced and he was taken to the medical reception station. His journey was an eventful one, for he was dropped twice and even on his arrival it was not realised how seriously ill he was. He then received treatment which was not only inappropriate but positively harmful and he died a couple of hours later. The Court Martial Appeal Court dismissed the appeal and Lord Parker CJ weighed up the various ingredients when he said:

> *It seems to the court that, if at the time of death the original wound is still an operating cause and a substantial cause, then the death can properly be said to be the result of the wound, albeit that some other cause of death is also operating. Only if it can be said the original wounding is merely the setting in which another cause operates can it be said that the death does not result from the wound. Putting it another way, only if the second cause is so overwhelming as to make the original wound merely part of the history can it be said that the death does not follow from the wound.*

These two earlier authorities came to be further considered in *R* v. *Cheshire* 1991 when the Court of Appeal dismissed an appeal by David Cheshire who had been convicted of murder. Cheshire had become involved in an argument in a fish-and-chip shop. He produced a gun and ran off after shooting his victim twice. The victim was taken to hospital where, in time, he developed respiratory problems and underwent a tracheotomy (that is, a tube was placed in the wind pipe to assist breathing). More than two months after the shooting the victim died as the result of a rare complication arising out of that tracheotomy and negligent medical care. The Court of Appeal held that Cheshire could not avoid responsibility unless the negligent medical treatment was so independent of his acts and in itself so potent in causing death that the jury were to regard the contribution made by his own acts (the shooting) as insignificant.

The 'malice aforethought' does not require a person actually to intend to cause death. A burglar's use of a cosh on a night watchman may not have been intended to kill the poor man. Nevertheless, if death was a natural consequence of the blows on the man's skull (and provided that the assailant foresaw that dreadful consequence) the charge would be one of murder. In practice, the courts can still be caused considerable difficulty over these seemingly simple issues. In three recent cases the House of Lords has been called on to consider just these points.

Firstly in the tragic case of *R* v. *Moloney* 1985, a young man's conviction for murdering his stepfather was set aside. After a dinner party to celebrate his grandparents' ruby wedding the appellant, a soldier, stayed up late with his stepfather. Much wine had flowed that evening and both men started talking about guns and their respective abilities to use them proficiently. To put the matter to the test two shotguns were fetched. The two men raced each other to load the guns and then aim them. The younger man, the soldier, not only won that contest but also pulled the trigger of a twelve-bore shotgun. His stepfather was killed instantly and the soldier stood trial for murder. Was he guilty of this crime as charged or guilty instead of manslaughter? The soldier told the police that he didn't aim the gun. He just pulled the trigger and his stepfather was dead. Later, in court, he told the jury:

> I never deliberately aimed at him and fired at him intending to hurt him, or to aim close to him intending to frighten him. I never conceived that what I was doing might cause injury to anybody. It was just a lark.

The House of Lords went on to lay down that in cases of murder trials, the jury had only to consider two questions. Firstly, was death or really serious injury a 'natural consequence' of the defendant's voluntary act? Secondly, did the defendant foresee that outcome as being a natural consequence of his act? The jury should then be told that if they answer 'yes' to both questions, it is a proper inference for them to draw that he intended that consequence.

Two months after this decision, two men stood trial at Cardiff Crown Court for murder in *R* v. *Hancock and Shankland* 1986. During the miners' strike in 1984 two Welsh miners, Hancock and Shankland had seen fit to drop two heavy lumps of concrete from a bridge as a taxi-driver, in a police convoy, drove inoffensively along the road under the bridge. In that taxi was a miner on his way to work whom Hancock disliked and whom Hancock had already tried to stop going to work by various unpleasant means. The concrete struck the taxi and the driver was killed in the wreckage. At trial, when Hancock and his helper were accused of murdering the driver, the prosecution alleged that the concrete was thrown into the path of the taxi at a time when the taxi could not avoid being struck. The defendants, on the other hand, contended that they intended merely to block the road and most certainly never had it in mind to kill or injure anyone at all.

At their trial, the judge directed the jury along the lines of the decision in *Moloney*. He directed them to consider the question of the defendants' intent by inviting them to ask themselves whether the defendants foresaw the fatal consequence of their action as a natural result of dropping 46- and 65-pound lumps of concrete into the path of traffic. Was this still the correct approach to this sort of case? Unlike Moloney, the men were convicted of murder and, on appeal, the Court of Appeal and later the House of Lords had to reconsider the earlier ruling in *Moloney*. The House of Lords held that, as well as considering the natural consequences of an act, the jury should also be asked to consider the 'probable consequences'. After all, the probability of death or serious injury resulting from a person's act may be critically important depending, of course, on the degree of probability. In practice, the greater the probability of a certain consequence the more likely it is that the consequence was foreseen and also intended. However, in *Hancock* the convictions for murder were set aside and convictions for manslaughter were substituted. The mandatory life sentences were also set aside and sentences of eight years substituted.

These two decisions were further considered in *R v. Nedrick* 1986. Ransford Delroy Nedrick had poured paraffin through the letter box of a woman's house. He then set the house alight without bothering to give any warning and a young boy died in the blaze. Nedrick later told the police that he had not wanted anyone to die. He added, when asked why he did it, that it was 'just to wake her up and frighten her'.

The judge's summing-up had been based on the law before the House of Lords cases of *Moloney* and *Hancock* so, through no fault of his, he had wrongly (in the light of those judgments) directed that Nedrick would be guilty of murder if he had known that it was highly probable that the act of setting fire to the house would result in serious bodily injury to someone inside. In the Court of Appeal, Lord Lane CJ confirmed the mental intent in murder in a few words:

> *What then do a jury have to decide so far as the mental element in murder is concerned? They simply have to decide whether the defendant intended to kill or do serious bodily harm. In order to reach that decision the jury must pay regard to all the relevant circumstances, including what the defendant himself said and did.*

Today, despite frequent calls for reform so as to allow the judge to sentence on the particular facts, such as the outcry in 2000 at the inflexibility of sentencing for murder upon the conviction of Tony Martin who shot dead a burglar, there is still only one course open to a court following a conviction for murder: the judge has no choice but to send the convicted murderer to prison for life. Quite how much of his life a prisoner will then spend in prison is determined by the Home Secretary in consultation with the trial judge, if available, and the Lord Chief Justice.

The Home Secretary has power to release the prisoner on licence and so after about a dozen years he or she may be let out; however he is always subject to recall and, therefore, may be sent back to prison at any time.

c) Manslaughter

Where a defendant has caused death by an act or omission, but without the 'malice aforethought' necessary for a conviction of murder, he or she may be convicted of a less serious form of homicide, called **manslaughter**. The *actus reus* obviously remains the same as in murder: it is the *mens rea*, or its lack, which determines the charge. Manslaughter takes many forms: we saw how a railway keeper was convicted of manslaughter when he forgot to close a gate and a man was killed as a result (see Unit 3.1a)). Similarly, parents may commit manslaughter if they fail to look after their children so that a baby dies from malnutrition or cold and it will be remembered how in *R v. Stone and Dobinson* 1977 (see Unit 3.1) the defendants were convicted of manslaughter when they allowed an elderly lady to die in circumstances of dreadful degradation.

The obligation to maintain life and, with it, the legality of euthanasia were brought tragically into sharp public focus in 1993 when the courts had to consider the plight of a young man gravely injured in the Hillsborough Stadium disaster nearly four years earlier (see Unit 2.3). In *Airedale NHS Trust* v. *Bland* 1993 the courts had been asked to approve a plan by the Airedale General Hospital to discontinue all life-sustaining treatment for Tony Bland who, because of his injuries, had

been in what was termed a 'persistent vegetative state' and was, therefore, without any hope either of recovery or improvement. Was this proposal to be viewed as an 'omission' to provide proper medical treatment
as in *R* v. *Stone and Dobinson*? Was it to be viewed as tantamount to
euthanasia which is unlawful under English law however well motivated
the person involved may have been – as a doctor discovered in Septem-
ber 1992 when Nigel Cox was convicted of attempted murder. The situation, therefore, had not changed since the famous trial of *Bodkin
Adams* in 1957 when the trial judge, Devlin J as he then was, directed
the jury trying that particular doctor for murder of his elderly parents
that 'no doctor, nor any man, no more in the case of the dying than of
the healthy, has the right deliberately to cut the thread of life'. In those
earlier cases it was alleged that drugs were administered actually to
shorten life. With the immediate dilemma, it was proposed only to withhold treatment which would preserve life. The House of Lords held that
a doctor who had in his care a patient who was incapable of deciding
whether or not to consent to treatment was under no absolute obligation to prolong the patient's life regardless of the circumstances or its
quality. The House of Lords went on to rule that, with the benefit of
responsible and competent medical opinion, treatment such as artificial
feeding and the administration of drugs could be lawfully withheld from
an insensate patient who was without hope of recovery.

What *mens rea*, if any, was required to found a conviction for
manslaughter was considered by the House of Lords in *Director of
Public Prosecutions* v. *Newbury* 1976. Two mindless youths had
dropped a paving stone from a bridge on to a train passing below. The
stone crashed through the driver's cab, struck the guard and killed him.
Both youths were convicted of manslaughter but appealed asking the
House of Lords to decide whether a defendant could be properly convicted of manslaughter if he did not foresee that his act might cause
harm to another. Their Lordships understandably spent few words in
dismissing the appeal. Lord Salmon was clear that manslaughter had
been committed in those circumstances and that

> *an accused is guilty of manslaughter if it is proved that he
> intentionally did an act which was unlawful and dangerous
> and that the act inadvertently caused death and ... it is
> unnecessary to prove that the accused knew that the act was
> unlawful or dangerous. This is one of the reasons why cases
> of manslaughter vary so infinitely in their gravity. They may
> amount to little more than pure inadvertence and sometimes
> to little less than murder.*

In *R* v. *Mitchell* 1983 the Court of Appeal had to consider the case of a
young man who had pushed his way into a queue at a post office and,
when he was spoken to by a pensioner also waiting to be served, struck
the poor man in the mouth. Obviously, that constituted the offence of
assault. Mitchell continued in his violence and his first victim fell against
a lady of nearly ninety. This lady was injured and later died in hospital.
Whatever could be said against the defendant it had to be said in his
favour that he had not intended this tragic result. Did the fact that the
defendant had not intended these fatal consequences mean that he was

not guilty of manslaughter? Secondly, as Mitchell's violence had been directly against the man and not this poor lady, should he be acquitted of causing her death by manslaughter? The Court of Appeal dismissed his appeal against his conviction at the Old Bailey. The court held that the prosecution had proved the four elements necessary to secure a conviction: firstly, there had been an act which was unlawful (that was the assault); secondly, that act had been dangerous in the sense that a sober and reasonable person would inevitably recognise that it carried some risk of harm; thirdly, the act was a substantial cause of death; and finally, the act had been intentional.

Recent figures published in 1999 have suggested that clinical negligence (the term now used for medical negligence) is the third major cause of death in this country after only heart disease and cancer. Negligent doctors may, therefore, find that they are faced with civil claims for damages for their errors. A much smaller number may even be prosecuted. One hospital doctor whose negligence caused the death of a patient during surgery was an anaesthetist who had failed to notice that a ventilator tube carrying oxygen had become disconnected. He also failed to note or respond to the self-evident distress of the patient on the operating table. In R v. Adomako 1994 the defendant anaesthetist admitted that he had been negligent. When tried for manslaughter, however, he denied that his admitted ineptitude was sufficiently grave to amount to the gross negligence which the prosecution needed to establish in order to secure a conviction of manslaughter. At trial, other doctors condemned the standard of care of this doctor as 'abysmal' and 'a gross dereliction of care'. The House of Lords upheld the conviction, declining strictly to construe words such as 'reckless' but emphasising that gross negligence such as this could also be a crime and, therefore, behaviour which, adopting the language of an earlier decision, 'went beyond a mere matter of compensation between subjects and showed such disregard for the life and safety of others as to amount to a crime against the State and conduct deserving punishment'. Disasters such as the sinking of the Herald of Free Enterprise ferry in 1987 with the loss of nearly 200 lives, the Clapham train crash, the Piper Alpha fire and the sinking of the pleasure boat, the Marchioness, with the death of 51 young people enjoying a summer evening on the Thames, have both individually and collectively led to calls for manslaughter prosecutions against the companies viewed as responsible. In practice, the prosecution of a company for what is commonly referred to as **corporate manslaughter** is a high mountain to climb. A company may only be convicted of manslaughter upon proof that a senior individual (known as the 'controlling mind') has been grossly negligent. It is for this reason that the larger the company the less chance there is of a conviction as the management structure grows increasingly complex with the size of the business. In smaller organisations the controlling mind can be readily identified so that, for example, the managing director of a company which organised outdoor activities was imprisoned for manslaughter after a number of sixth formers died in a canoe accident at Lyme Bay in 1993. At the time of writing, proposals have been put forward for a lesser test of corporate manslaughter where liability would be imposed where the company's activities fell far below what would reasonably be expected.

The point was recently underlined by the Court of Appeal in *Attorney-General's Reference (No. 2 of 1999)* 2000 following a ruling at the Old Bailey at the trial of a train company indicted for manslaughter following the disastrous collision on the approach to Paddington railway station when seven passengers died. The Court of Appeal was, therefore, asked to consider whether a non-human defendant could be convicted of manslaughter in the absence of evidence that established the guilt of a particular individual human being. In their judgment, the judges looked again at the decision in *R* v. *Adomako* when considering the sufficiency of gross negligence to found a conviction. Nevertheless, the Court of Appeal remained of the view that it was necessary to establish the guilt of an identified human individual and that any change in this law was a matter not for the courts but, rather, for Parliament.

At the time of writing, a Private Members Bill is before Parliament. The Corporate Homicide Bill, proposed by the Labour Member for Hendon and a solicitor, Andrew Dismore, would create a new offence of 'corporate killing' where a corporation would be guilty of the offence if (a) a management failure by the corporation is the cause or one of the causes of a person's death; and (b) that failure constitutes conduct falling far below what can reasonably be expected of the corporation in the circumstances. For these purposes it is further provided that:

(a) there is a management failure by a corporation if the way in which its activities are managed or organised fails to ensure the health and safety of persons employed in or affected by those activities; and
(b) such a failure may be regarded as a cause of a person's death notwithstanding that the immediate cause is the act or omission of an individual.

In particular, there are two ways in which a person on trial for murder may be convicted instead of the lesser alternative of manslaughter: **provocation** and **diminished responsibility**.

Provocation

It may be that the accused was provoked into attacking the victim. Such provocation will afford a defence where the defendant understandably 'flew off the handle'. A more definitive explanation is that of Devlin J in *R* v. *Duffy* 1949:

> *Provocation is some act, or series of acts, done by the dead man to the accused which would cause in any reasonable person, and actually causes in the accused, a sudden and temporary loss of self-control, rendering the accused so subject to passion as to make him or her for the moment not master of his mind.*

The *only* effect of provocation is to reduce a charge of murder to an act of manslaughter: it is not a defence to other charges. For example, it is no defence for a man charged with stealing a television set to say that he was provoked by jealousy because he did not have as big a screen as his neighbour or was provoked by the noise it made through the wall of his home. Neither is it a defence to other charges of assault, although obviously it is a matter which the court will consider in fixing a sentence.

The test is an objective one. Obviously not every petty irritation amounts in law to provocation. A man who shot his wife because there was no milk for breakfast has no defence of provocation. On the other hand, if he found that there was no milk for breakfast because his wife had run off with the milkman and, seconds later, seeing the offending dairyman next door, he hit the man with one of his bottles of Gold Top, the defendant might be able to show that he had been so provoked as not to have been master of his mind.

The test requires the jury to consider two points in particular: the nature of the instrument which the man used to kill his victim and whether a sufficient interval had elapsed since the provocation to allow a reasonable man to cool down. There is, of course, a lot of difference between the man returning home to find his wife in the arms of the milkman and furiously lashing out and one who, having sat down to join the couple for dinner, goes out to buy a gun and a week later shoots them both dead. In short, said Viscount Simon LC:

> the mode of resentment must bear a reasonable relationship to the provocation, if the offence is to be reduced to manslaughter.

The concept of the 'reasonable man' was reinforced by the Homicide Act 1957, which provides:

> Where on a charge of murder there is evidence on which the jury can find that the person charged was provoked (whether by things done or by things said or by both together) to lose his self-control, the question whether the provocation was enough to make a reasonable man do as he did shall be left to be determined by the jury; and in determining that question the jury shall take into account everything both done and said according to the effect which, in their opinion, it would have on a reasonable man.

How far the courts should recognise the individual characteristics of the character of a person who killed was more recently to occupy the House of Lords in R v. *Morhall* 1995. Alan Morhall had been sniffing glue when he killed another man by stabbing him several times. At his trial Morhall raised a multiplicity of different defences including provocation. The judge summed up to the jury on the conventional basis, namely whether the provocation relied upon was such as to make a reasonable man lose his self-control. The judge, however, did not specifically refer to any special characteristics of the defendant, such as his addiction to glue sniffing. The Court of Appeal had dismissed the appellant's appeal. However, and in a decision which caused some surprise, the House of Lords allowed the appeal saying that the appellant's addiction to glue sniffing should have been taken into account as affecting the gravity of the provocation to which he was exposed at the time of the killing.

The particular circumstances of the accused were relevant in R v. *Smith* 2000 when the House of Lords had to consider what characteristics could be properly attributed to the reasonable man when determining what standard of self-control should be exercised. Morgan Smith was tried for murder after he fatally stabbed a man after an argument over the alleged theft of some of Smith's carpentry tools. He raised a multiplicity of defences including provocation. In support of this particular limb of his case, Smith relied upon psychiatric evidence of a mental condition which had the effect of reducing his power of self-control. Was this particular mental impairment a characteristic to be attributed to the reasonable man? At his trial, the trial judge directed the jury that the effect of Smith's depression on his powers of self-control was 'neither here nor there'. Upon conviction Smith appealed and contended that this had been a misdirection by the trial judge. The House of Lords was to express the view that such a characteristic was to be so attributed and confirmed that the proper conviction was, therefore, one for manslaughter only.

In 1992 the concept of provocation had to be considered by the Court of Appeal in two cases where women had killed their partners after, it was claimed, themselves suffering long-term domestic violence. Firstly, in *R* v. *Thornton* 1992 the Court of Appeal ruled that provocative acts in the course of domestic violence over a period of time which did not cause 'sudden and temporary loss of self-control' did not by themselves amount to provocation in law. Such behaviour, however, might be considered as part of the background against which the defendant's reaction to provocative conduct should be judged by the jury. Later, in *R* v. *Ahluwalia* 1992 the Court of Appeal underlined that any change in the present law had to come from Parliament. Ahluwalia had been convicted of murdering her violent husband by throwing petrol over his duvet and setting fire to it. At her trial, her counsel had argued that the concept of a 'sudden and temporary' loss of self-control should be extended to cover long-standing violence and humiliation of women by their partners. Again, the appeal attracted much public interest but the Court of Appeal held that the trial judge had been right on the present law in directing the jury that the defence of provocation was only available if there had been a sudden and temporary loss of self-control.

Diminished responsibility

If a defendant is able to show that at the time he killed his victim he was suffering from diminished responsibility, he is entitled to an acquittal on a charge of murder; instead he will be convicted of manslaughter. This defence is of recent statutory creation and affords a defence to those unable or unwilling to prove insanity. As with provocation, it is a defence which may be raised only to a charge of murder.

A much publicised example of an effort to raise this particular defence was that advanced by lorry driver Peter Sutcliffe, the so-called 'Yorkshire Ripper', who stood trial at the Old Bailey in the Spring of 1981. Sutcliffe was tried for the murder of thirteen women between 1975 and 1980 and the attempted murder of another seven women. Sutcliffe admitted the killings but contended that he had been carrying out a divine mission to kill prostitutes. He alleged that he had heard voices impelling him to kill. The defence failed and Sutcliffe was convicted of murder.

Section 2 of the Homicide Act 1957 provides:

> Where a person kills or is a party to the killing of another he shall not be convicted of murder if he was suffering from such abnormality of mind (whether arising from a condition of arrested or retarded development of mind or any inherent causes or induced by disease or injury) as substantially impaired his mental responsibility for his acts and omissions in doing or being a party to the killing.

This section goes on to provide that, again exceptionally, it is up to the defendant to prove that he was suffering from diminished responsibility. As with insanity, however, the defendant need prove his case not 'beyond all reasonable doubt' but only on the lesser civil standard.

The crucial words are of course 'abnormality of mind' and their meaning was considered by Lord Parker CJ in *R* v. *Byrne* 1960 when he said that it meant

> *a state of mind so different from that of ordinary human beings that the reasonable man would term it abnormal. It appears to us to be wide enough to cover the mind's activities in all its aspects.*

It is, in fact, so wide that it covers a multitude of misfortunes including, for example, a depressed mother killing her new-born baby or a man killing the girl who jilted him for another.

The defence of diminished responsibility may also be raised in cases of so-called mercy-killing or euthanasia, where, for instance, the defendant is a mother who has smothered her young but appallingly deformed or handicapped child.

d) Rape

Few crimes attract as much emotive reaction or revulsion as rape. Today, specially trained police officers will investigate the allegations. Questions about judges' supposedly light sentences on rapists have been asked in Parliament and since then the Court of Appeal has laid down guidelines for judges who have to sentence such men.

The Criminal Justice and Public Order Act 1994 has further amended the statutory definition of rape originally set out in the Sexual Offences (Amendment) Act 1976, an Act which immediately followed the decision of the House of Lords in *Director of Public Prosecutions* v. *Morgan* 1976 (see Unit 3.1b)) so that the offence may now apply to offences committed against a man. Such change is now embodied in the statutory definition introduced by the 1994 Act so that:

> It is an offence for a man to rape a woman or another man.
>   A man commits rape if –
> (a) he has sexual intercourse with a person (whether vaginal or anal) who at the time of the intercourse does not consent to it; and
> (b) at the time he knows that that person does not consent to the intercourse or is reckless as to whether that person consents to it.
> A man also commits rape if he induces a married woman to have sexual intercourse with him by impersonating her husband.

More recently, the age for homosexual consent has recently been reduced to 18 years.

The aspect of the defendant's mental intent was looked at in Unit 3.1. At trial, the prosecution must prove some degree of penetration of the victim.

Traditionally it has been said that a husband could not be guilty of an act of rape upon his wife. Such immunity had been confirmed in 1736 when it was declared that 'by their mutual consent and contract the wife hath given herself in this kind unto her husband which she cannot retract.' Changing social attitudes and the wholly different status of women led to prosecutions of husbands who were estranged from their wives. In *R v. R (a husband)* 1991, the Court of Appeal described this eighteenth-century pronouncement as a common-law fiction which had become anachronistic and offensive. Their duty, said the judges, was to remove it from the law. The Court of Appeal and thereafter the House of Lords then dismissed an appeal by a husband who had sexual intercourse with his wife against her wishes a few days after she left him to return to her parents, even though the parties were still married.

Until recently it was presumed that a boy under the age of 14 years could not be guilty of rape. He could, however, always be convicted of the lesser offence of indecent assault. Such a presumption has been abolished by the Sexual Offences Act 1993.

Consideration whether consent had been given or withheld came in for consideration by the Court of Appeal in *R v. Linekar* 1995. The facts were somewhat unusual. A certain Mr G. Linekar (but not the Gary Lineker who once played for Tottenham Hotspur and other football clubs!) met the complainant when she was working as a part-time prostitute to supplement her social security benefits. Mr Linekar had agreed to pay £25 for her services but, after sexual intercourse had taken place, he made off without paying. The prostitute contended that she would not have agreed to sexual intercourse without payment. Had her consent been obtained by a false pretence that the customer would pay the money? The jury found that the woman's consent had been vitiated by fraud and, for that reason, had not been a valid consent. In quashing the conviction the Court of Appeal preferred the view that the reality of the woman's consent had not been destroyed by her customer's false pretences to pay money for her services.

Such a decision, however, was more recently distinguished by the Court of Appeal in *R v. Tabassum* 2000. The defendant, claiming to be carrying out research, asked several women to take part in a breast cancer survey. The defendant, devoid of any medical qualifications or training, nevertheless managed to persuade three of these women to allow him to feel their breasts under the pretence of instructing them how best to carry out a self-examination. At trial, it was argued that the women had undoubtedly consented and the court was asked to have regard to the earlier decision in *Linekar*. On the facts of this case, however, the Court of Appeal took the view that the fraudulent representation had vitiated the women's consent to what remained indecent assault for the apparent consent had not been true consent.

3.6 Offences against property

a) Theft   Stealing, nicking, pinching, half-inching, liberating, knocking off: call it what you will, almost everyone has some idea of what theft is. Most people would say that it is taking something which isn't yours. And so it is. It is also the most prevalent offence in England and Wales, be it pinching a packet of mints over Woolworth's counter or taking home a Canaletto to hide the damp patch in the front room. The definition of theft is a very full one, and takes up the first seven sections of the Theft Act 1968. Section 1 provides the working definition:

> *A person is guilty of theft if he dishonestly appropriates property belonging to another with the intention of permanently depriving the other of it; and 'thief' and 'steal' shall be construed accordingly.*

... a Canaletto to hide the damp patch ...

Here the *actus reus* is the appropriating of property belonging to another; the *mens rea* is the intention of doing so dishonestly and then of permanently depriving the owner of the property. The definition requires some further explanation, however, for before the prosecution may secure a conviction it must prove each of the following five ingredients mentioned even in the first section.

'Dishonestly'   Theft is not an offence of strict liability: it is a serious moral stigma to attach to someone and Parliament very properly requires proof of a guilty mind. So, for example, if Eleanor walks out of a shop with a tin of beans in her hand without paying for it, she will be guilty of theft only if it is proved that she was intending to do so. Absentmindedness, in this sense, would, therefore, afford Eleanor a defence.

Occasionally, however, difficulties have arisen when a defendant has a set of values which is different from those of most people. The point was resolved once and for all by the Court of Appeal in *R* v. *Ghosh*

1982. The defendant had been employed as a consultant surgeon. He had falsely represented that he had carried out an operation. He contended that there had been nothing dishonest about what he had done and that the medical fees claimed were properly payable to him. Until then judges had long told juries that it was up to them to set the standards of honesty. In the Court of Appeal, however, it was held that the test went a stage further.

Firstly, the jury (as representatives of society generally) must set the standards of honesty. After all, if dishonest people were allowed to decide what was honest or dishonest every thief would be acquitted automatically and, as one judge once said, 'Robin Hood would be no robber'. Next, said the Court of Appeal, the jury must go on to ask whether, if the act was dishonest by their standards, the particular defendant knew that his actions were dishonest by such standards. If he did know that then the prosecution will have proved that vital ingredient.

An honest belief does not also have to be a reasonable belief. For example, in *R* v. *Holden* 1991 the appellant, who worked for the local KwikFit garage, had been convicted of stealing scrap tyres. He had claimed that he had seen others taking such tyres and thought that it was permitted. The Court of Appeal held that the trial judge had been wrong to lay down that the test for the jury was whether the employee had a reasonable belief that he had a right to take the tyres.

Section 2 of the Theft Act further provides that a person will not be acting dishonestly if he appropriates property while fulfilling one of the following conditions:

1. He believes that he has a right to do so. For example, Tom believes that Dick owes him five pounds and so he relieves the strain on Dick's wallet by removing five pounds from it. In *R* v. *Clayton* 1920, Sam Clayton, who was separated from his wife, took 30 shillings (£1.50, quite a substantial sum at that time) towards the five pounds she owed him. He thought he had a right to take the money and the Court of Appeal quashed his conviction.
2. He believes that the other would consent; for example, Tom, who is staying the weekend at Dick's house, helps himself to one of his friend's cigarettes.
3. He believes that the owner cannot be found, for example, Dick finds a 50-pence coin in the sand on Brighton beach.

Money, it is said (by those who have none), cannot buy everything and certainly not happiness, and Parliament also expressed this sentiment by providing in section 2 that:

> a person's appropriation of property belonging to another
> may be dishonest notwithstanding that he is willing to pay for
> the property.

So if Tom takes Dick's Canaletto, it will do him no good to leave a £5 note on the table for, unless he believes that Dick is so stupid as to part with such a painting for that sum of money, Tom will be guilty of theft. If the law were otherwise no one would be sure of a fair price for his property.

'Appropriates' Essentially, this word means 'taking'.

Section 3 provides:

> Any assumption by a person of the right of an owner amounts to an appropriation and this includes where he has come by the property (innocently or not) without stealing it, any later assumption of a right to it by keeping or dealing with it as owner.

In practice, when someone is found in possession of stolen property he or she will often be charged with both theft and handling (see Unit 3.6i)). These are obviously alternatives but the aim is to prevent people being acquitted by saying quite simply: 'I'm not the thief, I'm the handler, please acquit me of theft.' As we shall see, a person is only guilty of handling stolen goods *if at the time he receives them* he knows or believes that they are stolen. If, having got them in good faith, he subsequently learns that they are, in fact, stolen he may not be able to get away scot-free. He could be caught by section 3's wide concept of 'appropriation'. In *Stapleton* v. *O'Callaghan* 1973 the defendant had been found in possession of a stolen driving licence. The stipendiary magistrate could not say for sure whether the man was actually the thief or actually the handler. Accordingly, although it was clear that the defendant had indeed been acting dishonestly, the learned magistrate acquitted him. The question arose whether that was the correct way out of the dilemma. In the Divisional Court Lord Widgery CJ took a different view. He held that as it had been proved that the defendant had dishonestly possessed himself of the licence and that he intended to keep the licence it followed that he had dishonestly assumed a right to the licence 'by keeping and dealing with it as owner', within the wording of section 3. Accordingly, the man should have been convicted and the case would have to be tried again.

Moreover, it is now clearly established that there is no need for the prosecution to prove that the appropriation was without the owner's consent: absence of such consent is not an ingredient of the act of appropriation. So in *Lawrence* v. *Metropolitan Police Commissioner* 1971 an Italian student who spoke little English arrived at Victoria Station. He went to Alan Lawrence, a taxi-driver, and showed him an address. The defendant said that the student's address was a long way away and the journey would be very expensive. The student handed over £1 but the taxi-driver said it was not enough and proceeded to lighten the student's still open wallet by a further £6. The correct fare was about 53 pence.

In court it was argued on behalf of the defendant taxi-driver that as the Italian student had consented to the taking of his £6 the defendant could not be guilty of theft. Before the Theft Act 1968 it was the law under the Larceny Act 1916 that, to be regarded as having been stolen, the property had to have been taken 'without the consent of the owner'. No such words appear in the Theft Act and the House of Lords, unanimously upholding Lawrence's conviction, were clearly of the view that the omission of that former requirement was deliberate policy: such a concept was of no importance today.

This decision was followed some years later in *R* v. *Morris* 1983 when the House of Lords had to consider the actions of a man who had found a way of cutting prices at a stroke. David Morris had gone into a self-service store. He removed price labels from cheap goods and stuck them over the correct labels on the more expensive items he wanted. He then paid for the goods at the lower prices. Did this 'do-it-yourself sale' amount to an act of appropriation within the meaning of section 3? The House of Lords held that there was no need for the prosecution to prove that possession was taken without the owner's consent or that the defendant had assumed all the rights of the true owner. The term 'appropriates' simply means taking possession of an item and assuming any of the owner's rights in it. It followed, on these facts, that Morris had appropriated the goods at the time he took them off the shelf in order to carry them to the check-out.

Both these decisions came to be further considered by the House of Lords in *R* v. *Gomez* 1993 when the courts again had to consider whether or not there had been an 'appropriation' in circumstances where the owner had consented to the removal of the goods. Edwin Gomez had been employed as an assistant manager at an electrical shop. He had been approached by an acquaintance, who also was later to be prosecuted, and asked by that acquaintance to accept payment for electrical goods in the form of two stolen building society cheques. Gomez then prepared a list of goods to be taken from the shop. He then told his manager that the order was genuine and further pretended that the bank had described those building society cheques as being 'as good as cash'. In this way electrical goods to a value in excess of £16,000 were removed from the shop with, it seemed at the time, the consent of the shop manager. Inevitably, the cheques were worthless and in due course Gomez and others were prosecuted for theft of those goods. At his trial Gomez sought to argue that he could not be guilty of theft as the shop owner had authorised the transaction and so, in those circumstances, there had been no 'appropriation'. The House of Lords rejected such argument, however, saying that such fraud, deception or false representation which induced consent on the part of an owner made the appropriation dishonest. In dealing with this appeal in the months following the scandal of the missing Maxwell Pension Fund monies, Lord Browne-Wilkinson commented:

> *I am glad to be able to reach this conclusion. The pillaging of companies by those who control them is now all too common. It would offend both common sense and justice to hold that the very control which enables such people to extract the company's assets constitutes a defence to a charge of theft from the company. The question in each case must be whether the extraction of the property from the company was dishonest, not whether the alleged thief has consented to his own wrongdoing.*

The correctness of these decisions in *Lawrence, Morris* and *Gomez* was recently confirmed by the House of Lords in *R* v. *Hinks* 2000. Karen Hinks had befriended a man of limited intelligence, described at her trial for theft as being naïve and trusting. This man, for whom Karen Hinks acted as carer, took some £60,000 from his building society accounts and handed over his inheritance to the woman whom he trusted. At her trial for theft of various sums of money, it was the prosecution case that this woman had simply taken this man for everything she could get. For her, it was argued that there could be no act of theft where the money had been a gift. Was the view of the judge that receipt of such money in such circumstances amounted to 'appropriation' correct? On appeal against her conviction (with a sentence of eighteen months' imprisonment for a mean crime) her lawyers argued that there could not be an appropriation unless the owner retained some interest or at least the right to recover some interest. Alternatively, they contended, the word 'appropriates' should be read so as to imply 'unlawfully' before the word. The House of Lords were unwilling to imply such additional words into 'the carefully crafted language of the Act of 1968' and further rejected the argument that would have required the owner to retain an interest.

Property
What may be stolen is defined in comprehensive terms by section 4 of the Theft Act:

> 'Property' includes money and all other property, real or personal including things in action and other intangible property.

Not everything is included within this definition, however; picnickers who gather flowers growing on the roadside or in the fields are specially protected because section 4 goes on to provide:

> A person who picks mushrooms growing wild on any land, or who picks flowers, fruit or foliage from a plant growing wild on any land does not (although not in possession of the land) steal what he picks, unless he does it for reward or for sale or other commercial purpose.

Quite what 'property' was covered by this definition fell to be considered by the Divisional Court in *Oxford* v. *Moss* 1978. In June 1976, as the universities' open season for examining their undergraduates was drawing near, a student (but not, of course, one reading law!) managed to get hold of the civil engineering examination paper. After he had had a good look at the questions he returned the examination paper, having seen all he wanted. He was, however, rumbled and later charged with theft of 'confidential information' from the Senate of Liverpool University. The court held that this confidential information did not fall within the definition of property in the Theft Act 1968.

A singularly more grisly form of theft involved the removal of parts of bodies from the Royal College of Surgeons in circumstances said by some to be reminiscent of Burke and Hare, the eighteenth-century body snatchers. In *R* v. *Kelly* 1998 over thirty body parts, used by doctors training to be surgeons, were removed. When prosecuted for theft, Kelly and a junior technician at the College argued that parts of bodies were not in law capable of being property and, for that reason, could not be stolen. The Court of Appeal ruled that parts of a corpse were capable of being property within section 4 of the Act.

'Belonging to another'
We have already mentioned the problems of a person who tries to steal his own umbrella while believing that he is stealing someone else's property (see Unit 3.3c)). Whom the property belongs to at the moment it is stolen is regulated by section 5 of the Theft Act:

> Property shall be regarded as belonging to any person having possession or control of it, or having in it any proprietary right or interest (not being an equitable interest arising only from an agreement to transfer or grant an interest).

Such a definition allows a man to be convicted of stealing what he owns. This happened in *R* v. *Turner* 1971 when the defendant had taken his car to be repaired. He said that he would come back the following day and pay for the work. A few hours later, however, he saw the car parked in the street. He drove it away without paying. The Court of Appeal dismissed the appeal against conviction and approved the direction of the trial judge when he told the jury that there were only two questions they had to decide: Had the garage proprietor possession or control of it? Had the defendant acted dishonestly?

'With the intention of permanently depriving'

Borrowing is not stealing. If Tom takes Dick's bike to get home because he has missed the last bus, he is not guilty of theft if his intention was only to borrow it for that purpose and if he planned to return it or, at the very least, tell Dick where he might collect it. Of course, if Tom delays returning it for many weeks the position may well change and, in this respect, section 6 provides:

> A person appropriating property belonging to another without meaning the other to lose the thing itself is nevertheless to be regarded as having the intention of permanently depriving the other of it if his intention is to treat the thing as his own to dispose of regardless of the other's rights; and a borrowing or lending of it may amount to so treating it if, but only if, the borrowing or lending is for a period and in circumstances making it equivalent to an outright taking or disposal.

Despite the ecological benefits of recycling paper, objection was taken by London Transport when Adrian Marshall and others sold unexpired tickets which they had obtained from passengers as they left the stations. In *R* v. *Marshall, Coombes and Eren* 1998 the defendant and others sold these used tickets on to others who, therefore, did not buy fresh tickets at any office which was still manned or any machine not already out of use. When prosecuted for theft, these entrepreneurs contended that they had had no intention of permanently depriving London Underground of the tickets. After all, such bits of flimsy cardboard would eventually be returned to London Transport. Such an argument failed in the Court of Appeal where the judges held that Marshall and the others had held the necessary intention of treating the tickets as their own to dispose of regardless of London Underground's rights. The implications of this decision would seem to go well beyond the last outpost of London Transport and have implications even for motorists who pass on or use unexpired parking tickets.

The maximum sentence for theft was ten years' imprisonment under the Theft Act 1968 but this term was reduced to seven years by the Criminal Justice Act 1991.

b) Robbery   When an act of theft is accompanied by violence or the threat of violence, it is translated into the offence of robbery.

Section 8 provides:

> A person is guilty of robbery if he steals, and immediately before or at the time of doing so, and in order to do so, he uses force on any person or puts or seeks to put any person in fear of being then and there subjected to force.

Robbery, of course, is an extremely serious offence and carries a maximum sentence of life imprisonment. It may only be tried in the Crown Court even if the property allegedly stolen is worth only a few pence.

c) Burglary   Many people still believe, quite erroneously, that burglary may only be committed at night, usually by a man (preferably dressed in a striped jersey and carrying a bag marked 'swag') up a ladder at a bedroom window. Since the 1968 Act, however, a burglary is committed whenever theft follows on from an act of trespass. Trespass is essentially an act of unlawful entry on to someone else's land.

... believe, quite erroneously, that burglary may only be committed at night.

Section 9 of the Theft Act provides:

> A person is guilty of burglary if –
> (a) he enters a building as a trespasser and with intent to commit any such offence as is mentioned in sub-section (2) below [grievous bodily harm, rape and criminal damage]; or
> (b) having entered any building or part of a building as a trespasser he steals or attempts to steal anything in the building or that part of it or inflicts or attempts to inflict on any person therein any grievous bodily harm.

The section thus covers the situation where a man intends to trespass and intends then to steal, as when someone sneaks in through the kitchen door in order to take the grocery money left on top of the fridge. Paragraph (b) covers the situation of, for example, a hotel guest who gets out of the lift on the wrong floor, lets himself in to what he thinks to be his room, and once inside sees a wallet lying on the bed and takes it.

The basis of the concept of burglary is thus that of the civil law of trespass. The mental element in trespass was considered by the Court of Appeal in the case of *R* v. *Collins* 1972, described by Edmund-Davies LJ as 'about as extraordinary a case as my brethren and I have ever heard either on the Bench or while at the Bar'.

Stephen Collins was convicted of burglary with intent to commit rape. The facts were such, said one judge, that

> *were they put into a novel or portrayed on the stage, they would be regarded as being so improbable as to be unworthy of serious consideration and as verging at times on farce.*

In the early hours of one Saturday morning a young lady went to bed, having spent the evening drinking with her boyfriend. She woke up a couple of hours later to see, at the open window, a man who had in fact just climbed up a ladder. She also noticed that he had no clothes on. She thought that it was her boyfriend paying her an ardent nocturnal visit. She sat up in bed; the man came in and sexual intercourse took place. Some time later the girl switched on the light and discovered (doubtless to her consternation) that the man in question was not her boyfriend at all, but the defendant. The question which arose was this: if the girl had invited him into the bedroom could he still be said to be a trespasser? The question, of course, was crucial because without trespass there can be no burglary. The Court of Appeal quashed the conviction and said:

> *We hold that, for the purposes of section 9 of the Theft Act 1968, a person entering a building is not guilty of trespass if he enters without knowledge that he is trespassing or at least without acting recklessly as to whether or not he is unlawfully entering.*

The Theft Act 1968 provided a maximum penalty of fourteen years' imprisonment for burglary. This maximum penalty has been retained but only in the case of residential burglary. In other cases of burglary, such as offices, the maximum sentence is now ten years.

d) Aggravated burglary

Section 10 of the Theft Act created the offence of aggravated burglary. This offence, even more serious than burglary itself, is committed if at the time of the burglary the accused has with him any firearm or other offensive weapon loaded or unloaded, real or imitation. On conviction for this offence a man may be sent to prison for life.

e) Taking a conveyance

A very real social menace today is the practice of joy-riding (or in contemporary parlance 'twoccing' from the offence of 'taking without consent') other people's cars. This is a specific offence; it is necessary to define it precisely because of the difficulty of proving the element of 'permanently depriving the owner' in a prosecution of the joy-rider for theft. A person so charged could readily say that he had only wanted to take the car in order to get home.

Section 12 creates two offences:

> ...a person shall be guilty of an offence if, without having the consent of the owner or other lawful authority, he takes any conveyance for his own or another's use or knowing that any conveyance has been taken without such authority, drives it or allows himself to be carried in it or on it.

By this section both the driver and any passengers commit an offence. **Conveyance** is defined so as to include transport for land, water or air, from milk-floats to hovercraft, excluding, however, pedal cycles.

For there to be a conviction it must be proved that something more than use alone took place. In *R* v. *Bogacki* 1973, three men went to a bus garage after they left a New Year's party. They boarded a bus and one of them, Stephen Bogacki, turned the engine over. The bus never moved but all three men were charged with attempting to take a motor vehicle without authority. All three were convicted but appealed. The Court of Appeal quashed their convictions and held that the mere unauthorised assumption of possession of a vehicle does not amount to any offence under section 12 – there must also be some movement, however slight, before the vehicle can be said to have been taken.

By the Criminal Justice Act 1988 the government saw fit to remove the right to trial by jury on this charge.

The Aggravated Vehicle-taking Act 1992 was introduced in response to what was perceived as a crimewave involving motor vehicles. Statistics showed that in twelve months more than half-a-million motor vehicles had been taken and there had been some 800,000 acts of theft from vehicles in that same period. Indeed, approximately one-third of all recorded serious crime related to motor vehicles. Today, therefore, a person who takes a conveyance without authority commits what is termed the 'basic offence'. If, after the vehicle is taken and before it is recovered, the vehicle is driven dangerously or causes an accident or other damage, the basic offence becomes aggravated. Such people can now be sent to prison for two years or five years if the vehicle is involved in an accident which causes death.

f) Obtaining by deception

Section 15 of the Theft Act 1968 provides:

> A person who by any deception dishonestly obtains property belonging to another, with the intention of permanently depriving the other of it, shall on conviction on indictment be liable to imprisonment for a term not exceeding ten years.

Deception is defined by the Act as 'any deception (whether deliberate or reckless) by words or conduct as to fact or as to law'. The ingredients of the offence are, of course, similar to those of theft and, again, each must be proved.

The sort of situation which section 15 covers is well illustrated by *R* v. *McCall* 1971. Paul McCall told an elderly and kind-hearted woman that he had to pay a fine of £310 and that if he did not do so he would be sent to prison. On the strength of that story, the woman lent the defendant that sum of money. In fact, the defendant put the money towards a more pleasurable use: he bought a car and went to Spain. The Court of Appeal upheld his conviction under section 15.

The gravitational principle 'What goes up, must come down' certainly applied to the boom and bust in the residential housing market of the late 1980s and early 1990s. In the boom days, when it seemed that prices would go on rising inexorably, there were many fraudulent applications to banks and building societies for mortgage finance. It was sometimes claimed that this was a 'victimless crime' because a man who dishonestly obtained, say £100,000 from a building society would be able both to repay that debt and pocket a tidy profit always provided that the value of the underlying asset purchased with the building society's money rose. The recent decision of the House of Lords in R v. *Preddy* 1996 concerned a number of men who had obtained substantial amounts of money from building societies or banks with such easy profits in mind. The application forms submitted by the appellants contained a number of false statements including, for example, their details as to employment and income. Preddy and the others contended that, while they had made false representations in these application forms, they had still not committed the offence charged because they had always intended to repay the advances in full when the houses were sold at a profit. Further, it was argued, no property belonging to the banks or building societies had been obtained or made the subject of any such attempt. The question for the court then arose whether the debiting of one bank account (the building society) and the corresponding credit of another bank's account (the defendant) brought about by dishonest misrepresentation amounted to obtaining property within section 15 of the Theft Act. The House of Lords quashed the convictions, accepting that section 15 did not legislate for this sort of deception. In particular, the debiting of one bank account and the corresponding crediting to another account did not mean that property 'belonging to another' was obtained by the person practising the deception. The arguments were very complex, centring upon the concept of a 'chose in action' but the victory enjoyed by these men had only a short life span because Parliament swiftly acted to pass the Theft (Amendment) Act 1996 which filled the gap exposed in Preddy's case by creating a new offence of 'Dishonestly retaining a wrongful credit'.

g) Obtaining a pecuniary advantage by deception

The first part of section 16 gave rise to so many difficulties that one judge was moved to call it a 'judicial nightmare'. In time, the report of the Criminal Law Revision Committee led to the Theft Act 1978. The Act, which replaces section 16.2(a) of the earlier statute, brought in three separate offences. They make it an offence to deceive someone as to the prospect of payment (Tom, who is out of work, tells Dick: 'I get paid on Friday. I'll settle up with you then'); or dishonestly to secure the remission of the whole or part of any existing liability to make a payment; or, knowing that payment on the spot is required, dishonestly make off without paying – as, for example, when Harry puts ten gallons of petrol in his car and races away from the garage forecourt.

Each section merits consideration in more detail.

(i) **Section 1** states that 'a person who by any deception dishonestly obtains services from another shall be guilty of an offence'. For example, in *R* v. *Halai* 1983 a prospective house-buyer wrote out a cheque for £40 to pay for a surveyor's report and valuation. He knew that his cheque would be dishonoured (as, inevitably, it was). He had dishonestly obtained the services of the surveyor and was convicted.

(ii) **Section 2** is a far more complex section which provides three ways in which a person may, by a deception, be guilty of an offence. The first is where by any deception he 'dishonestly secures the remission of the whole or any part of any existing liability to make a payment whether his own or another's'. For example, Tom borrows £100 from Dick on the promise that he will repay it when they meet for a pint next Sunday. At that lunchtime rendezvous Tom spins a long and pitiful yarn about how his only daughter urgently needs a life-saving operation in America. Dick, completely taken in by this hard-luck story, generously pleads with Tom to forget all about the debt and put it towards the poor girl's air fare.

The second situation arises where a person by any deception 'with intent to make permanent default in whole or part on any existing liability to make a payment, or with intent to let another do so, dishonestly induces the creditor or any person claiming payment on behalf of the creditor to wait for payment (whether or not the due date for payment is deferred) or to forgo payment.' For example, Tom tells Dick, to whom he owes £10,000, that his rich aunt is sending her favourite nephew a cheque next week and so Dick can have his money next Sunday. On this representation Dick waits a few more days before suing Tom, who then hops on a plane on the Saturday never to be seen again.

The third situation occurs where, by any deception, a person 'dishonestly obtains any exemption from or abatement of liability to make a payment'. This is illustrated in *R* v. *Sibartie* 1983, where a law student came face to face with the practical side of his studies. His journey to college from Acton to Hendon took in more stations than his season ticket on the underground authorised. He passed a ticket inspector at whom he was said to have 'flashed' his ticket so that the ticket inspector could not see it properly. The court held that by 'flashing' the season ticket in that way the student had suggested that he was the holder of a valid ticket authorising such travel without further payment. Such conduct, therefore, fell within the ambit of section 2 of the 1978 Act.

(iii) **Section 3** states that 'a person who, knowing that payment on the spot for any goods supplied or service done is required or expected from him, dishonestly makes off without having paid as required or expected and with intent to avoid payment of the amount due shall be guilty of an offence'.

This section obviously covers those cases where people quite literally run off without paying; for example, where the post-prandial calm of a restaurant is disturbed by the noisy rush of feet from the neighbouring table to the door, or where hotel guests do a midnight flit, or where motorists race away from petrol station forecourts with tanks full of unpaid-for lead replacement fuel.

The rest of the Act of 1968 remains unaltered so the remaining sub-sections (ii) and (iii) of that statute provide that a person commits an offence:

> (ii) Where, by his deception, he is allowed to borrow by way of overdraft or to take out any policy of insurance or annuity contract, or obtains an improvement of the terms on which he is allowed to do so.

For example, Ruth, an impecunious law student, goes to see her bank manager with terrible accounts of the cost of law textbooks these days. She asks to borrow money to buy a set of law reports and is then given an overdraft of £1,500. In fact, Ruth goes out and blows the lot on clothes.

> (iii) Where by his deception he is given the opportunity to earn remuneration or greater remuneration in an office or employment or to win money by betting.

For example, Ruth, who is aged seventeen and as yet unqualified, tells her employer that she is nineteen and has A-level law. Such are the compensations of age and benefits of education that the boss gives her a rise in pay. Ruth has obtained a pecuniary advantage by deceiving her boss about her age and qualifications.

h) Blackmail

Section 21 provides:

> A person is guilty of blackmail if, with a view to gain for himself or another or with intent to cause loss to another, he makes any unwarranted demand with menaces.

The Act further provides that a demand with menaces is unwarranted unless the person making it does so in the belief that

1. he has reasonable grounds for making the demand, and
2. the use of the menaces is a proper means of reinforcing the demand.

This section of the Act is really self-explanatory and, of course, covers the case where David threatens Frank that if he does not give him £50,000 he will tell Frank's wife, Theresa, all about her husband's secret and squalid life.

The only difficulty that can arise is whether what was said amounts to 'menaces'. The Court of Appeal has indicated that words or conduct amount to menaces if they are such as are likely to operate on the mind of a person of ordinary courage and firmness so as to make him accede unwillingly to the demand.

Blackmail has long been regarded as one of the most unsavoury offences and this is reflected in the maximum sentence of fourteen years' imprisonment.

i) Handling stolen goods

The peculiar phenomenon affecting articles being carried in the backs of lorries is viewed by physicists as yet another manifestation of Newton's Law of Gravity. Lawyers call it handling stolen goods.

Section 22 provides:

> A person handles stolen goods if (otherwise than in the course of the stealing) knowing or believing them to be stolen goods he dishonestly receives the goods, or dishonestly undertakes or assists in their retention, removal, disposal or realization by or for the benefit of another person, or if he arranges to do so.

The Court of Appeal has indicated that a mere failure to reveal the presence of goods of itself does not amount to handling; some more deliberate act of retention or assistance is required.

Once again, the element of dishonesty is essential. That the correct test is necessarily a subjective test was unequivocally emphasised by Lord Widgery CJ in *Atwal* v. *Massey* 1971. A thief had left a stolen kettle by the roadside for collection by Massey who had paid £1.50 for it. Massey was subsequently charged with handling stolen goods and the magistrates convicted him. They clearly took the view that the defendant ought to have known from these unusual circumstances that the kettle had been stolen. However, the Divisional Court quashed the conviction because the magistrates had incorrectly applied an objective test.

The Lord Chief Justice put the position clearly when he said:

> *If, when the justices say that the appellant ought to have known that the kettle was stolen, they mean that any reasonable man would have realized that it was stolen, then that is not the right test. It is not sufficient to establish an offence under section 22 that the goods were received in circumstances which would have put a reasonable man on his inquiry. The question is a subjective one: was the appellant aware of the theft or did he believe the goods to be stolen or did he, suspecting the goods to be stolen, deliberately shut his eyes to the consequences.*

j) Criminal damage

That which cannot easily be stolen, for example a car with locked doors and fitted with an alarm, can still be damaged very easily. Anyone who destroys or damages another's property may commit an offence under the aptly named Criminal Damage Act 1971, if either he or she intends to do such damage or is reckless whether or not such damage will be caused.

The so-called 'grudge-mark' deliberately scratched along the length of a new car would make the user of the penknife guilty of causing intentional damage. Equally, the college rugger team that decides to practise its drop-kicking or scrum-downs in the china department of a shop closely packed with fragile china would be held to be reckless about causing damage to the tiered displays of Dresden dinner services. It would be no defence for the team members to say that they were all too drunk after celebrating their smashing result on the rugger field that none of them appreciated the risk of a similar result in the china department.

. . . reckless about causing damage . . .

For example, in *R* v. *Caldwell* 1981, a man set fire to a hotel one night because he was very drunk and had a grudge against the owner. Fortunately, none of the ten people staying at the Hydro hotel was hurt. At trial James Caldwell told the jury at the Old Bailey that he was so drunk on the night that the thought that there might be people in the hotel whose lives might be endangered if it were set on fire had simply never crossed his mind. Lord Diplock said that a man would be reckless within the meaning of the Criminal Damage Act 1971 if:

(i) he does an act which in fact creates an obvious risk that property will be destroyed or damaged; and

(ii) when he does the act he either has not given any thought to the possibility of there being any such risk or has recognised that there was some risk involved and has nevertheless gone on to do it.

A couple of years after the fire in the Hydro hotel another minor conflagration blazed its way into the law reports when James Miller stood trial for an offence under the Criminal Damage Act 1971. In *R* v. *Miller* 1983, the defendant had left a fire which he had started unintentionally. As he told the police:

> *Last night I went out for a few drinks and at closing time I went back to the house where I have been kipping for a couple of weeks. I went upstairs into the back bedroom where I've been sleeping. I lay on my mattress and lit a cigarette. I must have fell to sleep, because I woke up to find the mattress on fire. I just got up and went into the next room and went back to sleep. Then the next thing I remember was the police and fire people arriving. I hadn't got anything to put the fire out so I just left it.*

He had not intended to start the fire. He was only enjoying a quiet smoke at bedtime. Could his failure to take steps to extinguish the fire make him guilty? Usually the criminal law punishes action rather than inaction. However, Lord Diplock expressed the view that if, before the resulting damage was complete, it would have been possible to take steps to put out the fire, or call the fire brigade, and the person who dropped the cigarette or had otherwise created the fire just did nothing, he was guilty of criminal damage.

It is of the essence in such a charge that the defendant acted 'without lawful excuse' in committing the damage. For example, obviously members of the fire brigade kicking down a door to save the lives of those in a burning house would not be prosecuted. What, though, of the vexed motorist who finds that his car has been immobilised by that loathsome device known politely as a wheel clamp? In *Lloyd* v. *Director of Public Prosecutions* 1992 Roger Lloyd had returned to a private car-park (where he had never been authorised to park) to find not only that his car had been clamped but that it would cost £25 to induce the security guards to release it. During the night the resourceful Mr Lloyd cut the padlock and drove away in his newly liberated car. When prosecuted for criminal damage to the device, Mr Lloyd argued that he had enjoyed a lawful excuse as the clamping had been an act of trespass, that the security guards were wrongly detaining the vehicle and that the sum of £25 was so high and so much in excess of any reasonable parking charge as to amount in law to a penalty (which would be unenforceable). Nevertheless, the judges rejected the arguments, saying that as a general rule if a motorist parked his car without permission on another's property and knew of the risk of clamping (for example, because of clear warning signs on display) he has no right to damage or destroy such a device. It may be of some consolation to those faced with similar problems that another motorist (in fact he was a barrister) who found his car similarly clamped on leaving court was able forthwith to return to the same court and, having issued proceedings under the Torts (Interference with Goods) Act 1977, obtained an order for the release of the car. Further consolation may be derived from a perusal of the decision in *Black* v. *Carmichael* 1992 of the Scottish High Court of Justiciary to the effect that, except where authorised by legislation, wheel clampers commit the offences of theft and extortion.

However, in *Arthur* v. *Anker* 1996 the purely civil consequences of wheel clamping came to be considered afresh by the Court of Appeal. Prominent notices had been displayed around some land. One such 'polite notice' (the word 'polite' always looking something like the word 'police') warned: 'Unauthorised vehicles will be towed away at their owner's risk and expense'. Another clearly displayed notice warned that a charge of £40 would be levied to release any vehicle which had been clamped. When David Arthur returned to find that his car had been clamped, he refused to pay and somehow managed to remove his car during the night. He sued the parking contractors for interference with his vehicle; the contractors then responded by suing for the cost of their lost clamp and padlocks! The Court of Appeal approved the approach of the County Court judge who had applied the maxim *volenti non fit injuria* (see Unit 6.7), holding that the motorist had known of and impliedly consented to the likely consequences of unlawful parking.

The range of offences committed under the Criminal Damage Act 1971 is, not surprisingly, very wide: the maximum penalty is one of ten years' imprisonment.

k) Trade descriptions

It may be an unappetising fact, but true, that those '100% Best British Beefburgers' just bought from the local butcher may also contain quantities of fat, bone, hair and water. Although misrepresentations as to terms have long given rise to civil actions for damages (see Unit 4.6), Parliament decided in 1968 that, in order to protect the vulnerable consumer more effectively, the application by a trader of a false trade description should be a criminal offence. Under section 1 of the Trade Descriptions Act 1968:

> Any person who, in the course of a trade or business –
> (a) applies a false trade description to any goods; or
> (b) supplies or offers to supply any goods to which a false trade description is applied;
> shall . . . be guilty of an offence.

Unusually, the offence is one of strict liability (see Unit 3.1b)) and a partner may even be liable for the acts of another partner even though he personally was not involved in applying the false trade description. Companies may also be liable as well as individual traders. In these ways, perfectly respectable businesses can be found guilty of slip-ups as well as those less fastidious independent entrepreneurs modelling themselves on 'Arthur Daley'.

The term 'trade description' is taken to refer to a long list of matters such as quantity, size, composition and method of manufacture. Misleading price indications on goods, services, accommodation or facilities are now also offences of strict liability under the Consumer Protection Act 1987.

Mere trade-puffs, however, do not amount to a trade description. So, in *Cadbury* v. *Halliday* 1975 the well-known chocolate manufacturers, Cadbury Limited, distributed some of their chocolate in wrappers marked with a flash with the words 'Extra Value'. In fact, these bars offered no greater value than other similar bars without the fancy wrapping. However, the court held that the words 'Extra Value' were not a trade description since they were not an indication of any of the matters listed in the Act.

Although holiday tour operators are not free from blame, it is the secondhand car-dealer who occupies a particularly conspicuous place in the line of cases on false trades descriptions. One motor trader even committed an offence not selling a car but actually buying one. So it was in *Fletcher* v. *Budgen* 1974 that Howard Budgen, a car-dealer, was negotiating for the purchase of an old Fiat motor car. Budgen told the Fiat's then owner that there was no possibility of repairing the car and that the only thing to do was to have it scrapped. Budgen then bought the Fiat for £2, did it up and advertised it for sale at £135. In the Divisional Court, Lord Widgery CJ commented on the wide ambit of the wording in the statute. The Lord Chief Justice held that even a buyer is covered by the Act provided, of course, that the buyer was conducting a trade or business. The genuine private seller (or even buyer) is not affected by the Act and even a man who repaired and then sold cars has been held to be carrying on a hobby and not a business.

In *Davies* v. *Sumner* 1984, a false car mileage reading led to a prosecution under the 1968 Act. John Davies worked as a self-employed courier and obviously drove many miles. When he came to part-exchange his old Ford for a new one he omitted to tell the garage that his car had, in fact, been round the clock and the mileage shown was a mere 100,000 miles out. Whatever the morality of this reluctance to disclose the true state of affairs, had he, as a self-employed courier, disposed of his old car in the course of 'trade or business'? The House of Lords took the view that the Act required a degree of frequency and continuity in any course of dealings. This trade-in of the old car was only a one-off sale of a capital asset and, accordingly, did not fall foul of the Act. Although the Act makes the offence one of strict liability so that the honest, if slipshod, trader is penalised as well as the unscrupulous rogue, the Act does, however, provide a defence in that the trader is allowed to apply a disclaimer to the goods. Of course, the disclaimer must be as compelling and precise as any description and it must not be lost in the small print. Garages especially rely on this disclaimer and will cover themselves over a car's mileage reading by disclaiming liability for any errors in that direction.

The fact that an individual is not acting in the course of a trade or business does not mean, however, that he or she has *carte blanche* to cheat and mislead when disposing of his old car. So, in *Olgeirsson* v. *Kitching* 1986 a police car developed a fault with its odometer and a new one was fitted when the car had covered about 64,000 miles. A month later the car was damaged in an accident and was later sold when the new odometer had a reading of 10,385 miles. Eventually a private individual, Einar Olgeirsson, bought it well aware that the car had covered something like 74,000 miles. When Olgeirsson sold it on to a dealer he played down the true mileage by saying that the odometer was only some 8,000 miles out. The dealer sold it in his turn and after some time the truth, as is its habit, came out. Olgeirsson was subsequently prosecuted on the basis that, when the first dealer had sold the car, he had committed an offence which, while one of strict liability, had been 'due to the act or default of another person' (namely Olgeirsson). Under the Trade Descriptions Act 1968, that other person is also guilty of an offence. The court rejected the argument advanced on appeal that such provision in the Act applied only to persons acting in the course of a trade or business. The words in that particular section had a plain and ordinary meaning and were not to be limited so as to exclude the private individual from possible liability.

3.7 *The prosecution process*

Today, we tend to think of the police as a nationwide organisation trained in the control of society generally and, in particular, in the prevention and detection of crime. Such a concept, however, is of comparatively recent origin. Indeed, it was not until the early nineteenth century that Sir Robert Peel, the then Home Secretary, set up the Metropolitan Police, which at that time patrolled only a few square miles of London and encountered both criticism and hostility in doing so. As the years went by, similar systems were adopted in other parts of the country and by about the mid-nineteenth century full-time police forces were to be found throughout most of England and Wales. This country, however, has never had a national police force although such a system has certainly been called for. So, today, a man on the run, say, from the Old Bailey and making good his escape along the M4 would be the object of unwelcome attention from the City of London Police, the Metropolitan Police and the Thames Valley Police – and all before he even reaches Reading.

England's supposedly characteristic love of the talented amateur rather than the trained full-time professional is perhaps responsible in part at least for the long-standing theory that the police are just ordinary citizens in blue suits. So, too, the English police forces have traditionally eschewed the more military appearance and structure of continental police forces now exemplified, for example, in the easy-going affability of the French Riot Police. The corollary to this theory is that if a policeman goes beyond his duty he, like anyone else, is liable for assault, false imprisonment and wrongful arrest.

The powers of the police, already very substantially increased in recent years, their conduct of investigations, the supervision of their behaviour and their role in the conduct of prosecutions are matters all considered by the Runciman Commission which reported in the summer of 1993. Set up on the day the Birmingham Six were freed after sixteen years in gaol and against a more general background of sadly diminished public confidence, stemming from cases such as that of Stefan Kiszko, in the ability of the English criminal process either to acquit the innocent or to convict the guilty, the Commission examined the criminal process from the early stages in police investigation to the point where all appeals have been exhausted. It is ironic that such inquiry, set up against the background of a major embarrassment to this country's system of justice, was the setting for so much of the Criminal Justice and Public Order Act 1994, which itself constituted a rejection of a pivotal part of the Commission's recommendations as to the citizen's 'right of silence'.

It is by the process of arrest that the ground is laid for many prosecutions. **Arrest** simply means imposing a restraint on a person's liberty. It was once described by one judge as the beginning of imprisonment. Such an act, of course, is a serious infringement of the liberty of the subject and is *prima facie* unlawful. The rules which govern arrest require some words of explanation.

Every citizen has a moral or social duty to assist the police but there is no legal duty to that effect. Equally, any police officer is as much as liberty to ask people questions as is, say, a butcher, baker or candlestick-maker. However, subject to certain exceptions to be found mainly in road traffic legislation, no one is obliged to answer such questions from the police any more than if such enquiry had come from one of those other three honest tradesmen.

One recent erosion of this principle is, however, now to be found in section 89 of the Terrorism Act 2000 which empowers a police officer to stop a person for as long as is necessary to question him about matters such as his identity, movements and knowledge of any recent explosion or recent incident endangering life. The section continues:

> A person commits an offence if he –
> (a) fails to stop when required to do so under this section;
> (b) refuses to answer a question addressed to him under this section;
> (c) fails to answer to the best of his knowledge and ability a question addressed to him under this section.

Another major erosion of this traditional right, however, is to be found in the Criminal Justice Act 1987, an Act intended to regulate the conduct of fraud trials and which established the Serious Fraud Office. Under this legislation the Serious Fraud Office has power to require someone whose affairs are to be investigated (or anyone else believed to have relevant information) to answer questions and to provide other information. Anyone refusing to do so runs the risk of imprisonment. Such legislation, however, was recently criticised by the European Court on Human Rights when it ruled that the trial of former Guinness chief, Ernest Saunders, had been unfair. Evidence which Saunders had been forced to give during a City investigation into the Guinness bid for Distillers should not have been used against him in his criminal trial. By a majority the judges found that the use of this material had constituted a 'remarkable departure from one of the basic principles of fair procedure'.

Similarly, anyone invited, cordially or otherwise, to accompany policemen to their station is entitled to decline such an invitation unless and until arrested. Nevertheless, recent years have seen a substantial increase in the powers granted to the police and new legislation enshrined in the Criminal Justice and Public Order Act 1994 allows the police to stop and search both citizens and their vehicles when it is feared that serious incidents of violence may take place in any locality. The same Act also provides a statutory basis for party-pooping so that the police are also now given power to remove people attending or preparing for a 'rave' (a word now even hallowed in Statute).

After carrying a report of some terrible crime, the press would often use the well-worn phrase: 'A man is helping the police with their inquiries.' Devlin J dispelled many a popular myth when, in a famous passage, he said:

> *You may sometimes read in novels and detective stories perhaps written by people not familiar with police procedure, that persons are sometimes taken into custody for questioning. There is no such power in this country. A man cannot be detained unless he is arrested.*

The message was forcefully brought home by Lawton LJ when he said:

> ... *it must be clearly understood that neither customs officers nor police officers have any right to detain somebody for the purposes of getting them to help with their inquiries. Police officers either arrest for an offence or they do not arrest at all. The law is clear. Neither arrest nor detention can properly be carried out without the accused person being told the offence for which he is being arrested. There is no such offence as 'helping the police with their inquiries'. This is a phrase which has crept into use, largely of the need for the press to be careful about how they report what has happened when somebody has been arrested but not charged. If the idea is getting about amongst either customs officers or police officers that they can arrest or detain people, as the case may be, for this particular purpose, the sooner they disabuse themselves of that idea the better.*

The situation was codified by the Police and Criminal Evidence Act 1984 which came into force on 1 January 1986 so that, under section 29:

> Where for the purpose of assisting with an investigation a person attends voluntarily at a police station or at any other place where a constable is present, or accompanies a constable to a police station or any other place without having been arrested:
> (a) he shall be entitled to leave at will unless he is placed under arrest;
> (b) he shall be informed at once that he is under arrest if a decision is taken by a constable to prevent him from leaving at will.

There is no magic formula governing the making of an arrest. What has to be done, however, is to make it clear to the suspect that he is being arrested and to give the reason for such arrest. More specifically, under section 28 of the same Act:

> An arrest is not lawful unless the person arrested is informed that he is under arrest as soon as practicable after his arrest. Further, no arrest is lawful unless the person arrested is informed of the ground for his or her arrest at the time of, or as soon as is practicable after, the arrest.

Any serious failure to make these matters clear to the suspect may found liability for wrongful arrest and false imprisonment (see Unit 6.6b)) as was the case in *Christie* v. *Leachinsky* 1947, when two Liverpool policemen arrested Mr Leachinsky. They suspected that he had stolen or dishonestly received some cloth and arrested him on a charge of 'unlawful possession' although such a charge required a warrant which the officers did not have. The House of Lords emphasised that it is a condition of lawful arrest that the party arrested knows the reason for this arrest.

Viscount Simon dealt with the constitutional importance of this rule in a free society when he said:

> *The matter is a matter of substance, and turns on the elementary proposition that in this country a person is, prima facie, entitled to his freedom and is only required to submit to restraints of his freedom if he knows in substance the reason why it is claimed that this restraint should be imposed. No one, I think, would approve a situation in which when the person arrested asked for the reason, the policeman replied 'that has nothing to do with you: come along with me'. Such a situation may be tolerated under other systems of law, as for instance of* lettres de cachet *in the eighteenth century in France, or in more recent days when the Gestapo swept people off to confinement under an over-riding authority which the executive in this country does not in ordinary times possess. This would be quite contrary to our conceptions of individual liberty.*

Quite what the concept of reasonable suspicion involved fell recently to be considered by the House of Lords in *O'Hara* v. *Chief Constable of the Royal Ulster Constabulary* 1997. Gerard O'Hara was arrested on suspicion of a terrorist murder in Northern Ireland. He was released some two weeks later without being charged with any offence and sued the police for wrongful arrest. The courts had to decide whether the arresting police officer, who was acting only on a briefing from a superior officer, had held reasonable grounds for suspecting O'Hara of terrorist activity. In the House of Lords it was said that the court need not look beyond what was in the officer's mind since it was the grounds which were in his mind at the time which were relevant. Such suspicion, the court said, need not be based upon the officer's own observations but, rather, could be based on what he had been told or, alternatively, upon information which had been given to him anonymously. Lord Steyn went on to emphasise that in order to have a reasonable suspicion, the police need not have evidence amounting to a *prima facie* case and, on that basis, even information from an informer or a tip-off from a member of the public may be enough.

Police officers also enjoy a statutory power to arrest members of the public for non-arrestable offences. The criteria for the so-called 'general arrest condition' is set out in section 23 of the Police and Criminal Evidence Act. The condition is satisfied where:

(1) the name of the suspect is unknown and cannot be discovered; or
(2) there are reasonable grounds for believing arrest is necessary in order to protect the suspect from:–
    a) causing physical injury to himself or some other person; or
    b) suffering physical injury; or
    c) causing loss or damage to property; or
    d) committing a public decency offence; or
    e) causing unlawful obstruction of the highway.

Quite apart from these 'general arrest conditions' specific Acts of Parliament will provide their own power of arrest. For example, section 29 of the Criminal Justice and Public Order Act 1994 provided police with the new power of arresting a person who has failed to answer to police bail. This new power obviates the need for the police to appear before a magistrate in order to obtain a warrant.

In another claim against the police for false arrest and wrongful imprisonment, the Court of Appeal in *Lewis* v. *Chief Constable of the South Wales Constabulary* 1991 held that an initially unlawful arrest became a lawful arrest from that moment when reasons for the arrest were at last given. In that claim this had the effect of shortening the period of time for which Elizabeth Lewis and her sister had been wrongfully imprisoned. The judges repeated earlier remarks that arrest is a continuing act which starts with the arrester taking a person into his custody and it continues until the person so restrained is either released from custody or is remanded into custody by the local magistrates.

The law governing the process of arrest was regularised by the Criminal Law Act 1967 which introduced the concept of the 'arrestable offence'. This concept was preserved and widened by the Police and Criminal Evidence Act 1984 which broadly defines 'arrestable offence' as one where the sentence is fixed by law (for example, murder) or where those aged 21 and over could be sent to prison for five years or more (for example, theft). Under this Act any person may arrest without warrant anyone committing an arrestable offence or anyone whom he or she has reasonable grounds for suspecting of committing such an offence. A police officer obviously has all these ordinary powers conferred on all citizens but is in a superior position to the ordinary citizen in that he or she may also arrest anyone whom he reasonably suspects to be about to commit an arrestable offence.

A less common form of arrest is an **arrest on warrant**. A warrant is an order of a court requiring the police to whom it is addressed to arrest the person whose name appears on the warrant and then bring him or her before the court. The warrant may also be **backed for bail**, which means that the man may be released on undertakings that he will turn up at court later. Such a warrant had been issued for unpaid fines in *R* v. *Purdy* 1974 when two police constables went to a dance, not for their own enjoyment, but in response to a call for assistance. At the scene of the disturbance, one of them saw the defendant, Van Purdy, for whom they had a warrant in their patrol car. The constable told Purdy that he had a warrant to arrest him for non-payment of fines. The defendant replied in monosyllabic crudities that brought out some dozen of his friends and a violent struggle ensued.

At his trial for causing an affray and assaulting the police, the defendant's counsel argued that, as the officer did not have the warrant in his actual possession at the time of the purported arrest, the defendant had been entitled to resist what, therefore, had been an unlawful arrest. The Court of Appeal dismissed his appeal against conviction and held that the warrant was in the constable's possession even though it had not been on him, for he still had control of it and could have easily produced it. The Police and Criminal Evidence Act 1984 now allows a police officer to execute a warrant (that is carry it out by arresting someone) even though he does not have the warrant in his possession at the time.

It requires only a little worldliness to realise that not everyone takes kindly to being arrested. For that reason Parliament has provided that reasonable force may be used to bring about an arrest and today the position is governed by the Criminal Law Act 1967, section 3:

> A person may use such force as is reasonable in the circumstances in the prevention of crime or in effecting or assisting in the lawful arrest of offenders or of a person unlawfully at large.

. . . not everyone takes kindly to being arrested.

Once arrested, a person should be taken to a police station or before the local magistrates as soon as reasonably practicable.

After arrest the police will usually be keen to question the prisoner in order to secure evidence. It is important that such interrogation complies with the Police and Criminal Evidence Act 1984 and its accompanying Code of Practice. While not every breach of this complex procedure will be fatal to the prosecution case at trial, the judge may so exercise his discretion as to exclude evidence obtained in any serious breach. After all, the aim of the procedure is to protect the citizen against bullying or sharp practice by the police, whose powers under the Police and Criminal Evidence Act 1984 are considerable.

As a historical matter of common law the traditional view of the court has been that it did not matter how evidence was obtained. If evidence was relevant it was admissible. Against this background, however, the courts were nevertheless prepared to exclude certain evidence, classically such as evidence of confessions where such confessions were not voluntary or had been obtained by some form of oppression. The Police and Criminal Evidence Act 1984 provides two separate routes by which evidence which the prosecution seek to rely upon can be excluded. At first blush, this may seem unfair on the prosecution who may have a ten-page signed confession. What better evidence could there be? Against this obvious question there is, sadly, all too much evidence that, for whatever reason, people do confess to crimes they simply have not committed. Sometimes this is the result of their own feeble intellect, perhaps aggravated by youth, inexperience or fear. One less attractive explanation is that the police have bullied, threatened or assaulted their prisoner in order to obtain what, and more so in days now gone, has all too often been viewed as the holy grail of police interrogation.

Where there is evidence that a confession was or might have been obtained as the result of oppression, or in circumstances that were likely to render such a confession unreliable, the court should exclude that confession in the absence of proof by the prosecution that such evidence was not so obtained. It should be emphasised that this is a strict approach of admissibility and so, at this early stage in the proceedings, it does not in fact matter whether the confession is true or not. For the purposes of judging admissibility the concept of 'oppression' is defined as including torture, inhuman or degrading treatment and the use or threat of violence.

The police officer should **caution** the suspect as soon as he or she has grounds for suspicion. This general rule is subject to exclusions so that, for example, no caution is required if it is impracticable to do so by reason of a person's condition or behaviour at the time. Even before the recent change in the words of the caution, crime writers would so often get it wrong. The recent expansion of the traditional words of the caution are significant for they are directly relevant to the concept of the citizen's right of silence.

Viewers of old black and white films will recall the arrival of the police (usually an inspector in a trenchcoat) who would enter the country house through the French windows to warn his man in terms:

> You do not have to say anything unless you wish to do so but what you say may be given in evidence.

Those more up-to-date with television portrayal of the police and even the change in men's fashions may already have become used to the new wording:

> You do not have to say anything. But it may harm your defence if you do not mention when questioned something which you later rely on in court. Anything you do say may be given in evidence.

This is far, far more than a mere change in wording. It reflects the rejection by the Conservative Government, and its then Home Secretary in particular, of the recommendations of the Runciman Commission and reflects a further shift away from the rights of the individual citizen in favour of an increase in police power. The debate had raged for years. The conflict remains a simple one. The easier it becomes rightly to convict the guilty, the easier it also becomes wrongly to convict the innocent. Those in favour of abolishing the centuries-old 'right of silence' have echoed the words of Jeremy Bentham:

> *If all criminals of every class had assembled, and framed a system after their own wishes, is not the rule the very first which they would have established for their security? Innocence never takes advantage of it. Innocence claims the right of speaking as guilt invokes the privilege of silence.*

On the other hand, the rights of the individual citizen to be protected from bullying or oppression especially when at risk through ignorance, fear or fatigue should not be ignored.

In 1981 the Royal Commission on Criminal Procedure advocated the retention of the right of silence and, in 1986, the Roskill investigation into fraud trials similarly came down in favour of its preservation as an integral part of the English criminal trial – a system which rightly tries to ensure that no innocent person is wrongly convicted.

Considerations of this right of silence, therefore, assumed a pivotal role in the Runciman Commission as its members debated whether such right was indeed a crucial safeguard for the suspect or whether, on the other hand, it has nothing more than an unacceptable obstacle to convicting the guilty. The Commission took account of the evidence of those with practical experience acquired over many years when solicitors pointed out that many people, suddenly confronted with the trauma of arrest, detention and questioning, find the experience both disorientating and intimidating. The Commission recognised that many suspects may be confused or unclear about legal concepts and definitions such as intent and dishonesty. Further, in some cases, suspects, while themselves innocent, may with some misplaced chivalry try to protect their family or friends. This may cause them either to remain silent or even falsely to confess their own guilt in order to protect others.

By a majority the Runciman Commission recommended the retention of the original caution and right of silence and further expressed the Commission's concern that there had already been too many cases of improper pressure being brought to bear on suspects when in police custody.

The response of the then Conservative Government, however, was to ignore such Report and to legislate in sections 34 to 37 of the Criminal Justice and Public Order Act 1994. This legislation allows adverse inferences to be drawn at trial in circumstances where a person has exercised his right to silence where there is *prima facie* evidence against him. Such inference may similarly be drawn if a suspect has failed to put forward defence facts or to explain either objects in his possession or his presence at a particular place.

Others would question what use a right is if one is to be penalised for exercising such right. The American lawyer Oliver Wendell Holmes had put the general issue well:

> *As soon as you interfere with a right it is no longer a right but a privilege enjoyed at another's sufferance.*

Inevitably, it could not be long before the courts were required to consider how the new legislation should be construed. The relevant section, section 34, provides:

1. Where, in any proceedings against a person for an offence, evidence is given that the accused –
   (a) at any time before he was charged with the offence, on being questioned under caution by a constable trying to discover whether or by whom the offence had been committed, failed to mention any fact relied on in his defence in those proceedings; or
   (b) on being charged with the offence or officially informed that he might be prosecuted for it, failed to mention any such fact,
   being a fact which in the circumstances existing at the time the accused could reasonably have been expected to mention when so questioned, charged or informed, as the case may be, sub-section (2) below applies.

The relevant sub-section then goes on to provide that:

   (c) the court, in determining whether there is a case to answer; and
   (d) the court or jury, in determining whether the accused is guilty of the offence charged,
   may draw such inferences from the failure as appear proper.

What inferences would be proper and what an accused person could reasonably have been expected to mention fell recently to be considered by the Court of Appeal in *R* v. *Cowan* 1995. The appellants had been convicted shortly after the new legislation came into force and all appealed, contending that a trial judge should exercise his discretion to direct the jury that they could draw adverse inferences from silence only in an exceptional case where there was no reasonable possibility of an innocent explanation for such silence. The Court of Appeal rejected this argument, saying that it was a matter for the jury to decide whether such inference could properly be drawn. The Court of Appeal went on to say that the jury should be reminded that the burden of proof remains on the prosecution and that an inference from a failure to give evidence (at the time of arrest) cannot on its own prove guilt. In other words, there must still be a case for the defendant to answer before that inference can properly be drawn. Judges who now sum up to juries the circumstances where an accused person has maintained his right of silence at trial may say something along the following lines:

> *The defendant has not given evidence. That is his right. But, as he has been told, the law is that you may draw such inferences as appear proper from his failure to do so. Failure to give evidence on its own cannot prove guilt but depending on the circumstances you may hold his failure against him when deciding whether he is guilty. . . . If you conclude that there is a case for him to answer, you may think the defendant would have gone into the witness box to give you an explanation or an answer to the case against him. If the only sensible explanation for his decision not to give evidence is that he has no answer to the case against him, or none that could have stood*

up to cross-examination, then it would be open to you to hold against him his failure to give evidence. It is for you to decide whether it is fair to do so.

Recently in *R* v. *Gill* 2000 the Court of Appeal emphasised the fundamental importance of a judge directing the jury that an inference by itself cannot prove guilt. It followed that the jury must still be satisfied of a *prima facie* case against the defendant. The jury could only consider whether to draw an inference adverse to the defendant whom they were trying if they had already rejected the explanation of the silence and had gone on to conclude that such failure to give evidence could only sensibly be attributed to the accused person having either no answer or no answer which would withstand cross-examination.

It is plain that the day which Lord Devlin hoped would never dawn, has arrived, such legislation having first been used in trials held in Northern Ireland. It will be interesting to see, once the Human Rights Act 1998 is in force, what view is taken of these statutory provisions and their arguable breaches of Article 6 of the European Convention for the Protection of Human Rights and Fundamental Freedoms.

In order to limit the scope for fabrication of false confessions (known traditionally, if colloquially, as 'verbals'), the 1984 Act and its Code lay down strict provisions over the recording of interviews. A full and accurate note is to be kept of any important conversation. The police will be keen to interview their suspect. The Runciman Commission emphasised the need at this stage for a thorough investigation of all evidence including any which may tend to exonerate the suspect. Such investigation also needs to be properly documented so that its quality may be gauged at trial. Investigation also needs to be conducted fairly in order to avoid the sort of oppressive questioning so roundly castigated by the Court of Appeal in the case of the *R* v. *Paris* 1993 where unreliable confessions had been obtained after many hours of hectoring interrogation. Such investigation, therefore, also requires sufficient supervision in order to restrict the scope for that kind of malpractice by certain police officers which has sadly been seen from time to time in the existence of palpably false confessions obtained in interview. When held at a police station such an interview is now almost certain to be tape-recorded. Such recording can afford valuable protection for all concerned and the tape may be played at trial. The Runciman Commission, approving this use of technology, also suggested that the use of video-recording should be further considered. If the police questioning is to be spread over many hours, it is important to protect a suspect against excessive fatigue and also to allow him or her sufficient rest periods. This is one of a number of responsibilities imposed on a police officer specially designated as the Custody Officer, who has a duty also to maintain a record known as the Custody Record, which times and records all important events during the prisoner's enforced sojourn in what is now generally if also delicately called the 'Custody Suite' of a police station.

The police are under an obligation to review periodically the continuing detention of all persons in police custody. Persons arrested may be detained at a police station without charge for up to 24 hours unless held in connection with what is known as a serious arrestable offence. In such cases the period of detention may be extended to 36 hours. Upon application to the local magistrates, a further period of detention up to a maximum 36 hours may then be sanctioned. Generally speaking, a prisoner should be allowed access to a solicitor and duty solicitors are available night and day throughout the year to assist and advise people so detained. This, however, is a right which the police are permitted in certain circumstances to withhold and, in any event, there is evidence that many people do not exercise this right.

The facility for an arrested person to have access to a solicitor was originally said to be a counter-balance to the increased powers granted to the police under the Police and Criminal Evidence Act 1984. The right of a person to consult a solicitor privately was enshrined in section 58 of the Act. This protection, however, is watered down because the police are permitted to delay access to a solicitor for 36 hours in specified cases such as a belief that other persons suspected of committing such an offence would be alerted. There is concern that this protection for people perhaps brought from their beds in the middle of the night is not as soundly based as the public were led to believe in 1984. There is substantial anecdotal evidence that the police often dissuaded prisoners from asking to see a solicitor on the basis that they would only be kept waiting even longer in a cell. A further worry is that a number of the people attending police stations to give advice to prisoners were, in fact, not solicitors but less qualified members of staff in solicitors' firms. The quality of the advice given in such circumstances is, as so often in the administration of justice now, intimately connected with the low levels of legal aid remuneration. Sadly, however, even when solicitors do attend police stations, there is also some evidence that they fail to assert themselves sufficiently and, therefore, to protect prisoners against aggressive police questioning.

Another worry has been an inconsistency in the approach of the courts to breaches by the police of the rules. Judges retain a discretion to exclude evidence which has been improperly obtained but recent decisions show an inconsistency of approach. In *R* v. *Samuel* 1988 the defendant was arrested for robbery at a building society. When arrested, he signed the custody record confirming that he did not 'want a solicitor at this time'. He was interviewed on two occasions and in the second interview asked to see a solicitor. The police denied him access to a solicitor. The interviews continued. In due course a solicitor instructed by the man's mother endeavoured to speak to the police on the man's behalf. After repeated bouts of questioning while denied access to a solicitor, Samuel confessed. Shortly afterwards he was allowed to see a solicitor. The Court of Appeal saw that there was a sinister side to what had happened. The police had, over a period exceeding 24 hours, interviewed this young man four times without obtaining any confession from him in respect of the robbery. Time was running out for them. Early in the next morning a solicitor would have to be permitted. The man would have to be taken before the local magistrates. The accused had been in police custody for over 24 hours and the Court of Appeal expected that a solicitor might well consider that, at least for that evening, enough was enough and that he ought to advise his client not to answer further questions at that time. The Court of Appeal took the view that Samuel had been denied improperly one of the most important and fundamental rights of a citizen and quashed the robbery conviction. This decision, however, does not sit comfortably alongside that in *R* v. *Alladice* 1988 when denial by the police of access to a solicitor was not viewed by the Court of Appeal as sufficiently serious to require statements made by the detainee to be excluded at his trial.

The recent trend in judges' approaches to irregularities in police investigation and questioning shows a hardening of attitude in favour of allowing evidence even when improperly obtained. For example, in *R* v. *Latif* 1996, the House of Lords had to consider the individual rights of a criminal and weigh them against the wider public interest in ensuring that those charged with grave crimes should be tried. Latif and another man were drug smugglers. They were involved in the export of heroin to the United Kingdom. The deal, struck in Pakistan, became known to the British Customs. In due course a Customs officer (carrying six bags of Horlicks rather than the genuine article!) delivered the bags to a man who was immediately arrested. The Customs officer had deceived Latif's co-accused into coming to London where he was arrested and put on trial. The trial judge declined to exclude the evidence and said:

> *Though no court will readily approve of trickery and deception being used, there are some circumstances in which one has to recognise, living in the real world, that this is the only way in which some people are ever going to be brought to trial, otherwise the courts will not get to try this sort of offence against people who are seriously involved in it.*

Upon appeal, the House of Lords expressed the view that there was nothing so unworthy or shameful in the conduct of the Customs that it was an affront to the public conscience to allow the prosecution to proceed.

A different view, however, had been taken by Runciman of the defendant's right to silence once there has been a fuller disclosure of the prosecution case. There were already rules for the advance disclosure of experts' reports and, of course, since 1967, a defendant who intends to raise a defence of **alibi** has been obliged to provide the particulars of that alibi to the prosecution. Alibi is Latin for 'elsewhere' and is defined as:

> Evidence tending to show that by reason of the presence of the defendant at a particular place or in a particular area at a particular time he was not, or was unlikely to have been, at the place where the offence is alleged to have been committed at the time of its alleged commission.

For example, say that Tom is charged with burgling a house in Birmingham last Saturday. He will say that at the time of that burglary he was at a party in Bristol. Tom must tell the police the identity of his host and the address of that party so that the police can check up on Tom's account.

Once their inquiries have progressed far enough, the police may **charge** their suspect. This means that they formally inform him that he is being prosecuted and once again he should be cautioned. Traditionally in England and Wales the decision whether or not to bring a person to trial was made by the police themselves. In some cases, such as minor assaults and shoplifting, the police were sometimes seen as reluctant to become involved so the private citizen with a black eye or the shopkeeper with the depleted shelves was obliged to bring a private prosecution. One such prosecution was that of Peter Hain, then the Leader of the Young Liberals but since appointed a Minister in the present Blair Government, for conspiring to disrupt the Davis Cup tennis tournament between South Africa and Britain in 1969 by throwing bags of flour during play. One court appearance, therefore, led to another.

Those who cynically jibe that lawyers are just actors manqué would have seen both occupations under the roof of the Old Bailey in 1982 when the indefatigable Mrs Mary Whitehouse launched her own prosecution against Michael Bogdanov for his stage production *The Romans in Britain* only to see the case brought to a halt by the issue of a *nolle prosequi* issued by the Attorney-General (see Unit 2.5d)). More recently, the family of Stephen Lawrence, brutally murdered in South London in 1993, pursued their own private prosecution against a number of youths later called to give evidence at the Inquiry conducted by Sir William Macpherson (see Unit 2.5f)).

For many years the decision whether or not to prosecute cases had been taken in the United States by District Attorneys and in Scotland by the Procurator Fiscal. A former Home Secretary, Alex Lyon, once explained the need for some independent critical judgment at this time:

> *If the police are actively engaged in the decision whether a case ought to be prosecuted there is a danger that in some cases a dispassionate view of the evidence may not prevail.*

Judges, too, were becoming concerned at the number of cases being tried in the Crown Court where, at the close of the prosecution case, they had to direct the jury to acquit the defendant as there was no evidence against him. It was against such movement for reform that Parliament passed the Prosecution of Offences Act 1985. This Act established a new **Crown Prosecution Service** (CPS) for England and Wales as advocated by the Phillips Commission on Criminal Procedure. Until then, prosecutions were either conducted by the police themselves (at least before local magistrates) or by solicitors either employed by that particular police force or in local private practice. In the Crown Court, in contrast, the conduct of such prosecutions has, until very recently, always been the province of the independent Bar.

This new system works under the superintendence of the **Director of Public Prosecutions** (the DPP). The holder of this office is appointed from among barristers and solicitors of at least ten years' standing. Working under the Attorney-General his duty was set out in the Prosecution of Offences Act 1985 as being 'to institute, undertake or carry on . . . criminal proceedings' and to advise and assist the police and magistrates' clerks on the conduct of proceedings. The Director also represents the Crown in proceedings on appeal from the High Court and the Crown Court and the DPP also has power to take over the conduct of proceedings brought by a private citizen.

There is evidence that the creation of the Crown Prosecution Service was affected adversely by a friction borne of the resentment felt by the police at the loss of their role as prosecutors. Moreover, a failure by the government to fund this new body properly also led at times to indifferent performance by the CPS, which then lacked sufficient numbers of lawyers for the work to be done.

Among its many duties the CPS must review all case papers sent to them by the police. Against the Code for Crown Prosecutors the CPS must decide whether to prosecute (or continue to prosecute) a person arrested or charged by the police. In most cases proceedings will already have been started by the police but the Crown prosecutor may prefer to change the charges or even drop the proceedings altogether. In determining what charges to prosecute the CPS is required to consider two specific stages. Firstly, does the case meet the evidential test? If the evidence is simply not there then, no matter how grave the allegation, the case should not continue. The Crown prosecutor must ask whether there is sufficient evidence to provide a 'realistic prospect of conviction' on any particular charge. The judgment may involve a consideration of the likely weight to be attached to the quality of evidence of identification (a notoriously weak area) or whether, for example, a particular witness is likely to have his or her own axe to grind so as to become unreliable. Secondly, the test requires a judgment to be made as to the public interest. Such consideration is likely to promote a prosecution where, for example, a victim of crime has been picked on because of race, sex or religious beliefs. Offences committed against people such as police or prison officers are traditionally viewed as serious and others who serve the public, such as nurses and bus drivers, receive similar consideration. On the other hand, if the result of any prosecution leading to conviction is likely to be no more than a very small or even only nominal penalty, where there has been long delay between the commission of the offence and the date of its discovery or perhaps where the defendant is elderly or unwell the decision may be made not to prosecute.

The relevance of these considerations has been recently underlined by the Director of Public Prosecutions in October 2000 when, in revised guidelines, prosecutors were also instructed to take into account the consequences for the victim of the decision to be made whether or not to prosecute and also consider the views of the complainant or the complainant's family.

3.8 Trial

A visit to a busy magistrates' court will reveal a large number of 'overnight charges' such as simple drunkenness which are dealt with straightaway, almost invariably on guilty pleas. Alternatively, the charge may be more serious or a witness unwell and the defendant will be **remanded** and the case put off to another day. A defendant remanded must turn up to court at the next hearing. He or she may be remanded either **on bail** or **in custody**. The decision is for the magistrates' court and may well be a difficult one. On the one hand, English law rightly presumes that every person is innocent until proved guilty and, of course, it would be wrong to lock up an innocent person. On the other hand, however, someone charged with a very serious offence and liable, on conviction, to many years in prison may feel that his interests would be best served by not turning up for trial. Some idea of the problem can be seen from the figures for 1974. In that year over 50,000 men and women were remanded in custody. Of that number over 2,000 were found not guilty and even of those convicted, over 16,500 were not sent to prison. Until October 2000 the European Convention for the Protection of Human Rights and Fundamental Freedoms had not been incorporated into English law but the underlying approach to the grant of bail was still well recognised if the national courts were to give effect to the principles set out in Article 5(3):

> Everyone arrested or detained . . . shall be brought promptly before a judge or other officer authorised by law to exercise judicial power and shall be entitled to trial within a reasonable time or to release pending trial. Release may be conditioned by guarantees to appear for trial.

Against these tenets and the numbers of prisoners on remand, Parliament sought to safeguard unconvicted defendants by passing the Bail Act 1976. There is, since then, a statutory presumption in favour of the grant of bail. Under the provisions of the Bail Act 1976 a court is required to grant bail to an accused person unless it is satisfied that there are good reasons to withhold that right. The same Act also makes it a fresh specific offence for a person granted bail to fail to arrive at court at the right time for the next hearing or, worse still, to abscond completely, for example by replacing trust in justice, truth and the dedication of his or her lawyers with fleet flight to the consoling climes of some foreign refuge. This risk is one of the many grounds upon which the police can object to a court granting bail. Other objections will include the likelihood of the person committing further offences or of breaking any condition as to bail. In most straightforward and more minor cases a person will simply be remanded on unconditional bail. Alternatively, the court may grant bail with conditions; for example, one that the defendant has to report at given intervals to the local police station, to surrender his passport, to live at a specific address or be subject to a curfew.

A potentially troublesome condition which can now be imposed under section 54 of the Crime and Disorder Act 1998 is one enabling a court to require the defendant to attend his or her solicitor for interview as a condition of his bail. While, of course, any adjournment brought about by the lack of representation would be unwelcome, this provision could cause a conflict of responsibility for the solicitor who would be the principal witness against his own client if the defendant failed to keep such an appointment.

One recent innovation has been the use of **electronic tagging** to monitor the movements of a defendant on bail. It was first used in the case of a man charged with theft and burglary whose home first had to be supplied with a telephone line before he, in turn, could be fitted with a tag to wear round his ankle so that his movements could be monitored were he to move more than 200 feet from the box connected to the telephone line. The police were later to bang on his door in the early morning after the sophisticated equipment had suggested that he had breached his bail condition. In fact, the man was still in his bed and was reported as saying, 'Perhaps there was a blind spot under the quilt.'

A more recent and less problematical application of modern technology to the grant of bail was seen in the case of a business tycoon accused of multi-million-pound theft. As a term of his bail he was ordered to carry a cordless telephone with him at all times so that the police could check on his movements, a form of remand more cellular than cell-like.

In more serious cases a defendant may be required to put forward another person who will stand as **surety** for the defendant's later attendance at court. This surety is required to guarantee the defendant's attendance by the pledge of a sum of money which he or she will have to pay if the defendant absconds. In some cases, where the charges are very serious, the court may require a number of different sureties who may have to pledge many thousands of pounds. It is important that the proposed sureties are acceptable to the police and, of course, are able to raise the money if called upon to do so. If, when the crunch comes, the surety is unable to raise money he is himself in danger of going to prison. Any agreement to indemnify a surety against loss by paying the money for him is in itself an offence under the Bail Act 1976.

The police may grant bail to a person arrested and brought to the police station either on the basis that that person will appear before a magistrates' court at a particular time and place or will attend a police station at a particular time. If, having been charged, a person is detained by the police he must be brought before the local magistrates' court as soon as is practicable. He may then apply for bail.

If the magistrates refuse bail the defendant is remanded in custody until a later hearing date. Usually the prisoner is kept on remand at a local prison where he enjoys certain privileges not given to convicted prisoners. As time served on remand is deducted from any prison sentence, this can be quite an agreeable way of passing one's sentence. Very occasionally, and usually because the police want to ask further questions, the accused may be remanded in police custody, where the prisoner simply extends his sojourn at the police station.

Home Office figures have revealed considerable disparity among magistrates' courts throughout the country on the grant or refusal of bail.

Until some years ago a person remanded in custody could make a further bail application when he next returned to the local magistrates' court. His plight might have attracted greater sympathy from a different set of magistrates. Such repetitious applications are now a thing of the past, since *R* v. *Nottingham Justices, ex parte Davies* 1980. Further applications are not now allowed unless the defendant can point to some new circumstances or some other such fresh consideration which ought properly to be taken into account.

After refusal of bail by magistrates, a further application may be made either to a judge of the High Court sitting in chambers or to the Crown Court. Similar rights of appeal against the grant of bail were conferred upon the prosecution by the Bail (Amendment) Act 1993.

Criminal offences may be tried in the magistrates' court or the Crown Court, and a defendant may not go straight to the Crown Court but must be sent there by the magistrates' court. Most committals today are conducted swiftly under the provisions of the Magistrates' Courts Act 1980. In the years before this system each witness was called, told his story, was cross-examined and the whole episode recorded by the clerk to the court. Until quite recently it was still open to either the prosecution or the defence to avail themselves of this old form of committal. Known colloquially as 'old style' committals the procedure allowed the defence to argue that, even taken at its highest, there was still insufficient evidence to justify committal for trial. This form of committal was laid to rest by section 47 of the Criminal Procedure and Investigations Act 1996 which requires evidence at committal to be limited only to documentary evidence. As a result it is no longer possible to call witnesses to give live oral evidence and, by definition, the defendant is deprived of his old opportunity of cross-examining those witnesses whose statements now represent the prosecution case. The right of a defendant to argue that the evidence does not justify committal has been preserved but, in practice, made more difficult as the defence have now been deprived of their opportunity of testing the evidence at an early stage.

A truncated form of committal may now be conducted where the defendant is legally represented, for the Magistrates' Courts Act 1980 provides:

> A magistrates' court inquiring into an offence as examining justices may, if satisfied that all the evidence before the court (whether for the prosecution or the defence) consists of written statements tendered to the court ... with or without exhibits, commit the defendant for trial for the offence without consideration of the contents of those statements.

The Criminal Justice Act 1991 further restricted the need for committal proceedings in cases involving children where the Director of Public Prosecutions may now simply serve a Notice of Transfer certifying that in his or her opinion there is sufficient evidence to put the accused on trial. The Act specifically excludes any right of appeal against such a decision by the prosecution.

Before a trial takes place in the Crown Court, there will have been a preliminary hearing known as **'pleas and directions hearing'**. The defendant will be reminded in terms that he or she will obtain a discount for pleading guilty at that stage and lawyers for both sides will agree or argue upon preliminary points in order to ensure that, by the time a jury is brought in to hear the case, no court time or public money will be wasted.

Of course, before any decision can be made as to admissibility of disputed evidence, the court and the parties must know what evidence the prosecution intend to rely upon. The unhappy record over quarter of a century of the English criminal justice system in dealing with terrorist trials has included the imprisonment for life in 1974 of a 25-year-old woman, suffering from mental disorder, upon her conviction for terrorist offences committed over the preceding couple of years. At trial, Judith Ward pleaded Not Guilty but was convicted upon evidence consisting substantially of her own confessions and scientific evidence including the evidence of the discredited Home Office forensic science chemist, Frank Skuse, the expert witness also involved in the trial of those accused of the Birmingham bombings. After almost two decades in prison, Ward's case was referred to the Court of Appeal by which time it had become known that the prosecution had failed at trial to disclose relevant evidence to the defence which cast doubt on the reliability both of the woman's admissions and of the scientific evidence adduced against her. Conscious that a grave miscarriage of justice had occurred, the Court of Appeal quashed the conviction.

The response, however, of the then Conservative Government was to pass the Criminal Procedure and Investigations Act 1996, an Act which, curiously against the background of such a miscarriage of justice, actually restricted the duty of the prosecution to disclose unused material. In *R* v. *Ward* 1993 the Court of Appeal had said that the defence should be given the opportunity to consider all the material evidence gathered by the prosecution. Later the same court made it clear that, if the prosecution were in doubt about materiality of information, the court should be asked to rule upon it. This approach was not welcomed by the police, who swiftly complained that their files were being subjected to 'fishing expeditions'.

In other ways, too, there was growing disquiet that excessive secrecy and material non-disclosure were inimical to the prospects of fair trials. The point was brought home to the public as a result of the same government's attempts to stop the full facts coming out in the so-called *Matrix Churchill* trial in 1992. After the invasion of Kuwait in 1990 by Iraq, the managing director of Matrix Churchill, an engineering company which had exported goods to Iraq, was prosecuted for exporting those machine tools in contravention of the constraints then applicable to such exports to such countries. The director, Paul Henderson, faced a jail sentence upon conviction. He contended that the government had approved the export of these machine tools. He also said that he had been asked to spy for MI6 on Iraqi military and scientific installations. In essence, he maintained that the government had secretly changed its own guidelines introduced at around the time of the outbreak of hostilities between Iraq and Iran. If this were true there would have been paperwork kept by the security forces and other government agencies which would either confirm his defence or, at a stroke, destroy it. His lawyers asked to see the files. They argued that justice required disclosure.

A number of ministers sought to prevent any disclosure on the ground that these documents were exempt from disclosure on the ground of 'Public Interest Immunity'. The evidence was to paint an unhappy picture of evasion and equivocality on the part of some civil servants and their ministers, one of whom, the late Alan Clarke, was upright enough candidly to admit having been 'economical with the *actualité*'. The sudden collapse of this prosecution forced the then government to set up the inquiry chaired by Lord Justice Scott, which was to report only three months before so many of those same politicians were driven from power but not before they had restricted the right of defendants in criminal proceedings brought by the State to disclosure of prosecution papers.

The new Act introduces a concept of **'primary prosecution disclosure'**, which is supposed to include unused material which might undermine the case. The next step requires **'defence disclosure'**, a step previously unknown in the criminal courts but standard practice in the civil jurisdiction. The defendant is now required to set out in writing the general nature of his case and, upon receipt of this document, the prosecution are then required to provide **'secondary prosecution disclosure'** which may include additional unused material which might reasonably be expected to assist the defence as disclosed. Some may still find it a curious situation that what might reasonably be expected to assist the defence is a matter not for the defence but, rather, for the prosecution.

Proceedings in the Crown Court are begun by the arraignment of the defendant. He (or she) is brought into the dock (where all accused persons must stay for the duration of their trial) and the charge is put to him. The Clerk of the Court reads out the charge which has by this stage been put into a document known as the **Indictment**. The defendant then **pleads** – that is, he says whether he is Guilty or Not Guilty. On a plea of not guilty the next step is to **empanel** (bring in) the jury who will try him. There are twelve jurors, all, in traditional phrase, 'good men and true'. The most recent statutory requirements essentially equate the right to vote with the duty to serve on a jury. Certain classes, however, are ineligible or disqualified or may be excused if they so choose (see Unit 2.2b)). The Criminal Justice Act 1988 has raised the maximum age of jurors to 70 years. Those summonsed for service after the age of 65 years may be excused service if they so wish. This extension in age will substantially enlarge the pool of potential jurors required to run the Crown Court system and may meet the objections of some who complained that younger jurors are prone to unreasonable acquittals.

Further criticism of acquittals by juries have prompted others to argue that such a trial is wholly inappropriate in complex cases involving alleged frauds. Such critics proclaim the benefits of trial by a judge sitting with expert assessors chosen because of their accountancy or City backgrounds. Indeed, it is thought likely that the Report of Sir Robin Auld will recommend so-called 'bench-trials' where those accused of offences such as fraud could elect to be tried by a judge sitting alone. Others have criticised jurors as being inexperienced and untrained in evaluating evidence and, therefore, prone either wrongly to acquit because of undue sympathy or wrongly to convict because of some prejudice.

Proposals in 1975 by the James Report would then have limited access to the Crown Court by reference to the value of property allegedly stolen. Such proposals were then followed by the Roskill proposal to remove fraud trials from the jury. In a famous passage Lord

Devlin once described the constitutional importance of the primacy of the jury system remarking that:

> *Trial by jury is more than an instrument of justice and more than one wheel of the Constitution: it is the lamp that shows that freedom lives.*

Since that lecture in 1956, however, Parliament has increasingly chosen to restrict the right of the citizen to trial by jury. For example, allegations of criminal damage of less than £2000 and taking motor vehicles without consent are just two recent additions to the long list of charges where defendants have increasingly been thwarted in their usual preference for trial by jury.

At the time of writing, Parliament has been debating the Criminal Justice (Mode of Trial) Bill, proposed legislation which, in cases triable either way, would take away a defendant's right to determine whether he or she is tried by a jury or rather by local magistrates and instead entrust that decision to the magistrates themselves. Those advocating the removal of such right see attractions in an expected saving of costs as trial by magistrates is a cheaper option than proceedings in the Crown Court.

Opponents, dismissed by the present Home Secretary as 'woolly-minded liberals', see trial by jury as the cornerstone of public justice combining, as the jury does, a cross-section of the community with the guidance of a judge. Of course, people are entitled to change their minds and some do profoundly. The Home Secretary himself, when in opposition, had spoken out forcefully against similar proposals put forward by the last Conservative government but the short walk from the opposition benches to those of government perhaps provided time to perceive merits in proposals not visible from the other side of the House.

Opponents of this latest attempt to restrict trial by jury were dismayed at the high-handed approach of the government during the passage of the Bill which had been subjected to a parliamentary guillotine so that a mere five hours were set aside for such debate. Those looking at the actions of a government with such a huge majority may reflect on the words of Lord Devlin:

> *every jury is a little Parliament ... The first objective of any tyrant in Whitehall would be to make Parliament utterly subservient to his will; and the next to overturn or diminish trial by jury.*

There is a considerable body of evidence that, whether rightly or wrongly, the conviction rate imposed by magistrates is much higher than that of a jury. Whether this is because magistrates become case-hardened or whether jurors are gullible is a matter of perennial debate. Many people, faced with summary trial, have tended to view magistrates as being unduly sympathetic to the prosecution and perceive the quality of justice in the Crown Court as superior. In commenting on the Royal Commission's Report in a public speech Lord Taylor CJ himself emphasised that it was essential not only for justice to be done but for those concerned to have confidence in the process:

> *We must have regard to our history, our culture and the per-*
> *ception of many that trial by jury is a fundamental right.*
> *More practically, when a store detective or police officer regu-*
> *larly gives evidence before the same court it is easy to see how*
> *a defendant may perceive the set up as too cosy.*

The point made by the respected late Lord Chief Justice was one lawyers hear all too often in discussing their clients' hesitations about trial before magistrates. Real evidence of bias was all too grossly obvious in *R* v. *Bingham Justices ex parte Jowitt* 1974. A motorist accused of a traffic offence gave a different account to that of a police officer. The futility of this stance was all too apparent when, unusually for lay magistrates, the chairman of the local magistrates purported to justify their finding in the ominous words:

> *Quite the most unpleasant cases that we have to decide are*
> *those where the evidence is a direct conflict between a police*
> *officer and a member of the public. My principle in such case*
> *has always been to believe the evidence of the police officer*
> *and, therefore, we find the case proved.*

The judges of the Divisional Court can barely have hesitated in quashing this conviction as a quite blatant example of bias.

Respect may also be shown to the views of Lord Denning MR who, while urging reform and greater selectivity among those who form the jury, was, nevertheless, a staunch defender of the system and praised its good sense:

> *It has been the bulwark of our liberties too long for any of us*
> *to seek to alter it. Whenever a man is on trial for serious*
> *crime ... or when one or other party must be deliberately*
> *lying, then trial by jury has no equal.*

Such tendency to the erosion of the citizen's rights to trial by jury shows how farsighted was the warning, more than two centuries ago, of Sir William Blackstone:

> *So that the liberties of England cannot but subsist so long as*
> *this Palladium remains sacred and inviolate; not only from all*
> *open attacks (which none will be so hardy as to make), but*
> *also from all secret machinations, which may sap and under-*
> *mine it. ... though begun in trifles, the precedent may gradu-*
> *ally increase and spread, to the utter disuse of juries and*
> *questions of the most momentous concern.*

The waiting jurors are then called into court to be 'empanelled'; that is to say, they enter the jury box and take their oath that they will 'faithfully try the defendant and give a true verdict according to the evidence'. Until recently not every prospective juror got even that far for he or she could be rejected by the defendant's counsel calling out 'Challenge!' This was an exercise of what was called 'the peremptory challenge' and no reason was required for its use. In practice, it was not uncommon in cases of a sexual nature for some women (especially those wearing tweed skirts and sensible shoes) to be challenged in the belief that they might be irrationally censorious of some of the issues to be raised.

Historically, there was a right to challenge seven jurors, but the Criminal Law Act 1977 reduced that number to three. This was still too much for the government, and for one back-bencher in particular, who complained that such a right was an abuse. In fact there is evidence not only showing that the right was not greatly exercised but also suggesting that its use coincided with a higher than average conviction rate.

A defendant still retains the right to challenge prospective jurors if he can show cause to reject them; for example, if he should find the parents of the girl he is accused of raping sitting among those who are to try him. It is obviously important that there is confidence in the jury system and in recent years there have been complaints from, say, young black defendants that they have no confidence in a jury composed of middle-aged Anglo-Saxons. Such hesitancy or even distrust about the ethnic composition of a jury does not give rise to grounds to challenge for cause.

The prosecution has always had a right to remove potential jurors by asking them to 'stand-by for the Crown'. No reason had to be given. The prosecution retains this right while the effect of section 118 of the Criminal Law Act 1988 has been, in one short sentence, to remove this ancient right from accused persons. It remains to be tested whether the removal of one right from the defence and the retention of a corresponding power on the part of the prosecution (even one so sparingly used) could amount to a breach of the European Convention on Human Rights.

Finally, when each juror has been accepted, he or she then takes an oath that he will faithfully try the defendant and give a true verdict according to the evidence.

The next step is for prosecuting counsel to open his (or her) case. He will give the jury an outline of what led to the defendant being charged and offer them an idea of what the relevant law is. It is not his job to go hammer and tongs at a defendant to secure a conviction. His duty has been likened to that of a 'minister of justice', whose job is dispassionately to lay the facts before the jury.

He will then call his witnesses and ask them questions. This is known as **examination-in-chief** and is the way in which each side tells its tale. Counsel will examine the witness on the basis of what is already written down in the statements served on the defence so both sides have a good idea of the answer before the question is even asked although it is, of course, all fresh to the jury.

Almost all witnesses give their evidence on oath or after affirmation and do so publicly in the witness box. Some years ago a practice started of allowing those children who were alleged to be victims of sexual misconduct to give their evidence from behind a screen protecting them from having to see their alleged attacker. The Criminal Justice Act 1991 allows evidence of children to be given by live television links so that the child is filmed sitting in another room and the pictures displayed in court. It is now common practice for such allegations to be produced in evidence by showing a video recording of the child being questioned by some suitably sympathetic-sounding woman police officer or social worker. Care obviously needs to be taken in these video interviews to comply with the Code of Practice which cautions against the use of the leading question which is examined later in this Unit.

There has also been recent discussion of allowing not only television screens but even television cameras into the court room. Criminal trials are held in public unless there are exceptional reasons (such as those of national security) for excluding the public and the press. Hearing criminal cases in public has been said to be 'a safeguard against judicial arbitrariness or idiosyncrasy' which 'maintains the public confidence in the administration of justice'. Moreover, as a result of changes introduced by the Criminal Justice Act 1991, all children under the age of fourteen now give evidence unsworn (without taking the oath). Children over that age automatically give sworn evidence without judges any longer having to embark on their traditional inquiry as to whether or not the child attends Sunday School and understands the importance of telling the truth and the significance of the oath.

There are certain rules for examining witnesses, most of which are outside the scope of this book, but two in particular require attention: that which restricts the use of the **leading question** and the rule against **hearsay**. 'When are you going to start doing some work?' may indeed be an unwelcome enquiry but, contrary to a widespread but erroneous belief, it is not a leading question. A leading question is one which itself suggests the answer. To take a hypothetical case, rather than ask a police officer who arrested the defendant: 'As you turned the corner did you see the defendant sprawling in the gutter, unable to stand or talk coherently, and did you form the impression that he was drunk?' a lawyer would ask a series of questions: 'Where did you go?' 'Did something attract your attention?' 'Was the defendant doing anything at this time?' Hearsay is an old exclusionary rule classically defined as laying down the rule that 'an assertion other than one made by a person while giving oral evidence in the proceedings is inadmissible as evidence of any facts asserted'. While of fundamental importance, it is not always immediately obvious in practice whether proposed evidence is hearsay or not. However, the rule does clearly prohibit one witness saying what he or she has heard another person say. For example, in a trial of alleged theft from a shop a police officer cannot give evidence to the effect that he heard the store manager being told by the store detective that she had seen the defendant pick up a tin of baked beans. The prosecution must bring the store detective to court for her to give such evidence and then be cross-examined upon her account. Only in this way can the validity of that witness's allegations be properly tested.

Lord Normand put it more profoundly in *Tepler* v. *R* 1952 when he said:

> *It is not the best evidence and it is not delivered on oath. The truthfulness and accuracy of the person whose words are spoken to by another witness cannot be tested by cross-examination, and the light which his demeanour would throw on his testimony is lost.*

The situation, incidentally, is now different in the civil courts because the Civil Evidence Act 1995 provides that evidence shall not be excluded in civil proceedings on the ground that it is hearsay. Even though such evidence may, therefore, become admissible the fact that such evidence is of a hearsay nature may still influence the weight which a judge will attach to such account.

Once a witness has been examined by the side calling him, he may be **cross-examined** by the other side. This is another term commonly misunderstood, for it has nothing to do with the pleasantness or otherwise of the person asking the questions. In cross-examination the aim is to weaken or destroy the harmful effect of the earlier evidence. A second and separate purpose of cross-examination is to ensure that the contrary case is 'put' to the other side. This allows the real issues to be swiftly identified and allows each party the opportunity of commenting upon the other's case. It is for this reason that various suggestions and allegations will be put to witnesses in order to allow their comment, rejection and occasionally even acceptance. So, for example, in a case involving an allegation of assault where the defendant relies upon self-defence, it is likely that it will be 'put' to the alleged victim that he started the trouble and was the first to use or threaten violence. No one really expects the complainant immediately to fall backwards out of the witness box only to pick himself up and immediately confess to having perjured himself for the last half-an-hour of his evidence. The procedure is, nevertheless, important because it will be assumed that the defendant is putting forward a false account as he thinks it up in the witness box if these particular challenges have not earlier been put to the witnesses called against him as they were cross-examined.

The right to cross-examine an accuser has recently been taken away from accused persons in cases involving allegations of sexual offences or offences said to have been committed against children. The relevant provisions of the Youth Justice and Criminal Evidence Act 1999 specifically outlaw an accused person cross-examining such witnesses in person. In such circumstances, the court must appoint a lawyer of its choice to cross-examine the witness. Quite how such a lawyer is able to do so properly in the absence of sensible instructions from the defendant (to whom he is specifically not responsible) remains to be seen as does the impact upon such restriction of the Human Rights Act 1998.

The legislation of 1999 extends the restrictions upon the range of matters properly to be canvassed in cross-examination in cases involving allegations of sexual offences so that, for example, except with the judge's permission, no evidence may be called or any questions asked in cross-examination about any sexual behaviour of the complainant.

Of course, our hypothetical defendant charged with being drunk and disorderly can only be tried in the magistrates' court and is most unlikely to obtain legal representation (and inconceivably so from public funds) but the principles remain the same. Any lawyer so instructed for the alleged inebriate would cross-examine the police officer on the instructions of his client (for lawyers do not make it all up as they go along) and is allowed, in cross-examination only, to ask as many leading questions as he chooses. For example, he might ask:

> 'It's correct, is it not, that when a diabetic goes without his insulin he may well appear rather drunk?'
> 'Can't really say.'
> 'And it's also correct, is it not, that when you arrested the defendant he told you that he needed his insulin injection?'
> 'Don't have a note of it.'

In this way the defence has tried to weaken the prosecution case so as to leave in the court's mind that element of reasonable doubt.

The third and final stage is called **re-examination**. The side which called the witness may now try to repair any damage done in cross-examination by asking more questions which arise out of the earlier cross-examination. Similar principles apply to those of examination-in-chief, so once again, the leading question is not permissible. So the prosecuting lawyer might now ask the police officer:

> *'Officer, when you arrested the defendant for being drunk and disorderly, did you do anything else?'*
> *'I searched him, Sir.'*
> *'Did you find anything?'*
> *'An almost empty bottle of Scotch, Sir.'*

The pendulum has swung the other way and the prosecution case has been restored to health.

However, by the end of the prosecution case it may well be apparent that the case against the defendant has simply not held up. Prosecution witnesses may have been shown to be unreliable and the full picture may be far less impressive than the story first appeared when put down on paper. Specifically, for example, in the case of a prosecution dependent upon identification evidence, it may turn out that the star witness had nothing more than a fleeting glance in poor light of a man whom he had never seen before and even then on a foggy night and without his glasses on. In other circumstances, a judge may have refused to allow the prosecution to call some piece of evidence on the basis that it was inadmissible for one or more reasons. In these circumstances, it is always open to the defence, upon closure of the prosecution case, to seek to persuade the trial judge that there is **no case to answer**. It is important to bear in mind that it is not for the judge to usurp the function of a jury. Rather, however, the judge must still ensure that there is at the very least a minimum sufficiency of evidence which justifies the trial continuing. The matter was put more profoundly by the Court of Appeal in *R* v. *Galbraith* 1981 when Lord Lane CJ posed the question: 'How then should the judge approach a submission of "no case"?' and then answered his own question as follows:

> *If there is no evidence that the crime alleged has been committed by the defendant, there is no difficulty. The judge will of course stop the case. The difficulty arises where there is some evidence but it is of a tenuous character, for example because of inherent weakness or vagueness or because it is inconsistent with other evidence. Where the judge comes to the conclusion that the prosecution evidence, taken at its highest, is such that a jury properly directed could not properly convict upon it, it is his duty, upon a submission being made, to stop the case. Where however the prosecution evidence is such that its strength or weakness depends on the view to be taken of a witness's reliability, or other matters which are generally speaking within the province of the jury and where on one possible view of the facts there is evidence upon*

which a jury could properly come to the conclusion that the defendant is guilty, then the judge should allow the matter to be tried by the jury.... There will of course, as always in this branch of the law, be borderline cases. They can be safely left to the discretion of the judge.

In the event that the submission is upheld the jury (who will have been asked to retire to their room to allow argument to continue in their absence) will be brought back into court and will be directed to return a verdict of Not Guilty on any count in the indictment upon which such successful submission had been based. If the submission has failed then the trial must continue.

When all the prosecution witnesses have been examined, cross-examined and re-examined, the defendant formerly had three courses open to him:

1. to give evidence on oath in the witness box;
2. to make an unsworn statement from the dock;
3. to keep his lips tightly sealed.

The first option not only remains, but is positively encouraged. The second option – a halfway house between total silence and full exposure under oath to cross-examination by the prosecution and, indeed, also by any co-defendant – was abolished by the provisions of the Criminal Justice Act 1982. Anything a defendant wishes to say must now be said from the witness box. The third option is also now a more risky course than ever. We have already seen how the Criminal Justice and Public Order Act 1994 allows a court to draw adverse inferences from silence. Under the new regime a judge will enquire of a defendant's counsel whether he or she has advised the client that the time has now come for the defendant to give evidence. If the accused person is unrepresented the judge will call upon him to give evidence. In circumstances already considered the jury may think it proper to draw adverse inferences from a failure then to give evidence.

If a defendant does elect to give evidence it is normal practice for such evidence to be given before any other witness is called on his or her behalf. This is based not so much on a consideration of his own feelings but, rather, upon the more cynical view that he should not be allowed to hear other witnesses give their evidence before deciding what to say. It is rare for the defence to make opening speeches and, indeed, the defence is restricted in its ability to make opening speeches because the defendant may only open his case if he calls evidence other than his own as to the facts in dispute.

When the defendant, and any witnesses that he may wish to call, have been examined, cross-examined and re-examined, both sides may address the jury. The prosecution makes the first speech and the defence has the last word.

The judge then sums up to the jury. He will remind them of some evidence, put the defence case to the jury, direct them on the relevant law and, in particular, will warn them that they must acquit unless persuaded that the prosecution has proved its case so that they feel sure of the defendant's guilt. Lord Diplock described the role of the judge at this stage in this way:

> *A summing up is not meant to incorporate abstract disquisitions on the general law relating to the offence with which the accused is charged. It ought to be tailored to the evidence that has been adduced in the particular case. It should explain to the jury what facts they must find to be established by the evidence and, where appropriate, what opinion they must form about those facts, in order to justify in law their bringing in a verdict of guilty or not guilty.*

The jury then retires and elects a foreman, and then considers its verdict. Until recently, once a jury had retired it had to stay together until the verdict had been returned or the jury discharged so that, in long cases, jurors would traditionally be advised to bring a toothbrush and might spend several nights in a hotel. Section 43 of the Criminal Justice and Public Order Act 1994 now allows the judge to permit a jury to separate after retirement.

It is desirable that any verdict, whatever it be, will be unanimous. After a minimum time of 2 hours 10 minutes (the minutes being added to allow the jury time to walk to their room and back!) it is open to a judge to accept a majority verdict where at least ten of the jury have reached the same verdict.

Of course, if the jury returns a verdict of Not Guilty, the defendant is free to go and cannot normally be tried again on the same charge. Concern about bribery or intimidation of jurors (known colloquially as 'jury nobbling') led to the creation of a new criminal offence. The Criminal Justice and Public Order Act 1994 created a new offence of intimidation of witnesses, of jurors and of others. Upon the conviction of a person for this offence, anyone acquitted by the jury so nobbled or by a jury which heard evidence from an intimidated witness may now face retrial upon the original indictment.

Traditionally, it has always been the case that such acquitted defendant could not be tried again upon the same charge. As part of the Macpherson Report in the Stephen Lawrence Inquiry there was a recommendation that consideration should be given to permitting prosecution after an acquittal where fresh and viable evidence is presented. This particular hot potato was handed to the Law Commission in the summer of 1999 and led to a Consultation Paper entitled 'Double Jeopardy'. The recommendation subsequently put forward for further discussion was that, subject to certain exceptions, this old rule against double jeopardy should be retained. However, the Law Commission advocated that, as with convictions, acquittals could also be quashed on the grounds of new evidence where there was a very high probability of conviction following the gathering of new evidence which made the prosecution case substantially stronger than at the first trial.

Of course, if the jury convicts or if the defendant had earlier pleaded guilty upon arraignment, the judge must proceed to consider what sentence is appropriate.

3.9 *Sentence*

Two hundred years ago the range of possible sentences was much more limited and the policy much more restricted than today. Hanging, flogging and assisted one-way passages to Australia were the order of the day. Flogging has now been abolished, no one has been hanged in England since 1964 and Australia has imposed immigration controls.

So, too, the policy of the courts and their more individualised approach to sentencing have changed radically. It is not easy to say exactly what effect a court hopes to achieve by adopting any particular course. This question was considered by the Wolfenden Committee on Homosexuality and Prostitution in 1957:

> *It is, we understand, now generally accepted that apart altogether from any consideration of retribution the object-ives of penal sanctions are deterrence, prevention and reformation. Thus the law provides for the punishment of certain acts in the hope that persons will be deterred from committing such acts. Where the law itself has not proved a sufficient deterrent, it may be necessary, for the protection of others, to prevent the offender from doing further wrong even by putting him in prison. And for the common good it is desirable that an offender should be subjected to such form of treatment as is most likely to improve his character and make him a better citizen.*

In recent years the nature of sentences, their claimed purpose and their severity have proved a tempting target for politicians anxious for votes. In the run up to the 1997 general election it was noticeable how the politicians vied with each other to be (or at least to appear to be) 'tough on crime, tough on the causes of crime'. It was soon noticeable how, upon election, the Labour Party ran with the Tories' clothes as they not only enthusiastically embraced the Crime (Sentences) Act 1997 but also went on to introduce further stern legislation in the Crime and Disorder Act 1998. Claimed by the government as the 'biggest crime cutting initi-ative in the world', it will be interesting in due course to see how much of this legislation will also be open to attack after implementation of the Human Rights Act 1998.

Most recently, in particular, the politicians have sought to impose straitjackets upon judges by requiring them to pass minimum sentences upon a range of specified offenders. The principal purpose behind such legislation appears to be based upon retribution and deterrence.

The offence of rape, for example, is a particularly sensitive offence and one which seems at times also to have attracted a measure of polit-ical correctness even to the extent of the suggestion that, exceptionally in this offence alone, the burden of proof should be reversed. Rape and attempted rape are defined as a 'serious offence' so that under the provi-sions of the recently introduced Powers of Criminal Courts (Sentencing) Act 2000 a second offender is automatically subject to life imprison-ment.

The unrelenting resolve of the Tory Government to adopt discredited sentencing practices of the United States met with sustained opposition from the judges expected to impose mandatory sentences without choice. The point that a man might as well be hanged for a lamb as well as for a foot-and-mouth-diseased sheep was made more profoundly by Lord Justice Rose, speaking extra-judicially, when he said:

> *Mandatory life for a second offence of rape will mean fewer pleas of guilty and more murders. You are not going to plead guilty if you commit an offence which carries a mandatory life sentence. And so far as more murders are concerned, rapists will think they may as well kill their victims – there is no point leaving them alive if the sentence is the same.*

On the other hand, some outside the Palace of Westminster have much less confidence in heavy sentencing as a deterrent to crime and would place much more confidence in likelihood of detection as an effective form of deterrent against criminal behaviour. Others will share the sentiments of Oscar Wilde:

> *One is absolutely sickened not by the crimes the wicked have committed but by the punishments the good have inflicted.*

Traditionally, retribution and deterrence are only two of a number of factors which the courts have borne in mind when determining the appropriate sentence. Lawton LJ once referred to the classic principles of sentencing as comprising 'retribution, deterrence, prevention and rehabilitation'.

Ever since the then Home Secretary, Michael Howard, received a rapturous reception from his party faithful by decreeing: 'Prison works!' there has been a noticeable increase both in the use of imprisonment and the length of sentences. In this way the courts are seen to be responding to the perceived wish of the public as well as recent legislation such as Criminal Justice Act 1991 and Crime (Sentences) Act 1997 as now re-enacted in the Powers of Criminal Courts (Sentencing) Act 2000.

Any court about to impose sentence must, therefore, consider not just the seriousness of the offence but ought also to have some regard to the purpose behind any sentence. Among many considerations regard will be paid to the following principles.

Punishment Put simply, this is society getting its own back upon the offender. Such philosophy has assumed greater significance in English penal thinking in recent years. The popular demand that there should be some nexus between offending and retribution is hallowed not only in the belief that such punishment may satisfy the victim but also in the hope of the offender that he or she might obtain some prospect of spiritual salvation. The link, of course, was apparent to the Russian novelist Dostoyevsky whose aptly entitled work *Crime and Punishment* was to draw heavily upon this theme.

Protection of the public Society, as judges so often say in passing sentence, has a right to be protected from the violence and dishonesty of others. This purpose and the need to protect women in particular has recently been emphasised by judges dealing with rapists. This point was put on a statutory footing by the Criminal Justice Act 1991 which, while perceived by many as Parliament going soft on recidivist criminals and emasculating the courts' powers with young offenders in particular, has clearly emphasised that offences of a violent or sexual nature may require long terms of imprisonment where such a sentence 'in the opinion of the court is necessary to protect the public from serious harm from the offender'.

Deterrence The policy of the courts in imposing deterrent sentence has mirrored the social and economic difficulties of British life over the last three decades. In the mid-1970s, reflecting the petrol shortage, the courts imposed deliberately heavy sentences on those who siphoned other people's petrol. A year later it was heavy fines for foreign shoplifters in the West End of London. A decade or so later public revulsion of sexual abuse of children was reflected in some long prison sentences on such molesters, and after more terrorist attacks in London in the 1990s those who made hoax bomb calls received no mercy. As the decade drew to an end the courts mirrored public concern about air safety. Those who over-indulged from the drinks trolley's duty frees at 30,000 feet soon found themselves brought sharply down to earth as the courts imposed deterrent prison sentences on those whose boorish or violent behaviour endangered the safety of everyone else on the flight.

Enthused by the American concept of 'three strikes and you're out' (so that, for example, in America a man was jailed for 25 years for stealing a pizza), the government passed the Crime (Sentences) Act 1997. While extolled by the politicians keen to be seen to be 'tough on crime, tough on the causes of crime', those with a life-time of experience in the courts were far from supportive. The then Lord Chief Justice, Lord Taylor, was scathing in his remark that:

> *Never in the history of our criminal law have such far-reaching proposals been put forward on the strength of such flimsy evidence.*

His successor, Lord Bingham CJ, was equally unimpressed, commenting that:

> *If, as the century and the millennium slide to a close our penal thinking is to be judged by the thinking which animates this Bill, then I for one will shrink from the judgment of history.*

The Act, now re-enacted already in the Powers of Criminal Courts (Sentencing) Act 2000, introduced mandatory minimum sentences unless the court is of the opinion that there are exceptional circumstances. Under the Act, anyone over the age of eighteen already convicted of a 'serious offence' (as listed) will automatically be jailed for life. Minimum sentences of seven years would be imposed for repeat drugs offences and those convicted of a third domestic burglary would be sent to prison automatically for a minimum of three years. What the politicians ignore is that the courts already show a determination to impose substantial terms of imprisonment upon those convicted of serious offences of these kinds and that, by imposing a blanket sentencing policy, such legislation not only deprives the courts of the chance of doing individual justice but even perhaps requires judges to impose injustice.

Reform The more adventurous and liberal approach to sentencing has been based on a desire to reform the offender. The sentence imposed is aimed at teaching the offender the error of his or her ways and assisting him to lead a purposeful and industrious life. This is further reflected in the training and education which the prison service supplies.

Even when the aim is clear, the court still has to decide in which way to achieve its declared objective. The Wolfenden Report already quoted continued:

> The courts are faced with the problem of reconciling, in an individual case, these ... main objects which are not always compatible. It is not enough to look only to the details of the offence or the circumstances of the offender. In doing justice to the individual offender the courts cannot overlook their duty to protect other citizens and to ensure respect for the criminal law and they must necessarily ask themselves in every case which of these three objectives should be paramount before considering the method most likely to be successful in a particular case. Thus, for example, when a particular offence is rife at a particular time or in a particular place, it may be right for the courts to attach more weight to the deterrent and preventive aspects than would otherwise be the case. At the same time, the ultimate purpose is more likely to be achieved if the treatment of the offender is constructive and not merely punitive, and it follows that the personality of the individual offender must be a decisive factor in determining the appropriate treatment.

In deciding what sentence to impose the court will have regard to what is said by the defendant's counsel or solicitor, by way of **mitigation**. In this way the defendant's representatives will, as far as they are able, indicate to the court what led to the man's appearance in the dock, for example, shortage of money, marriage difficulties or drink, and what lies in the future for him – perhaps he is about to marry and settle down, or has plans for a new job or a new home elsewhere. The court will often also have the benefit of a **pre-sentence report**, prepared by a local probation officer and based on a recent interview with the defendant. In some cases, however, the reality is that there is little to be said by way of mitigation which would much affect the outcome. Indeed, said Watkins LJ, when dealing with a case of major drugs importation 'in such cases there is seldom, if ever, room for mercy'.

With all this information at hand, the judge or the magistrates will have to decide which sentence is the most appropriate, bearing in mind the court's duty to the public, but at the same time its responsibility to the defendant.

A judge's sentencing is a skilled task. The approach of judges is probably becoming more uniform every year. This tendency is partly attributable to the sentencing conferences which judges attend and the special reporting of decisions of the Court of Appeal when criminals have appealed against their sentences. The former Lord Chief Justice, Lord Lane, in particular in a number of appeals took the opportunity to offer other judges guidelines in cases such as rape, drugs importations, company fraud and causing death by reckless driving. Lord Lane's observations in *R* v. *Boswell* 1984 illustrate the variety of different factors that a judge has to consider in this sort of case where a man has killed another through reckless driving. Some factors add to the gravity and criminality of the offence. The use of drink or drugs (and especially what the Court of Appeal once described as a 'motorised pub crawl'), showing off to others (by racing or by the use of grossly excessive speed or by ignoring warnings from passengers), persistent and prolonged bad driving (such as jumping one set of red lights after another) would all aggravate the offence, as would a bad previous record or committing such offences in an attempt to avoid detection or apprehension by the police.

Other cases, though still resulting in death, would be less serious. A motorist of good character, with a previously unblemished record, may after a long, tiring day, momentarily doze off at the wheel. He or she may plead guilty (always a form of mitigation) and may be truly full of remorse. These factors all go to help the defendant receive a lesser sentence.

Similarly in *R* v. *Aramah* 1982 the Court of Appeal considered the general level of sentences appropriate for all drug smugglers and since then revised by the same court in *R* v. *Ronchetti* 1998. In *R* v. *Barrick* 1985 the Court of Appeal considered at length the multiplicity of factors which both aggravated and mitigated the offence of theft when committed by an employee. The courts have long regarded thefts by employees as an aggravated form of dishonesty because of the 'breach of trust' which such theft necessarily involves. The well-known 'Barrick Guidelines' have been kept up to date by the Court of Appeal so that in *R* v. *Clarke* 1998 the court was also able to amend the guidelines by taking into account the fall in the value of money since 1985 and the reduction since then in the maximum term of imprisonment for theft. Against the background of these offences, it is generally said that only a sentence of immediate imprisonment will be appropriate. The protection of an employer's money (or for that matter the money of, say, the members of a club) is generally thought more important than the personal tragedy which such dishonest employees may well suffer. The latter consideration was not lost on the then Lord Chief Justice, Lord Lane, who said of such an offender:

> *He will usually, as in this case, be a person of impeccable character. It is practically certain, again as in this case, that he will never offend again and, in the nature of things, he will never again in his life be able to secure similar employment with all that that means in the shape of disgrace for himself and hardship for himself and his family.*

The court then went on to consider those matters which would aggravate the offence and which would serve to reduce the sentence. Such factors will include:

1. the quality and degree of trust placed in the offender;
2. the period over which such thefts were committed (that is the longer the offending went on the worse for the defendant);
3. the use to which the money was put;
4. the effect upon the victim;
5. the impact on the public and public confidence;
6. the effect upon fellow employees;
7. the effect on the offender himself;
8. the offender's own history;
9. matters of mitigation special to the offender; and
10. the help, if any, given to the police.

The court then went on to offer guidelines for imprisonment so that, for example, upon conviction of such theft of money between £17,500 and £100,000 the appropriate range after a contested hearing is said to be between two and three years. Whereabouts in this bracket the sentence is finally determined is, of course, a matter for the judge upon consideration of all the various individual factors. It is a matter of common sense that in case of assault it will also be relevant to know whether the defendant had been provoked and whether there was one blow only or a series of blows. Common sense further dictates that the use of weapon would be viewed as an aggravating feature.

a) Custodial sentences

Prison

Now that hanging has been abolished the harshest sentence which a court may impose is imprisonment. The courts lean over backwards to avoid such a drastic course if at all possible. In particular, a first offender will not be imprisoned if this course may be responsibly avoided.

Such is the notorious present level of overcrowding in Her Majesty's prisons that Her Majesty's judges would be taking this course even without such encouragement from Parliament. Indeed, in R v. *Bibi* 1980 the Lord Chief Justice sought to lay down guidelines for other judges to follow in order to ensure uniformity of approach. Mindful of prison overcrowding, Lord Lane urged the courts to ensure that if an immediate sentence of imprisonment is necessary it should be as short as possible consistent, of course, with the duty of the court to protect the interests of the public and also to punish and deter the criminal.

A prison sentence is not without its incidental problems, and may harm innocent people, such as the prisoner's family. Moreover, it goes without saying that a prisoner is going to mix with criminals – many of whom will be more accomplished and more hardened than he is. Rather than be reformed, he may in this so-called 'University of Crime' receive instruction in the finer points of safe-blowing and forgery. Even so, in 1985 the courts imprisoned a record number in England and Wales so that the prison population reached over 48,000 for the first time. By the summer of 2000 the prison population had risen to 65,222 inmates.

The sentence is also appallingly expensive to implement: figures for 1998–9 showed an average cost per prisoner of £22,649 per annum. It also puts a person in danger of losing his ties with his family and with his work. His family may then have to be cared for out of the public purse, further increasing the cost and often stretching the already over-burdened social services. No doubt creditably with these disadvantages in his mind, in the summer of 2000 the Home Secretary mooted his proposals for 9 a.m. to 5 p.m. imprisonment which would have the benefit of economy in the prison building programme which would no longer need to cater for sleeping accommodation. A more cynical eye might observe that the proposals would nevertheless keep men out of work during the day but free them to go out burgling at night.

The approach of any court to sentence is now governed by the provisions of the Powers of Criminal Courts (Sentencing) Act 2000 and the so-called 'threshold criteria'. Other than in a case where the sentence is fixed by law or where a mandatory minimum sentence must be passed, section 79 of the Act provides:

> The court shall not pass a custodial sentence on the offender unless it is of the opinion –
> (a) that the offence, or the combination of the offence and one or more offences associated with it, was so serious that only such a sentence can be justified for the offence; or
> (b) where the offence is a violent or sexual offence, that only such a sentence would be adequate to protect the public from serious harm from him.

The Court of Appeal, when considering identical wording in earlier legislation, offered judges further guidance in determining whether an offence is so serious that the custody threshold has been crossed. In *R v. Howells* 1998 Lord Bingham CJ advised courts to consider:

(a) the nature and extent of the defendant's criminal intention;
(b) the nature and extent of any injury or damage to the victim;
(c) whether the offence was deliberate or premeditated, or involved an excessive response to provocation;
(d) that an offence which inflicted personal injury or mental trauma, particularly if permanent, would usually be more serious than one which inflicted financial loss only;
(e) any previous convictions of the offender or failure to respond to previous sentences; and
(f) whether the offence was committed on bail (an aggravating factor now referred to in section 151 of the Powers of Criminal Courts (Sentencing) Act 2000).

The court went on to consider what further thought should be given where an offender was only on the border-line of such threshold. His plight would be materially assisted by factors such as:

(a) an admission of responsibility, particularly if evidenced by an early plea of guilty and accompanied by hard evidence of genuine remorse;

    (b) where the offending had been fuelled by addiction to
        drink or drugs and practical steps were being taken
        towards addressing that addiction;
    (c) youth and immaturity;
    (d) previous good character; and
    (e) the fact that an offender had never served a custodial sen-
        tence before.

Lord Bingham CJ was referring to one factor specifically canvassed in section 48 of the Criminal Justice and Public Order Act 1994 which, for the first time, placed on a statutory basis the well-established principle of 'discount' for a plea of guilty. The wording of this section has since then been re-enacted in the Powers of Criminal Courts (Sentencing) Act 2000. Under the new regime of 'pleas and directions hearings' in the Crown Court specific enquiry is made ahead of trial whether or not a defendant has been made aware of these provisions. It has long been the well-known standard practice of the criminal courts to reflect a plea of guilty by a reduction in the sentence of about one-third of the sentence which would have been passed after conviction following a trial. The saving of court time and, perhaps above all these days, expense are the reasons behind this long-standing approach. In cases of sexual offences and particularly those involving children this discount is due to an offender because, by a guilty plea, witnesses have been spared the ordeal of re-living their experience.

    Section 152 of the Powers of Criminal Courts (Sentencing) Act 2000 now specifically provides:

    (1) in determining what sentence to pass on an offender who
        has pleaded guilty to an offence in proceedings before
        that or another court, a court shall take into account –
        (a) the stage in the proceedings for the offence at which the
            offender indicated his intention to plead guilty, and
        (b) the circumstances in which this indication was given.
    (2) If, as a result of taking into account any matter referred
        to in sub-section (1) above, the court imposes a punish-
        ment on the offender which is less severe than the punish-
        ment it would otherwise have imposed, it shall state in
        open court that it has done so.

This discount can, therefore, be reduced if the guilty plea is tendered only at the last minute. Similarly, there is a progressive reduction in the discount if the evidence against the defendant is so overwhelming that, in practice, and perhaps also upon advice, he really has no realistic alternative but to plead guilty. Against this background the judge must then consider whether the offence is indeed 'so serious that only such a sentence can be justified for the offence' before imposing any sentence of imprisonment. Quite how a court is to approach the 'so serious' test is less easy to lay down. Attempts to do so have in practice proved rather circular but it has been said that such an offence is one which 'would make all right thinking members of the public, knowing all the facts, feel that justice had not been done by the passing of any sentence other than a custodial one'.

Even against this background an offender may still just avoid hearing the clanging of the prison gates by a consideration of mitigation which is peculiar to his or her own circumstances.

Although it has increasingly been the practice of judges to give reasons when sentencing, there is now a specific requirement under the Act for a court 'to explain to the offender in open court and in ordinary language why it is passing a custodial sentence on him'. Not only does this promote public confidence but is also important for a prisoner and his lawyers to know the basis upon which a sentence was passed so that, if necessary, the sentence can be further considered by the Court of Appeal at which hearing the judge's reasons would need to be closely examined.

Where immediate loss of liberty is inevitable the prisoner will be sent to the appropriate prison, where he or she will be classified according to risk and the likelihood of attempted escape. In particular, prisoners inside because of offences of a sexual nature and especially those against children may well be segregated because of the hostility shown to such offenders by other inmates, who have a strict, if at times curious, moral code. Those who are in prison because of their violence or who may otherwise represent a threat to the public will be incarcerated in an ordinary prison, also known self-evidently as a **closed prison**. Other prisons, especially 'white-collar' criminals such as bankrupt bank-managers, perjured police-officers and less than accurate accountants will usually be sent to an **open prison** such as Ford Prison in Sussex where security is far less strict. People such as these, who have fallen from grace, nevertheless generally prefer not to take advantage of the opportunities for escape because, when caught, they will be sent back to an ordinary prison.

The Criminal Justice Act 1991 abolished remission but introduced new rules for early release. Prisoners serving four years or less (known as 'short-term' prisoners) are released on licence after serving half their sentence. Those sentenced to twelve months or less will be released halfway through the sentence but are released unconditionally. Those released on licence must comply with conditions relating to compulsory supervision by a probation officer. Long-term prisoners (those serving more than four years) may be released on licence after serving two-thirds of their term. Such a prisoner would also be eligible for **parole** after serving half the sentence. The grant of parole lies in the province of the Secretary of State upon the recommendation of the Parole Board which advises on early release. The Board is particularly involved in the decision to release those serving sentences of life imprisonment.

Suspended sentence   A suspended sentence is nothing to do with hanging. It means that so long as the defendant keeps out of trouble for an operational period he or she will hear no more about the offence. If he is convicted of any sub-sequent offence during that period, however, he is in the gravest danger of not only being sent to prison for the original offence but also having some other period added on in respect of the second offence. For example, suppose that in January 2000 Tom received a sentence of twelve months' imprisonment suspended for two years. In December 2002 he is caught doing his Christmas shoplifting. The court could then send him to prison not only for the original twelve months but for a few extra months as well in respect of the second offence. This was a very common sentence both in the Crown Court and in the magistrates' courts and was known in the colloquial parlance of those spared immediate incarceration as a 'bender'. Such a sentence, however, was often seen as a soft option and fell out of favour. The Criminal Justice Act 1991 imposed very severe restraints upon the ability of the courts any longer to suspend sentence of imprisonment. While it was often viewed as a 'let off' it also sat uncomfortably alongside the dichotomy between sentences of imprisonment and 'community sentences'. The relevant section is re-enacted by section 118 of the Powers of Criminal Courts (Sentencing) Act 2000:

> A court shall not deal with an offender by means of a suspended sentence unless it is of the opinion –
> (a) that the case is one in which a sentence of imprisonment would have been appropriate even without the power to suspend the sentence; and
> (b) that the exercise of that power can be justified by the exceptional circumstances of the case.

In other words, the offender had firstly to cross the custody threshold. As a general rule today if an offender has crossed that Rubicon he will go to prison. By definition 'exceptional circumstances' will be rare indeed. For example, a mother who has young children at home is not an exception to the rest of her sex. While there has been some recent evidence that the courts are becoming more willing to find 'exceptional circumstances' the history of the legislation shows that a strict test is applied. For example, Lord Taylor CJ found it easier to say what did not amount to exceptional circumstances than to identify them. In *R* v. *Okinikan* 1993 the Court of Appeal indicated that neither on their own nor in combination could attributes such as good character, youth or early plea of guilty be held to constitute exceptional circumstances. Less academic and far more tragic a background was that in *R* v. *Lowery* 1993 where a police officer with many years' service pleaded guilty to offences of false accounting. His personal circumstances were tragic. His wife was disabled and the money had been taken in order to meet some of the costs of making alterations to the defendant's police house. The consequences of his dishonesty were profound: his employment and home were lost. His pension rights were frozen and he made attempts upon his own life. The Court of Appeal nevertheless took the view that, despite these catastrophic consequences, the seriousness of the offence merited an immediate sentence of imprisonment. Although this may seem a harsh result in some ways, it is to be borne in mind that the courts are merely complying with the specific provisions of the legislation passed by the politicians acting, presumably, upon their perception of the public mood.

Young offender institution

The traditional means of dealing with troublesome youths aged between 15 and 21 who were either convicted of serious criminal offences or were convicted of not such serious offences but who had records of previous offences, was to order the miscreant to undergo a period of borstal training. Such establishments were envisaged as

> Places in which young offenders ... may be given such indus-
> trial training and other instruction, and be subjected to such
> disciplinary and moral influences as will conduce to their
> reformation and the prevention of crime.

The length of stay was not fixed and was theoretically dependent on the trainee's own response. In practice, it was also influenced by the lack of sufficient space for the newcomers and consequently the stay was usually not more than about nine months. The system was riddled with problems for the judges whose hands were tied by various statutory restrictions on sentencing young persons and the sentence of borstal training was abolished by the Criminal Justice Act 1982, which intro-duced a new concept called **youth custody**. Offenders under the age of 21 years who satisfy the criteria for imprisonment of those over that age may be sent to a Young Offender Institution.

For the offender it remains to be seen how different it all is. The same sort of courses are held by the authorities in various skills and trades. The same problem exists with some inmates who are exposed to the unofficial courses in cheque fraud, lock-picking and 'hot-wiring' other people's motor cars. The old jibe about borstals being the 'Colleges of Further Education for Crime' is almost certainly as true now as it was under the old regime as society still tries to grapple with the heady mix of youthful energy and testosterone, a potent combination even in the days of Shakespeare's Old Shepherd:

> *I would there were no age between sixteen and three-and-*
> *twenty, or that youth would sleep out the rest; for there is*
> *nothing in the between but getting wenches with child,*
> *wronging the ancientry, stealing, fighting.*
> *The Winter's Tale* (Act III Scene 3)

Detention and training orders

Younger miscreants under the age of 18 who commit offences which, were they over the age of 21, would merit imprisonment, will be the subject of a 'detention and training order'. It has become difficult to lock up the younger offenders so that, in particular, those under the age of 15 may only be the subject of such an order if the court is of the opinion that the youth is a persistent offender. Further, where the offender is under the age of 12 the court must specifically be of the opinion that only a custodial sentence would be adequate to protect the public from further offending by him.

Over the years, different philosophies over criminal offending have led to correspondingly different approaches to the treatment of such youthful offenders. Traditionally, during his enforced sojourn, the youth would be subjected to a strict and vigorous life with early starts to the day, physical exertion and frequent inspections. The efficacy of such a regime (once hailed by the then Home Secretary as a 'short, sharp shock') was soon in doubt. With the high cost of each place and a his-toric 70 per cent reconviction rate within a couple of years, the main achievement of such establishments was once said to be to turn out fit young burglars able to run faster than the police.

b) Community sentences

The Criminal Justice Act 1991 introduced the concept of the 'community sentence'. This concept of punishment in the community may avoid some of the disadvantages of imprisonment such as the effect on innocent members of the offender's family and the consequent substantial cost to the public purse. If the court is not of the view that the offence is 'so serious that only a custodial sentence can be justified' the court must then consider whether the offence is still 'serious enough' to warrant a community sentence. Such a sentence could take the form of any of the following orders.

Probation order

Under section 41 of the Powers of Criminal Court (Sentencing) Act 2000 the court may impose such an order where a person aged over sixteen is convicted of an offence and the court is of the opinion that supervision is desirable in the interests of:

(a) securing his rehabilitation, or
(b) protecting the public from harm from him or preventing the commission by him of further offences.

The offender must then keep in touch with the probation officer and comply with any particular conditions or requirements. In June 2000 Parliament began to consider the Criminal Justice and Court Service Bill by which Parliament proposed changing the Powers of Criminal Courts (Sentencing) Bill before that particular piece of legislation had even been implemented so as to rename this probation order as a **Community Rehabilitation Order**.

Community service order

This term is similarly likely to be replaced with the new term of **Community Punishment Order** if the new Bill is brought into effect. Such came into being through the Powers of Criminal Courts Act 1973 as an alternative to prison. Section 46 of the Powers of Criminal Courts (Sentencing) Act 2000 empowers the court, when dealing with offenders over the age of sixteen, to require them to perform unpaid work for not less than 40 and not more than 240 hours. The nature of the work will obviously vary with the local needs and any special skills of the offender. It might include, for example, gardening, clearing up waste ground or painting and carpentry at old people's or children's homes.

... even after completing her allotted time.

In one early case, a musically trained shoplifter had her skills put to good use when she was ordered to play the piano at an old people's home for 100 hours. Early investigations indicated a very encouraging response generally on the part of these offenders. In particular, the lady pianist was reported as saying that she might go on playing the piano even after completing her allotted time. More recently, in 1995, the footballer Eric Cantona, spent part of his community service order for assaulting a Crystal Palace fan by teaching a boys' football club how to tackle and dribble.

Combination order This term is also likely to be abolished by the imposition of a new term of **Community Punishment and Rehabilitation Order**. The old term of 'combination order', as was self-evident in its name, represented a combination of probation and community service. The present legislative background is to be found in section 51 of the Powers of Criminal Courts (Sentencing) Act 2000, which allows a court dealing with those over the age of sixteen years both to place them under supervision and require them to work unpaid, although this particular approach leads to a reduction in the maximum hours to one hundred.

Curfew order Where an offender over the age of sixteen has neglected to pay earlier fines or, alternatively, simply would not have sufficient means to pay a fine, the court may make a curfew order as a way of dealing with persistent petty offenders. The idea had been introduced by the Criminal Justice Act 1991 so as to require an offender to remain at a specified place during specified times of not less than two hours and not more than twelve hours.

Supervision order Offenders under the age of eighteen may be placed under the supervision of the local authority, a probation officer or a member of a youth offending team. Section 63 of the Powers of Criminal Courts (Sentencing) Act 2000 further provides that the offender shall reside in a particular area of a local authority and such residence may last for up to three years. During that time the supervisor shall advise, assist and befriend the offender. Such offenders may also enjoy the benefits of character-building activity during this period.

Attendance centre orders A traditional course taken in the case of youthful offenders, such as the less virulent breed of football hooligans, is to pass upon such offenders an order requiring them to spend so many hours (often twelve but up to thirty-six hours) at an attendance centre. Conveniently, for the rest of society if not so much for the delinquent, these centres are open on Saturdays and at times remarkably similar to kick-off times at the local football stadium.

Section 60 of the Powers of Criminal Courts (Sentencing) Act 2000 provides that such orders may be made upon those under the age of 21 years who commit offences punishable with imprisonment. The Act allows the court to pass a sentence of less than twelve hours where the offender is under the age of fourteen or where twelve hours would be excessive having regard to the offender's age or any other circumstances.

Deferred sentence   A court may feel that the offender is likely to mend his ways in the immediate future. He may, for instance, be leaving school, changing jobs, getting married or moving home. Rather than act immediately the court may wish to wait and see how he turns out.

The Powers of Criminal Courts (Sentencing) Act 2000 provides in section 1 that the court may defer passing sentence on an offender in order to have regard to the offender's conduct after conviction (including where appropriate, the making by him of reparation of his offences) or to any change in his circumstances. This particular course requires the consent of the offender. The offender may be brought back at any time up to six months after the hearing, and what happens to him then will depend largely on his own efforts in the intervening period. Obviously it is desirable that the same judge and counsel should deal with the case the second time around. Moreover, in dealing with this provision as enacted in legislation passed in 1973 the Court of Appeal indicated in *R* v. *Gilby* 1975 that where the probation report is not unfavourable to the offender a court should not impose any substantial custodial sentence. Further, in *R* v. *George* 1984 the Court of Appeal indicated that the offender upon whom sentence is deferred, should be told what conduct is expected of him during the period of deferment. If, when he returns to court for sentence, the offender has attempted substantially to conform with those expectations, an immediate custodial sentence will not be passed.

Fine   Almost every offence may be punished by the imposition of a fine, and, in the lower courts particularly, fining is very common. Figures for 1999/2000 show that the Treasury was enriched to the extent of over £435 million from fines imposed by the courts. Indeed, the fines imposed by the Crown Court may be very substantial and may even be imposed in addition to any other order. For example, in 1996 a fine of no less than £4 million was levied against the Milford Haven Port Authority for pollution caused when the *Sea Empress* oil tanker ran aground at the entrance to the harbour.

Section 128 of the Powers of Criminal Courts (Sentencing) Act 2000 requires that the court should enquire into the financial circumstances of any individual offender and then go on to fix the fine in such sum, as in the opinion of the court, reflects the seriousness of the offence. This enquiry into an offender's means is assisted by the court making what is now termed a 'financial circumstances order' with respect to him. Anyone who declines to provide such information is fined for such refusal and even faces imprisonment if he does not make candid disclosure.

It is, of course, self-evident that magistrates who impose a fine of £100 on, say, a television licence dodger, will bring about a very different impact on a millionaire and on a student living on a loan. In a short-lived attempt to impose comparable hardship, the Criminal Justice Act 1991 introduced the concept of unit fines which, in the example given, would reduce the £100 on the student and very greatly increase it for the now luckless plutocrat. Offenders were required to furnish details of income and expenditure in order to allow the courts to calculate the disposable weekly income. This figure was to be treated as the 'unit'. A view then had to be formed as to the seriousness of the offence. Such a view would be reflected in the number of units which the offender is fined. For example, a person with a disposable income of £50 with a ten unit fine would pay £500 while one with only five units would escape at £250. There were suggested penalties so that, for example, the guideline fine for shoplifters was 15 units. The poor thief who took a tin of baked beans from a local shop with a minimum unit of £4 would then have to find £60 – by deduction from Income Support if necessary. The next shoplifter, at the other end of the unit scale, with a maximum of £100 per unit would then have had to write a cheque for £1,500 as a fine for stealing, say, a bar of chocolate. As with so many new ideas, the apparent social justice was soon shown to be less real in practice. Recidivist criminals, eschewing work and declaring low incomes, escaped with pitifully modest penalties which offer no deterrent. On the other hand, honest, hardworking motorists, without hire-purchase commitments or other means of reducing their disposable incomes, found themselves fleeced for the most venial infringements of the increasingly stern road traffic legislation. These absurdities soon gained widespread press coverage and the new legislation was swiftly and roundly discredited. The press rightly highlighted the disparity between two neighbours each prosecuted for driving without insurance but one being fined a mere £75 and the other as much as £1,500. More absurd still was the much-publicised fine of £1,200 upon a man who endangered society by dropping a crisp packet! Within months the politicians had to negotiate the sort of violent U-turn which, if committed by a motorist on the roads, would have been judged worthy of the highest number of units. The Criminal Justice Act 1993 killed off the unit fine and restored some common sense to the courts, which are now required to enquire only into the financial circumstances of the offender and then to fix any fine so as to reflect the seriousness of the offence.

In the spring of 2000, however, the Magistrates' Association turned their attention to a slightly refined version of the old idea by setting out specific fines for particular bands of income. Some would view the very suggestion that such rigidity needs to be built into the process of sentencing as itself providing evidence that too many of that particular association's members have simply not properly applied the existing rules, which require that regard be had to an offender's means and which if adhered to could, so to speak, bring a new meaning to the idea of 'fine-tuning'.

A convicted defendant is almost invariably allowed time to pay, often 28 days. If, after that time, a defendant declines to provide the cash he is in jeopardy of a spell in prison. The Powers of Criminal Courts (Sentencing) Act 2000 provides a table for periods of imprisonment in default of payment. The very high level of fines imposed by the Crown Court in major crimes (such as first division robberies, City fraud and large-scale drug deals) is itself reflected in the provisions of the Act, which provides that those who default on payment of fines above £1 million should serve ten years in prison. Punishment on this scale had been seen in the *Guinness* fraud trial in 1990 when one very rich man was fined £5 million.

Discharge

Rather than actually punish an offender, a court may discharge him or her. In particular, section 12 of the Powers of Criminal Courts (Sentencing) Act 2000 provides for two forms: the *absolute* and the *conditional* discharge.

A **conditional discharge** means that so long as the offender keeps out of further trouble for a specified period (up to three years) he will hear no more about it. If he does get into trouble within that time, however, he will be in danger not only of being punished for the second offence, but also of being dealt with for the initial crime. In that respect, of course, a conditional discharge resembles a suspended sentence, although in the former case no sentence is laid down for the initial offence in the event of a further appearance before the court.

The alternative **absolute discharge** allows a court to discharge a man or woman where no real blame can attach to what he or she did so that, in the words of section 12 of the Powers of Criminal Courts (Sentencing) Act 2000 it is thought 'inexpedient to inflict punishment' – for example, such a course would be appropriate in Tom's offence (mentioned in Unit 1.2) of failing to display a tax disc on his windscreen.

c) Other orders

Compensation

The victim of theft or criminal damage has long been able to take the road to the civil courts and sue for the value of the goods stolen or damaged. The criminal courts have long had power to deal with simple cases and the present framework is to be found in section 130 of the Powers of Criminal Courts (Sentencing) Act 2000 which authorises a court 'instead of or in addition to dealing with' an offender in any other way to make a compensation order requiring the offender to pay compensation for any personal injury, loss or damage resulting from the offence. Indeed, the judge is even required to explain his reasons for not making a compensation order if money is sought.

Although repayments of money stolen will obviously be potent mitigation, it is to be remembered that, in the words of Scarman LJ in *R v. Inwood* 1974:

> *Compensation orders were not introduced into our law to enable the convicted to buy themselves out of penalties for crime. Compensation orders were introduced into our law as a convenient and rapid means of avoiding the expense of resorting to civil litigation when the criminal clearly has the means to enable the compensation to be paid.*

Confiscation

A burglar whose car is found crammed with stolen goods is in danger not only of losing the goods but also of saying goodbye to his car. In this regard section 143 of the Powers of Criminal Courts (Sentencing) Act 2000 empowers the court to deprive a criminal of property which had been used for the purpose of committing crime.

Disqualification

Under the new legislation to be found in section 146 of the Powers of Criminal Courts (Sentencing) Act 2000 a person convicted of an offence may, instead of or in addition to any other sentence, find that he is disqualified from driving.

3.10 A free country

'It's a free country – I can do as I like.' Such comment is more appropriate as a somewhat naive political slogan than as an exposition of modern English law on the liberty of the individual. Nevertheless, it does have the essential merit of being at least part right. The adult citizen of the United Kingdom today still retains certain essential freedoms such as the general liberty to vote in free elections, to live and travel where he or she wants, and generally to enjoy a life where freedom has long been the tradition and which, no longer resting just on the common law, is now specifically preserved by the European Convention on Human Rights (see Unit 1.8).

On the other hand, of course, the very existence of our law prevents the citizen from doing exactly as he or she might like. Some restraint on individual liberty is essential if any society is to emerge from primeval anarchy. This need for law and some fundamental regulation of society was considered in Unit 1.1. The need to limit individual liberty was well expressed in the nineteenth century by John Stuart Mill in his work *Liberty*:

> *The liberty of the individual must be thus far limited; he must not make himself a nuisance to other people.*

The threat to our society both from hostile forces abroad and from insidious factions at home adds to the difficulties of balancing security for the community at large against the rights of the individual. Terrorism in Northern Ireland has exemplified the difficulty and was recognised as a justification for some limitation on personal freedom by Lord Gardiner in his Report:

> *While the liberty of the subject is a human right to be preserved under all possible conditions, it is not, and cannot be, an absolute right, because one man may use his liberty to take away the liberty of another and must be restrained from doing so. Where freedoms conflict, the state has a duty to protect those in need of protection.*

The problem is illustrated on an everyday level by the frustration felt by a motorist trying to drive through central London at the same time as a march of banner-waving demonstrators takes place. Their proper freedom to protest inevitably interferes with the freedom of other citizens to use the same streets for an equally lawful purpose.

English common law has traditionally adopted a generally permissive approach to the rights and freedoms of the individual. Rather than lay down a list of things citizens may do, our society has preferred its law merely to proscribe in a shorter list that which the citizen may not do. In other words, English law has recognised that everything is allowed unless it is specifically restricted or forbidden. Other countries have taken a different approach and have drafted statements of fundamental freedoms and essential rights to be enjoyed by their citizens. Magna Carta ('Great Charter') 1215 and the Bill of Rights 1688 went some way towards defining and limiting the power of the Sovereign but, of course, these can have only limited influence in today's very different society.

It can be instructive to examine the wording of the European Convention and then to investigate how far English law gives and intends to give practical effect to the spirit of the Convention's laudable aims.

This topic is deliberately examined in detail for in the words of Lord Hope in *R* v. *D.P.P. ex parte Kebilene and Others* 1999:

> *It is now plain that the incorporation of the European Convention ... into our domestic law will subject the entire legal system to a fundamental process of review and, where necessary, reform by the judiciary.*

Article 2 provides:

> Everyone's right to life shall be protected by law. No one shall be deprived of his life intentionally save in the execution of a sentence of a court following his conviction of a crime for which this penalty is provided by law.

Although the death penalty was abolished in cases of murder in the 1960s it was nevertheless retained in cases of treason by British citizens and not abolished for all purposes until section 36 of the Crime and Disorder Act 1998 came into force. It is to be noted that Article 1 of the Sixth Protocol had long since sought to abolish the death penalty within Europe.

Article 3 provides:

> No one shall be subjected to torture or to inhuman or degrading treatment or punishment.

In 1993 the European Court of Human Rights considered the complaint by fifteen-year-old Jeremy Costello-Roberts who, when seven years old, had been hit by his head teacher with a gym shoe. At the time Jeremy was a pupil at a private boarding school in Devon. In *Costello-Roberts* v. *United Kingdom* 1993 Jeremy's mother had complained that this treatment was 'degrading' and therefore constituted breach of Article 3. By a slender majority the judges ruled that, despite Jeremy's age and despite the formalised nature of a long delayed punishment, this beating was not severe enough to fall foul of the Convention. Ironically, at the time of judgment, such punishment would have been unlawful under English law in a state school since the Education (No. 2) Act 1986 came into force. Until recently, corporal punishment of the young remained a privilege of private education but even this elitism has been brought to an end. Such change followed the decision in *A* v. *The United Kingdom* 1998. The minor, born in 1984, had been repeatedly hit with a garden cane by his stepfather and had even been placed on the local authority Child Protection Register. The stepfather was charged with assault occasioning actual bodily harm but was acquitted when the jury accepted that he had done no more than impose reasonable chastisement. The European Court of Human Rights was later to accept that the beating with a garden cane amounted to 'inhuman or degrading treatment or punishment' and fell the wrong side of permissible punishment.

Article 4 outlaws slavery along with compulsory labour.
Article 5 provides:

> Everyone has the right to liberty and security of person. No
> one shall be deprived of his liberty save in the following cases
> and in accordance with a procedure prescribed by law.

No one may be deprived of his freedom save by lawful arrest. A person
being arrested must be told the reason for his or her arrest. All arrests
are *prima facie* unlawful unless and until the arrest is justified. These
matters are examined in greater detail in Unit 3.7. A person taken under
arrest to a police station is entitled to have someone notified of his arrest
and detention. He ought usually to be allowed to consult privately with
a solicitor. A person is also entitled to have a solicitor present at any
police interview. Further restrictions are imposed on the police where
the suspect is under eighteen years of age.

People may not be detained by the police or anyone else unless actually arrested and the old ambiguity about people staying at police stations 'helping with inquiries' has been cleared up by the Police and
Criminal Evidence Act 1984, which states unambiguously that a person
who has attended voluntarily at a police station is entitled to leave at
will unless placed under arrest when the police may then use 'reasonable
force' in effecting the arrest and handcuffs may be applied if needed to
prevent escape or restrain violent behaviour. On arrest a suspect may be
searched. One of the many controversial aspects of the Police and Criminal Evidence Act 1984 involves the general power now given to the
police to stop and search people in the streets in order to look for stolen
or prohibited goods such as drugs or offensive weapons. The Act
requires the police officers conducting such searches to keep a record of
the search and limits such searches to outer clothing only. The police
may retain items of evidential value found either on the person of an
arrested person or in his home. Further, the police have a statutory right
to search a private home if they are in possession of a search warrant:
this is just one of the statutory limitations on the right of a householder
to shut the door to unwelcome visitors. This matter is looked at again in
Unit 6.7. The citizen may even be stopped while driving home, as the
police also have the right to carry out road checks involving the stopping of vehicles and then searching them.

After arrest, a suspect has the right under the Bail Act 1976 to bail.
This right may only be withheld on establishment of one or more of the
specific statutory exceptions (see Unit 3.8). The Act has long required
that magistrates set out their reasons for the refusal of bail and, in everyday practice, this has long been done by the simple and quick expedient
of ticking the relevant box on a standard pro-forma record sheet. It is
open to question whether this short form of reasoning will stand
scrutiny under Article 5 and the values of the Convention taken as a
whole. More obviously objectionable was the outright prohibition on
the grant of bail to anyone already convicted of homicide or rape and
now facing a second such allegation. This blanket ban could never have
been consonant with the Human Rights Act and bail may now be
granted in exceptional circumstances.

Before releasing him the police may take photographs and fingerprints from their reluctant guest but these should be destroyed if the suspect is not convicted at court. As a general rule, however, a person acquitted after trial will have no automatic redress against those who prosecuted him unless he can prove malicious prosecution and/or false imprisonment. Such claims are not always easy to prove. The recent proposals of the Law Commission on 'Double Jeopardy' have been considered in Unit 3.8 but it is convenient at this juncture also to note the European perspective which, by Article 4 of the Seventh Protocol, grants a right to the citizen not to be tried or punished twice.

Article 6 of the European Convention lays down that:

1. In the determination of his civil rights and obligations or of any criminal charge against him, everyone is entitled to a fair and public hearing within a reasonable time by an independent and impartial tribunal established by law. Judgment shall be pronounced publicly but the press and public may be excluded from all or part of the trial in the interests of morals, public order or national security in a democratic society, where the interests of juveniles or the protection of the private life of the parties so require, or to the extent strictly necessary in the opinion of the court in special circumstances where publicity would prejudice the interests of justice.
2. Everyone charged with a criminal offence shall be presumed innocent until proved guilty according to law.
3. Everyone charged with a criminal offence has the following minimum rights:
    a) to be informed promptly, in a language which he understands and in detail, of the nature and cause of the accusation against him;
    b) to have adequate time and facilities for the preparation of his defence;
    c) to defend himself in person or through legal assistance of his own choosing or, if he has not sufficient means to pay for legal assistance, to be given it free when the interests of justice so require;
    d) to examine or have examined witnesses against him and to obtain the attendance and examination of witnesses on his behalf under the same conditions as witnesses against him;
    e) to have a free assistance of an interpreter if he cannot understand or speak the language used in court.

The requirement that a lawyer's services should be provided without charge to the defendant if this is necessary in the interests of justice may increasingly prove an embarrassment to this country as the government cuts and cuts again at the grant and scope of pubic funding. To its credit, however, the government acted speedily to confirm the independence of judges after the recent Scottish decision in *Starrs* v. *Procurator Fiscal* 1999 when it had been held that the system of part-time Sheriffs was unlawful, for these part-time judges, like the English Recorders, had no security of tenure of office and were therefore not 'independent' within the meaning of Article 6 of the European Convention. In England, Recorders now are appointed for no less than five years. Less easy to control, however, is the rogue juror. In the summer of 2000 the European Court of Human Rights ruled in *Sander* v. *United Kingdom* that the Asian defendant had been denied his rights to a fair trial under Article 6 because the trial judge had not taken sufficient steps to deal with an allegation of racial prejudice among the jury at Birmingham Crown Court.

In *T* v. *United Kingdom* 2000, proceedings brought after the decision of the House of Lords in *R* v. *Secretary of State for the Home Department, ex parte Venables and Thompson* (see also Unit 2.3b)) the European Court of Human Rights held that Thompson, one of two ten-year-old boys convicted of murdering a young child, had not received a fair hearing. It was found that Article 6 of the Convention had been breached because Thompson had not been able properly to participate in his Crown Court trial at the age of eleven years. As also seen in Unit 2.3b)) steps have already been taken by means of the relevant Practice Direction to reform the trial of young persons in the Crown Court.

Nevertheless, the same Article does recognise that there may be circumstances in which the press and the public should be excluded from the court – for example where public order, national security or the interests of juveniles are concerned. A common application of this principle is the restriction placed on the freedom of the press to report the names of any juveniles involved in an office. There are related restrictions on the naming of adult parties in cases of alleged rape.

Constraints upon the freedom of the press are to be found in the Contempt of Court Act 1981 which itself limits freedom of expression.

A court has further power to restrict press reporting under the provisions of the Contempt of Court Act 1981. Under section 4 of the Act the court may order the postponement of reports of any case 'where it appears necessary for avoiding a substantial risk of prejudice to the administration of justice'. For example, a man may be awaiting trial on two sets of charges. If Tuesday's morning paper contains widespread coverage of Monday's trial there is a risk of prejudice to the defendant if his next trial starts on Wednesday for the jurors will probably see the press coverage and possibly be influenced by it. As Wills J said in *R* v. *Parke* 1903:

> It is possible very effectively to poison the fountain of justice before it begins to flow.

Salmon LJ was also deeply critical of the 1967 television interview by David Frost of Emil Savundra, the disgraced former chairman of the crashed Fire, Auto and Marine Insurance Company, at the time of his appeal against his conviction for fraud:

> On any view, the television interview with the Savundra was deplorable. With no experience of television, he was faced with a skilled interviewer whose clear object was to establish his guilt before an audience of millions of people. None of the

ordinary safeguards for fairness that exist in a court of law were observed, no doubt because they were not understood. They may seem prosaic to those engaged in the entertainment business, but they are the rocks upon which freedom from oppression and tyranny have been established in this country for centuries. . . . Trial by television is not to be tolerated in a civilized society.

Neither may jurors sell their account of the trial to the press as the inside story. Such opportunistic journalism, if indeed it can properly be described as journalism, is outlawed by section 8 of the Act which provides that it is contempt of court to disclose opinions advanced by a jury in the course of its deliberations. The dangers of trial by the tabloid media were again in the mind of the Court of Appeal in *R* v. *Taylor* 1993. Two sisters, Michelle and Lisa Taylor, had been convicted on circumstantial evidence of the murder of a bank clerk with whose husband Michelle Taylor had enjoyed an affair. The girls appealed against those convictions complaining firstly, as their lawyers subsequently discovered, that the police had suppressed evidence which weakened the prosecution case, and secondly that prejudicial press reporting had deprived them of a fair trial. Headlines such as 'Cheats Kiss' and 'Captured on Video . . . the murder case mistress at her lover's wedding' were condemned by McCowan LJ as 'unremitting, extensive, sensational, inaccurate and misleading' and also as reporting matters not even said in court. The Lord Justice added:

What the press did was not reporting at all. It was comment, and comment which assumed the guilt of the two girls in the dock. . . . The press is no more entitled to assume guilt in what it writes during the course of a trial than a police officer is entitled to convince himself of a defendant's guilt and suppress evidence.

When *The Mail on Sunday* carried an article on the *Blue Arrow* fraud trial in which jurors' thoughts were published (including one juror's view that another juror showed a complete lack of understanding, wanting to drag the case out and only agreeing with others about the verdict so he could go home!) the court fined the newspaper for contempt of court. In *Attorney-General* v. *Associated Newspapers* 1993 Beldam LJ rejected the argument that such publication made a valuable contribution to the debate on whether juries should decide complex fraud trials. He said:

We consider that the free, uninhibited and unfettered discussion by a jury in the course of their deliberations is essential to the proper administration of justice, which includes trial by jury.

Punishment of such contempt could bring those same jurors face to face with the man they convicted as they are reunited in prison.

The press may also be excluded where the interests of national security require the court to sit *in camera* – a phrase indicating not that photography is encouraged but rather that the public is excluded. Considerations of national security often arose in cases of spying and other prosecutions under the Official Secrets Act 1911. For example, little detail became known to press and public in the 1984 trial at the Old Bailey of the MI5 spy, Michael Bettany.

The Official Secrets Act 1911, however, had now become a widely discredited piece of legislation because of the very wide scope of its prohibitions. Matters which could have no possible significance to national security were nevertheless classified as official secrets. The absurdity of some prosecutions was illustrated in March 1985 when, after a wait of many months, the prosecution against civil servant Alan Lowther was dropped. Lowther had been prosecuted for allegedly passing on to a departmental colleague information on the manufacture of toy typewriters in prison workshops – scarcely the sort of militarily sensitive or otherwise vital information which Parliament no doubt had in mind when it rushed the Act on to the statute book shortly before the First World War.

Reform of the Official Secrets Act had been recommended in 1972 by a committee headed by Lord Franks. Nevertheless, the Act had recently been invoked to deal with the enthusiasm of some civil servants to 'leak' information to the press. For example, in 1984 a young civil servant, Sarah Tisdall, passed secret information to *The Guardian* newspaper. In fact, the information she leaked was scarcely a threat to national security but was a ministerial minute on how best to handle a CND protest against cruise missiles. Miss Tisdall's offence led to a prison sentence.

Another and much publicised prosecution was that of the civil servant Clive Ponting who had passed documents from his department of the Ministry of Defence to an opposition Member of Parliament who had been a persistent critic of British conduct during the Falklands war of 1982 and, in particular, the sinking of the enemy cruiser *General Belgrano*. In particular, there was a dispute whether this warship represented a danger to our shipping. At Ponting's trial in 1985 the jury had to consider the meaning of the phrase 'the interests of the State'. The jury's verdict of Not Guilty surprised many people for it effectively ignored the judge's direction in law that the interests of the State were to be equated with 'the policies of the State'. This sort of refusal by juries to convict, coupled with the *Spycatcher* debacle, led to the introduction of the Official Secrets Act 1989.

A less draconian and more subtle way in which the government can seek to restrict publication of matters touching upon national security is by means of the D-notice. This is a voluntary form of censorship accepted by the press which is contained in a notice issued by a committee consisting of press and government representatives.

Relations between the press and government came to be further considered by the House of Lords in *Brind* v. *Secretary of State* 1991. The Home Secretary, exercising powers under the Broadcasting Act 1981, had issued directives to the BBC and IBA preventing them from carrying the words of various persons in Northern Ireland. A number of journalists complained that the Home Secretary had acted outside his powers (*ultra vires*) and that he had also breached Article 10 of the European Convention on Human Rights in seeking to deny what the politicians called 'the oxygen of publicity' to the IRA and others. The House of

Lords pointed out that as the Convention had not been incorporated into English domestic law it could not be a source of rights and obligations. There was, said Lord Bridge, an important competing public interest sufficient to justify a restriction on the right to freedom of expression:

> *In any civilized and law-abiding society the defeat of the terrorist is a public interest of the first importance.*

If the citizen's right to read what he wants and view what he chooses is controlled by law what, then, of his right to free speech?

Article 10 of the European Convention recognises that:

1. Everyone has the right to freedom of expression. This right shall include freedom to hold opinions and to receive and impart information and ideas without interference by public authority and regardless of frontiers. This Article shall not prevent States from requiring the licensing of broadcasting, television or cinema enterprises.
2. The exercise of these freedoms, since it carries with it duties and responsibilities, may be subject to such formalities, conditions, restrictions or penalties as are prescribed by law and are necessary in a democratic society, in the interests of national security, territorial integrity or public safety, for the prevention of disorder or crime, for the protection of health or morals, for the protection of the reputation or rights of others, for preventing the disclosure of information received in confidence, or for maintaining the authority and impartiality of the judiciary.

In 1987 the courts, both in Australia and Britain, had to consider just what duties and responsibilities were relevant when Peter Wright, a former member of the British security service MI5, shot to the top of the best-seller list in America and elsewhere with revelations of alleged misconduct by MI5 officers, recounted in his book *Spycatcher*. After a long hearing against the Australian publishers – lost by the British government, whose principal witness admitted to having been 'economical with the truth' – the Attorney-General applied to the English courts for an injunction restraining certain British newspapers from publishing extracts from the book, which was by now freely available for sale outside Britain.

Of course, Wright had long been subject to the restraints of the Official Secrets Act 1911 and he appeared, therefore, to have broken his duty of confidentiality to the British government. Was Wright wrong? What price freedom of the press? In *Attorney-General* v. *Guardian Newspapers Ltd* 1988, the House of Lords was seriously divided. Three judges favoured an interim ban on publication. Lord Ackner spoke for them:

> *To refuse to allow the injunction to be continued … would have established a Charter for Traitors to publish on the most massive scale in England whatever they managed to publish abroad.*

The minority view of the other two judges was expressed by Lord Bridge, a former Chairman of the Security Commission:

> *What of the other side of the coin and the encroachment on freedom of speech? Having no written constitution, we have no equivalent in our law to the First Amendment to the Constitution of the United States of America.*
>
> *Some think that puts freedom of speech on too lofty a pedestal. Perhaps they are right. We have not adopted as part of our law the European Convention on Human Rights to which this country is a signatory. Many think that we should. I have hitherto not been of that persuasion, in large part because I have had confidence in the capacity of the common law to safeguard the fundamental freedoms essential to a free society including the right to freedom of speech.*
>
> *Freedom of speech is always the first casualty under a totalitarian regime. Such a regime cannot afford to allow the free circulation of information and ideas among its citizens. Censorship is the indispensable tool to regulate what the public may and what they may not know.*
>
> *The present attempt to insulate the public in this country from information which is freely available elsewhere is a significant step down that very dangerous road.*
>
> *Maintenance of the ban, as more and more copies of* Spycatcher *enter this country and circulate here, will seem more and more ridiculous. If the Government are determined to fight to maintain the ban to the end, they will face inevitable condemnation and humiliation by the European Court of Human Rights in Strasbourg. Long before that they will have been condemned at the bar of public opinion in the free world.*

At the full hearing the House of Lords expressed the view that the earlier injunction should be discharged since publication of *Spycatcher* abroad had destroyed any secrecy as to its contents. The memoirs of Peter Wright had clearly greatly annoyed the government, which responded by passing the new Official Secrets Act 1989. This Act imposes on members of the security services a life-long duty of confidentiality. It makes actions such as those of Wright an offence and prohibits both past and present members of such services from disclosing without lawful authority any information, document or other article which has ever been in their possession. At the time of writing concern about the contents of an autobiography by former head of MI5, Dame Stella Rimmington, have prompted calls for her arrest under this same Act.

Also at the time of writing a former MI5 officer, David Shayler, stands charged with two separate offences under the Official Secrets Act in respect of allegations made in a Sunday newspaper about incompetence and drunkenness within the British security forces. Any trial would itself be a test of the extent to which freedom of expression can properly be restricted in the interests of national security and such considerations may even inhibit any prosecution.

Some restraint on crudity of expression is to be found in section 5 of the Public Order Act 1986, which makes it an offence to use threatening, abusive or insulting words or behaviour within the hearing of a person likely to be caused harassment, alarm or distress by such behaviour. As will be seen in Unit 6.10, the law of defamation provides protection and remedies for those about whom untrue and damaging remarks are made.

The importance of both the English common law of freedom of expression and Article 10 of the European Convention in proceedings for alleged defamation fell to be considered by the House of Lords in *Derbyshire County Council* v. *Times Newspapers* 1993. *The Sunday Times* had published articles with titles such as 'Bizarre deals of a Council Leader and the Media Tycoon' in which journalists questioned the propriety of certain investments made by the Council in its superannuation fund. The county council and its leader sued for libel. The courts rejected the right of the local authority to sue for defamation. The House of Lords held that it would be contrary to public policy for organs of government, whether central or local, to have such a right for it was of the highest public importance that a government body should be open to uninhibited public criticism. To allow such bodies a right to sue for defamation would impose an undesirable fetter on freedom of speech.

One problem with secrecy and in particular the compilation of secret files is that information contained in those files may be wrong. The increasing use of computers to store and transmit information (and the prospect of electronic intrusion by 'hackers' and possible alteration of records) has caused its own problems and led to the Data Protection Act 1984, now replaced by the 1998 Act of the same name.

The Act applies to 'data' which is defined as 'information recorded in a form in which it can be processed by equipment operating automatically in response to instructions given for that purpose'. The Act confers on an individual the right to look at such data held on him or her, provided that he pays the necessary fee. The individual is then entitled to have any inaccuracies in that data corrected and to receive compensation for any losses resulting from such inaccuracies.

There are, however, a number of exceptions to this general right which apply to data concerned with:

1. the prevention or detection of crime; or
2. the apprehension or prosecution of offenders; or
3. the assessment or collection of any tax or duty.

People will not, therefore, be allowed to inspect data held on them in the cavernous Police National Computer which houses records not only on criminals but also on all motorists.

The Act therefore is similar in concept to the more limited right conferred by the Consumer Credit Act 1974 which, in section 158, requires a credit reference agency to provide a copy of a person's file if that person pays £1. The individual may correct any errors in that file (for example, a suggestion that he has left a trail of debt wherever he has gone) and may even draft his own notice of correction.

The Access to Personal Files Act 1987 allows an individual to inspect a manual file in much the same way that the Data Protection Act 1984 gave the citizen a right to examine relevant computerised records.

Postmen are assumed to have an implied licence to walk up the garden path in order to deliver the morning post. Such post, however, must not contain any indecent or obscene articles even in the proverbial plain brown wrapper. The Postal Services Act 2000 makes it an offence to send indecent or obscene articles through the post.

Obscenity is another controversial and unsatisfactory area of English law. So much of the practical difficulty (as opposed to any moral principle) stems simply from difficulties of definition.

The test applied by the courts in deciding whether some article is obscene is that laid down in the Obscene Publications Act 1959. An article is deemed to be 'obscene' if its effect, taken as a whole, is such as to tend to deprave and corrupt persons who are likely to see it. Ever since 1961 when members of an Old Bailey jury were asked by prosecuting counsel if D. H. Lawrence's book *Lady Chatterley's Lover* was the sort of book they would want their wives and servants to read, it has been clear that the whole book must be considered on its merits and not just one or two isolated 'juicy' passages. The issue is nevertheless far from straightforward. Some would echo the sentiments of Oscar Wilde:

> *There is no such thing as a moral or an immoral book. Books are well written or badly written.*

In the *Lady Chatterley* trial the judge told the jury:

> *...to deprave means to make morally bad, to pervert, to debase or corrupt morally. The words 'to corrupt' mean to render morally unsound or rotten, to destroy the moral purity or chastity of, to pervert or ruin a good quality, to debase, to defile ... just as loyalty is one of the things which is essential to the well-being of the nation, so some sense of morality is something that is essential to the well-being of a nation, and to the healthy life of the community. ... and, accordingly, anyone who by his writing* tends *to corrupt that fundamental sense of morality is guilty of an obscene libel.*

In 1968 specific censorship of the theatre was removed by the Theatres Act and two years later nudity on stage was seen in *Oh! Calcutta!* Nevertheless, stage performances are still subject to the general law. In 1977 a private prosecution was launched against a man called Lemon and a publication entitled *Gay News*, of which Lemon was editor. Lemon was later convicted of the offence of **blasphemous libel** in respect of a distasteful poem about Christ. Lord Scarman accepted as still accurate the old definition of blasphemy:

> Every publication is said to be blasphemous which contains any contemptuous, reviling, scurrilous or ludicrous matter relating to God, Jesus Christ, or the Bible, or the formularies of the Church of England as by law established. It is not blasphemous to speak or publish opinions hostile to the Christian religion, or to deny the existence of God, if the publication is couched in decent and temperate language.

The publication in 1988 of Salman Rushdie's book *The Satanic Verses* (winner of the Whitbread Prize for Literature, but later banned in every Muslim country) caused offence to Muslims living in the United Kingdom. Some attempted to prosecute the author for the offence of blasphemous libel, but the court refused to issue the necessary summons. On appeal, in *R* v. *Chief Metropolitan Stipendiary Magistrate, ex parte Choudhury* 1991 the Divisional Court held that the common-law offence of blasphemy was confined to protecting the Christian religion and was not to be extended to other religions.

Freedom of thought, conscience and religion is guaranteed by **Article 9** of the European Convention. This right expressly includes a person's 'freedom to change his religion or belief, and freedom, either alone or in the community with others and in public or private, to manifest his religion or belief, in worship, teaching, practice and observance'.

English law recognises religion as a charitable cause and confers various reliefs from iniquities such as taxation. Such relief is not confined to the Church of England for as one judge said:

> As between different religions the law stands neutral, but it assumes that any religion is at least likely to be better than none.

Article 8 provides:

> Everyone has the right to respect for his private and family life, his home and his correspondence.

One addition to the embarrassingly long list of cases where the United Kingdom has been found to have been in breach of the Convention involved the 'tapping' of private telephone conversations. In *Malone* v. *Commissioner of Police (No. 2)* 1979 the then Vice-Chancellor, Sir Robert Megarry, remarked that this was 'not a subject on which it is possible to feel any pride in English law'.

When James Malone, an antiques dealer, discovered that the police had been having his private telephone calls monitored he asked the High Court to declare that such 'tapping' had violated Article 8 of the European Convention not then transformed into English law.

Sir Robert Megarry VC went on to dismiss Mr Malone's claim for such declaration. The court held that this Article did not confer any direct right on the citizen. At that time the courts had to bear in mind that the Convention did not actually form part of English law and the courts were limited in the inquiries they could make into such complaints. In the words of Sir Robert Megarry VC:

> The United Kingdom, as a High Contracting Party which ratified the convention on 8 March 1951, has thus long been under an obligation to secure these rights and freedoms to everyone. That obligation, however, is an obligation under a treaty which is not justiciable in the courts of this country. Whether that obligation has been carried out is not for me to say. It is, I suppose, possible to contend that the de facto practice in this country sufficiently secures these rights and freedoms, without legislation for the purpose being needed. It

is also plainly possible to contend that, among other things, the existing safeguards against unbridled telephone tapping, being merely administrative in nature and not imposed by law, fall far short of any rights and freedoms 'secure' to anyone. However, as I have said, that is not for me to decide. All that I do is to hold that the Convention does not, as a matter of English law, confer any direct rights on the plaintiff that he can enforce in the English courts.

The judge went on to comment that the whole subject of telephone tapping cried out for legislation. Some attempt to heed that cry was made in the Interception of Communications Act 1985 which offered some, but only limited, reassurance to the citizen whose telephone calls were being monitored. The substance of the legislation is now re-enacted in the Regulation of Investigatory Powers Act 2000 which, by Section 1 makes it an offence to intercept a communication intentionally in the course of its transmission by post or by means of a public telecommunication system. The Act provides for a penalty of two years' imprisonment for such offences.

The Act, nevertheless, envisages that telephone tapping may be authorised. Section 2 empowers the Secretary of State to grant a warrant requiring another to intercept telephone or postal communications and pass them (or a record of them) to interested parties, such as the Customs or the police, through the National Intelligence Services' so-called 'Tinkerbel Unit' (from 'bell', a slang term for telephone and 'tinker', meaning to meddle with). Such intrusion by the State is said to be required:

1. in the interests of national security; or
2. for the purpose of preventing or detecting serious crime; or
3. for the purpose of safeguarding the economic well-being of the United Kingdom.

Recently, the European Parliament (see Unit 1.8) announced an inquiry into a worldwide monitoring set-up known as 'Echelon', whose listening stations are said to be able to process millions of messages an hour and to have listened in on calls, according to reports of former employees, between revolutionary figures such as the Pope and Mother Teresa of Calcutta as well as charities such as Amnesty International and Christian Aid.

People who suspect that their communications are being intercepted may apply to a tribunal of lawyers set up under the Act. Unless the request is frivolous or vexatious this tribunal will investigate the complaint and report on it both to the individual and also to the Prime Minister. One unusual aspect of the statute, however, is that there is no appeal from the decision of the tribunal, whose conduct cannot be questioned in the courts and whose activities, therefore, are 'judge-proof'. There are further exceptional restrictions on the conduct of court proceedings for the Act provides that, in court, no questions may be put to those persons specified in the Act which would tend to suggest that an offence under section 1 has been committed. Such restriction is ironic for it was only inspection of a police officer's notebook in a criminal trial involving James Malone which revealed that his telephone was being tapped in the first place.

The Interception of Communications Act 1985 did not apply to private telephone networks or to the interception of calls made internationally or upon cordless telephones. The Police Act 1997 further extends the power of the police to bug telephones where it is said that they believe that such interference is likely to be of substantial value in the prevention or detection of serious crime and that other means do not permit the obtaining of such evidence. The already modest level of protection for the individual citizen's privacy was further diminished by section 92 of the Police Act 1997 which effectively represents a licence to the police to commit trespass and criminal damage in order to bug homes, offices or cars where a senior police officer grants such authorisation. Those whose homes have been broken into or damaged will be without remedy as, under section 92:

> No entry on or interference with property or with wireless telegraphy shall be unlawful if it is authorised by an authorisation having effect under this Part.

The police were again eavesdropping in *R* v. *Khan* 1996. On this occasion, however, the surveillance had been by means of a listening device planted in the suspect's home and not, as with Malone, by tapping the telephone. Sultan Khan appealed against his conviction on drugs offences, contending that the evidence of the tape recording should not have been allowed because it involved the commission of trespass by the police and was a breach of his rights to respect for private and family life accorded by the European Convention on Human Rights. In rejecting the appeal the House of Lords adhered firmly to the traditional rule of English law that relevant evidence was admissible in a criminal trial even if it had been obtained improperly or unlawfully.

Even so, concern was expressed at the lack of any statutory control over such use of surveillance devices by the police. Such regulation was subsequently included in the Police Act 1997 which specifically provides for covert entry upon and interference with property by the police, Customs and others. Some four years after the House of Lords dismissed Khan's appeal the European Court of Human Rights unanimously held that his right to respect for private and family life, as guaranteed by Article 8 of the European Convention, had been violated. So, too, in *Khan* v. *United Kingdom* 2000 the European Court found that there had been a breach of Article 13 of the Convention. The relevant Article provides:

> Everyone whose rights and freedoms ... are violated shall have an effective remedy before a national authority notwithstanding that the violation has been committed by persons acting in an official capacity.

Such Article was found to have been breached on the ground that the English courts should have taken into account the fact that the evidence obtained by the secret listening device had been obtained in breach of the Convention.

The growth of the cellular telephone market has made it increasingly easy for others to eavesdrop on supposedly private telephone calls. In 1992–3 some conversations in particular attracted much attention in the press with the publication of the so-called 'Squidgy' and 'Camillagate' tapes, said to be recordings of telephone conversations of members of the Royal Family. This sort of intrusion into that family's privacy followed earlier publication of photographs of the Duchess of York sunbathing nude. Over the same months various politicians such as Paddy Ashdown, Virginia Bottomley and, most ironically, David Mellor, also found themselves under sustained public scrutiny of their private lives. Such events provided the backcloth for the publication in January 1993 of the Calcutt Report. Ironically, this Report by Sir David Calcutt QC entitled *Review of Press Self-Regulation* had been commissioned by the then Heritage Secretary, David Mellor, at a time when the minister warned the press (as if they had never heard the warning before) that they were 'drinking in the last-chance saloon' and faced statutory control. The Calcutt Report concluded that self-regulation of the press had failed to curb the wilder excesses of some newspapers. Calcutt recommended the creation of new criminal offences which would outlaw any unauthorised entry onto private property and would further outlaw telephone tapping. These restrictions would apply to the press rather than to individuals. The newspaper or magazine concerned should then be able to rely upon the defence that such an act was carried out to counter anti-social conduct or crime, to prevent the public being misled by an individual or to protect public health and safety. The High Court should have power to grant injunctions restraining publications of photographs or recordings illegally obtained. The Report also recommended the creation of a new tort of infringement of privacy. This was in marked contrast to the Report in 1972 of the Younger Committee which had rejected the introduction of the general right to privacy and instead concluded that:

> the best way to ensure regard for privacy is to provide specific and effective sanctions against clearly defined activities which unreasonably frustrate the individual in his search for privacy.

Unsurprisingly, the Report received a mixed reception. The press was hostile to the Report and complained that it represented a draconian attempt to gag the British press. Lawyers have criticised the Report for its failure to balance the proposed new offences with any corresponding law to protect freedom of expression. Others have condemned the proposals as being little more than a shield for the rich and powerful which would prevent disclosure of cant or corruption. Investigative journalism, such as that of television presenter Roger Cook, would no longer be able to confront tricksters and fraudsters as they collected their morning milk or to pursue that sort of investigation which has so often uncovered serious criminal activity. Others would say that the proposals do not go far enough and in particular wholly fail to tackle the squalid 'kiss and tell' disclosures made by discarded mistresses as, of course, unprompted by any payments, they publicly profess their love for some public figure.

One public figure who, at different times, received both welcome and unwelcome attention from the press was the late Princess of Wales who featured prominently in the *Sunday Mirror* when in 1983 it published photographs taken secretly by the manager of a gym showing Diana at exercise. Was this really 'in the public interest' or merely 'of public interest'? On the one hand, this gym was open to anyone willing to pay a subscription; on the other, did not this manager have a duty to respect his patrons' right to privacy? This issue was all too similar to the thoroughly distasteful way in which the *Sunday Sport* had photographed the *Allo! Allo* actor, Gorden Kaye, when seriously ill in hospital. In *Kaye* v. *Robertson* 1991 the Court of Appeal needed to say it only once to underline the impotence of English law to restrain this sort of gross intrusion into the private suffering of a public person. Whether the later claim against the *Sunday Mirror* would have advanced the claimed rights of the citizen for protection against this sort of press intrusion must remain a matter for speculation as the Princess's claim was settled without a hearing.

In a Consultation Paper published in the summer of 1993 the government proposed that a right to privacy should be recognised in law. Matters such as a person's health, communications, family and relationships would all enjoy a 'right to be free from harassment or molestation'. Those who could show that they had suffered the sort of substantial distress that a person of ordinary sensibilities would have suffered would be able to claim damages up to £10,000. Defences to such actions include consent, lawful authority, privilege and intrusion in the public interest. Such proposed recourse to the courts therefore differed from the recommendation of the Calcutt Report which had earlier recommended the creation of a complaints tribunal. In contemplating that prospect the editor of *The Sun* had been characteristically forthright:

> *I'm not going to have some clapped-out judge and two busybodies deciding what our readers want to read.*

One member of the government who would have had access to such report was Jonathan Aitken, later sent to prison after his conviction for conspiracy to pervert the course of justice in his libel action against the *Guardian* newspaper. In his subsequent bankruptcy the trustee in bankruptcy was keen to sell Aitken's private correspondence in which he expected much press interest and also some money which could be applied towards payment of Aitken's debts. Although the decision in *Haig* v. *Aitken* 2000 was reached on the basis of the provisions in the Insolvency Act 1986 argument had also been addressed upon Article 8 and the judge was also clearly of the mind that such a breach was strongly arguable in the case.

It was, therefore, somewhat ironic that, in the same month that the Human Rights Act 1998 was brought into force in October 2000, the new Regulation of Investigatory Powers Act 2000 also came into force. The latter statute erodes the protection afforded by the former. This Act repeals much earlier legislation and brings a wider range of communication under control. For example, the Act deals more specifically with communication other than through the public telecommunications system (now also more widely defined) by including mobile telephones and pagers. In particular, the Act is already best known for authorising the reading of employees' e-mails but, on a broader scale, the Act makes further wide-ranging provision for the grant of warrants for interception of communications.

Article 11 provides:

> Everyone has the right to freedom of peaceful assembly and to freedom of association with others, including the right to form and join trade unions for the protection of his interests.

The civil insurrection caused by riots in the early 1980s in Brixton, Toxteth and later Tottenham's Broadwater Farm Estate was evidence of the need to revise the law on public order (which in practice usually means public disorder). A report prepared by Lord Scarman after the Brixton riots of 1982 led to the Public Order Act 1986.

The Act replaces old common-law offences such as riot and affray with specific new statutory offences to curb violent public disorder.

The new statutory offence of riot is committed where twelve or more persons who are present together use or threaten unlawful violence for a common purpose and where their conduct (taken together) is such as could cause a person of reasonable firmness present at the scene to fear for his personal safety. In this definition Parliament has blended together most of the ingredients of the old offence found necessary by the courts over many years. The new statutory offence provides for a maximum sentence of an unlimited fine and ten years' imprisonment. This is obviously a major offence against public order and any prosecution will require the consent of the Director of Public Prosecutions (see Unit 3.7).

The old common-law offence, however, was committed where only three or more persons were present in some tumultuous disturbance. This lower number is preserved in the new lesser statutory offence of violent disorder. Such offence carries a maximum sentence in the Crown Court of five years' imprisonment or, as always, a maximum in magistrates' courts for six months' imprisonment. The other ingredients required to be proved are those also required in the principal offence of riot.

Numbers of likely defendants continue to dwindle as the Act progresses and in section 3 Parliament has preserved the old offence of affray but, as with all these offences, puts it on a purely statutory basis. The offence of affray (from the old French word *effrayer* – 'to frighten') is committed where a person uses or threatens unlawful violence towards another and where his or her conduct is such as would cause a person of reasonable firmness present at the scene to fear for his or her personal safety. As with the other new offences there is no need at all for this person of reasonable firmness (the same sort of person who travels on the Clapham omnibus) actually to be present at the scene of such violence.

Sections 4 and 5 make it an offence to use 'threatening, abusive or insulting words or behaviour' or to display 'any written sign or other visible representation' which is threatening, abusive or insulting. These sections obviously cover demonstrations where controversial views are promulgated either in churlish chant or provoking placard. These offences are similar to those created by the Public Order Act 1936 which have long provided the police with a wide range of reasons for arrest when a citizen's natural inhibitions have worn thin. The Public Order Act 1986, however, specifically emphasises that offences under sections 4 and 5 are only committed where the person responsible either intends his words or behaviour to be insulting or is aware that they may be threatening, abusive or insulting. While the intake of alcohol may often lend added colour to personal expression the 1986 Act specifically rules out self-induced intoxication (see Unit 3.4e)) as a defence.

The Act recognises that prevention may be better than cure. Freedom to demonstrate may be an obvious public manifestation of the citizen's right to voice complaint or dissent but its date, time and place are all subject to control. Anyone planning to hold a public procession intended to demonstrate support for or opposition to the views or actions of others, or seeking to publicise any cause or commemorate some event, must give notice to the local police. Details of date, time and route and the identity of the organisers must be given not less than six clear days before the event to the police in the area where the procession will start. Failure to give such notice (or then to depart either from the route or timing) would normally make the organisers guilty of an offence for which they may be fined. Once the details are known, a senior police officer may lay down conditions as to time or place if he is fearful that the procession would result in serious public disorder, serious damage to property or serious disruption to the life of the community. Such control would be used to avoid the sort of violent disruption experienced in the mid-1970s when the National Front paraded through areas of London with a high immigrant population. In cases where the police believe that even their powers to lay down conditions as to route and time will be insufficient they may apply to the local council for an order banning public processions for up to three months. The police in London have special powers so that the Commissioner may, with the Home Secretary's approval, prohibit all public processions for up to three months. The conduct of the Metropolitan Police in its unlawful suppression of legitimate protest was the subject of much criticism and subsequent litigation in 2000 after the police had repressed lawful protest by Tibetans against China's lamentable record of human rights and political repression during the ceremonial visit of Jiang Zemin, the Chinese president, who, perhaps, would have been made to feel quite at home by what he saw or, preferably for his hosts, did not see.

The Public Order Act 1986 reached the statute book at a time when many Cabinet Ministers had spoken out against the mayhem that occurred at so many football matches. The Act tackles this problem by adding to the sentences open to the courts dealing with a hooligan convicted of violence at the match or on his way to or from it. The courts may make an exclusion order prohibiting the offender from entering any football ground prescribed by the court for any given period of not less than three months. A police officer may arrest anyone attending a football match in breach of such order and place the offender not merely offside but actually outside. The recent Football (Offences and Disorder) Act 1999 strengthens these powers so that the courts may even make orders preventing such offenders from travelling abroad so as to ensure that one particularly unwelcome British export will not leave the docks – or at least not those at the ports.

Although admission to the universities is traditionally less easy than admittance to football stadia, recent years have shown a sad lack of tolerance quench some students' supposed thirst for knowledge. The intellectual thrust of reasoned, articulate debate was replaced by less cerebral attempts to shout down speakers, whether lecturers or visitors, whose views were perceived as being inimical to political preconception. The Education (No. 2) Act 1986 seeks to deal with this problem by imposing on the academic authorities a duty to take steps to ensure that freedom of speech within the law is secured for members, students and employees of the establishment and for visiting speakers. If implemented properly this recent provision should help to ensure, as Disraeli saw it a century ago, that a university should be a 'place of light, of liberty and of learning'.

Since the days of Disraeli, however, successive governments have increasingly eroded individual freedom. The citizen has only to look at the so-called 'ring of steel' in the City of London to see how a supposedly short-term response to sudden emergency has not only become a permanent barrier to access to the capital city but has even been extended so that motorists face being stopped and searched as they drive home, to realise that freedom, once removed by the State, is not lightly restored. The year 1984 came and went without the fulfilment of Orwell's prophecy but experiences suffered by those countries affected by military takeover and other forms of high-handed control show just how delicate a flower individual freedom can be. Such freedoms as modern British society still enjoys have their roots in history and this country's traditional distaste for State control.

Those who have grown accustomed to a steady erosion of individual freedom will have rejoiced not only at the decision of the House of Lords in *DPP* v. *Jones* 1999 (see Unit 6.6a)) but more especially perhaps at the stance of the Divisional Court in *Redmond-Bate* v. *DPP* 1999 when the court had to consider the conviction by local magistrates of a Christian fundamentalist arrested at the steps of a cathedral for a supposed breach of the peace and later convicted of obstructing the police. In quashing the magistrates' conviction (which seems wholly incompatible with the values of the Convention which recognises freedom of thought, conscience and religion along with freedom of expression) Sedley LJ was robust in his wish to respect such values:

> *Free speech includes not only the inoffensive but the irritating, the contentious, the eccentric, the heretical, the unwelcome and the provocative provided it does not tend to provoke violence. Freedom only to speak inoffensively is not worth having ... From the condemnation of Socrates to the persecution of modern writers and journalists, our world has seen too many examples of state control of unofficial ideas.*

In this celebrated judgment, Sedley LJ provides comfort to those who see a growing trend of the State to watch over and control the citizen. It is a judgment which carries on the liberal traditions of this country's common law and demonstrates the resolve of the courts and the lawyers to give effect to the words of the nineteenth-century Lord Chief Justice, Lord Ellenborough:

> *The law of England is a law of liberty.*

3.11 Questions

1. Discuss the criminal liability of *A* in the following unrelated circumstances:

   A persuades his eleven-year-old nephew to bring him any unattended bicycles which his nephew may find. *A* resprays bicycles brought to him by his nephew and sells them in his bicycle shop as second-hand models.

   A, the wife of *Y*, steals from her employer because *Y* has threatened that unless she does so he will divorce her.

   A, under threat of harm to his family, helps *X* to plant a bomb in a pub. The bomb explodes and kills several people.

2. a) Define the crime of rape.
   b) Mr *A* has recently given an undertaking to a court not to molest his wife, Mrs *A*. Yesterday he had sexual intercourse with Mrs *A* against her will. What is his criminal liability, if any?
   c) *X* has sexual intercourse with Miss *Z*. She later discovers that *X* was suffering from AIDS, a virulent communicable disease, and she tells you that she would not have consented to sexual intercourse had she known of this. Advise Miss *Z* as to *X*'s liability for rape.

3. Assess the impact of the European Convention on Human Rights on civil liberties in the United Kingdom.

4. For what reasons are custodial sentences given? Discuss the effectiveness of such sentences.

5. *A* is getting married and the previous day goes drinking with his friends by way of a celebration. They all get drunk. *A*'s friends take off his clothes and tie him to railings outside a girls' school where he is seen by the girls returning for the afternoon session. A police officer releases him, but *A* is so drunk and confused that he attacks the police officer, knocking off his helmet. To what extent should the criminal law intervene and punish such conduct?

6. Joe misses the last bus home late one night and sets out to walk the five miles to his home. On the way he passes a house with the garage doors open and he enters the garage to see if there is anything worth taking. He notices that the ignition keys have been left in the car which is in the garage. He decides to borrow the car to drive home but after a short distance collides with another car which has been parked on the road without lights. Joe then abandons the car and begins to walk home but is arrested by a police officer who has seen the accident. What interests have been infringed by Joe's actions? With what criminal offences may Joe be charged in the protection of these interests?

7. Prudence is a novelist who has strong views about morality in public life. In order to show up what she believes to be immoral behaviour by politicians, she writes a thinly disguised novel about a well-known politician called Fred Wheeler whom she calls Frank Dealer. Part of the novel contains explicit descriptions of Dealer's behaviour which shows him and other leading politicians, also with slightly altered names, to be men of sadistic and cruel pursuits. Prudence's only aim is to show how she believes Wheeler behaves. The book is seized by the police from many bookshops and Prudence is arrested and charged with publishing an obscene article.

   A meeting is held in a public square to protest at Prudence's arrest. A large number of persons attend and become excited as a result of an inflammatory speech made by Prudence's brother Victor. The police intervene to halt the meeting and arrest Prudence's brother. It later appears that Prudence's telephone has been tapped to obtain information about the meeting and that Victor has had documents seized by the police which have nothing to do with Prudence or the meeting.

Consider what issues for civil liberties are raised by the above facts.

8. Harry and Ian had already had a few drinks in a bar when Harry slipped a tablet of 'powerblast' (a drug which increased feelings of strength and aggression) into Ian's drink whilst he was not looking. Shortly afterwards, John and Karl entered the bar. Ian and John knew each other and some good-natured banter developed, which ended with Ian challenging John to an arm-wrestling contest to which John readily agreed. During the contest, Ian suddenly exerted a great deal of strength, twisting John's arm very awkwardly and severely damaging tendons in John's wrist.

Two days later, Ian's wife, Laura, returned home to find that the message, 'Ian you are scum you will die' had been sprayed on the front door. Subsequently, telephone calls were made at various times during the night, in which no one spoke but screaming could be heard, as if a person was in terrible pain. Laura became anxious and depressed, and imagined she was about to be attacked whenever she was out in the street. On one such occasion, she lashed out with her bag at Martin, a perfectly innocent pedestrian who happened to be walking past her. Martin suffered a heart attack and died. It was later established that Karl was responsible for the message and the telephone calls.

a) Considering any defence(s) that he may raise, discuss Ian's criminal liability for the injury to John.
b) Considering any defence(s) which Laura may raise, discuss her criminal liability for the death of Martin, and discuss the criminal liability of Karl arising out of his actions.
c) How satisfactory is the law on intoxicated defendants?

(AQA)

9. It has been said that justice must not only be done but it must also be seen to be done. What are the reasons for this? When might it be justifiable to exclude the public from the courtroom, or to restrict the reporting of a case by the media?

4 Law of contract

4.1 What is a contract?

Fiona asked Stephen to decorate her house and promised to pay him £1,500 when the job was completed. Stephen accepted and worked hard for two weeks. As he was putting the finishing touches to his labours, Fiona announced that she had not really meant what she had said about the £1,500 and that, in short, Stephen could whistle for his money.

Andrew invited Catherine to dinner at a restaurant. They arranged to meet for drinks at 7.20 but Catherine did not arrive until 8.15.

Common sense dictates that Stephen should be able to get at least some of his money but that Andrew will simply have to learn to live with Catherine's fine disregard for the clock.

A lawyer would differentiate between these two examples by saying that in the first there is a contract but that in the second there is nothing more than an agreement. Every contract involves an agreement but not every agreement amounts to a contract: the element which converts an agreement into a legally enforceable contract is the intention of the parties to enter into legal relations and thereby bind themselves to carry out the agreement.

Of course, if there is a failure by one party to carry out an agreement there may well be a dispute as to whether the parties had intended to enter into legal relations in the first place. To deal with this problem the courts have established certain tests.

Initially, the courts look at the nature of the relationship between the parties. This much is clear from *Rose & Frank Co. v. J. R. Crompton & Bros* 1923, where Scrutton LJ explained:

> Now it is quite possible for parties to come to an agreement by accepting a proposal with the result that the agreement concluded does not give rise to legal relations. The reason of this is that the parties do not intend that their agreement shall give rise to legal relations. This intention may be implied from the subject-matter of the agreement but it may also be expressed by the parties. In social and family relations such an intention is readily implied, while in business matters, the opposite result would ordinarily follow.

So it is that the courts presume that members of a family do not normally intend to be legally bound by their domestic arrangements whereas if two large companies come to some commercial pact they will find it difficult to show that they did not intend to be bound by it.

This principle had already been established by the Court of Appeal in *Balfour* v. *Balfour* 1919, where a husband, who was working abroad, promised to send his wife an allowance of £30 per month. Some time later, when the marriage had deteriorated, the husband neglected to keep up the payments. The wife sued but failed to recover any money because, in the words of Atkin LJ:

> *It is quite common ... that the two spouses should make arrangements between themselves ... by which the husband agrees that he will pay to his wife a certain sum of money. ... To my mind those agreements, or many of them, do not result in contracts at all ... and they are not contracts because the parties did not intend that they should be attended by legal consequences ... Their promises are not sealed with seals and sealing wax.*

This presumption can be rebutted, however, if husband and wife are no longer living happily together. This was the case in *Merritt* v. *Merritt* 1970, where the husband had deserted his wife. He agreed to pay her £40 per month and she, in turn, agreed to discharge their mortgage. In addition, the husband undertook in writing to transfer the house into her name but failed to do so. The Court of Appeal held that the husband's promise could be enforced because, here, there was a contract. Lord Denning MR, referring to earlier cases such as *Balfour*, said:

> *I do not think that those cases have any application here. The parties there were living together in amity. In such cases their domestic arrangements are ordinarily not intended to create legal relations. It is altogether different when the parties are not living together in amity but are separated or about to separate. They then bargain keenly. They do not rely on honourable undertakings. They want everything cut and dried. It may safely be presumed that they intend to create legal relations.*

The same principles govern agreements between parent and child. For example, in *Jones* v. *Padavatton* 1969 a mother informally promised to pay her daughter a monthly allowance if she would come to England to read for the Bar. A dispute over money arose after the daughter had been in England for some time. In the Court of Appeal, Danckwerts LJ held that there had been no contract between mother and daughter:

> *There is no doubt that this case is a most difficult one, but I have reached a conclusion that the present case is one of those family arrangements which depend on the good faith of the promises which are made, and are not intended to be rigid, binding agreements. Balfour v. Balfour was a case of husband and wife, but there is no doubt that the same principles apply to dealings between other relations, such as father and son, and daughter and mother.*

Although, in general, domestic arrangements are not intended to be legally binding, this principle can be rebutted as happened in *Parker* v. *Clark* 1960. An elderly couple (the Clarks) invited a younger couple (the Parkers) to live with them at their house and in return for some domestic help the Clarks promised to leave the Parkers some property in their wills. Unfortunately, difficulties arose between them and the Clarks asked the Parkers to find somewhere else to live.

The Clarks argued that, as in *Balfour* v. *Balfour*, the original agreement had been a purely social or domestic one. However, the judge distinguished the earlier decision and held, on the evidence of the Parkers' moving into the Clarks' house, that an arrangement binding in law had been intended by both sides. The Parkers were accordingly entitled to damages for the loss they had suffered by the Clarks' abrogation of the agreement.

Where there is a commercial element in the agreement it will be difficult to show that no legal relationship had been intended. This line of defence, therefore, failed in the well-known case of *Carlill* v. *Carbolic Smoke Ball Company* 1893.

The company, as its name suggests, sold a medicinal preparation known as the 'carbolic smoke ball'. They claimed that inhaling its fumes would prevent influenza and other colds. The company was so confident in the prophylactic quality of its product that it inserted an advertisement in the *Illustrated London News*:

> £100 reward will be paid by the Carbolic Smoke Company to any person who contracts the increasing epidemic influenza, colds or any disease caused by taking cold after having used the ball three times daily for two weeks according to the printed directions supplied with each ball.

The advertisement went on to say:

> £1,000 is deposited with the Alliance Bank, Regent Street, showing our sincerity in the matter.

The plaintiff bought one of these balls and used it. Unfortunately, it did not do her much good and she still caught a cold. Now she was asking to have her money. The company's argument that there was no binding contract was rejected by the Court of Appeal, which held that the words of the advertisement showed an intention to be legally bound. The court applied an objective test: would the man in the street have thought that the company intended to be legally bound by its promise as set out in the advertisement?

Now she was asking to have her money.

Both the decision in *Carlill* and specifically the words already cited from the judgment of Scrutton LJ in *Rose & Frank Company* v. *J.R. Crompton & Brothers* were considered against the background of the 1970 World Cup in *Esso Petroleum Ltd* v. *Commissioners of Customs and Excise* 1976. The petrol company had devised a scheme to promote its sales by producing millions of coins with a likeness of one of the members of the England Soccer Team. One coin would be given away to every customer who left the forecourt with four gallons of fuel. The eyes of the Customs & Excise fell upon these coins as something else they could tax and they contended that the coins had been 'produced in quantity for general sale' and, as such, were chargeable to Purchase Tax (a not greatly liked forerunner of VAT but with a then more limited application). In determining whether the coins had been produced for sale or by way of gift, the courts had to consider whether either Esso or its football enthusiast drivers intended that there should be a legally binding contract to supply the coins. If the coins were a gift, no tax could be due, but if there existed a legally binding obligation, Esso would end up writing a cheque for about £200,000. In answering the question, the judges looked at the negligible intrinsic value of the coin and the lack of any attempt by Esso even minimally to increase the cost of the petrol. The scheme was viewed as so trivial that the judges could not accept either that Esso intended to create a legal contractual relationship or that their customers could so view it.

Finally, it is to be noted that sometimes the intention to be legally bound is specifically excluded. For example, when parties are negotiating for the sale of a house the prospective purchaser will usually put down a 10 per cent deposit but he will take care to obtain a receipt marked 'subject to contract'. So, if a survey proves unfavourable or if a better property becomes available he is free to withdraw from the sale without incurring any liability. Neither, of course, is the vendor (the seller) bound to sell, as many potential purchasers found out, literally to their cost, in the so-called 'gazumping' scandals seen in the rising property market of recent years.

4.2 How a contract is made: offer and acceptance

Can a shopkeeper refuse to serve you? The answer depends upon an analysis of the essential elements of a contract. One party has to make an offer to the other who, in turn, must accept the offer, so formulating an agreement.

When next you present your groceries at the check-out of the local supermarket you might reflect that, as a matter of law, you are making an offer to buy the contents of the trolley. The extra-polite customer might say: 'I would like to buy these, please', while the regulars will just pile their tins of sealed-in nourishment on to the conveyor belt. The extra-polite customer is making his offer in express terms while the regular shopper's offer will be implied from his conduct.

The important point here is that it is the would-be customer who makes an offer to buy the goods and not the shopkeeper who offers to sell them by stacking them high on the shelves. The shopkeeper may then accept the offer (which he may do by scanning or ringing the price into the till) or he may reject it. In *Pharmaceutical Society of Great Britain* v. *Boots Cash Chemists Limited* 1952 the question arose whether a contract with a self-service store was made when a customer placed a bottle in the wire basket provided or only when the cashier rang up the price. The matter was important because of the statutory requirement that the sale of some medicines must be supervised by a qualified pharmacist.

Lord Goddard CJ was clear that the contract was made only at the check-out:

> ...*in my opinion, the mere fact that a customer picks up a bottle of medicine from the shelves in this case does not amount to an acceptance of an offer to sell. It is an offer by the customer to buy, and there is no sale effected until the buyer's offer to buy is accepted by the acceptance of price.*

As the offer and acceptance, and therefore the contract, were made at the till the statutory requirement had been satisfied.

What then is the position where a shop window is decorated with colourful posters announcing an 'Amazing Offer!!'? The shopkeeper might not thank you for pointing out, albeit quite accurately, that the 'Amazing Offer!!', of which he is so proud, is really, however amazing, in law only an invitation to treat and not an offer at all: it is the would-be customer who makes the offer.

This point was stressed by Lord Parker CJ in *Fisher* v. *Bell* 1960. A police officer saw a flick-knife in Mr Bell's shop window. With the knife was a ticket printed with the words: 'Ejector knife 4/-' (20 pence). The shopkeeper was prosecuted under the Restriction of Offensive Weapons Act 1959, which made it an offence for a person to 'offer for sale or hire' a flick-knife. The Lord Chief Justice was emphatic.

> *It is clear that, according to the ordinary law of contract, the display of an article with a price on it in a shop window is merely an invitation to treat. It is in no sense an offer for sale the acceptance of which constitutes a contract.*

A similar point was raised in another appeal from conviction in a magistrates' court. In *British Car Auctions Ltd* v. *Wright* 1972, the appellants had sold a car which did not comply with the safety regulations: the steering mechanism and one of the tyres were defective. Under the Road Traffic Act 1972 it was unlawful to sell such a car and the appellant auctioneers were convicted of 'offering to sell' such a vehicle. Although the court expressed its regret at doing so, the conviction was quashed.

The Lord Chief Justice, Lord Widgery, was clear about the legal position although, as he said:

> *I confess that, free of authority, I should have thought that the colloquial acceptance of an auctioneer as a person who offers the goods for sale is so strong that the use of a phrase such as 'offer for sale' in a statute of this kind might readily be construed as including the function of the auctioneer when he carries out an auction in the ordinary way. But, of course, as a matter of strict law of contract, forgetting for the moment the colloquial meaning of the phrase 'offer for sale', the auctioneer when he stands on his rostrum does not make an offer to sell the goods on behalf of the vendor; he stands there making an invitation to those present at the auction themselves to make offers to buy. In the strict law of contract there is no doubt whatever that has always been the law, that when an auction sale takes place, the offer comes from the bidder in the body of the hall and the acceptance is communicated by the fall of the auctioneer's hammer. It is technically incorrect to describe an auctioneer as offering the goods for sale for that reason.*

Neither is a statement of price by itself an offer: for example, a greengrocer may tell you the price of his sprouts but that does not mean that he has to sell them to you. This was seen in *Clifton* v. *Palumbo* 1944, where the plaintiff wrote:

> *I am prepared to offer you my Lytham estate for £600,000.*

The Court of Appeal held that this was not an 'offer' in any real sense and that it amounted to no more than a statement of price as a guide to the defendant of the sort of terms on which the plaintiff might agree to sell his estate.

However, the Court of Appeal distinguished that earlier decision in *Bigg* v. *Boyd Gibbins Ltd* 1971, where the plaintiff wrote: 'For a quick sale. I would accept £26,000', to which the defendant replied: 'I accept your offer.' The defendant then refused to go through with the deal. The Court of Appeal held that, on the evidence contained in the letters passing between them, the parties had struck a bargain for the sale and purchase of the property.

Nevertheless, problems of construction do still arise and a so-called 'test case' (where a large number of others are affected as well as the actual parties to the dispute) came before the House of Lords in *Gibson* v. *Manchester City Council* 1979. Ralph Gibson worked in the works department of Manchester City Council and was keen to buy his council house home as soon as the council started to sell to its tenants. He filled

in a form headed 'Application to buy a council house' and signed a declaration that he wished to purchase his council house. The city treasurer
had already written to Mr Gibson indicating that the council (then
under the control of the Conservative Party) 'may be prepared to sell the
house to you at the purchase price of £2,725 less twenty per cent equals
£2,180 (freehold)'. Unfortunately for Mr Gibson, there was a change of
political power after the local council elections and political control
shifted to the Labour Party, who then stopped such council sales. Not
only was Mr Gibson affected but so were some 350 other tenants who
were also trying to buy their homes. The House of Lords held that there
had been no binding contract requiring the council to sell Mr Gibson his
house. The judges said that there had never been an offer capable of
acceptance. The city treasurer's comment that his council 'may be prepared to sell' and his subsequent invitation to Mr Gibson to make an
application to buy were not in law an offer to sell. They were merely an
invitation to treat and so Mr Gibson would have to go on paying rent to
the council.

We are now able to answer the question posed at the start of this
section: can a shopkeeper refuse to serve a customer? It is clear that the
customer may properly be refused service, though not on grounds of
race or creed (under the Race Relations Act 1976) or on grounds of sex
(under the Sex Discrimination Acts 1975 and 1986). Neither will he
have any remedy for his wasted time, travel or effort.

Most offers are either **accepted** or **rejected** but an offer can be
revoked or it may **lapse**. It is easiest to consider the rule concerning each
of these one by one.

An offer may be revoked   A shopper may decide that he would rather buy some peas and not the
tin of beans he has already put into the wire basket. At any time until
the price has been rung up at the check-out he may replace the beans on
the shelf and thereby avoid having to buy them. This is because, as a
matter of law, an offer may be revoked at any time up until the moment
of acceptance.

For example, it is clear from *Payne* v. *Cave* 1789 that a bid at an
auction (which, of course, in law is an offer) may be withdrawn at any
time before the auctioneer brings the hammer down (which is an acceptance). Moreover, the Sale of Goods Act 1979, section 57 specifically
provides:

> A sale by auction is complete when the auctioneer announces
> its completion by the fall of the hammer, or in another cus-
> tomary manner; and until the announcement is made any
> bidder may restrict his bid.

An offeror (the party who makes the offer) can revoke his offer even if
he has promised to leave the offer open for a time. This promise could
only be enforced if a would-be customer had put down a deposit, as, of
course, is usual when buying a house.

Neither does it matter how the offeree (the party receiving the offer)
hears about the revocation. For example, in *Dickinson* v. *Dodds* 1876
Dodds had signed and given to Dickinson a document about the contemplated sale of some property. After his signature Dodds added: 'P.S.

This offer to be left over until Friday 9 o'clock a.m.' On Thursday afternoon Dickinson learned, through a third party, that Dodds was negotiating with someone else. Nevertheless, later that Thursday, Dickinson purported to accept the offer. The Court of Appeal held that the document amounted only to an offer which could be withdrawn at any time before acceptance. A sale to a third party amounted to a revocation of the offer.

An interesting question is raised where, to take an imaginary example, MacStinge offers £100,000 to the first Scotsman to climb Ben Nevis in a kilt. MacPick is 10 feet from the summit when MacStinge shouts out that he is revoking the offer. A strict application of the theory advanced by the courts in the nineteenth century would allow MacStinge to save his money.

Such a problem has yet to come before the courts, but one possible solution might be based on the existence not only of the express offer by MacStinge to pay the money to MacPick but also of a promise implied by the law that for a reasonable time he will not revoke the offer once MacPick has started his climb.

An offer may lapse

An offer will lapse if it is not accepted within a specified time (for example: 'please let me have your answer by next Saturday') or, where no time is specified, when it is not accepted within a reasonable time.

The lapse of an offer was considered in *Ramsgate Hotel Co. Ltd* v. *Montefiore* 1866. Montefiore applied for some shares in the plaintiff company. His application was made on 8 June but it was not until 23 November that the plaintiff company purported to allot the defendant his shares, which Montefiore then refused to take up. It was held that, although no time limit had in fact been specified, the allotment should have been made within a reasonable time and that a wait for more than five months was not reasonable. Accordingly, the offer had lapsed.

It seems likely that, in general, death will cause an offer to lapse with the results that the deceased's personal representatives will not be able to accept any offer on behalf of the estate.

An offer may be rejected

As a shopper presents a packet of sausages at the till, the shopkeeper may quite properly refuse to serve him. In so doing, the shopkeeper (the offeree) has rejected the offer of the would-be customer (the offeror).

In such a situation the rejection is **express**. Rejection of an offer could also be **implied**, where, for instance, there has been a counter-off (as where the parties are haggling over price) or where acceptance has only been conditional (for example, on the arrangement of finance by one of the parties). Such implied rejection arose in *Hyde* v. *Wrench* 1840, where the parties were negotiating for the sale of the defendant's farm. The defendant wanted £1,000; the plaintiff offered £950 but when that proved too low he agreed to pay £1,000. The court held that the plaintiff could not compel the defendant to sell him his farm for £1,000 because, in trying to save £50, he had impliedly rejected the offer originally made.

Nearly a century and a half later the principle was to be applied in *Butler Machine Tool Co. Ltd* v. *Ex-Cell-O Corporation* 1979, a case where, it was said in court, the documents amounted to a 'battle of forms'. In brief, what had happened was that on 23 May 1979 the sellers, Butler's, quoted a price and delivery date on a machine tool. Their quotation contained various conditions in the small print including a price variation clause. Under this clause, the buyers would have to pay the price actually prevailing at the date of delivery which, of course, might be higher than that mentioned in May. On 27 May the buyers, Ex-Cell-O Corporation, placed an order but did so on their own terms and conditions. These were materially different from those of Butler's. On 5 June Butler's acknowledged the order, returning a tear-off acknowledgement with the words: 'We accept your order on the Terms and Conditions stated thereon'. By the time the machine tool was delivered Butler's had put their price up by nearly £3,000. Could they charge this extra sum? Obviously they could if the buyers had accepted the sellers' terms. Equally, the buyers said that the sellers had accepted their order on 5 June on the buyers' terms and, accordingly, no price increase was payable.

The Court of Appeal held that the order from the buyers of 5 June constituted a counter-offer which destroyed the offer made in the sellers' quotation of 27 May. Instead, the sellers had accepted the buyers' terms on 5 June when they acknowledged the order.

Similarly, as in *Northland Airlines Ltd* v. *Dennis Ferranti Meters Ltd* 1970, the insertion of fresh terms will operate as a rejection of an offer. The parties were negotiating the sale of aircraft and exchanged telegrams by which the plaintiff company sought to introduce fresh terms relating to delivery and payment. The defendant company then discovered that a better price could be obtained elsewhere and called the agreement off. The Court of Appeal held that the last telegram was not an acceptance of the offer because of the new terms which it had sought to incorporate into the contract.

An offer may be accepted

When an offeree wishes to accept an offer he or she must unconditionally agree to all the terms of the offer – there must be no 'ifs' or 'buts'. He must also make it clear to the offeror that he accepts the offer: silence is not enough. That quiescence is not acquiescence can be seen from *Felthouse* v. *Bindley* 1862 where the plaintiff wrote to his nephew:

> *If I hear no more about him I shall consider the horse mine at £30 15s.*

The nephew did not answer the letter and the court held that the plaintiff's offer had not been accepted. To decide otherwise would, of course, in effect sanction confiscation under the guise of legitimate contract.

Parliament has acted in an attempt to deflate high-pressure selling techniques where, for example, companies unload their merchandise on naive and often frightened householders who have neither ordered the goods nor have the slightest wish to receive them. The Unsolicited Goods and Services Act 1971 allows the recipient a choice of action. He may simply sit back for six months and, after that time has elapsed, treat the goods as an 'unconditional gift' to himself. Alternatively, he may serve a notice on the person (and it is most likely to be a company) inviting the sender to come and collect the goods. If, after a month, the sender has not bothered to collect them they become the property of the recipient.

The post Certain rules apply to offer and acceptance where the parties have relied on the post or the telephone. Even in the nineteenth century the postal services were not free from flaw and the courts were soon called upon to decide whether or not a contract had in fact been concluded. In order to do this certain rules were evolved which, relying on business convenience rather than on logic, are necessarily artificial.

Generally speaking, an offer is accepted once notice of acceptance is put into the post-box. Of course, the letter must be properly addressed and stamped but, once posted, neither delay nor even non-delivery will invalidate that acceptance. For example, in *Henthorn* v. *Fraser* 1892, Fraser offered to sell some houses to Henthorn who went away. At 3.50 p.m. on the following day he posted to Fraser a letter in which he accepted the offer. By then a letter was already on its way to Henthorn from Fraser revoking the offer. The Court of Appeal held that there was a contract and that it had been made when Henthorn posted his letter of acceptance at 3.50 p.m., because, as Lord Herschell LC said:

> *Where the circumstances are such that it must have been within the contemplation of the parties that, according to the ordinary usages of mankind, the post might be used as a means of communicating the acceptance of an offer, the acceptance is complete as soon as it is posted.*

The rules relating to revocation, however, are different from those of acceptance; although the letter of revocation had already been posted the offer could still be accepted. Revocation is only effective when the letter of revocation arrives.

So, in *Byrne* v. *Van Tienhoven* 1880 the defendant posted a letter containing an offer on 1 October. A week later, he wrote to the plaintiff revoking the offer but on 11 October, before receiving this second letter, the plaintiff accepted the offer. The letter of revocation was not received until 20 October. The court held that there was a contract concluded on 11 October, because revocation, unlike acceptance, actually has to be communicated to the offeree.

Telephone and telex Where two parties are negotiating over the telephone it is vital that the acceptance is heard; if the line goes dead before then, there can be no acceptance.

The same principle can be applied to telex, a system which may appear outdated in days of alternative electronic communication but which enables a message typed by a clerk in one office to be simultaneously and automatically typed out by the machine in another office: the acceptance must be received before the contract can be regarded as having been made. Thus in *Entores Ltd* v. *Miles Far East Corporation* 1955 a company in London was in communication by telex with another in Amsterdam. The English company made an offer, which was accepted by the Amsterdam company by telex which, said Birkett LJ:

> *does not differ in principle from the cases where the parties negotiating a contract were actually in the presence of each other.*

The Court of Appeal was presented with a novel problem for that time: it was necessary to determine the time and place at which the contract was made, whether in the Amsterdam office where the acceptance was expressed, or in the London office where it was received. Denning LJ, as he then was, distinguished contracts made by post when he said:

> My conclusion is, that the rule about instantaneous communications between the parties is different from the rule about the post. The contract is only complete when the acceptance is received by the offeror; and the contract is made at the place where the acceptance is received.

Parker LJ summarised the rules of the telephone and telex when he said:

> Where, however, the parties are in each other's presence or, though separated in space, communication between them is in effect, instantaneous, there is no need for any such rule of convenience. To hold otherwise would leave no room for the operation of the general rule that notification of the acceptance must be received. An acceptor could say: 'I spoke the words of acceptance in your presence, albeit softly, and it matters not that you did not hear me'; or 'I telephoned to you and accepted and it matters not that the telephone went dead and you did not get my message' ... So far as Telex messages are concerned, though the dispatch and receipt of a message is not completely instantaneous, the parties are to all intents and purposes in each other's presence just as if they were in telephonic communication, and I can see no reason for departing from the general rule that there is no binding contract until notice of the acceptance is received by the offeror.

That being so, and since the offer was made by the plaintiffs in London and notification of the acceptance was received by them in London, the contract resulting from that exchange had been made in London.

These principles were approved by the House of Lords in *Brinkibon Ltd* v. *Stahag Stahl GmbH* 1982. The English company was a buyer of steel bars. The company sent a telex from London to Vienna accepting the foreign seller's terms of sale. The contract was never carried out and the buyers (Brinkibon Ltd) sued for breach of contract. It was necessary to decide where the contract had been made. The House of Lords confirmed the old rule about telex communications. As before, where there was instantaneous communication between the offeror and the offeree the contract was made where and when the acceptance of the offer had been received by the offeror. It followed, on these facts, that the contract had been made in Austria. The House of Lords, evidently no novices at the marvels of late twentieth-century communications, did bear in mind the possibility of delays in the telex reaching the intended recipient because, for example, the message is sent at night or out of office hours or, for some other reason, the machine is unattended. In those circumstances, said Lord Wilberforce:

> No universal rule can cover all such cases; they must be resolved by reference to the intentions of the parties, by sound business practice and in some cases by judgment where the risks should lie.

4.3 Consideration

Consideration is generally thought of as a quality which parents try to imbue in their children. It has the connotation of being kind to dumb animals and of seeing old ladies across busy roads.

In law, consideration consists of some gain to one person or some loss to the other. For instance, when a customer buys some sausages in a supermarket, the consideration is the gain to the shop of the customer's money and also the customer's prospect of having something to eat when he arrives home.

Equally, each side has parted with something – the customer with his cash and the shopkeeper a kilo of his best chipolatas. More than this, consideration is that vital element which imprints on an agreement the willingness of the courts to give effect to the intention of the parties. Without that consideration, what the parties promised remains a *nudum pactum* ('a bare promise') which cannot be enforced through the courts.

The classic definition of consideration is that of Lush J in *Currie* v. *Misa* 1875, when he said:

> *A valuable consideration, in the sense of the law, may consist either in some right, interest, profit or benefit accruing to the one party, or some forbearance, detriment, loss or responsibility given, suffered or undertaken by the other.*

A more recent, briefer and probably simpler definition is that of Sir Frederick Pollock which was approved by the House of Lords in *Dunlop* v. *Selfridge & Co. Ltd* 1915 as being:

> *an act of forbearance of one party or the promise thereof is the price for which the promise of the other is bought and the promise thus given for value is enforceable.*

Over the years, but again principally in the nineteenth century, the courts have laid down various tests for an alleged act of consideration. It is undeniable that, as with the rules of offer and acceptance, the rules of good consideration are somewhat artificial. The most important are set out below.

Consideration must be real Essentially, this simply means that consideration must have some value. It follows that anyone seeking to rely on an alleged act of consideration must prove that he did something *over and above* what he was already obliged to do. The point is clear from the decision of Lord Ellenborough in *Stilk* v. *Myrick* 1809. A sailor had agreed to join the crew of a ship sailing from London to the Baltic and back again. On the way, two other sailors deserted and when the master was unable to replace them he promised to divide the deserters' wages among the rest of the crew. The master did not pay out the extra money and the sailor sued him.

However, he failed, as the court held that the matelot had already agreed to do all that he in fact did. After all, said Lord Ellenborough, if any part of the crew had died would not the remainder have been forced to work the ship home? If those deaths would have left them liable to do the whole work without any extra pay why should not desertion also require the crew to do the same? The only way, said the judge, that the master would have to pay the crew extra, would have been if the voyage had ended: in that case the sailors would have been free to make a fresh bargain.

That point was successfully taken by another sailor in *Hartley* v. *Ponsonby* 1857 after a voyage from Liverpool to Australia. Again, the ship had become short-handed after arrival in port and the captain was unable to recruit any new crew. The difference in this case was that the crew was so depleted that it had become dangerous to set sail. The defendant, the captain, promised the remaining members of the crew an extra £40 if they would take the ship on to Bombay.

Following Myrick's example, Ponsonby refused to pay the extra money but enjoyed little sympathy from Lord Campbell CJ, who took the view that the voyage involved a risk to life which excused the crew from going on to Bombay. On that basis, they had been in a position to dictate fresh terms to their captain by which he would be bound.

Nearly 200 years later this decision was approved by the Court of Appeal in *Williams* v. *Roffey Brothers* 1990, where the defendant builders had engaged the plaintiff as a sub-contractor to carry out carpentry work on some new flats. The builders would have been liable to pay heavy damages under a penalty clause if the flats were not ready on time. They promised to pay £575 extra per flat if the plaintiff finished work on time. The builders failed to pay and argued that the plaintiff had not provided good consideration as he was only carrying out an existing contractual obligation. However, the argument failed as the Court of Appeal held that the defendant builders had secured a practical advantage as they had avoided liability under the penalty clause.

A duty may, of course, be imposed by the law from which persons may not escape, such as a duty to attend court when ordered to do so. This was the case in *Collins* v. *Godefroy* 1831, where the plaintiff had been subpoenaed to give evidence. A **subpoena** is an order of the court requiring a person to attend court to give evidence: he may be punished if he does not turn up because, as the Latin implies, he will be under (*sub*) a penalty (*poena*) if he fails to attend. Collins attended court for six days and sought to charge Godefroy for his time and trouble. However, he went without his money because the court held that there had been no consideration: the plaintiff did only what he had been obliged to do. Lord Tenterden explained the principle:

> *If it be a duty imposed by law upon a party regularly subpoenaed to attend from time to time to give his evidence, then a promise to give him any remuneration for loss of time incurred in such attendance is a promise without consideration.*

On the other hand, the dangers of exaggerating another's duty were brought home to the owners of a colliery in *Glasbrook Brothers* v. *Glamorgan County Council* 1925. There was 'trouble at t' pit'; the colliery was being picketed and ugly scenes were developing. The owners' manager asked for police protection. He took the view that the only way to look after the colliery properly was to billet a police force at the colliery itself. The local police superintendent refused to arrange this unless the colliery paid for the police: all he would agree to was the provision of a mobile force. The manager agreed to the superintendent's terms but then refused to pay up. The county council sued for £2,000, which was the cost of providing the police protection. The colliery owners refused to pay and counterclaimed for £1,330, the cost of housing and feeding the police officers who had been provided. They argued that there had been no consideration for the manager's promise to pay – after all it was the council's duty to them as ratepayers to provide a police force to protect life, limb and property. The question, then, for the House of Lords to decide was how far this duty went.

The House of Lords held that although the police were bound to provide sufficient protection to life and property without payment, an individual must pay for protection or assistance outside the scope of the police's public duty. In the words of Viscount Finlay:

> If a particular person gets special police protection in a particular form on his promise to pay for it, he is bound by his contract legally as well as morally.

This reasoning was recently applied in *Harris* v. *Sheffield United Football Club* 1987 when the provision of police officers inside the football ground to maintain order at weekend matches was held to have gone beyond the general duty of the police to enforce the law. The club was accordingly required to pay for these 'special police services'.

Consideration must move between promisor and promisee

Basically, this means that if Tom sells Dick a kilo of beef sausages which turn out to be mouldy, Harry, who was not a party to the contract, cannot do anything about it. This principle is closely related to the doctrine of privity of contract which is examined in Unit 4.14. The implication of Harry being poisoned by the beef sausages is a matter not of contract but of tort and is looked at in Unit 6.3.

The principle is an ancient one and was looked at in *Price* v. *Easton* 1833. William Price owed John Price £13 and agreed to work for Mr Easton on the understanding that Easton would pay off his debt on his behalf. Although William did work for Easton, John Price never got his money. Price, however, was unable to proceed against Easton because no consideration had passed between them and no contract could be held to have bound them; the court said that no privity could be shown between the plaintiff and the defendant.

Lord Denman CJ explained the need for consideration to pass between promisor and promisee when he said:

> I think the declaration cannot be supported, as it does not show any consideration for the promise moving from the plaintiff to the defendant.

Consideration must not be illegal

The whole topic of illegality in contracts is looked at in detail in Unit 4.12.

Consideration need not be adequate

Although consideration must be real (which means that it must have some value) English law has traditionally been anxious to allow parties to strike whatever bargain they choose. Of course, any extreme price may well indicate some form of fraud or oppression (see Unit 4.10) but, unless some vitiating factor is proved, the contract will remain good and one which the courts will recognise. So, if Edward buys a house for £250,000 on Monday and on Tuesday agrees to sell it to Timothy for £5,000, Tuesday's low price is no reason for setting the contract aside. Indeed, in 2000 the German car-makers BMW sold the entire Rover group for the sum of £10, rather less, in fact, than the cost of air-conditioning or even a car radio in one of their older models.

The irrelevance of a realistic market price was emphasised by the House of Lords in *Chappell & Co. Ltd* v. *Nestlé Co. Ltd* 1959.

Nestlé, the chocolate manufacturers, were anxious to advertise their products. They did this by selling copies of a record called *Rockin' Shoes* for 1/6d (7½ pence) on receipt also of three wrappers from their chocolate bars. In doing so, however, they upset Chappell & Co., who owned the copyright of the record and were, therefore, entitled to a royalty. Nestlé then offered Chappell a percentage of the 1/6d but Chappell maintained that the money was only part of the consideration and that their royalties should, accordingly, be more. They argued that the wrappers, which Nestlé only threw away, were also part of the consideration. The House of Lords favoured their argument. The reason for their decision was neatly put by Lord Somervell:

> *I think that they are part of the consideration. It is said that when received, the wrappers are of no value to the respondents, the Nestlé Co. Ltd. This I would have thought to be irrelevant. A contracting party can stipulate for what consideration he chooses. A peppercorn does not cease to be good consideration if it is established that the promisee does not like pepper and will throw away the corn. As the whole object of selling the record, if it was a sale, was to increase the sale of chocolate, it seems to be wrong not to treat the stipulated evidence of such sales as part of the consideration.*

Consideration must not be past

In *Roscorla* v. *Thomas* 1842, for example, the plaintiff bought a horse from the defendant. After the money had been handed over Thomas said to Roscorla 'that the horse ... was sound in wind and limb, perfect in vision and free from vice'. The horse was, in fact, particularly vicious and the plaintiff sued for breach of this term. However, the court held that Thomas's promise could not be enforced because the assurance had been given only after the sale had been completed.

Lord Denman CJ emphasised the general rule that:

> *...it may be taken as a general rule subject to exceptions not applicable to this case that the promise must be co-extensive with the consideration.*

... particularly vicious ...

The artificial nature of the rule surrounding this doctrine has long attracted criticism and various attempts at reform have been made from Lord Mansfield in the eighteenth century to the report of the Law Reform Committee in 1937. In its sixth interim report the Committee put forward its proposals 'to cut away those difficulties of the doctrine of consideration' and, among other measures, recommended the abolition of the rules that past consideration is no consideration. After all, said the Committee, the fact that the promisor had already received consideration for his promise before he made it, far from enabling him to break his promise, seemed rather to form an additional reason for making him keep it. Other tests of ascertaining the parties' intentions have also been advanced ranging from the reduction of the contract to writing to straightforward reliance by the promisee.

Over sixty years have elapsed since that investigation. Clearly, too much water has flowed under the bridge since then for any wholesale introduction of those recommendations. It is not inconceivable, however, now that national law is subordinate to that of the EC that a fresh impetus might be given to rationalising the doctrine. English law's criterion for distinguishing enforceable contracts from bare promises might then bear more resemblance to that adopted long ago by the continental jurists such as, for example, in the French *Code Civile*, which defines a contract as:

> an agreement by which one or several persons bind themselves in favour of one or several other persons, to give, or to do, or not to do, something.

4.4 Capacity

Anyone under the age of eighteen years who has tried to buy a car, open a bank account or obtain any form of credit will almost certainly have found it a difficult business. This is because any person under eighteen is in law an **infant** or a **minor**, and, as such, is protected by the law against himself and his inexperience. In terms of the law of contract, he does not yet enjoy full **capacity**.

Some contracts made by minors can, however, be binding. Some will be void and others voidable. A contract which is **void** is one which is treated by the law as never having existed: it follows that neither side has acquired any rights or liabilities under it. A contract which is **voidable** is something less insubstantial. It means a contract from which one or other of the parties can choose to withdraw but which is otherwise binding. In the context of contracts made by minors it means an agreement that will develop into a binding contract after a reasonable time unless the minor has taken steps to repudiate (avoid) the contract either before his eighteenth birthday or shortly afterwards. As Lord Watson explained in *Edwards* v. *Carter* 1893, when the House of Lords held four years to be too long a delay to allow repudiation:

> *The law gives this minor the privilege of repudiating the obligations which he had undertaken during his minority within a reasonable time after he comes of age. It laid not obligations upon him – it merely conferred upon him a privilege of which he might or might not avail himself, as he chose. If he chooses to be inactive, his opportunity passes away; if he chooses to be active the law comes to his assistance.*

For example, the lease of a flat is binding upon a minor (which means that he will have to pay the rent for the period agreed) unless he repudiates it within a reasonable time after attaining his majority.

Over a hundred years ago Parliament intervened to protect minors by passing the Infants' Relief Act 1874. Section 1 of that Act provides that

> ...all contracts entered into by infants for the repayment of money lent or to be lent, or for goods supplied or to be supplied (other than contracts for necessaries) and all accounts stated with infants, shall be absolutely void.

This legislation means that if a sixteen-year-old buys goods (or borrows money to buy those goods) which he or she does not really need, the law will treat that contract as never having been made. This will be so even where the minor has lied about his age. In *Leslie* v. *Sheill* 1914, for instance, the infant defendant had lied about his age to the plaintiffs, who were money-lenders, and in this way the money-lenders were fraudulently induced to advance him £400. When the money-lenders wanted their pound of flesh, the infant refused and raised the defence of infancy. The Court of Appeal upheld the infant's defence, saying that there was no liability on the defendant to repay the money.

The corollary of this was that anyone who had guaranteed an infant's contract could not be compelled to honour that guarantee, as a bank discovered literally to its cost in *Coutts & Co.* v. *Browne-Lecky* 1946.

In this claim, the guarantor had undertaken to pay off the infant's overdraft if he himself would not do so but the court would not enforce the payment.

Parliament further reinforced this protection by passing the Betting and Loans (Infants) Act 1892 which provided that if an adult agrees to pay back money which he had borrowed when an infant, that agreement cannot be enforced: under the Act it is 'absolutely void'.

The position today, however, could well be different since the advent of the Minors' Contracts Act 1987, another statute to be based on recommendations made by the Law Commission to remedy the weaknesses of outdated nineteenth-century legislation. The position now is that, after attaining the age of majority, a young person has the option, if he or she so wishes, of ratifying contracts which would otherwise be unenforceable against him. Also since the Act came into force it is possible for a guarantee given in respect of a minor's contract (for example, as a guarantee for a loan) to be enforced against the guarantor even when the main contract (for the repayment of the loan) cannot be enforced against the lucky minor.

At first glance, therefore, this unit might appeal to anyone under eighteen anxious to dress in designer labels, holiday in the sun, eat cordon bleu meals, drink fine wine and drive fast cars all at another's expense. He would, however, do well to look again at the provisions of the Theft Act 1968 relating to obtaining property by deception (see Unit 3.6f)) and, further, to note well the exception in the 1874 Act relating to **necessaries**.

No definitive list can be compiled of what is 'necessary'. Some statutory assistance is afforded by section 3 of the Sale of Goods Act 1979, which provides:

> 'necessaries' means goods suitable to the condition of life of the minor or other person concerned and to his actual requirements at the time of the sale and delivery.

The authorities show that the courts will decide what is necessary to a minor by looking not only at his actual requirements but also at what has rather quaintly been called his 'rank' or his 'station in life'. For example, as long as indecent exposure remains an offence, clothing is obviously necessary to everyone. A minor would thus have to pay for a pair of ordinary shoes if he had nothing else to walk around in but the shopkeeper would find it hard to prove (as he would have to) that the minor really needed his fiftieth pair of fleece-lined alligator-skin slippers.

The relevance of the infant's finances and background was repeatedly emphasised by the nineteenth-century courts. For instance, in *Peters* v. *Fleming* 1840 Baron Parke, in deciding whether an infant undergraduate (whose father was described as 'a gentleman of fortune as well as an MP') had to pay for some gold jewellery, explained the importance of the family resources:

It is perfectly clear, that from the earliest time down to the present, the word 'necessaries' was not confined, in its strict sense, to such articles as were necessary to the support of life, but extended to articles fit to maintain the particular person in the state, station and degree in life in which he is.

The message was underlined by Baron Alderson, who added:

It has been ruled that an infant may be liable for schooling, and if it became a question how much schooling is necessary, then you must inquire what situation in life he is required to fill. A knowledge of the learned languages may be necessary for one, a mere knowledge of reading and writing may be sufficient for another. The real question would be, whether or not what he has contracted for be such as a person in his station and rank of life would require. The articles must be for real use, and such as would be necessary and suitable to the degree and station in life of the infant. The question in these cases is this – Were the articles bought for mere ornament? If so, they cannot be necessaries for anyone. If, however, they are bought for real use then they may be necessaries provided they are suitable to the infant's age, state, and degree.

The strictly ordered structure and somewhat patronising attitude of Victorian society is further reflected in a judgment in *Chapple* v. *Cooper* 1844, again that of Baron Alderson:

. . . the subject-matter and extent of the contract may vary according to the state and condition of the infant himself. His clothes may be fine or coarse according to his rank; his education may vary according to the station he is to fill; and the medicines may depend on the illness with which he is afflicted, and the extent of his probable means when of age. So again, the nature and extent of the attendance will depend on his position in society; and a servant in livery may be allowed to a rich infant, because such attendance is commonly appropriate to persons in his rank of life. But in all these cases, it must first be made out that the class itself is one in which the things furnished are essential to the existence and reasonable advantage and comfort of the infant contractor. Thus, articles of mere luxury are always excluded, though luxurious articles of utility are in some cases allowed . . . In all cases there must be personal advantages from the contract derived to the infant himself.

When trying to recover money from an infant on the grounds that the goods supplied were necessary, a claimant must prove that the infant had actually needed them. So, if the infant had enough of the goods already, the supplier will go away empty-handed. This was why in *Nash* v. *Inman* 1908 the plaintiff, a Savile Row tailor, did not get paid for eleven fancy waistcoats which he had supplied to an infant undergraduate in the days when it was the distinguishing mark of a gentleman not to pay his tailor. The undergraduate's father (who was an architect with two houses) gave evidence that when his son had gone up to university he had already sufficient clothes. The Court of Appeal held that the plaintiff had to prove not only that the goods supplied were suitable to the condition in life of the infant (hence the relevance of the father's wealth) but also that the infant was not sufficiently supplied with goods of that class at the time he bought them.

The authorities clearly show that education is a 'necessary' – although the level of education must, so to speak, remain a matter of degree. Neither is it confined to formal academic instruction. The prospect of proficiency at billiards was held to be a 'necessary' by the Court of Appeal in *Roberts* v. *Gray* 1913, even if such a skill is traditionally associated with a misspent youth; it was held to be for the benefit of the infant defendant to learn the game which could well lead, even then, to a highly profitable career as a professional billiards player.

The prerequisite of benefit to the infant was emphasised in *De Francesco* v. *Barnum* 1890, litigation which concerned an infant who had been apprenticed to the plaintiff to be taught stage-dancing. The obligations on the parties were by no means equal. The girl could not accept any professional engagement without permission. On the other hand, the plaintiff could put an end to the agreement if the girl was no good or if she broke any of the engagements or in any way misconducted herself. Nor did he have to provide her with any engagements or support her when she was unemployed. The court held that the contract was unenforceable as it was not for the infant's benefit. After reviewing the parties' respective duties, Fry LJ commented:

> *Those are stipulations of an extraordinary and an unusual character, which throw, or appear to throw, an inordinate power into the hands of the master without any correlative obligation on the part of the master. I cannot, therefore, say that on the face of this instrument it appears to be one which the court ought to hold to be for the benefit of the infant.*

It is clear from the decision of the Court of Appeal in *Chaplin* v. *Leslie Frewin (Publishers) Ltd* 1965 that, in examining the question of whether the contract is beneficial, the crucial time to be considered is the date when the contract is made.

An infant does not forfeit the protection of the courts when he enters into a commercial agreement from which he intends to profit. For example, in *Cowern* v. *Nield* 1912 an infant sold some hay and clover to the plaintiff. The clover was so rotten that the plaintiff was entitled to reject it. The court held that, although the contract was of a trading nature, the infant defendant was not bound to hand back the money, as the trading contract did not fall within any exception to the 1874 Act.

The point was emphasised by the Court of Appeal in *Mercantile Union Guarantee Corporation Ltd* v. *Ball* 1937. Ball, an infant, was in business as a haulage contractor. He obtained a lorry on hire-purchase but could not afford to keep up the instalments. The finance company sued for its arrears and Ball raised the defence of infancy. The Court of

Appeal held that, firstly, even though the infant was carrying on a business, the contract could not be enforced as it was not a contract for necessaries. Secondly, said Finlay J:

> *Even if it be assumed, contrary to our view, that the contract is one of the class by which an infant could be bound, we find it quite impossible to differ from his [the judge's] view that a contract for a large and expensive lorry, on onerous hire-purchase terms, was not a contract for the benefit of the infant.*

People contracting with infants will encounter obvious risks even though it may sometimes be possible to award compensation. In *Stocks* v. *Wilson* 1913, for example, the judge held that an infant, who had obtained goods – not 'necessary' goods – by misrepresenting his age and who had later sold them, was accountable for the proceeds of sale. This particular decision, however, rests largely upon the imposition of a trust and the general principle remains today as it was in *Barnes* v. *Toye* 1884, when Lopes J said:

> *A contract by an infant for the supply of goods to him cannot be enforced unless the articles be necessaries, the policy of the law being directed to the protection of infants. In point of fact, a tradesman dealing on credit with an infant does so at his peril, and must lose his money (that is, if the infant does not voluntarily pay him) unless he can prove that the goods supplied were necessaries for the infant according to his station in life.*

4.5 Terms

Dennis goes to a garage showroom and talks to the salesman about a sports car which is on sale. The salesman tells Dennis that it is a 1999 model with only one previous owner – an old lady who never drove faster than 20 mph – that it has never been damaged and that it has covered only 2,000 miles. Dennis is so enthusiastic that he buys the car immediately. Later, he discovers that the car had been manufactured in 1996, its mileage recorder has been 'clocked', it has been frequently and extensively damaged and, in its time, it has been rallied over most of Europe.

Sandra goes to the hairdresser and asks for blonde highlights to be put in her hair. When she emerges from the drier her hair has turned green.

What redress, if any, Dennis or Sandra may have against the garage or the hairdresser will depend on what the terms of the contract in question were, that is to say, those contents of the contract which determine the rights and liabilities of the parties, such as Sandra's obvious right to have her hair blonde rather than green.

In the case of Dennis the terms are said to be express, because he and the garage salesman have expressly discussed the car's qualities – its age and mileage, for instance.

Sandra is unlikely to have discussed the subject of hair colour at any great length but she would still be entitled to rely on terms which will be implied by the law.

For example, in the absence of any express provision as to time the courts will imply into a contract a term that the contract will be performed 'within a reasonable time'. Similarly, the courts will imply terms needed to add 'business efficacy' to a contract. This practice was explained by Lord Wright in *Luxor* v. *Cooper* 1941 when he said:

> ...*there may be cases where obviously some term must be implied if the intention of the parties is not to be defeated, some term of which it can be predicated that 'it goes without saying', some term not expressed, but necessary, to give the transaction such business efficacy as the parties must have intended ... The implication must arise inevitably to give effect to the intention of the parties.*

The concept of the 'officious bystander' was introduced by MacKinnon LJ when, in *Shirlaw* v. *Southern Foundries* 1939, he set out to explain when the courts will imply a term:

> Prima facie *that which in any contract is left to be implied and need not be expressed is something so obvious that it goes without saying. Thus, if while the parties were making their bargain, an officious bystander were to suggest some express provision for it in their agreement they would testily suppress him with a common: 'Oh, of course!' At least it is true, I think, that if a term were never implied by a judge unless it could pass that test he could not be held to be wrong.*

Indeed, such caution was seen in *Lancaster* v. *Bird* 1999 when the Court of Appeal held that, whilst there may be a custom in the construction industry that prices quoted exclude VAT, the officious bystander dealing with a consumer contract would say that it was not the parties' intention that VAT should be paid on top of the price quoted.

The courts must be cautious in their approach to implying additional terms into the contract before them. Other terms may be implied by statute, such as those terms relating to quality and fitness for purpose implied by the Sale of Goods Act 1979 and the Supply of Goods and Services Act 1982 (see Unit 4.6). More recently, the Late Payment of Commercial Debts (Interest) Act 1998 implied into a contract to which it applies (and it certainly does not apply to every contract but only a qualifying debt as defined) a term that the unpaid debt carries simple interest.

Not everything, of course, that is said by the parties before a contract necessarily becomes a term. For example, a tailor may advertise his suits as having the 'millionaire touch'. The tailor simply wishes to advertise the quality of his suits and no one really imagines that the worsted has in fact been caressed by some plutocrat with a seven-figure bank-balance. This sort of advertisement is not a term but is known as a 'mere puff'. Of course, the position was otherwise in *Carlill* v. *Carbolic Smoke Ball Co.* 1893 (see Unit 4.1) because the company's claim that its smoke ball would also cure snoring and hay-fever were definite promises and not just glib advertising banter.

The question whether what was said amounted to a term (by which that party intended to be bound) or was only sales-talk (intended to induce the contract but not intended to be binding) is to be answered by finding out the precise intentions of the parties. Would a reasonable man say that they had intended what they said to give rise to legal obligations? In order to decide this point the court has to examine all the surrounding circumstances leading to the contract and to consider both what was said and what was written. However, some limitation was imposed by the House of Lords in *Prenn* v. *Simmonds* 1971, when their Lordships indicated that although, in construing a written agreement, the court is entitled to take account of the surrounding circumstances and object of that agreement, it ought not to look at the prior negotiations of the parties as an aid to construing the written agreement which later resulted from those negotiations.

Nonetheless, the court was able to consider both oral and written evidence in *Couchman* v. *Hill* 1947, where the plaintiff bought the defendant's heifer at a cattle auction. The heifer was described in the sale catalogue as a 'red and white stirk heifer, unserved'. The sale catalogue also contained the disclaimer that:

> The lots are sold with all faults, imperfections, and errors of description, the auctioneers not being responsible for the correct description, genuineness, or authenticity of, or any fault or defect in any lot, and giving no warranty whatever.

Just before the sale, the plaintiff asked the defendant and the auctioneer whether they could confirm that the heifer was, indeed, 'unserved'. This they both did. However, a couple of months later the heifer died as a result of carrying a calf when she was too young. The plaintiff now claimed damages for the breach of warranty and the problem for the court was, of course, what effect, if any, the catalogue's disclaimer would have. The Court of Appeal held that the conversation between the parties before the sale had priority over the catalogue's disclaimer and that the contract had been made on the basis of the later representation.

In deciding whether what was said amounted to a term the court will apply various tests. The judge will need to know, firstly, what was said or written and, further, whether the other party acted in reliance on those words. What was said must be certain and so meaningless advertising and sales-patter will be ignored. Such words were used in *Nicolene* v. *Simonds* 1953, when the plaintiff wrote to the defendant accepting an offer and said:

> *I assume that we are in agreement that the usual conditions of acceptance apply.*

In fact, there were no such 'usual conditions' in operation between the parties and, after the defendant had failed to deliver the goods, the Court of Appeal had to construe the terms of the agreement. The court held that since there were no 'usual conditions' and, accordingly, nothing to which the clause could apply, it was indeed meaningless and should, therefore, be disregarded. Denning LJ, as he then was, resolved the difficulty in this way:

> *In my opinion, a distinction must be drawn between a clause which is meaningless and a clause which is yet to be agreed. A clause which is meaningless can often be ignored, while still leaving the contract good, whereas a clause which has yet to be agreed may mean that there is no contract at all, because the parties have not agreed on all the essential terms.*

The principle of the meaningless clause was applied twenty years later in *Richards* v. *St Saviours* 1975 when, as the result of a clerical error, the words 'subject to contract' appeared on the written acceptance of a tender for the sale of land. As these words were meaningless (for the contract was clearly made) the court ruled that they should be expunged.

The second kind of clause mentioned by Denning LJ was relevant in *Foley* v. *Classique Coaches* 1934, where the respondent coach company had agreed to buy their petrol from the appellant 'at a price to be agreed by the parties in writing and from time to time'. The Court of Appeal held that, although no price had in fact been agreed upon, there was, nevertheless, a contract to supply petrol at a reasonable price that still had to be agreed between the parties.

Conditions and warranties

Some terms are more important than others. The would-be buyer of a secondhand car may be told that it was last owned by a famous pop-star. He may well never have heard of the pop-star and not like pop-music anyway and so the history of the car's ownership may not interest him at all. The car's age and mileage are his concerns: those are the factors which influence him to complete the purchase.

The law divides terms in 'conditions' and 'warranties'. Whether a term is a condition or a warranty becomes important if something goes wrong so that there is a **breach** (see Unit 4.19) of the contract. A **condition** is the major term and is so important that, if the condition is broken, the injured party may refuse to go on with the contract. A **warranty** is a less vital term. If a warranty is broken, the injured party will still have to go on with the contract but he may be compensated for that breach by an award of damages.

This distinction was codified by the Sale of Goods Act 1979, which provides that a condition is a term which, if broken, 'may give rise to a right to treat the contract as repudiated'. A warranty is defined as a term 'collateral to the main purpose' of the contract and which, if broken, would not allow the injured party to put an end to it but which 'may give rise to a claim for damages'.

The Sale of Goods Act 1979 also helps to determine whether implied terms – such as those relating to title, quiet possession, quality and fitness for purpose – are conditions or warranties. The word used to describe any specific term is by no means conclusive for the Act provides:

> a stipulation may be a condition, though called a warranty in
> the contract.

The courts therefore have to look at all the circumstances surrounding the contract. Another illustration from the world of cattle auctions helps to explain this elasticity of terminology. In *Harling* v. *Eddy* 1951 the defendant had noticed that bidders were being put off buying a heifer because she looked rather unwell. He went on to tell the crowd that there was nothing wrong with her, that he would absolutely guarantee her and, further, that he would be willing to take her back if she proved to be other than as he stated. The plaintiff bought the heifer which died four months later from tuberculosis. The plaintiff now claimed damages but, somewhat predictably, came up against a disclaimer in the sale catalogue:

> No animal, article or thing is sold with a 'warranty' unless
> specially mentioned at the time of offering and no warranty
> so given shall have any legal force or effect unless the terms
> thereof appear on the purchaser's account.

The Court of Appeal rejected this line of defence. The court held that the defendant's statement at the sale amounted not just to warranty but to a condition. The disclaimer related only to a warranty and was, accordingly, of no effect. Sir Raymond Evershed MR explained the decision:

> *It has been said many times . . . that whether any statement is to be regarded as a condition or a warranty must depend on the intention to be properly inferred from the particular statement made. A statement that an animal is sound in every respect will,* prima facie, *be but a warranty, but in this case the learned judge found as a fact that the defendant went further and promised that he would take the animal back if she was no good. . . . The defendant's statement having, therefore, included words to the effect: 'If there is anything wrong I will take it back', seems to me plain that the language he used could not have been intended merely as a warranty, for a warranty would give no right of rejection to the purchaser. The final words involve necessarily a right to the purchaser to reject, that is, to return the animal. They convert the statement, to my mind, from a warranty to a condition.*

The Court of Appeal was again called upon to decide whether a term was a condition or warranty in *Wickman Ltd* v. *L. Schuler A.G.* 1972, where the agreement provided that it was a 'condition' that Wickman Sales should send one of their representatives to various firms at regular intervals. The agreement further provided that the agreement might be determined if either party 'shall have committed a material breach of its obligations'. Wickmans did not send a representative to the firms as frequently as Schuler would have chosen and Schuler then put an end to the contract. Had they been entitled to do so?

The case obviously turned on the use of the word 'condition'. Lord Denning MR examined the various ways the word is commonly used:

> *. . . was this requirement (sending of a representative every week) 'a condition of the agreement' in this sense, that it was a prerequisite to the* very existence *of the agreement? . . . I do not think the word 'condition' was used in that sense in this clause. Even if Wickman Sales did not send the representative every week, the contract would not be void. That is obvious.*
>
> *Alternatively, I ask myself, was this requirement (sending of a representative every week) a 'condition of the agreement' in this sense, that it was a prerequisite to the* right to recover *on the agreement? So that, if Wickman Sales did not fulfil the requirement, they could not sue Schuler for a breach of the agreement? . . . I do not think the word 'condition' was used in that sense in this clause. For instance, if Wickman Sales introduced a purchaser and became entitled to commission, Schuler could not resist payment on the grounds that Wickman Sales had failed to make one weekly visit. . . .*
>
> *The second meaning of 'condition' is the common meaning which receives little attention in the Oxford English Dictionary: 'a provision, a stipulation'.*
>
> *The word is frequently used by laymen and lawyers in this sense. When an agreement is made for the sale of land, it is always subject to 'conditions of sale'. The Law Society's*

> *'Conditions of Sale' are in everyday use. When a building contract is made, it is usually subject to the RIBA conditions. Whenever a quotation is given or invoice sent the printed form invariably says it is subject to the 'conditions' on the back. In all these cases the word 'conditions' simply means terms of the contract.*
>
> *I must turn to the third meaning of 'condition'. It is the meaning given to it by lawyers as a term of art. A 'condition' in this sense is a stipulation in a contract which carries with it this consequence: if the promisor breaks a 'condition' in any respect, however slight, it gives the other party a right to be quit of his future obligations and to sue for damages. . . . A 'condition' in this sense is used in contrast to a 'warranty'. If a promisor breaks a warranty in any respect, however serious, the other party is not quit of his future obligations. He has to perform them. His only remedy is to sue for damages.*

The Court of Appeal held that should the word 'condition' be construed as a term of art meaning that any breach of the clause, however trivial, would entitle the other company to cancel the contract, the consequences would be so astonishing that the court should not confirm that the word had that meaning unless it was clear beyond doubt. The court should adopt a construction which would lead to a reasonable result.

Again, the Master of the Rolls said:

> *This difference is, I think, to be resolved by these principles. Where a word like this word 'condition' is capable of two meanings, one of which gives a reasonable result, and the other a most unreasonable one, the court should adopt the reasonable one. In addition, if one of the meanings is an ordinary meaning, and the other is a term of art, then it should be given its ordinary meaning, unless there is evidence from the surrounding circumstances that it was used by both parties as a term of art.*

On that basis, it was held Schuler had not been entitled to put an end to the agreement for any trivial breach.

Shortly thereafter, in *Cehave* v. *Bremer* 1975, a German company had agreed to sell a Dutch company 12,000 tons of citrus pellets to be used in cattle food. A clause in the contract stated: 'Shipment to be made in good condition'. When the pellets arrived at Rotterdam, part of the cargo had been overheated and damaged in the process. The damaged citrus left a sour taste in the mouths of the Dutch buyers who rejected the goods. The Court of Appeal eventually had to decide whether the wording of the contract ('Shipment to be made in good condition') had amounted to a condition (allowing the buyers to reject the pellets) or only a warranty (giving rise only to a claim for damages).

In fact, although they were by no means in what could be described as 'good condition', the pellets were still suitable for use in cattle food. It followed, said Lord Denning MR in the Court of Appeal, that the buyers had not been entitled to reject the whole lot. Their remedy lay only in a claim for damages for the difference in value between the damaged goods and the sound goods on arrival at Rotterdam.

Incidentally, this claim had initially been referred to arbitration, but as the arbitrators had failed to agree the matter had been referred to an 'umpire' (see Unit 2.4).

Two further classic examples of the distinction between a condition and a warranty both concern singers who turned up late because of ill-health in the same year. In *Bettini* v. *Gye* 1876 the plaintiff singer had agreed to be in London at least six days before the first performance to allow time for adequate rehearsals. As the result of illness he arrived only three days before the first performance and the defendant, who was the director of the Italian Opera, refused to accept his services. However, the court treated this late arrival lightly and held that the stipulation as to rehearsals was not a condition precedent for it did not go to the root of the matter.

An even later arrival by another plaintiff – this time in Milan – led to a different result in *Poussard* v. *Spiers* 1876. This particular diva had not been able to attend any rehearsals at all and so her understudy had to take over. She turned up eventually but the defendant refused to accept her services at his theatre. When the plaintiff sued for wrongful dismissal the court adopted a more stringent attitude. The court held that the singer's inability to perform at the early performances went to the root of the contract and that the defendant had, therefore, been entitled to act as he did.

More personal and more poignant was the distress experienced by a woman who paid a doctor to make her sterile and later found that she had become pregnant. In *Eyre* v. *Measday* 1986 Mary Eyre and her husband had decided against having any more children. She consulted the defendant, a gynaecologist, and paid him to perform an operation for her sterilisation. The doctor did explain to her before the operation that, even after the operation there would still be a very small risk (put at less than one per cent) of her becoming pregnant. The following year, the plaintiff discovered that she had become pregnant. She felt that the doctor had made a mess of it. She sued the defendant doctor alleging that he had contracted to make her irreversibly sterile and that the doctor had, in fact, warranted to her that the operation would completely sterilise her. The Court of Appeal rejected her claim. The judges said that the contract with the doctor was to carry out a certain operation: it had not been a contract guaranteeing to make the lady completely sterile. The doctor's description of the operation as being 'irreversible' meant literally just that: it could not be reversed. The word was not to be construed as meaning that the doctor was guaranteeing absolute sterility. In law, said the court, such a warning about the operation could not be treated as a warranty for, as Slade LJ put it:

> *On the facts of the present case, I do not think that any intelligent lay bystander (let alone another medical man), on hearing the discussion which took place between the defen-*

*dant and the other two parties, could have reasonably drawn
the inference that the defendant was intending to give any
warranty of this nature. ... But, in my opinion, in the
absence of any express warranty, the court should be slow to
imply against a medical man an unqualified warranty as to
the results of an intended operation, for the very simple
reason that, objectively speaking, it is most unlikely that a
responsible medical man would intend to give a warranty of
this nature. Of course, objectively speaking, it is likely that he
would give a guarantee that he would do what he had undertaken to do with reasonable care and skill; but it is quite
another matter to say that he has committed himself to the
extent suggested in the present case.*

Collateral contracts

A convenient and possibly less complex approach can be seen where
courts have relied on the existence of a so-called collateral contract. This
is the name given to a contract which is subsidiary to, and which gives
rise to, the principal contract and which can itself be enforced, and, said
Lord Moulton, the 'consideration for which was the making of some
other contract'.

Of this concept there are many examples, most of them the result of
unfortunate car deals during the years after the Second World War. One
of them, *Andrews* v. *Hopkinson* 1956, is memorable in its irony. The
plaintiff visited the defendant's car showrooms, where the sales manager
showed him a secondhand car and commended it in these prophetic
words: 'It's a good little bus, I would stake my life on it.' He didn't but
the plaintiff nearly had to do just that. A few days later the plaintiff was
driving the car when the steering failed and he was badly injured. The
accident had been caused by a defect of long standing and one which
any competent mechanic could easily have discovered. The plaintiff now
sued for damages for breach of warranty. The court held that the relevant words amounted to a warranty that the car was in good condition
– these words and their acceptance comprising the collateral contract in
this instance – and that the plaintiff was thus entitled to damages for
breach of that warranty and also for his own injuries.

A similar situation had arisen with another defective secondhand car
in *Webster* v. *Higgin* 1948, where the foreman at the defendant's garage
told the plaintiff that, if he were to buy a car, the defendant vendor
would guarantee that it was in good condition and that he would have
no trouble with it. However, all these good intentions could not stand
with a clause in the hire-purchase agreement which the plaintiff signed:
this included, *inter alia*, the words:

> ...any statutory or other warranty, condition, description or
> representation whether express, or implied, as to the state,
> quality, fitness or roadworthiness being hereby expressly
> excluded.

The absurdity of this inconsistency was spelt out by Lord Greene MR:

> *We therefore have this curious position analysing the words again:*
>
> *'If you the purchaser will sign this contract which contains an exclusion of every guarantee I will guarantee the car.'*
>
> *Of course, that is nonsense but parties often make nonsensical arrangements. If the contract meant that, we should be bound to give it that meaning but whether or not it has that effect must in my opinion be a pure question of construction of the contract.*

The Court of Appeal went on to hold that the wording in the hire-purchase agreement was not clear enough to do away with the separate collateral contract constituted by the foreman's offer of a guarantee.

Words spoken again triumphed over print in *City and Westminster Properties* v. *Mudd* 1958. A tenant had been living for some years at the back of an antique shop which he rented from the property company. He was reluctant to sign a lease which expressly forbade him from using the premises except 'for his business' and which required him 'not to let them become a dwelling-house'.

During negotiations the tenant was clearly opposed to the clauses and the representative of the property company told him that the landlords would not really object to his living on the premises if he would sign the lease in its original form. Some years later, the landlord company claimed that the lease should be forfeited because the tenant was living on the premises and that, as the tenant was in breach of his convenant, the company was entitled to possession. Harman J, however, gave judgment for the tenant. He accepted that the tenant had only gone through with the lease because of the overriding oral promise made to him by the company's representative. That promise had amounted to an enforceable contract from which the landlords could not resile.

4.6 *Consumer contracts*

a) Sale of goods

'Is it guaranteed?'

'Yes, it's fully guaranteed.'

Such elevating snippet of conversation, common all over the country, may instil ephemeral confidence in trusting shoppers but its very vagueness (as well so often as its superfluousness) would evoke only scepticism in the mind of any sharp-eared lawyer further down the queue.

The vagueness of such conversation is self-evident as the precise scope and duration of this supposed guarantee remain unknown, probably to shopper and shopkeeper alike. The superfluous nature may be readily divined by an examination of the Sale of Goods Act 1979 which aims to give protection to the vulnerable shopper by implying into contracts for the sale of goods certain implied terms. The Supply of Goods and Services Act 1983 similarly ensures that repairs and services generally are properly carried out.

The Sale of Goods Act 1979 replaced the old 1893 statute of the same name. That nineteenth-century legislation remains a classic example of codification (see Unit 1.5) of commercial and trade practice existing at that time. The 1979 legislation also takes account of intervening legislation such as the Supply of Goods (Implied Terms) Act 1973. This statute grappled with the misleading appearance and insidious effect of some so-called guarantees. Until 1973 the consumer could actually be worse off by registering a guarantee and thereby accepting its application to his contract. Such guarantees, like any contract at that time, might actually exclude the benefits intended to be confirmed on shoppers since 1893. For example, a bicycle might be 'guaranteed' but the 'guarantee' would specifically exclude 'all and any moving or mechanical parts'. The saddle and the basket might be covered but if anything else went wrong the cyclist would find himself taken for a ride in one sense only. The 1973 legislation outlawed this sort of trickery and, since then, guarantees may only add to the basic protection afforded by statute. It is this legislative development which is alluded to on products' labels or wrapping which say: 'Your statutory rights are not affected'.

The rights which are not affected are those set out in the Sale of Goods Act 1979. First of all, it is helpful to note that a contract of sale of goods is defined as

> a contract by which the seller transfers or agrees to transfer the property in goods to the buyer for a money consideration, called the price.

This is not as pedantic as it may seem for it excludes contracts for the transfer of property based on exchange or barter. These forms of measuring the value of alternative kinds of consideration are now governed by the Supply of Goods and Services Act 1982.

The price itself may be fixed by the contract but section 8 of the Sale of Goods Act 1979 provides that it

> may be left to be fixed in a manner agreed by the contract or may be determined by the course of dealing between the parties.

Once the goods have been sold the vendor will want to see the colour of his money. Traders will often incorporate terms such as 'Payment: 30 days' and will include in the contract a term requiring dilatory payers to add interest to their bills. In this regard, section 10 provides:

> Unless a different intention appears from the terms of the contract stipulations as to time of payment are not of the essence of a contract of sale.

Where there is a contract of sale the Sale of Goods Act 1979 deals specifically with three important aspects – title, description and quality.

Title Title, that is to say, who owns the goods up for sale, is protected by section 12 which, in its material part, as amended, provides simply enough that

> there is an implied term on the part of the seller that in the case of a sale he has a right to sell the goods.

In other words, the seller says (or at least is taken as saying) that the goods belong to him and that there is no reason why he should not hand them over to the purchaser. The purchaser is, accordingly, protected if, for example, the goods turn out to be stolen. The goods will still belong to the victim of the theft (who may have lost immediate physical possession but still retains ownership in law) but at least the purchaser is entitled to his money back.

The Act also recognises that the seller may wish to retain title to the goods until certain conditions are fulfilled – for example, garages may have notices on the petrol pumps to the effect that the motion lotion in question remains their property until it has been paid for, even though the lead replacement fuel is splashing around in the customer's car before he queues up to pay.

Clauses of this sort in contracts are known formally as 'retention of title clauses' but are increasingly known also as 'Romalpa clauses' after the case: *Aluminium Industrie Vaassen BV* v. *Romalpa Aluminium Ltd* 1976. More recently, in *Clough Mill Ltd* v. *Martin* 1984 the Court of Appeal had to consider a clause not allowing the sellers to dispose of yarn 'until payment in full for all the yarn has been received...'. The buyers, who were fabric manufacturers, became insolvent before they had paid for all the yarn and the sellers tried to get their product back. To cut a long story (or yarn) short the Court of Appeal held that, under section 19 (which concerns the right of disposal), the sellers were entitled to retain title in the goods even after delivering them to their customers.

If goods are bought from a thief the purchaser cannot usually get good title because, as a general rule, no one can pass better title to goods than he or she already has. Good sense and good law are conveniently united in the legal maxim *nemo dat quod non habet* – 'no one gives what he does not have'.

The point is reinforced by section 21 of the Sale of Goods Act 1979 which provides:

> ...where goods are sold by a person who is not their owner, and who does not sell them under the authority or with the consent of the owner, the buyer acquires no better title to the

goods than the seller had, unless the owner of the goods is by his conduct precluded from denying the seller's authority to sell.

Unsurprisingly, however, in a flexible system of law there are a number of exceptions to this general rule, which are now considered separately.

Estoppel

Where the true owner so negligently or intentionally conducts himself as to lead an innocent purchaser to believe that the seller is acting with the authority of the true owner then the innocent purchaser does acquire good title. The true owner is prevented (or 'estopped') from saying that the seller had no authority.

Mercantile agents

A mercantile agent (an agent who in the course of his everyday business has authority to buy or sell goods) may pass title to goods as though he were expressly authorised by their owner to carry out such sales on his behalf. Under section 2 of the Factors Act 1889 a purchaser in good faith acquires good title.

Sale under voidable title

Under section 23 of the 1979 Act:

> When the seller of goods has a voidable title to them, but his title has not been avoided at the time of the sale, the buyer acquires a good title to the goods, provided he buys them in good faith and without notice of the seller's defect of title.

This was the position experienced by the two students arguing over Robin Hood's Mini in *Lewis* v. *Averay* 1971 (see Unit 4.8).

Seller in possession

Section 24 of the Sale of Goods Act 1979 provides that where a person, having sold goods, nevertheless retains them, the delivery of those goods or of any document of title in respect of those goods to a third party will pass good title to that third party provided he or she acts in good faith. Such requirement of good faith is intended to protect the honest purchaser while avoiding conferring protection on any rogue. For example, Tom sells a video recorder to Dick who keeps it still in Tom's home. Tom then takes money off Harry for the same video recorder. Provided Harry has acted in good faith the machine will belong to Harry and Dick can sue Tom for the return of his money.

Market overt

Whilst thieves are supposed to go about their nefarious business at night, there is a corresponding, if reverse, argument that what is done openly is also done honestly. Against this principle there was an old exception that applied to open markets (known as 'markets overt') where goods were openly displayed for sale between sunrise and sunset. A buyer who bought in good faith and without notice of any defect or want of title on the part of the seller would, from such venue, obtain good title. This centuries-old rule of law, once enshrined in the Sale of Goods Act 1979, was abolished by the Sale of Goods (Amendment) Act 1994.

Description

'Didn't your mother tell you never to buy anything you hadn't seen?'

Such unhelpful comment will be of small consolation to people fleeced of their money in return for goods not matching what was said about them. It is a matter of legitimate complaint if what were advertised as 'luxury fur-lined real leather gloves' turn out to be thin, brittle PVC mittens. Quite apart from any possible criminal liability under the Trade Descriptions Act 1968 (see Unit 3.6k)) the rogue seller is liable to refund the cash into the cold hands of his disappointed customer.

Under section 13 of the Sale of Goods Act 1979 there are implied conditions in cases of sale by description. Therefore:

1. Where there is a contract for the sale of goods by description, there is an implied condition that the goods will correspond with the description.
2. If the sale is by sample as well as by description it is not sufficient that the bulk of the goods correspond with the sample if the goods do not also correspond with the description.

The wording of a similar section in the old Sale of Goods Act 1893 came to be considered by the Court of Appeal in *Beale* v. *Taylor* 1967 when Laurence Beale paid £160 for a car advertised as a 'Herald Convertible, white, 1961, twin carbs'. It was true enough that the Herald did have two carburettors. Unfortunately, it also had two parts of other cars in it as well: in a 'cut and shut' operation the halves of two Herald cars had been welded together. The court held that the sale had been by way of description and that the seller had, therefore, been in breach of section 13 of the old Act. The Court of Appeal quoted the words of another judgment and held that

> there is a sale by description even where the buyer is buying something displayed before him on the counter.

Quality and fitness for purpose

All too often, whether from ignorance or some less excusable reason, shopkeepers will still try to avoid their legal liability for having sold shoddy goods. The customer is fobbed off with counterfeit sympathy and advised to take the matter up with the manufacturers (or, indeed, anyone as long as he leaves the shop and stops causing trouble). The dissatisfied customer is entitled to more than merely the manufacturer's telephone number: he is entitled to the return of every single penny of his money together with damages if additional loss has been incurred.

Essential protection is given to those who buy from shopkeepers and other dealers in the course of trade. Under section 14 there is no general condition as to fitness where there is a private sale (Tom selling his old car to his next-door neighbour, for example) but where the seller sells goods *in the course of a business*

> there is an implied condition that the goods supplied under the contract are of merchantable quality, except that there is no such condition–
> (a) as regards defects specifically drawn to the buyer's attention before the contract is made; or
> (b) if the buyer examines the goods before the contract is made, as regards defects which that examination ought to reveal.

The section also goes on to lay down that where the buyer makes known, either expressly or by implication, the purpose for which the goods are being bought

> there is an implied condition that the goods supplied under the contract are reasonably fit for that purpose...

Not only are private sales excluded (which is why some motor traders masquerade as private sellers) but so is the sale of land, for this is 'real property' and not 'personal property'. In each case the buyer must make his own enquiries (for example, by arranging a survey) and generally heed the maxim *caveat emptor* – 'let the buyer beware'.

Section 14 of the 1979 Act continued to use language first appearing in 1893 when the statute implied a term that the goods were of 'merchantable quality'. This language was abandoned by the Sale and Supply of Goods Act 1994 which has substituted the phrase 'satisfactory quality'. This implied term is set out in the new statute:

> For the purposes of this Act, goods are of satisfactory quality if they meet the standard that a reasonable person would regard as satisfactory, taking account of any description of the goods, the price (if relevant) and all the other relevant circumstances.
>
> For the purposes of this Act, the quality of goods includes their state and condition and the following (among others) are in appropriate cases aspects of the quality of goods–
> (a) fitness for all the purposes for which goods of the kind in question are commonly supplied;
> (b) appearance and finish;
> (c) freedom from minor defects;
> (d) safety; and
> (e) durability.

Judicial confirmation of the everyday economic reality that you get what you pay for was given by Lord Denning MR when he dealt with the problems of a secondhand car in *Bartlett* v. *Sidney Marcus* 1965:

> *A buyer should realize that, when he buys a second-hand car, defects may appear sooner or later; and, in the absence of an express warranty, he has no redress. Even when he buys from a dealer the most that he can require is that it should be reasonably fit for the purpose of being driven along the road.*

Just what sort of teething problems the purchaser of a brand-new car has to put up with was one of the issues raised in *Bernstein* v. *Pamsons Motors (Golders Green) Ltd* 1987, a case which attracted considerable publicity as a test case supported by the Automobile Association and which reflected the unfortunate irony of the then advertising slogan of Nissan UK: 'They don't half work'. Unfortunately, such a fraction proved unduly optimistic for Leslie Bernstein who bought a brand-new Nissan Laurel car for some £8,000. The car broke down on the M3 motorway after covering only 142 miles. A piece of loose sealing compound in the engine (present at the time of sale) had caused it to seize up. The oil flow to the camshaft had been cut off, causing a major breakdown. The garage was willing to repair the car but Leslie Bernstein demanded his money back. The judge was in effect being asked to lay down guidelines of wider application than this particular case and was quoted as asking the lawyers:

> *Are you saying you want a judgment saying what makes a car fit for its purpose? You will be lucky. It's like defining a sausage.*

Nevertheless, the judge reviewed a small number of different aspects of the claim, including the time the repair took, the risk of knock-on effects and the price of the car (the merest cosmetic blemish on a new Rolls Royce might render that car unmerchantable whereas it might not on a humbler model). The judge held that the car had not been of merchantable quality on delivery and had been still less fit for its purpose. Nevertheless, Leslie Bernstein did not get all his money back because the judge also found that Mr Bernstein had left it too late to complain because he had kept the car and used it for three weeks before the engine seized up – he had failed to reject the new car within a reasonable time (a case, perhaps, of resting on his Laurel).

Such a decision may well have appeared harsh for Mr Bernstein. Purchasers of defective goods in the twenty-first century may be better able to draw both comfort and support from the more recent decision of the High Court in *Truk (UK) Limited* v. *Tokmakidis GmbH* 2000 where in a dispute between two companies over lifting machinery the court extended the term for rejection to a full year to allow the buyer a reasonable time not only to inspect the goods, but also to permit a period of use in which defects might appear.

In *Wormell* v. *R.H.M. Agriculture (East) Ltd* 1987, the courts had to consider not only the goods themselves but also the instructions which came with them. Peter Wormell was a farmer. Unlike those young men who strive to sow their wild oats, this farmer wanted only to kill those wild oats which intruded his land. He bought from the defendants a pugnacious-sounding herbicide called *Commando*, which he applied at too late a stage in the growth of the unwelcome oats. He complained that the instructions supplied with the herbicide regarding time of application were unclear and, on that account, in breach of section 14.

The Court of Appeal held that the farmer could not complain that his own misunderstanding of the warning in the instructions about the time of application had rendered the weedkiller unfit for the purpose for which it had been supplied.

Sale by sample

A person may look at a sample of cloth before ordering a new suit. If decorating, he (or she) will want to look through various samples of wallpaper. In either case, he will be let down if, when the yards of worsted or flock arrive, they do not match the samples in the books. In such a case there will have been a breach of the implied terms:

(a) that the bulk will correspond with the sample in quality;

(b) that the transferee will have a reasonable opportunity of comparing the bulk with the sample; and

(c) that the goods will be free from any defect, making their quality unsatisfactory, which would not be apparent on reasonable examination of the sample.

4.7 *Exemption clauses*

Often one party to a contract may wish to limit or exclude his liability for possible failure to comply with a condition or warranty. He will then seek to incorporate another term into the contract – known as an **exemption** or **exclusion clause**.

The next time you buy a railway ticket avert your eyes from the price and look at the small print:

> Travel on Train Companies' trains is subject to the National Rail Conditions of Carriage. This ticket is not transferable . . .

The aim of these words is to incorporate into the contract between the train company and you, the passenger, certain terms which limit or exclude their liability to the travelling public. For example, however uncomfortable your journey or however late your train's arrival (or should the 'Network' simply not work) the passenger will only have limited opportunity of redress because the standard conditions provide:

> . . . The Train Companies do not accept liability for any loss (including consequential loss) caused by the delay and/or cancellation of any train, by any missed connection or by the closure of the railway.

Where there is a dispute between the parties to a contract, the court may have to decide whether or not the terms of the contract, drafted as they were by the company for its own protection and not for the customer's benefit, successfully excluded or limited the company's liability in contract or tort (the latter is defined in Unit 6.1).

In order to succeed on this point, the company will have to show that the document relied on had become part of the contract. This was where the defendants failed in *Chapelton* v. *Barry UDC* 1940. The council hired out deck-chairs. Vacant deckchairs were stacked next to a notice saying: '. . . hire of chairs 2d per session of 3 hours'. Mr Chapelton received two tickets on which were the words: 'the Council will not be liable for any accident or damage arising from hire of chairs'. He put the tickets in his pocket without reading them and settled down in his deckchair. Unfortunately, the chair collapsed under his weight and Mr Chapelton was injured.

The Court of Appeal refused to allow the council to rely on the words on the ticket for its defence. It held that Mr Chapelton had been entitled to assume that all the conditions of hire had been contained in the notice near the stack of chairs. The effect of the ticket was only to furnish proof of payment. Goddard LJ said:

> *I think that the ticket he received was nothing but a receipt for his 2d, a receipt which showed him how long he might use the chair.*

In other words, once the contract has been made, one party cannot try to add on additional terms such as an exemption clause. All the terms must be clear at the time the contract is made. This principle is illustrated in *Olley* v. *Marlborough Court* 1949, when two guests booked into an hotel. When they reached their bedroom they saw, for the first time, a notice to the effect that the hotel would not accept responsibility for any articles which might be lost or stolen. A thief entered the bedroom and the wife's fur stole was stolen. The Court of Appeal held that, as the contract had been made at the reception desk, the hotel's attempt to exclude liability had been too late to be effective.

The result might have been different had the plaintiffs been regular guests at the hotel; they would then have known of the notice and might, by returning, be thought to have agreed to the exemption. A restricted approach to this erosion of the rule can be seen in the decision of the Court of Appeal in *Hollier* v. *Rambler Motors Ltd* 1972, where the court took the view that only three or four transactions in the course of five years would not be sufficient to establish a course of dealings.

It is the duty of the party seeking to rely on the exemption clause to prove that all reasonable steps had been taken to make the other party aware of it; this was emphasised by Lord Denning MR in *Thornton* v. *Shoe Lane Parking* 1971. A motorist drove into an automatic car park and took a ticket from a machine but did not read it. That ticket, in fact, referred to conditions which were displayed elsewhere in the car park. The plaintiff motorist was injured and the defendants sought to rely on an exemption clause among their conditions. The Court of Appeal held that the exemption clause failed because insufficient steps had been taken to draw the attention of the customer to those conditions. Further, it was said, when a customer causes a ticket to be issued from a machine an irrevocable step is taken and so no more conditions could be subsequently incorporated into the contract.

If the exemption clause is contained in the notorious 'small print' of an order form, then a customer who has signed the form will have difficulty in establishing a claim. This was the predicament of Mrs L'Estrange in *L'Estrange* v. *Graucob Ltd* 1934. Mrs L'Estrange ordered a cigarette-vending machine. She signed an order form but did not read the conditions which included the words:

> any express or implied condition is hereby excluded.

The machine did not work properly but when Mrs L'Estrange claimed damages under the old Sale of Goods Act 1893, the Court of Appeal was persuaded by a certain Mr A.T. Denning of counsel that the defendant company had successfully excluded any terms implied by the statute, for example, that the machine would be of merchantable quality. The court made it clear that, in the absence of fraud, once such a document had been signed it made no difference that the customer had not read it.

A more cautious approach was displayed by the plaintiff in *Curtis* v. *Chemical Cleaning and Dyeing Company* 1951. She brought a wedding-dress into the defendants' shop for dry-cleaning and was given a piece of paper to sign. When she asked what it was for, she was told by the shop assistant that it contained a clause excluding liability for damage to the beads and sequins. In fact, it went much further and sought to exclude 'any damage'. When the dress came back it was stained. The Court of Appeal refused to allow the defendant cleaners to escape liability because, although the plaintiff customer had signed the form, its effect had been misrepresented by the assistant.

A verbal assurance again overrode a printed set of conditions in *Mendelssohn* v. *Normand Ltd* 1969, where a customer very reluctantly left his Rolls-Royce unlocked, after a car-park attendant had instructed him to do so, adding that he, the attendant, would lock it after he had parked the car. Some luggage was stolen from the car and, when sued, the defendant company sought to rely on its conditions which purported to exclude such liability. However, the Court of Appeal decided that it could not do so because the oral assurance by the attendant took priority over the written conditions.

In *Evans & Son Ltd* v. *Andrea Merzario Ltd* 1976 the Italian defendants had contracted with English importers to send machinery to the United Kingdom. The defendants assured the plaintiffs that the machinery would be shipped under deck. The plaintiffs had been worried that, if the machinery were carried on deck, it was likely to rust. In the event, the plaintiffs need not have worried about minor matters such as some superficial ferric oxide for the whole load fell overboard in a swell. When sued, the defendants sought to rely on their standard written terms which gave them complete freedom as to how goods were transported. The Court of Appeal refused to allow this avenue of escape. The court held that the oral assurance overrode the printed conditions.

In order to be effective, then, the exemption clause must have been brought to the notice of the customer and incorporated into the contract. Even if such a term has passed these tests, however, it may still fail. One reason may be that the customer is proceeding against another party not protected by the clause in the contract, or proceeding otherwise than on the contract, for example in tort.

One such case was *Adler* v. *Dickson* 1954, where the plaintiff was a passenger on board a ship. The ticket issued by the shipping company carried the warning 'passengers are carried at passengers' entire risk'. The gangway moved and the plaintiff fell 16 feet on the wharf. The plaintiff sued the master and boatswain of the ship rather than the company and did so not in contract but in tort for their negligence in allowing the gangway to move. The judge held that the defendants, who were not parties to the contract, could not enjoy its protection. Neither had the company been acting under any implied agency on behalf of the defendants.

An exemption clause may also fail if a claimant is able to plead a **fundamental** breach, that is, where the actual performance of the contract is wholly different from that intended so that, in the example of Lord Abinger in *Chanter* v. *Hopkins* 1838; 'if a man offers to buy peas of another, and he send him beans, he does not perform his contract.'

Under this doctrine, where the performance of the contract is wholly different from that contemplated, an exemption clause will not protect the party in breach. For example, in *Harbutt's Plasticine Ltd* v. *Wayne Tank and Pump Co. Ltd* 1970, the defendant company agreed to install equipment for storing and dispensing stearine (a greasy wax used in the manufacture of plasticine) at temperatures of 120–160 °F. The piping used proved unsuitable for that temperature range, a fire broke out, and the plaintiffs' factory burned down. The question then arose whether the defendants could rely on a clause in the contract which sought to limit their liability to a sum substantially lower than the plaintiffs' losses.

The Court of Appeal, stressing the need to have regard not only to the breach itself but also to the events resulting from that breach, held that the purported exemption clause was of no force.

The reluctance of the courts to allow reliance on such wide-ranging exemption clauses is again clear from the decision of the Court of Appeal in *Farnworth Finance Facilities Ltd* v. *Attryde* 1970. Mr Attryde obtained a motor-cycle under a hire-purchase agreement which provided that the vehicle supplied was

> subject to no conditions or warranties whatsoever express or implied.

Mr Attryde can have derived little pleasure from that bike: among other faults its head-light failed, it was unstable at high speed and the final straw came when its rear chain broke. It was, as one witness said, 'disgusting for a new machine'. The Court of Appeal held that the defects in the bike were such as were likely to cause an accident. They were, accordingly, a fundamental breach of the contract and the finance company, which of course owned the bike, was barred from relying on the exemption clause. Fenton Atkinson LJ quoted with approval the words of Lord Dunedin, who had said in *Pollock and Co.* v. *Macrae* 1922:

> *Now, when there is such a congeries of defects as to destroy the workable character of the machine, I think this amounts to a total breach of contract, and each defect cannot be taken by itself separately so as to apply the provisions of the conditions of guarantee and make it impossible to claim damages.*

Every day the individual citizen is faced with the bleak choice of either accepting goods and services on the supplier's own terms or simply going without. The long-suffering commuter who, in a triumph of hope over experience, tries to persuade the railway booking clerk to accept legal liability for consequent loss from the half-hour delay on the 8.20 to Waterloo will get little joy. Either travel on the railway's terms or walk would be the probable response. Dry-cleaners often put notices up in their shops seeking to limit liability for their errors to a sum of money far below the true replacement cost of the garments ripped or shrunk. Similarly, garages dealing with motorists often ask the driver to sign a standard form in which he not only agrees to pay the garage charges but also accepts that he has no claim against them should their mechanic reverse the car into a brick wall. The inequality, and indeed iniquity, of this freedom of contract came to be reviewed by Lord Denning MR as he gave judgment in *George Mitchell* v. *Finney Lock Seeds* 1983:

> *None of you nowadays will remember the trouble we had, when I was called to the Bar, with exemption clauses. They were printed in small print on the back of tickets and order forms and invoices. They were contained in catalogues or timetables. They were held to be binding on any person who took them without objection. No one ever did object. He never read them or knew what was in them. No matter how*

unreasonable they were, he was bound. All this was done in the name of 'freedom of contract'. But the freedom was all on the side of the big concern which had the use of the printing press. No freedom for the little man who took the ticket or order form or invoice. The big concern said, 'Take it or leave it'. The little man had no option but to take it. The big concern could and did exempt itself from liability in its own interest without regard to the little man. It got away with it time after time. When the courts said to the big concern, 'You must put it in clear words', the big concern had no hesitation in doing so. It knew well that the little man would never read the exemption clauses or understand them.

Parliament rallied to the protection of the consumer when it tackled this sort of unfair trading term in the Unfair Contract Terms Act 1977. This statute, largely the result of a Law Commission report (see Unit 1.9), greatly restricts the power of the stronger party to impose exemption clauses on the weaker party to the contract. Although some exemption clauses, such as any term seeking to exclude liability for death or personal injury arising from negligence (see Unit 6.3) are absolutely outlawed, the majority of such clauses fall simply to be judged by the test of reasonableness. For the private citizen buying goods and ordering services, the most important section is section 3 which applies, however, only where one of the parties is dealing with the other as a consumer. A party is said to 'deal as consumer' if:

(a) he neither makes the contract in the course of a business nor holds himself out as doing so; and
(b) the other party does make the contract in the course of a business; and
(c) ...the goods ... are of a type ordinarily supplied for private use or consumption.

In these circumstances the section provides:

As against that party, the other cannot by reference to any contract term –
(a) when himself in breach of contract, exclude or restrict any liability of his in respect of the breach; or
(b) claim to be entitled–
  (i) to render a contractual performance substantially different from that which was reasonably expected of him, or
  (ii) in respect of the whole or any part of his contractual obligation, to render no performance at all,
except in so far as (in any of the cases mentioned above in this subsection) the contract term satisfies the test of reasonableness.

In determining whether the disputed exemption clause is reasonable or not the courts are enjoined to have regard to a number of considerations in the Act itself. Included are factors such as the strength of each party's bargaining position.

Consider, for example, the case of a lady who takes a roll of film to a large chain of chemists to have it developed and printed. The film contains the only photographs taken at her grand-daughter's wedding. The shop ruins the film and those important memories are lost for ever. Is it fair to allow the shop to rely on a term to the effect that any customer's loss is limited to the cost of the film itself – perhaps only £5 or so? In practice, attempts by photographic shops to rely on this sort of clause have already fallen foul of the test of reasonableness as frustrated photographers have sued. The judge would have to consider whether the customer could have gone elsewhere to a business without such terms, whether the customer even knew of the full extent of the exemption clause and also whether the goods were manufactured to the special order of the customer. In any event, it is for the shop or manufacturer (that is to say, the party seeking to rely on the exemption clause) to satisfy the court that the clause in question satisfies the test of reasonableness.

. . . those important memories are lost for ever.

This burden remains on the trader whether the exemption clause was incorporated into the contract by a document signed by the customer (as when motorists book their cars into the garage for a service) or whether the term appeared on a notice – such as a notice at the entry to a car-wash with wording to the effect that if their rolls mangle your Rolls it is nothing to do with them.

These examples have covered problems faced by individual consumers who are particularly dependent on this legislation. Big businesses, dealing at arms' length with other such businesses, are far better able to bargain from a position of strength and consequently do not receive such protection as 'consumers'.

Just how the courts should approach exemption clauses in contracts made between businesses was considered by the House of Lords in *Photo Production* v. *Securicor* 1980. The defendant security company sought to avoid payment of some £615,000 in respect of a fire caused by one of their guards whose job it had been actually to protect the factory in Kent where Photo Production Limited made Christmas cards. The security guard was later sent to prison for arson and Photo Production looked to his employers for compensation on the basis that he had been acting in the course of his employment at the time he threw the match on to some cardboard (see Unit 6.8b)). The security company relied on a clause in the contract exempting them from 'any injurious act or default by an employee'. In the House of Lords, Lord Wilberforce considered what effect should be given to the 1977 Act in this sort of case

> *This Act applies to consumer contracts and those based on standard terms and enables exemption clauses to be applied with regard to what is just and reasonable. It is significant that Parliament refrained from legislation over the whole field of contract. After this Act, in commercial matters generally, when the parties are not of unequal bargaining power, and when risks are normally borne by insurance, not only is the case for judicial intervention undemonstrated, but there is everything to be said, and this seems to have been Parliament's intention, for leaving the parties free to apportion the risks as they think fit and for respecting their decisions.*

The judge went on to look at what each party got out of the contract. Photo Production had their premises inspected for 26 pence per visit, but Securicor did not agree to provide equipment. It would have no knowledge of the value of Photo Production's factory. That value and the efficacy of their fire precautions would, however, be known to Photo Production. In those circumstances nobody could consider it unreasonable that, as between these two equal parties, the risk assumed by Securicor should be a modest one or that Photo Production should carry the substantial risk of damages or destruction.

The House of Lords went on to say that although Securicor was in breach of their obligation to operate their service with due and proper regard to the safety and security of their customer's premises, the exemption clause in question was clear and unambiguous. In those circumstances, the security company was spared from paying any of the £615,000.

Whether a fundamental breach of contract could negative the effect of an exclusion clause was one of the issues which concerned the Court of Appeal in *George Mitchell* v. *Finney Lock Seeds* 1983, the last case heard by Lord Denning MR before his retirement. Finney Lock, seed merchants, had supplied some farmers with cabbage seed. The crop was a failure and the seed was shown not to have been the variety agreed upon. In any event, the stuff was not of satisfactory quality. The seed merchants relied on a clause in their contract of supply which purported to limit their liability to a refund of the purchase price. In this case, however, the farmers were claiming a sum in excess of £60,000 more than the price paid for the seed itself. After all, the farmers had lost a full year's production from over sixty acres. The court reviewed all the factors. What was the ratio between the purchase price of the faulty seeds and the lost profit? Was the clause negotiated between persons of equal bargaining power or was it just inserted by the seed merchants?

Did the buyers have any opportunity of discovering that the seed delivered was no good? Could such a mistake over packing and labelling have taken place without there having been serious negligence on the part of the seed merchants? Having considered all these factors the Court of Appeal, and later the House of Lords, held that it was not reasonable to allow the seed merchants to rely on this clause in this contract. Lord Denning MR took the opportunity to consider the general effect of the Unfair Contract Terms Act 1977:

> *What is the result of all this? To my mind it heralds a revolution in our approach to exemption clauses; not only where they exclude liability altogether and also where they limit liability; not only in the specific categories in the Unfair Contract Terms Act 1977, but in other contracts too . . . Just as in other fields of law we have done away with the multitude of cases on 'common employment', 'last opportunity', 'invitees' and 'licencees' and so forth, so also in this field we should do away with the multitude of cases on exemption clauses. We should no longer have to go through all kinds of gymnastic contortions to get round them. We should no longer have to harass our students with the study of them. We should set about meeting a new challenge. It is presented by the test of reasonableness.*

In 1995 the new Unfair Terms in Consumer Contracts Regulations came into force. These regulations, which had been based upon a European Directive, complement the Unfair Contract Terms Act and have since been replaced by the later 1999 Regulations. While the statute itself is concerned with the reasonableness of exemption clauses, the regulations go further and deal with the overall fairness of all contract terms. For example, insurers will now be less able to wriggle out of their obligations because of some insignificant non-disclosure in a proposal form (see Unit 4.11). In general terms the regulations prevent a party from relying on unfair contract terms where an 'unfair term' is defined as:

> Any term which contrary to the requirement of good faith causes a significant imbalance in the parties' rights and obligations under the contract to the detriment of the consumer.

Further protection for the consumer against tortuously drafted contracts or gobbledegook is further provided in regulation 6 requiring written contract terms to be expressed in 'plain, intelligible language'. Any doubt as to the meaning of the written term will be construed in a way most favourable to the consumer.

4.8 Mistake

As a general rule, once two parties have reached a lawful agreement, supported by consideration, then they have made a contract. It is important to remember that, in considering how a contract is affected if one or both of the contracting parties enters into it under some mistaken belief or misunderstanding, we are concerned only with the exceptions to this rule. It may be, indeed often will be, that because of the interplay of commercial circumstances, or even because of some chance, one party will do better out of the deal than the other, but the law does not forbid such profit or loss.

For example, suppose Claude, a keen but none-too-knowledgeable collector of antiques, sees a vase on a market stall which he believes to be a priceless relic of the Ping Pong dynasty of Ancient China. Eagerly, he buys it for £5 in the hope of selling it later at a vast profit. In fact, while he is not so very far out geographically, the vase was made last year in Hong Kong. Claude, disappointed as he will be, has no remedy: it was his mistake and he must at least learn, if not profit, by it. The law simply says *caveat emptor* – 'let the buyer beware'.

This example is not as far-fetched as might be imagined for in *Leaf* v. *International Galleries* 1950 a man had bought an oil painting depicting Salisbury Cathedral, which he erroneously believed to be the work of the English landscape painter, John Constable.

Five years later he realised his mistake and wanted his money back. He did not get it. Denning LJ said:

> *Such a mistake, however, does not avoid the contract. There was no mistake as to the subject-matter of the sale. It was a specific picture of 'Salisbury Cathedral'. The parties were agreed in the same terms on the same subject-matter, and that is sufficient to make a contract.*

There are, however, those exceptional cases where the mistake is so fundamental that it negatives or nullifies consent. The mistake is so important that it goes to the root of the contract. Such a mistake is known as an **operative mistake**: it prevents the formation of a true contract and any apparent contract is void (not binding in law) *ab initio* (from the outset).

There are four varieties of operative mistake.

Mutual mistake Say that Claude and the stall-holder were discussing vases. Claude was talking about a small blue one. The stall-holder thought that he was referring to the large red one. The parties, of course, were at cross-purposes: in law they are said to have been **mutually mistaken**. This kind of confusion arose in *Raffles* v. *Wichelhause* 1864 where the defendants had agreed to buy '125 bales of surat cotton to arrive ex *Peerless* from Bombay'. Unfortunately, there happened to be two ships called the *Peerless* sailing from Bombay. The plaintiffs were referring to the one sailing in December. The defendants had in mind the other, leaving in October.

In the circumstances the court held that there was no contract. The parties had different ships in mind; there was, in lawyers' language, no *consensus ad idem* – no 'meeting of the minds'.

Common mistake A different problem arises when both parties make the same mistake. For example, Claude encounters the stall-holder in a public house at 1 p.m. Over some jars they discuss some vases and Claude agrees to buy the blue vase which he has heard about. They walk back to the market together, only to discover that the vase had fallen off the stall at 12.30 p.m. and is now lying, smashed to a thousand tiny pieces, in the dustbin. At the time of the agreement, the vase was no longer in existence and both parties were wrong in assuming that it had been: they are said to have made a **common mistake**. The vase was *res extincta* (a thing no longer in existence) at the relevant time and the Sale of Goods Act 1979 section 6 provides:

> Where there is a contract for the sale of specific goods, and the goods without the knowledge of the seller have perished at the time when the contract is made, the contract is void.

In this section 'specific goods' are goods which have been individually identified – for example, 'that blue vase on your stall' as opposed to any old Ancient Chinese blue vase.

Common mistake may occur otherwise than in connection with the sale of specified goods. This (and the fact that truth can be stranger than fiction) was demonstrated in *Galloway* v. *Galloway* 1914 where the plaintiff and the defendant, each believing that he or she was married to the other, entered into a deed of separation by which the 'husband' was to pay maintenance to the 'wife'. It then transpired that they had never been married in the first place so the 'husband' stopped paying. The 'wife' sued him but failed to recover any of the money said to have been due under the deed. The court held that the separation deed was void and said that, as a matter of general principle, if the parties to any agreement make a mistake of fact which is both material and mutual then that agreement is void.

At first sight the nomenclature is perhaps a little confusing but in essence:

1. If the parties are *at cross-purposes*, that is *mutual mistake*.
2. If the parties both make *the same mistake*, that is *common mistake*.

Mistake as to identity Normally, of course, a shopkeeper is happy to sell you his goods, no matter what your name is. He is interested in your money, not in your ancestry. Of course, if you ask for credit, pay by cheque, or charge the bill to an account, then your identity does become important. Are you credit-worthy? Is that really your cheque-book? Do you have an account at that shop? Say that Sebastian buys a television set and asks the newly appointed shop assistant to put it on his account. He tells her that he is Lord Snookes, who, according to the credit control book, is an old and respected customer. In fact, Sebastian is a notorious con-man without a penny to his name (except that he now has a brand-new television set in his drawing-room). Who owns the set? Who pays for it?

The courts have dealt with questions like these on many occasions and it is not possible to reconcile all decisions in this area.

In *Phillips* v. *Brooks* 1919, the judge held that the shopkeeper jeweller was contracting with the man in the shop, whatever his name was, whom he had 'identified by sight and hearing', and not with the respected and well-known Sir George Bullough whom the con-man had pretended to be. Accordingly, the 'rogue' (to use the traditional, if still a little benign, language of the courts) obtained a good title (legal right) to the goods which he had been allowed to take away. This was important because, as the rogue had good title, he in turn could pass title on to the person who, in good faith, had bought the valuables from him. The loss, therefore, fell on the jeweller who had been deceived in the first place and not on the innocent purchaser.

The facts in *Ingram* v. *Little* 1960 were virtually indistinguishable from these but the outcome was different.

A rogue called on three old ladies who were selling a car. He gave a false name and address, claiming to be a certain P.G.M. Hutchinson who lived (as the real Mr Hutchinson did, indeed, live) at Stanstead House, Caterham, Surrey. The old ladies checked the name and address in a telephone directory and, thus reassured, handed over the car in return for a cheque. The cheque bounced. The Court of Appeal said that the ladies had not meant to contract with the con-man whom they actually spoke to but only with the real P.G.M. Hutchinson. It followed that the rogue could not have acquired any title to the car and so the old ladies were entitled to get it back from whoever was in possession of it. In fact, this was the person who had in good faith paid the rogue for it.

The law was thus in a state of uncertainty, if not complete confusion, when Robin Hood himself, no longer as discriminating in his victims, robbed rich and poor alike when he cheated a man out of his car. In *Lewis* v. *Averay* 1971 Keith Lewis was a postgraduate chemistry student at Bristol. A little over a hundred miles away, in Bromley, Kent lived Anthony Averay, a music student.

Mr Lewis owned a Mini 'S' Cooper which he advertised for sale at £450. A man came along and offered to buy it. He introduced himself as Richard Greene, the actor who then took the lead part in the ITV television series *Robin Hood*. He was not that famous actor at all, however, but simply yet another rogue. In order to persuade Mr Lewis to accept a cheque he produced an admission pass to Pinewood Studios, in the shape of a card bearing Richard Greene's name and address together with the rogue's photograph. On the strength of that Mr Lewis let the rogue take the car away. He took it to Anthony Averay who bought it for £200. That must have represented a quick profit of around £250 for the rogue, because, in the meantime, not a thousand miles away, his rubbery cheque for £450 had bounced high and hard.

The awkward situation was that the rogue was better off by some £250, Mr Averay had a Mini 'S' Cooper to drive around in but all Mr Lewis had was a worthless forgery of an actor's autograph. Which student now owned the car? One or them was bound to lose. Mr Lewis claimed that the Mini still belonged to him and so sued Mr Averay.

The question which the Court of Appeal had ultimately to decide was whether or not there had been a contract of sale under which ownership of the car had passed first to the rogue and then from him to Mr Averay.

The court followed the *Phillips* decision and expressed doubt about *Ingram* v. *Little*. Lord Denning MR explained the law when he said:

> . . .*when two parties have come to a contract – or rather what appears, on the face of it, to be a contract – the fact that one*

party is mistaken as to the identity of the other does not mean that there is no contract, or that the contract is a nullity and void from the beginning. It only means that the contract is voidable, that is, liable to be set aside at the instance of the mistaken person, so long as he does so before third parties have in good faith acquired rights under it.

Mistake as to documents As already seen in Unit 4.7, as a general rule, a person is bound by what he or she signs. You should read the small print before you sign anything: if you don't like it, don't sign it. For instance, if you have signed a so-called 'delivery note' stating that the furniture has arrived in perfect condition it may be just tough luck if you take the wrapping off your new mattress to find the springs sticking out: you have, so to speak, made your bed and now you must lie on it as best you can.

What would be the position if a man, who had broken his glasses, were asked to sign a 'delivery note', which was in fact a cheque made out in favour of the delivery man? Does he have to honour what would be a very expensive tip? A cheque and a delivery note are, of course, very different documents. In such a case the man may be able to avoid liability by saying *non est factum* ('it was not my deed'). He must, however, prove three things:

1. that he was not negligent in signing the document;
2. that he signed it as the result of a fraudulent inducement; and
3. that what he thought he was signing and what he actually did sign were fundamentally different.

These principles are clear from the leading case of *Saunders* v. *Anglia Building Society* 1970, when the House of Lords considered the sad plight of a 78-year-old widow, the victim of planned dishonesty. A Mr Lee had given the lady a piece of paper to sign. The widow had broken her glasses and believed him when he told her that it was a deed of gift in favour of her trusted and loved nephew. In fact it was a deed of assignment of her house to the Anglia Building Society to provide security for a loan taken out by Lee himself. Nevertheless, the Court of Appeal and House of Lords emphasised the limitations of the doctrine of *non est factum* when they both held that the widow was bound by what she had signed – after all the piece of paper had obviously been a legal document.

In the Court of Appeal Lord Denning MR had this to say:

Whenever a man of full age and understanding, who can read and write, signs a legal document which is put before him for signature – by which I mean a document which it is apparent, on the face of it, is intended to have legal consequences – then, if he does not take the trouble to read it but signs it as it is, relying on the word of another as to its character or contents or effect, he cannot be heard to say that it was not his document.

The House of Lords also stressed the need to keep the plea of *non est factum* within narrow limits and said that, although it was not limited to the blind or the illiterate, the plea was unlikely to be available to a person who signed a document without informing himself of its meaning. For the plea to succeed the person raising it would have to show, firstly, that, although he had signed a document the true meaning of which was unknown to him, he had still acted with reasonable care. Secondly, he must show that there was a radical or fundamental difference between what he reasonably believed that he was signing and what he actually did sign.

The widow's evidence failed to satisfy these tests because as Lord Reid said:

> *The pleas cannot be available to anyone who was content to sign without taking the trouble to try to find out at least the general effect of the document.*

a) The consequences of mistake

In *Solle* v. *Butcher* 1949 Denning LJ discussed the consequences of mistake when he said:

> *...mistake is of two kinds: first, mistake which renders the contract void, that is, a nullity from the beginning which is the kind of mistake which was dealt with by the courts of common law, and, secondly, mistake which renders the contract not void but voidable, that is, liable to be set aside on such terms as the court thinks fit, which is the kind of mistake which was dealt with by the courts of equity.*

Although, of course, today the administration of law and equity is fused, it is convenient to deal with the remedies separately.

Mistake of common law

Where there has been an operative mistake the contract is void and no property can pass. It follows that the original and true owner will be able to recover either the property or damages in its place from whoever is in wrongful possession. Denning LJ, in the case already cited, went on to say:

> *...once a contract has been made, that is to say, once the parties, whatever their inmost states of mind, have to all outward appearances agreed with sufficient certainty in the same terms on the same subject-matter then the contract is good unless and until it is set aside for breach of some condition expressed or implied in it, or for fraud, or on some equitable ground. Neither party can rely on his own mistake to say it was a nullity from the beginning no matter that it was a mistake which to his mind was fundamental and no matter that the other party knew he was under a mistake.*

Mistake in equity

Denning LJ went on to say:

> *Let me next consider mistakes which render a contract voidable, that is, liable to be set aside on some equitable ground. While presupposing that a contract was good at law, or at any rate not void, the court of equity would often relieve a party from the consequences of his own mistake, so long as it could do so without injustice to third parties. The court had power to set aside the contract whenever it was of the opinion*

*that it was unconscionable for the other party to avail himself
of the legal advantage which he had obtained ... This branch
of equity has shown a progressive development. It is now
clear that a contract will be set aside if the mistake of the one
party has been induced by a material misrepresentation of the
other, even though it was not fraudulent or fundamental.*

In particular, equity will intervene in three ways to provide discretionary
remedies where the common law would have otherwise held the contract good.

<u>Rectification</u>   Firstly, equity may rectify the contract so as to ensure
that the second time round it accurately expresses what the parties had
actually agreed.

For example, in *Craddock Bros.* v. *Hunt* 1923 there had been an oral
agreement to sell some land. That agreement was put into writing but, by
mistake, the conveyance omitted any reference to part of the land which
had, in fact, been paid for. The Court of Appeal pointed out that ever since
the Judicature Act 1873 the court had jurisdiction to rectify the conveyance.

<u>Refusal of specific performance</u>   Secondly, the court may refuse an
order of specific performance (see Unit 4.19c)) where to make such an
order would be unjust to the party who had made the mistake.

For example, in *Grist* v. *Bailey* 1966 Mrs Bailey had agreed to sell a
house to Frank Grist for £850. The price was very low because Mrs
Bailey believed that she had a statutory tenant living at the house. She
was mistaken because, in fact, the tenant had died. Obviously, with
vacant possession, the house was worth very much more. When she
realised that her mistake was likely to cost her about £1,500 Mrs Bailey
not surprisingly refused to sell. The court found that there had been a
common mistake of fact between the plaintiff and the defendant. Goff J
held that there was an equitable jurisdiction to set aside the sale agreement for common mistake. Moreover the court refused to order Mrs
Bailey to sell at such an inadequate price.

<u>Setting aside</u>   Thirdly, the court may set the agreement aside on terms
which are fair to all the parties.

For example, in *Solle* v. *Butcher* 1949 the plaintiff rented a flat from
the defendant at £250 per annum for seven years. In fact, there had been
a common mistake because the Rent Restriction Acts provided that the
maximum rent allowed was £140. The Court of Appeal refused to give
the plaintiff back his money but did set the lease aside.

Such decision came also to be examined in *Clarion Limited* v.
National Provident Institution 2000 when the court rejected an argument advanced by the insurance company suggesting that an agreement
with financial advisers should be set aside in equity on the grounds of
mistake. The court took the view that the mistake had not centred upon
the subject-matter of the agreement but only concerned its commercial
consequences and effect. Such mistake, therefore, had not related to the
terms of the contract but merely to its potential for commercial exploita-
tion. While the insurers may have made a bad bargain, the court would
not set it aside on grounds of mistake.

4.9 Misrepresentation

We saw in Unit 4.5 how what the parties said in their negotiations leading up to the contract may have become a term of the contract. A **representation** is not a term but, rather, a statement of fact made by one party to the other, during their preliminary negotiations, which was intended to induce the other party to enter into the contract and which did so induce the other party to enter into that contract.

This requires some words of explanation.

(i) **'Statement of fact'** The statement must be of fact and not of opinion. To go back to Claude and his Chinese vase, mentioned in Unit 4.8: if the stall-holder tells Claude that the vase is of the Ancient Chinese Ping Pong dynasty, that is a statement of *fact*. If he tells Claude that the vase will look good in the hall, that is a statement only of *opinion*. For example, in *Bisset* v. *Wilkinson* 1927 the Privy Council expressed the view that a remark that some land in New Zealand would support 2,000 sheep was only an expression of opinion and not a representation of fact.

Such a decision, however, must now be read in the light of the judgment of the Court of Appeal in *Esso Petroleum Co. Ltd* v. *Mardon* 1976 where liability was imposed on an opinion.

Philip Mardon was the tenant of a petrol station in Southport. He decided to take on the site after he had been told by the local manager for Esso that its 'estimated annual consumption' of petrol was likely to be some 200,000 gallons. At first, Mr Mardon was sceptical but he was persuaded by Esso's figures and took the tenancy at a substantial yearly rental. Unfortunately, the business never really got off the ground, the turnover was nothing like 200,000 gallons and Mr Mardon's financial position became parlous. Business did not improve and Esso eventually claimed possession of the petrol station. Philip Mardon was in straitened circumstances. In Lord Denning's words:

> He had tried for four years to make a success of it. It was all wasted endeavour. He had lost all his capital and had incurred a large overdraft. It was a financial disaster.

Mr Mardon now tried to get back his money. He claimed that Esso ought to have known that he was relying on their judgment of the likely annual consumption of petrol and that they had been negligent in rendering such advice and information to him. Esso argued that what had been said about 200,000 gallons was only an opinion and did not amount in law to a warranty.

The Court of Appeal rejected such a defence for, although what had been said did not *guarantee* that the annual consumption would be 200,000 gallons, it was nevertheless a forecast made by a party, Esso, who had special knowledge and skill. Lord Denning MR commented:

> It seems to me that if such a person makes a forecast – intending that the other should act on it and he does act on it – it can well be interpreted as a warranty that the

*forecast is sound and reliable in this sense that they made
it with reasonable care and skill ... It is very different
from the New Zealand case where the land had never
been used as a sheep farm and both parties were equally
able to form an opinion as to its carrying capacity.*

It followed that what the Esso manager had said about the likely
petrol sales had become a warranty and that Esso were liable in
damages to Mr Mardon for their breach.

Of course, a trader's puff does not amount to a term or a
representation; *simplex commendatio non obligat* ('simple praise,
by itself, has no binding force').

(ii) **'Made by one party to another'**   Usually a representation will be
what the seller said to the buyer; what the buyer was led to believe
by someone else does not become a representation. This, of course,
is related to the doctrine of privity (see Unit 4.14).

(iii) **'During negotiations'**   The statement must have induced the other
party to make the contract. From this it will be obvious that, to
pursue the earlier example, if, after Claude had bought the vase, the
stall-holder said: 'Oh, by the way, that's Chinese, the Ping Pong
dynasty', those words would not amount to a representation
because they were said after the contract had been made.

(iv) **'Intended to induce'**   If what was said was not intended to persuade the other party to enter into the contract, then, again, there
will not have been a representation. For example, if, on hearing the
dealer's words about the Ping Pong dynasty, Claude said that he
was only looking for a door-stop and didn't care what it looked
like, the remark did not induce the contract and was not, therefore,
a representation.

... only looking for a door-stop ...

A **misrepresentation** is simply a representation which is false. Misrepresentation comes in three shapes and sizes: it may be *fraudulent, negligent* or *innocent*.

(i) *Fraudulent misrepresentation*   To say that a misrepresentation has
been made fraudulently is a very serious allegation and the clearest
proof is required. In the leading case of *Derry* v. *Peek* 1889 Lord
Herschell said that

> *fraud is proved when it is shown that a false representation has been made knowingly, or without belief in its truth, or recklessly, careless whether it be true or false.*

(ii) *Negligent misrepresentation* This occurs when the party gets the matter wrong because he has not bothered to look into it properly.

(iii) *Innocent misrepresentation* This takes place where the party, acting in good faith, just slips up.

Remedies for misrepresentation

The remedies available are part common law and part statutory. The possible courses depend on the nature of the misrepresentation.

Any form of misrepresentation will allow the injured party to **rescind** (cancel) the contract, provided that *restitutio in integrum* is still possible. That simply involves putting both sides back in the position where they were before the contract was made in the first place. It follows that this equitable and, therefore, discretionary remedy will not be available where such *restitutio in integrum* is no longer possible, for example, where a third party has become involved.

On the other hand, for example, where the misrepresentation is not particularly serious, the injured party may prefer to go on with the contract and recover damages to compensate: he is then said to **affirm** the contract.

The Misrepresentation Act 1967

This Act extended the available remedies for misrepresentation. An injured party had long been able to recover damages for fraudulent misrepresentation which, at common law, is also a tort.

Section 2(1) of the Act allows an injured party to recover damages for misrepresentation which has caused loss, unless the other party

> proves that he had reasonable ground to believe and did believe up to the time the contract was made that the facts represented were true.

In other words, this is another exceptional situation in which a defendant is required to prove that he is not to blame.

Section 2(2) further provides that, in cases other than fraudulent misrepresentation, the court may award damages instead of allowing the injured party to rescind the contract. In this way the court is empowered to

> declare the contract subsisting and award damages in lieu of rescission, if of the opinion that it would be equitable to do so, having regard to the nature of the misrepresentation and the loss that would be caused by it if the contract were upheld, as well as to the loss that rescission would cause to the other party.

In *Gosling* v. *Anderson* 1972, Lord Denning MR pointed out that before 1967 the plaintiff would have been without any remedy unless she had been able to prove fraud. Instead a retired schoolmistress was awarded damages for innocent misrepresentation that the flat she was buying had planning permission for a garage.

Finally, section 3 restricts the way in which parties may exclude liability for misrepresentation. Such a proposed exemption clause will have no more effect than the court may allow as being 'fair and reasonable in the circumstances of the case'.

4.10 Duress and undue influence

Where an individual is induced to enter into a contract by means of pressure brought to bear upon him so as to influence his own independent judgment, the courts will refuse to enforce that contract. In the extreme case of violence or threats of violence being offered ('sign here or I'll break your legs') such pressure is described as **duress**; but it need by no means take so crude a form. The most subtle kind of improper pressure is that known as **undue influence** which equity recognises as allowing the pressurised party to avoid the contract at his option. That influence may even be presumed to arise in a relationship such as that of parent and child, solicitor and client, doctor and patient. For example, in *Lancashire Loans Ltd* v. *Black* 1934 the Court of Appeal indicated that there is no rule of law that just because a daughter marries and leaves home, she is no longer under the domination of her parents. The case concerned a mother who was very extravagant and frequently borrowed from money-lenders. When her married daughter came of age she raised some £2,000 to help to pay off her mother's debts. The only advice (even then hardly independent) which the daughter received was from the solicitor who also acted for her mother.

On that evidence, the Court of Appeal held that the daughter had still been under the influence of her mother when she had entered into that unfortunate transaction and, moreover, had received no independent advice. For those reasons, the court held that the transaction must be set aside.

Much of the case-law on this area has arisen out of proceedings brought by banks for possession of land upon which their lending has been secured. In the Court of Appeal, Lord Denning MR rallied to the support of an elderly farmer when Lloyds Bank wanted his farm in order to clear his son's overdraft at the bank. In *Lloyds Bank* v. *Bundy* 1974 the father had mortgaged the farm to help out with his son's business. Although the bank obtained the advantage of this security for their loans to the son, they never advised the farmer to obtain independent advice. Such an omission proved fatal for their case and Lord Denning MR held that such cases rested on what he termed 'inequality of bargaining power'. English law, he said will give relief to one who, without independent advice, enters into a contract on terms which are very unfair or where a man transfers property for a consideration which is grossly inadequate, when his bargaining power is grossly impaired and undue influence or pressure is brought to bear on him by or for the benefit of another.

Ten years later, however, the National Westminster Bank asked the House of Lords to review the earlier decision in *Lloyds Bank* v. *Bundy*. So, in *National Westminster Bank plc* v. *Morgan* 1985 Janet Morgan had been persuaded by the bank manager to sign a charge over the house in Somerset which she and her husband owned jointly. The charge gave the bank security for its lending to the husband in his contracting business. Although the bank manager acted in good faith he made a mistake in explaining the effect of the charge to the wife. Neither did she receive any proper independent advice from someone such as a solicitor. The bank did not receive the repayments due and sought possession of the house. The wife argued that she had signed the charge (the security) because of undue influence on the part of the bank and, she said, for that reason the charge should be set aside. Should this agreement be set aside as had that of Farmer Bundy or had the Court of Appeal gone too far a decade earlier?

The House of Lords, in a more restrictive approach to the issue, held that a transaction could not be set aside on the grounds of undue influence unless it was shown that the transaction was actually to the 'manifest disadvantage' of the person subjected to that influence. A confidential relationship by itself would not necessarily give rise to a presumption of undue influence. Further, and contrary to the views of Lord Denning MR, the doctrine was not based simply on inequality of bargaining power.

The parade of litigation brought by high street banks against their former customers continued in *Barclays Bank* v. *O'Brien* 1993. By then eleven similar cases had been before the Court of Appeal in the preceding eight years and had led to a difference of judicial opinion. Mr O'Brien had guaranteed a company's overdraft with its bankers by granting Barclays a second charge over the home which he jointly owned with his wife, Bridget O'Brien. The bank staff failed to advise the O'Briens to take independent legal advice and the wife signed the documents at the bank without reading them. All too predictably, the company overdraft was not repaid and the bank sought to enforce its security upon the charge over the O'Briens' matrimonial home. The wife raised a number of issues contending both that her husband had put undue pressure on her to sign and that he had misrepresented the effect of the legal charge (another name for mortgage). The House of Lords held that if there had been undue influence by the principal debtor then, unless the creditor (i.e. here the bank) had taken reasonable steps to satisfy himself or itself that the obligation had been entered into freely and in knowledge of the true facts, the creditor (the bank or other financial institution) would be unable to enforce that obligation. On the particular facts of this case, the judges said that Barclays Bank, knowing that the parties were husband and wife, should have been put on inquiry as to the circumstances in which the wife had agreed to stand as surety for her husband's debt. The bank's failure, moreover, to warn the wife about the consequences of signing such documents or to advise her to take independent legal advice meant that the bank should be taken as knowing of the husband's misrepresentation. In those circumstances, Mrs O'Brien was entitled to set aside the charge on her home.

Any wife or girlfriend who jointly owned her home and who thought that bank borrowing could be lightly avoided by her playing the role of the dumb blonde should note the juxtaposition in the law reports of this decision with the claim of another financial institution in *CIBC Mortgages plc* v. *Pitt* 1994. The Pitts owned a valuable house with a small building society mortgage upon it. They borrowed £150,000 on the security of their home saying, among other things, that they wanted to use the money to buy a holiday home. Mr Pitt then used the money borrowed upon this remortgage to buy shares. Initially he was very successful, indeed becoming a millionaire, but lost a lot of money in the Stock Market crash of 1987.

When the mortgagees (CIBC) tried to enforce the security upon the Pitts' matrimonial home, Mrs Pitt alleged that the charge had been procured by her husband's misrepresentation and undue influence (as with Mrs O'Brien). The result, however, was different because as far as CIBC were concerned the transaction consisted of a joint loan to a married couple to allow them to clear their existing mortgage and to buy themselves a holiday home. There was nothing in the transaction to indicate that this was anything other than a normal advance for the joint benefit of a married couple living together in apparent marital harmony. The mere fact, said the House of Lords, that there was a risk of undue influence because one of the borrowers was a wife was, by itself, not enough to put the lenders on inquiry. In effect, the judges took the view that it would be commercially unrealistic to impose knowledge of undue influence upon banks and similar institutions where a borrower was married. As Lord Browne-Wilkinson remarked:

> ...such transactions would become almost impossible. On every purchase of a home in joint names, the building society or bank financing the purchase would have to insist on meeting the wife separately from the husband, advise her as to the nature of the transaction and recommend her to take legal advice separate from that of her husband. If that were not done, the financial institution would have to run the risk of a subsequent attempt by the wife to avoid her liabilities under the mortgage on the grounds of undue influence or misrepresentation. To establish the law in that sense would not benefit the average married couple and would discourage financial institutions from making the advance.

This harsh test was the subject of considerable criticism. Yet another dispute between a high street bank and borrower came before the Court of Appeal in *Barclays Bank* v. *Coleman* 2000 when the judges, themselves anxious about the binding force of the House of Lords' approach in *National Westminster Bank* v. *Morgan* 1985, seized the opportunity of considering what the concept of 'manifest disadvantage' actually involved. Indeed, following the earlier decision of the House of Lords in *CIBC Mortgages plc* v. *Pitt* 1994 a claimant who proved actual undue influence was no longer under the further burden of proving that the transaction was manifestly disadvantageous. Such a test, however, remained before any presumption of undue influence could arise. The Court of Appeal was, of course, bound by the approach of the House of Lords. Nevertheless, the judges did go on to water down the approach holding that even small manifest disadvantage would be sufficient.

4.11 *Contracts* uberrimae fidei

Next time you insure your car, your house or yourself, have a look at the declaration you will almost certainly be asked to sign. More often than not you end up declaring that the answers you have given 'shall form the basis of the contract'. This means that if you have not presented a complete picture on which the insurance company can assess you as a risk, and thus decide whether they want the business at all and, if they do, at what premium, it may not pay up in the event of a claim: in short, it will **repudiate** the policy.

A company may do this because there are some contracts which are said to be *uberrimae fidei* ('of the utmost good faith'). In *Bell* v. *Lever Brothers Ltd* 1932, Lord Atkin discussed such agreements:

> *There are certain contracts expressed by the law to be contracts of the utmost good faith, where material facts must be disclosed: if not, the contract is voidable. Apart from special fiduciary relationships, contracts for partnerships and contracts of insurance are the leading instances. In such cases the duty does not arise out of contract; the duty of a person proposing an insurance arises before a contract is made, so of an intending partner.*

The most obvious everyday example remains the insurance proposal. It is no secret that a middle-aged man with a twenty years' no-claims bonus, driving a small family saloon, is a more attractive risk to an insurance company than a seventeen-year-old learner who mows down old ladies on zebra crossings in his flash foreign GT sports coupé with 'go faster' stripes down the side. So if the latter either conceals any information or actually lies about himself (such as his age, occupation and driving record) or his car and especially any alterations made to it, hoping to shave a few pounds off his premium, it may well prove to be an expensive false economy: his insurers will decline to pay up when he subsequently knocks Auntie Flo off her bicycle.

For example, in *Locker and Woolf Ltd* v. *Western Australian Insurance Co. Ltd* 1936 a client seeking fire insurance was faced with the question: 'Has this or any other insurance of yours been declined by any other company?' and answered 'no'. In fact, the company had been declined insurance on cars some time earlier. The Court of Appeal held that the non-disclosure of this refusal of the motor-car insurance was the non-disclosure of a material fact in the proposal for the fire insurance and this entitled the insurers to avoid the policy.

More recently, another insurance company accepted the premium money on a policy which was to cover the insured against the risk of fire, among other risks. However, when faced with a claim for £30,000 (after the house in question was burned down), the company sought to avoid liability. In *Woolcott* v. *Sun Alliance and London Insurance* 1978 George Woolcott had bought a house in 1972 called 'Greenacres' in Kent. He obtained insurance cover from the Sun Alliance. On the relevant form one open and rather vague question asked: 'Are there any other matters which you wish to be taken into account?' Woolcott said 'no'. He did not say (for he did not think he was being asked about his moral character) that in 1960 he had been sentenced to twelve years' imprisonment for robbery. Some two years later 'Greenacres' was destroyed by fire. Mr Woolcott now claimed on the policy and for the first time the Sun Alliance learned of his criminal past. They refused to pay contending that a criminal conviction increased the moral hazards of the risk they were insuring.

The court held that Mr Woolcott had been under a duty to disclose his criminal record for that affected the moral hazard which the insurers had to assess. Such material non-disclosure allowed the insurance company to avoid paying up the policy.

It now seems unlikely, following the implementation of the Unfair Terms in Consumer Contract Regulations 1994, as amended, that minor omissions in the insurance proposal form would allow insurers to repudiate liability on grounds of non-disclosure.

Similar requirements of absolute good faith are further reflected in the Companies Act 1985, which makes special provisions as to the sort of information which must be contained in any company prospectus (a document advising the investing public about the company). Failure to include this information will allow a prospective shareholder to rescind the contract.

The obvious need to know what one is buying or becoming involved in is further reflected in contracts such as the sale of land and partnership agreements, where all material facts, whether advantageous or not, must be disclosed to a prospective purchaser or would-be partner. The same principles are also applied to family settlements and similar domestic arrangements.

4.12 Illegality

Gangster films sometimes refer to 'underworld' disputes where one member has made himself sufficiently unpopular for a rival gang to put out a so-called 'contract' for that unfortunate's premature demise. What redress would there be then if the assassin, having performed his task, were not paid his fee? Obviously it would be abhorrent for the courts to give effect to an agreement which so clearly threatens society. The reason for the law's refusal to uphold such agreements is commonly put in the Latin maxim *ex turpi causa non oritur actio* ('no claim arises from a base cause').

This policy was well summarised by Lord Mansfield CJ in the eighteenth century when he declared:

> *No court will lend its aid to a man who founds his cause of action upon an immoral or illegal act. If the cause of action appears to arise* ex turpi causa ... *the court says he has no right to be assisted.*

Although less obvious and less dramatic than our hypothetical example, there are many kinds of agreement which the courts will refuse to recognise. They are best examined one at a time.

Agreements involving crime

That the courts will not give effect to an agreement which involves the commission of a crime can be seen from the decision of the Court of Appeal in *Berg* v. *Sadler and Moore* 1937. Mr Berg sold cigarettes and was a member of the Tobacco Trade Association. One object of that association was to prevent price-cutting and to secure price maintenance. Each trader, when supplied with the tobacco, agreed that he would not sell it at below the minimum retail price. Mr Berg nevertheless cut his prices and, when the association found out, they refused to supply him with any more cigarettes. He was also placed on their 'stop-list'.

Mr Berg tried to find a way around this ban. He approached another member of the association, Mr Reeve, who was still able to obtain supplies. Mr Reeve then ordered cigarettes in his own name and subsequently passed them on to Mr Berg.

One day Mr Reeve ordered some more cigarettes from the defendants. To pay for those cigarettes Mr Berg provided £70 which was handed over to the defendants. One of the defendants, Mr Moore, became suspicious and refused to hand over the goods immediately. Mr Berg demanded the return of the £70 but the defendants refused, and their refusal was supported by the Court of Appeal. The court said that, in deceiving the defendants about the destination of the cigarettes, Mr Berg had attempted to obtain goods by false pretences. This of course was an offence under the Larceny Act 1916. As Romer LJ said:

> *The money was paid by the plaintiff to the defendants in the course and for the purpose of an attempt on the part of the plaintiff to defraud the defendants ...*
>
> *...it is abundantly plain that no court in this country would lift a finger to help the plaintiff to recover from the defendants the money which the plaintiff paid to them.*

That was a case where a specific statute, the Larceny Act 1916, had been breached. An act may be illegal even though no particular statute has been broken, but because it is nevertheless contrary to public policy. *Gray* v. *Barr* 1971 is a tragic example.

Mr Gray and Mr Barr were fighting. Mr Barr was carrying a loaded shotgun, and in the course of the struggle the gun went off and one of the shots killed Mr Gray. Mrs Gray, the deceased's widow, claimed damages from Mr Barr under the Fatal Accident Acts legislation: her husband had been a farmer and Mrs Gray looked to Mr Barr to compensate her for the loss of her husband's earnings. Mr Barr admitted that he was liable to pay damages. However, he had taken out a 'hearth and home' insurance policy in respect of his possible liability for 'bodily injury to any person ... caused by accidents'. Could Mr Barr claim on this insurance policy for the £6,000 damages awarded against him? The policy was, of course, intended to cover risks such as that of the milkman tripping over a loose paving-stone in Mr Barr's garden.

The Court of Appeal held that the insurance company did not have to indemnify Mr Barr. The court took the view that Mr Barr's conduct had been blameworthy and it agreed with the trial judge when he had said:

> *In the present case there was certainly a deliberate and intentional assault and probably also an unlawful battery committed by the defendant. The death of the deceased resulted from those actions which were an essential ingredient in the course of events leading to the death, and the defendant, therefore, is not entitled to the indemnity which he seeks from the third party.*

In the Court of Appeal, Salmon LJ was quite emphatic about the dangers to public policy of allowing such an indemnity, when he said:

> *Although public policy is rightly regarded as an unruly steed which should be cautiously ridden, I am confident that public policy undoubtedly requires that no one who threatens unlawful violence with a loaded gun should be allowed to enforce a claim for indemnity against any liability he may incur as a result of having so acted.*

More recently, a bank was to rely upon the maxim *ex turpi causa non oritur actio* when sued by a disgruntled customer whose cheque had been paid into the wrong account. In *Thackwell* v. *Barclays Bank plc* 1986 the plaintiff claimed damages from Barclays when the bank had wrongly credited a cheque in the sum of £44,227 to the wrong account after the bank had failed to notice that the endorsement on the cheque had been forged. The money represented the dishonest proceeds of a fraud on a finance company. Against such an unedifying background, the judge refused to allow Raymond Thackwell to recover a penny of the money because it was contrary to public policy to allow the plaintiff the use of moneys which had been obtained by fraud in the first place.

The music hall comedian's warning to potential bigamists that the maximum penalty for such an offence is two mothers-in-law would not have greatly amused the Court of Appeal when, in *Whiston* v. *Whiston* 1998, they had to consider the rights of a bigamist wife to claim financial relief upon annulment of such ceremony of marriage. Although the offence was perhaps not treated as seriously as had once been the case, being said to 'involve an outrage upon public decency by the profanation of a solemn ceremony', Maria Whiston had still committed an imprisonable offence. In those circumstances, the Court of Appeal held that it was offensive to public policy to allow a bigamist to avail herself of financial provision afforded to those who had contracted valid marriages.

Agreements which would corrupt public life

At the end of the year 2000 there was renewed public concern at the grant of knighthoods and at the elevation to the peerage of some rich businessmen who had earlier made massive donations or loans to the funds of both main political parties. The press were keen to investigate the nexus, if any, between these payments of millions of pounds and the inclusion of the politicians' benefactor in the subsequent New Year's Honours list. These concerns are not new for there is still debate about the so-called 'Lavender List' prepared by the Labour Prime Minister, Harold Wilson, at the time of his surprise resignation in 1976 and the inclusion in the resignation honours list of some party funders. A decade later there were allegations that, during the 1986 Westland affair, a knighthood had been promised to one businessman in return for his support in opposing the European bid for the company.

One attempt to influence the honours system had already been that of Colonel Parkinson in *Parkinson* v. *College of Ambulance Ltd* 1925. The secretary of the defendant college had intimated to Colonel Parkinson that he, the secretary, was in a position to influence the granting of honours. The secretary had further promised to obtain a knighthood for the plaintiff if he were prepared to donate £10,000 to the college. The plaintiff did, in fact, hand over £3,000 but when no knighthood was forthcoming, he tried to get his money back.

The court held that, even though the money might have been put to a commendable purpose, the agreement was an improper one and was illegal. Consequently, the plaintiff would not be able to recover his money from the college.

As Lush J said:

> The contract, in my opinion, is one that could not be sanctioned or recognized in a court of justice ... a contract for the purchase of a title, however the money is to be expended, is itself an improper contract.

This case led to Parliament itself taking action by passing the Honours (Prevention of Abuses) Act 1925, which made such efforts a specific offence, punishable with imprisonment.

Agreements against the interest of justice

We saw in Unit 3.8 that a person who had been granted bail subject to the taking of sureties is, theoretically at least, in the custody of his sureties. They must, for example, ensure that he attends his trial and, if he fails to do so, they may be called upon to part with some or all of the money they agreed to put up. This threat, of course, acts as a considerable incentive for sureties to take their duties seriously. If they were only to lose someone else's money that fear would be taken away and this aspect of criminal procedure would take on the appearance of a game with paper money.

Such factors were unlikely to have weighed over-heavily on the mind of a man who stood surety in *Herman* v. *Jeuchner* 1885. In order to protect that surety from losing his money in the event of the accused defaulting, the latter deposited some of his own money with the surety. When he subsequently asked for it back, the Court of Appeal held that he could not recover his cash, because the contract had been an illegal one. As Brett MR said:

> When the object of either the promise or the consideration is to promote the committal of an illegal act, the contract itself is illegal and cannot be enforced ... To my mind, it is illegal because it takes away the protection which the law affords for securing the good behaviour of the plaintiff.

Moreover, it is clear from the decision of the Court of Criminal Appeal in *R* v. *Porter* 1910 that such an agreement also involves the commission of a criminal offence. Mr Porter stood surety for an accused person who, in depositing £50 with Mr Porter, had agreed to indemnify him against any loss in the event of a breach of bail. The implications were explained by Lord Alverstone CJ when he said:

> ...the agreement entered into by the appellant was an illegal contract, not only in the sense of being unenforceable, but also as being one which clearly tended to produce a public mischief and that it amounted to criminal conspiracy.

Sexually immoral agreements

It is against the policy of English law to promote sexual licence. One manifestation of this attitude is the refusal of the courts to uphold agreements founded upon an immoral consideration, for example, an agreement for future cohabitation or otherwise involving immorality. For example, in *Pearce* v. *Brookes* 1866 some coach-builders hired a coach to a woman whom they knew to be a prostitute and who wanted it to attract her customers. When the plaintiff coach-builders sued for their money, the court held that, as they had known that the coach was to be used for immoral purposes, they were unable to recover their money. Immorality was fatal to the plaintiffs' claim for, as Baron Bramwell said:

> Nor can any distinction be made between an illegal and an immoral purpose; the rule which is applicable to the matter is ex turpi causa non oritur actio *and whether it is an immoral or an illegal purpose in which the plaintiff has participated, it comes equally within the terms of that maxim, and the effect is the same.*

More recently Parliament has acted in response to an emotive public reaction to the Warnock report into Human Fertilisation and Embryology, which considered the issue of surrogacy, a practice where a woman will bear a child for a couple unable to start a family themselves. On birth, the mother hands the baby to the father for him and his wife to bring up as their own. Difficulties of all sorts could arise if the mother declined to hand the baby over in accordance with her agreement. Since the Surrogacy Arrangements Act 1985 came into force, commercial surrogacy agreements are illegal. It seems likely, therefore, that a court would refuse to order the natural mother either to part with her new-born child or to refund her fees for such so-called 'rent-a-womb' service.

Agreements to defraud the Revenue

Tax avoidance, while allegedly one feature of the unacceptable face of capitalism, is no crime. Indeed, it has been judicially stated that every person has a right to arrange his or her affairs so as to attract the minimum liability for tax. Tax evasion is very different, however: it is a criminal offence and so any agreement intended to facilitate such evasion is illegal, as was the arrangement in *Napier* v. *National Business Agency* 1951. Mr Napier was employed by the defendants at a salary of £13 per week (which was, of course, taxable). He was also allowed expenses. Expenses are not taxable because they are intended only to reimburse an employee for what he has spent on his employer's behalf. Mr Napier's expenses did not, in fact, exceed £1 per week but his employers allowed him £6 per week. This arrangement came to light when Mr Napier was sacked and he sued his former employers, the defendants, for wages in lieu of notice.

The Court of Appeal showed Mr Napier little sympathy and clearly took the view that the aim had been to mislead the Revenue. That illegality had so tainted the whole contract that Mr Napier not only failed to recover his £6 per week expenses but also was unable to recover one penny of his legitimate wages. As Denning LJ said:

> *The insertion of a fictitious figure for expenses in order to defraud the Revenue is illegal. It vitiates the whole remuneration and disentitles the servant from recovering any part of it. He cannot recover either the part described as expenses or even the part described as salary.*

a) The effects of illegality

We have seen that, as a general principle, an agreement which is tainted with illegality is void – a claimant will be unable to compel performance, to recover any property or to obtain damages. In *Ashmore Ltd* v. *Dawson Ltd* 1973, for instance, a large piece of machinery, a 'tube-bank', was to be transported from the plaintiffs' factory to a port. The plaintiffs' transport manager was present when the tube-bank was loaded on to the defendants' vehicle. The weight of the lorry then exceeded the maximum weight permitted by the regulations by some five tons. The manager was aware of such regulations. On the way to the port, the tube-bank fell off the lorry and was damaged. The plaintiffs now claimed damages, alleging negligence and/or breach of contract. The Court of Appeal held that, on the evidence, the plaintiffs' manager must have realised that the weight was in breach of the regulations and that the plaintiffs had, therefore, participated in an illegal act and so were now unable to recover any damages for their loss.

There are, however, some exceptions to this rule.

In pari delicto, potior est conditio defendentis

This piece of lawyers' Latin means: 'Where the parties are equally at fault, the defendant is in the better position', and it expresses the general rule applying to otherwise void contracts. Lord Denning MR made this clear when he said in *Ashmore Ltd* v. *Dawson Ltd*:

> *I know that Dawsons were parties to the illegality. They knew, as well as Mr Bulmer, that the load was overweight in breach of the regulations. But in such a situation as this, the defendants are in a better position.* In pari delicto, potior est conditio defendentis.

It follows from this that a claimant might be able to recover where he could show that he was at fault to a lesser degree than the defendant. He could show this by proving that he had entered into the agreement under some form of oppression (for example, an employer's economic superiority over his servant) or, as in *Hughes* v. *Liverpool Victoria Legal Friendly Society* 1916, that he had acted on a fraudulent misrepresentation. In that case, the plaintiff was able to recover the premiums which she had paid to take over an insurance policy which was illegal and void. This was possible because the defendants' agent had fraudulently told her that the policy would be legal.

Class-protecting statutes

Some Acts are specifically intended to protect a particular group in society. They are commonly referred to as class-protecting statutes. Members of such a class are in a privileged position. Even though the contract may be illegal, members of the class so protected will, nevertheless, be able to recover any property exchanged under the agreement. For example, in *Bonnard* v. *Dott* 1906 the plaintiff had borrowed some money. The lender had not been licensed as required by the Moneylenders Act 1900, an Act which provided that any agreement made with an unlicensed moneylender was illegal and void. The plaintiff, who was a member of the class which the Act was intended to protect from usury, sought to recover the share certificates which he had deposited as security. The court held that, as a member of that class, the plaintiff would be able to get back his share certificates.

Severance

Where the illegal content is minimal, it may be possible to take a 'blue pencil' and strike out the offending words. However, the test is a strict one and the remainder of the agreement must still make proper sense and be capable of being lawfully fulfilled. For example, in *Fielding and Platt Ltd* v. *Najjar* 1969 the parties allegedly agreed that the plaintiff company should render false invoices so as to deceive the Lebanese authorities into admitting a press into the country under import licences which did not, in fact, cover those goods. The Court of Appeal held that the arrangement for invoicing the goods was not a term of the contract but that, even if it were a term of the contract which would be void for illegality, it was severable and would leave the remainder of the contract capable of being performed legally.

Repentance

Before an illegal agreement is actually carried out, one party may decide not to go through with it. If that 'repentance' is both genuine and early enough, that party may, so to speak, wash off that illegality and then be able to recover any property transferred.

A claim other than in contract

A party to an illegal agreement may still be assisted by the courts if he is able to found his action otherwise than on the illegal agreement, for example, in tort. This was the case in *Bowmakers Ltd* v. *Barnet Instruments Ltd* 1944, where the defendants sold some tools which they had acquired under certain hire-purchase agreements. Those agreements contravened the wartime licensing regulations. The defendants, in selling goods which did not belong to them, had committed the tort of conversion. In this way the plaintiffs were able to recover damages in tort, although they would not have been able to recover if they had been obliged to rely on the illegal agreement.

4.13 *Void and voidable agreements*

It remains to look at the effect of other agreements which are not actually illegal and which do not breach morality but which will still not be enforced by the courts because of their potentially adverse effects on the public. They are best examined separately because, as Bowen LJ said in *Mogul Steamship Co.* v. *McGregor Gow & Co.* 1892:

> ...*the term 'illegal' here is a misleading one. Contracts, as they are called, in restraint of trade are not in my opinion illegal in any sense except that the law will not enforce them. It does not prohibit the making of such contracts; it merely declines after they have been made to recognize their validity.*

More recently, in *Bennett* v. *Bennett* 1952, Denning LJ, as he then was, considered a promise made by a wife involved in divorce negotiations that she would not take proceedings for maintenance on behalf of her child. He said:

> *In solving this problem, a useful analogy may be drawn from covenants in unreasonable restraint of trade. Such covenants offend public policy just as the covenants of a wife may do. They are not 'illegal' in the sense that a contract to do a prohibited or immoral act is illegal. They are not 'unenforceable' in the sense that a contract within the Statute of Frauds is unenforceable for want of writing. Those covenants lie somewhere in between. They are invalid and unenforceable. The law does not punish them. It simply takes no notice of them. They are void, not illegal.*

Incidentally, the Child Support Act 1991 now specifically provides that this sort of promise not to claim maintenance for a child is void.

Into this class fall two different kinds of agreement which are thought to constitute a possible danger to the public: agreements to oust the jurisdiction of the courts (as with child maintenance) and agreements in unreasonable restraint of trade.

a) Agreements to oust the jurisdiction of the courts

We saw in Unit 2.4 that it is an important principle that all citizens enjoy the right of unimpeded access to the courts. Any attempt, for example by way of arbitration, to deprive any persons of that right will be rejected by the courts.

Such an attempt failed in *Czarnikow* v. *Roth, Schmidt & Co.* 1922, where a contract for the sale of sugar provided that if any dispute arose it should be referred to arbitration and that no party would be allowed to refer the matter to the court. The Court of Appeal held that the clause was contrary to public policy and of no effect because it purported to oust the jurisdiction of the courts.

b) Agreements in unreasonable restraint of trade

Such agreements cover a multitude of ways in which one of the parties agrees to restrict the way in which his business is to be carried on. For example, the seller of a business might agree with the buyer that he will not compete with his successor within a certain district or for a certain time after the sale.

The general attitude of the courts, however, is that such an agreement will be void unless the party seeking to rely on the clause can prove that it is reasonable. That, said Lord Parker in *Attorney-General for Australia* v. *Adelaide Steamship Co.* 1913, was a question for the court:

> to be determined after construing the contract and considering the circumstances existing when it was made. It is really a question of public policy and not a question of fact upon which evidence of the actual or probable consequences, if the contract be carried into effect, is admissible.

In deciding what is reasonable the court must, of course, have regard to the circumstances surrounding each case. Factors which are relevant will obviously include the subject-matter, the length of time the restraint is to run, its area and the nature of the relationship between the parties

The subject-matter of the agreement was important in the leading case of *Nordenfelt* v. *Maxim Nordenfelt Guns and Ammunition Co. Ltd* 1894. Nordenfelt, who in 1866 had invented a machine-gun called the 'Maxim', covenanted with the company to which he had sold the patent that he would not be involved in the manufacture of guns for 25 years, unless it was on the company's behalf. The House of Lords held that the covenant (which, of course, was quite unrestricted as to area) was not wider than was reasonably required for the company's protection, considering the specialised nature of the business and the limited number of customers involved. As Lord Herschell LC explained:

> If the covenant embraced anything less than the whole of the United Kingdom, it is obvious that it would be nugatory. The only customers of the respondents must be found amongst the Governments of this and other countries, and it would not practically be material to them whether the business were carried on in one part of the United Kingdom or another.

The views of another judge in that case were reviewed by Lord Parker in *Herbert Morris Ltd.* v. *Saxelby* 1916, when he said:

> It will be observed that in Lord Macnaghten's opinion two conditions must be fulfilled if the restraint is to be held valid. First, it must be reasonable in the interests of the contracting parties, and, secondly, it must be reasonable in the interests of the public. In the case of each condition he lays down a test of reasonableness. To be reasonable in the interests of the parties, the restraint must afford adequate protection to the party in whose favour it is imposed; to be reasonable in the interests of the public it must be in no way injurious to the public.
>
> With regard to the former view, I think it is clear that what is meant is that for a restraint to be reasonable in the interests of the parties, it must afford no more than adequate protection to the party in whose favour it is imposed.

The confidential and personal nature of a solicitor–client relationship was held to be in need of protection in the important case of *Fitch* v. *Dewes* 1921. Mr Fitch, a solicitor's clerk, who later qualified as a solicitor, covenanted with Mr Dewes, an already established solicitor, that, if he were ever to leave Mr Dewes' employment, he would not practise as a solicitor within a radius of seven miles of Tamworth Town Hall. The House of Lords upheld that agreement because, although no time limit was involved, the covenant did not exceed what in the circumstances was reasonably required for the protection of Mr Dewes. Neither did such a covenant operate against the public interest.

It is an accepted fact that many people in trade, such as shop assistants, hairdressers and milkmen, form special relationships with customers and that the employing company's interests may not always be uppermost in the minds of all concerned. Against this background, there is a need for protective covenants, an example of which can be seen in the case of *Home Counties Diaries Ltd* v. *Skilton* 1970. Mr Skilton was a milkman. He agreed with his employers that, for a year after leaving Home Counties Diaries, he would not 'serve or sell milk or dairy produce to, or solicit orders for milk or dairy produce from, any person or company' with whom he had dealt in the last six months of his employment.

. . . form special relationships with customers . . .

After leaving his employers, Mr Skilton found similar work and again worked as a milkman on his former round where, of course, he enjoyed the goodwill of his old customers. He was, in the words of Harman LJ, 'a familiar and probably influential character, well known to every householder in the road'. When the former employers sought an injunction to stop Mr Skilton working his old round, the Court of Appeal had to consider the defence put forward that the clause was too wide and, therefore, invalid as being in restraint of trade. The court rejected that argument because the clause referred only to trading as a dairyman and the employee would not, therefore, be prevented from working otherwise than as a dairyman – for example, selling butter and cheese or in a restaurant. Secondly, said the court, the clause relating to service of previous customers was not unreasonable since the employer could reasonably hope that any errant customer might well return.

In *Clarke* v. *Newland* 1991 the Court of Appeal had to consider the validity of an agreement between two doctors which had proscribed (rather than prescribed) the junior partner setting up his own surgery 'in the practice area' within three years of any termination of the partnership. When the assistant planned to practise round the corner the senior partner sought an injunction. The junior doctor sought to dispense with that agreement, saying that it was completely one-sided and applied only to him. Looking at the nature of the partnership and viewing the object of the clause as the protection of the senior doctor's practice, the Court of Appeal held that the clause was enforceable.

4.14 Privity

We saw how, in *Adler* v. *Dickson* 1954, a passenger was able to recover damages against the master and the boatswain of a ship because the passenger's contract had been made with the shipping company and, therefore, only the shipping company could take shelter behind an exemption clause (see Unit 4.7). The officers and crew, who of course had not been parties to that contract, could not take advantage of it. This is an obvious example of the long-standing refusal of English law until very recently to recognise rights or obligations of third parties; there is, it is said, no **privity of contract**. In its simplest form this doctrine means that if Tom and Dick make a contract, Dick's friend Harry has nothing to do with it – he has no interest: he cannot incur liability under it or take advantage of it.

This rule was clearly established by the early nineteenth century. For example, in *Price* v. *Easton* 1833 the court held that no one could be bound by the terms of a contract to which he was not an original party.

That this was still the case, even where the contract had been made for the express benefit of some third party, was confirmed in *Tweddle* v. *Atkinson* 1861. A father and a father-in-law had agreed with each other to pay some money to the lucky husband. The father-in-law did not pay up, however, and so the husband, for whose benefit the contract had of course been made, sued for that money. The judge dismissed the claim and held that, in the absence of consideration, the plaintiff husband could not succeed. The judge said that

> ...*it is now established that no stranger to the consideration can take advantage of a contract, although made for his benefit.*

The topic came in for the definitive pronouncement of the House of Lords in *Dunlop* v. *Selfridge & Co. Ltd* 1915. Dunlop sold car-tyres to a wholesaler, Dew & Co., who in return for discount agreed not to sell the tyres to a retailer at a price below Dunlop's list price. They further agreed to obtain similar undertakings from any other dealers to whom they in turn sold the tyres. Selfridges, however, undercut the market by selling tyres below the list price, and the manufacturers then tried to obtain an injunction (an order of the court) preventing them from doing so. The House of Lords held that there was nothing that Dunlop could do. The contract which contained the relevant term had been made between the manufacturers and the wholesaler: it had not been made between the manufacturers and any retailer. The wholesaler (Dew) was bound, but the retailer (Selfridge), as a stranger to the contract, was not bound by it. Viscount Haldane LC, in declaring that there was no contract between Dunlop and Selfridges, was emphatic:

> *My Lords, in the law of England certain principles are fundamental. One is that only a person who is a party to a contract can sue on it. Our law knows nothing of a* jus quaesitum tertio *arising by way of contract. Such a right may be conferred by way of property, as, for example, under a trust, but it cannot be conferred on a stranger to a contract as a right to enforce the contract* in personam.

This had long remained the law and attempts to vary or erode the rule were not approved by the House of Lords in *Scruttons Ltd* v. *Midland Silicones Ltd* 1962.

The liability of a firm of carriers was limited under the contract to $500 per day in the event of loss, damage or delay. Some drums of chemicals were shipped from America to London and a drum was damaged in transit. The actual damage amounted to much more than $500. Scruttons, who were stevedores engaged by the carriers (but not parties to the initial contract), tried to limit their liability to $500, but the House of Lords held that the stevedores had no right to rely on that clause.

An interesting application of the rule is to be found in the decision of the House of Lords in *Beswick* v. *Beswick* 1967. Peter Beswick was a coal merchant. He sold his business to his nephew, John, who agreed to pay his uncle £6/10s (now £6.50) per week during Peter's lifetime and then £5 per week to his aunt after his uncle's death. The uncle died but John refused to hand over the weekly £5 to his aunt. The aunt now sued for her money. She did so, of course, in a dual capacity: firstly, she was the administratrix of her late husband's estate, and, secondly, she was suing in a personal capacity as the person for whose benefit the contract had been made. The House of Lords disallowed her claim in her personal capacity but held that she could obtain specific performance of the contract in her capacity as administratrix. They took into consideration the effect of the Law of Property Act 1925, section 56(1), which provides:

> A person may take an immediate or other interest in land or other property, or the benefit of any condition, right of entry, covenant or agreement over or respecting land or other property, although he may not be named as a party to the conveyance or other instrument.

In *Drive Yourself Hire Co.* v. *Strutt* 1953, Denning LJ had suggested that the effect of this section was to do away with the rule in *Tweddle* v. *Atkinson*, leaving the courts free, in cases respecting property, to go back to the old common law whereby a third party can sue on a contract made expressly for his benefit.

However, in *Beswick* v. *Beswick*, the House of Lords said that 'property' in this section meant 'real property' (which is the name lawyers give to land as opposed to, say, a television set, which is a form of 'personal property').

A number of other exceptions to this rule will crop up later in the book. One important exception concerns agency (discussed in more detail in Unit 4.15): where a contract has been entered into by an agent, the principal may sue on that contract. This, of course, is not surprising because the whole point of agency is that the acts of the agent are treated in law as being those of the principal.

Some hint of further erosion was to be seen in the decision of the Court of Appeal in *Jackson* v. *Horizon Holidays Ltd* 1975. Mr Jackson took his wife and three young children to Ceylon on a Horizon holiday. They were badly disappointed with the hotel. In particular, there was no mini-golf, no swimming pool, no beauty salon or hairdressing salon, the food was distasteful and the walls were decorated with fungus and mildew. Mr Jackson had paid £1,200 for a four-week holiday. On returning home, Mr Jackson sued the company, and the only dispute was what the measure of damages should be – how much cash could he get?

The Court of Appeal held that, where a person had entered into a contract for the benefit of himself and others who were not parties to the contract, he could sue on the contract for damages for losses suffered not only by himself but also by the others as a result of a breach of contract. It made no difference that the contracting party was not a trustee for the other. In short, the father could recover damages for the discomfort of his wife and children, even though the claim had to be brought in his own name.

The potential injustice of this doctrine that a person who is not a party to a contract may not enforce it (even when for that person's benefit) had led to sustained criticism even before the Law Commission's Report in 1996. The new Contracts (Rights of Third Parties) Act 1999 now allows a third party beneficiary to enforce a contract in certain situations. Under section 1 of the Act a third party may in his own right enforce a term of the contract if:

(a) the contract expressly provides that he may, or
(b) the term purports to confer a benefit on him.

The third party must be expressly identified in the contract by name, or as a member of a class or as answering a particular description. Even then, however, the third party still will have no rights to enforce the contract if 'on a proper construction of the contract it appears that the parties did not intend the term to be enforceable by the third party'.

4.15 Agency

The examples of contracts so far examined have all been relatively straightforward cases of the kind where, for instance, Edward goes to the shop to buy a kilo of sausages from Eleanor, both contracting parties being together in the shop.

Of course, to require both parties always to be present together in the shop or in the factory would do little to boost British exports. The managing directors of all our leading companies would have to travel the country ordering a packet of paper clips here, a ton of coal there, and so on. It would be absurd.

This is why the law recognises the doctrine of **agency**. Agency, in law, has nothing to do with the way a garage sells petrol (even though it may describe itself as, say, a Shell or Esso 'agency') and the real-world contractual agent is far removed from the celluloid glamour of the Big Screen and James Bond. Rather, he is simply someone who is authorised to act on behalf of another, who, in turn, is known as the **principal**. In this way, the agent has power to enter into contracts on behalf of his principal. That contract is then that of the principal – the agent is not himself a party because it was not personally his contract for English law recognises that *qui facit per alium, facit per se* ('he who does something through another does it himself').

Of course, for this reason, it is obviously vital that the principal enjoys full contractual capacity. The role of the agent, however, is different and, as the contract is not his, he may be under eighteen. In law the effect is the same as if the principal had actually gone along in person to make the contract.

This general rule, however, is subject to the doctrine of the **undisclosed principal**, which is considered further in the paragraph on 'Agency by ratification' below. In outline, this doctrine will apply where an agent does not disclose the fact that he is acting for a principal. In such a case, two particular limitations may apply:

1. If something goes wrong, the other party has a choice between suing either the principal or, exceptionally, the agent.
2. If something goes wrong on the other side, the principal may only sue if the agent had in fact been properly authorised at the time of the contract – subsequent ratification is not good enough. Indeed, an undisclosed principal cannot ratify a contract.

For example, in *Keighley, Maxsted & Co.* v. *Durant & Co.* 1901, the House of Lords said that a contract made by a person intending to contract on behalf of a third party (but without that party's knowledge) cannot later be ratified by that third party so as to allow him to sue or be sued on that contract, unless that person had revealed that he was acting on behalf of the third party in question. Lord Macnaghten explained:

> As a general rule only persons who are parties to a contract acting either by themselves or by an authorized agent can sue or be sued on the contract. A stranger cannot enforce the contract nor can it be enforced against a stranger.

The relationship of principal and agent may arise in a variety of ways.

Agency arising expressly

Once again, the law will look at the intent rather than the precise jurisprudential form. For example, suppose that Robert is busy at his office when he suddenly remembers his wife's birthday. He has no idea what to get her so he sends Susan, his secretary, round to Harrods and tells her to pick up something suitable for him to take home. Here, Robert is the principal and Susan is his agent. The contract is, in fact, between Robert and Harrods, even though it was Susan who actually went into the shop and chose the present.

Agency arising impliedly

Robert's account at that emporium in SW1 may be thrown even further into the red by his wife, Ann. The law recognises that a wife has an implied power to pledge her husband's credit. Before the current vogue for emancipation, the courts (composed of male judges) had imposed certain limitations on this concept.

Firstly, the couple must be living together at the relevant time. Secondly, what the wife actually orders must be 'necessaries', which means substantially the same as it does in the case of infants (see Unit 4.4). A husband may, nevertheless, avoid paying for his wife's purchases if he can show that he had told her not to pledge his credit, or that he has told the shop in question that they are not to serve his wife as his agent.

Similarly, Susan, in her capacity as Robert's secretary, has authority to pledge Robert's credit for what is necessary to her work – for example, if she calls in someone to repair the photocopier her boss will have to pay for such service.

The extent to which a secretary (although a different sort of secretary from Susan) may bind his company was considered by the Court of Appeal in *Panorama Developments Ltd* v. *Fidelis Furnishing Fabrics Ltd* 1971. The plaintiffs ran a car-hire business, renting out prestigious cars. The defendant company had as its company secretary a Mr Bayne. This gentleman, who ended up in prison, ordered a number of cars from the plaintiffs and signed himself 'R.L. Bayne – company secretary'. The car company now wanted their money. The defendants knew nothing of these cars and argued that they could not be liable because Mr Bayne was only a secretary and, as such, had no authority to make contracts for the company. The Court of Appeal rejected the defence and Lord Denning MR, in distinguishing earlier authority, said:

> But times have changed. A company secretary is a much more important person nowadays than he was ... He is an officer of the company with extensive duties and responsibilities. This appears not only in the modern Companies Acts, but also by the role which he plays in the day-to-day business of companies. He is no longer a mere clerk ... He is certainly entitled to sign contracts connected with the administrative side of a company's affairs, such as employing staff, and ordering cars, and so forth. All such matters now come within the ostensible authority of a company's secretary. Accordingly I agree with the judge that Mr R.L. Bayne, as company secretary, had ostensible authority to enter into contracts for

> *the hire of these cars and, therefore, the company must pay for them. Mr Bayne was a fraud. But it was the company which put him in the position in which he, as company secretary, was able to commit the frauds. So the defendants are liable.*

Trade may be carried on not only as a company but also as a partnership. The partnership is a fine example of the relationship of principal and agent because each partner is liable for the acts of his fellow partners, and each partner is *prima facie* the agent of the firm and each other partner. This is because the Partnership Act 1890, section 5 provides:

> Every partner is an agent of the firm and his other partners for the purpose of the business of the partnership; and the acts of every partner who does any act for carrying on in the usual way business of the kind carried on by the firm of which he is a member bind the firm and his partners, unless the partner so acting has in fact no authority to act for the firm in the particular matter, and the person with whom he is dealing either knows that he has no authority, or does not know or believe him to be a partner.

Agency by ratification

One year Robert completely forgets his wife's birthday. Fortunately, for his safe return to the matrimonial home that evening, his efficient secretary Susan, on her own initiative, goes out to Harrods and buys a bracelet for the occasion, explaining to the shop assistant that it is for her boss. Robert returns to the office and is greatly relieved when Susan tells him of her thoroughness. At the time when Susan ordered the bracelet, she had no authority as Robert's agent – he did not know what she was doing and the bracelet was not essential to her work as a secretary. Nevertheless, Robert may so approve that he ratifies Susan's contract with Harrods, so that the contract is now between Harrods and him.

As we have seen, this ratification is only possible where the agent has said who the principal is; this ensures that one party cannot be deceived into contracting with someone with whom he would prefer not to do business.

Further, of course, it must now be that same principal who seeks to ratify the contract. For example, if Charles is starting up a new company he should wait until the company has been incorporated before he starts buying office furniture. This is because the company, as a separate entity, cannot ratify what he did as agent until it actually exists, and so until incorporation Charles will be personally liable on the debts. Thus in *Kelner* v. *Baxter* 1866, Erle CJ held the defendant personally liable on a contract made before the company had come into an existence independent of its members.

The effect of ratification is to endow that contract with all the force it would have enjoyed had the agent been so authorised before the contract had in fact been made.

Agency arising by necessity

When Robert and Ann go away for a weekend at the coast, they leave their son with Susan, whose secretarial duties have now extended to baby-sitting. While Robert and Ann are enjoying the sun and air on the beach, their own son and heir is taken ill. Susan cannot get in touch with the parents but calls in their family doctor whom she pays out of her own purse. Can Susan now recover the doctor's fees from Robert and Ann?

Where it is not possible for a person looking after someone else's property or animals to take instructions from the owner, he may act in this kind of emergency as an **agent of necessity**. In short, the law presumes that if Robert and Ann had known of the boy's illness they would naturally have wanted him to receive proper medical attention. This approach is illustrated in *Great Northern Railway* v. *Swaffield* 1874 when the defendant sent a horse by rail but failed to meet the animal at the station. The railway company sent the horse to a livery stable. The court held that the company had acted reasonably in doing what they did and, moreover, that since the defendant had failed to meet the horse, he was liable to the plaintiffs for all the stable charges which they had paid. In dealing with the problems raised by the horse, Baron Piggot said:

> *Then what were the carriers to do? They were bound from ordinary feelings of humanity to keep the horse safely and feed him; and that became necessary in consequence of the defendant's own conduct in refusing to receive the animal at the end of the journey according to his contract.*

Even so, because an agent is in a sense playing with someone else's money, the courts have adopted a restrictive attitude to this doctrine. For example, in *Prager* v. *Blatspiel Stamp & Heacock Ltd* 1924, both parties were fur merchants, the defendants operating in Bucharest and the plaintiffs in London. During the First World War, the defendants bought some skins for the plaintiffs. When the Germans invaded Rumania, however, the defendants were no longer able to send the skins to England; indeed they could not even get in touch with the plaintiffs. After the war the plaintiffs asked for their skins but the defendants wrote to say:

> *We thought it best to realize your goods as they were getting stale and there was no knowing how long these troublous times might last.*

When sued, the defendants argued that they were agents of necessity. However, the judge held that on the facts no such necessity had existed. What the defendants should have done was to store the furs until communication was once again possible.

The strictness of the doctrine was further considered by the Court of Appeal in *Sachs* v. *Miklos* 1948. In 1940 Mr Sachs stored his furniture at the house of Mrs Miklos. In 1944 Mrs Miklos wanted him to collect the furniture, but, despite considerable effort, she was not able to get in touch with him. In July 1944 she sold his furniture at an auction for £13. A couple of years later Mr Sachs sued her for the value of the furniture which he said had been more than just £13. The Court of Appeal rejected all contention that the bailee was an agent of necessity and Lord Goddard CJ favoured a restrictive interpretation of the doctrine:

Agents of necessity, until very modern times, were confined to two classes of persons, those who accepted bills of exchange for the honour of the payee and masters of ships who found themselves in foreign parts and unable to get immediate instructions from their owners when they wanted money, for unlooked-for expenses and so forth. They then had power to pledge, sell or hypothecate [mortgage] the ship, and, in some cases, to deal with the cargo as agents of necessity. ... When it becomes impossible, or commercially impossible, or extra-ordinarily difficult, as may happen in the case of a strike or breakdown of communications, for a carrier to communicate with the owner of goods, there is no reason why he should not be entitled to sell or dispose of them in the same way as a master of a ship ... I think it is clear ... that the courts should be slow to increase the number of classes of people who can be looked on as agents of necessity. They are selling or disposing of other people's goods without the authority of the owners, and certain it is that they have never been entitled so to act unless there is a real emergency. In this case, what-ever else there might have been, there was no emergency. It was not a case of the house being destroyed and the furniture left exposed to thieves and the weather. There was nothing perishable here in the sense in which that term is used when applied to goods. The fact was that Mr and Mrs Miklos wanted to get rid of this furniture which was in their way.

a) The relationship between principal and agent

Duties of an agent

The law imposes duties upon principals and agents which extend beyond those that are purely contractual.

An agent must act honourably. He must not abuse the trust of his principal and must not take advantage of any confidential information which may come his way – any such wheeling and dealing, backhanders in brown envelopes and other such incidental emoluments or pourboires should be handed over to the principal, who will now also have a power to put an end to the agency. For instance, in *Reading* v. *Attorney-General* 1951 Mr Reading was an army sergeant stationed at Cairo. He found that his army uniform deterred the local constabulary from searching his lorry and so he put that sartorial advantage to good use in smuggling about £20,000 worth of drinks. On each expedition he was given a large sum of money but when he was caught the authorities inconveniently confiscated this cash. The House of Lords said that any position which enabled a servant to earn money by its use gave the master a right to take that money. In this case, the appellant was using his army stripes to obtain that money and so the Crown, as his employer, was entitled to relieve him of the cash.

Moreover, an agent must always put his principal's interests first. The agent is there to promote the interests of his principal. As part of that duty he is, of course, obliged to keep in touch with his principal and follow his instructions. Neither must he lie down on the job. For instance, in *Keppel* v. *Wheeler* 1927 some estate agents failed to tell a client that they had received a higher offer for the house he wanted to sell. The Court of Appeal held that the agents' duty was not finished when they accepted one offer – they should have told their client of the higher offer. It followed that they were liable in damages for the difference in price between the two offers.

Duties of a principal

In return for the dutiful discharge of these responsibilities the agent is entitled to protection and remuneration from his principal. The principal must indemnify the agent against any liability entered into during the course of the agency. He must also pay any commission as agreed between them or whatever other sum is reasonable in the circumstances.

b) Termination of agency

Since the relationship between principal and agent is, in part at least, contractual, the relationship may in general be terminated in any of the ways that a contract is discharged – be it subsequent illegality, lapse of time, death, insanity or frustration. In rare and exceptional cases, however, the agency may be expressed as being irrevocable.

If, after the termination of his agency, an agent continues to contract with third parties he does so at his peril and in all likelihood at his expense. He should bear in mind two considerations in particular:

Firstly, an agent will be liable in damages to compensate anyone whom he misleads. For example, in *Starkey* v. *Bank of England* 1903 a stockbroker in good faith believed that he was a client's agent, although his supposed authorisation had in fact been forged. The House of Lords held, nonetheless, that the broker must have given an implied warranty that he had authority to act, and was accordingly liable to indemnify the Bank of England for any loss it had been caused.

Secondly, an agent will still be personally liable even if he did not know that his authority had been revoked. For example, in *Yonge* v. *Toynbee* 1910 some solicitors were instructed by a client. The client, however, was subsequently certified as of unsound mind. Unaware of this, the solicitors embarked on litigation. When the case did not proceed to trial, the question arose as to who was to pay the costs of the aborted litigation. The Court of Appeal held that the solicitors must pay those costs themselves because they had impliedly warranted that they were duly authorised when, in fact, their agency had ceased when their client was certified.

4.16 Part performance

Every time you get on a bus you make a contract. No special words are necessary – indeed, where there is a ticket machine you are unlikely even to open your mouth – neither do you have to write anything. As a general rule, a perfectly valid contract may be formed in any way the parties choose, although there are a few exceptional cases where the contract must be evidenced in writing, for example, hire-purchase agreements. Even if such a contract is not in writing it is not *ipso facto* void or even voidable. The contract itself is good: the difficulty would be in proving its existence and its terms. Without that writing there will not be the necessary evidence and, without that evidence, the contract must remain unenforceable at common law. This rule dates back to the seventeenth century when the Statute of Frauds 1677 provided:

> No action shall be brought whereby to charge any executor or administrator upon any special promise to answer damages out of his own estate; or whereby to charge the defendant upon any special promise to answer for the debt, default or miscarriage of another person; or to charge any person upon any agreement made upon consideration of marriage; or upon any contract of sale of lands, tenements or hereditaments, or any interest in or concerning them; or upon any agreement that is not to be performed within the space of one year from the making thereof, unless the agreement upon which such action shall be brought, or some memorandum or note thereof shall be in writing and signed by the party to be charged therewith or some other person thereunto by him lawfully authorized.

The most important practical consequence of this statute was the necessity for having written evidence of contracts for the sale of land and this was emphasised by the Law of Property Act 1925, section 40:

> No action may be brought upon any contact for the sale or other disposition of land or any interest in land unless the agreement upon which such action is brought, or some memorandum or note thereof, is in writing and signed by the party to be charged or by some person thereunto by him lawfully authorized.

However, looking at the intent rather than the form, the courts were still allowed to consider acts done in performance of the requirements of the contract, known as **acts of part performance**. This was another example of the way in which equity would not allow a statute to be used as an instrument of fraud. The provisions of section 40 of the Law of Property Act 1925 were repealed by section 2 of the Law of Property (Miscellaneous Provisions) Act 1989, which now provides:

> A contract for the sale or other disposition of an interest in land can only be made in writing and only by incorporating all the terms which the parties have expressly agreed in one document, or, where contracts are exchanged, in each.

This change does not affect earlier contracts and the courts may still be asked to grant an **order for specific performance,** which is an order compelling a party to a contract to perform his side of the agreement and which is discussed further in Unit 4.19.

The remedy is discretionary and the student should know something of the four requirements listed by Fry LJ in his leading textbook on the subject:

1. *'The acts of part performance must be such as . . . to be referable to a contract such as that alleged'.* For example, in *Kingswood Estate Co.* v. *Anderson* 1962 a woman was persuaded by a property company to move home on the company's assurance of the grant of another tenancy. She moved into another flat but the landlords later sought possession. In the Court of Appeal, Willmer LJ said that, where the question is whether there was an agreement for a tenancy:

   > *I cannot imagine any better evidence of part performance than the fact of the tenant going into actual occupation.*

   Upjohn LJ went rather further and summed up the principle of the rule when he said:

   > *The true principle of the operation of acts of part performance seems only to require that the acts in question be such as must be referred to some contract, and may be referred to the alleged one; that they prove the existence of some contract and are consistent with the contract alleged.*

   The acts relied on had failed to meet this stringent test in *Maddison* v. *Alderson* 1883. John Alderson had promised to leave his house to Elizabeth Maddison if she would act as his unpaid housekeeper. She worked for Mr Alderson for many years, but the will which Mr Alderson had made was defective and Elizabeth Maddison claimed an order of specific performance to give effect to John Alderson's oral promise. The House of Lords refused to grant the order. They held that although she had clearly worked for Mr Alderson for a considerable time, her services were not unequivocally or uniquely referable to any particular contract. Today, this sort of injustice would be avoided by allowing the disappointed party to rely on the doctrine of 'equitable estoppel'. For example, in *Gillett* v. *Holt* 2000 the Court of Appeal recognised the detriment suffered by Geoffrey Gillett who, upon assurances from an older farmer that he would in due course inherit the farming business, worked for some forty years at the farm.

   The eagerness of the courts to distinguish such precedents where obvious injustice would be caused was also clear from the decision in *Wakeham* v. *Mackenzie* 1968. Mr Ball was an elderly man in poor health. He promised his neighbour, Mrs Wakeham, that if she would move into his house and look after him she could have the property on his death. Mrs Wakeham did give up her council flat and moved into Mr Ball's house. On his death, however, it became clear that Mr Ball had failed to leave his house to Mrs Wakeham as he had promised. She now sued Mr Mackenzie, Mr Ball's executor. The court held that Mrs Wakeham's giving up her flat, moving into Mr Ball's house and looking after him and his house were all acts of part performance which had to be referred to some contract, and in particular to the one which she relied on.

2. The acts must be *'such as to render it fraud in the defendant to take advantage of the contract not being in writing'.* Such had been the danger in *Rawlinson* v. *Ames* 1925. Mrs Ada Ames had agreed to rent Mrs Rawlinson's flat near Richmond. However, the rented housing market was then better stocked than it is now and Mrs Ames was able to insist on certain alterations being made. In fact, she even came round to inspect the way the work was going and among other matters discussed the partitioning of a large room and the decoration. Mrs Ames eventually decided against taking the flat, and when sued upon her agreement, relied on the Statute of Frauds as a defence. The judge now had to decide whether there had been sufficient acts of part performance.

Romer J held that the alterations undertaken by Mrs Rawlinson at the express request of Mrs Ames did amount to acts of part performance. The judge considered the second requirement:

> *It only remains to consider whether the acts of the plaintiff were such as to render it a fraud in the defendant to take advantage of the contract not being in writing. As to this I can feel no doubt. I am satisfied that had the plaintiff laid out the flat in the manner that she herself wished, it would, when constructed, have differed materially from what it is at present. As a result of acceding to the requests and suggestions of the defendant, she is now possessed of a flat which is not likely to commend itself to tenants. It would cost her a sum of about £177 to alter the flat to a condition in which it would be possible for her to let it to other persons. She has, therefore, in carrying out her part of the contract, materially changed her position for the worse.*

3. The contract *'must be such as to be in its own nature enforceable by the court of equity'.* It follows that this remedy, which is discretionary, will be refused, for example, where the plaintiff's conduct has been improper – equity has long required that 'he who comes to equity must come with clean hands'.

Moreover, as we shall see in Unit 4.19, the courts will not award specific performance to certain contracts, for example, contracts of personal service, or contracts which would require constant supervision by the court.

4. *'There must be proper parol* [that is, oral] *evidence of the contract which is let in by the acts of part performance.'* Put simply, this means that the court must hear from the parties and any witnesses who come to court to tell the tale.

4.17 Discharge

When a contract is at an end it is said to have been **discharged**. Most contracts are discharged by proper performance – the taxi-driver takes you to the station, the milkman delivers the required number of pints and the chef cooks your steak as you ordered it. You, in turn, pay for the ride, the milk or the meal. This is known as **discharge by performance**.

Not all contractual duties, however, are done as well as the steak: the taxi-driver might not turn up, the milk might be sour or the chef might instead serve up best Alsatian. This is known as **discharge by breach**.

A third possibility would be that both parties might think better of the whole deal and agree to release each other from their respective obligations. This is known as **discharge by agreement**.

Finally, it may prove impossible to carry out the contract, giving rise to what is called **discharge by frustration**.

There are other ways in which a contract may be discharged but these four are the most common and most important. Each form of discharge merits separate attention.

a) A contract may be discharged by performance

This means that both sides do what they agreed to do when they agreed, where they agreed and as they agreed. Most cases on discharge by performance concern situations where one party claims that he has discharged his half of the bargain by doing what he said he would do, or by supplying what he said he would supply and is accordingly entitled to be paid.

The old common-law rules were once applied so very strictly that they could result in injustice, as, for example, in *Cutter* v. *Powell* 1795. Powell promised to pay Cutter, a seaman, thirty guineas (£31.50 pence) provided he proceeded, continued and did his duty as second mate on a voyage from the West Indies to England. Unfortunately, Cutter died just before the ship reached Liverpool. His widow tried to get at least some of the money from Powell but, although Cutter had done most of the work he had promised to do, she failed in her attempt. The court held that as Cutter had not in fact done everything he had agreed to do his widow could not recover one penny of the thirty guineas. The contract was an entirety: unless and until Cutter had performed the whole of his duties under it he was not entitled to be paid anything at all. Like patriotism, partial performance was not enough.

This general, if harsh, rule was still the law a hundred years later in *Sumpter* v. *Hedges* 1898, where the plaintiff was a builder who had agreed to put up a couple of houses and a stable on the defendant's land, for which he was to be paid a lump sum of £565. Sumpter did about half the work but, because of 'cash-flow' problems, was unable to complete so Hedges finished the job off himself. Even though the work which Sumpter had done was worth £333, the judge, Bruce J, held that as he had abandoned the contract by not completing the buildings, he was not entitled to be paid a farthing for his work. The Court of Appeal agreed with that decision; in the words of A.L. Smith LJ:

> The law is that where there is a contract to do work for a lump sum, until that work is completed, the price of it cannot be recovered.

Obviously, this rule could be the subject of abuse; for instance, a customer could turn round to a builder who had left one screw undone on his new £180,000 house and refuse to pay one penny of the price.

In order to avoid such possible injustices and at the same time to prevent unfair manipulation of the old rules, the courts have recognised two doctrines: that of the **divisible contract** and that of **substantial performance**.

The divisible contract   A builder may have ordered a certain number of bags of cement to be delivered each week. Such a contract may be said to be **divisible** and so the builder must pay for every delivery actually made.

Substantial performance   A builder who has just completed a new house but has left out one small nail in a kitchen cabinet has nevertheless **substantially performed** the contract. The courts now say that, in such a case, the customer must pay up for all the work actually done, although of course he may knock a few pence off the bill to take proper account of the missing nail.

In *Dakin* v. *Lee* 1916 the Court of Appeal indicated that where a builder has done work under a lump-sum contract but that work has not complied exactly with the contract, he is entitled to be paid something for his labours unless:

1. the work he did was of no benefit to the customer; or
2. the work he did was entirely different from what he had agreed to do; or
3. he had abandoned the work and left it unfinished.

Lord Cozens-Hardy MR explained the common sense behind the rule when he said:

> *Take a contract for a lump sum to decorate a house; the contract provides that there shall be three coats of oil paint, but in one of the rooms only two coats of paint are put on. Can anyone say that under those circumstances the building owner could go and occupy the house and take the benefit of all the decorations which had been done in the other rooms without paying a penny for all the work done by the builder, just because only two coats of paint had been put on in one room where there ought to have been three?*

That decision, however, was distinguished by the Court of Appeal in *Bolton* v. *Mahadeva* 1972, where the plaintiff had agreed to install a central-heating system for £560. The defendant refused to pay anything at all because, he argued, the installation was defective. The judge in the County Court found that there was a defective flue which affected the operation of the system and reduced the amount of heat generated. He went on to hold that the defendant was accordingly entitled to deduct £174.50 but had to pay the balance of the bill. The Court of Appeal went further, saying that the doctrine of substantial performance applied only where the defects were so trifling that they could be disregarded under what lawyers called the *de minimis* rule, from the Latin tag *de minimis non curat lex* ('the law does not concern itself with trifles'). In this case, the court held that the defects were such that the system as a whole did not effectively perform its intended function: it did not heat the house properly and, worse still, it gave off fumes. These defects could not be put right either easily or cheaply: accordingly, it was impossible to say that the contract had been 'substantially' performed. Cairns LJ suggested that in deciding whether there has in fact been substantial performance, one should take into account both the nature of the defects and the relation between the cost of rectifying them and the contract price.

b) A contract may be discharged by agreement

Generally speaking, what two people agree to do, they may later agree not to do. In lawyers' language, this process is known as **waiver**: the parties agree to waive (give up) their rights and responsibilities under the contract. Normally, as each party is released from his contractual obligations each both gives and receives consideration – he gives the other's discharge and receives his own. However, it may happen that one party has already made a start on his side of the contract. In such a case his waiver must be supported by fresh consideration. Such situation is known as 'accord and satisfaction', the **accord** being the agreement to discharge the contract and the **satisfaction** the fresh consideration offered by the other party to the contract in exchange for that agreement.

For instance, in *D & C Builders* v. *Rees* 1965 the plaintiffs were jobbing builders who had carried out some work for Mr Rees, who now owed the firm £482 for this work but preferred not to pay. After some months Mrs Rees, who knew that the builders were short of cash, offered them £300 on a take-it-or-leave-it basis. The builders took it. They also gave Mrs Rees a receipt in completion of the account. The plaintiffs were now suing for the balance of £182. A preliminary point which had to be decided was whether this action was barred by 'accord and satisfaction'.

The Court of Appeal held that the plaintiffs were not barred from recovering the balance of the debt. In the first place there was no true accord because Mrs Rees had put pressure on the builders to accept the lower sum of £300 by threatening that otherwise they would get nothing. Moreover, to constitute proper accord the agreement to waive one's contractual rights must itself be binding in law: that could not be the case where, as here, the agreement was neither under seal nor supported by fresh consideration. The plaintiffs had received nothing in exchange for forgiving the Rees family £182 of the debt.

Such decision was more recently applied in *Ferguson* v. *Davies* 1997. When sued for money the defendant had sent a cheque for a much smaller amount indicating that such cheque was offered as full payment. The plaintiff nevertheless continued with his action. In the Court of Appeal it was emphasised that acceptance by a plaintiff (or claimant) from a defendant of a lesser sum than the amount claimed did not constitute accord and satisfaction unless the plaintiff also received some additional benefit by way of consideration. In those circumstances the presentation of the cheque had not compromised the claim.

c) A contract may be discharged by frustration

Traditionally the common law always expected people to perform their contracts come war, flood or civil insurrection. For instance, in *Paradine* v. *Jane* 1647 a tenant, thrown out of his house by soldiers during the Civil War, was not discharged from continuing to pay his rents.

Over three hundred years later in *National Carriers Ltd* v. *Panalpina Ltd* 1981 other tenants sought to avoid paying rent on a warehouse in Hull because of the closure by the local authority of the street which led to the warehouse. A nearby building was in a dangerous condition and, pending its demolition, the street was likely to be blocked off for a couple of years. The lease on the warehouse was for ten years at a rental of £6,500 for the first five years and £13,300 for the second five years. In other words, the tenants might have to pay thousands of pounds for a warehouse they could not even get in to. Had the contract for the rental been frustrated by the street closure? In the House of Lords it was held that the disruption of two years as against the overall length of the lease was not sufficiently grave to amount to a frustrating event. Lord Wilberforce, while readily appreciating how inconvenient it all was for the tenants, said:

> But this does not approach the gravity of a frustrating event. Out of ten years they will have lost under two years of use; there will be nearly three years left after the interruption has ceased ... The obligation to pay rent under the lease is unconditional...

In the nineteenth century, however, the courts evolved the doctrine of **frustration**. This exception to the old rules applies where some disaster has happened or the law has been changed so that the contract can no longer be carried out. For example, in *Taylor* v. *Caldwell* 1863 the plaintiffs agreed to hire a music-hall but before the date of the planned concert the hall was destroyed by fire. The court held that the destruction of the hall discharged both parties from performance of their contractual obligations.

A change in the law may also discharge a contract. Thus in *Baily* v. *De Crespigny* 1869 a tenant had covenanted (that is, he had promised) that he would not allow anything to be built on a paddock which he was renting. His landlord was most upset, therefore, when he discovered that nothing less than a railway station had been built there. Nevertheless, when sued upon the covenant, the tenant was able to point to the London, Brighton and South Coast Railway (New Lines) Act 1862 which empowered the private railway company to grab land on a compulsory purchase basis. The court accordingly held that the defendant tenant had been discharged from his covenant.

The sudden illness of King Edward VII in 1902 gave rise to a barrage of litigation in the course of which the doctrine of frustration was carefully considered. What had happened was that an extravagant coronation procession and other celebrations had been arranged for 26 and 27 June 1902. Just before this patriotic saturnalia was scheduled to take place, the King fell ill and so the festivities had to be postponed. In *Krell* v. *Henry* 1903, the defendant had agreed to hire a flat in Pall Mall for two days so that he could watch the coronation procession. The Court of Appeal held that as it was obvious that the occasion of the procession was the foundation of the contract, the plaintiff could not get any money once the procession had been cancelled and the defendant no longer had any use for the flat.

On the other hand, in *Herne Bay Steamboat Co.* v. *Hutton* 1903 the defendant had arranged to hire the boat *Cynthia* to take passengers from Herne Bay 'for the purpose of viewing the naval review and for a day's cruise round the fleet' at Spithead. The review had been planned as part of the coronation celebrations and had similarly been cancelled, although the fleet itself was still there. The court held that Mr Hutton must pay the hire charges.

At first sight, it is difficult to see why Krell lost, but the steamship owner won; if Hutton could have had a day's outing looking at seagulls, surely Henry could have sat in the flat watching pigeons. The answer seems to be that Hutton could still go on a cruise of sorts but that Henry would have been out of his senses to pay good money to sit in someone else's flat for the afternoon in any normal circumstances.

In order to frustrate a contract there must always be something more than mere inconvenience or financial inadvisability. For instance, in *Davis Contractors Ltd* v. *Fareham UDC* 1956 the building company had contracted to build seventy-eight houses within eight months. Largely because of the shortage of skilled labour, the eight months stretched to twenty-two. Building costs rose in those extra fourteen months and the company now claimed that they should be paid more than had initially been agreed; they argued that the original contract was no longer applicable because it had been discharged by the impossibility of recruiting suitable workmen. However, the House of Lords rejected this contention and emphasised the need to keep the doctrine of frustration within very narrow limits. Viscount Simonds put the point tersely when he said:

> But it by no means follows that disappointed expectations lead to frustrated contracts.

The effect on shipping of the long-running war between Iraq and Iran which began in 1980 had to be considered in *Finelvet A.G.* v. *Vinava Shipping* 1983 where charterers appealed against the result of an arbitration (see Unit 2.4). It seemed at one point that the ship, which had become one of sixty or so ships caught at the Iraqi port of Basrah, would be stuck there for several months. If the contract was frustrated no further hire charges would be due to its owners. On the other hand, if the contract remained in force the charterers would remain liable for a much longer period for the hiring charges on the vessel. The court held that there was no presumption in law that the mere declaration of war prevented the performance of a contract on which the war had a direct bearing, unless, of course, the war had made the contract illegal because it would involve trading with the enemy. One had to look in particular at the effects of the war and then decide whether the contract was frustrated. On these facts the judge held that the outbreak of war between Iraq and Iran had not automatically frustrated the contract.

The effect of frustration

Obviously, frustration will bring a contract to an end. What happens, though, about any work already done and any money already spent?

The original doctrine was that, as the frustration put an end to the contract, any losses lay where they fell. Now, however, the Law Reform (Frustrated Contracts) Act 1943 provides that any money which changed hands before the occurrence of the frustrating event may be recovered. Equally, any sums which were payable before that event are no longer due. Nevertheless, if one party has been put to expense, he may be allowed by the court to withhold a reasonable sum – up to the limit of what he has in fact spent – from the money he would otherwise have to return to the other party. Finally, where one party gained a benefit from the contract before it was frustrated, the court may make him pay a reasonable sum to the other party in compensation for any expense borne by him.

The Act, however, does not apply to certain contracts such as charter-parties (a form of shipping contract), insurance contracts or contracts for the sale of 'specific goods' (goods which have actually been defined – for example, 'a Ford Mondeo with the registration number BUY 1', rather than 'a new car'), or, unsurprisingly, where the doctrine of frustration was expressly excluded by agreement between the parties in their original contract.

d) A contract may be discharged by breach

When a party fails to do what he agreed to do or does not do it properly, he is said to be **in breach** of the contract, and will be liable to pay damages to the aggrieved party to compensate him for any loss occasioned. Of itself, a breach does not discharge the contract. Thus 'discharge by breach' is something of a misnomer.

However, if the breach is such a serious one that, as the lawyers say, 'it goes to the root of the contract', the aggrieved party may, if he wishes, treat the contract as having been terminated by the breach; this is called **repudiation**. The aggrieved party will then be discharged from the further performance of his side of the bargain.

He may, however, still be able to claim damages for any loss occasioned by the breach and also to claim some payment for as much of the contract as he has so far performed. This is known as a claim on *quantum meruit* ('as much as he has earned').

For example, in *Planché* v. *Cockburn* 1831 an author had been commissioned to write a book for the proprietors of *The Juvenile Library*. Before the book was finished, the publishers told him that the *Library* was to be discontinued and, accordingly, the book was no longer required. The author chose to repudiate the contract and the court held that the publishers were obliged to pay the author a reasonable sum for what he had in fact written. Alternatively, the author could have elected to consider the contract good, completed the book and sued the publishers for the whole fee.

The right to treat a contract as discharged by breach and to sue for damages may even arise before the time for performance had actually arrived. The doctrine of **anticipatory breach** allows the injured party to take action as soon as the other party has announced his intention to breach the contract. For example, in *Hochster* v. *De La Tour* 1853 Hochster had been engaged to work for De La Tour, beginning on

1 June. In May, De La Tour told Hochester that the deal was off. Hochster was able to sue De La Tour straight away: he did not have to wait until 1 June, the day he was to have started work.

The failure of a firm of solicitors to refer a client to a member of the firm who was, in fact, admitted as a solicitor has recently been held sufficient to entitle the disappointed client to treat his contract with the solicitors as discharged by the firm's breach. In *Pilbrow* v. *Pearles de Rougemont & Co.* 1999 a man telephoned a firm of solicitors asking for an appointment to see a solicitor about a family matter. As a matter of widespread practice, solicitors' firms employ people who, while not fully qualified as solicitors, are nevertheless well equipped to handle much of the routine work. It was to such an employee that the client was referred. In due course the client refused to pay a bill and, when sued for the fees, discovered for the first time that he had not seen a solicitor. In the Court of Appeal the judges had to decide whether this was a question of defective performance of a contract or complete non-performance of a contract. The court preferred the latter construction. With interesting comparisons in his judgment Schiemann LJ remarked:

> *In my judgment a firm of solicitors which is asked for a solicitor and, without telling the client that the adviser is not a solicitor, provides an adviser who is not a solicitor, should not be entitled to recover anything. I would come to the same conclusion in relation to a case where a person goes into a doctor's surgery, asks for a doctor and a receptionist refers him to a nurse who thereafter, perfectly competently, handles his problems. These situations are not to be equated with situations where a drinker asks for a pint of one make of bitter but is mistakenly provided with a pint of another make and does not discover the difference until he has drunk the glass dry.*

4.18 Contracts of employment

'A fair day's work for a fair day's pay', while conceived as a political slogan against low wages, is nevertheless a broadly accurate if somewhat basic exposition of one of the fundamental aspects of the relationship between employer and employee. Each party enters into a contract with the other and, as with any other contract, each has rights and duties under that agreement.

a) Employer and employee

Sometimes, it can be difficult to know whether a person carrying out work for another is employed by that person or whether he or she is only offering services as a self-employed person. The lawyer would say that the first, the employee, has a **contract of service** but that the second, the self-employed, operating as an **independent contractor**, has a **contract for services**. This matter is considered in detail in Unit 6.8b) because of the way in which employers may be liable for the acts and omissions of their employees.

Assuming that one party to the contract does actually employ the other, the courts have long been willing to imply into that contract certain terms such as the duty of the employer to pay wages and the duty of the employee to obey proper instructions. The twentieth century, however, has seen enormous legislative inroads into employment law in order better to protect those who, in less happy times, would have been exploited by being sent down polluted pits or up choked chimneys. Children and young people especially have been safeguarded and there are various restrictions today on the hours those under the age of sixteen may work. Indeed, as a general rule, children under the age of thirteen may not be employed at all.

Current legislation: sex discrimination

Modern legislation begins to affect the law of employment even before the employer and employee have shaken hands on their agreement. No longer may an applicant for a job be turned away because of sex or race, save only in certain defined circumstances.

The position of women was protected by the Sex Discrimination Act 1975 which provided that a person discriminates against a woman if:

(a) on the grounds of her sex he treats her less favourably than he treats or would treat a man; or
(b) he applies to her a requirement or condition applied also to men but where the number of women who can comply with it is considerably smaller than the number of men who can comply.

Even men – provided they are married – are protected because discrimination on grounds that the job applicant or employee is married is also forbidden. It is specifically unlawful for an employer or prospective employer to discriminate against a woman in deciding to whom to offer the job or the terms on which he offers that job. Employers must similarly offer women equal treatment by way of training and opportunity for promotion.

. . . treats her less favourably . . .

Certain exceptions are now provided for in the Sex Discrimination Act 1986, as where the employer is a private household or where being a man is a genuine occupational qualification because of either the physical strength required for the job or considerations of decency. After all, an advertisement such as: 'Wanted: Circus strongman (male or female)' might raise some laughter. Ever sensitive male modesty may well cause some red faces among bathers undressing in the changing rooms of the local swimming baths where the new attendant wears a bikini. Even though Christmas pantomime tradition allows a girl to play the part of Prince Charming some restraint on sexual equality for parts in dramatic performances is provided for in the Act, which recognises that *Hamlet* with a woman in the title role would indeed be 'Hamlet without the Prince'.

Even advertisements for vacancies can fall foul of the Sex Discrimination Act 1975 unless the advertisement makes it clear that both men and women may apply. The 'sits vac' column of the local paper may now contain advertisements such as 'Waitress wanted (man or woman)' or 'Girl Friday wanted (male or female)'.

In order to superintend this legislation the Act created the **Equal Opportunities Commission** to work towards the elimination of discrimination and also to keep the workings of the Act under review. The Commission may carry out investigations into alleged discrimination and has power to require employers to furnish information about their conduct. Such discrimination is not a criminal offence but would be subject to possible complaint to an Employment Tribunal (see also Unit 2.4a)).

Current legislation: racial discrimination

In broad terms, the Race Relations Act 1976 similarly outlawed discrimination on grounds of race unless the job actually requires a particular race as a genuine occupational qualification, for example:

1. in the case of stage or screen where authenticity is required as in Shakespeare's *Othello*;
2. in the case of modelling or photographic work similarly requiring authenticity, as when a Japanese girl is required to model a kimono; or
3. where authentic waiters are required in a restaurant – after all a tall Nordic blond might look a little out of place serving the chop suey; or
4. where members of a particular racial group can best provide welfare services to their own group, for example as a community social worker.

Complaints about alleged racial discrimination will be investigated by the Commission for Racial Equality which has aims, duties and powers broadly similar to those of the Equal Opportunities Commission, including the power to issue a non-discrimination notice requiring the employer to comply with the legislation.

One unusual application of this Act was seen in *Showboat Entertainment Centre Ltd* v. *Owens* 1984 when the Industrial Tribunal (the old name for the Employment Tribunal) had to consider the claim of a white man who alleged that he had been dismissed from his job at an amusement centre because of his refusal to carry out racially discriminating instructions to exclude young black people from the centre. On appeal, the Employment Appeal Tribunal (see Unit 2.4a)) held that this sort of conduct also fell within the scope of the Race Relations Act because the complainant's unfavourable treatment was caused by racial discrimination in the first place.

Current legislation: disability discrimination

Subsequent efforts to outlaw discrimination by prospective employers were enacted by the Disability Discrimination Act 1995 so that it is unlawful for an employer to discriminate against a disabled person:

(a) in the arrangements which he makes for the purpose of determining to whom he should offer employment;
(b) in the terms on which he offers that person employment; or
(c) by refusing to offer, or deliberately not offering, employment.

Even when the disabled candidate has succeeded in obtaining that employment, it is further specifically unlawful for the employer then to discriminate:

(d) in the terms of employment which he offers him;
(e) in the opportunities which he affords him for promotion, a transfer, training or receiving any other benefit;
(f) by refusing to afford him, or deliberately not affording him, any such opportunity; or
(g) by dismissing him, or subjecting him to any other detriment.

These provisions do not, however, apply to employers with fewer than twenty employees. The exemption for small businesses was a necessary feature of the legislation, which also requires employers to take a number of steps in relation to disabled employees which include, but are by no means limited to, making adjustments to the work premises.

b) Rights at work

Once the applicant has actually landed the job he or she will be entitled to receive written details of his or her employment. The Employment Rights Act 1996 provides that, within two months of starting the job, the employee must be given a document setting out details such as the name of the employer, the date when the employment began, pay, hours of work and the employee's entitlement to holidays and holiday pay. The document should also state what period of notice the employee is entitled to receive. Under the Act the employee is entitled to certain minimum periods of notice. These will vary according to the length of service, so that an employee is entitled after one month in the job to at least a week's notice but after being in the job for two years he is entitled to a minimum of one week's notice for every year worked up to a maximum of twelve weeks.

The written contract of employment will also outline what courses of action are open to the employee if he feels he has a grievance. The nature of the grievance procedure will tend to vary from employer to employer and will usually become more formal as the size of the workforce increases.

Once in the job the employee is under a duty to obey lawful instructions and to serve the employer faithfully. During the hours of work the employee should stay at his post, doing the work himself and not working also for others. If the employee does undertake work on the side he must account to the employer for his profits (see Unit 4.15). Further, the employee should carry out the job with reasonable care. For most people the dignity of labour alone is not sufficient reward for the sweat of the brow. A principal obligation on the employer, therefore, is to pay the wages agreed.

An employer must also provide a safe system of work for his employers. This has long been held to require

> the provision of a competent staff of men, adequate material and a proper system and effective supervision.

Indeed, the Health and Safety at Work Act 1974 imposes on every employer the general statutory duty.

> ...to ensure so far as reasonably practicable, the health, safety and welfare at work of his employees.

The employer's duty to provide and maintain a safe system of working may incorporate many different aspects. They will probably include regular inspections of the premises and machinery, correct maintenance and regular servicing of machinery, the provision of guards on dangerous equipment, the provision of any necessary protective clothing and proper ventilation to remove fetid fumes.

Failure to take proper care of employees' safety may involve the employer in the commission of an offence for breach of his statutory duty (see Unit 6.8a)). For example, the Factories Act 1961 makes widespread provision for the creation and maintenance of decent, safe working conditions in factory premises. The Act regulates matters such as cleanliness, overcrowding, temperature, ventilation, lighting and drainage. Dangerous machinery must be fenced and handrails must be provided on staircases.

Although an employer does not have any duty to take care of his employees' own possessions (as where thefts take place from lockers) an employer must take reasonable care of the employees themselves and must not expose them to any unnecessary risks. This does not mean that an employee injured at work will automatically receive compensation, but if he can prove either negligence or breach of statutory duty (see Unit 6.8a)) he has a better chance than most people of seeing the colour of his money. After all, employers (like car-drivers) are required to take out insurance to cover accidents at work. Certificates of the insurance taken out must be displayed at the place of work where employees can see them.

The Health and Safety at Work Act also requires the employer to prepare a written statement of his general policy on health and safety at work. This statement must be made available to the workforce where there are more than four employees. Trade unions also have a role to play, for they may nominate members to act as 'safety representatives' whom the employer must consult over health and safety at work.

The political nature of much of the legislation introduced in employment law was again seen when the National Minimum Wage Act 1998 outlawed the pitifully low levels of pay suffered by some vulnerable employees. The new Act requires that employers should pay at a rate which is not less that the national minimum wage, a rate which will be varied from to time and, which, at the time of writing, has been set at £3.70 per hour.

Employees generally have a right to belong to a **trade union**. The officials of a recognised trade union must also be allowed time off work to carry out trade union activities concerned with industrial relations with the employer or to undergo approved training to help carry out trade union duties. Employees who have other interests (such as those who are local lay magistrates) must be allowed time off for such public duty.

c) The sack

Complaints of unfair dismissal are heard by the Employment Tribunal (see Unit 2.4a)). The right of an employee not to be unfairly dismissed is now enshrined in section 94 of the Employment Rights Acts 1996. Not every employee, however, is eligible. The employee must first show that he or she has been employed long enough to have acquired protection from unfair dismissal. The qualifying periods are something of a political yo-yo and have been altered in the past after changes of government. At the time of writing an employee must have been continuously employed for a period of twelve months immediately prior to the effective date of termination of employment.

In calculating this period, it is sometimes necessary to decide whether a previous period of employment can be taken into account. Problems arise when a business is taken over by a new employer. Is the new boss buying the bricks and mortar of the factory or shop alone or is he taking over the whole business? In order to answer this question the courts tend to look at whether the new employer took over a 'going concern' at the time of transfer.

In any event, it is important that the dismissed employee presents his complaint to the Employment Tribunal within three months of his dismissal. This period may also be altered and care should always be taken to check time limits in this sort of case.

Assuming that the Employment Tribunal has jurisdiction to hear the application it is then the job of the employer to prove that the dismissal was fair. As examined already in Unit 2.4a), it is not the duty of the employee to prove that he was unfairly dismissed. The respondent employer has to satisfy the tribunal that there was a proper reason for the dismissal and that in all the circumstances (including the size and administrative resources of the employer's undertaking) the employer had acted reasonably in treating that reason as a sufficient reason for dismissing that employee.

Some reasons will be doomed from the start. For example, dismissal on grounds of pregnancy alone or the employee's involvement in trade union activities would be obviously unfair. A dismissed employee is entitled to receive in writing the stated reasons for his dismissal. The reason may or may not later be shown to have been sufficient.

More often than not in practice those reasons relate to the conduct or capability of the employee or to his qualifications to hold such a position. Under the umbrella of those grounds will be many different allegations such as theft of or damage to company property, abuse or violence to the employer or other employees, poor timekeeping, absence from work (including absence on grounds of ill-health) and disobedience to a reasonable instruction. The employee's own individual record and the existence of any prior warning (whether oral or written) will be relevant factors in determining the fairness of the dismissal. It is, of course, only fair that the employee should have an opportunity to learn what allegations are made about him and should be allowed to put his own side of the story to the employer before any decision is taken. It is desirable, whenever possible, that the employee be accompanied by a representative of his union.

Special difficulties sometimes arise when an employee is accused of a criminal offence, for example, dipping into the till. The employee may be prosecuted by the police but may have to wait many months before his case is tried in the Crown Court. There is no need for the employer to wait to learn the jury's verdict. In *British Home Stores* v. *Burchell* 1978 an employee was dismissed for alleged dishonesty relating to staff purchases. The Employment Appeal Tribunal (see Unit 2.4a)) held that in such cases the employer had only to show that he entertained a reasonable suspicion amounting to a belief in the guilt of the employee concerning that misconduct at the time. In practice, this will require the employer to have made sufficient investigation into the matter before dismissing the suspected employee.

Sometimes the employee will have left his job, without being told to go, because his employer's conduct drove him away (for example, by asking him to cover up criminal offences). In such circumstances, if the applicant can show some breach of the contract of employment on the part of the employer which entitled him to leave, the applicant can proceed to the Employment Tribunal on grounds of what is called **constructive dismissal**. If, at the end of the hearing, the employer has failed to prove the dismissal to have been fair, the applicant will be entitled to damages unless the employer reinstates him in his old job or re-engages him in another job as near as possible to the old one. The award falls into two parts:

1. basic award; and
2. compensatory award.

The **basic award** is calculated simply by having regard to the age of the applicant, his wages and the number of years worked. The **compensatory award** is a more complex figure for calculation as it takes into account factors such as loss of net earnings, estimated loss of future earnings and the costs of finding future employment.

The Employment Tribunal has power to reduce its award to take account of the applicant's own conduct (even to the extent of one hundred per cent) but will only make an order for costs if the losing party has acted frivolously, vexatiously or otherwise unreasonably.

Sometimes, through no fault of his own, an employee loses his job because of **redundancy**. This is said to take place when the employer has ceased or intends to cease carrying on the business for the purposes of which the employee is employed – in other words the job itself has gone. An employer with more than ten employees on his books, who is faced with the prospect of making redundancies, is under a duty to give details to any recognised union. An employee losing his job because of redundancy will be entitled to a redundancy payment based on terms and calculations similar to those already considered. Further explanation is therefore at least otiose if not redundant.

4.19 Remedies

Breach of contract is not a problem reserved solely for Hollywood film stars. If your clothes are not properly dry-cleaned, your car is not properly serviced, and your new television set blows up when you switch it on, you have been the unfortunate victim of three separate breaches of contract. You were entitled to have your scrambled-egg stains removed; it was an implied term that the garage would exercise all proper skill and due care; and the Sale of Goods Act 1979 (see Unit 4.6) provides that your television set should be of satisfactory quality and fit for its purpose. You have lost out: what can you do about it?

The victim of a breach of contract will have to decide which of three possible courses is most appropriate. He may sue for damages, he may treat the contract as discharged or he may seek a discretionary remedy.

a) Damages

The expression **damages** means money. By awarding the innocent party a sum of money, the court does what it can to put the innocent party in the position he would have been in had the contract been properly carried out. Compare this aim with the rule in tort (see Unit 6.2).

'How much?' is, obviously, the pressing question. For instance, say that David buys a new table light which is faulty. David decides to take it back to the shop and on the way dents his new sports car. If the light had worked in the first place, David would not have used his car again that day and the accident would not have happened. Is the electrical shop therefore liable to pay for the cost of repairing David's dents? In short, what is the measure of damages?

Unsurprisingly, perhaps, David will not recover one penny for the dents: that loss, says the law, is 'too remote' from the breach.

How much money (what lawyers call the *quantum*) an injured party may recover was considered in the nineteenth-century leading case of *Hadley* v. *Baxendale* 1854. The plaintiffs were millers in Gloucester. Their mill had broken down and the defendant was given the faulty shaft to take to Greenwich for repair. The defendant said that he would deliver it on the following day. In fact, he was over-optimistic and it took him nearer a week. The plaintiffs now argued that because of the defendant's delay the mill had been out of action for longer than necessary and that they had consequently lost profits.

The court held that this loss was too remote. In delivering the judgment of the court, Baron Alderson established the fundamental principles of the assessment of damages for breach of contract:

> Now we think that the proper rule in such a case as the present is this: where two parties have made a contract which one of them has broken, the damages which the other party ought to receive in respect of such breach of contract should be such as may fairly and reasonably be considered either arising naturally, i.e. according to the usual course of things, from such breach of contract itself, or such as may reasonably be supposed to have been in the contemplation of both parties, at the time they made the contract as the probable result of the breach of it.

Baron Alderson went on to apply that rule to the facts then before the court and held that:

> The loss of profits here cannot reasonably be considered such a consequence of the breach of contract as could have been fairly and reasonably contemplated by both parties when they made this contract.

This common-law rule was later codified in the Sale of Goods Act 1979. The Act, dealing with breach of contract to sell goods, provides in section 50(2) that:

> The measure of damages is the estimated loss directly and naturally resulting, in the ordinary course of events, from the buyer's breach of contract.

Another claim for loss of profit came before the Court of Appeal in *Victoria Laundry (Windsor) Ltd* v. *Newman Industries Ltd* 1949, where the defendant engineering company had agreed to sell the plaintiff laundry a new boiler, which they knew was required for immediate use. Delivery was delayed because of damage in transit.

The Court of Appeal held that damages to compensate for a loss of profits could be recovered if it were obvious to the party in breach, as a reasonable person, that such loss would be caused by delay. On the facts before the court, the engineering company had been aware of the likely loss of profit and was, therefore, liable to compensate the laundry for the profit it would have made had the boiler been working on time.

To be successful, a claim for possible loss of profit must have been reasonably foreseeable by the party in breach. For instance, in *Diamond* v. *Campbell-Jones* 1960 Buckley J refused to allow the plaintiff to claim for the profit he might have made on converting some property. The court took the view that it was not reasonable to hold that the defendant had known of these speculations and, accordingly, the possible profit was not recoverable when the defendant refused to sell after all.

The longevity of these principles was more recently confirmed by the Court of Appeal in *Kpohraror* v. *Woolwich Building Society* 1996 when a 'self-employed exporter/importer' sought additional damages from the building society with which he banked after the building society refused to pay a cheque on the ground that the cheque had been reported lost. The plaintiff had wanted to ship goods to Nigeria and claimed damages for the wrongful dishonour of his cheque. The defendants accepted that their refusal had been based upon an error on their part. The plaintiff then appealed seeking an increase in damages on the basis that he had suffered trading losses because of the delay in shipment of the goods. In dismissing the appeal, the Court of Appeal followed the earlier decision in *Hadley* v. *Baxendale* finding that the claim for damages was too remote because there was nothing to indicate that a one-day delay in payment would cause the loss of the transaction or, alternatively, even a substantial trading loss. As Evans LJ encapsulated the principle:

> I would prefer to hold that the starting point for any application of *Hadley* v. Baxendale *is the extent of the shared knowledge of both parties when the contract was made.*

In the last few decades some considerable judicial ingenuity has been concentrated on the question of pre-contract expenses. For example, in *Lloyd* v. *Stanbury* 1971 the parties were negotiating for the sale of the defendant's farmhouse and land. The plaintiff had agreed to provide a caravan for Mr Stanbury to live in while his new bungalow was being built. The plaintiff went into occupation of the farmhouse before completion. He installed a new power circuit and put up a television aerial. He also paid for a caravan to be brought from Dorset to Exeter. Rather inconveniently after these efforts the defendant backed out of the sale.

The defendant argued that the plaintiff's damages should be limited to expenses incurred under or in reliance on the contract. Nevertheless, Brightman J allowed the plaintiff to recover the cost of moving the caravan but not the cost of the new power circuit or the television aerial.

The extent to which pre-contract expenses may be recovered was further considered by the Court of Appeal in *Anglia Television* v. *Reed* 1971. Lord Denning MR made the background appear intriguing:

> *Anglia Television Ltd were minded in 1968 to make a film of a play for television entitled 'The man in the wood'. It portrayed an American married to an English woman. The American has an adventure in an English wood.*

The British screen heritage will be ever the poorer because the American actor, Robert Reed, had been double-booked and could not cross the Atlantic to make the film. Anglia Television had already spent some £2,750 in employing a director, designers and a stage-manager and in other pre-contract expenses. Although the plaintiff company made no claim for loss of profit, it did claim for the £2,750 as wasted expenditure.

The Court of Appeal approved the award of £2,750 and held that where a plaintiff, as here, elected to claim for his wasted expenditure instead of his loss of profit (for he could not claim for both – he had to choose), he was not limited in his claim to money spent after the contract had been concluded. He was allowed to claim pre-contract expenditure provided that such expenditure was reasonable, bearing in mind that it was likely to be thrown away should the contract ever be broken.

An attempt to recover expenditure incurred before any contract was reached failed in *Regalian Properties* v. *London Dockland Development Corporation* 1995. The plaintiff property company had paid some £3 million in professional fees in respect of a proposed development in the old London Docks. The property company had entered into negotiations with the relevant Corporation to build new homes. The LDDC accepted the offer but did so 'subject to ... contract ...' and other conditions. For various reasons no contract was concluded and the site was never developed. The property company wanted its money. The plaintiffs argued that where parties to a proposed contract had a mutual understanding that there would be a contract between them and, in reliance on that understanding, one party incurred expense, that party could recover his wasted costs from the other. The words 'subject to contract' proved fatal to the claim and the judge held that any costs incurred by one party in preparation for the intended contract would be incurred at that party's own risk.

Over the last few years the courts have shown themselves more willing to award damages for the distress and disappointment so often brought about by breach of contract. It all started when a lawyer had a rotten holiday. In *Jarvis* v. *Swan Tours* 1973, a solicitor's annual fortnight's holiday was spent skiing in Switzerland. The basic cost was £63. The holiday was a great disappointment to Mr Jarvis in many different ways. The brochure itself had been inaccurate and there was obviously a good claim for damages against the holiday company. What, though, was the proper measure of damages? Was it limited to £63 at most? The old cases were a hundred years old. Lord Denning MR brought the law up to date. The Court of Appeal held that damages for mental distress could be recovered in an action for breach of contract. Such damages were no longer to be restricted to the issue of physical inconvenience but should take proper account of emotions such as annoyance and disappointment. The solicitor's damages were, therefore, increased to £125.

The work of lawyers often involves dealing with people who are already under stress when they seek help. In *Heywood* v. *Wellers* 1976 Sheila Heywood went to a firm of solicitors for help in stopping a policeman, Mr Marrion, with whom she had once been friendly, from molesting her. The solicitors' clerk who dealt with her case failed to do so properly. Because of the clerk's negligence Mrs Heywood suffered more annoyance from her ex-friend that was probably avoidable. She sued the solicitors and, on top of other money, she recovered £150 for the distress which she had been caused by the failure of her solicitors to deal properly with her case. In the Court of Appeal, Lord Denning MR said this of the negligent solicitors:

> *So here, Mrs Heywood employed the solicitors to take proceedings at law to protect her from molestation by Mr Marrion. They were under a duty by contract to use reasonable care. Owing to their want of care she was molested by this man on three or four occasions. This molestation caused her much mental distress and upset. It must have been in their contemplation that, if they failed in their duty, she might be further molested and suffer much upset and distress.*

More recently, in *Perry* v. *Sidney Phillips* 1982 the court had to consider a claim brought against a firm of surveyors. Ivan Perry was thinking about buying a house in the West Country which had been described as a 'most attractive detached freehold residence'. Some local surveyors were instructed to prepare a full report on the house for Mr Perry. Those instructions obviously amounted to a contract between Mr Perry and the surveyors. When the report came back from the surveyors it seemed that the house was a reasonable buy at £27,000. In fact, the surveyors had not done their work properly and there were a number of faults with the house which, in the worst traditions of such cases, only became clear once the new owner had moved in. The surveyors had been at fault and had not properly carried out their duties under the contract. What though was the proper measure of damages? Was it to be limited to the cost of employing workmen to deal with problems such as beetle infestation and damp? The court held that Mr Perry was also entitled to damages for the anxiety, discomfort and distress which he suffered. As Lord Denning MR said:

> It seems to me that Mr Perry is entitled to damages for all the vexation, distress and worry which he has been caused by reason of the negligence of the surveyor. If a man buys a house for his own occupation on the surveyor's advice that it is sound and then find out that it is in a deplorable condition, it is reasonably foreseeable that he will be most upset. He may, as here, not have the money to repair it and this will upset him all the more. That, too, is reasonably foreseeable. All this anxiety, worry, and distress may nowadays be the subject of compensation. Not excessive, but modest compensation.

Where the dividing line was to be drawn between modest and excessive compensation was considered by the Court of Appeal in *Watts* v. *Morrow* 1991, another claim against a negligent surveyor. After the purchasers moved into their new home, Ian and Mary Watts found substantial defects which required urgent correction. These extended from the roof down to the very floorboards. The new owners had obviously paid more than the house was worth. It was agreed that they had paid £15,000 too much. However, the cost of the repairs came to nearly £34,000. Were the new owners entitled to the full £34,000 or only the £15,000? The Court of Appeal held that the damages should reflect the diminution in value rather than the higher cost of repair. For their distress and inconvenience the couple were not entitled to damages, said the judges, but were each entitled to £750 as compensation for physical discomfort suffered by them when living in what in evidence they had described as a 'building site'.

Tour companies, solicitors, wedding photographers and hirers of wedding limousines all have been held liable to pay damages for distress and disappointment when they have failed to discharge properly their contractual obligations to their customers or clients. Although since *Jarvis* v. *Swans Tours* 1973 holiday tour operators seem to occupy a particularly large number of pages in the law reports, much smaller businesses have been held liable for the sort of distress suffered in *Cole* v. *Rana* 1993. No fewer than 250 guests from all over the word were attending a wedding estimated to cost £30,000. The defendants were to provide Rolls Royce and Mercedes limousines. In fact, only one car (and even then a dirty one) arrived so that the parties and their many guests had to use a succession of taxis and mini-cabs, arriving only late and dishevelled at the ceremony, which was further marred by the bride fainting on this most special day. The court recognised that a day which should, indeed, have been a special one had been turned into a nightmare. The judge took the view that a claim for a ruined wedding, a once in a lifetime event (hopefully at least but see Unit 5.3!) was on an altogether higher scale than one for a spoilt holiday and awarded general damages of £2,500.

Mitigation   Certain factors must be considered before damages can be calculated. One of these factors is the role of the injured party following the breach of the contract: he is expected to do what he can to look after his own interest. After all a young wife whose marriage has broken up cannot just sit back and expect her former husband to support her in the manner to which she had hoped to become accustomed. She must attempt to find work and make the best of her difficulties (see Unit 5.8).

So it is with breaches of contract. The injured party, lawyers would say, must **mitigate his loss**. Suppose that Andrea contracts with Nigel for the sale of 1,000 loaves at £400. When the time comes, Nigel refuses to buy them and is, therefore, in breach. However, Andrea may not just sit back on her bread mountain – she must do her best to sell it to someone else. For instance, she may unload the stale carbohydrate on to the local college canteen for £100. In this way, she has mitigated her loss and may now sue Nigel for the other £300 of the contract price.

Penalty clauses   In the more substantial contracts – for instance, contracts for the building of a school, hospital or hotel – the local authority or hotel company may well wish to insert clauses into the contract with the builders to the effect that for every day the building is late for completion, the builders shall pay so many pounds in compensation.

If this contract is later the subject of litigation, the court must decide whether that clause represents a genuine pre-assessment of damages or, on the other hand, whether it is what is termed a **penalty clause**. Although people talk loosely of such clauses, the courts will not enforce them since they are void. The courts will only enforce genuine pre-estimates of likely loss.

How then does a judge tell them apart? He may well be guided by what Lord Dunedin had to say in *Dunlop Tyre Co.* v. *New Garage Ltd* 1915. Dunlop sold tyres to the New Garage. The garage agreed to sell them according to certain terms and undertook that, if they sold tyres otherwise than in accordance with their contract, they would pay Dunlop £5 per tyre by way of liquidated damages for breach of contract. What the House of Lords had to decide was whether this was really a genuine pre-estimate (which would be valid) or a penalty clause (which would be void).

Lord Dunedin put forward a number of tests:

1. Whether it is called 'damages' or 'penalty' is not the end of the matter . . . The court must find out whether what the payment stipulates is in truth a penalty or liquidated damages.
2. The essence of a penalty is a payment of money stipulated as *in terrorem* of the offending party; the essence of liquidated damages is a genuine covenanted pre-estimate of damage.
3. The question whether a sum stipulated is penalty or liquidated damages is a question of construction to be decided upon the terms and inherent circumstances of each particular contract, judged of as at the time of the making of the contract not as at the time of the breach.
4. It will be held to be a penalty if the sum stipulated for is extravagant and unconscionable in amount in comparison with the greatest loss that could conceivably be proved to have followed from the breach.

5. It will be held to be a penalty if the breach consists only in not paying a sum of money and the sum stipulated is a sum greater than the sum which ought to have been paid.

6. There is a presumption (but no more) that it is penalty when a single lump sum is made payable by way of compensation on the occurrence of one or more or all of several events, some of which may occasion serious and others but trifling damages.

Taxation

Where the profits of a business deal or a person's wages would have been subject to income tax, the courts are obliged to take that liability into account in awarding damages.

The drastic effect of this rule may be seen in *British Transport Commission* v. *Gourley* 1955. Mr Gourley, a civil engineer, was badly injured in a railway accident. He was no longer able to earn as much money as he could before the accident. The judge awarded him £37,720 but did not take his tax liability into account.

The House of Lords, however, held that liability to income tax was not so remote that it should be disregarded. They then went on to reduce Mr Gourley's damages by the amount of income tax which he would have had to pay, as much as £6,695.

b) Treat contract as discharged

This right of the innocent party to treat the contract as discharged has already been examined in Unit 4.17d).

c) Discretionary remedies

Injunction

An injunction is a discretionary order of the court compelling someone to do or not to do something. It is a remedy which is often used to prevent the commission of a tort – for example, a judge may order noisy and inconsiderate neighbours not to play their records at 3 a.m. so as to wake up the people in the downstairs flat. It may also become important in contract.

Say, for example, that a company called 'Scrubbits' is about to market a new detergent powder. The 'new improved formula' with 'DK 69' is a closely guarded secret. However, Mr White, the head chemist, is offered a better job with a rival company, Foamo Ltd, who would obviously like to learn what 'DK 69' really is. If they find this out, however, all the research Scrubbits has done will be wasted. Scrubbits will not want Mr White to reveal the formula and will do its best to deter the gent from doing the dirty on the company. It will, therefore, apply for an injunction to prevent him from disclosing trade secrets.

An injunction will not be granted where an award of money would be sufficient to compensate the injured party. It is, of course, an equitable, and therefore a discretionary, remedy and so, for example, the soap company must come with clean hands (see Unit 1.7).

Such a course was considered appropriate in *Hivac Ltd* v. *Park Royal Scientific Ltd* 1946, when Hivac, which manufactured thermionic valves for use in hearing-aids, had discovered that some of the company's highly skilled employees were working for a rival firm in their spare time.

Specific performance   Specific performance is another equitable and, therefore, discretionary remedy. It is, in a sense, the opposite of an injunction: it is an order of the court compelling someone to do what he agreed to do. Over the years, the courts have indicated that, in addition to the normal limitations of any equitable remedy, they will not grant specific performance in two particular cases: contracts of personal service, and contracts which require supervision.

<u>Contracts of personal service</u>   The courts will not attempt to compel one party to an agreement to go though with it against his will, where to do so would be to enforce some special relationship. For example, the courts will not enforce agreements between partners in a firm.

This, said Lord Jessel MR in *Rigby* v. *Connol* 1880, is because:

> *The courts have never dreamt of enforcing agreements strictly personal in their nature, whether they are agreements of hiring and service, being the common relation of master and servant, or whether they are agreements for the purpose of pleasure, or the purpose of scientific pursuits, or for the purpose of charity or philanthropy.*

<u>Contracts requiring supervision</u>   The sort of problems inherent in such a contract were reviewed in *Ryan* v. *Mutual Tontine Westminster Chambers Association* 1893. A man was employed as a resident porter in a block of flats. He rarely attended to his duties and instead employed boys and charwomen to do his work for him, while he worked elsewhere as a chef. Would the court compel the chef to carry out his duties as a porter? The court refused to enforce the contract and Kay LJ indicated that the reason was twofold: firstly, because damages, in such cases, are usually an adequate remedy: and, secondly, because the court is unable to see that the work is, in fact, properly carried out.

Lopes LJ emphasised that:

> *. . . it is such a contract that, in order to give effect to it by an order for specific performance, the court would have to watch over and supervise its execution. But it is a recognized rule that the court cannot enforce a contract by compelling specific performance where the execution of the contract requires such watching over and supervision by the court.*

4.20 *Survival of actions in contract*

The law has long refused to allow people to bring actions before the courts many years after the events in dispute first arose. Best CJ summed up the attitude of the courts in *A'Court* v. *Cross* 1825 when he said:

> *Long dormant claims have often more of cruelty than of justice in them.*

For this reason the Limitation Act 1980 provides that a claim under a simple contract must be brought within six years of the cause of action arising. So, in the unlikely event of a plumber delaying six years before sending his customer a bill the claim for payment has gone down the drain.

Different considerations apply to claims relating to land. Under the Limitation Act 1980 (which re-enacts earlier legislation) claims to recover land must be brought within twelve years of the date when the cause of action accrued. After twelve years a person who has been in adverse possession of land acquires title (or as it is popularly known, 'squatters' rights') against the original owner. However, if that person in occupation acknowledges the original owner's title the limitation period starts to run afresh. The position of limitation periods in tort is examined separately in Unit 6.9.

One particular difficulty has arisen where defects in a house's construction only appear long after the builder has left the site. Under the Limitation Act that defect might not have manifested itself until after the expiry of the six-year period for such claim. However, the Latent Damage Act 1986 has come into force and is of general application allowing the normal six-year period to be extended so as to enable an action to be started within three years from the date when the claimant knew or ought to have known of the damage in question.

4.21 *Questions*

1. Outline the transactions which may legally be entered into by a person under the age of eighteen. Do you think sufficient protection is given to adults dealing with under eighteen-year-olds? Justify your answer.

2. Three months ago Rashid bought a second-hand car from Modern Motors Ltd. He paid £3,000. In the contract of sale (which he read but did not sign) there was a clause which stated: 'All conditions and/or warranties, express or implied, are hereby excluded.' Yesterday the engine seized up and the car is now worthless. Advise Rashid as to his legal rights.

3. State the legal position in the following situations:
   a) Gary sells a motor cycle to Wayne for £800, delivery to be made in a week's time. Before delivery the motor cycle is destroyed when Gary's garage catches fire without negligence on the part of anyone.
   b) Kevin orders one hundred cases of tinned fruit from Linda. The order is accepted by Linda, but she only delivers fifty cases.

4. a) When will mistake as to the identity of the other party affect the validity of the contract?
   b) Jerry Builder submits an offer to build one hundred houses for Lowtown Corporation. The offer is accepted and a contract is drawn up and signed. Later Jerry Builder discovers that he had made a mistake in his offer by deducting an item twice and would like the contract rectified. Lowtown Corporation refuse to rectify the contract and Jerry Builder commences proceedings against them. Consider the likely outcome of the case.

5. 'As a result of a combination of EU directives, decisions of the European Court of Justice and national legislation it can be said that women have legal, if not actual, equality with men as far as obtaining work and remuneration for that work is concerned.' Discuss.

6. An hotel, which takes a pride in its Victorian atmosphere, advertises for additional staff to assist with its 'Dickensian Christmas' festivities. *K* is subsequently appointed even though his experience is more limited than that of the other two applicants, *L* and *M*. From what was said at the interview *L* believes that he was not appointed because his West Indian origin would not fit the hotel manager's idea of what should be the appropriate background for the festivities. *M* was told that the work would be too heavy for her but she believes that the real reason is that she disclosed at the interview that she had recently become pregnant. To what extent and in what ways may the law become involved in this situation?

7. Albert, a houseowner, contacts Bill, a painter and decorator, and asks him to give an estimate for the decoration of Albert's house. Bill provides the estimate. Albert writes to Bill asking him to do the work in accordance with the estimate and adds 'you can start immediately'. Bill at once buys the necessary materials and goes to Albert's house. Albert meets him on the doorstep and says that he has changed his mind. Advise Bill.

8. Donald agrees with Louise that for a fee of £5,000, plus expenses, Donald will travel to Farlandia to report on employment relationships in that country. The day before Donald is due to leave, Louise tells Donald that she no longer requires the report. Nevertheless, Donald travels to Farlandia and in due course submits his report to Louise who refuses to accept it or to pay Donald any money. Advise Donald. How would your answer differ if after the agreement was made Farlandia prohibited the entry of foreign nationals because of the outbreak of civil war?

9. a) Distinguish between an offer and an invitation to treat.
   b) On 1 December Jim wrote to Sasha offering to sell his house to Sasha for £90,000 and asking for Sasha's reply to be made in writing to reach him before 9 December. On 7 December Sasha sent a letter to Jim accepting his offer, but due to industrial action at the Post Office the letter did not reach Jim until 11 December. On 6 December Jim wrote to Sasha revoking his original offer. Sasha received this letter on 8 December. On 7 December Jim sold his house to Tom. Advise Sasha.

10. a) The law imposes a duty of utmost good faith on proposers for a life assurance contract. Why does this duty exist and what does it entail?
    b) In proposing for a policy on his own life, P stated that he had not received any medical treatment in the last five years. In fact he had recently undergone a series of hospital check-ups for a suspected liver complaint and subsequently died of liver failure. The life office accept that P honestly believed at the time of proposal that the check-ups were not material. What is the life office's position?

11. a) How may the relationship of principal and agent arise?
    b) Jenny employs a manager to run her jewellery shop. The manager regularly buys jewellery in Jenny's name from Gina for sale in the shop. The manager leaves Jenny's employment but continues to order jewellery in her name from Gina and has now absconded with it without paying. Advise Gina.

12. a) 'Consideration must be real but it need not be adequate.' Discuss with special reference to those areas where the adequacy of the consideration is in doubt.
    b) Consider the adequacy of the consideration in the following instances:
       (i) Helen makes a claim against the Reliable Airfreight Company for goods damaged in transit. She is offered £3,000 'in full and final settlement' and she accepts the offer. The carriers are now refusing to pay, stating that 'your claim was invalid and therefore there was no consideration for our promise to give you £3,000.'
       (ii) Mary asks Paul, a mechanic, to repair her car. He does so and Mary promises him '£50 for your trouble'. She now refuses to pay on the grounds that the consideration was past.

13. a) Discuss and illustrate 'injunction' and 'specific performance' as remedies for a breach of contract.
    b) P, a painter, agreed to paint a portrait of Miss X, the Managing Director of a small but prosperous airline. However, after hearing what he considered to be scandalous reports about Miss X's private life, P told her that he had changed his mind about painting her portrait. Advise Miss X.

14. Discuss briefly:
    a) the distinction between common and mutual mistake in the law of contract;
    b) the doctrine of *non est factum* (it is not my deed) in the law of contract;
    c) the duties of an agent in relation to his principal.

Law and the family

5.1 *From this day forth*

a) Marriage as a contract

Once the champagne has been drunk, the cake scoffed and the confetti swept away it would be accurate, even if a little prosaic, to reflect that the whole ceremony has been just another contract.

The classic definition of marriage has remained unaltered for over a century since Lord Penzance's words in *Hyde* v. *Hyde* 1866 that, in English law, marriage was:

> *the voluntary union for life of one man and one woman to the exclusion of all others.*

Such a definition involves a number of different ingredients, each of which must have been present at the time of the ceremony. For example, as with any contract, each party must have capacity to enter into the agreement. This means that each party must be free to marry in the sense that he or she is not already married and is over the age of sixteen years. Persons who are under the age of 18 must have the consent of their parents, or, if those parents are divorced, of the parent in whose favour a Residence Order has been made. Such definition further requires that the parties to the marriage are respectively male and female for English law does not recognise homosexual marriages nor, indeed, the sort of regulated partnership open to homosexual partners in Scandinavian countries.

If, because of the refusal of parental consent or the dawning realisation that one's intended is not the person with whom to spend the rest of one's life, the proposed marriage is called off, the legal consequences are no longer very substantial. Although a marriage is itself a contract there is no longer the old action of **breach of promise to marry** which provided the setting for the Gilbert and Sullivan opera *Trial by Jury*. Almost a hundred years after the comic opera's first night Parliament abolished such action in the Law Reform (Miscellaneous Provisions) Act 1970. Today, the spurned bride's only consolation may be no more than being able to keep the ring. Such jewellery is presumed to have been an absolute gift, subject only to evidence that there had been some term (express or implied) that it should be returned if the marriage did not take place.

b) Void and voidable marriages

Any breach of the requirements as to the parties' capacity would render the marriage invalid. The Matrimonial Causes Act 1973 (which is the statute which, until, if ever, the Family Law Act 1996 is brought into force, still regulates nearly all modern matrimonial law) provides that marriages may be declared either **void** or **voidable**, in the various situations specified in the Act. If the marriage is declared to have been void it is viewed as never having taken place. If, on the other hand, it is declared to have been only voidable the marriage is treated as having been good and valid unless and until one of the parties successfully takes steps to have the marriage annulled. This is far more than a mere academic distinction and has important practical application where, for example, the validity of a will is challenged. A will is normally revoked on marriage but the testator's original will may still prevail if the marriage was invalid.

The distinction between void and voidable marriages was considered by Lord Greene MR in *De Reneville* v. *De Reneville* 1948 when he said:

> *The substance, in my view, may be thus expressed: a void marriage is one that will be regarded by every court in any case in which the existence of the marriage is in issue as never having taken place and can be so treated by both parties to it without the necessity of any device annulling it; a voidable marriage is one that will be regarded by every court as a valid subsisting marriage until a device annulling it has been pronounced by a court of competent jurisdiction.*

The situations which render a marriage void are set out in section 11 of the Matrimonial Causes Act 1973. Each merits separate consideration.

Firstly, a marriage will be void where:

1. the parties are within the prohibited degrees of relationship; or
2. either party is under the age of sixteen; or
3. the parties have intermarried in disregard of certain requirements as to the formation of marriage.

The Marriage Act 1949 contains a list of those who may not marry each other. The new Marriage (Prohibited Degrees of Relationship) Act 1986 has made amendments to the old list and has since November 1986 allowed a man, brave enough to do so, to marry his mother-in-law. Reciprocal provision allows a woman to marry her father-in-law as well as allowing marriage between step-parents and step-children. Such marriages, however, may not be entered into at sixteen years of age and in-laws may only marry if the former spouse has died.

Traditionally, the Marriage Act 1949 required that marriages took place in a building suitably recognised for such ceremonies, that marriages were conducted by persons so authorised and took place between the hours of 8 a.m. and 6 p.m. in circumstances which allowed the public to be present. Such ceremonies no longer need take place in the village church or local Registry Office. The Marriage Act 1983 allowed marriages to take place in other buildings where (because, for example, of medical disability) one of the parties was housebound or detained (say, because the groom is in prison). There was new business for hotels and many other places including Kew Gardens when the Marriage Act 1994 enabled the local authorities to approve a wider range of premises for civil marriages. The Act still requires two witnesses to be present. One couple whose marriage was celebrated as they ran the London Marathon in 1999 would have had no difficulty in finding at least two witnesses and must also have breathed a sigh of relief as they ran the distance that the Marriage Ceremony (Prescribed Words) Act 1996 had truncated the words to be spoken (or perhaps gasped) at such a ceremony. No doubt the happy couple were also relieved that not all 30,000 competitors crossed the finishing line to attend the reception.

Secondly, a marriage will be void on the ground that at the time of the marriage either party was already lawfully married. Such a defect would also render the recidivist Romeo liable to criminal penalties under the Offences Against the Person Act 1861 which, in addition to the draconian prospect of two mothers-in-law, provides for a penalty of seven years' imprisonment.

Thirdly, a marriage will be void on the ground that the parties are not respectively male and female. The fact that the law does not recognise homosexual marriages is of more than prurient or academic interest. For example, in *Corbett* v. *Corbett* 1970 the court had to consider the legality of a ceremony of marriage between Arthur Corbett and his bride, April Ashley. Some three years before that ceremony 'April' had in fact been known as 'George'. Having been registered at birth as a boy and even having served with the Merchant Navy before finding employment as a female impersonator in a night club, 'George' underwent a so-called 'sex change' operation. Was this ceremony of marriage valid? The judge (who was also medically qualified) held that this ceremony of marriage had been void. The court held that the validity of the marriage had to be determined by the sex of the parties, and such matters were determined at birth and not by any subsequent surgery.

In *Rees* v. *United Kingdom* 1987 the European Court rejected a claim by Mark Rees, a transsexual who had been born a girl, that English law, since Corbett's case, violated his right to respect for his private life under the European Convention on Human Rights (see Unit 3.10). A related complaint came before the European Court of Human Rights in *Cossey* v. *United Kingdom* 1991. The applicant had been born a male but subsequently underwent surgery and thereafter lived as a woman. She complained that she had been refused a birth certificate showing her to be female and further complained that under United Kingdom law she could not marry a man. She complained that the United Kingdom was in breach of Articles 8 and 12 of the Convention. The complaints were rejected as it was said that the birth certificate was merely a statement of facts known to exist at a certain time. They could not, it was said, be altered to suit subsequent developments. Further, the applicant's claim to have a right to marry a man was rejected on the ground that the majority of the contracting Member States also prohibited marriage between members of the same sex.

Fourthly, in the case of a polygamous marriage (that is, one with more than one spouse) entered into outside England and Wales, the marriage will be void if either party was at the time of the marriage domiciled in England and Wales. As Lord Penzance's definition suggests, English marriage is monogamous. Whether English law will recognise a polygamous marriage depends on a consideration of where the parties to that polygamous marriage were domiciled at the time of the ceremony. **Domicile** is the description of the place or country where a person has made his or her permanent home. The concept has particular relevance to family law, not only because of its relevance to whether or not the English courts will recognise a foreign marriage but also because, if things do go wrong, the party seeking a divorce (known as the **petitioner**) should be domiciled in England and Wales. In the latter situation efforts will be made to satisfy the court that the petitioner is domiciled in the jurisdiction.

Most people stay in the country of their birth, having acquired a **domicile of origin** at the time of their birth. If a child is legitimate he or she takes the domicile of the father at the date of birth. If the child is illegitimate (that is, the parents are not married) then the child will acquire the domicile of the mother.

Some years later the child may decide to go abroad to live and work. If he makes his permanent home abroad he will acquire in his new country a **domicile of choice**. That same person may, however, regain his domicile of origin if he returns permanently to the country of his birth. Domicile is a more profound concept than mere residence and is not lost or gained just by working temporarily abroad, let alone by a two-week package tour in the sun.

Such independent domicile can only be enjoyed by persons over the age of sixteen. Until then the child enjoys a **dependent domicile**, which is usually that of the father. Until quite recently, married women were treated in the same way as children under sixteen and were incapable of enjoying their own independent domicile. Instead, they automatically acquired the domicile of their husband along with their husband's income-tax returns. In 1973, however, this dependent domicile of married women was abolished and they now have their domicile determined by the usual criteria and independently of their husbands.

The position of voidable marriages is also regulated by the Matrimonial Causes Act 1973 which, in section 12, lists those problems which would allow a court to annul a marriage if asked to do so.

1. The first ground is that the marriage has not been consummated owing to the incapacity of either party to consummate it. **Consummation** has been defined as sexual intercourse which is ordinary and complete and not partial and imperfect.

2. The second and related ground is that the marriage has not been consummated owing to the 'wilful refusal' of the respondent to consummate it. The person petitioning for the decree of nullity or divorce is known as the **petitioner**. The other party is called the **respondent**. In this regard **wilful refusal** is said to involve 'a settled and definite decision come to without just excuse' but the whole history of the marriage must be looked at.

3. The third ground is that either party to the marriage did not validly *consent* to it, whether in consequence of duress, mistake, unsoundness of mind or otherwise. Although it might readily be thought that no great perspicacity is normally required to understand that one is getting married, problems can and do still arise. The Old Testament tells how Jacob, hoping to marry Rachel, worked for seven years for her father, Laban, in order to gain his consent to the wedding. After the ceremony Jacob found it was not his beloved Rachel but her elder sister Leah whom he had married.

Mistakes of this sort (but not mistakes such as the health of a future partner's bank balance) would render the marriage voidable, as would drunkenness where, after a rather good night out, a person stirs from a drunken slumber to discover that he or she is married. Mistakes as to the nature of the ceremony would render the marriage voidable. For example, in *Mehta* v. *Mehta* 1945 a woman teacher went through a ceremony in India. The ceremony was conducted in Hindustani, a language which Mrs Mehta did not understand.

She had thought that it was a religious ceremony involving her conversion to the Hindu faith. She found out later that she had acquired not only that faith but also a husband whom she had married according to the rites of that Hindu sect. The court, which had regard to earlier but similar legislation, held that as the lady had no intention of marrying, the marriage was voidable.

Duress, as where the other partner's family gather with their trigger fingers twitching nervously at a so-called 'shotgun' wedding, is another reason to annul a marriage. For example, in *Buckland* v. *Buckland* 1967 a British man working in the dockyards at Malta married a local girl only in order to escape prosecution there on charges of 'minor corruption'. This choice of either marrying the girl or going to prison was such as to allow the court to annul the marriage.

The court may also annul a marriage on the ground either that the respondent was suffering from **venereal disease** at the time of the marriage or, at that time of the marriage, the **respondent was pregnant** by a man other than the petitioner.

In all such cases other than grounds relating to consummation, however, the court would not annul the marriage if the respondent satisfies the court that the petitioner led the respondent to believe that he or she would not take steps to annul the marriage and that it would be unjust to the respondent to grant such a decree.

5.2 *To have and to hold*

a) The rights and duties of husband and wife

The Church of England wedding ceremony itself gives an indication of some of the mutual rights and duties which each spouse has as regards the other. Even the independently spirited bride who omits obedience in one of her vows still promises 'to love and cherish in sickness and in health'.

The wife's duties in the marriage have traditionally included the domestic responsibilities of running the home, cooking, cleaning and shopping. There is, of course, equality between spouses these days but in most cases it is still the husband who is the main breadwinner even if no longer the head of the household. The husband's position has clearly changed over the last two centuries and no longer can legal writers say, as they did 200 years ago, that a husband could beat his wife so long as he did it with a stick no bigger than his thumb. His duties today include providing financially and materially for his wife. This liability is reflected in the general principle that a wife has authority to pledge her husband's credit and to act as his agent (see Unit 4.15) for the purchase of necessaries such as food and clothing. Just what the husband will be required to pay for would depend on the general standard of living and financial strength of the family.

Any wilful neglect to maintain a wife may be the subject of complaint to the court under section 27 of the Matrimonial Causes Act 1973. Husbands may also apply to the court under the same section and the court has power to order either regular payments, known as periodical payments, or a lump sum.

Even after divorce a husband (and, on his death, his estate) may still have to maintain a dependent wife. This often bitter aspect of matrimonial breakdown is considered later in Unit 5.8.

By convention a woman will usually take the surname of her husband whose name she is said to have assumed 'by repute'. Some women in business or carrying on a professional practice as, say, a lawyer, dentist or doctor, may prefer to practise under their own name. A woman may retain her married name even after divorce, whatever displeasure this may cause either to her ex-husband or to any of her successors in the home.

A wife's position in the home is also protected. The duty of a husband to provide for the wife also requires him to allow the wife proper and free use of their home, even if it is in the husband's sole name. The Matrimonial Homes Acts of 1967 and 1983 protected the position of a wife. For example, the Matrimonial Homes Act 1983 protected a wife's rights of occupation in the matrimonial home. Further, where the home is not registered also in the wife's name the Act confers upon the wife a statutory right of occupation. The Act further allows the courts to declare, enforce, restrict or terminate rights of occupation and the court has power to exclude a spouse from his or her home. This aspect is considered later in Unit 5.4.

Even where the parties are still living happily together, each may sue the other. For example, a husband who was injured as a passenger in a car carelessly driven by his wife may sue her. In practice, of course, it is not a case of the wife having to scrimp and save out of the housekeeping to pay any damages but rather an insurance company having to dig into its coffers. Until 1962 a wife and husband could not sue each other in this way. However, the Law Reform (Husband and Wife) Act 1962 provides that each of the parties to a marriage has the same rights of action in tort against the other as if they were not married. Nevertheless, the court still has power to stop such a case from proceeding if it seems that no substantial benefit would accrue to either party or if the dispute could be more conveniently dealt with under the Married Women's Property Act 1882, an Act which gave women full proprietary rights and allowed married women to hold property as if they were not, in fact, married. A decade after the passing of this statute saw the production of Oscar Wilde's play *A Woman of No Importance*. Mrs Allonby had her own view of the topic:

> *All men are married women's property. That is the only true definition of what married women's property really is.*

Otherwise, there have long been restrictions on the ability of one spouse to give evidence against the other and, indeed, each partner is expected to preserve marital confidences. The Police and Criminal Evidence Act 1984 provides in section 80 that an accused's spouse may be compelled to give evidence either for or even against the other spouse unless they are jointly charged in the same proceedings. This new Act, therefore, changes the old common law under which a wife could very rarely be made to give evidence against her husband or vice versa. The exception to this general rule was usually to be found in cases of violence towards the wife. Within the marriage each party is entitled to sexual intercourse and a wife is deemed to have consented to intercourse. Such is just one of the consequences of a ceremony, the effect of which was acerbically noted by the seventeenth-century law student turned comic dramatist William Congreve as being:

> *Tho' marriage makes man and Wife one flesh, it leaves 'em still two fools.*

5.3 *Putting asunder*

It is a sad fact that today there is a very high rate of divorce in England and Wales. Figures for 1998 showed that the great majority of divorce petitions were issued by wives. Of the 165,870 such petitions, some three-quarters were issued by wives and of those most were based on the husbands' behaviour.

Within the sadness of such matrimonial breakdown is, of course, a wide range of problems but many lawyers working in this area detect problems over money and sex as common features in marital discord. To those who see a divorce rate (where approximately four in ten marriages now taking place will end in divorce) as an indication of a more wide-spread deterioration in the fabric of modern society generally three points must be borne in mind. Firstly, it is only since 1882 that married women have been able to hold property in their own right and only very much more recently that women have been able to obtain substantial financial assistance after divorce. No longer does a divorced woman retreat into the life of a penurious recluse or social outcast. Secondly, until 1857 only the very rich could afford to obtain a divorce as nothing less than a private Act of Parliament was required to dissolve a marriage. Moreover, only a narrow approach was allowed and the position of a wife was especially inferior. Thirdly, many years ago (when some would paint a golden age for the traditional family) a number of women would die in child-birth and life expectancy was generally much lower for both parties.

Today, the aim of the legislation and of the courts which apply it is to crush the empty legal shell of a failed marriage with the maximum fairness and the minimum bitterness, distress and humiliation. Some suggestions have been made that under the modern law it is too easy for people to dissolve their marriages. In one much publicised, if perhaps unguarded, judicial aside during a sitting of the Family Division of the High Court, the late Mr Justice Faulks commented that to obtain a divorce you needed only to:

> *fill your wife with gin, give her a complacent lodger and file your petition next day ... Or a husband might say he found it intolerable to live with his wife because she wears pink knickers – or nothing at all.*

... fill your wife with gin ...

A less informal appraisal of the effect of the modern legislation is that of Lord Denning MR in *Wachtel* v. *Wachtel* 1973:

> *When Parliament in 1857 introduced divorce by the courts of law, it based it on the doctrine of the matrimonial offence. This affected all that followed. If a person was the guilty party in a divorce suit, it went hard with him or her. It affected so many things. The custody of the children depended on it. So did the award of maintenance. To say nothing of the standing in society. So serious were the consequences that divorce suits were contested at great length and at much cost.*
>
> *All that altered. Parliament has decreed: 'If the marriage has broken down irretrievably, let there be a divorce.' It carries no stigma, but only sympathy. It is a misfortune which befalls both. No longer is one guilty and the other innocent. No longer are there long contested divorce suits. Nearly every case goes uncontested. The parties come to an agreement, if they can, on the things that matter so much to them. They divide up the furniture. They arrange the custody of the children, the financial provision for the wife, and the future of the matrimonial home. If they cannot agree, the matters are referred to a judge in chambers.*

The modern law, which stems from the Divorce Reform Act 1969, is now to be found in the Matrimonial Causes Act 1973, as amended.

The continuing pivotal relevance of this legislation, still the guiding statute some years after the passing of the Family Law Act 1996, speaks all too powerfully of the limitations of successive governments properly to understand the subtlety of matters of family law. The Major Government encountered sustained opposition from all sides when its then Lord Chancellor, Lord Mackay, with whom the legislation is intimately linked, introduced the Bill which was to become the Family Law Act 1996. No one could resist the theoretical benefits to distressed families of the avowed aims of the legislation in strengthening the institution of marriage and minimising hostility and bitterness between the parties when marriage broke down. In practice, however, there was criticism that the politicians had overlooked the fact that divorce remained a legal process. So, too, others feared that the new legislation would, as with earlier attempts at reforming divorce law, lead to an upsurge in couples seeking divorce in a country which already had the highest rate of marital breakdown in Europe.

Much of the thinking that animated the approach to the Bill was that, by ridding the process of lawyers and substituting mediators, the sting of litigation would be replaced by a calm antiseptic balm of mediation. The threat of denying the grant of legal aid to couples who did not attend a mediation further exposed the characteristic cost-savings endeavours of that government's perception of the importance of a citizen's access to advice. Ironically, in the months before the present Lord Chancellor announced that the main thrust of the Family Law Act had been effectively shelved, statistics showed that, far from being less likely to consult solicitors, those couples who had attended mediation were more likely to do so.

The future of the Family Law Act's proposals is, therefore, very much uncertain at the start of the new millennium but an outline account remains appropriate if only as a cautionary tale.

The starting point (or in modern jargon 'mission statement') could scarcely be faulted when, in section 1, the general principles establish:

(a) that the institution of marriage is to be supported;
(b) that the parties to a marriage which may have broken down are to be encouraged to take all practical steps, whether by marriage counselling or otherwise, to save the marriage;
(c) that a marriage which has irretrievably broken down and is being brought to an end should be brought to an end –
    (i) with minimum distress to the parties and to the children affected;
    (ii) with questions dealt within a manner designed to promote as good a continuing relationship between the parties and any children affected as is possible in the circumstances;
    (iii) without costs being unnecessarily incurred in connection with the procedures to be followed in bringing the marriage to an end; and
(d) that any risk to one of the parties to a marriage, and to any children, of violence from the other party should, so far as reasonably practicable, be removed or diminished.

Neither, had the legislation been brought into force, could the behaviour of either the husband or wife ever be faulted for the Act would have removed the concept of fault in this jurisdiction. Critics of this approach nevertheless contend that the removal of fault serves only to undermine the moral basis of a serious legal process which represents a major event in anyone's life. Such opponents of the legislation would see as unfair the dissolution of a marriage where a dutiful and loving wife is consigned to history where her only 'fault' is to have allowed her youthful allure to fade.

Whether, in practice, couples who may have grown to hate each other are best served by the in-built delay which is central to this legislation (and which in every other area of litigation is viewed as objectionable) remains seriously open to question.

Under the Act, which may now never be brought into force, the unhappy spouse (and perhaps even both spouses) would first have to attend an **information meeting**. Fortunately, at least some common sense prevailed in Parliament so as to allow couples who would not even sit in the same room without abuse or violence to attend separate meetings. Legal advice would not be available at such a meeting. At such a meeting the parties would then receive the sort of advice their lawyers would give them anyway.

The parties seeking a divorce would then have to wait for at least three months before filing a **statement of marital breakdown** at court. Thereafter, further delay is built into the proposed process so as to allow (and in practice require) a **period for reflection and consideration** and which will last for between a further nine to fifteen months. The role of mediation underlined the approach to the legislation. As with the porcine-led chant in Orwell's *Animal Farm* where two legs were seen as bad and four legs were seen as good, proponents of this approach extolled mediators as skilled in speedily resolving problems and con- demned lawyers as equally skilled in speedily causing them. On the other hand, the weakness of mediation (which is by no means free or cheap) is that people undergoing a legal process need advice and those who are being asked to enter into perhaps complex financial agreements require proper disclosure of the other party's financial circumstances. The present Lord Chancellor rightly recognised the limits of this approach in parliamentary debate:

> *Mediation is an anodyne word but the lot of a fearful and intimidated wife in the mediation process will not be a happy one, despite prior legal advice on the skills and courtesy of the mediator. She will have been told what her legal goals should be; but, unrepresented, in the real world it is unlikely that she will ever be able to present her case effectively.*

During this enforced hiatus in the divorce process the parties would be required to spend time reflecting on their future. They should explore the prospects of reconciliation and, at worst, plan for their future lives if they did decide to go their separate ways. Some, of course, may just find it somewhat condescending to suppose that sensible husbands and wives had not really given thought to these considerations before consulting solicitors who, in any event, as a matter only of routine good practice, have long canvassed the prospects of reconciliation with clients.

Only after this lengthy delay could the unhappy spouse file with the court his or her **application for a divorce order** upon further specific assurances (which may seem otiose after a period of such delay) that the marriage cannot be saved. The application would also need to set out confirmation as to the arrangements for financial matters.

In the early part of 2000, the present Lord Chancellor announced that the government was not proposing to bring these provisions into force for the foreseeable future. It is, however, to be noted that other parts of the Act had been brought into force before this announcement. For example, Part IV of the Act introduces new measures in respect of domestic violence and, in doing so, substantially replicates much of what had initially been separate proposed legislation set out in the earlier Family Homes and Domestic Violence Bill of 1995. These provi- sions are examined in greater detail in Unit 5.4.

Even without the complications afforded by contentious and failed legislation, all too often people still have a flawed understanding of the true basis of modern divorce law. For example, reports in the Sunday papers often suggest that a wife's 'grounds for divorce' were that her husband knocked her about, or drank too much, or chased other women (usually the pretty ones), or played too much golf or indulged some other weakness of character. Such reports confuse the **grounds** for the divorce with the **evidence** called to prove that ground.

Today, there is still only one ground for divorce. Under section 1 of the Matrimonial Causes Act 1973:

> ... a petition for divorce may be presented to the court by either party to a marriage on the ground that the marriage has broken down irretrievably.

If the marriage has not broken down irretrievably there can be no divorce. Such a requirement excluded the occasional lovers' tiff and similar little local difficulties within such a demanding relationship. Another aspect of Parliament's attempts to prevent people rushing head-long into the divorce courts is that under the Matrimonial and Family Proceedings Act 1984 there is an absolute ban on divorce petitions being presented within one year of the marriage.

A spouse caught up in a marriage which seems to have broken down irretrievably must present a **petition** to the court. That spouse is now known as the **petitioner**. The other spouse is referred to as the **respondent**. The petition must set out the history of the marriage and outline the reasons why the petitioner claims that the marriage has broken down. An example of a petition is given in Figure 5.1.

In order to prove the fact of irretrievable breakdown a petitioner must rely on any one of five matters set out in the Matrimonial Causes Act 1973. These are examined individually below. The court must then consider the allegations and any comments of the other spouse in respect of those allegations. If the court is satisfied that, on those allegations, the petitioner has proved irretrievable breakdown it will grant a decree of divorce dissolving the marriage. The Matrimonial Causes Act 1973 provides that the court

> ... shall not hold the marriage to have broken down irretrievably unless the petitioner satisfies the court of one or more of the following facts.

The Act then lists five separate matters.

1. 'that the respondent has committed adultery and the petitioner finds it intolerable to live with the respondent'
There are two separate issues here. Firstly, the petitioner must prove that the respondent has committed adultery. **Adultery** has been defined as 'voluntary sexual intercourse between a married person and a person of the opposite sex, the two persons not being married to each other'. Secondly, the petitioner must still find it intolerable to live with the respondent. Further, in order to protect so-called 'wife-swappers' or erring partners whose wanderings have been forgiven, a petitioner may not rely on this adultery if he or she lives with the erring partner for a period or periods totalling six months after learning of the adultery.

Under the Act the next ground is **behaviour**. A petitioner could alternatively allege:

2. 'that the respondent has behaved in such a way that the petitioner cannot reasonably be expected to live with the respondent'
This is not to be confused with the old concept of the 'matrimonial offence' of 'cruelty'. Certainly, no particular intention of ill-will is required and it follows that people who are mentally ill or unable to help their behaviour may still be divorced by their spouses. On the other hand, the courts must not take a prudish or moralistic stance of the idiosyncrasies and whims of human behaviour. The courts must consider the personalities of the spouses involved. This approach was imaginatively described in *Ash* v. *Ash* 1972 when the judge said of an identical provision in the Divorce Reform Act 1969:

> *... it seems to me that a violent petitioner can reasonably be expected to live with a violent respondent; a petitioner who is addicted to drink can reasonably be expected to live with a respondent similarly addicted; a taciturn and morose spouse can reasonably be expected to live with a taciturn and morose partner; a flirtatious husband can reasonably be expected to live with a wife who is equally susceptible to the attractions of the opposite sex; and if each is equally bad, at any rate in similar respects, each can reasonably be expected to live with the other. This conclusion seems to me to be consonant with what have been said to be the objects of the 1969 legislation, which are not, in my view, simply to make divorce easier but, to quote from one source: '(i) to buttress, rather than to undermine the stability of marriage; and (ii) when, regrettably, a marriage has irretrievably broken down, to enable the empty legal shell to be destroyed with the maximum fairness, and the minimum bitterness, distress and humiliation.'*

The modern approach to the concept of behaviour was outlined by the Court of Appeal in *Buffery* v. *Buffery* 1988. The correct test to be applied today is for the court to ask whether a right-thinking person, looking at the particular husband and wife, would ask whether the petitioner could reasonably be expected to live with that respondent taking into account all the circumstances of the case and the respective characters and personalities of the two parties concerned. The conduct alleged does not need to be either grave or weighty. The need to consider the particular petitioner and particular respondent was further outlined in *Birch* v. *Birch* 1992 when the subjective nature of the test was underscored when one judge remarked:

> *In matrimonial cases we are not concerned with the reasonable man as we are in cases of negligence. We are dealing with this man and this woman.*

A third alternative is for the petitioner to allege **desertion** and say:

3. *'that the respondent has deserted the petitioner for a continuous period of at least two years immediately preceding the presentation of the petition'*
Desertion is said to be separation from the other party with the intention of bringing the relationship to an end and doing so without the consent of the other spouse or reasonable excuse.

Where one spouse's behaviour has been such as to drive the partner out of the home this expulsive conduct is said to amount to **constructive desertion**.

Fig. 5.1 Example of a divorce petition

IN THE

SOUTH LONDON   COUNTY COURT

IN THE _____

No. SL 2001 D 1001

(1) On the 14th day of February 1994 the petitioner who was then Gertrude Ingrid Black was lawfully married to Thomas John White (hereinafter called 'the Respondent') at the South London Registry Office, London SW27

(2) The Petitioner and Respondent last lived together as husband and wife at 101 South London Road, London SW27

(3) The Petitioner is domiciled in England and Wales, and is by occupation a Solicitor's Secretary and resides at 69 South London Road, London SW27 and the Respondent is by occupation a Barrister's Clerk and resides at 101 South London Road, London SW27

(4) There are no children of the family now living *except*
Darren White, born 2nd May 1994
Wayne White, born 21st December 1997
and Tracy White, born 22nd June 1999

(5) No other child, now living, has been born to the Petitioner during the marriage.

(6) There are or have been no other proceedings in any court in England and Wales or elsewhere with reference to the marriage (or to any child of the family) or between the Petitioner and Respondent with reference to any property of either or both of them.

(7) There are or have been no proceedings in the Child Support Agency with reference to the maintenance of any child of the family.

(8) There are no proceedings continuing in any country outside England and Wales which are in respect of the marriage or are capable of affecting its validity or subsistence.

(9) The said marriage has broken down irretrievably.

(10) The Respondent has behaved in such a way that the Petitioner cannot reasonably be expected to live with the Respondent.

(11) <u>Particulars</u>

1. The Respondent is a man of violent disposition who, on occasions too numerous to particularise herein, has assaulted the Petitioner. On New Year's Day 2001 the Respondent threw a bottle at the Petitioner when they were at a party. On their return home the Respondent again assaulted the Petitioner and knocked her down the stairs. The Petitioner had to crawl to a neighbour's house and was taken by ambulance to hospital where examination revealed a broken wrist and extensive bruising. On learning of the nature and the extent of the Petitioner's injuries the Respondent merely remarked that as the Petitioner was so fat she should have bounced.

2. The Respondent is a man of crude disposition and vulgar expression who, on occasions too numerous to particularise herein, has greatly distressed the Petitioner by his frequent use of intemperate language in public. Throughout the said marriage the Respondent has belittled and ridiculed the Petitioner in terms that she was a 'fat cow', 'silly bitch', 'dippy tart' and an 'old slag'.

3. The Respondent is a man of libidinous disposition who, throughout the said marriage, has distressed the Petitioner by his philandering and various improper associations with other women. At Christmas 2000, the Petitioner returned home early from her needlework classes to discover the Respondent naked in the shower with the Au Pair. The Respondent merely told the Petitioner that she would have to use the bath instead.

4. By reason of the Respondent's behaviour as aforesaid, the Petitioner has suffered great distress. She has been obliged to seek medical help for anxiety and depression. On New Year's Day 2001 and in consequence of the said assault as set out above the Petitioner left the matrimonial home with the said children of the family and sought refuge at a neighbour's house.

Fig. 5.1 Example of a divorce petition

Prayer

The Petitioner therefore prays:

   (1) The suit
     That the said marriage be dissolved.

   (2) Costs
     That the Respondent may be ordered to pay the costs of this suit.

   (3) Ancillary relief
     That the Petitioner may be granted the following ancillary relief:

     a) an order for maintenance pending suit
        a periodical payments order
        a secured provision order
        a lump sum order
        a property adjustment order in respect of 101 South London Road, London, SW27
        an order pursuant to section 25B and C Matrimonial Causes Act 1973, as amended

     b) For the children
        a lump sum order
        a property adjustment order as above

Gertrude White   Signed

The names and addresses of the persons to be served with this petition are:–

Respondent:– Thomas John White.
             c/o his Solicitors,
             Wright Shambles & Crooks,
             1 London Road,
             London SW27

Co-Respondent (adultery case only):–

The Petitioner's address for service is:– c/o her Solicitors,
                                      Stinking, Filthy & Rich,
                                      2 London Road.
                                      London SW27

Dated this   14th   day of   February 2001

Address all communications for the court to: The Court Manager, County Court.
The Court office at } 3 London Road, London SW27
is open from 10 a.m. to 4 p.m. on Mondays to Fridays.

Probably the most amicable way to obtain a divorce is for the petitioner to prove **two years' separation and consent**. The fourth possible evidential burden is:

4. *'that the parties to the marriage have lived apart for a continuous period of at least two years immediately preceding the presentation of the petition ... and the respondent consents to a decree being granted'*
It is even possible, where the husband and wife have split the home into two camps and have limited communication to curt missives left on the kitchen table, for the court to hold that these warring spouses have been living separate and apart under the same roof.

One of the novel and most controversial aspects of the modern legislation was the provision allowing one spouse to divorce the other, who may be blameless in every way, after **five years' separation** for the final aspect is:

5. *'that the parties to the marriage have lived apart for a continuous period of at least five years immediately preceding the presentation of the petition'*
This practical application of the common-sense recognition that a marriage where husband and wife have lived separate lives for five years cannot be much of a marriage is tempered by protection for the respondent. Under section 5 of the Act a respondent to such a petition may oppose the grant of a divorce on the ground that the dissolution of the marriage would result in 'grave financial or other hardship ... and that it would in all the circumstances be wrong to dissolve the marriage'.

For example, in *Banik* v. *Banik* 1973 the court declined to grant a husband a divorce even though it had been many years since he and his wife last lived together in India. The wife gave evidence that as a Hindu she would become a social outcast in a society where divorce was regarded as anathema on religious and moral as well as social grounds.

Whichever particular complaint is put forward the petitioner must serve the respondent with a copy of the petition. The respondent will be asked to complete a form known as the **Acknowledgement of Service**. In this document the respondent will say whether he or she wishes to defend the petition. If the respondent intends to defend the petition it will be necessary to serve a form of defence known as the **Answer**.

In undefended cases a petition proceeds under the so-called **Special Procedure**. If the district judge is satisfied about the matter he will grant a certificate and in due course the circuit judge will formally pronounce the decree *en bloc* with many others listed that day. Initially, the court will pronounce a **decree nisi** which is the first stage in the dissolution of the marriage. After six weeks the petitioner may obtain a **decree absolute** and the parties are now free to marry again. The only contact the petitioner and respondent need have with each other will concern finances and, of course, their children, if any.

5.4 Domestic injunctions

Most accidents are said to happen in the home. So, sadly, does much deliberate violence within marital or other relationships. The last quarter of a century has seen a sea-change in the way such domestic hooliganism is treated. The police no longer dismiss assaults between spouses or cohabitants as merely a 'domestic' in their own colloquial jargon and instead may prosecute. Parliament acted in passing the Domestic Violence and Matrimonial Proceedings Act 1976 to give the courts power to grant injunctions to prevent one party molesting the other or a child in the home. The significance of such legislation was that there was no longer any need for the applicant (the name given to the person seeking the protection) to have instituted proceedings for divorce. Within the main suits for divorce the courts had already evinced a willingness to grant such orders and even to grant so-called **ouster injunctions** – orders requiring a violent or otherwise disruptive spouse out of the home. Until 1976, such protection was not, however, available where the parties were not married. The Act also empowered a judge to grant a power of arrest which would authorise the police to arrest the respondent (the name given to the other party) if he, and sometimes also she, nevertheless went on to assault or molest the applicant.

Further legislation was enshrined in the Matrimonial Homes Act 1983 which empowered the court to declare, enforce, restrict or terminate a spouse's rights of occupation in a matrimonial home. In practice, this usually meant that a violent or disruptive husband might be forced to leave his own home if the circumstances (and the welfare of the children perhaps especially) so warranted. Local magistrates had also been given some limited powers by virtue of the Domestic Proceedings and Magistrates Courts Act 1978 which allowed magistrates (sitting in what is termed a Family Proceedings Court) to make **personal protection orders** and even **exclusion orders**. Under section 16 of the Act where the applicant had proved actual or threatened violence against himself or herself or a child and had also satisfied the court that an order was necessary for his or her protection the court could order the respondent not to use or threaten violence against the applicant or any child.

The passing of three different Acts of Parliament within seven years led to a farrago of legislation and difficulties for, as Lord Scarman remarked in *Richards* v. *Richards* 1983:

> *The statutory provision is a hotchpotch of enactments of limited scope passed into law to meet specific situations or to strengthen the powers of specified courts. The sooner the range, scope and effect of these powers are rationalised into a coherent and comprehensive body of statute law, the better.*

These apposite criticisms were examined by the Law Commission whose proposals found their way into the Family Law Act 1996, following the demise of the original Family Homes and Domestic Violence Bill. Part IV of the Family Law Act 1996 now grants the courts jurisdiction to make **occupation orders** and **non-molestation orders** under sections 33 to 37 of the Act. The court has power under section 33 to regulate the occupation of a home by either or both parties. In practice this may often mean the court requires the respondent to the application (usually, but by no means always, the man) to leave the home or, less severely, to leave at least a defined area (perhaps a bedroom). These, of course, are powerful weapons in a dispute between cohabitants where one party may see such a procedure as little more than part of the routine preliminary barrage before the main battle. As a safeguard, therefore, the judge is specifically enjoined to consider all the circumstances including:

1. the housing needs and housing resources of each of the parties and any relevant child;
2. the financial resources of the parties;
3. the likely effect of any order, or of any decision by the court not to exercise any of the above powers, on the health, safety or well-being of the parties and of any relevant child; and
4. the conduct of the parties in relation to each other and otherwise.

Even against these criteria, the court is required to make an order if the applicant or any relevant child is likely to suffer significant harm which is attributable to the conduct of the respondent unless the respondent or any relevant child is also likely to suffer significant harm upon the order being made and where such harm is as great as that likely to be suffered by the applicant or child. Even children may apply for occupation orders although some additional safeguard against teenage rebellion is provided by section 43 which requires a child under the age of sixteen to obtain permission from the court before making such application.

5.5 Children

The courts do everything possible to protect the interests and welfare of children who can so easily be caught up in their parents' continuing wrangling. In all cases, the first consideration to which the courts must have regard is the 'welfare' of the child, which has long been held to be the 'paramount' (that is to say, above all others) consideration.

This long-standing approach has been preserved by the Children Act 1989 which came into force in October 1991.

Until then, as the courts had worked on the basis that until the child was old enough to take care of himself one of the parents must assume responsibility for that child's upbringing, one parent would often obtain an order for **custody**. In more recent years the trend has developed of recognising that both parents should properly be involved in making important decisions. Such approach was reflected in the tendency often to make an order for **joint custody** of a child.

However, as the parents were now divorced and living separately, one parent would need to have the day-to-day care of the child. This regime was known as an order for **care and control**. Under the old law the parent who was no longer to have care and control would, nevertheless, almost invariably obtain an order for **access**. In that way it was hoped that the bond between parent and child would be maintained for there is disturbing statistical evidence that all too many fathers lose contact with their children upon divorce. Fortunately, many parents could agree the periods and times of access, for example, with 'staying access' on alternate weekends and often for half of the school holiday periods. In such cases, the courts would merely say that there should be an order for **reasonable access**. On occasions, however, and in some cases because the parents would do little more than continue their own wrangling as spouses through their children, the courts would have to lay down dates and times for such contact. Such an order would then provide for **defined access**.

Human nature has sadly shown little change of heart since then but the terminology of court orders has been altered by the Children Act 1989. The long-standing paramountcy of the child's welfare is confirmed by section 1. The Act, however, now provides that the courts should be more circumspect about making orders for the future welfare of the children and the court is now required not to make any order at all 'unless it considers that doing so would be better for the children than making no order at all'.

The courts are also required by Parliament to act speedily in determining any question of a child's upbringing and, despite the shortage of judges to cope with the volume of work, to recognise the common-sense principle 'that any delay in determining the question is likely to prejudice the welfare of the child'.

Although the parents are no longer husband and wife, they remain for ever the only parents their children will have. In the language of the 1989 Act, each retains **parental responsibility** for their children if they were married at the time of birth. Where the mother was not married at the time of the birth, she alone will have parental responsibility unless and until the father takes the steps to acquire such responsibility in accordance with the Act. This new concept of parental responsibility replaces the old idea of 'parental rights and duties' – a concept with more duties than rights and one in which the balance would vary as the child grew older. A parent's right to custody of a child would end on the child's eighteenth birthday. As Lord Denning MR said in *Hewer* v. *Bryant* 1969:

> ...*and even up till then, it is a dwindling right which the courts will hesitate to enforce against the wishes of the child, the older he is. It starts with a right to control and ends with little more than advice.*

The modern concept of parental responsibility is defined in section 3 of the Children Act 1989 as meaning:

> ...all the rights, duties, powers, responsibilities and authority which by law a parent of a child has in relation to the child and his property.

This nebulous farrago of a definition will still require consideration of the decision of the House of Lords in *Gillick* v. *West Norfolk and Wisbech Area Health Authority* 1985 when the courts were called upon to consider whether parental consent was required before daughters under the age of sixteen years could be prescribed the contraceptive pill. The plaintiff, who had five daughters under the age of sixteen, had sought an assurance from her local health authority that none of her daughters would be given advice or treatment on contraception without the plaintiff's prior knowledge and consent. The authority refused to give the mother such an assurance. In such circumstances, could a doctor properly provide contraception to a girl still too young to give valid consent to sexual intercourse without obtaining her parents' agreement? In considering this question the judges had to take account of wider issues of parental rights generally. They said that, having regard to the reality that a child became increasingly independent as he or she grew older and also that parental authority dwindled correspondingly, the law did not recognise any rule of absolute parental authority until any fixed age. Rather, said the House of Lords, parental rights were recognised by the law only as long as they were needed for the child's protection. Even those rights had to make way once the child had reached a sufficient understanding and intelligence to be capable of making up his or her own mind. Against that background, it could not be said that a girl under the age of sixteen lacked legal capacity to consent to contraceptive advice merely because of her age. Doctors, therefore, should have a discretion whether or not to put such a girl on the pill. The practical need for the law to keep in step with changing social conditions was well recognised by Lord Fraser:

> *It is, in my view, contrary to the ordinary experience of mankind, at least in Western Europe and the present century, to say that a child or a young person remains in fact under the complete control of his parents until he attains the definite age of majority, now eighteen in the United Kingdom, and*

that on attaining that age he suddenly acquires independence. In practice most wise parents relax their control gradually as the child develops and encourage him or her to become increasingly independent. Moreover, the degree of parental control actually exercised over a particular child does in practice vary considerably according to his understanding and intelligence and it would in my opinion be unrealistic for the courts not to recognize these facts. Social customs change, and the law ought to, and does in fact, have regard to such changes when they are of major importance.

Almost inevitably some parents who are divorcing may disagree where and with whom their children should live in the future. Either party may then apply to the court for an order detailing with whom the children should reside and, therefore, known logically as a **residence order**. This is one of a number of orders which the court has jurisdiction to make under section 8 of the Children Act 1989 and was intended to remove any impression given by the old **custody** order that one parent was interested and worthy while, in contrast, the other parent aspired to neither virtue. A residence order means:

> An order settling the arrangements to be made as to the person with whom a child is to live.

The order is wider than the old custody concept and is the basis behind recent characteristically extravagant newspaper headlines of children 'divorcing' their parents. Under section 10 of the Act, a child who is deemed to have 'sufficient understanding' is able to ask the court to make a residence order so that, for example, a child unhappy at home may be able to obtain such an order for him or her to live at the home of a favourite aunt.

As the needs of the individual children will remain as they were before October 1991, the old law on custody and access will remain of background relevance. Indeed, the worth of principles established over the years by the courts is enshrined in the new legislation. Before making any order under section 8, the court is required to consider the statutory checklist laid down in section 1 and pay regard in particular to:

1. the ascertainable wishes and feelings of the child concerned (considered in the light of his age and understanding);
2. his physical, emotional and educational needs;
3. the likely effect on him of any change in his circumstances;
4. his age, sex, background and any characteristics of his which the court considers relevant;
5. any harm which he has suffered or is at risk of suffering;
6. how capable each of his parents, and any other person in relation to whom the court considers the question to be relevant, is of meeting his needs;
7. the range of powers available to the court under this Act in the proceedings in question.

Against such a list of factors, the courts must weigh all sorts of considerations. Among them is the principle that young brothers and sisters should, where possible, be brought up together. As Purchas LJ said in *C v. C* 1988:

> It is really beyond argument that unless there are strong features indicating a contrary arrangement, brothers and sisters should, wherever possible, be brought up together, so that they are an emotional support to each other in the stormy waters of the destruction of their family.

Although in practice younger children are much more likely to be with their mothers, it is to be stressed that this is not a presumption. At every stage the court must ask what is in the child's best interests. In most cases, however, the young child will have been cared for by the mother and it is thought that any change in the continuity of such care is best avoided. For example, in *D v. M* 1982 the Court of Appeal said:

> continuity of care is a most important part of a child's sense of security ... disruption of established bonds is to be avoided whenever it is possible to do so. Where, as in this case, a child of two years of age has been brought up without interruption by a mother ... it should not be removed from her care unless there are strong countervailing reasons for doing so.

Even though today's modern man and caring father is more widely expected to play a close role in bringing up his children, it is undeniable that mothers are statistically more likely to obtain residence orders. It remains important, nevertheless, that children maintain close and affectionate ties with both parents and, with this commendable aim in mind, it is possible for a court to make an order for **joint residence**. It has been said that such an order removes the impression that one parent is good and responsible whereas the other possesses neither quality. Even so the courts had been cautious about making such orders and would long do so only where the circumstances were exceptional or, more recently, were viewed as unusual. So it was that in *A v. A (Minors) (Shared Residence Order)* 1994 the Court of Appeal had thought that a shared residence order would be unlikely to be appropriate if there were still issues such as contact or education to be resolved between the parents. However, very recently, in *Re D (Children) (Shared Residence orders)* 2001 the Court of Appeal expressed the view that where a child was spending a substantial amount of time with both parents a shared residence order could well be the answer.

The parent with whom the child is no longer living full-time can apply for a **contact order**. This is defined in section 8 as an order:

> ... requiring the person with whom a child lives, or is to live, to allow the child to visit or stay with a person named in the order, or for that person and the child otherwise to have contact with each other.

Again, the old approach of the courts to access orders will afford helpful guidelines. Generally, it is thought that a child should grow up knowing both parents. This view was well explained by Latey J in *M* v. *M* 1973 when he spoke of the long-term advantages to the child of:

> *keeping in touch with the parent concerned so that they do not become strangers, so that the child later in life does not resent the deprivation and turn against the parent who the child thinks, rightly or wrongly, has deprived him, and so that the deprived parent loses interest in the child and therefore does not make the material and emotional contribution to the child's development which that parent by its companionship and otherwise would make.*

This principle should not be abrogated solely on account, say, of past violent or sexual abuse by a parent of the child. Of course, such misconduct would be an extremely important factor but the court would, nevertheless, have to consider whether the child may benefit from knowing that parent. Mothers or fathers who ignore their children for years may find that it is too late suddenly to seek an order for contact: despite the biological link such a parent would, after a number of years' absence, be a stranger to the child and a court may well say that such an order for contact would be distressing and, therefore, harmful to the child.

It remains the aim of the courts at least always to minimise the risk of harm to a child, a point recently emphasised by the Court of Appeal in *In Re L and Others* 2000. In considering a number of linked appeals by fathers who had been unable to obtain orders for direct contact, the judges recognised that in such applications where domestic violence had been alleged the court must consider the conduct of both parties towards each other and, of course, towards the children. Indeed, the government's 'think tank' in this area, the Family Advisory Group, have gone so far as recently to suggest that, where a mother alleges violence, the father should be deprived of contact with the children where such a result enjoys the approval of the court welfare officer.

In considering these and other such delicate matters, the court is assisted by a report prepared by a **court welfare officer**. This officer acts as the eyes and ears of the court. He or she will see the parents, whether separately or together, will see the children and may speak to others such as teachers, child minders and health visitors in order to form a view as to what is in the child's best interests. The court will always pay the greatest attention to these reports and a judge must give reasons for not following any recommendation they contained. Such a report may well offer some indication as to the child's own wishes in the matter.

In practice, once the child is a teenager it is unlikely that a judge would do other than give effect to his or her own wishes, especially since the decision of the House of Lords in *Gillick*.

In the case of younger children the courts must consider whether or not any particular child is of such an age as to be able to make a wise choice in his or her own interests. In giving the judgment of the Court of Appeal in *Re S (a Minor)* 1993 Sir Thomas Bingham MR outlined the principles upon which judges should consider the views of children caught up in their parents' disputes:

First is the principle, to be honoured and respected, that children are human beings in their own right with individual minds and wills, views and emotions, which should command serious attention. A child's wishes are not to be discounted or dismissed simply because he is a child. He should be free to express them and decision-makers should listen. Second is the fact that a child is, after all, a child. The reason why the law is particularly solicitous in protecting the interests of children is because they are liable to be vulnerable and impressionable, lacking the maturity to weigh the longer term against the shorter, lacking the insight to know how they will react and the imagination to know how others will react in certain situations, lacking the experience to measure the probable against the possible. Everything of course depends on the individual child in his actual situation. For purposes of the 1989 Act, a babe in arms and a sturdy teenager on the verge of adulthood are both children, but their positions are quite different: for one the second consideration will be dominant, for the other the first principle will come into its own. The process of growing up is, as Lord Scarman pointed out in Gillick's case, a continuous one. The judge has to do his best, on the evidence before him, to assess the understanding of the individual child in the context of the proceedings in which he seeks to participate.

A disappointed parent will have only a very limited prospect of success in any appeal against the judge's decision. These difficult decisions involve a balancing exercise and the use of considerable discretion on the part of the judge. In G v. G 1985 the House of Lords underlined how difficult it is for an appellate court to say that the judge's decision was wrong even in cases where that higher court would have itself preferred a different result. Moreover, in *Clarke-Hunt* v. *Newcombe* 1983 Cumming-Bruce LJ well appreciated the difficult task such decisions present the judges:

The problem of the judge was to appreciate the factors pointing in each direction and to decide which of the two bad solutions was the least dangerous, having regard to the long-term interests of the children, and so he decided the matter. Whether I would have decided it in the same way if I had been in the position of the trial judge I do not know. I might have taken the same course as the judge and I might not, but I was never in that situation. I am sitting in the Court of Appeal deciding quite a different question: has it been shown that the judge to whom Parliament has confided the exercise of discretion, plainly got the answer wrong? I emphasize the word 'plainly'.

Even when residence and contact orders have been made, the parents may still be in dispute over other aspects of the child's life – for example, which particular school little Johnny should attend. Differences of this sort may be resolved by the court making a **specific issue order**. This is further defined in section 8 as an order giving directions for the purpose of determining a specific question which has arisen, or which may arise, in connection with any aspect of parental responsibility for a child.

The parent who has failed to achieve any of the orders of any sort may decide to take drastic measures. Such a parent may even remove the child not only from the home of the other parent but also from England and Wales. Some safeguard against these snatches may be found in the last order available under section 8 of the Children Act. The **prohibited steps order** is defined as

an order that no step which could be taken by a parent in meeting his parental responsibility for a child, and which is of a kind specified in the order, shall be taken by any person without the consent of the court.

Such an order may be appropriate also for comparatively minor matters such as medical treatment or removal from school. Where, however, there is a risk of abduction, international co-operation has recently produced an increasingly effective means of restoring children to the other parent.

Quite apart from the old common-law offence of kidnapping, those who move children from the lawful custody of another parent may commit an offence under the Child Abduction Act 1984. The removal of children from the country can be impeded by the emergency procedures which the police and immigration authorities operate as a 'port alert'.

Within England and Wales the courts have wide powers to trace children. For example, television news programmes will occasionally give publicity to **search and recovery** orders. The Family Law Act 1986 gives officials a statutory power to search premises and section 50 of the Children Act 1989 introduced the **recovery order**. This further confers wide powers to order the production of and removal of a child unlawfully taken. The Family Law Act 1986 further allows the court to order any person who may have relevant information to disclose it.

If, despite the port alert procedure, the child has been removed from the jurisdiction, the deprived parent will be able to draw on international co-operation made possible since the Child Abduction and Custody Act 1985. This statute ratified two international conventions known as the Hague Convention and the European Convention. These Conventions are intended to provide a short summary procedure for returning children to their home countries before they put down roots in the country to which they have been taken. In England and Wales the Lord Chancellor's Department will help the deprived parent to apply to the country where his or her child has been taken unlawfully. Other countries which are signatories to the Conventions will then take the various steps laid down in the Conventions with a view to ensuring the prompt return of the child to the United Kingdom. The courts of England and Wales offer reciprocal procedures to ensure the child leaves these shores as soon as possible. The courts specifically avoid entering into any dispute between the parents as to the way in which that child is being cared for and express the view that such matters should be considered by the national court.

5.6 *Legitimacy*

The discussion of children's upbringing so far in this Unit has assumed that the child in question is the legitimate offspring of the divorcing couple. Traditionally, a child is said to be legitimate if his parents were married at the time of his birth. The old problems and disadvantages encountered by illegitimate children have now disappeared. Such progress is the result of changing social views and lifestyle, factors which have increasingly been recognised by the legislation passed over half a century and which led to the Legitimacy Act 1976, which confirms and adds to earlier legislation. For example, the Legitimacy Act 1926 provided that a child born to unmarried parents could be legitimated by the later marriage of those parents. The Legitimacy Act 1976 now confirms that position in section 2, which provides that:

> Where the parents of an illegitimate person marry one another, the marriage shall, if the father of the illegitimate person is at the date of the marriage domiciled in England and Wales, render that person, if living, legitimate from the date of the marriage.

What, though, of children born to parents who entered into a marriage later found to have been either void or voidable? This position is also governed by the Legitimacy Act 1976, which in section 1 provides that if at the time of the child's conception the parents reasonably believed that they were properly married to each other the child must be treated as their legitimate child.

Section 22 of the Family Law Reform Act 1987, an Act which implemented recommendations of the Law Commission (see Unit 1.9), provides that, where necessary, a person may apply to the High Court or County Court for a declaration as to his or her legitimacy. Such procedure may be necessary if the applicant is concerned to obtain British nationality or to accede to some title (and, through it, maybe also to an estate).

In other respects the distinction between legitimate and illegitimate children has become increasingly blurred over the last half century. For example, the Family Law Reform Act 1969 allowed illegitimate children to inherit the property of either parent where that parent had died intestate (that is, without leaving a will – see Unit 5.9). Further, such children are now able to obtain financial provision from the estates of their deceased parents if those children qualify as dependants at the time of the parent's death. This matter is specifically examined in Unit 5.9. These children are also allowed to claim as dependants under the Fatal Accidents Act 1976 and so may sue the person responsible for causing the death of one or both parents.

In order to help determine the issue of paternity in disputed cases, the court has long had power to order that **blood tests** should be carried out. Recent developments now permit much more sophisticated tests to be ordered. The old blood test could never positively establish that a man (known as a **putative father**) was in fact the natural father of the particular child. Such a test could only either exclude the man as a father by saying that it was impossible for a man with such a blood group to father a child of such a blood group or, alternatively, indicate the statistical range of men who could be the father. For example, the tests might have shown that only 17 per cent of the country could have fathered the child; but, as well as the putative father, the butcher, baker and candlestick-maker might also come within this range. Today, the courts acknowledge the use of **DNA profiling**, which offers virtually certain identification of parentage. DNA (deoxyribonucleic acid) is extracted from blood or other body tissue and separated into bands. Each of us inherits about half our DNA bands from each parent and analysis of the putative father's DNA will determine whether those bands not maternally inherited have come from him. It has been claimed that the chances of a non-biological father possessing the true biological father's bands is so remote as to be some many millions to one.

Where the parents are not married, the mother may apply to the courts under the Children Act 1989 for an order for periodical payments or other financial benefit to be paid by the father for the support of the child. Under this legislation the court has once again wide powers also to make lump sum orders and even orders for the settlement of property in favour of those under the age of eighteen years.

Recent figures show that more children than ever before are now being born to mothers not married to the father of the child. Such evidence, fortunately, also indicates that the children are nevertheless being born to parents who, although not married, enjoy a close and stable relationship. For some unfortunate single mothers, however, the prospect of bringing up a child on their own may persuade them that the best hope for the baby lies in allowing another family to **adopt** the baby and bring the child up as a full member of that family.

5.7 Adoption

Adoption, first known in England and Wales in 1926, extinguishes the rights of the natural parents over their child and transfers parental responsibility to the new adoptive parents. It is a fundamental change over the lives of the children concerned who exchange one set of parents for another.

Commonly, anyone applying to the court to adopt a child will be married and living with his or her spouse. The categories both of those who may adopt and those who may be adopted are set out in the Adoption Act 1976, as amended by the Children Act 1989. A married couple will each have attained the age of twenty-one years. A person on his or her own may also adopt a child provided that the applicant is over twenty-one years and domiciled in the United Kingdom. Married couples face similar requirements as to their domicile but would usually find it easier to adopt a child. The child to be adopted must be under the age of eighteen years and never have been married. In practice, a single man aged twenty-one would have scant prospect of adopting a seventeen-year-old girl however willing he might be to take care of her.

A court must in any event be satisfied that the applicants are suitable people to adopt the child. The court must then also consider the welfare of the child and the Adoption Act 1976 requires that the first consideration should be given to the need to safeguard and promote the welfare of the child throughout his childhood. The court should also discover the child's own wishes and feelings, having regard of course to the child's age and understanding.

Because of the fundamental change of parental roles brought about by the making of an adoption order, it is usually necessary to obtain the consent of the natural parent to the proposed adoption. Understandably, this may be a desperately difficult decision for a natural parent to make but a reasonable parent is expected to consider not only his own feelings but also the long-term welfare of the child. For that reason, a court is empowered to dispense with the consent of the natural parent where the court is satisfied that the natural parent's consent to the proposed adoption is being unreasonably withheld.

Once made, the effect of the adoption order is as set out in section 12 of the Adoption Act 1976 which defines such order as

> an order vesting the parental rights and duties relating to a child in the adopters...

From then on the adopted child is treated in law as if it were not anyone's child other than the child of the adopter. The parental responsibility for that child is now that of the adopters. It follows that the new member of the family is no longer illegitimate and will have full rights to inherit the property of the new parents, a procedure known as **succession**.

5.8 Divorce: dividing the spoils

The newly married couple returning from honeymoon may reflect on the difficulties of getting a quart into a pint pot as they struggle to squeeze into their suitcases such essential souvenirs as bottles of Scotch whisky. The divorcing couple would look wearily at the same principle of physics from a different angle as the impossibility of getting a quart from a pint pot proves as self-evident but more serious a problem.

On divorce, a typical family which for years has led a comfortable life on the husband's salary in, say, a three-bedroomed suburban semi-detached house must suddenly share out the assets so as to make two new homes out of one old home. One income may now have to support two separate homes. Such fundamental revision of the parties' lives is usually difficult, and often impossible, to achieve without varying degrees of hardship. In practice, it is such disputes which are very often the most bitter and hard fought vestiges of an unhappy marriage as the spouses turn their attention from matrimony to just plain money.

Under the principle of the old law, to be found in section 17 of the Married Women's Property Act 1882, a wife could, on divorce, get out of her home only what she had put into it. So, for example, a wife who had provided half the purchase price could look forward to receiving half the sale price. Equally, a wife who had contributed only 10 per cent of the purchase price could obtain only 10 per cent of the sale price. Not many late-nineteenth-century wives could afford divorce. A wife's position on divorce has improved beyond recognition since the introduction of the new approach to divorce brought about by the Divorce Reform Act 1969. The later Matrimonial Causes Act 1973 embodied the spirit of a new approach and required the court to exercise its discretion:

> ...so to exercise those powers as to place the parties, so far as is practicable and, having regard to their conduct, just to do so, in the financial position in which they would have been if the marriage had not broken down and each had properly discharged, his or her financial ... obligations and responsibilities towards the other.

Obviously, this sort of instruction to the courts was never going to be easy to implement. After all, if the marriage had not broken down each party would perhaps be sharing a comfortable home, eating well, enjoying holidays, dining out and running a car. On divorce, the wife and children would probably want to stay on in the matrimonial home. Unless there is also a crock of gold upon which the family can draw, the husband will often find it very difficult to buy another home. Out of his income the man would be expected to pay **maintenance** for his ex-wife and children. Even if he were to remarry he may still have to make regular payments for his ex-wife and their children. In practice, the stability of a second marriage can quite easily be threatened by this constant strain and drain.

Of course, many wives would richly deserve proper provision both by way of capital (such as a **lump sum payment**) and by way of regular payments of income (often called **periodical payments**). For example, a wife who had not paid any money towards either the deposit on a house or towards the building society repayments on the mortgage but rather, for forty years, had helped the husband in his business as well as cooking, cleaning, ironing and bringing up four children would, in common justice, merit something better than being made homeless and merely pointed in the direction of the nearest social security office. After all, even if she had not made any direct financial contributions the wife had done her share in building up the home. The common-sense justice of such a proposition was reinforced by Sir Jocelyn Simon, a past President of the old Probate Divorce and Admiralty Division of the High Court (dealing, it was said, with 'Wills, Wives and Wrecks'), when he used this telling metaphor:

> *The cock can feather the nest because he does not have to spend most of his time sitting on it.*

He went on to say:

> *In the generality of marriage the wife bears and rears children and minds the home. She thereby frees her husband for his economic activities. Since it is her performance of her function which enables the husband to perform his, she is in justice entitled to share in its fruits.*

Parliament's noble intention in 1973 of placing each party in the position he or she would have been in had the marriage continued soon proved to be unrealistic. Some amendment to this impossible dream was called for. The Matrimonial and Family Proceedings Act 1984 amended the Matrimonial Causes Act 1973 by deleting the reference to putting the parties in the position they would have been in but for the divorce. Today, the courts are nevertheless clearly still required to give first consideration to the welfare of any child under the age of eighteen.

Under the modern legislation there is a wide range of orders available to the courts by which to grant either spouse what is called **ancillary relief** – that is to say 'ancillary' (or secondary) to the decree of divorce itself. It is noteworthy that today there is equality at the judgment seat and so a husband is perfectly entitled to claim ancillary relief from his ex-wife if she is better off than him. In practice, all too sadly, there is a shortage of rich women and usually it is the wife who seeks financial support from her former husband. Such provision can include claims for maintenance (also known more formally as periodical payments), a property transfer order, transferring say a home to the wife and children and a requirement for one spouse to pay the other a cash sum (known as a lump sum order).

In all proceedings for financial relief the court is required to consider the criteria set out in section 25 of the Matrimonial Causes Act as amended:

(a) the income, earning capacity, property and other financial resources which each of the parties to the marriage has or is likely to have in the foreseeable future, including in the case of earning capacity any increase in that capacity which it would in the opinion of the court be reasonable to expect a party to the marriage to take steps to acquire;

      (b) the financial needs, obligations and responsibilities which each of the parties to the marriage has or is likely to have in the foreseeable future;

      (c) the standard of living enjoyed by the family before the breakdown of the marriage;

      (d) the age of each party to the marriage and the duration of the marriage;

      (e) any physical or mental disability of either of the parties to the marriage;

      (f) the contributions which each of the parties has made or is likely in the foreseeable future to make to the welfare of the family, including any contribution by looking after the home or caring for the family;

      (g) the conduct of each of the parties, if that conduct is such that it would in the opinion of the court be inequitable to disregard it.

One convenient and long-standing starting point for calculating whether or not any payment of maintenance is due from one spouse to the other has been the so-called **one-third rule**, a fraction which had its roots in the awards of the old Ecclesiastical courts. Although today this is an old-fashioned approach and one which ought not to be regarded as anything more than just a starting point (and most certainly not as a rule as such) the court could add up the respective incomes and say that the wife should receive one-third of that aggregate net sum. Say, for example, that Martin works as a doctor. His wife, Susie, is a nursing sister at the same hospital. Martin earns £46,000 net per annum. Sister Susie earns a more modest £14,000 net per annum. Together they earn £60,000 and so Martin ought to pay Susie £6,000 to raise her annual income to one-third of their joint net incomes, that is £20,000 per annum.

It should be remembered that the so-called 'one-third rule' was only ever a rough guideline which could be altered either upwards or downwards according to the weight which the court gives to other factors set out in the Act. Nevertheless, as a starting point only it had some relevance and especially so in the earlier days of modern divorce law. In *Wachtel* v. *Wachtel* 1973 the Court of Appeal had to consider the financial positions of a couple upon their divorce.

The case laid down various principles and Lord Denning MR took the opportunity of considering the 'one-third rule' in a case where the husband was a dentist and the child attended a public school so that the family was reasonably comfortable in its finances.

There was, we think, much good sense in taking one-third as a starting point. When a marriage breaks up, there will thenceforward be two households instead of one. The husband will have to go out to work all day and must get some woman to look after the house – either a wife, if he remarries, or a housekeeper, if he does not. He will also have to provide maintenance for the children. The wife will not usually have so much expense. She may go out to work herself, but she will not usually employ a housekeeper. She will do most of the housework herself, perhaps with some help. Or she may remarry, in which case her new husband will provide for her. In any case, when there are two house-holds, the greater expense will, in most cases, fall on the husband rather than the wife. As a start has to be made some-where, it seems to us that in the past it was quite fair to start with one-third ... But this so-called rule is not a rule and must never be so regarded. In any calculation the court has to have a starting point. If it is not to be one-third, should it be one-half? or one-quarter? ...

The ages of the parties is relevant as, of course, is the length of the mar-riage itself. Obviously, a wife aged sixty whose marriage of forty years has just ended is in a much more vulnerable position than, say, a twenty-year-old divorcee who walked out on her husband after only a year of marriage. The Matrimonial and Family Proceedings Act 1984 (which prevents young wives claiming that their marriages gave them a 'meal ticket for life') now allows the court to order payment of mainte-nance for a fixed term.

For example, a wife aged forty-five may have worked until her mar-riage at the age of eighteen. She could get a job as a secretary but needs to polish her skills and to learn all about the intricacies of word-processing. She is starting a secretarial course and needs maintenance until she has found herself a job. In these circumstances her ex-husband may be ordered to pay her maintenance for, say, two years only, allow-ing her time to get herself back on her feet.

The correct approach to the distribution of the capital assets of a marriage has recently been considered by the House of Lords in *White* v. *White* 2001. While reviewed in the popular press as hailing much larger payouts for wives, it is not yet certain how far this decision on its own facts will affect the more modest family. The Whites had farmed in the West Country as partners in the traditional sense of the word for many years. They were worth some £4.6 million. Depending on the terms of any relevant partnership deed, ex-partners in a business may well share the assets equally. Did this rule from the Partnership Act 1890 entitle Pamela White to say, as do so many wives, that she wanted 'her half'?

The trial judge had awarded her only another £800,000 to add to the £200,000 she already had in her own right. In this approach, he had fol-lowed the traditional route of assessing a wife's 'reasonable needs' rather than any pre-ordained strictly arithmetical division, whether a *Wachtel* one-third or a partnership style one-half. The judge, therefore, had followed the approach of the Court of Appeal in *Dart* v. *Dart* 1996, where the wife of an exceedingly rich man worth no less than £400 million received a mere 2.5 per cent of his fortune. Even so, with an award of some £10 million Christine Dart could at least meet those needs which, by the standards of that family's enormous wealth and lifestyle, were thought to have been 'reasonable'.

The Court of Appeal increased Pamela White's lump sum to £1.5 million and now neither party was satisfied, so each appealed to the House of Lords. While dismissing each appeal, the House of Lords took the opportunity of reviewing the development of ancillary relief claims over some thirty years. The House rejected the approach of assessing 'reasonable needs' as a judicial gloss on the Act and called upon judges to discontinue such practice. While stopping short of any principle of automatic equality (for all the section 25 factors already examined in this Unit still require attention by judges who in this area have a wide discretion) Lord Nicholls was nevertheless to move in that direction:

> Sometimes, having carried out the statutory exercise, the judge's conclusion involves a more or less equal division of the available assets. More often this is not so. More often, having looked through all the circumstances, the judge's decision means that one party will receive a bigger share than the other. Before reaching a firm conclusion and making an order along these lines a judge would always be well advised to check his tentative views against the yardstick of equality of division. As a general guide, equality should be departed from only if, and to the extent that there is good reason for doing so. The need to consider and articulate reasons for departing from equality would help the parties and the court to focus on the need to ensure the absence of discrimination.

Where there is sufficient capital it sometimes happen that a husband will hand a large capital sum over to the wife, who agrees to accept this capital lump sum in full and final settlement of all her claims. In this way she cannot come back to court in five years' time to ask for an increase in her maintenance. Such an approach, known as a **clean break**, has become more popular as it allows each party to start afresh. Section 25A of the Matrimonial Causes Act 1973 requires the court to consider the appropriateness of a clean break but the courts need not strive to achieve it so as to ignore all other factors.

Before any such agreement is made it is, of course, essential that each spouse knows how much money the other spouse is earning and what savings he or she may have. The Family Proceedings Rules 1991 allow one spouse to require the other to produce various documents and other information. By requiring production of, say, business accounts, income-tax returns, bank statements, credit card statements, passports and mortgage application forms, it is sometimes possible to flush out the truth from those who prefer to avoid close scrutiny of their business affairs. These new Rules can also be used to secure the attendance of ex-spouses' new partners and production of their paperwork so that it is made more difficult for, say, cash traders to launder their money through their girlfriends' accounts.

A former husband will be vigilant to discover whether his ex-wife is likely to remarry because her entitlement to receive periodical payments will end upon such remarriage. Her cohabitation without the formality of remarriage, however, does not automatically bring her maintenance claim to an end because she does not acquire rights of support against any cohabitant merely by sharing his life and their home but obviously this can play an important part in any application the husband may make to stop or very substantially reduce such support.

Traditionally, the court would also decide what level of **periodical payments** (maintenance) should be paid to the children by the parent who would no longer be looking after them on a daily basis (usually the father). In this way the district judge would be able to do overall justice in an area of litigation where the court's first consideration was always the welfare of relevant children. The court could take into account in its discretion that wide range of factors such as the capital contribution which the father was making to the children's future, for example, by transferring the home into his ex-wife's name so as to save her paying mortgage instalments or paying rent on a new home for her and the children. Other fathers might be prepared to take on the debts on credit cards and other bills and in this way relieve the children's mother of making those payments. In such cases, the justice of the case might lead the court to make a small order for the weekly support of a man's children which, for those reasons, might well be below the direct economic cost of caring for them. Jurisdiction to make these orders, however, was removed from judges by the Child Support Act 1991 which came into force in April 1993. Since then, the sums to be paid by an absent parent are calculated by adherence to a strict algebraic formula. Any father, for it is usually him, will in this way easily be able to calculate his liability provided he has either ready access to a specialised computer program or is already employed as a rocket scientist. The well publicised difficulties experienced by the Child Support Agency itself have provoked nationwide anger at even their inability to calculate assessments properly. Indeed, recent evidence indicates that some four out of ten assessments are wrong. In 1999 the government, around whose head the CSA hung like the proverbial albatross, proposed a different approach but one which, as before, would still cause injustice and anger because of its inflexibility. The present indication is that such proposals, now set out in the Child Support, Pensions and Social Security Act, will not be carried into effect until the end of 2001 and, even then, only in respect of new cases. One minister let the cat out of the bag by announcing the politicians' wish to turn payment of child support into a 'tax on fathering'. Under the new Child Support, Pensions and Social Security Act 2000, as with income tax, standard rates would apply so that an absent parent would pay 15 per cent of his net income for the first child and 20 per cent for the second with a top rate of 25 per cent for three or more children. While this has a certain simplistic ease of calculation it fails to take any account of the income of the other parent and wholly ignores one other important fact: the payment is not linked in any way to the needs of the child, the cost of meeting those needs or the ability of the other parent to contribute also. The point was well made by one Member of Parliament who noted that, unless the final figure was to be capped (as was eventually agreed contrary to the government's initial proposals in the Bill) in the case of Microsoft's Bill Gates his liability under the formula would exceed the gross domestic product of Luxembourg!

5.9 Succession

a) The will The optimist's confident assertion that 'Where there's a will there's a way' might well be amended by lawyers dealing with the distribution of a deceased's estate to the comment that 'Where there's a will there are relatives'.

The sadness caused by the death of a near relation can be turned to bitterness and feuding as members of the family quarrel over their respective shares in Auntie Flo's estate. The position can be all the more difficult to resolve if Auntie Flo has not left a will (and is, therefore, said to have died 'intestate') or if she has left all her money to the local cats' home. In such cases the courts must decide who is to succeed to the money and other property. When property is transferred by reason of death it is said to pass under the rules of succession.

A lot of trouble, let alone cost, could be avoided if everyone made a will. People are often hesitant about doing so, either because they believe that they have insufficient wealth to justify a will or perhaps because they do not like to think of their own mortality. A will is often a simple document and can be prepared by a solicitor at very modest cost. Substantial difficulty and distress can be caused by people who fail to leave a will at all or who leave a home-made and possibly unclear will. In addition, some proper advice may also later avoid the payment of unnecessarily large amounts of tax. Good health and long life would be suitable toasts to many of those who make their own wills, for the law reports are full of cases where a **testator** (that is a person making a will) has failed to identify properly the property which is to pass – be handed over to other people – or to identify the intended beneficiaries clearly enough, for example by vague terms such as 'I leave everything to the family' or 'all to Mother' (a phrase which in some families means not the man's 'mother' but his 'wife'). Sometimes, a will is found to be invalid because it has not been properly witnessed as required by the Wills Act 1837.

A will is the formal expression of a person's wishes as to what should happen on or after his or her death. It may also give details as to the desired funeral arrangements and specify how that person's home and other property should be distributed.

In order to ensure that these wishes are properly carried out, the testator will appoint people known as **executors** to carry out (or 'execute') the terms of the will. It is common practice for the surviving spouse or children to be appointed to carry out this work. It is also common to appoint a solicitor as an executor and in practice, of course, the main burden will fall on him or her. Banks also carry out this work, for which it is necessary to obtain what is called the **grant of probate**, but banks tend to be quite a bit more expensive than a family solicitor.

The legal requirements for a will's validity are set out in the Wills Act 1837 as amended by the Administration of Justice Act 1982, the Wills Act 1968 and other statutes. Under the amended section 9 of the 1837 Act no will shall be deemed valid unless it is in writing and signed by the testator. This signature must be made or acknowledged by the testator in the presence of two or more witnesses present at the same time. Problems can arise from time to time over this requirement as to witnesses.

For example, in *Re Gibson (deceased)* 1949 the court held that a will was invalid when it was known that one of the two witnesses was blind and had, therefore, been unable to witness the testator's signature properly. More recently, in *Re Colling (deceased)* 1972 a hospital patient was making his will a few days before his death. One of the witnesses, a nursing sister, was called away to attend another patient. Unfortunately, the testator completed his signature in her absence and the court held that the requirements of the Wills Act 1837 had not been complied with. The precise position of a signature upon a will, however, is less important and in *Wood* v. *Smith* 1992 the Court of Appeal regarded a testator's writing at the top of his will as sufficient.

Of course, the reasons for such requirements are related to the need to prevent fraud by greedy people with dishonest designs on a person's estate. Any potential beneficiary who tries to bring his intended benefit forward by murdering the testator is similarly disentitled from inheriting and thus benefiting from his crime.

It is important to note as well that the witnesses must not be intended beneficiaries under the will or even the spouse of such proposed beneficiary. Anyone asked to witness a will, therefore, will learn at an early stage that there is nothing in it for him.

Of course, the testator should know what he is doing. Newspapers, and to a lesser extent the law reports, sometimes carry accounts of an elderly man making out a new will just days before his death and leaving the family fortune to some shapely blonde with her own particular charms for the testator and not to the deceased's children, grandchildren, nieces and nephews.

The testator must have capacity to make a will and be of sound mind and understanding at the time he signs the will. A will may be set aside by a court in the event of proof of undue influence (see Unit 4.10) having been brought to bear on the testator. In practice, considerable suspicion can attach to death-bed revocations of earlier wills.

More often in fiction but also in life, additional drama is sometimes provided by the last-minute discovery that the deceased has left a later will, signed after the one which is causing all the fuss. A will may be revoked at any time prior to the testator's death. A will is said to 'speak from death' and until then it is said to be **ambulatory**, that is, to have no fixed effect. Until death, then, a will may be altered in part or revoked completely.

Obviously, the testator must actually intend to revoke the will. He may, for example, execute another will in which he will say that he is expressly revoking all former wills. Alternatively, he may add some fresh writing, by way of a postscript, which will give further instructions in the will. This addition is known as a **codicil**. A more dramatic way of revoking a will would be by burning it, tearing it or otherwise intentionally destroying it. A mutilated will is *prima facie* evidence of an intention to revoke a will but it is not conclusive of the matter. However, in *In Re Adams (Deceased)* 1990 a lady who had called for the return of her will from her solicitors and then used ink heavily to score out certain lines was held sufficiently to have destroyed her own will.

Where there are difficulties over the construction of a will (that is, how it should be interpreted) application may be made to the court for rectification of the will. The Administration of Justice Act 1982 allows the court to order rectification where the court is satisfied that either because of a clerical error or a failure properly to understand a testator's instructions, the will, as drafted, does not carry out the testator's genuine intention. In such circumstances, the court may order rectification of the will.

Wills are also revoked by subsequent marriage unless the will was made in contemplation of that marriage.

As a general rule, only persons over the age of eighteen years may make a valid will. The old restrictions on a woman's right to make her own will have now passed and adult women now have full testamentary capacity. Generally, however, the property of those who die under the age of majority (eighteen years) will pass to the parents. An exception to this rule is to be found in the case of members of the armed forces who are in actual military service. Such servicemen are allowed to make a so-called **privileged will**. Such a will need not be in writing or witnessed in the normal way. By the Wills (Soldiers and Sailors) Act 1918, brought in during the closing stages of the carnage of the First World War, it was declared that any soldier in actual military service had always been able to dispose of his personal estate without strict compliance with the Wills Act 1837. The Act also applied to sailors and would now also include those serving with the Royal Air Force.

Whether the important concept of the soldier being 'in actual military service' applied to internal anti-terrorist operations had to be considered in *Re Jones* 1981 where a young soldier was shot while on patrol with his unit in Northern Ireland. On his way to hospital the soldier said, 'If I don't make it, make sure Anne gets all my stuff.' Anne was his fiancée. Later on, the court had to decide whether Anne was indeed to inherit or whether the soldier's property should pass to his mother under the terms of an earlier written will. The court held that those words amounted to an effective declaration of what is called a **nuncupative** will (that is one which had been spoken by the deceased in the presence of a credible witness).

b) Administration of the estate

Although the Hollywood picture of a family sombrely gathering in the dusty office of an equally dusty solicitor as the old family lawyer slowly reveals the astounding contents of grandfather's will is an improbable spectacle, it is nevertheless some indication of the work that needs to be done in order to administer the deceased's estate. It is at this stage that the **personal representatives** of the deceased must start on their task and obtain the necessary **grant of probate** after which they must distribute the estate among the named beneficiaries.

If the deceased left a will and there is enough money left over after satisfying the deceased's debts to pay out to the named beneficiaries, the matter is comparatively straightforward. If, on the other hand, the deceased foolishly left no will, the procedure is governed by the Administration of Estates Act 1925, as amended. This Act lists the classes of people who will inherit and places them in pecking order. For example, a surviving spouse would inherit the whole residuary estate (that is, everything left after tax and debts) if there are no children.

At present, if the deceased dies intestate leaving children the general rule is that the widow or widower takes personal possessions absolutely,

£125,000 and a life interest in half the residue of the estate. The other half is held on trust for the children, who become entitled to the capital upon reaching their majority. These figures are, however, liable to change from time to time even if there is not wholesale revision of these rules in the near future.

It should be noted that these inheritance rights do not apply automatically to cohabitants, who should take proper steps to regulate their financial dealings by clear testamentary expression.

As a last resort, where there are no relations to inherit the money, the deceased's estate will be classed as *bona vacantia* (ownerless property) and pass to the Crown – another vivid and salutary warning to those who do not make out a proper will. Even at death the demands of the State bite upon family finances and inheritance tax is now levied on all estates in excess of £234,000 (figure for 2000/01 tax year) at nothing less than 40 per cent upon money already taxed during the deceased's lifetime, an unhappy confirmation of Benjamin Franklin's fatalistic view:

> But in this world nothing can be said to be certain, except death and taxes.

One problem which the personal representatives may have to deal with is that of the insolvent estate, where the deceased's debts and desired bequests actually exceed his assets. In such a case, some creditors take precedence over others. Funeral and testamentary expenses must be paid first. The demands of the State by way of rates and taxes then fall to be paid. Outstanding wages are then to be paid to any employees. One prudent safeguard against late claims on the estate is for advertisements to be placed in the *London Gazette* and a local newspaper, inviting claims to be made promptly. In some cases where there is not enough money to pay out the desired sums to the desired beneficiaries an intended beneficiary may receive nothing at all. In these circumstances the proposed gift is said to 'abate' and there are special rules for determining the order in which such **abatement** is to take place.

c) Claims upon the estate

One particularly difficult claim with which the personal representatives may have to deal is a claim by a dependant of the deceased who seeks further financial provision from the estate. For example, Tom leaves all his property to the barmaid at the Dirty Dog public house where he spent so many happy hours in such convivial company. Tom's wife and six children are completely forgotten in Tom's will and will have neither a home to live in nor income to live on. In such circumstances, the wife and children will be able to make a claim on Tom's estate under the provisions of the Inheritance (Provision for Family and Dependants) Act 1975. As a rule, such claims should be brought within six months of the grant of probate or grant of letters of administration.

. . . such convivial company.

The categories of persons who may apply are set out in section 1 of the Act as:

(a) the wife or husband of the deceased;
(b) a former wife or former husband of the deceased who has not remarried;
(c) a child of the deceased;
(d) any person (not being a child of the deceased) who, in the case of any marriage to which the deceased was at any time a party, was treated by the deceased as a child of the family, in relation to that marriage;
(e) any person (not being a person included in the foregoing paragraph of this subsection) who immediately before the death of the deceased was being maintained, either wholly or partly, by the deceased.

This last category, introduced by the 1975 Act (which replaces earlier legislation passed in 1938), would apply to a mistress of the deceased who had been looked after by him. Since then the position of cohabitants has been protected as a result of the latest category introduced by the Law Reform (Succession) Act 1995, which extends jurisdiction to any person who 'during the whole of the period of two years ending immediately before the date when the deceased died was living in the same household as the deceased, and as the husband or wife of the deceased'.

Applications under the Act are made either to the Family Division of the High Court or to the County Court in the case of smaller estates. The court has wide powers to order reasonable financial provision to those who need it. Such provision may be by way of capital or income. It is, however, most important to bear in mind that the Act is not intended to assist those who feel, whether rightly or wrongly, that they could have done better under a will. The Act is concerned only to ensure that specified persons receive reasonable provision. It follows that if members of a deceased's family and any other dependant are already comfortably off they may well receive no further provision through the courts. Indeed, until 1938, when the first Act was passed, a testator had complete freedom to prefer the needs of his feline friends at the cats' home to those of his wife or children.

The court must embark upon a two-stage test. Firstly, the judge must ask whether reasonable financial provision has been made for the applicant either under the will or under the rules of intestacy. Only when that first question has been answered in favour of an applicant must the judge go on to consider what order to make. Different categories of applicant will receive different standards of award. For example, the surviving spouse would have her (or his) provision judged by the standards of what 'would be reasonable in all the circumstances of the case for a husband or wife to receive'. All other applicants must set their sights lower for they will receive only 'such financial provision as it would be reasonable in all the circumstances of the case for the applicant to receive'.

In considering all the circumstances the court is specifically enjoined to have regard to those matters set out in section 3 of the Act. This section broadly repeats the same sort of considerations which, under the Matrimonial Causes Act 1973, a court must consider in deciding maintenance and capital provision for a divorced spouse. In this way, the courts aim to meet the Act's objective – one summarised by Waite J in *Moody* v. *Stevenson* 1992:

> *The objective is that the acceptable minimum posthumous provision for a surviving spouse should correspond as closely as possible to the inchoate rights enjoyed by that spouse in the deceased's lifetime by virtue of his or her prospective entitlement under the matrimonial law.*

Such approach, however, has been criticised on the basis that it would leave insufficient provision for the surviving spouse. After all, in proceedings after divorce the courts must consider the needs of *two* former spouses. In inheritance applications, it is self-evident that only one of those spouses has a continuing need and in cases such as *Re Besterman* 1984 the Court of Appeal thought that the matrimonial analogy was a useful cross-check but the main consideration for the judges remained the determination of what was reasonable.

Such a judgment requires that the financial resources and needs of an applicant be considered along with the needs and resources of other beneficiaries.

Until the turn of the twentieth century it used to be thought that adult children would receive little provision under the Act in the absence of a clear moral obligation on the part of the deceased but in *Re Hancock (deceased)* 1998 the Court of Appeal has recently made clear that such a concept is not to be viewed as any form of threshold criteria and is nothing more than a weighty factor. So, for example, an unmarried but elderly daughter who, at considerable personal sacrifice, had cared for an aged parent over many years and say, worked for a low wage in the family business, would have an almost unanswerable claim. On the other hand, an adult child who had failed to maintain contact with a parent for many years, and was well able to earn his or her own living, would receive little, if indeed any, provision. The size and nature of the estate must also be considered by the court in work which acts as a salutary reminder to all of us how profoundly the law continues to affect our lives from first to last.

5.10 Questions

1. Pat and Gerry have been married for five years. They have two children. Two years ago Gerry started going out with Monica, a girl from his office. He has now moved out of their council flat and gone to live with Monica. Pat is devastated. She seeks your advice about obtaining a divorce.
   a) What are the facts on which a divorce must be based, and on which particular 'ground' would you advise Pat to rely?
   b) Which court is likely to hear the petition?
   c) How and when will the court decide what is to happen to the children?
   d) As Pat has never worked and wants to stay at home while her children are young, what financial provisions can she expect will be made?

2. Ruth's husband is an alcoholic who beats her from time to time when he is drunk. She wishes to leave him, taking with her her daughter aged four, but she has no capital or income of her own, nor has she anywhere else to live. What are Ruth's legal rights in this situation and how may they be enforced?

3. Mrs Parkinson has been married for thirty years and has three children; her elder daughter Olga is now married, her adult son Patrick is working and has left home, and her younger daughter Felicity is still at school and living at home. Mrs Parkinson's husband has recently died and it has now been discovered that he has left all his property by will to a charity. On what grounds may the will be challenged?

4. Natalie has two children aged ten and twelve. She has been deserted by her husband and is seeking a divorce. What factors ought the court to take into account when settling the future financial arrangements for Natalie and the two children?

5. Mr Burns wishes to divorce his wife to whom he has been married for twenty years. He states that because she is a very successful business woman she is often away from home for long periods of time; that she works late every night, often not returning home until 11 o'clock at night; that she works at home at weekends. He states that in the last six months his wife has become increasingly indifferent towards him and that she has only consented to sexual intercourse twice in the last nine months. Advise him.

6. Mrs Patel aged seventeen requests your advice as to the validity of her marriage celebrated some six weeks ago. She states that the marriage was arranged by her parents; that she had not met Mr Patel before the ceremony and that her parents had threatened to throw her out of their house if she refused to comply with their wishes.

7. Roberto died unexpectedly seven months ago. He had been married to Penny for 25 years. Together they had built up a successful restaurant which allowed them to enjoy many holidays abroad and to afford private education for their three daughters, the eldest of whom is now reading Law at university.

Penny is now distraught to have discovered that for the last two years Roberto had been having an affair with Jenny, a teenage waitress in the restaurant, and that a week before his death he had signed a new will leaving the family home (which had been in his sole name) and all his lifetime savings to Jenny after she had falsely told him that she was expecting his baby. Advise Penny.

6.1 *What is a tort?*

A **tort**, as those fluent in old French will readily appreciate, is a civil wrong. The remedy for a tort is primarily a sum of money paid by way of damages as compensation. If, while you are sitting in your car waiting for the traffic lights to change, a van impales itself on your rear bumper, the van driver (or his employer) will have to compensate you for the tort of his negligent driving. If, during the ensuing pleasantries, the van driver punches you on the nose he has committed the torts of assault and battery. Finally, if, as he leaves you, he loudly airs his views on your driving, your morality and your family history (and gets at least some of it wrong!) he may have committed the tort of defamation.

Of course, in punching you, the driver commits not only a tort but also a crime – for example, assault occasioning actual bodily harm which is an offence under section 47 of the Offences Against the Person Act 1861 (see Unit 3.5a)). There is often a considerable degree of overlap between tort and crime, as we saw in Unit 1.3 in the hypothetical instance of the careless driver Dick and, indeed, also between tort and contract. We have already seen that if a road accident is caused as the result of a garage mechanic's failure to fit new brake-pads properly, then he (or his employers) will be liable either in contract (for breach of an implied term that he would take all due care and exercise proper skill) or in tort for his negligence. Indeed, there may also be an overlap between a tort and a breach of trust.

It was considerations such as these that led Sir John Salmond, one of the two major authorities in this field of law, to define a tort as

> a civil wrong for which the remedy is a common law action for unliquidated damages and which is not exclusively the breach of a contract or the breach of a trust or other merely equitable obligation.

The other great name in tort, Professor Winfield, took the view that

> *tortious liability arises from the breach of a duty primarily fixed by the law; this duty is towards persons generally and its breach is redressible by an action for unliquidated damages.*

The study of this branch of the law has been greatly influenced by both these jurists. They approached the topic in different ways.

Salmond was of the opinion that there was a *law of torts* – that there is a limit to the number of ways in which the law will compensate injury or loss. A claimant would have to bring his claim under an existing tort or be without a remedy. As Salmond argued:

> *Just as the criminal law consists of a body of rules establishing specific offences so the law of torts consists of a body of rules establishing specific injuries. Neither in the one case nor in the other is there any general principle of liability.*

Winfield, however, adopted a different approach. He argued that there was a general *law of tort* so that

> *all injuries done to another person are torts, unless there is some justification recognized by law.*

If Winfield's view is correct then the courts may recognise new torts as and when the need arises.

In practice, the attitude of the courts in this well trammelled arena has not been entirely consistent. For example in *Perera* v. *Vandiyar* 1953 the Court of Appeal refused to recognise a tort of eviction when a landlord, anxious to wave farewell to his tenant, cut off the gas and the electricity supplies. Moreover, on two separate occasions since then the courts have declined to recognise the existence of a tort of perjury (although this, of course, is also an offence). On the other hand, in *Khorasandjian* v. *Bush* 1993 the Court of Appeal was prepared to recognise the existence of the tort of harassment.

The topic came before the House of Lords in *Rookes* v. *Barnard* 1964, when a trade union had used its great power to persuade BOAC to dismiss a draughtsman who had resigned from the union. The House of Lords recognised a new tort of intimidation because, as Lord Reid said:

> *It has often been stated that if people combine to do acts which they know will cause loss to the plaintiff, he can sue if either the object of their conspiracy is unlawful or they use unlawful means to achieve it. In my judgment, to cause such loss by threat to commit a tort against a third person if he does not comply with their demands is to use unlawful means to achieve their object.*

A few years later Lord Reid was again called upon to consider the flexibility of the law of tort (or torts) and its aptitude for expansion in *Home Office* v. *Dorset Yacht Co. Ltd* 1970. Because of damage done to a yacht by some Borstal boys on the run, the House of Lords had to decide whether Borstal officers owed any duty to any member of the public to take care to prevent Borstal trainees under their control from injuring him or damaging his property. Although it is unlikely that, as they set about smashing up someone else's yacht, the escapees debated at any great length the implications of their vandalism on English jurisprudence, the House of Lords had, as a result of their activities, to consider the wide basis of the law of tortious conduct.

Lord Reid analysed the competing theories:

> *About the beginning of this century most eminent lawyers thought that there were a number of separate torts involving negligence, each with its own rules, and they were most unwilling to add more. They were of course aware from a number of leading cases that in the past the courts had from time to time recognized new duties and new grounds of action. But the heroic age was over; it was time to cultivate certainty and security in the law; the categories of negligence were virtually closed.*

Next he summarised and preferred Winfield's arguments:

> *In later years there has been a steady trend towards regarding the law of negligence as depending on principle so that, when a new point emerges, one should ask not whether it is covered by authority but whether recognized principles apply to it.* Donoghue *v.* Stevenson *may be regarded as a milestone, and the well-known passage in Lord Atkin's speech* [see Unit 6.3] *should I think be regarded as a statement of principle. It is not to be treated as if it were a statutory definition. It will require qualification in new circumstances. But I think that the time has come when we can and should say that it ought to apply unless there is some justification or valid explanation for its exclusion.*

The matter really depends on the way in which the courts assess the public's need to be protected from loss or injury at the hands of the careless or the wrongdoer. Earlier, when the same case had been before the Court of Appeal, Lord Denning MR indicated as much when he said:

> *It is, I think, at bottom a matter of public policy which we, as judges, must resolve. This talk of 'duty' or 'no duty' is simply a way of limiting the range of liability for negligence.*

Such considerations of public policy had to be taken into account when one burglar sued another burglar. In *Ashton* v. *Turner* 1980 Philip Ashton had gone out on a burglary with Kevin Turner after a night of drinking. They were pursued from the scene of the crime in their getaway car but Turner crashed it. Ashton was very seriously injured. Turner, as well as raising the defence of *volenti non fit injuria* (see Unit 6.7) based on Ashton having got into the car of a drunk driver, contended that, as a matter of public policy, Ashton had no right of action against him: he raised an argument along the lines of *ex turpi causa non oritur actio* (see Unit 4.12). The judge went on to hold that, as a matter of public policy, English law would, in certain circumstances, refuse to recognise the existence of a duty of care owed by one criminal to another participant in that same crime in respect of acts done to further that offence. On the facts of this case, said the judge, the driver of the getaway car did not owe a duty of care to his fellow burglar either in the course of the burglary itself or in their flight from the scene of the crime.

Even if there is such a general law of tort, that is not to say that everything which causes damage or loss is, *ipso facto*, a tort.

For example, old Bill has been running his little corner shop for over 30 years. Last week Rippoffs, a shiny new supermarket, opened its doors in Bill's street and since then Bill has been on a one-way ticket to the Bankruptcy Court. His business has been wiped out but can he sue the supermarket? The answer is no. This can be seen from the related problem in *Mogul Steamship Co.* v. *McGregor Gow & Co.* 1892. One shipping company had cut its rates and put pressure on others not to load the ships of its rival company, which now claimed damages alleging a conspiracy to injure its trading interests. The House of Lords held that what the other company was doing was only to extend its trade and thus to increase its profits. There was nothing the injured company could do because, as one judge had already said:

> All commercial men with capital are acquainted with the ordinary expedient of sowing one year a crop of apparently unfruitful prices, in order by luring competition away to reap a fuller harvest of profit in the future.

This sort of misfortune is known as *damnum sine injuria* ('a loss without any cause of action').

Economic loss has been one such example. For instance, in *Electrochrome Ltd* v. *Welsh Plastics* 1968 a lorry ran into a fire-hydrant on an industrial estate near the plaintiff's factory. The water supply was cut off for some hours and the plaintiff lost a day's work and profits. The court, however, held that there was no cause of action: once again, *damnum sine injuria*.

The rule is sometimes reversed: there may be a cause of action without any real harm having been done. Then there is said to be *injuria sine damno* – for instance, putting your foot on someone else's land is still trespass even though you do not do any harm to the ground or anything on it.

Those principles still apply even where someone is acting maliciously. This may be relevant to the measure of damages but otherwise, except in a handful of special torts, malice is irrelevant.

For instance, in *Bradford Corporation* v. *Pickles* 1895 Mr Pickles wanted the local corporation to buy some of his land. In order to encourage them not to delay further he sank a shaft on his land. This interfered with the flow of water percolating under his land and running into some adjoining corporation land. The corporation was now trying to obtain an injunction against Mr Pickles from continuing to sink that shaft or otherwise polluting the water.

The House of Lords held that Mr Pickles could do what he liked with his land, no matter how improper or unworthy his motives might be. As Lord Macnaghten emphasised:

> It is the act, not the motive for the act, that must be regarded. If the act, apart from motive, gives rise merely to damage without legal injury, the motive, however reprehensible it may be, will not supply that element.

This general rule is subject only to malice (meaning improper motive) having an essential ingredient in the torts of malicious prosecution and malicious falsehood; it will also remove the defence of fair comment in actions for libel or slander (see Unit 6.10).

6.2 *Remoteness of damage*

In Unit 4.19 we considered liability for breach of contract. In that area, the courts have indicated that the damages which the innocent party may recover should be those either arising naturally from the breach itself or such as were reasonably in the contemplation of both parties. Any loss not falling under one of those heads is said to be **too remote**.

The remedy sought by an injured party in tort is also essentially an award of damages. Obviously, those damages must be assessed by the judge – for example, how much is that broken leg worth, how much is the proper award to compensate the beauty queen for the scars on her face? The damages claimed are, therefore, said to be **unliquidated** because no one knows precisely how much the judge will award.

There is a difference, however, between the principles followed in awarding damages in contract and in tort. While damages in contract are intended to place the innocent party in that position which he would have been in had the contract been carried out, the aim in tort is to put the victim (so far as possible) in the position he would have been in had, for example, his car not been dented or his house not been burned down.

Nevertheless, the courts have emphasised that it would be unjust to make a person pay for every misfortune which could conceivably be connected in some fanciful way with his initial tortious act. For example, say that as Luke is driving to work the side of his new car is scraped when Neil tries to slip through a very small gap to get to the head of the queue. That was Neil's fault and he must pay for the cost of repainting the car. But if, because of the delay, Luke is now in such a hurry that he jumps a red light to hit Carl coming the other way, then it is Luke who must pay up. It may be that if Luke had not been held up earlier by Neil he would not now be in a hurry and would not have raced the lights; Neil's carelessness is, nevertheless, too remote for him to be liable for the second collision.

The law, once again, refuses to make a person liable *ad infinitum*. How then are the courts to decide what is recoverable and what is too remote? Over the years lawyers have disputed between two competing theories of remoteness of damage.

a) The directness test

Initially, a person was liable for all damage which flowed directly from his tortious act. This test was considered by the Court of Appeal in *Re Polemis* 1921. A ship was in harbour at Casablanca and some local stevedores were shifting some cans of benzene out of the hold. The workmen had not made a proper job of the sling and one of its wooden planks fell into the hold. Unfortunately, there were some inflammable vapours down there and as the plank went down so the flames came up. The ship was burned out.

The Court of Appeal held that the stevedores and their employers were liable for all the direct consequences of their negligence, even though their drastic nature could not reasonably have been foreseen.

The strictness of this rule was made clear by Scrutton LJ:

> *But if the act would or might probably cause damage the fact that the damage it in fact caused is not the exact kind of damage one would expect is immaterial, so long as the damage is in fact directly traceable to the negligent act, and not due to the operation of independent causes having no connection with the negligent act except that they would not avoid its results.*

In a later case Viscount Simonds summarised the effect of the rule:

> *There can be no doubt that the decision of the Court of Appeal in* Polemis *plainly asserts that, if the defendant is guilty of negligence, he is responsible for all the consequences, whether reasonably foreseeable or not.*

b) The reasonable foreseeability test

The more modern and more restrictive school of thought considers that a defendant should be liable solely for that loss which was not only caused by his act or omission but which was also reasonably foreseeable as being the result of that act or omission. The workings of this doctrine and its effect on the *Re Polemis* decision were considered at length by the Privy Council in yet another case known simply by the name of the ship involved, *Wagon Mound* 1961. The S.S. *Wagon Mound* was at Sydney, Australia. Some of its oil was spilt in the bay and drifted some 200 yards to a wharf where a ship was being repaired. The oil had become mixed with some floating cotton waste. This was rather unfortunate because only a short distance away some workmen were welding and some molten metal fell on to the oil and cotton mixture. In the ensuing conflagration, the wharf was extensively damaged. Obviously, the fire would not have happened if the S.S. *Wagon Mound* had not discharged any oil. So, clearly, the damage to the wharf was the *direct* result of the oil leak.

The Privy Council now said that the test of liability for the damage done to the wharf was that of foreseeability of injury by fire. On the facts of the case, a reasonable man would not have foreseen such damage and it necessarily followed that the defendants were not liable to the wharf owners even though their servants' negligence was the *direct* cause of the damage.

Viscount Simonds extolled the virtue of the new test:

> *Enough has been said to how that the authority of* Polemis *has been severely shaken, though lip-service has from time to time been paid to it. In their Lordships' opinion, it should no longer be regarded as good law. It is not probable that many cases will for that reason have a different result, though it is hoped that the law will therefore be simplified, and that in some cases, at least, palpable injustice will be avoided. For it does not seem consonant with current ideas of justice or morality that, for an act of negligence however slight or venial, which results in some trivial foreseeable damage, the actor should be liable for all consequences, however unforeseeable and however grave so long as they can be said to be 'direct'.*

He went on to point out the weakness of the old law:

> *After the event even a fool is wise. Yet it is not the hindsight of a fool but it is the foresight of the reasonable man which alone can determine responsibility. The* Polemis *rule by substituting 'direct' for 'reasonably foreseeable' consequences leads to a conclusion equally illogical and unjust.*

The courts have had to consider the rules of remoteness of damage in one particular class of tortious act – that is, where the injuries sustained have been quite exceptionally severe and much more serious than could have been expected. For example, as Mark and David discuss their respective claims on the affections of a certain young lady, Mark reinforces his argument with a swift and dextrously aimed left hook to David's nose. Unknown to Mark, David is a haemophiliac and, of course, his bleeding nose puts him into very serious danger. David's mother comes into the room and is so worried by what she sees that it proves too much for her already very weak heart and she suffers a cardiac arrest on the spot. It was not foreseeable that David was a haemophiliac or that his mother had a weak heart but is Mark liable?

As with the criminal law, the general rule is that a defendant takes his victim as he finds him even if, as lawyers say, he has an 'eggshell skull'. The question was decided in *Dulieu* v. *White* 1901. The defendant had driven his coach and horses into a public house (though not one of that name). The barmaid suffered a form of nervous shock which had been exacerbated by her pregnant state. Kennedy J asked:

> *But what does that fact matter? If a man is negligently run over or otherwise negligently injured in his body, it is no answer to the sufferer's claim for damages that he would have suffered less injury, or no injury at all, if he had not had an unusually thin skull or an unusually weak heart.*

Similarly, in *Smith* v. *Leech Brain & Co. Ltd* 1961 a workman had been splashed on his lip by some molten metal. Unfortunately, the man already had a pre-malignant condition and the burn proved to be the promoting agent of a cancer that caused his death some three years later.

The deceased's employers were held responsible. It was held that the risk of a workman being splashed by molten metal was foreseeable and so was the type of injury, if not also the eventual death. Lord Parker CJ approached the problem in this way:

> *The test is not whether the employers could reasonably have foreseen that a burn would cause cancer and that he would die. The question is whether these employers could reasonably foresee the type of injury he suffered, namely the burn. What, in the particular case, is the amount of damage which he suffers as a result of that burn depends upon the characteristics and constitution of the victim.*

The eggshell skull principle has also been applied to cases of 'eggshell personality', as in *Malcolm* v. *Broadhurst* 1970. Ian and Jean Malcolm were injured in a road accident. They sued Charles Broadhurst, the other driver. Ian Malcolm sustained some head injuries and these caused a personality change: from being a quietly controlled man he became irritable and occasionally violent. This greatly upset Jean Malcolm, who, even before the crash, had a nervous disposition which was aggravated partly by the accident and partly by her husband's changed behaviour. The court held that Mrs Malcolm was entitled to damages for the exacerbation of her nervous condition as this was a foreseeable consequence of the injury. As the judge said:

> The defendant must take the wife as he finds her and there is no difference in principle between an eggshell skull and an eggshell personality ... Exacerbation of the nervous depression was a readily foreseeable consequence of injuring her.

The imposition of liability for events which are reasonably foreseeable was considered in *Brice* v. *Brown* 1984. Sheila Brice was involved in an accident when she was a passenger in a taxi which was struck by a bus. Although not seriously injured, Sheila Brice was badly affected by the experience and her mental state deteriorated. She sued both the drivers involved and contended that, although the precise extent of her mental disorder might not have been foreseeable, the nervous shock which she suffered as a result had been reasonably foreseeable. The drivers replied that they could only be held liable for her nervous shock if its precise nature and extent had been foreseeable. The judge held that once nervous shock was shown to have been a reasonably foreseeable consequence of such negligent driving the plaintiff was entitled to damages – whether or not the full extent of her problems had been precisely foreseeable. The poor lady obviously suffered a very great deal and, apart from other moneys to pay for the cost of past and future nursing care, she recovered £22,500 for her suffering.

In *Hevican* v. *Ruane* 1991 the father of a boy killed in a road traffic accident recovered damages even though he had not been present at the scene of the collision. He learned of the accident at a police station and then travelled to the mortuary. The effect of the tragedy was to cause continuing depression which prevented him working. The judge held that, although it was not foreseeable that the nervous shock suffered would result in continuing psychological illness such as the depression, each link in the chain which caused the nervous shock was foreseeable. In any event, said the court, it was irrelevant that the degree of psychological illness could not have been foreseen.

The range of people who could claim damages for nervous shock was considered by the House of Lords in *Alcock* v. *Chief Constable of South Yorkshire Police* 1991. In April 1989 Liverpool played Nottingham Forest in the FA Cup Semi-Final at the Hillsborough Stadium in Sheffield. The local police, responsible for crowd control, crammed supporters into pens in such numbers that, in the resulting crush, 95 people were killed and over 400 were physically injured. This ghastly scene was shown live on television and then shown again in later recorded broadcasts. Friends and relations of the dead and injured watched the disaster on television and a number of them sued the police for nervous shock which had led to their suffering psychiatric damage. The police admitted that they owed the dead and injured a duty of care but denied that this duty extended to their friends and family. Were these friends and relations 'persons who are so closely and directly affected' (on the *Donoghue* v. *Stevenson* test: see Unit 6.3) by the negligence of the police? The House of Lords considered their earlier decision in *McLoughlin* v. *O'Brian* 1982 which had established that a claim for psychiatric illness resulting from shock caused by negligence could be made without the plaintiff having to show that he had been injured or even put in fear of personal injury. Should the range of persons able to claim for psychiatric illness now be extended, bearing in mind that there was now a better understanding of mental illness and its relation to shock? The House of Lords considered each claim on the particular facts of family relationship and the nature of the friendship. A number of claims were rejected because of insufficient evidence of any particular close tie of love or affection. As Lord Keith explained:

> The mere fact of the particular relationship was insufficient to place the plaintiff within the class of persons to whom a duty of care could be owed by the defendant as being foreseeably at risk of psychiatric illness by reason of injury or peril to the individuals concerned.

The judges said any claimant had to satisfy the test of 'reasonable foreseeability' that he would be affected by psychiatric illness and also to show that this relationship with the primary victim (the dead or injured) had been sufficiently close. In other words, the courts would look at the quality of the relationship and any claimant would have to prove the existence of a close relationship. In certain cases (such as husband and wife or parent and child) the law would presume that a close relationship existed. In other cases this would have to be established at trial.

The adequacy of the common law to deal with claims for nervous shock (or, in contemporary parlance, 'post-traumatic stress disorder' or PTSD) was fully stretched by the horror and magnitude of this football disaster being broadcast live on television. Clarification of the law could, thought some of the judges, be better provided by way of legislation.

Without such statutory guidance, however the courts were once again required to consider a claim for psychiatric harm in *McFarlane* v. *E.E. Caledonia Limited* 1994. In 1988 the North Sea Oil Rig Piper Alpha was engulfed in flames with massive loss of life. The plaintiff was on one of a number of vessels that had gone to assist in the rescue. Francis McFarlane had not been burnt or physically injured at all but, as a result of what he saw that dreadful night, he suffered psychiatric injury. Did the owners and operators of Piper Alpha owe Francis McFarlane a duty to exercise reasonable care to avoid causing him psychiatric injury? Guided by the decision in *Alcock* the Court of Appeal held that there must be a sufficiently close tie of love and affection between the plaintiff and the victim. Moreover, said the court, reactions to horrific events were entirely subjective and, noted one of the judges, some people actually gather to witness calamities.

Such decision came to be considered by the Court of Appeal in *Vernon* v. *Bosley* 1997. Quite some years earlier the plaintiff's children had been involved in a road traffic accident when their nanny lost control of the car. The parents, Mr and Mrs Vernon, were called to the scene of the accident where they watched the attempts of the emergency services to save their children. Prior to this ghastly experience, the plaintiff had been a successful businessman with a fulfilling social and happy family life. He suffered a severe grief reaction and developed post-traumatic stress disorder as a result of what he witnessed. His life simply fell to pieces. The Court of Appeal, while remarking that damages for normal grief and bereavement suffered as a result of another's negligence were not recoverable, held that such a plaintiff as Peter Vernon could recover damages for PTSD provided that two preconditions for recovery of damages for psychiatric illness were satisfied. Firstly, such a plaintiff had to be in a close and loving relationship with the primary victim (in this case his two children) and, secondly, he had to be connected with the accident in time and place (that is, as in this case, as an observer of the rescue attempt). The cataclysmic effect upon this poor father led to an award in excess of £1 million.

Since then, in another case involving a claim by police officers against their chief constable, sued as their employer, the House of Lords in *White* v. *Chief Constable of the South Yorkshire Police* 1999 rejected the suggestion that an employer/employee relationship was sufficient to make individual police officers who had witnessed the disaster at Hillsborough Football Stadium primary victims.

What, though, would be the position when a fresh act on the part of someone else intervenes in the chain of events? Is the person responsible for starting the chain off still responsible for everything from then on? In Unit 3.5 we saw how seriously wrong medical treatment led to the death of a man who had been stabbed. In that criminal case, the court cleared the defendant of murder on the ground that the subsequent negligence on the part of the doctors had amounted to what lawyers call a *novus actus interveniens*, that is to say, a new act that intervenes in the chain of events.

As is often the case, there are similarities between the civil law of tort and English criminal law. The police themselves were involved in *Knightley* v. *Johns* 1982 when PC Knightley, a police motor-cyclist, had been seriously injured while on duty. Earlier that day there had been a bad road accident in a tunnel in Birmingham caused by the negligent driving of a man called Thomas Johns who had turned his car over. The police attended the accident and a police inspector sent PC Knightley to close the tunnel to incoming traffic. This very unwise order required PC Knightley to ride back against the flow of traffic. Unfortunately, PC Knightley was in collision with a car being driven into the tunnel. The officer sued the driver of the car that struck him, the inspector who had sent him the wrong way down the tunnel, the Chief Constable as the inspector's employer (see Unit 6.8b)) and the man Johns whose negligent driving had started all the problems in the first place. Johns did not deny that he had been negligent in overturning his car but he argued that the negligence of the others had caused PC Knightley's injuries. The Court of Appeal held that in such a case one has to consider whether the chain of causation between the original tort and any subsequent damage had been broken by any *novus actus interveniens*. A court had to ask whether the damage done was natural and probable (and, therefore, reasonably foreseeable) in the sense that something similar to what happened had been likely to happen. On this test, and on the particular facts of the case, the Court of Appeal held that it had been the police inspector's own negligence in not closing the tunnel to traffic earlier and his ordering the plaintiff to drive the wrong way down the tunnel which had been the real cause of PC Knightley's injuries. This negligence on the part of the police inspector had made the constable's injuries too remote from the original act of Johns' turning his car over to have been a consequence of Johns' negligence. It follows that it was not Johns who was liable but, rather, the plaintiff's own superior officers.

Another claim by a police officer against the police force came before the courts in *Costello* v. *Chief Constable of the Northumbria Police* 1999. Julie Costello was a woman police constable who was attacked and injured by a female prisoner. A police inspector had been standing nearby but did not come to the WPC's assistance. The Chief Constable (who, of course, would be vicariously liable and obliged to pay any damages) argued that police officers did not owe each other a duty of care in the event of one of them being attacked. The responsibility of the police for incompetence generally was already severely limited by the decision in *Hill* v. *Chief Constable of West Yorkshire* 1987 to the effect that the police are under no general duty of care to members of the public for their activities in the investigation and suppression of crime. Moreover, in *Alexandrou* v. *Oxford* 1993 a shopkeeper's claim against the police failed when he sued the police for the value of goods stolen from his shop after two police officers failed to inspect the rear of the shop after burglar alarms had been activated. In Costello's claim, however, the inspector accepted that he had been under a duty to help his junior officer if she needed help. The inspector had given evidence that he had heard no noise of any commotion and, therefore, had had no reason to go to the plaintiff's help. It was this particular point which persuaded the Court of Appeal that the inspector's acknowledged breach of police duty should be seen incrementally also as a breach of a legal duty of care. That duty, said May LJ was 'a duty to comply with a specific or acknowledged police duty where failure to do so will expose a fellow officer to unnecessary risk of injury. Public policy considerations were not as widely affected.' May LJ continued:

> *An ingredient of my conclusion is the close relationship between Inspector Bell and the plaintiff. They were police colleagues and he was in close attendance for the specific purpose of coming to her help if she needed help. It would not therefore follow from this analysis that I would also have found a duty of care owed by a police officer to a member of the public in otherwise similar circumstances. The balance of public policy could, depending on the circumstances, then be different.*

6.3 Negligence

'Don't blame me: it wasn't my fault – it was an accident. It could have happened to anyone.'

Such sentiments, common as they are, do not afford much consolation to someone who has been hurt, for example, because a lorry driver chose not to stop at a zebra crossing. Whether or not that injured pedestrian has any redress against the lorry driver will depend on whether or not he can prove that the driver had been **negligent**.

Almost everyone, of course, has some idea that being negligent means being careless, not doing something properly and making a mess of a job. Obviously, the courts have to be rather more precise than this. For example, Professor Winfield thought of this particular tort as 'the breach of a legal duty to take care which results in damage undesired by the defendant to the plaintiff'.

The necessarily objective attitude of the courts to this tort is made clear in what Baron Alderson said in *Blyth* v. *Birmingham Waterworks* 1856:

> *Negligence is the omission to do something which a reasonable man, guided upon those considerations which ordinarily regulate the conduct of human affairs, would do, or doing something which a prudent and reasonable man would not do.*

If we examine the ingredients of Professor Winfield's definition we can see that a party who alleges negligence will have to prove:

1. that the defendant owed him a duty of care; and
2. that the defendant broke that duty; and
3. that the claimant suffered a loss.

It is important to realise at the outset that each of these requirements is a hurdle and that if the claimant falls at any hurdle he will lose and be without any remedy. Each hurdle requires detailed consideration.

1. The claimant must prove that the defendant owed him a duty
It is not particularly hard to see that a lorry driver owes a duty to other road users not to kill or maim them, but does he also owe a duty to the ambulancemen who may be called out on their rest-day to witness harrowing scenes of carnage? No one, in law, owes a duty to the whole world. The line has to be drawn somewhere. For example, in *Bourhill* v. *Young* 1942 a motor-cyclist, John Young, had collided with a car and was killed. Unfortunately, the plaintiff, a pedestrian who was then some eight months' pregnant, was badly frightened by witnessing the collision. Worse still, and because of the severe shock sustained, she subsequently gave birth to a stillborn child. There was no question that the motor-cyclist had owed a duty of care to others driving on the road or that, by colliding with the car, he had broken that duty. The question arose, however, whether the motor-cyclist had also owed any duty to the woman pedestrian. Should he, as a reasonable man, have contemplated the likelihood of her also being injured?

The House of Lords held that John Young had owed no duty to the plaintiff because he could not be held to have reasonably foreseen the likelihood of her being affected by his negligence. Lord Porter was clear when he said:

> In the case of a civil action there is no such thing as negligence in the abstract: there must be neglect of the duty of care towards a person towards whom the defendant owes the duty of observing care.

Lord Macmillan agreed that:

> She was not so placed that there was any reasonable likelihood of her being affected by the deceased's careless driving.

Sometimes public policy may be an important factor in deciding whether or not a duty was owed, as it was in *Home Office* v. *Dorset Yacht Co. Ltd* 1970 (discussed in Unit 6.1) where the House of Lords held that the prison authorities did, after all, owe a duty of care to the public to protect them from escaped prisoners. Policy had also been relevant in the decision of the House of Lords in *Rondel* v. *Worsley* 1967, when it was decided that a barrister then owed no duty of care to his client in the presentation of his case in court (but now see Unit 2.5).

Clearly, the courts have somehow to decide where to draw the line. On the one hand it is important not to allow suffering to go uncompensated, yet it would be just as wrong to hold a man responsible for every trivial complaint of the fussy, the malcontent or the rabidly litigious.

How far the courts are prepared to extend this 'duty of care' was decided, in part, by a decomposing snail in the leading case of *Donoghue* v. *Stevenson* 1932.

One August evening in 1928, Mrs May Donoghue and a friend went out to an Italian café in Paisley near Glasgow. Mrs Donoghue's friend bought her a bottle of ginger beer. As she poured herself a second helping, the revolting remains of a decomposing snail floated into her glass. The unhappy combination of this nauseating sight and the impurities in the ginger beer she had already drunk produced both shock and gastro-enteritis for which Mrs Donoghue had to go to hospital in Glasgow.

. . . this nauseating sight . . .

What could the woman do about it? Obviously if it had been her friend's ginger beer he would have been able to sue the café-owner. He had bought it. He had made a contract with the café owner and, of course, could have sued the owner for breach of that contract. The woman, however, had not made any contract: she had been treated to the drink.

Her canny Glaswegian solicitor, however, was up to the challenge and, on his advice, Mrs Donoghue sued a local beer merchant, David Stephenson.

So, ultimately, the question for the House of Lords to decide was this: if a company has manufactured a drink and sold it to a distributor, was it under any legal duty to the ultimate purchaser or consumer to take reasonable care that the article was free from defect likely to cause injury to health?

To a large extent, the decision in this case represents the basis of the modern law of negligence. Lord Atkin contented himself with pointing out that in English law there must be, and is, some general conception of relations giving rise to a duty of care of which the particular cases found in the books are but instances.

He went on to lay down the basis of the present law in the doctrine of the 'neighbour' principle in this much-quoted passage:

> The rule that you are to love your neighbour becomes in law, you must not injure your neighbour; and the lawyer's question, 'Who is my neighbour?' receives a restricted reply. You must take reasonable care to avoid acts or omissions which you can reasonably foresee would be likely to injure your neighbour. Who, then, in law, is my neighbour? The answer seems to be – persons who are so closely and directly affected by my act that I ought reasonably to have them in contemplation as being so affected when I was directing my mind to the acts or omissions which are called in question.

This test has proved the foundation upon which countless cases of alleged negligence have been tried and continue to be judged. In what direction the courts will move in the future is less easy to assess with certainty. That it must, as with law in general, reflect the needs of society, can perhaps be detected in a judgment of Lord Denning MR, when in *S.C.M. Ltd* v. *Whittall* 1970 he had to decide whether economic loss as opposed to physical loss was too remote; he asked:

> Where is the line to be drawn? Lawyers are continually asking that question. But the judges are never defeated by it. We may not be able to draw the line with precision, but we can always say on which side of it any particular case falls...
> ...Only where in the particular case the good sense of the ...judge decides.

A claim against a hospital illustrates the point well. In *Sidaway* v. *Bethlem Royal Hospital Governors and others* 1985 the House of Lords had to consider the extent of a doctor's duty of care to his patients. Mrs Sidaway suffered persistent pain in her neck and shoulders. A surgeon advised surgery but he never warned her of possible danger to the spinal cord. Tragically, the operation went wrong and the poor lady ended up badly disabled. She sued the surgeon, alleging that he had been in breach of the duty of care he owed her because he had failed to warn her of all the possible risks inherent in the operation. The court had to consider, firstly, whether a patient has a legal right to know the risks inherent in the recommended treatment. Secondly, did a doctor have a legal duty to disclose those risks to the patient? The plaintiff failed in her claim. The House of Lords held that all the doctor had to do was to act in accordance with a practice accepted at the time as proper by a responsible body of medical opinion. When advising a patient about proposed treatment the doctor does have a duty to provide the patient with enough information to allow the patient to make a balanced judgment but subject at all times to the doctor's overriding duty to have regard to the best interests of the patient. In other words, it was for the doctor to decide what information should be given to the patient and how that information should be couched.

In *Hill* v. *Chief Constable of West Yorkshire* 1987 the Court of Appeal was asked to consider what duty of care, if any, the police owed to the community both collectively and individually in detecting criminals and thereby preventing the commission of further offences. The litigation arose out of the many murders committed by Peter Sutcliffe, the so-called and infamous 'Yorkshire Ripper'. Sutcliffe had murdered thirteen women and had attempted to murder another eight. The plaintiff was the mother of one of the murder victims. She complained about the competence (or, rather, alleged lack thereof) which the police had displayed in their long investigation, during which Sutcliffe had been interviewed and then released, thereby freeing him to kill yet again. Mrs Hill alleged that the police had owed a duty of care to exercise all reasonable skill and care in detecting this mass killer and that the police had been in breach of their duty in failing to detect Sutcliffe before the murder of her daughter. The Court of Appeal rejected her claim. The court held that the police owed no special duty of care to any individual member of the public. Neither, said the House of Lords in *Calveley* v. *Chief Constable of the Merseyside Police* 1989, does the police force owe its own individual officers any duty of care in the way it carries out disciplinary investigations. The plaintiffs had all been former police officers who had been the subject of disciplinary investigation and who complained that the proceedings had been misconducted and the subject of very great delay.

On the other hand, the traditional illegibility of doctors' handwriting led to a doctor being sued when his particular style of calligraphy led a pharmacist to prescribe the wrong drug to the plaintiff. In *Prendergast* v. *Sam and Dee* 1989 a doctor was held to have been negligent when his handwriting on a prescription was so bad that the pharmacist dispensed a wholly different drug which had a very serious effect upon the poor patient.

Rather than go on filling up library shelves reinforcing each camp of authority, some more general test was required. Until recently it seemed that the matter had been settled by the decision of the House of Lords in *Anns* v. *London Borough of Merton* 1977 where the tenants of a block of flats in south-west London sued the local council when their homes literally started to crack up. The tenants alleged that the council's building inspectors had been negligent in approving faulty foundations. The House of Lords was, therefore, required to consider whether the local council owed any duty of care to the men and women who would have to live in the homes which the council's building inspectors allowed to be put up. This was then the latest in a series of claims against negligent builders and councils who had allowed faulty buildings to be erected. In *Anns*, the House of Lords held that the council had been under a duty to take reasonable care to ensure that a builder did not cover in foundations that did not comply with the relevant bye-laws. Lord Wilberforce was to lay down a famous two-stage test, which was later to be criticised by the House of Lords itself as not proceeding on the basis of any principle at all but as constituting a remarkable example of judicial legislation which was to engender a vast spate of litigation. The test as propounded by Lord Wilberforce was:

> *First one has to ask whether, as between the alleged wrongdoer and the person who has suffered damage, there is sufficient relationship of proximity or neighbourhood such that, in the reasonable contemplation of the former, carelessness on his part may be likely to cause damage to the latter, in which case a prima facie duty of care arises. Secondly, if the first question is answered affirmatively, it is necessary to consider whether there are any considerations which ought to negative, or to reduce or limit, the scope of duty or the class of persons to whom it is owed or the damages to which the breach of it may give rise.*

Such a test was adopted shortly afterwards in *Ross* v. *Caunters* 1979. A firm of solicitors had drawn up Mr Philp's will. Under the Wills Act 1837, a will has to be signed by the testator and witnessed. It is quite well known that a witness cannot be a beneficiary under the will. What is less well known is that the Wills Act 1837 also provides that the gift shall similarly 'be utterly null and void' if the beneficiary's wife or husband is a witness. One of the witnesses who signed Mr Philp's will was the husband of a lady to whom Mr Philp wanted to leave some property. The solicitor failed to notice this until after the death of his client, Mr Philp, when it became clear that the gifts to Mrs Ross were void. She claimed damages for negligence against the solicitors. The solicitors, in turn, very properly admitted that they had been negligent but argued that they could be liable only to their own client and not to someone else such as an intended beneficiary. At trial, therefore, the judge had to decide whether or not the testator's solicitors owed a duty of care to the beneficiary. In upholding the claim against the solicitors, the judge found, in Lord Wilberforce's phrase, that there had been a 'sufficient relationship of proximity or neighbourhood'.

In *White* v *Jones* 1995 the House of Lords dealt with the claim against a firm of solicitors brought by disappointed prospective beneficiaries. A father had instructed solicitors to prepare a new will to include gifts to his two daughters whom he had earlier cut out of his will. The father died two months later but the solicitors had not by then prepared the new will. The daughters, each now disappointed in their hopes of inheriting £9,000, sued the solicitors. The House of Lords held that a solicitor could owe a duty to such prospective beneficiaries and, in this case, each daughter recovered £9,000 from their late father's solicitors. This decision was later followed by the Court of Appeal in *Carr-Glynn* v. *Frearsons* 1998 where it was held that a solicitor preparing a will owed a duty of care to an intended beneficiary to ensure that effect was given to the testator's testamentary intentions.

Lord Wilberforce's test in *Anns* v. *London Borough of Merton* seemed also to do away with the older distinction between physical loss and economic loss. Over the years, the courts have often had to consider claims by claimants for the loss of profit or some other form of purely economic (rather than physical) loss. For example, Tom and Dick are digging holes in the road one afternoon when Dick's drill burrows its way a little too deep and strikes not oil but rather an electricity cable. The whole area is suddenly plunged into darkness. Worse, a nearby factory is forced to close down. Damage is done to the machinery itself as it suddenly grinds to a halt. Moreover, the factory is unable to meet a deadline and so loses a valuable order. Can the owners sue for this loss of profit as well as the purely physical damage done to the equipment? Traditionally, in such cases the courts had said that such 'economic loss' was 'too remote'.

On Lord Wilberforce's test, however, it seemed that the courts would simply look to see if there was a sufficient proximity between the parties and then consider whether there was any good reason either to limit the scope of the duty owed by the defendant to the claimant or to reduce the damages to be awarded. Such an approach was taken in *Junior Books Ltd* v. *Veitchi Co. Ltd* 1982. Veitchi were sub-contractors brought in to lay a concrete floor in a factory. As they were sub-contractors, there was no direct contractual link between the owners of the factory and Veitchi. This prevented the factory owners suing the sub-contractors direct in contract. After a couple of years the concrete floor laid by Veitchi began to crack. The business then being run by Junior Books was obviously disrupted by the inconvenience caused when a new floor had to be laid. After all, the employees still wanted to be paid and other such business overheads were present as usual; it was only the work that stopped. Could Junior Books recover their economic losses as well as the cost of the new floor itself? The House of Lords favoured Junior Books and said that where the proximity, as here, between a workman and the person who was to use the product was sufficiently close then the workman owed a duty to avoid faults being present in the work carried on or the article manufactured.

This decision was pregnant with possibility as to how far the age-old doctrine of privity (see Unit 4.14) was to be affected but, logically, it seemed that a dissatisfied customer might now be able to sue the manufacturer rather than merely the shopkeeper with whom the sale contract was actually made. This concept of 'product liability' was one of a number of concerns raised in the later case of *Murphy* v. *Brentwood District Council* 1990 when the House of Lords decided that *Anns* had been wrongly decided. The case centred on a semi-detached house, in this case one bought some years earlier by Thomas Murphy. The plans had been approved by the local council and, as with the other cases, cracks were to develop. Mr Murphy, therefore, sued the council for the negligence of its engineers in approving the original design. On the old law as established in the *Anns* case the council had owed a duty of care to the plaintiff to see that his house was properly built. The door (if that much of the house was left standing) was, therefore, open to claims not just against any slapdash builder but also against the local authority for passing the builder's plans. In practice, of course, local authorities are likely to be better able to meet any damages awarded than some small local builder already in hock to his bank manager. This time, however, the House of Lords recognised that the earlier case of *Anns* had been subject to much criticism. The House of Lords rejected Lord Wilberforce's two-stage test and substituted is own 'incremental' approach. One judge adopted the words of an Australian judge who had earlier criticised Lord Wilberforce's test, saying:

> It is preferable, in my view, that the law should develop novel categories of negligence incrementally and by analogy with established categories, rather than by a massive extension of a prima facie duty of care restrained only by indefinable 'considerations which ought to negative or to reduce or limit the scope of the duty or the class of persons to whom it is owed'.

Later judicial criticism of the two-stage test formulated by Lord Wilberforce in the *Anns* case was to include the diplomatic remark of Lord Keith that such two-stage test 'for determining the existence of a duty of care in negligence has been elevated to a degree of importance greater than its merits, and greater perhaps than its author intended'.

The new approach is, therefore, now to ask firstly whether the damage or harm to the claimant was reasonably foreseeable by the defendant. If so, secondly, was the relationship between them 'sufficiently proximate' to give rise to a duty of care? Thirdly, is it in all the circumstances just and reasonable to impose this duty? The House of Lords did not think it proper to change the law by what was termed 'judicial legislation' and was not to be seduced by concepts of public policy. As Lord Bridge said:

> There may be cogent reasons of social policy for imposing liability on the authority. But the shoulders of a public authority are only 'broad enough to bear the loss' because they are financed by the public at large. It is pre-eminently for the legislature to decide whether these policy reasons should be accepted as sufficient for imposing on the public the burden of providing compensation for private financial losses.

Quite apart from protecting the coffers of the local authorities and their council-tax payers, one immediate consequence of this decision is in the field of economic loss. In this case the House of Lords held that Mr Murphy's loss was a purely economic one. The House of Lords also narrowed the claim for economic loss to loss sustained through reliance on negligent mis-statement, an area long established by the House of Lords in *Hedley Byrne & Co.* v. *Heller* 1963. The plaintiffs, who were advertising agents, lost some £17,000 when one of their customers went into liquidation (the company equivalent of an individual's bankruptcy). The plaintiffs sued some bankers for negligence in giving them references about their mutual customer which actually gave a false impression as to that other company's creditworthiness. The House of Lords held that, even in the absence of any contractual relationship, anyone who gave such information in the course of a business or profession, where he must know that his skill or judgment was being relied upon, accepted a legal duty to exercise care in giving out such views or references and would be liable for any financial loss brought about by his carelessness.

In *Yianni* v. *Evans* 1981 surveyors were sued by the Yiannis who had bought a house in North London which the defendant firm had surveyed at the request not of the plaintiffs but rather of the Halifax Building Society which wanted to know if the Society should lend Mr and Mrs Yianni the money with which to buy it. Nevertheless, the Halifax let the Yiannis see the surveyor's report but warned the couple in terms that the Halifax did not warrant that the purchase price was reasonable, that the valuer's report was confidential to the building society and that, if the Yiannis required a survey of the house for their own information, they should instruct an independent surveyor. The Yiannis nevertheless went ahead with the purchase of the house without having their own survey carried out. Nine months later they discovered cracks in the foundations which would cost some £18,000 to repair. The Yiannis sued the surveyors, alleging negligence in their statement to the Halifax that the house was adequate security for a loan of £12,000. The surveyors argued that they had not owed any duty of care to the Yiannis themselves but only to the Halifax. Nevertheless, the court held the surveyors liable. The judge said that there had been a sufficiently proximate relationship between the Yiannis and the surveyors for the surveyor to be aware that the Yiannis would rely on the valuation in deciding whether or not to buy the house.

The intrusion of burglars into a London flat led the Court of Appeal to consider whether the owners of that flat owed any duty of care to their neighbours to keep out vandals, tramps and, of course burglars. In *Perl (Exporters) Ltd* v. *Camden London Borough Council* 1983 the burglars had quite literally broken in through a common wall from the flat next door, which had been left unoccupied and unsecured by Camden Council. Other flats in the block had been burgled but, despite complaints, the local authority still did nothing to improve security. The victim of this particular burglary argued that Camden Borough Council owed their tenants a duty of care, even though the damage had been done by third parties – the actual burglars, however, had evidently not been tempted to play any part in the proceedings! The Court of Appeal took the view that Camden were not liable to compensate Perl for their loss. The court held that Camden owed no duty of care to an occupier of neighbouring premises to protect its own premises or to prevent another (such as a burglar) from gaining access to its own premises and, from those premises, getting in to the neighbouring premises. Similarly, in *King* v. *Liverpool City Council* 1986 the Court of Appeal rejected Mary King's claim against her landlords when her flat had been flooded after vandals damaged pipes in the flat next door.

The question of liability for another's carelessness which allowed criminals to injure innocent people came before the Court of Appeal in

Topp v. *London Country Bus (South West) Ltd* 1993. A bus had been left unattended outside a public house for nine hours with the keys left in the ignition. A thief took that bus and killed the plaintiff's wife. The Court of Appeal rejected the claim, saying that as the parked bus did not fall within any special category of risk the defendants had owed no duty of care to the plaintiff's wife.

Even in the absence of contract or reward, the courts have held that there may be a duty of care on friends who give gratuitous advice. So it was in *Chaudhry* v. *Prabhakar* 1988 when the plaintiff asked a friend who had some knowledge of cars to find her a suitable secondhand car. Sometime later it became clear that the car he recommended had been unroadworthy. The plaintiff sued both the man who sold it to her and her friend who had advised her. The Court of Appeal held that as the friend knew the plaintiff was relying on him he owed her a duty of care.

The concept of 'duty of care' had to be considered in *Hughes* v. *National Union of Mineworkers and others* 1991. A police officer had been injured while on duty at the scene of a Yorkshire colliery during the miners' strike in 1984. The officer, Anthony Hughes, sued his Chief Constable (as his employer) complaining that the officer in charge at the time had deployed his forces negligently so that the plaintiff had been exposed to an excessive and avoidable risk of injury. The Chief Constable, however, argued that he owed PC Hughes no such duty of care in the operational control of police officers dealing with violent public disorder. The court struck the plaintiff's claim out, saying that it was bound to fail. The judge held that as a matter of public policy senior police officers were generally not liable to their junior officers since, if they were held to owe such a duty of care, it would be detrimental to the control of public order as there would often be little time for considered thought. Those senior officers might, therefore, be handicapped in making difficult decisions if they were to be worried about potential negligence claims against them by their subordinates injured at demonstrations.

In other ways, the current trend of the courts has been to restrict liability in areas such as careless mis-statement. In *Caparo Industries plc* v. *Dickman* 1990, Caparo Industries had bought heavily on the stock market in the shares of a company called Fidelity. They later complained that their share purchases had been made in reliance on accounts prepared by chartered accountants and that those accounts had been inaccurate and misleading in a number of respects. Caparo complained that had they known that an apparent pre-tax profit of some £1.3 million was going to turn out to be a loss of over £400,000 they would not have acted as they did. Caparo accordingly sued, among others, the chartered accountants who had audited the accounts, claiming that they were negligent in certifying, as they had done, that the accounts showed a true and fair picture of Fidelity's position. In the House of Lords, it was held that the auditor of a public company owed no duty of care to a member of the public at large who relied on those accounts to buy shares in the company. In what has become the classic exposition of modern negligence, the House of Lords viewed three criteria as of overwhelming importance. Firstly, was the damage foreseeable? Secondly, what was the proximity between the parties? Thirdly, was it reasonable in all the circumstances to impose liability?

A major consideration to be applied by the courts in determining whether or not a duty of care exists will, accordingly, be found in considerations of public policy. Such consideration no doubt had played a substantial factor in the decision in *Hill* v. *Chief Constable of West Yorkshire* 1987 and featured in the approach taken by the Court of Appeal in *Osman* v. *Ferguson* 1993. A schoolmaster formed an unhealthy attachment to a teenage male pupil and even changed his name to that of the boy. The teacher harassed the pupil even after being dismissed from his teaching post and went so far as to warn the police that he feared he might do something criminally insane. Some time later the teacher rammed a car in which the boy was a passenger and, almost a year after his dismissal, visited the boy's home where he shot his former pupil and killed the boy's father. The mother of the injured boy sued the police for negligence, contending that, during the year in which they had known about this teacher, they had failed to apprehend him, interview him, search his home or charge him with anything more serious than a minor road traffic offence arising out of the earlier collision. This particular case was, therefore, different on the facts from *Hill* because in *Osman* v. *Ferguson* there were specific examples of deviant, criminal and disturbing behaviour committed on specified occasions by a clearly identified man. The identity of the Yorkshire Ripper had not been as easy to discover. The judges were clearly able to see a number of failures in the police investigation but the Court of Appeal followed the earlier approach of the House of Lords' decision which had been taken on grounds of public policy. It followed that, under national law as it then stood, the claim had to be dismissed.

Six years later, however, in *Osman* v. *United Kingdom* 1999 the European Court of Human Rights was to view this dismissal on the grounds of public policy as a breach of Article 6, being a disproportionate restriction on the citizen's right of access to the courts.

At around the time of the decision of the Court of Appeal in *Osman* and in *Ancell* v. *McDermott* 1993 the Court of Appeal also rejected another claim in negligence against the police, holding that the police were under no duty of care to warn motorists about or protect road users from hazards discovered by the police on the highway. In that case, the plaintiff's wife died after losing control in a skid on diesel fuel left on the road after an earlier spillage. The earlier impact and fuel spillage had been known to the police. The judges in the Court of Appeal stepped back from imposing liability, remarking that, if imposed, such a duty of care would impose on police potential liability of almost unlimited scope.

Not every single act of incompetence by the police, however, goes uncompensated. Where the consequences of imposing a duty of care are narrow, the courts have indicated a willingness to uphold the requirement as to proximity. Another form of public interest (the need to protect police informers and to encourage them to come forward without fear that their identities will become known to suspects) played an important role in the decision of the Court of Appeal in *Swinney* v. *Chief Constable of the Northumbria Police* 1996. Mary Swinney and her husband ran a public house and were able to pass on to the police information about a fatal road accident. She gave this information in confidence and did not want anyone else to know of her involvement. These concerns were rightly noted by the police, who were also said to know of the violent and ruthless characters of the people involved. It was, therefore, at least unfortunate that documents confirming the source of such information were left in an unattended police vehicle. Even worse, the vehicle was broken into and the relevant documents found their way into the very hands of the suspect. The plaintiff and her husband were subsequently threatened with violence and arson and suffered great distress and psychiatric harm. The application of the modern law to the particular facts appears clearly from the straightforward judgment of Ward LJ, as he identified the considerations emerging from the decision in *Caparo Industries* v. *Dickman*:

> *It seems to me that it is indeed properly arguable that:*
> (1) *the risk of theft of one of the documents from the police car is foreseeable, it being conceded that the harm to the plaintiffs and consequence of the theft is also foreseeable;*
> (2) *there is a special relationship between the plaintiffs and the defendant, which is sufficiently proximate. Proximity is shown by the police assuming responsibility, and the plaintiffs relying upon that assumption of responsibility, for preserving the confidentiality of the information which, if it fell into the wrong hands, was likely to expose the first plaintiff and members of her family to a special risk of damage from the criminal acts of others, greater than the general risk which ordinary members of the public must endure with phlegmatic fortitude; and*
> (3) *it is fair, just and reasonable that the law should impose a duty, there being no overwhelming dictate of public policy to exclude the prosecution of this claim.*

However, neither the Stock Market loss in *Caparo Industries* nor the now comparatively minor sum of £17,000 in *Hedley Byrne* v. *Heller* came remotely near the cataclysmic losses suffered by a number of Lloyd's Names who had invested their wealth in the London Insurance Market, entrusting their money to their Members' Agents and then to their Managing Agents. A series of natural disasters and other losses such as Piper Alpha, coupled with gross ineptitude by some Lloyd's professionals, led to ruinous trading losses in the early 1990s even to the extent that the entire future of the Lloyd's market was brought seriously into question. A number of impoverished Names then sued the Agents alleging both breach of contract and negligence. In the House of Lords, it was accepted by the judges that an assumption of responsibility by a person rendering professional services, coupled with a concomitant reliance by the person for whom the services were rendered, could give rise to a tortious duty of care irrespective of whether or not there was also a contractual relationship between those parties. In his speech, Lord Goff turned immediately to the earlier decision in *Hedley Byrne* v. *Heller* and said that once the case was identified as falling within that principle 'there should be no need to embark upon any further enquiry whether it is "fair, just and reasonable" to impose liability for economic loss . . .'.

In a case which attracted some media attention the Court of Appeal had to consider whether the ambulance service owed a duty of care to those in need of care from the emergency services. In *Kent* v. *Griffiths* 2000 Tracy Kent had suffered an asthmatic attack which required immediate hospital treatment. Although records found at trial by the judge to have been falsified indicated that an ambulance arrived after 22 minutes, the emergency services took 40 minutes to reach Mrs Kent. The London Ambulance Service argued that it owed no duty of care and relied on other cases in which it had been held that the Police and Fire Services owed no duty of care in answering 999 calls. The Court of Appeal felt able to distinguish those other cases by holding that the Ambulance Service, as part of the Health Service, was to be regarded as providing services of the category provided by hospitals rather than the general protection of the public to be provided by the other emergency services. It followed that an ambulance service could owe a duty of care to a member of the public and, on the facts of this case, the service was required to justify its failure to attend within a reasonable time.

2. *The claimant must prove that the defendant went on to break that duty owed to him*

The mere occurrence of some misfortune does not, as a rule, make someone automatically liable. The exceptions to this general rule are looked at in Unit 6.8. The judge must look at the evidence and decide whether or not the defendant did something he or she ought not to have done or, alternatively, had failed to do something which he ought to have done. How then is the judge to decide whether the defendant is liable? What tests can the judge apply?

Many cases in tort which come before the courts arise from so-called 'running-down' incidents – road-traffic accidents, where it sometimes seems that the judge is being asked to decide whether or not there was negligence on one side or the other when two allegedly stationary cars managed to collide at 70 mph. Once some of the facts have been clarified the judge will have to consider what each driver should have done. He may well look, for instance, at the Highway Code, though it will not necessarily settle the matter, because in *Powell* v. *Phillips* 1972 the Court of Appeal held that failure to be guided by the Highway Code does not automatically amount to negligence. Nevertheless, the Road Traffic Act 1988, section 38(7), provides:

> A failure on the part of a person to observe a provision of the Highway Code shall not of itself render that person liable to criminal proceedings of any kind, but any such failure may in any proceedings ... be relied upon by any party to the proceedings as tending to establish or to negative any liability which is in question in those proceedings.

So, to refer again to the example in Unit 1.3, when Tom sues Dick, he may wish to refer the judge to rules in the Highway Code (1999 edition) such as:

> Rule 104: The speed limit is the absolute maximum and does not mean it is safe to drive at that speed irrespective of conditions. Driving at speeds too fast for the road and traffic

conditions can be dangerous. You should always reduce your speed when:

- the road layout or condition presents hazards, such as bends;
- sharing the road with pedestrians and cyclists, particularly children, and motor cyclists;
- weather conditions make it safer to do so;
- driving at night as it is harder to see other road users.

Rule 202: In wet weather, stopping distances will be at least double those required for stopping on dry roads. This is because your tyres have less grip on the road.

However, liability cannot always be as easily decided. For instance, there is no such thing as the Highway Code to offer guidance when suing accountants who have failed to claim allowances or expenses for their clients, or doctors who have failed to detect serious illness. How then is the judge, who is neither accountant nor doctor, to decide whether the defendant has been negligent?

His first course is to call in the assistance of the 'Reasonable Man'. This mythical creature of jurisprudence has been introduced to myriads of law students as 'the man on the Clapham omnibus', and is known across the Atlantic as 'the man who takes the magazines at home, and in the evening pushes the lawn-mower in his shirt sleeves'. He is, of course, a figment of judicial ingenuity but a necessary one: he is there to provide an objective criterion of what the claimant and the defendant would or would not have done had each been acting reasonably. If, on his journey to or from Clapham, the Reasonable Man would have acted with greater care or prudence than the defendant has shown, then the courts will say that the defendant has been negligent.

It is convenient now to review some of the more memorable achievements of this guest at almost every court up and down the land and to examine his character.

... dynamite and a walking stick ...

Firstly, the Reasonable Man will always bear in mind the magnitude of the risk which he can reasonably foresee; as Professor Winfield remarked: 'No reasonable man handles a stick of dynamite and a walking-stick in the same way.' Such considerations were emphasised by the House of Lords in *Bolton* v. *Stone* 1951. During the course of a cricket match the batsman had excelled himself not only scoring six, but in doing so by hitting the ball over a fence some 17 feet high above the pitch and the best part of a hundred yards away. This particular effort was, on all the evidence, quite exceptional, having happened only half-a-dozen times in 30 years. The only difficulty arose when the ball fell to earth and injured Miss Stone who was outside her house.

The House of Lords refused to hold the cricket club liable because, they said, such strokes were exceptional and the risk of injury in such a place was, therefore, so remote that a reasonable person would not have anticipated it. Lord Reid balanced the risks when he commented:

> *I think that reasonable men do in fact take into account the degree of risk and do not act on a bare possibility as they would if the risk were more substantial ... In the crowded conditions of modern life even the most careful person cannot avoid creating risks and accepting others. What a man must not do, and what I think a careful man tries not to do, is to create a risk which is substantial ... In my judgment the test to be applied here is whether the risk of damage to a person on the road is so small that a reasonable man in the position of the appellant, considering the matter from the point of view of safety, would have thought it right to refrain from taking steps to prevent the danger.*

However, the Reasonable Man will not allow himself to be lulled into any sense of complacency and will view every fence and every ball-game on its facts. His help was required, for example, in *Hilder* v. *A.P.C.M.* 1961. The defendants allowed young children to play football on some of their land which was alongside a busy road. Some embryonic cup-finalist lobbed the ball over a low wall and into the path of a motor-cyclist who was knocked off his bike and died from his injuries. Factors such as the busy road and the low wall prompted the court to find that the defendants had indeed been negligent.

So, too, will the Reasonable Man take into account the peculiar needs or susceptibilities of those with whom he comes into contact. In *Paris* v. *Stepney Borough Council* 1951, for instance, the defendants knew that a man whom they employed as a fitter's mate had only one good eye. At work one day, this man tried to remove a bolt which had rusted on. He struck it with a hammer and a metal chip flew off and blinded his good eye. The House of Lords held that this special risk of injury should have been a relevant consideration in the minds of the employers when considering the nature and extent of the precautions they should have taken for the safety of each individual workman. It followed that their failure to discharge this special duty of care to Mr Paris amounted to negligence on their part.

The Reasonable Man, however, does not just stand on the side-lines the whole time. Even the Reasonable Man can expect to find himself in situations of emergency. He will then take into account not only the risks that he will run but also those to which he may expose others. In his pressured deliberations, however, the Reasonable Man will also weigh those risks against the importance of the object to be attained. This point was made clear by Asquith LJ in *Daborn* v. *Bath Tramways Ltd* 1946 when he said:

> *In determining whether a party is negligent, the standard of reasonable care is that which is reasonably to be demanded in the circumstances. A relevant circumstance to take into account may be the importance of the end to be served by behaving in this way or in that. As has often been pointed out, if all the trains in this country were restricted to a speed of five miles an hour, there would be fewer accidents, but our national life would be intolerably slowed down. The purpose to be served, if sufficiently important, justifies the assumption of abnormal risk.*

This principle was applied by the Court of Appeal a few years later in *Watt* v. *Hertfordshire County Council* 1954, where a fireman had been injured by a heavy jack which slewed forward and caught his ankle when the lorry in which he was travelling braked suddenly. The Court of Appeal had no doubt that the fire authorities had a duty to take reasonable care to avoid exposing their firemen to unnecessary risks but held that they had not been negligent in requesting their employees to take abnormal risks when they were out on an emergency call.

Denning LJ, as he then was, looked at the object of the exercise:

> *It is well settled that in measuring due care you must balance the risk against the measures necessary to eliminate the risk. To that proposition there ought to be added this: you must balance the risk against the end to be achieved. If this accident had occurred in a commercial enterprise without any emergency, there could be no doubt that the servant would succeed. But the commercial end to make profit is very different from the human end to safe life or limb. The saving of life or limb justifies taking considerable risks and I am glad to say that there have never been wanting in this country men of courage ready to take those risks, notably in the fire service.*

Nevertheless, in whatever position the Reasonable Man finds himself, he will always bear in mind what would have to be done to minimise any risk. Moreover, if such steps can be reasonably taken the Reasonable Man will be sure to take them. As long as he does that he cannot be said to be negligent even if something still goes wrong. This principle was applied in *Latimer* v. *A.E.C.* 1953. As the result of an exceptionally heavy rainstorm, a factory was flooded. The water had become mixed with some grease and an oily film was left over the floors. The defendant company put down some sawdust. Even so, one of its employees slipped and was injured. The House of Lords had to consider whether the company had done all that it could be reasonably expected to have done. Obviously, it could have gone further – it could, for instance, have closed the factory. The court held that the company had not been negligent because it had taken every step that an ordinary prudent employer would have taken to secure the safety of the workforce.

In *Tremain* v. *Pike* 1969, after an employee had fallen ill in the course of his work, the question arose whether or not his employer had taken all reasonable precautions for his safety. William Tremain was a herdsman employed by Edward Pike, a farmer whose farm had become infested by large numbers of rats. Mr Tremain now claimed damages because, he said, he had developed a very rare disease, leptospirosis (Weil's disease), which is contracted through contact with rats' urine. The judge held that the disease was so very rare that the farmer had not been in breach of his duty to Mr Tremain in having taken no steps to avoid exposing him to the risk of contracting so very uncommon an infection.

In most fields of human endeavour there is said to be a right way to do it and a wrong way to do it. If there is a proper and standard procedure or a widely accepted practice you can be sure that the Reasonable Man will follow it, on the basis that if the drivers of 99 cars going northwards down a one-way street meet one car coming southwards, it is more likely than not that they are right and the other driver is wrong. The principle was summarised more profoundly by Lord Alness in *Vancouver General Hospital* v. *McDaniel* 1934 when he said:

> *A defendant charged with negligence can clear [himself] if he shows that he has acted in accordance with general and approved practice.*

Two decades later in *Bolam* v. *Friern Hospital Management Committee* 1957 McNair J offered the following test for the standard of care required of a doctor:

> *A doctor is not guilty of negligence if he has acted in accordance with a practice accepted as proper by a responsible body of medical men skilled in that particular art ... Putting it another way round, a doctor is not negligent, if he is acting in accordance with such a practice, merely because there is a body of opinion that takes a contrary view.*

The principle applied equally, of course, to other skilled occupations so that in *Simmons* v. *Pennington & Son* 1955, when the plaintiff sued his solicitors alleging that they had been negligent in some conveyancing work, the Court of Appeal rejected his claim because the solicitors had acted in accordance with a long-established general practice which had worked well in the past.

The test in *Bolam* v. *Friern Hospital* was recently reconsidered by the Court of Appeal in *Michael Hide & Associates Limited* v. *J.D. Williams & Company Limited* 2000 where the court noted that there were different views of acceptable practice within the architectural profession. In such circumstances, ruled the court, the competence of a professional person was to be gauged by the lowest acceptable standard.

Establishing negligence on the part of the medical profession is still very far from easy and attempts to do so must be considered in the light of the much publicised case of *Whitehouse* v. *Jordan* 1981 where a gynaecologist's actions came in for close scrutiny. A pregnant woman went into a Birmingham hospital for what had been expected to be a troublesome birth. When attempts to bring the baby into the world with forceps failed, the defendant gynaecologist switched to a Caesarean section which, in the event, was performed most skilfully. Sadly, however, the baby, Stuart, was born with severe brain damage and was crippled. The mother blamed the defendant doctor. She said that he had been negligent in that he had pulled too long and too hard with the forceps. She alleged that the doctor had been guilty of such want of care that he had caused the poor baby's cerebral haemorrhage. Eminent medical men gave evidence to the effect that how hard a doctor should pull on forceps and how often he should use them were really matters of clinical judgment based on experience. Both the Court of Appeal and later the House of Lords agreed that a simple error of clinical judgment did not amount to negligence on the part of a doctor. Neither was the fact that a child was born with brain damage in itself evidence of negligence. Rather, what had to be shown was that the doctor had failed to measure up to the special skill of his profession generally. As Lord Edmund-Davis put it shortly:

> If a surgeon fails to measure up to that standard in any respect ('clinical judgement' or otherwise) he has been negligent and should be so adjudged.

Later on, in *Clark* v. *Maclennan* 1983 the court had to consider the actions of another gynaecologist at an Oxford hospital. The doctor carried out an operation on the mother within a month or so of the birth in order to relieve some bladder trouble. The operation was not a success and the lady was left permanently, if not too seriously, disabled. It was normal practice among gynaecologists generally not to perform such operations until at least three months after the birth. For day after day, doctor followed doctor into the witness box. The judge attached weight to the evidence of this departure from the normal approach of other gynaecologists. The judge held that, although it is usually the claimant who has to prove that the defendant had been negligent, where there has been a failure to take a recognised precaution intended to prevent the damage caused, the burden of proof lay on the defendant to show either that he had not breached any duty of care or, alternatively, that no damage flowed from such breach.

While every surgeon has to have his first cut, it is no defence for a negligent doctor to say that, because of his or her inexperience, he was not negligent. In *Wilsher* v. *Essex Area Health Authority* 1986 a junior and inexperienced doctor placed a catheter into a vein rather than an artery. The Court of Appeal rejected the doctor's argument that his inexperience afforded a defence by requiring him to discharge his duty merely according to his actual experience. Instead, said the Court of Appeal, the standard was to be determined by having regard to the status of the doctor rather than the doctor himself.

3. *The claimant must prove that, because the defendant broke his duty of care, he has been caused loss*
Such a loss could be a physical one (for instance, a broken leg) or loss of money, but is always subject to the rules already explained relating to remoteness of damage.

a) *Res ipsa loquitur* Much of this section has been concerned with what a claimant has to prove before a court will hold a defendant negligent. In Unit 1.3 we saw how the Civil Evidence Act 1968 allows a claimant to rely on a defendant's conviction as evidence – for example, of his careless driving. Thus, in practice, in such circumstances the defendant will have little chance of defeating any claim arising out of the same incident.

There is another way in which a claimant's task will be made easier: this time the basis is simply one of common sense. This is the doctrine of *res ipsa loquitur* ('the thing speaks for itself'). For instance, the law recognises that it is not usual for a car to cross the central reservation of a motorway at 100 mph – the driver will have some explaining to do. In other words, the courts are prepared to draw certain inferences of negligence from the accident itself where the cause of the damage has been under the defendant's control.

This doctrine first saw the light of day in *Scott* v. *London and St Katharine Dock Co.* 1865, a case which concerned the fall of six bags of sugar on to a Customs officer who was in a warehouse.

Erle CJ looked at the fall of the bags and then inferred negligence on the part of the defendant. He put forward this test:

> *There must be reasonable evidence of negligence. But where the thing is shown to be under the management of the defendant or his servants, and the accident is such as in the ordinary course of things does not happen if those who have the management use proper care, it affords reasonable evidence, in the absence of explanation by the defendants, that the accident rose from want of care.*

The practical effect is that unless the defendant is able to offer a reasonable explanation of how the accident could have happened, the judge would draw the inference that the defendant had been negligent. Of course, if a reasonable explanation is provided by the defendant, the claimant must go on (as before) to prove that the defendant had been negligent.

6.4 Occupiers' liability

If the postman cuts his hand on your rusty gate, if your milkman is hit on the head by a passing roof-slate or if the friendly encyclopaedia sales-man falls under the weight of his learning on your icy doorstep, you, the householder, may have to pay up.

Occupiers of land have long had a common-law duty to look after their visitors and these duties were codified in the Occupiers' Liability Act 1957, as now amended by the later 1984 Act of the same name and by the Defective Premises Act 1972. The term **visitors** used in these Acts is defined more loosely than the terms employed before 1957 and denotes people who are lawfully on the premises. The position of tres-passers is looked at later on.

The Occupiers' Liability Act provides in section 2:

> An occupier of premises owes the same duty, the 'common duty of care', to all his visitors, except insofar as he is free to and does extend, restrict, modify or exclude his duty to any visitor or visitors by agreement or otherwise.

The Act also defines that duty:

> The common duty of care is a duty to take such care as in all the circumstances of the case is reasonable to see that the visitor will be reasonably safe in using the premises for the purposes for which he is invited or permitted by the occupier to be there.

This duty is imposed on the **occupier** of premises. Although this term is not defined it may be taken to mean a person exercising control over those premises. **Premises** are, in turn, extended to cover

> any fixed or movable structure, including any vessel, vehicle or aircraft.

Parliament has still allowed the occupier to restrict that duty of care 'so far as he is free to do so'. For example, he may decorate his garden gate with signs reading 'Private', 'Keep Out', or 'No hawkers or traders'. If a hawker or trader does then venture across the threshold, he will be a trespasser and the occupier's duty to him is a lesser one.

Similarly, as in shops or hotels, the occupier may impose some partial limitation – for example, by a STAFF ONLY sign. As Scrutton LJ neatly phrased it:

> *When you invite a person into your house to use the staircase you do not invite him to slide down the banisters.*

An occupier may also try a more blanket approach in an attempt to exclude liability by warnings. The Act takes a cautious view of this and provides that:

> The warning is not to be treated without more as absolving the occupier from liability, unless in all the circumstances it was enough to enable the visitor to be reasonably safe.

So, for example, the warning, if given in writing, must have been prominently displayed, legible and, where necessary, lit up. If given orally, it must have been audible and understandable.

Further, the attempt at excluding such liability must be one which is permissible under the Unfair Contract Terms Act 1977 (see Unit 4.7). Although the title of that statute would suggest a concern with contract, it does nevertheless also govern attempts at excluding liability in tort for negligence. Under section 2, no notice will exclude liability for death or personal injury resulting from negligence. In the case of other loss or damage, a person cannot exclude or restrict his liability for negligence except in so far as the notice is shown to have been reasonable. Further, the Act specifically provides that, where such a notice is put up, a person's agreement to or awareness of it is not of itself to be taken as indicating his voluntary acceptance of any risk.

While the keynote of the Occupiers' Liability Act is what is reasonable, Parliament has afforded specific guidance on two particular classes of visitor, namely children and workmen. Section 2(3) provides:

> The circumstances relevant for the present purpose include the degree of care, and of want of care, which would ordinarily be looked for in such a visitor, so that (for example) in proper cases –
> (a) an occupier must be prepared for children to be less careful than adults; and
> (b) an occupier may expect that a person, in the exercise of his calling, will appreciate and guard against any special risks ordinarily incident to it, so far as the occupier leaves him free to do so.

Quite what degree of risk was covered by this sub-section was considered in *Salmon* v. *Seafarer Restaurants Ltd* 1983 when a man forgot to turn off the gas flame under a chip-fryer in an Essex fish and chip shop. The sign 'frying tonight' soon applied literally to the shop itself. Worse still, the heat of the resultant conflagration led to a gas explosion and Gary Salmon, a fireman attending the blaze, was badly injured. The fireman claimed damages for those injuries and alleged that the shop's employee had been negligent in leaving the gas on. The chip shop relied on this sub-section in the Occupiers' Liability Act 1957 and contended that it was not liable for Mr Salmon's injuries as the accident to him had been the result of an ordinary risk necessarily incident to a fireman's often dangerous work. Nevertheless, the court held that the restaurant had owed firemen who might be called out in an emergency the same duty of care as it owed other visitors under the Act. Because the explosion was of a kind that might result from the fire which had been caused by the negligence of the shop's employee, the 'chippy' was liable and Gary Salmon recovered £58,000 damages.

The same sub-section goes on to deal with the position of workmen who are 'independent contractors' (see Unit 6.8). For example, suppose that your staircase has only just been repaired by Messrs Cheape & Nastie, builders to the gentry, and your weekend guest trips on a loose board and falls headlong down the whole flight; are you still liable or is it the fault of the builders?

The Act provides:

> Where damage is caused to a visitor by a danger due to the faulty execution of any work of construction, maintenance or repair by an independent contractor employed by the occupier, the occupier is not to be treated without more as answerable for the danger if in all the circumstances he had acted reasonably in entrusting the work to an independent contractor and had taken such steps (if any) as he reasonably ought in order to satisfy himself that the contractor was competent and that the work had been properly done.

In short, a court would regard it as reasonable to employ a well-known long-established firm to undertake your staircase repairs, but not to entrust the job to a couple of Scouts on a bob-a-job basis.

What, though, if that same independent contractor is swinging from the banisters knocking the last nails into the staircase when suddenly down come hammer, nails, independent contractor and all? The law, as made clear in paragraph (b) of section 2(3) quoted above, expects workmen to know what they are doing. So, for example, in *Roles* v. *Nathan* 1963 the Court of Appeal held that the defendant occupiers were not liable for the deaths of two chimney-sweeps who had ignored warnings and had been overcome by carbon monoxide fumes. Not only had the expert's warning, had they heeded it, been sufficient to make them reasonably safe but, said Lord Denning MR:

> *When a householder calls in a specialist to deal with a defective installation on the premises he can reasonably expect the specialist to appreciate and guard against the dangers arising from the defect. The householder is not bound to watch over him to see that he comes to no harm.*

a) Children

We have already seen that the Act warns that an occupier must be prepared for children to be less careful than adults. Traditionally children and trespassers (so often one and the same) have presented the courts with difficult decisions. Children are less readily able to recognise danger than are adults and are, perhaps, unable to read any warnings. In particular, such is their curiosity that, like burglars, if they really want to get into someone's premises they will usually find a way. That children must be especially protected from their own curiosity where any 'allurement' is involved is clear from *Glasgow Corporation* v. *Taylor* 1922, where a seven-year-old boy had died as a result of eating poisonous berries growing in a public park in Glasgow. The House of Lords held the local corporation liable for its negligence. Lord Sumner approached the problem on the basis that

> *Infancy as such is no more a status conferring right or a root of title imposing obligations to respect it than infirmity or imbecility; but a measure of care appropriate to the inability or disability of those who are immature or feeble in mind or body is due from others, who know of or ought to anticipate the presence of such persons within the scope and hazard of their own operations.*

Lord Atkinson emphasised the special care which an occupier must take to protect children from allurements:

> *The liability of defendants in cases of this kind rests, I think, in the last resort upon their knowledge that by their actions they may bring children of tender years, unable to take care of themselves, yet inquisitive and easily tempted, into contact, in a place in which they, the children, have a right to be, with things alluring or tempting to them, and possibly in appearance harmless, but which, unknown to them and well known to the defendants, are harmful or dangerous if meddled with.*

In short, precautions which would exclude liability to adult visitors may have to be heightened in order to make children reasonably safe. In *Pearson* v. *Coleman Bros* 1948, for example, which concerned a seven-year-old girl who had been mauled by a circus lion when, in her search for a lavatory, she crawled under a rope barrier, the court held that such a barrier, though sufficient to keep adults out of danger, was inadequate to protect children. As Lord Greene MR emphasised:

> *But we are not dealing here with an adult but with a child who is not moving about out of mere curiosity or without any reason. We are dealing with a child in a condition which the proprietors must have contemplated as reasonably possible, namely the condition of being under an urgent necessity to find a quiet place in which to relieve herself.*

b) Trespassers

Because, by their very definition, trespassers are not lawful visitors, the courts have traditionally accepted that an occupier's duty to such unwelcome entrants was a low one, essentially a duty not to injure them intentionally – by littering the flower-beds with man-traps underneath the rhododendrons, for instance. The rigours of this doctrine were applied by the House of Lords in *Addie* v. *Dumbreck* 1929. A four-year-old boy was crushed in the wheel of a haulage system at the defendant's colliery. There was no doubt that the defendant's supervision had been 'casual and ineffective' or, indeed, that the wheel was an 'allurement' and an intrinsically dangerous one at that. The crucial question was whether the child was what is now known as a 'lawful visitor' or whether, on the other hand, he was only a trespasser who, said Lord Dunedin,

> *is he who goes on the land without invitation of any sort and whose presence is either unknown to the proprietor or, if known, is practically objected to.*

The House of Lords held that the boy was only a trespasser: the defendants, accordingly, were not liable for his death. Lord Hailsham LC distinguished law and sentiment when he concluded:

> *The sympathy which one cannot help feeling for the unhappy father must not be allowed to alter one's view of the law, and I have no doubt that in law the respondent's son was a mere trespasser.*

Today, however, the law relating to trespassers, and child trespassers in particular, has to be read in the light of the decision of the House of Lords in *British Railways Board* v. *Herrington* 1972. Peter Herrington, then aged six years, was playing near a railway line at Mitcham. He managed to get through a fence that had not been properly maintained. He was injured when he came into contact with the live electric rail. Lord Reid explained:

> *His age was such that he was unable to appreciate the danger of going on to the railway line and probably unable to appreciate that he was doing wrong in getting over the fence.*

Peter was a trespasser, and if it had been 50 years earlier he would not have been able to claim one penny damages. Was that still good law? The House of Lords was no longer bound by its own decisions. The law must reflect the standards of society. The railways argued that they owed no duty to Peter. Peter's lawyers argued that it was time to reconsider the law.

Lord Reid discussed the obvious dilemma:

> *Child trespassers have for a very long time presented to the courts an almost insoluble problem. They could only be completely safeguarded in one or other of two ways. Either parents must be required always to control and supervise the movements of their young children, or occupiers of premises must be required to take effective steps to keep them out or else to make their premises safe for them if they come. Neither of these is practicable. The former course was practicable at one time for a limited number of well-to-do parents but that number is now small. The latter, if practicable at all, would in most cases impose on occupiers an impossible financial burden.*
>
> *Legal principles cannot solve the problem. How far occupiers are to be required by law to take steps to safeguard such children must be a matter of public policy.*

The House of Lords went on to indicate that public policy had indeed changed over the last half-century and that social justice now required a more humanitarian approach, so that the railways did owe a duty to Peter and were, therefore, liable.

Lord Reid summed up that duty as depending on

> *whether a conscientious humane man with his knowledge, skill and resources could reasonably have been expected to have done or refrained from doing before the accident something which would have avoided it. If he knew before the accident that there was a substantial probability that trespassers would come, I think that most people would regard as culpable failure to give any thought to their safety.*

Special allowance was also made for the youthful age of a fourteen-year-old boy in *Jolley* v. *London Borough of Sutton* 2000 when the House of Lords had to consider whether it was reasonably foreseeable that an accident would occur if the local authority failed to remove an old boat from a grass area where children played. Justin Jolley was severely injured when a derelict boat fell on him after he had jacked it up in order to renovate it. The boat had been left lying in the grounds of a block of council flats owned by the London Borough of Sutton. All the local authority had done was to place a sticker on the boat which was in the form used by the council for abandoned cars. Justin and his friend had hoped to repair it and then take it to Cornwall to sail it. Tragically, the boat collapsed trapping the young claimant who was severely injured. The local authority argued that Justin had been engaged in an activity very different from normal play and that they should not be liable because it was not reasonably foreseeable that such an accident could occur as a result of children deciding to work under a propped up boat. In the House of Lords, however, the judges noted that the ingenuity of children in finding ways of doing mischief to themselves should never be underestimated. As Lord Hoffmann put it with now unfashionable classical erudition:

> *In the present case, the rotten condition of the boat had a significance beyond the particular danger it created. It proclaimed the boat and its trailer as abandoned,* res nullius, *there for the taking, to make of them whatever use the rich fantasy life of children might suggest.*

It is unlikely in 1972 that the House of Lords had given much thought to the regular summer intrusion into anyone's back garden airspace of bees in search of pollen. Nevertheless, problems of bees flying over another's land came before the courts in *Tutton* v. *Walter* 1985 when some Sussex beekeepers sued A.D. Walter Ltd, a farming company, in respect of the loss of their bees. In a field near the plaintiffs' beehives the defendants grew oil-seed rape, a yellow plant which when in flower is very attractive to foraging bees. One summer's day, the defendants sprayed the field with pesticide which killed the plaintiffs' bees as they buzzed their way to the rape. The plaintiffs sued the defendant farmers for negligence in spraying as and when they did. In their defence the farmers contended that, since *Herrington's* case, their only duty to trespassers (and this term was intended by the defendants to include bees) was to refrain from deliberately or recklessly carrying out acts which would injure them. However, the judge refused to view these winged honey-producers as trespassers. Instead, he applied the basic principles laid down in *Donoghue* v. *Stevenson* 1932 and held that the spraying of the pesticide was clearly likely to injure the buzzing little *apis mellifera*. As the defendants well knew that there were beehives in the adjoining field, the farmers owed the plaintiffs a duty of care which they had failed to discharge and were, therefore, liable for the loss of the bees.

Since *Herrington's* case was decided, Parliament has enacted two new statutes.

In 1972 the Defective Premises Act was passed. Section 4 of that Act provides that, where a landlord is obliged under the terms of the lease to carry out necessary repairs and maintenance, he will be liable if anyone is injured because of some defect in the property. Parliament has now provided that a landlord:

owes to all persons who might reasonably be expected to be affected by defects in the state of the premises a duty to take such care as is reasonable in all the circumstances to see that they are reasonably safe from personal injury or from damage to their property caused by a relevant defect.

In 1984, Parliament passed a new Occupiers' Liability Act. This Act provided specific statutory rules which reapplied the old common-law rules such as those in *Herrington's* case. No doubt, however, in practice the courts will still have regard to the old cases to judge just how well the occupier of land has discharged his new statutory duty to someone who is not classed as a visitor (such as a trespasser). Under section 3 an occupier owes such people a duty of care if:

(a) he is aware of the danger or has reasonable grounds to believe that it exists;

(b) he knows or has reasonable grounds to believe that the other is in the vicinity of the danger concerned or that he may come into the vicinity of the danger (in either case, whether the other has lawful authority for being in that vicinity or not); and

(c) the risk is one against which, in all the circumstances of the case, he may reasonably be expected to offer the other some protection.

The Act goes on to provide that the duty owed is a duty

to take such care as is reasonable in all the circumstances of the case to see that he does not suffer injury on the premises by reason of the danger concerned.

Signs such as 'Danger! Loose rocks' or 'Keep out: Quicksand' may well be sufficient in most cases to avoid any liability to persons hit on the head by a lump of chalk who then fall over and are sucked into slippery sands.

One trespasser who was hit not on the head but rather in the chest was Mark Revil. In *Revil* v. *Newbery* 1996 the plaintiff tried to break in to a brick shed belonging to pensioner William Newbery. Within the shed Mr Newbery had rigged up sleeping quarters and had been in the habit of sleeping there to protect his property from the vandals and thieves who had been all too active in that area. In the middle of the night, Mr Newbery was woken by the noise of the plaintiff trying to break open the shed. The defendant took a shotgun, put the barrel through a hole in the door and fired. What duty was owed at common law to an intruder who comes onto premises in the middle of the night? On the evidence heard, the judge found as a fact that Mr Newbery had not in fact intended to hit the burglar. Nevertheless, the court held that Mr Newbery owed some duty to Mark Revil and had breached such duty. Neither trespassers nor criminals were to be treated as outlaws. Rather, the duty of care owed by an occupier to a trespasser under the Occupiers' Liability Act 1984 was to take such care as was reasonable in all the circumstances to see that the trespasser did not suffer injury on the premises. Such statutory duty applied even when the trespasser was involved in criminal endeavour.

6.5 Nuisance

Jane is stuck in a traffic-jam for over an hour just because some idiot lorry driver has parked his oil-tanker by a narrow hump-back bridge.

Richard returns home to his house unable to find a clean cup and has to spend even longer washing up the week's dishes.

Alice, meanwhile, is being blasted out of her flat for the third time this week by the noise of her neighbour's new stereo.

In a sense all three could have described their experiences as being something of a nuisance (if not worse). In law the definition of a nuisance is more restricted and more precise. At the outset, however, it is necessary to note that a nuisance may be either 'public' or 'private'.

In *Attorney-General* v. *P.Y.A. Quarries Ltd* 1957, Romer LJ described a **public nuisance** as being something

> which materially affects the reasonable comfort and convenience of a class of Her Majesty's subjects.

So, for example, the lorry driver's lack of consideration and road sense has materially affected the comfort and convenience of all those who were held up in the traffic, including Jane.

A **private nuisance** is more limited. The courts have approved the definition of Professor Winfield when he said it was

> unlawful interference with a person's use or enjoyment of land, or some right over or in connection with it.

Alice has a right to some degree of peace and quiet in her own home and, by his persistent stereophonic cacophony, her neighbour is committing a private nuisance.

Richard, on the other hand, will just have to buy a dishwasher.

a) Public nuisance

Public nuisance is not only a tort; it is also a crime. It includes obstruction of the highway (also an offence under a number of statutes, including the Highways Act 1980), selling or serving food in unhygienic conditions (which could transgress the various public health regulations) and brothel-keeping (which infringes the Sexual Offences Act 1956). The list is very long and one judge has said that it covers a 'multitude of sins'. The offender runs two risks: firstly, he may be prosecuted (for example, by the Public Health Inspector) and, secondly, he may be taken to the civil courts which may grant an injunction to stop him from carrying on that nuisance and may in addition award damages to anyone who has been particularly affected.

In order to avoid hitting the offender too hard, however, and also to avoid the danger of a multiplicity of actions inundating the courts, a judge will only award damages to an individual if he can prove that he was particularly harmed by that nuisance: he must have suffered something over and above what everyone else has undergone. So, in *Castle* v. *St Augustine's Links Ltd* 1922, George Castle, the plaintiff, had been driving his taxi near a golf course when a player 'sliced' the ball and sent it smashing through the plaintiff's windscreen. The judge held that the slicing of golf balls on to the highway amounted to a public nuisance.

The plaintiff, however, had been particularly affected: he had lost an eye in the accident. That particular loss allowed him to claim damages to compensate him for his injury.

Noise is just one topical matter (atmospheric pollution is another) which may amount to a public nuisance if it affects a sufficient number of people – if it has a 'public' ingredient.

Just when a nuisance does become 'public' was considered by the Court of Appeal in *Attorney-General* v. *P.Y.A. Quarries Ltd* 1957, when the Attorney-General (who as a law officer of the Crown may apply for an injunction in such a case) asked for an injunction against the defendant company to stop them from blasting. How many members of the public had, as individuals, to be regarding the noise from the quarry as a nuisance before the court would grant an injunction? No one could really say. Romer LJ, describing the sphere of the nuisance as 'the neighbourhood', said:

> The question whether the local community within that sphere comprises a sufficient number of persons to constitute a class of the public is a question of fact in every case. It is not necessary, in my judgment, to prove that every member of the class has been injuriously affected; it is sufficient to show that a representative cross-section of the class has been so affected for an injunction to issue.

Neither was Denning LJ, as he then was, prepared to be tied down:

> The classic statement of the difference is that a public nuisance affects Her Majesty's subjects generally, whereas a private nuisance only affects individuals. The question, 'When do a number of individuals become "Her Majesty's subjects generally"?' is as difficult to answer as the question 'When does a group of people become a crowd?' Everyone has his own views ... I prefer to look at the reason of the thing and to say that a public nuisance is a nuisance which is so widespread in its range or is so indiscriminate in its effect that it would not be reasonable to expect one person to take proceedings on his own responsibility to put a stop to it, but that it should be taken on the responsibility of the community at large.

b) Private nuisance

People can commit private nuisance in a vast number of ways. Anyone living in a block of flats knows only too well that noisy music, extravagant parties and a staple diet of curried onions do little enough for good-neighbour relations. Smell, noise and dirt have all long been the subjects of action in the courts. Traditionally the law's advice to neighbours has been: *sic utere tuo ut alienum non laedas* ('use your own land so as not to harm another's'). This maxim must, of course, now be read in the light of modern living conditions.

Obviously in any crowded country some occasional discomfort is almost inevitable. Your green-fingered neighbour will probably have a couple of bonfires every year. Once a year he may have a few friends round to celebrate his birthday. Smoke and laughter, whether together or separately, will probably intrude into your home and garden. By itself, that is not enough to amount to a nuisance. On the other hand if it happened every day your neighbour would be committing a private nuisance. Where the line is to be drawn is a matter for the judge to decide in the light of all the surrounding circumstances. As Lord Wright remarked:

> *It is impossible to give any precise formula, but it may broadly be said that a useful test is perhaps what is reasonable according to the ordinary usages of mankind living in society.*

The locality, the nature of the irritation, the reason for it, its duration and the damage done are all relevant considerations.

Locality What the luckless inhabitants of the industrial areas of London are expected to suffer may be different from what the residents of the choicer parts of SW1 may have to tolerate – as Thesiger LJ remarked in *Sturges* v. *Bridgman* 1879:

> *What would be a nuisance in Belgrave Square would not necessarily be so in Bermondsey.*

Whatever welcome the good folk of Bermondsey would give a 'sex centre and video club' the residents of Pimlico SW1 certainly objected when an old dress shop in a quiet residential area was converted into a so-called sex shop and cinema. Ironically, the interests of this establishment's prospective clientele were likely to be precisely the reverse of the couturier's visitors who had come actually seeking clothes to put *on*. In *Laws* v. *Florinplace Ltd* 1981 the court granted an injunction against the emporium in question after local residents complained about the nuisance which the area would suffer from such an establishment drawing, as it was said, 'a number of men of sleazy and unprepossessing mien'.

. . . 'a number of men of sleazy and unprepossessing mien'.

The court accepted that the law of nuisance covered not only cases of physical harm but also the use of property which would amount to an affront to the reasonable susceptibilities of ordinary men and women.

Some few years later and even fewer miles down the road from SW1, a number of residents of the East End found that their television reception suffered interference after construction of the Canary Wharf Tower.

The Court of Appeal rejected the argument that the presence of this contribution to the elegance of London's skyline could amount to either a public or private nuisance. The unwelcome presence of this structure was no more relevant than the unwelcome absence of a particular view. As Pill LJ remarked:

> *I accept the importance of television in the lives of very many people. However, in my judgment the erection or presence of a building in the line of sight between a television transmitter and other properties is not actionable as an interference with the use and enjoyment of land. The analogy with loss of prospect is compelling. The loss of a view, which may be of the greatest importance to many householders, is not actionable and neither is the mere presence of a building in the sight line of a television transmitter.*

Reason for the act Your neighbour may claim that his bonfires save his fellow council-tax payers expense in sparing the services of the refuse disposal operatives. He may claim that his parties are given for the purpose of taking his friends' minds off their problems. Such unlikely altruistic motives are irrelevant: the question is whether or not the acts are reasonable. For example, in *Adams* v. *Ursell* 1913 the plaintiff lived next door to a fried-fish shop. His house was permeated with the smell of batter and oil. The defendant made two points: firstly, he said that he used all the most modern equipment and tried to keep the smell down; secondly, he also argued that he was performing a public service in providing dinner for the poor people of that area. Neither argument prevented the judge from granting an injunction to put an end to 'frying tonight'.

Exceptionally, indeed, an improper motive may be relevant in deciding whether the actions were reasonable. In *Christie* v. *Davey* 1893 Mr Davey had been driven to desperate revenge on his neighbour who gave music lessons at her semi-detached house in Brixton. He had tried writing to complain about 'the frantic effort of someone trying to sing to piano accompaniment' which, he said, he had 'at first thought were the howlings of your dog'. When his sarcasm fell on deaf ears he tried banging on the wall with a tin tray. His revenge went sour, however, when a judge granted an injunction against Mr Davey because he had set out to be unreasonable.

The damage done Some people are unable to face life without the constant companionship of their transistor radios. Others find the faintest sound of Radio One an insult to their finer musical training and sensitivity. Neither the intellectual bluntness of one person nor the nervous sensitivity of another is a proper criterion to decide whether the damage is reasonable. A highly sensitive spirit receives no extra protection: instead he just has to suffer rather more.

This kind of problem arose in *Robinson* v. *Kilvert* 1889, where the defendant landlord kept the temperature in his cellar very high. The plaintiff, his tenant, stored brown paper above that cellar. The brown paper was dried out by the rising heat and consequently went down in value, although ordinary paper was not affected.

... he just has to suffer rather more.

It turned out that the plaintiff's brown paper was particularly sensitive to changes in the temperature. The Court of Appeal rejected the plaintiff's complaint of a private nuisance; Lopes LJ said:

> *I think the plaintiff cannot complain of what is being done as a nuisance. A man who carries on an exceptionally delicate trade cannot complain because it is injured by his neighbour doing something lawful on his property, if it is something which would not injure anything but an exceptionally delicate trade.*

Once a nuisance has been alleged the person inconvenienced will ask for damages as compensation. He will also ask the court to grant an injunction ordering the defendant not to go on with the nuisance. Before the claimant can sue he must show that he has a proprietary interest in the land affected. Any proprietary interest is sufficient; a tenant is, therefore, able to sue a neighbour without the need to resort to his landlord. On the other hand if the landlord has let a flat in which a nuisance already existed, or if he has just stood by and in some way sanctioned the nuisance, the tenant may have to join his landlord as another defendant.

An **injunction** is a discretionary remedy, that is to say, the court may grant an injunction in one case but not in another. In practice, a judge has to ask himself whether the payment of damages alone would be an adequate remedy. In addition, a judge must consider the balance of convenience between granting the injunction and refusing it. Whether an injunction should be granted was the principal issue in *Miller* v. *Jackson* 1977. Mr and Mrs Miller had moved into a house on a new housing estate which had been built near a village cricket ground in County Durham where bat and ball had entertained the local villagers for well over half a century. In the two years following their move to their new home Mr and Mrs Miller were troubled by several cricket balls landing in their garden during the twenty-week cricket season. Their house was struck and damaged on four occasions because of the batsmen's prowess. The Millers complained to the club, which made various efforts to stop this nuisance. The Millers were still unhappy and sought an injunction to put a long stop to the cricket. At trial, the club contended that they had taken all reasonable steps to protect the plaintiffs and their home but fairly conceded that occasionally balls would end up in the Millers' garden.

The Court of Appeal held that as there was a foreseeable risk of injury to the Millers, the club was liable in negligence and would have to pay for any damage done. On the other hand, the court refused to grant an injunction which would put a stop to play. Lord Denning MR balanced the competing views and conflicting interests:

> *This case is new. It should be approached in principles applicable to modern conditions. There is a contest here between the interest of the public at large and the interest of a private individual. The* public *interest lies in protecting the environment by preserving our playing fields in the face of mounting development, and by enabling our youth to enjoy all the benefits of outdoor games, such as cricket and football. The* private *interest lies in securing the privacy of his home and garden without intrusion or interference by anyone. In deciding between these two conflicting interests, it must be remembered that it is not a question of damages. If, by a million-to-one chance, a cricket ball does go out of the ground and cause damage, the cricket club will pay. There is no difficulty on that score. No, it is a question of an injunction. And in our law you will find it repeatedly affirmed that an injunction is a discretionary remedy. In a new situation like this, we have to think afresh as to how discretion should be exercised.*

Lord Denning MR considered where each party might be able to move to in order to get away from the other. On balance, however, he said that the public interest should prevail over the private interest and the Millers were refused their injunction.

As a general rule an injunction will not be granted where damages (the payment of money as compensation) is a sufficient remedy. The receipt of money was, however, clearly insufficient as a remedy in *Tetley v. Chitty and others* 1986. In 1981 a borough council had granted a go-kart club the lease of some council land. Christopher Tetley, a schoolmaster, was one of a number of local residents much troubled by the noise made by these machines which, no doubt, made the disgruntled pedagogue wish that the karts would indeed go. For its part, the go-kart club agreed not to continue using the site but at trial the local council tried to argue that they were not liable in nuisance because they had neither created nor permitted any nuisance to be caused. The council further contended that Mr Tetley had failed to show that the nuisance was a likely consequence of the use to which the land was put.

At trial, however, the judge took the view that the noise caused by the go-karts was an ordinary and natural consequence of the use of such go-karts. It followed that Mr Tetley was entitled to an injunction. Damages, in such a case, said the judge, would be a wholly insufficient remedy.

In addition to the usual defences to tort a defendant to an action in private nuisance may raise the defence of *prescription*: that is he may be able to show that the nuisance has been going on for at least twelve years. Such a defence only works for private nuisance. A public nuisance is a crime as well and the passage of time can never hallow its commission for, it is said, time does not run against the Crown.

6.6 *Trespass*

a) Trespass to land

Buckingham Palace has long received many distinguished visitors from all over the world. Christopher Robin, loyal friend of Winnie the Pooh, is said to have gone there with Alice. Neither, however, got into the Queen's private bedroom. Fact can sometimes be stranger than fiction and headline news was made in July 1982 when Michael Fagan managed to shin up a drainpipe and slip into the Queen's bedroom for a chat about life. At the time there was popular surprise that Fagan could not be prosecuted for his nocturnal wandering in Buckingham Palace – not even when all prosecutions in the Crown Court are conducted in the name of the Queen! Trespass, as mentioned in Unit 1.1, is not generally a crime: normally it is merely a civil wrong. In the wake of the Fagan incident, suggestions were made that the law should be changed to bring some forms of trespass within the criminal law. The cries for reform had only just died down when, at Christmas 1985, a young Australian lawyer, anticipating somewhat prematurely the annual Yuletide rooftop present-delivery service of Santa Claus, went from down under to up over and indeed on to the roof of the Prime Minister's residence in Downing Street. Frantic police activity interrupted this learned antipodean's activities but, once removed, he could still not be prosecuted. Once again, such actions were a matter only for the civil courts. Mrs Thatcher, as occupier, could have sued him for damages – indeed, as might have been said in the then Prime Minister's famous phrase: 'There is no alternative!' The only remedy would lie in a civil action for trespass – that is, the unjustifiable and direct interference with another's possession of land.

Such interference can take many forms: walking across a farmer's field or climbing your neighbour's apple trees would be obvious examples. The trespass could also involve the soil under another's land if you went burrowing under the garden fence looking for oil or buried treasure. Even interference with the air above another's land could be trespass, as when branches of a tree intrude over the owner's back-garden fence into the neighbouring garden. A less natural intrusion was that of an advertising sign in *Kelsen* v. *Imperial Tobacco Company* 1957. John Kelsen owned a tobacconist's shop in Islington. The next door premises were owned by the cigarette manufacturers who erected an advertisement for their product saying 'Players Please'. Evidently, the sign itself certainly did not please Mr Kelsen because it projected into the airspace above his single-storey shop. The court held that Mr Kelsen was entitled to an order requiring Imperial Tobacco to remove their sign. This was because, in theory at least, the occupier is entitled to the enjoyment both of the air above his land and the soil underneath. This proposition is traditionally summed up in the old Latin phrase: *Cujus est solum ejus est usque ad caelum et ad inferos* (which might be loosely translated as meaning that the landowner has the air above up to the heavens and also the earth down below to the other place).

Since those cultured days when Latin was more readily understood the situation has become less straightforward. After all, if this principle was rigidly and literally applied, air-fares would rise sky high just to cover the cost of claims brought by vexatious occupiers of semidetacheds around every airport in the country. Attempts to sue a low-flying photographer failed in *Bernstein* v. *Skyviews* 1977. Lord Bernstein had objected when a pilot, employed by a company whose business was taking aerial photographs of people's houses for future sale to the proud owners, flew over his estate. The court held that the defendants were protected by the statutory exemption given to civil aircraft and now re-enacted in the Civil Aviation Act 1982 which provides:

> No action shall lie in respect of trespass or in respect of nuisance, by reason only of the flight of an aircraft over any property at a height above the ground, which having regard to the wind, weather and all the circumstances of the case is reasonable...

It might well be different, and so one could distinguish the *Bernstein* case if a flying-machine repeatedly crossed low over someone's home – for example, if some scoop-hungry journalist in a helicopter hovered over a film-star's private swimming pool as she cavorted naked in what she thought was the privacy of her own grounds. Such an example raises also questions of privacy examined in Unit 3.10, breach of which is all the easier to achieve with modern technology which now allows aerial photographs of anywhere in the country to be downloaded from the internet.

Some consolation for the outraged householder whose greenhouse is demolished as a loose wheel falls 30,000 feet from a jumbo jet is offered by the Act which goes on to provide that the airline will be strictly liable to pay for the damage done. In other words, the householder need not actually prove negligence on the part of the airline. He will, however, still have the task of identifying the airline. Once the damage is done and the culprit identified the airline must pay up, even if there was no evidence of negligence either in the pre-flight inspection or maintenance generally.

As the Act's title suggests, it is concerned with civil aeroplanes rather than military flights. So if a bomb drops from a Royal Air Force Tornado jet, the aggrieved occupier of what little may be left of the ancestral home will still have to prove negligence in the usual way.

Trespass is said to be actionable *per se*: that is, there is no need to prove damage. Neither does a claimant have to prove any intention on the defendant's part to have committed the trespass. This is not to say that the paper boy who cuts across a householder's front drive to deliver next door's newspapers will be made to pay thousands of pounds for this trifling infringement – such litigation would receive a very cool reception indeed. Sometimes, however, the court may grant quite substantial damages. For example, if Messrs Hippy, Happy and Hoppy trespass and start squatting in a person's house the court may award a sum approximately equivalent to what would have been a reasonable rent.

Parliament has already intervened in the Animals Act 1971 to regulate the position of straying animals which wander on to other land. The farmer need only stop his tractor and pick up his copy of the Animals Act to see that, under section 4, where livestock stray on to land owned or occupied by another and then do damage, the owner of that livestock is responsible not only for the cost of the damage actually done but also for payment of any reasonable expenses incurred in keeping the live-stock until they can be restored to their owner.

One means of self-help available to those having to deal with persons who, although previously invited or allowed on to land, decline to leave when asked to do so, or misbehave while on the land, is the reasonable use of force. For example, in *Harrison* v. *Duke of Rutland* 1893 the defendant owned a grouse moor which, in turn, was crossed by a highway. When the plaintiff tried to drive the grouse away by waving his handkerchief and opening and shutting an umbrella the defendant's servants removed Harrison from their noble employer's lands. Harrison later sued for this assault and the Duke contended that his men's actions had been justified because Harrison was a trespasser. The defence succeeded because, as Kay LJ said in the Court of Appeal:

> *The plaintiff went upon this highway, not for the purpose of exercising as one of the public his right of passage, but of interfering with the grouse drive by placing himself upon the soil of the highway so as to prevent the grouse from flying over the butts.*

Several years later, the courts had to deal with the activities of a racing tout in *Hickman* v. *Maisey* 1900 when the tout walked up and down a highway from where he could observe some horses in training. He strolled up and down and back and forth for about an hour and a half, taking notes as he went of the horses' form. The trainer objected and sought a court order to stop any further observations. In those days, juries sat in the civil courts and the judge explained to them that in law the tout was perfectly free to use the highway for the purpose of passing and repassing. However, he was not entitled to stop on the highway for the purpose of carrying on his business, reviewing the progress and performance of horses in training. The jury awarded damages of only one shilling (five new pence) but, more importantly, the plaintiff also obtained the injunction he sought.

In cases of trespass, it is often an injunction to restrain further acts of trespass which is the most important aspect of the claim. For example, in *League Against Cruel Sports* v. *Scott* 1985 the plaintiff League (and self-evidently no friends of blood-sports) owned land on Exmoor where wild deer could move freely. The Devon and Somerset Staghounds had different interests. The League complained about acts of trespass by the hunt and its hounds (even though no damage had actually been done) and asked the court for an injunction ordering the hunt not to come on to the League's land. At trial, the court awarded the plaintiff League only £100 in all but did grant them an injunction stopping both horse and hound from entering on to the League's own land.

It will be remembered from Unit 1.2 that trespass has traditionally been a civil wrong and not a matter appropriately the subject of criminal sanction. Recent legislation has, however, increasingly penalised trespass so that, for example, trespassory assemblies by twenty or more persons are outlawed under the provisions of the Public Order Act 1986. Further, in order to inhibit protests against hunting or the construction of new roads, the Criminal Justice and Public Order Act 1994 created the new offence of 'aggravated trespass'.

The gathering of Druids each June at Stonehenge had been enjoyed for many years before the creation of this new offence under the Public Order Act. In *DPP* v. *Jones* 1999 the House of Lords had to consider the limits of the public's right of access to the highway. The order under the Act could only be made in respect of land to which the public had no right of access or only a limited right of access. Moreover, the European Convention for the Protection of Human Rights and Fundamental Freedoms specifically required that there was a right of assembly on the public highway. Margaret Jones was one of a number of people outside the perimeter fence at Stonehenge one June evening. She was arrested for taking part in a trespassory assembly. On appeal, the House of Lords had to decide whether the law should recognise that the public highway is a public place on which all manner of reasonable activities may go on. The judges considered the earlier cases such as *Harrison* v. *Duke of Rutland* and *Hickman* v. *Maisey* but disagreed as to the extent to which the public could use public roads. By only a narrow majority, the view of the Lord Chancellor himself prevailed as he concluded, upon an analysis of the earlier authorities, that the public have the right to use the public highway for such 'reasonable and usual activities as are consistent with the general public's primary right to use the highway for purposes of passage and re-passage'. Lord Irvine LC continued:

> Nor can I attribute any hard core of meaning to a test which would limit lawful use of the highway to what is incidental or ancillary to the right of passage. In truth, very little activity could accurately be described as 'ancillary' to passing along the highway; perhaps stopping to tie one's shoe lace, consulting a street-map, or pausing to catch one's breath. But I do not think that such ordinary and usual activities as making a sketch, taking a photograph, handing out leaflets, collecting money for charity, singing carols, playing in a Salvation Army band, children playing a game on the pavement, having a picnic, or reading a book would qualify. These examples illustrate that to limit lawful use of the highway to that which is literally 'incidental or ancillary' to the right of passage would be to place an unrealistic and unwarranted restriction on commonplace day-to-day activities. The law should not make unlawful what is commonplace and well accepted.

Such a decision is both a consolation for those concerned at the tendency of politicians to erode individual freedom and a reassurance in the way lawyers and judges still value traditional freedoms.

b) Trespass to the person

It may be of little consolation to the man rolling in the gutter (even if looking at the stars) to reflect that the blow which knocked him down and blacked his eye is a classic example of the overlap between criminal law and the law of tort. An **assault**, as considered in Unit 3.5a), is a criminal act as well as a civil wrong. In its criminal context it is often defined somewhat loosely as the deliberate or reckless application of unlawful force to another. Speaking more strictly, an assault is any act which causes another to fear infliction of a battery. A **battery** is the intentional (or arguably reckless) application of actual force. In other words, raising your fist to the man who gets to the bar before you is an assault. The battery is committed when your clenched fist makes contact with the fleshy tip of the man's nose. There can be an assault without a battery, as where no blow is actually struck. There can even be a battery without an assault, as where a man is struck suddenly from behind and without warning.

... rolling in the gutter (even if looking at stars) ...

Words alone, however, cannot amount to an assault although they could today be construed as an offence of 'insulting behaviour'. For example, the restraining effect of a judge's visit to a town on assizes (the old criminal court which preceded the Crown Court, see Unit 2.2b)), could be seen in *Tuberville* v. *Savadge* 1669 when a man's action in putting his hand to his sword was mellowed by his comment that 'if it were not assize time I would not take such language from you'. Such reservation prevented his action from being held to have been an assault. In other words, no assault would be committed by Bill saying to Ben: 'If it weren't for all those large policemen over there looking at us I would ram your teeth down your throat.' Shaking a fist from a fast-moving train at a person standing on a railway platform would probably be held not to be an assault because the man on the platform would not reasonably be put in fear of immediate violence as the Inter-City sped away into the distance.

Most black eyes are the result of a deliberate blow to the victim's face. It is, however, essential for a claimant to prove that what the doctor would imaginatively diagnose as 'periorbital haematoma' was caused intentionally or, at least, negligently. In *Fowler* v. *Lanning* 1959 the defendant shot the plaintiff at a shooting party at Corfe Castle in Dorset. It had not been the aim of the party for guests actually to shoot *each other* and the shooting was quite unintentional. The court held that the plaintiff could have no claim for his injuries on the basis of trespass to the person if the injury had been caused unintentionally and without negligence on the part of the defendant.

A similar point came before the Court of Appeal in *Letang* v. *Cooper* 1964. The plaintiff, Doreen Letang, sued Frank Cooper in respect of her personal injuries sustained when Cooper drove his Jaguar car over her as she was sunbathing in the grounds of a Cornwall hotel. Doreen Letang proceeded on grounds of trespass to the person. However, the Court of Appeal rejected the claim. Lord Denning MR put the matter shortly and clearly:

> *If one man intentionally applies force directly to another the plaintiff has a cause of action in assault and battery or, if you please to describe it, in trespass to the person. 'The least touching of another in anger is battery.' If he does not inflict injury intentionally, but only unintentionally, the plaintiff has no cause of action today in trespass. His only cause of action is in negligence, and then only on proof of want of reasonable care. If the plaintiff cannot prove want of reasonable care, he may have no cause of action at all.*

Questions of intention and proof of hostility in cases of alleged trespass to the person came in for consideration by the Court of Appeal in *Wilson* v. *Pringle* 1986. Two schoolboys were involved in some form of horseplay in a school corridor. Unfortunately, Peter Wilson sustained an injury to his hip. Peter sued Ian Pringle, alleging trespass to the person. Peter (who, as a minor, sued through his mother) argued that he had to prove nothing more than an intentional application of force on the part of the other boy. The defendant contended that such simple horseplay could not be classified as trespass to the person and required proof of an intention to cause injury.

The Court of Appeal looked at cases going right back to *Tuberville* v. *Savadge* 1669 and thought that this case showed that some sort of hostile behaviour was required. It would follow, therefore, that innocently touching another person did not, by itself, amount to trespass. The Court of Appeal went on to hold that, while an intention to injure was not an essential ingredient in trespass, an intention to touch had to be shown to have been a hostile intention as, for example, in punching, stabbing or shooting.

Sportsmen regularly get battered, especially those who participate in the so-called 'contact sports'. Sportsmen such as rugger-players, wrestlers and boxers consent to the risk of injury and any claim against other players would be met by the defence *volenti non fit injuria* considered in Unit 6.7. Team games and field sports also assume that the players consent to the risks incidental in the particular sport, whether it be 'bouncers' aimed at Rudyard Kipling's 'flanelled fools at the wicket' or a late tackle on one of his 'muddied oafs at the goal'.

In normal circumstances an injured player will be without remedy. There is, however, a limit on the risks to which such participants are deemed to have consented, as can be seen in the decision of the Court of Appeal in *Condon* v. *Basi* 1985. James Condon had been playing one Sunday in a football league. An opposing player, Basi, tackled Condon in such a way that the plaintiff broke his leg. The referee had given evidence in the County Court that the defendant had challenged Condon (who then pushed the ball away) by sliding in from a distance of about three to four yards. This slide tackle came later and was made in what the referee had considered to be a reckless and dangerous manner of play for which Basi was shown the red card. The Court of Appeal upheld the award of nearly £5,000 against Basi and said that if one participant injures another he will be liable in negligence if it can be proved that he failed to exercise a degree of care appropriate to the match. This degree of care would obviously be different in a Sunday league from that expected at the top of the Premier League.

The remedy for assault and battery lies in an action for damages. One very real problem, however, is that many people who could be sued are simply not worth pursuing through the courts. They are what lawyers call 'men of straw' and not worth powder and shot in the courts. Some consolation to those who have suffered such personal violence is to be found in the **Criminal Injuries Compensation Authority**. Formerly known as the Criminal Injuries Compensation Board when set up in 1964, the Authority administers a compensation scheme making payments to people who have sustained personal injury attributable to:

(a) a crime of violence (including arson, fire raising or an act of poisoning); or
(b) an offence of trespass on a railway; or
(c) the apprehension or attempted apprehension of an offender or a suspected offender, the prevention or attempted prevention of an offence, or the giving of help to any constable who is engaged in any such activity.

The Authority has the right to reduce or even withhold a payment where:

(a) the applicant failed promptly to inform the police;
(b) the applicant failed to co-operate with the police;
(c) the applicant failed to assist in the processing of an application;
(d) the applicant's conduct, whether before during or after the incident, makes it inappropriate for a full award or any award at all to be made; or where
(e) the applicant's character makes it inappropriate that a full award or any award at all be made.

These are not new conditions so that, for example, in cases where the applicant's own character or way of life is tainted the Authority may take this factor into account, as in *R* v. *Criminal Injuries Compensation Board, ex parte Thompstone and Crowe* 1984 when the scope of the earlier scheme fell to be examined by the courts. Two men applied for compensation. Each had been assaulted in separate incidents. Thomas Thompstone had been stabbed. George Crowe sustained a broken leg. Neither, however, was given any money because each had a long list of convictions and the Board had felt that it would be inappropriate to award compensation from public funds having regard to the 'character, conduct and way of life' of the two men. Even though there was no connection between the backgrounds of the applicants and the injuries they had suffered the Court of Appeal was unwilling to say that such decision had been plainly wrong.

The Court of Appeal has also ruled that train drivers who suffer psychiatric injury in the form of shock and depression after seeing people commit suicide by jumping in front of trains do not qualify for such compensation. In *R* v. *Criminal Injuries Compensation Board, ex parte Warner* 1986 the Court of Appeal rejected the argument that such distress had been caused by a 'crime of violence' which the scheme had been intended to cover.

Injuries caused by bad driving are excluded from the scheme, as are minor injuries with a value less than the Authority's traditional minimum award of £1,000. Until recently, awards above that sum were assessed in the same way that a judge would calculate an award for personal injury in the civil courts.

Victims of violent crime faced a double blow when the Conservative government introduced new cost-cutting measures (of course, all too predictably claimed at the time as intended only to speed up compensation) by replacing the old common-law damages scheme with a 'tariff system', introduced by the Criminal Injuries Compensation Act 1995. Although such payments are now made as of right, the amounts of such compensation are no longer decided by lawyers working on traditional common-law principles but, rather, by claims officers who authorise payment by reference to this tariff. Few doubt that the dominant purpose was to reduce the cost of the scheme and virtually every piece of the human body now carries its own price tag. For example, at the lowest end of the scale, a deviated nasal septum would attract a standard award of £1,000, a fractured femur £3,000, a fractured patella (kneecap) with full recovery £7,500, rape £7,500, loss of an ear £10,000, loss of sight in one eye £25,000 and, at the maximum possible pay-out, injuries with extremely serious and permanent brain damage £250,000.

In some cases of assault the alleged assailant may be arrested by the police. In this sort of offence, as in any other, it is essential that the police officer (or others such as Customs officers and store-detectives) acts properly in making the arrest and does so with reasonable suspicion that the person has committed the offence for which he is arrested. From that moment the person arrested suffers a loss of liberty. He will be taken to the police station and placed in either a cell or an interview room. In the vast majority of cases such treatment is absolutely reasonable and authorised by law. As Viscount Haldane LC said over half a century ago, 'by the law of this country no man can be restrained of his liberty without authority in law'. Where such loss of liberty (and that would probably include being taken back into a shop by a store-detective if there was any great delay in sorting the matter out) is not so authorised by law the person so detained will have a claim for **false imprisonment**. In practice, claims for false imprisonment are often linked with claims for **malicious prosecution** where a person, cleared at trial of the charge against him or her, complains that the prosecution had been carried on maliciously, that is without reasonable and probable cause. This is the principal way in which an innocent man may obtain compensation for the trauma of a criminal trial.

It is a serious step to deprive a person of his or her liberty. The gravity of the situation is recognised by the fact that the tort of false imprisonment is said to be actionable *per se* (that is without proof of damage) and also by the approach of the court in *Meering* v. *Grahame-White Aviation* 1919 when a young aeroplane designer was asked by the works police of the defendant company to stay in a waiting room at the aviation works. He did not know as he waited there that works police were also waiting outside the door. The court held that the plaintiff had still been falsely imprisoned although his lack of knowledge would be relevant to the measure of damages.

Nevertheless, the restraint upon liberty must be total and be such as to prevent the person leaving. In other words, it would not be sufficient to lock the front door if the back door were left open. For example, in *Bird* v. *Jones* 1845 part of Hammersmith Bridge had been fenced off in order to provide some special seating for a regatta on the Thames. The plaintiff tried to climb over this fence and a clerk of the bridge company tried to stop him. Two policemen were then called and they prevented him from going any further. Indeed, he was arrested for breach of the peace and spent a night in the cells. The plaintiff's claim for false imprisonment failed because he was always free to leave the bridge by going back the way he had come. As the judge explained, the restraint had not been total:

> *I have no doubt that in general, if one man compels another to stay in any given place against his will, he imprisons that other just as much as if he locked him up in a room ... But I cannot bring my mind to the conclusion that, if one man merely obstructs the passage of another, in a particular direction, whether by threat of personal violence or otherwise, leaving him at liberty to stay where he is or to go in any other direction if he pleases, he can be said thereby to imprison him ... But imprisonment is, as I apprehend, a total restraint of the liberty of the person, for however short a time, and not a partial obstruction of his will, whatever inconvenience it may bring on him.*

Neither can a person complain about false imprisonment if he or she has agreed to terms in a contract which impose certain obligations as to when or how he may leave. An attempt to sue an Australian ferry company failed in *Robinson* v. *Balmain New Ferry Ltd* 1910 when a man insisted on leaving a ferry when he learned that there was to be a twenty-minute delay in its journey across the harbour. He was asked to pay a penny and was prevented from leaving when he refused. There had been a notice erected as to the ferry company's terms:

> A fare of one penny must be paid on entering or leaving the wharf. No exception will be made to this rule, whether the passenger has travelled by the ferry or not.

A few years later the House of Lords considered the claim of a miner who had been stuck down the pit. In *Herd* v. *Weardale Steel Coal and Coke Co.* 1915 a miner asked to come up in the cage before the end of his shift. There was some delay in taking him to the surface and, when sued for false imprisonment, his employers relied on the principle of *volenti non fit injuria* and argued that Herd was only entitled to use the cage on the terms on which he was allowed to go down. Viscount Haldane LC, rejecting Herd's claim, drew this parallel:

> If a man gets into an express train and the doors are locked pending its arrival at its destination, he is not entitled, merely because the train has been stopped by signals, to call for the doors to be opened to let him out. He has entered the train on the terms that he is to be conveyed to a certain station without the opportunity of getting out before that, and he must abide by the terms on which he has entered the train.

The principle of *volenti* can also be extended to those who willingly give up their freedom to leave. Many a solicitor will have spent time locked in a police cell (naturally only as a visitor to his criminal client) and could not claim for false imprisonment in those circumstances although it might be different if some prankster in a blue serge suit and silver buttons pretended to forget that the solicitor was also behind the adamantine lock of the cell door.

The solicitor's client himself may not succeed in any claim for false imprisonment just because he is released from the police station without charge. For example, in *Mohammed-Holgate* v. *Duke* 1983 the plaintiff sued the police for false imprisonment after she had been arrested on suspicion of having stolen some jewellery. It was found that the police officer who arrested her had acted in good faith. She was questioned at the police station and released after about six hours. The Court of Appeal held that where the police have reasonable cause for suspecting that a person had committed an arrestable offence they could detain that person under arrest not only to see if those suspicions were justified but also to seek further material evidence.

Neither would that solicitor's client have any claim against the prison governor if he were imprisoned after a properly conducted lawful trial. Judges, as seen in Unit 2.5, enjoy an immunity from this sort of action at the hands of disgruntled defendants. Teachers at school, who are said to stand *in loco parentis* (in the place of a parent), traditionally had the implied consent of the parents themselves not only to keep the little cherubs later after school in that widespread form of juvenile imprisonment known as detention but also to inflict violence on their children during the supposedly happiest days of their lives. These practices of flogging the nation's young gentlemen, long hallowed as part of school culture even before Tom Brown's schooldays, have now been brought to an end firstly in state schools and, more recently, even in those establishments where corporal punishment had remained a privilege of the few.

Rather than just sitting back and counting the tiles on the wall until one is eventually released – and then suing – the law recognises two other forms of remedy. Firstly, a person falsely imprisoned may resort to **self-help**. In other words, if smashing windows, climbing down drainpipes or barging a locked door off its hinges would secure escape such attempt is proper. A more judicial remedy is that made available by one of the most ancient forms of writ known to English law. By a writ of *habeas corpus* (Latin for 'you have the body') the courts are enabled to inquire into the legality of a person's detention. Magna Carta itself recognised the right of the individual not to be unlawfully detained and this principle was further enshrined in Habeas Corpus Acts dating back to 1679. Application may be made to the High Court for an order directed to whoever is responsible for the applicant's detention (and it is usually the police, a prison governor or the immigration authorities) to produce that body at court. Whenever the liberty of the subject is at stake such cases take precedence over all others. Indeed, in cases of emergency an application for habeas corpus could even be made at night to a judge at his home. In practice, however, it is rare for a court to order the immediate release of a person from police custody.

c) Trespass to goods

The thief who steals another's property obviously commits an offence under the Theft Act 1968 (see Unit 3.6). At the same time he commits a civil wrong in depriving the owner of his property and converting it to his own use – either by using it or perhaps by selling it. This is just one example of the ways in which unlawful interference with goods can be committed. Property may be stolen or destroyed or simply not returned on time. In their own ways, these problems were all the subject of separate consideration in this old area of English law. Trespass to goods may be regarded as the direct physical interference with another's possession of goods without lawful justification. **Possession** is all that is required for a claimant to have a right of action. It is not necessary that the claimant is actually the **owner** of those goods. For example, if Tom kindly lends Dick his car for the evening it is Dick who is in possession of it but Tom remains the owner. Just how far the old childhood saying 'Finders keepers, losers weepers' accurately reflects contemporary English jurisprudence had to be decided by the Court of Appeal in *Parker* v. *British Airways Board* 1982. Alan Parker was an obviously honest man. One day he was in the international executive lounge at Heathrow Airport which was operated by British Airways. Mr Parker found a gold bracelet and handed it to an employee of British Airways (in the words of their advertising slogan, the 'world's favourite airline') along with a note of his own name and address. Mr Parker asked the airline to return the bracelet to him if it was not claimed by the true owner. Unfortunately, the airline forgot another part of its own advertisement and failed to 'take more care'. They simply sold the bracelet and kept the proceeds of £850. They certainly were not Mr Parker's favourite airline and he sued them for the £850. The difficulty on these simple facts was that, on one argument, Mr Parker had enjoyed possession of the bracelet because he picked it up. On the other hand, British Airways also had possession of the bracelet because they also had possession of the whole lounge. The Court of Appeal considered the nature and extent of the control exercised by the airline over their departure lounge and held that the airline had no superior claim to that of Mr Parker. As Donaldson LJ, as he then was, put it:

> As the true owner has never come forward, it is a case of 'finders keepers'.

Trespass to goods is said to be actionable *per se*: that is, the person in possession need not show that he actually suffered any loss. He must, nevertheless, show that the defendant's actions were other than purely accidental – they must be shown to have been intentional or at least negligent.

Some of the law on this topic is extremely old. For example, in considering the claim of Mr Parker against British Airways, the Court of Appeal also had regard to an old case heard in 1722 when a chimney sweeper's boy found a jewel. One old form of trespass to goods was known as **detinue**, the wrongful retention of goods. For example, Amy borrowed Gillian's dress to go to a party but then refused to give it back. In practice, there was often overlap between detinue and another form of trespass to goods known as **conversion**, which involves dealing with another person's goods in a way which is inconsistent with that other person's title to those goods. For example, Amy now sells Gillian's dress to Helen.

Although the old principles are still relevant to the modern law the present position is now governed by the Torts (Interference with Goods) Act 1977, another piece of legislation stemming from a report of the Law Commission (see Unit 1.9). This Act abolished the old action of detinue but the scope of conversion is now extended to cover cases of loss or destruction of goods. The term 'wrongful interference with goods' covers conversion, trespass to goods and negligence so far as it results in damage to goods or to an interest in goods. Under the Act, the court may give certain specific relief to a claimant. A judge may make any one of the following three orders:

1. an order for delivery of the goods and for payment of any consequential damages; or
2. an order for delivery of the goods, but giving the defendant the alternative of paying damages by reference to the value of any goods, together in either alternative with payment of any consequential damages; or
3. damages.

Where a claimant receives damages on the basis that he is being compensated for the whole of his interest in the goods, his interest in the goods is extinguished by payment of those damages.

Problems and potential injustice can arise where the person sued for wrongful interference has actually improved the goods in question. For example, if Tom has acted in the mistaken but honest belief that he had good title to Dick's car there is provision in section 6 of the Act for Tom to receive an allowance for any increase in the value of the car, for example, through Tom respraying it.

6.7 Defences

Unit 3.4 demonstrated the need for the criminal law to provide some form of defence in order that a person may avoid unmerited punishment and possible social opprobrium. The law of tort (or torts), the concepts of which are closely allied to parts of the criminal law, similarly requires some defence to claims which might otherwise be unfairly brought against the citizen.

As with criminal defences, most of the defences in tort can be raised to meet any kind of claim. Some, however, are more specific and more limited. For instance, just as diminished responsibility is a limited defence in that it may only be used to reduce a charge of murder to manslaughter (see Unit 3.5), the defence in tort of 'fair comment' is by its very nature only a defence to a claim in defamation (see Unit 6.10).

In allowing the defence of **inevitable accident,** the law recognises that even the Reasonable Man can be involved in an accident despite all his characteristic efforts to take reasonable precautions. The law expects people to consider prudently any reasonable probabilities but, said Lord Dunedin, 'they are not bound to guard against fantastic possibilities'.

As in criminal law, **self-defence** is a valid defence and may be raised in reply to an action for assault and battery. **Necessity** affords a defence to an otherwise tortious act where the immediate situation was very grave. The severe limitations on this defence to a criminal charge are again present, and in *Southwark London Borough Council* v. *Williams* 1971 the Court of Appeal held that necessity was no defence to a claim for possession of a house – even if the squatters had nowhere else to live, they could not live there. Lord Denning MR had an eye on public policy when he warned:

> *The doctrine so enunciated must, however, be carefully circumscribed. Else necessity would open the door to many an excuse.*

A more thoroughly tried and tested defence is that of **statutory authority**. This doctrine is based on the concept of Parliament as the supreme source of law: if our rulers, in their infinite understanding of what is good for us, lend their approval to what would otherwise be a tort, the courts are powerless to intervene. For example, there is no legal way to prevent a small army of civil servants from committing what would be trespass were anyone else in their shoes: policemen, VAT officials, Customs officers and television-licensing officials are just a handful of the many people whom Parliament now refuses to allow you to show the door.

In the nineteenth century, the railways had good reason to be grateful for this defence for it allowed them to commit various acts which would otherwise have been trespass or nuisance. So it was in *Vaughan* v. *Taff Vale Railway Company* 1860, when a spark from a locomotive set five acres of the plaintiff's woodland ablaze. The court held that, because of the protection afforded by the Railway Consolidation Act 1845, the railway company was not liable for the damage done.

More recently, in *Department of Transport* v. *North West Water Authority* 1983 a water main had burst under a main street which suffered damage as a result. When the water authority was sent the bill for the cost of repairs they were able to rely on the Public Utilities Street Works Act 1950 which absolved them from liability for the nuisance caused by the burst main.

The defence of *volenti*, unknown to the criminal law, requires close attention. This line of defence rests on the fact that the law still allows some freedom of individual choice and recognises that people should be allowed to run certain risks.

Before being put under the surgeon's knife a patient in hospital will be asked to sign a form by which he or she consents to the operation. The legal effect of this form is to excuse the surgeon from what might otherwise have been a serious assault and battery in removing a patient's appendix. The patient's consent prevents him from suing because, put in the traditional Latin, *volenti non fit injuria* ('no cause of action arises to someone who voluntarily accepted the risk').

Some of the considerations applying to this doctrine were also relevant to exemption clauses examined in Unit 4.7. As with exemption clauses, there is no need to show that the claimant signed anything: his acceptance of the risk may be deduced from his behaviour. For example, if you insist on charging round a muddy field carrying an oval-shaped ball there is a good chance that some heavily built prop-forward will do his best to relieve you of the ball with little ceremony and, as you soak the resulting bruises in a bath afterwards, you may reflect that by taking part in the game you had voluntarily accepted the risk of injury.

Even spectators at some sports have to accept the risk of injury. For instance, in *Wooldridge* v. *Sumner* 1962, a horse left the arena at the White City Stadium and injured Edmond Wooldridge, a photographer. The Court of Appeal held that Mr Wooldridge was not entitled to damages for as Diplock LJ explained:

> *A person attending a game or competition takes the risk of any damage caused to him by any act of a participant done in the course of and for the purposes of the game or competition, notwithstanding that such act may involve an error of judgment or a lapse of skill, unless the participant's conduct is such as to evince a reckless disregard of the spectator's safety.*

It is vital to note that a person may appreciate the presence of some risk but may still not consent to it. Knowledge is not to be taken as consent. For instance, a pedestrian knows that he runs a risk every time he crosses the road but that does not mean that he consents to being run down with the same monotonous regularity. The point was made more profoundly by the House of Lords in *Smith* v. *Baker* 1891. Smith was employed by Baker and was cutting holes in a rock. Nearby, some fellow-employees were operating a crane to lift stones. Every now and then they swung one over Smith's head without warning. Smith was aware of the danger but went on working for some months. Almost inevitably, the day came when a stone succumbed to the inexorable force of gravity because it had not been properly tied up. Smith now sued his employers. The House of Lords held that *volenti* did not apply and that, although Smith went on working when he knew of the danger, such work did not stop him recovering damages from his employers because of their negligence.

The Court of Appeal confirmed that mere knowledge of the danger is some steps removed from a voluntary acceptance of the risk in *Nettleship* v. *Weston* 1971. Mrs Weston wanted to learn to drive and so asked Eric Nettleship, a friend, to give her lessons. He checked on her insurance policy and then agreed to supervise her. During the third lesson, Mrs Weston panicked badly; the car ended up around a street lamp and Mr Nettleship injured his leg. It was argued for Mrs Weston that Mr Nettleship had voluntarily accepted the risk of injury when he agreed to give her lessons. The Court of Appeal rejected that defence, holding that a driver was not entitled to claim the defence of *volenti* merely on the ground that his passenger knew of the risk of injury or was willing to take that risk. Rather, it had to be shown that the passenger accepted for himself the risk of injury arising from the driver's lack of experience. The fact that Mr Nettleship had been careful to check that Mrs Weston's insurance was in order afforded good evidence that he was not just prepared to accept the risk of injury. The test was made clear by Lord Denning MR:

> *Knowledge of the risk of injury is not enough. Nor is willingness to take the risk of injury. Nothing will suffice short of an agreement to waive any claim for negligence. The plaintiff must agree, expressly or impliedly, to waive any claim for any injury that may befall him due to the lack of reasonable care by the defendant: or more accurately, due to the failure of the defendant to measure up to the standard of care that the law requires of him.*

The continuing relevance of this principle was confirmed by the Court of Appeal in *Morris* v. *Murray* 1990. Gary Morris and Harry Murray had spent much of the day drinking. Harry Murray, who held a pilot's licence, then suggested that he and Gary should go for a flight in Harry's light aircraft. The flight was short and chaotic. The plane crashed; the pilot was killed and Gary Morris was severely injured. The Court of Appeal held that the pilot's drunkenness had been so extreme and so glaring that the claim brought by Gary Morris was barred by the defence of *volenti non fit injuria* because, in such circumstances, the passenger had implicitly waived his right to damages.

The courts will not normally admit the defence of *volenti* in a case where a person has been hurt while going to the rescue of someone in danger. Common morality and public policy require that such a person should be praised and certainly not prevented from recovering damages for any injuries he may have suffered on account of his gallantry. As an American judge remarked:

> *Danger invites rescue. The cry of distress is the summons to relief. The law does not ignore these reactions of the mind in tracing conduct to its consequences. It recognizes them as normal.*

The rescuer will not, therefore, normally be regarded as having freely consented to the risk of danger. For example, in *Haynes* v. *Harwood* 1934 the plaintiff was a police officer who, while he was on duty in the police station, saw some runaway horses charging down a busy street full of young children. He bravely rushed out and managed to stop the horses but was injured in doing so. He now sued the owner of the horses who had left his van unattended.

The Court of Appeal held that in leaving the van unattended the defendant's servant had been negligent. The defendant now raised the defence of *volenti*. In rejecting that defence Maugham LJ said:

> *In my opinion the police constable was not in any sense a volunteer ... There is a general duty to protect the life and property of the inhabitants ... In my opinion they [the police] are not mere lookers-on when an accident takes place, or seems likely to take place ... At any rate, they have a moral duty to intervene in such a case as the present where it appeared, and rightly appeared, to the plaintiff that there was a reasonable chance of preventing a most serious accident.*

Nevertheless, not everyone who interferes will be able to recover damages. Before refusing to recognise the defence of *volenti* the judge must decide how seriously the public had been endangered. That is why in *Cutler* v. *United Dairies Ltd* 1933 the plaintiff rescuer was unable to recover. A runaway horse was stopped by Mr Cutler, who was injured as a consequence. This time, however, the horse was not in a busy London street, nor was there any crowd; it was in a meadow and not endangering anyone. Against such a factual background, the court held that the horse's owners could raise the defence of *volenti* and decided that Mr Cutler had freely undertaken to run the risk of injury.

The courts' refusal to allow people to escape the direct consequences of their negligence is seen clearly in the decision of the Court of Appeal in *Baker* v. *T.E. Hopkins & Son Ltd* 1959. The defendants were a small firm of contractors who had been given the job of cleaning out a well. They brought in a petrol-driven pump to help them but that produced a lethal concentration of carbon monoxide in the well and two workmen were overcome by the fumes. A doctor was summoned and, against all advice, insisted on going down the well. He too, succumbed to the fumes and died as a result. His widow, Mrs Baker, now sued the contractors. Had her husband freely consented to the risk? Ormrod LJ (himself a doctor as well as a lawyer) thought not:

> *The important word is* volenti *and not* scienti. *Dr Baker may well have had knowledge of the risk he was running, but that is wholly different from saying that he freely and voluntarily took the risk. He was a member of the medical profession, schooled in the tradition to do all he could to save life and relieve suffering. In addition, he was a brave man and, in my view, he acted under the compulsion of his instincts as a brave man and a doctor. This would, I think, be sufficient to dispose of the defence of* volenti non fit injuria *but in any event the doctrine would not, in my judgment, apply in a case of an attempted rescue when the act was the natural and foreseeable result of the negligence of the defendants.*

The defendants had caused the danger; they must pay for the consequences. Morris LJ summarised the reasons for the decision:

> ...*what he did was brought about and caused by the negligence of the company. In those circumstances the company cannot say that he was a volunteer.*

The liability of a person rescued to compensate those injured through rescuing him was considered in *Harrison* v. *British Railway Board* 1981. The plaintiff, Robin Harrison, was employed as a guard on the Southern Region. As a train was pulling out of Weybridge station, the plaintiff guard saw a man hanging on to a door handle of one of the moving coaches. In fact it was the station foreman, who should have known better. Mr Harrison signalled to the driver to stop. Very bravely, the guard then jumped from the train to the platform in the hope of being able to support the station foreman. In the event, Mr Harrison was thrown across the platform and sustained serious injury. The station foreman had very foolishly tried to board a moving train but, when sued, argued that he had not owed his rescuer any duty of care. At trial, the court held that the foreman had created a dangerous situation through lack of reasonable care for his own safety. Further, said the judge, the foreman ought reasonably to have foreseen that the guard might come to his aid. For those reasons, the foreman was held liable for the plaintiff's injuries which, after a deduction of 20 per cent for his own contributory negligence (see below), were worth £5,320.

The position of an injured rescuer was considered again by the House of Lords in *Ogwo* v. *Taylor* 1987. Michael Ogwo, a fireman, was called to a fire at the home of the defendant who had set fire to his house by his use of a blowlamp to remove some old paint. The fireman was injured and suffered very serious burns. Even accepting that he had been negligent in setting fire to his home, did Taylor have any responsibility in law to a fireman? Ought Taylor reasonably to have foreseen that Michael Ogwo would be injured in helping to save Taylor's home? The House of Lords held that a person who negligently started a fire was liable for any injury sustained by a firefighter, even though a firefighter undertook to bear the ordinary risks of his calling. In any event, said the judge (applying the earlier case of *Haynes* v. *Harwood* 1934) the householder was also liable on the principle that a person, who by negligence created some peril to the life or safety of others, owed a duty to a third person who, acting reasonably, came to the rescue.

a) Contributory negligence

A defendant who has raised the defence of *volenti* may well cover himself by further alleging that the claimant was guilty of contributory negligence – meaning that the claimant was also to blame because his own negligence contributed to his miseries.

Before the Second World War, such an allegation could be a complete defence to the claim. Of course, this could be very unfair to a claimant who was, say 1 per cent to blame while the defendant was 99 per cent responsible, for the more negligent party could then avoid all liability.

This injustice was remedied by the more logical Law Reform (Contributory Negligence) Act 1945. Where the claimant is found to have been partly at fault, the effect of this Act is to allow the judge to knock off a certain proportion of the damages he would have awarded, so as to take account of the claimant's own negligence.

Section 1 provides:

> Where any person suffers damage as the result partly of his own fault and partly of the fault of any other person or persons, a claim in respect of that damage should not be defeated by reason of the fault of the person suffering the damage, but the damages recoverable in respect thereof shall be reduced to such an extent as the court thinks just and equitable having regard to the claimant's share in the responsibility for the damage.

'Fault' is defined so as to include not only common-law negligence but also breach of statutory duty or other act or omission. The concept of 'negligence' remains unaltered and so the standard of care required of the claimant is not changed. 'Damage' in this context includes personal injury.

Say, by way of illustration, that O'Reilly, a builder's labourer of no great intellectual capacity, forgets that his boss told him always to wear a safety helmet. O'Reilly is sitting down for his mid-afternoon break one fine day, wondering how many lumps to put in his tea, when a particularly large lump appears on his head as a half-brick bounces off his exposed cranium. Even if O'Reilly manages to prove that his employers had been negligent in failing to provide a safe system of work, the court will deduct an amount from the damages that reflects his own negligence in not wearing the helmet provided.

This bit of everyday common sense has been placed on a statutory footing under the Health and Safety at Work Act 1974 which, in section 7, makes it the duty

> of every employee while at work to take reasonable care for the health and safety of himself and of other persons who may be affected by his acts or omissions at work.

There are two kinds of case where the courts are reluctant to make findings of contributory negligence: those involving workers and children.

The courts appreciate how noise, heat and sheer boredom can exert a spectacularly comatose effect on the workers on a production line and, therefore, they do not penalise every unwise move by the employee as negligence.

Similarly (as we saw when considering occupiers' liability in Unit 6.4), the courts appreciate that young children, in their endless capacity for adventure and mischief, are less likely than adults fully to recognise the attendant dangers and, on this account, findings of contributory negligence against young children are rare.

The Act requires the court to reduce the claimant's damages

> to such an extent as the court thinks just and equitable having regard to the claimant's share in the responsibility for the damage.

The percentage to be deducted is a matter for the judge. Some indication of the way in which the courts work may be gleaned from looking at some decided cases such as *Sayers* v. *Harlow UDC* 1958. Mrs Eileen Sayers had entered a lavatory cubicle. Unfortunately, the door jammed and she was unable to leave. After some time spent shouting to no avail she tried to climb over the top of the cubicle door. In her struggles to escape, she rested her right foot on the lavatory roll and fixture. True to its mechanical function the roll rolled and Mrs Sayers lost her balance and fell. The Court of Appeal held that, while the local council had certainly been negligent so had Mrs Sayers in allowing her balance to depend on the roll. The court, accordingly, reduced her damages by 25 per cent so as to take account of her own carelessness.

One common application of the principle of contributory negligence is to be found in what lawyers call 'running-down' cases – where, on the evidence called, it often must seem that two cars, each travelling on the correct side of the road at 30 mph, have collided head on. One motorist may have been less negligent than the other but still be found to have contributed either to the initial collision or to any injuries sustained.

For many years it has been held to be contributory negligence for a passenger injured in a road accident to have accepted a lift from a driver who was affected by drink. More recently, the courts had to consider whether any deduction should be made for a claimant's failure to wear a seat belt. At first, there were conflicting decisions but in *Froom* v. *Butcher* 1975 the Court of Appeal laid down guidelines for other judges as to the amount to be deducted for failure to wear a seat belt in the days, of course, before the wearing of such contraptions was made compulsory. In giving judgment, Lord Denning MR first of all reviewed the relevant principles:

> *Negligence depends on a breach of duty, whereas contributory negligence does not. Negligence is a man's carelessness in breach of duty to* others. *Contributory negligence is a man's carelessness in looking after* his *own safety. He is guilty of* contributory *negligence if he ought reasonably to have foreseen that if he did not act as a reasonable prudent man, he might hurt himself.*

Lord Denning MR then went on to lay down what are today regarded as the correct deductions for such contributory negligence. If the use of a seat belt would have prevented altogether the injuries suffered by the claimant then the court would deduct 25 per cent of the damages which would be due on full liability. If, on the other hand, the use of the belt would only have made a considerable difference then the court would deduct 15 per cent as reflecting the injured party's own contributory negligence.

6.8 *Special classes of liability*

We have already seen how the criminal law, by dispensing in some instances with the ingredients of *mens rea*, has provided for the conviction of people who are morally blameless (see Unit 3.1). Similar principles operate in certain circumstances in tort. So it is that, for reasons of social convenience and economic necessity, a man may be liable in damages for events that took place while he personally was miles away.

a) Breach of statutory duty

In Unit 1.3, we saw how Dick was still liable to pay damages to Tom even though he had just had to pay £750 in fines in the magistrates' court. Criminal sanctions do not generally extinguish civil remedies – on the contrary, they are evidence in those fresh proceedings. That is particularly so where one party has been in breach of statutory duty: that is, where he has failed to comply with obligations imposed on him by Act of Parliament.

Cases involving industrial accidents are obvious applications of this rule. Parliament has long been rightly concerned with the health, comfort and convenience of employees whose working day may be spent amid noisy, smelly and potentially dangerous machinery. Prolonged exposure to noise helps only to boost the sale of hearing-aids, nasty smells may be much more than a mere olfactory inconvenience for they may well mask the presence of poisonous gas, and the butcher who does not put a guard on his bacon-slicer may even find that his employee literally has a finger in every pie.

In attempts to protect workmen from the attendant risks at work, Parliament has, over the years, passed a number of Acts to compel employers to take proper precautions for the safety of those who work for them. In particular, present-day employers must pay particular heed to the provisions of the Factories Act 1961, the Offices, Shops and Railway Premises Act 1963 and the Health and Safety at Work Act 1974.

Under these and other similar statutes an employer who fails to meet Parliament's requirements of him is liable to conviction and punishment in the criminal courts. So, if on her first day at work with Mr Lamb, the local butcher, Dotty is rashly allowed to operate a bacon-slicer that has no protective guard on it, Mr Lamb might be fined in the magistrates' court for his breach of statutory duty in failing to comply with section 14 of the Factories Act 1961, which provides that:

> Every dangerous part of any machinery ... shall be securely fenced unless it is in such a position or of such construction as to be as safe to every person employed or working on the premises as it would be if securely fenced.

That conviction will be good evidence for Dotty if she subsequently sues her employers for any injury she has sustained; she must, of course, be able to prove that her injuries were the direct result of that breach.

Moreover, a claimant must prove that he or she was one of the people whom Parliament intended to protect by the passage of the Act then being considered by the court. This requirement was raised in *Hartley* v.

Mayoh & Co. 1954. The fire brigade was called to a factory fire. The electric wiring at this factory did not comply with complex regulations laid down by Parliament to cover all appliances which were 'of such a nature as to cause risk of bodily injury to the persons employed'. One of the firemen was electrocuted. The Court of Appeal held that, as the fireman was not one of the 'persons employed' whom the regulations were intended to protect, the defendants were not liable for their obvious breach. It would, of course, have been different had one of the employees been electrocuted; any widow would then have been able to recover damages for his death.

Finally, a claimant must also prove that the injury suffered was the sort of damage that the regulations had been intended to prevent. In *Gorris* v. *Scott* 1874 the defendant was a ship-owner who had agreed to bring the plaintiff's sheep to England. Unfortunately, some of the sheep were washed overboard and drowned. The plaintiff now sought to rely on regulations that required every place being occupied by animals being brought to the United Kingdom to be divided into pens. There were no such pens on board the defendant's ship. Nevertheless, the court held that, as the order had been intended only to prevent the spread of disease, the plaintiff had no case, for, as Kelly CB said:

> *The Act was passed merely for sanitary purposes, in order to prevent animals in a state of infectious disease from communicating it to other animals with which they might come into contact ... But the damage complained of here is something totally apart from the object of the Act of Parliament.*

b) Vicarious liability

In Unit 2.6 it was suggested that because the van-driver might be a 'man of straw' a claimant would be on safer ground if he sued the driver's employer as well. That an employer is liable for the tortious acts of his or her employees is one common example of how someone who was miles away from the accident is still liable to pay for the errors of another. Such liability for the acts of another is said to be **vicarious** (meaning 'substituted').

The capitalist economic system requires that there should be some differential between the contribution made by an employee to the success of the business and his wage. The corollary of this is that an employer who stands to benefit from his employee's labours should also be required to compensate anyone who is injured by that employee's actions. Of course, an employer will only be liable for the acts or omissions of his employees while they were acting in the course of their employment. If, on the way home from work or while out on a Sunday afternoon drive to the country, a man runs down an old lady on a zebra crossing she must look to that driver (and in practice his insurance company) for compensation. His employer is then in no way liable. On the other hand, if the old lady were knocked down by a firm's van between 9 a.m. and 5 p.m., Monday to Friday, she should normally look to the employer for redress. In such a case the old lady would have to prove two things: that the driver was the employer's servant and that the driver was acting in the course of his employment.

Who is a servant? Any building company will seek to justify the astronomical cost of its houses by blaming the high cost of labour today. People work for the company, however, in different ways. At its head office there will be architects, secretaries and cleaners. On site there will be carpenters, bricklayers and plumbers. In law, their status differs as much as their wages. For example, the secretary will be paid so much money per annum and from that her take-home wage is calculated, deductions being made for tax and National Insurance contributions. This is because she is an employee – a servant of the company, whose contract is said by lawyers to be a **contract of service**.

Bricklayers and similar craftsmen are more likely to be self-employed, offering their services to whoever will pay the asking price. As a matter of law they are not employees but **independent contractors** whose contract with the builders is said to be a **contract for services**.

Such a contract is relatively straightforward. The need to differentiate the categories more precisely has led the courts to employ two tests in distinguishing the servant (whose negligence can cost his employer dear) from the independent contractor (who generally must still pay for his own mistakes although European law has recently made some inroads into this principle). The difficulties which faced the courts were neatly examined by Denning LJ, as he then was, when, in *Stevenson* v. *McDonnell* 1952, he said:

> *It is often easy to recognize a contract of service when you see it, but difficult to say wherein the distinction lies. A ship's master, a chauffeur and a reporter on the staff of a newspaper are all employed under a contract of service; but a ship's pilot, a taxi-man, and a newspaper contributor are all employed under a contract for services.*

Two particular tests require examination.

The contract test   Initially, the courts ask what degree of control was exercised over the way in which a person did his or her job. If he was told what to do, where and when to do it and, indeed, how to do it there is some evidence that the person was a servant. The difficulty in this test, however, is growing increasingly apparent: for example, accountants and solicitors may well be the servants of a company even though the complex and intricate nature of their work is such that the managing director is scarcely in a position to dictate how these highly trained servants are to discharge their duties and also to do so in compliance with their own professional standards. This test's inherent weakness became particularly obvious in the so-called 'hospital cases', where its application exculpated hospitals for the negligence of doctors on the basis that the medically unqualified hospital administrator was scarcely in a position to stand over the surgeon as he wielded his scalpel and advise him, say, how best to remove an appendix.

The integration test   In the early 1950s Denning LJ, as he then was, put forward this alternative test. Having already reflected on the different contractual implications of a ship's master and a ship's pilot, he continued:

> *One feature which seems to run through the instances is that, under a contract of service, a man is employed as part of a business, and his work is done as an integral part of the business; whereas under a contract for services, his work, although done for the business, is not integrated into it but is only accessory to it.*

In practice, the courts have shown that both tests are relevant, as indeed are matters such as the nature of the work, how much say the company has over its progress, who supplies the equipment, how payment is made (in particular, whether tax is deducted by the company under the 'Pay As You Earn' scheme or whether it is attended to by the recipient when he prepares his year's accounts on a 'Schedule D' basis) and, of course, whose is the power of hiring and firing.

When is he a servant? Having determined who is a servant, the courts must then be satisfied that he was acting 'in the course of his employment' before his employer can be held liable in respect of his actions. Needless to say, no employer actually engages people to run down old ladies on zebra crossings but if he employs someone to deliver his products he must take the blame if, while on his way, the driver has an accident. It is a different matter, however, if when employed to deliver goods to various shops in town, the driver prefers to take his girlfriend to the seaside (when, as lawyers say, he is on a 'frolic of his own').

There is no clear-cut test for deciding when a servant is or is not acting in the course of his employment. Some indication, however, may be gleaned by comparing the court's approach to some old problems at petrol pumps.

In *Century Insurance Co. Ltd* v. *Northern Ireland Transport Board* 1942 the driver of a petrol lorry was transferring his load to the underground petrol tanks when he lit a cigarette and threw away the match with consequences too self-evident to require elaboration. The House of Lords held that this careless act had been done in the course of the driver's employment and his employers must pay up.

The unfortunate selection of men employed to supply petrol to the motoring public came before the courts again a few years later. *Warren* v. *Henlys Ltd* 1948 concerned a petrol-pump attendant who wrongly thought that a customer was driving off without paying and who expressed his doubts rather too freely for the customer's liking. On being threatened by the customer with having his behaviour reported to his boss, the attendant, as he explained to the police later, 'gave him one on the chin to get on with'. When the customer sued the garage for his injuries the court held that the employer was not liable for this act of personal vengeance by the pump attendant.

What, though, if the employee wilfully disobeys a particular instruction as to what he may or may not do or, alternatively, how he may or may not do his job? What if a hitch-hiker is injured in a road accident caused by a lorry driver who is specifically told not to give lifts to hitch-hikers? Many operators of such vehicles have notices in and around the driver's cab to the effect that no hitch-hikers are allowed to ride in that vehicle. A similar problem had arisen in *Rose* v. *Plenty* 1976 when a teenager, Leslie Rose, sued a milkman whom he had helped on the milk rounds. One day, Leslie Rose was injured as a result of Mr Plenty's negligent driving of the milk-float. Clearly, the milkman himself was responsible for his negligence. As seen in Unit 2.6 it is usually wise to sue the employers as well where one defendant is their employee – after all, the employer usually has the money to meet any judgment. In this case, Leslie Rose's lawyer had also sued the dairy itself, the Co-op. They denied liability. After all, they said, there was a notice at their depot:

> Children and young persons *must not in any circumstances be employed by you* in the performance of your duties.

Nevertheless, by a majority the Court of Appeal held that the Co-op must pay. The court held that these specific instructions did not actually limit or define the scope of the milkman's employment: all it did was govern the way in which the employee carried out his defined duties of delivering pintas and collecting the money. As Lord Denning MR explained:

> *In the present case it seems to me that the course of Mr Plenty's employment was to distribute the milk, collect the money and to bring back the bottles to the van. He got or allowed this young boy, Leslie Rose, to do part of that business which was the employer's business. It seems to me that although prohibited, it was conduct which was within the course of the employment; ... this case falls within those in which the prohibition affects only the conduct within the sphere of the employment and did not take the conduct outside the sphere altogether.*

Whether a fellow employee was acting in the course of his employment or had embarked upon a frolic of his own fell to be decided in *Harrison* v. *Michelin Tyre Company Limited* 1985. The plaintiff, Frederick Harrison, worked with a man called Smith at the defendant's company. The plaintiff, a tool grinder, was at his machine one December day as Mr Smith, then acting in the course of his employment, tipped the plaintiff off his board by way of a joke. In holding the employers liable, the judge took the view that Mr Smith had, in the middle of his employment, and for a matter literally of seconds only, done something that amounted to an act of complete folly. Such general skylarking was not so divergent from his employment for Mr Smith to have been on a frolic of his own. Accordingly, the employers were liable for a fellow employee's particular concept of a practical joke.

Independent contractors If the person responsible for the damage is not a servant but, rather, is an independent contractor his customer will not generally be held vicariously liable.

The position, however, is different in certain circumstances.

<u>Where the activity was ultra-dangerous</u> In *Honeywill* v. *Larkin Brothers* 1933 a firm of acoustics specialists called in independent contractors to take flash photographs of the inside of a cinema where they had done some work. They wanted the photographs for publicity purposes. The

photographer operated an old-fashioned flash-gun which used magnesium powder. The powder exploded rather too near the stage curtains which went up in smoke. The Court of Appeal held that, because of the hazards involved in flash photography at that time, the acoustics firm was liable for the damage caused by their photographer. Slesser LJ explained the position when he said:

> *The principle is that if a man does work on or near another's property which involves danger to that property unless proper care is taken, he is liable to the owners ... for damage resulting to it from the failure to take proper care, and is equally liable if, instead of doing the work himself, he procures another whether agent, servant or otherwise, to do it for him.*

Where the activity was carried on on the highway   The defendant in *Tarry* v. *Ashton* 1876 rented a house in the Strand in London. On the front of the house there was a large and heavy lamp which he had asked an experienced gas-fitter to examine. About a year later the lamp fell on the plaintiff. The court held that the defendant had a duty to keep the lamp in proper repair and was liable for failing to discharge that duty even though he had relied on the gas-fitter.

Where the selection of independent contractor was negligent   We have already examined a common application of this exception when dealing with occupiers' liability (see Unit 6.4).

c) Animals

Every dog, it is said, is allowed his first bite. The second may come rather more expensive for his owner, because liability for damage done by animals is 'strict'. The postman savaged by a pet poodle does not have to prove negligence on the part of the owner.

The law used to impose liability on the owner of an animal belonging to a dangerous species (when it was said to be *ferae naturae*) such as lions and tigers, and also on the owner of an animal of a species not normally dangerous (*mansuetae naturae*) who, nevertheless, knew of that animal's uncharacteristic propensity for violence.

... uncharacteristic propensity for violence

This concept (if not also the Latin terms) was retained by Parliament when it codified the law in the Animals Act 1971 which replaced the old common-law rules.

Section 2 of this Act provides that, in the case of an animal belonging to a dangerous species, the keeper is liable for any damage done. It further provides that the keeper of an animal which does not belong to a dangerous species shall be liable if:

(a) the damage is of a kind which the animal, unless restrained, was likely to cause or which, if caused by the animal, was likely to be severe; and

(b) the likelihood of the damage or of its being severe was due to characteristics of the animal which are not normally found in animals of the same species or are not normally so found except at particular times or in particular circumstances; and

(c) those characteristics were known to that keeper or were at any time known to a person who at that time had charge of the animal as that keeper's servant or, where that keeper is the head of a household, were known to another keeper of the animal who is a member of that household and under the age of sixteen.

The Act does not offer any exhaustive list of what is and what is not a dangerous species. However, section 6(2) does provide:

A dangerous species is a species –

(a) which is not commonly domesticated in the British Islands; and

(b) whose fully grown animals normally have such characteristics that they are likely, unless restrained, to cause severe damage or that any damage they may cause is likely to be severe.

A doting owner may believe that little Fido would not hurt anyone but if one day Fido goes for the postman the owner must be on his guard from then on. He now knows of his pet's vicious streak and he must protect people from the sharpness of its teeth. Edmund-Davies LJ, as he then was, explained the position in *Draper* v. *Hodder* 1972 when, in dealing with a claim by a young boy who had been viciously savaged by a pack of Jack Russell terriers, he said:

> A *person keeping an animal* mansuetae naturae *which he knows has a propensity to do a particular kind of mischief is under an absolute duty to prevent it from doing that kind of mischief and is therefore liable without proof of negligence for any damage caused by the animal's acting in accordance with that known propensity. But to render the defendant liable, proof must be directed to his knowledge regarding the propensity of the individual animal whose activities have given rise to the institution of legal proceedings.*

A decade later in *Wallace* v. *Newton* 1982 Mr Justice Park (who had also tried *Draper* v. *Hodder*) had to consider the characteristics of 'Lord

Justice'. The offending beast was not some frisky member of the Court of Appeal but, rather, was a skittish horse with this eminent judicial title as his name. Elaine Wallace worked as a groom at the defendant's stables. One day, Lord Justice (who was known to be nervous and unpredictable) became violent and uncontrollable. The equine leapt forward and crushed the young groom's arm. The injury was a serious one and Miss Wallace sued. At the hearing she obviously had to prove under section 2(2)(a) of the statute that the damage which she had suffered had been of a kind which Lord Justice was likely to cause. What was it, though, that the plaintiff had to prove under section 2(2)(b) in order to establish that the likelihood of the damage 'was due to the characteristics of the animal which are not normally found in animals of the same species'? If it meant that Miss Wallace had to show that Lord Justice had a vicious tendency to injure people by attacking them her claim would fail. On the other hand, if the Act only required her to show that her injuries were due to a characteristic of Lord Justice which was unusual in a horse, she would recover substantial damages. This was an example of a judge's duty to interpret the meaning of a statute (see Unit 1.6). The judge held that the words were to be given their ordinary natural meaning and so Miss Wallace went on to win her case and recover £10,000 for her injuries.

The Act further goes on to provide a wide definition of 'keeper' so that a person is a keeper of an animal if

   (a) he owns the animal or has it in his possession; or
   (b) he is the head of a household of which a member under the age of sixteen owns the animal or has it in his possession.

In addition to making provision for the usual defence of *volenti*, and taking account of contributory negligence where this is appropriate, the Act recognises the role of guard dogs so that an owner will not be liable for injury sustained by a trespasser if it is proved that keeping the dog was not unreasonable.

The Guard Dogs Act 1976 further requires a capable handler to be present on the premises to keep the dog under control unless it is chained up. Adequate warning of the dog's presence must also be displayed; failure to comply with these requirements is an offence punishable with a fine. As the Roman satirist, Juvenal, asked nearly 2,000 years ago: 'But who is to guard the guards themselves?'

d) *Rylands* v.
**   *Fletcher***

It may be of some small consolation to anyone who lives next door to an oil refinery or a chemical plant, that if his house is blown up because of something escaping from his neighbour's land, the neighbour will be strictly liable for all damage done. This principle is known as the 'Rule in *Rylands* v. *Fletcher*' from the 1868 case of that name.

In that case, the defendant was a mill-owner who had brought in independent contractors (who were perfectly competent at their work) to build a reservoir on his land so that he could have water-power to run his mill. What neither the defendant nor the contractors had known at the time was that underneath that land lay an old mineshaft which led to the plaintiff's mine on neighbouring land. The reservoir was filled with water which escaped down the shaft and flooded the mine. The mine-owner could not prove any negligence on anyone's part. Nevertheless, the court held that the mill-owner was strictly liable for the damage to the mine.

Blackburn J propounded his test which was later approved by the House of Lords and is now regarded as definitive:

> *We think that the true rule of law is, that a person who for his own purposes brings on his lands and collects and keeps there anything likely to do mischief if it escapes, must keep it in at his peril, and if he does not do so, is* prima facie *answerable for all the damage which is the natural consequence of its escape.*

The irrelevance of negligence on the part of a defendant faced with a claim under the *Rylands* v. *Fletcher* principle was recently emphasised by the House of Lords in *Cambridge Water Company Limited* v. *Eastern Counties Leather plc* 1994. A leather manufacturer had allowed small amounts of solvent to spill onto the floor of the tannery. Over the years this solvent seeped into the soil below the tannery floor until, after a slow and long journey, it finally percolated into the strata from which the local water company extracted water through a borehole. This pollution cost the defendants over £1 million but, on appeal, the House of Lords held that strict liability could only arise if the defendant knew or ought to have foreseen that the thing which escaped might cause damage. While the storage of substantial quantities of chemicals on an industrial premises was an almost classic case of non-natural use even in an industrial complex it could not, on these facts, be said that the defendants could reasonably have foreseen that such seepage would cause pollution of the plaintiff's borehole.

In practice, if this rule is to apply, proof is required that the defendant brought something on to his land, that 'the thing' was likely to do mischief if it escaped, and that 'the thing' did in fact escape. Each constituent part of the principle requires examination.

<u>The thing was brought on to land</u>   This essentially concerns the concept of non-natural use of land – for instance, the presence of some water on land is perfectly natural but the accumulation of enormous quantities in a reservoir is not natural.

<u>The thing was likely to do mischief</u>   The vast range of such 'things' includes petrol, fire, gas, electricity, oil and explosives. It has even been extended to cover an unsavoury collection of dirty caravan-dwellers.

<u>The thing must have escaped</u>   Without actual escape from the premises there can be no liability. This limitation is illustrated by the decision in *Read* v. *Lyons* 1946. During the Second World War, a Ministry of Supply inspector was visiting a factory which made explosive shells when a shell exploded and injured her. She was not able to prove negligence on the part of the factory and instead attempted to rely on this rule. However, the House of Lords held that *Rylands* v. *Fletcher* had no application in this case because there had been no escape, the accident having happened inside the factory premises.

6.9 *Survival of actions in tort*

We saw in Unit 4.20 how claims for breach of contract have generally to be brought within six years from the date of the cause of action. Similar principles govern claims in tort although the periods are not identical. Nevertheless, the aim behind the principle is similar and Parliament has given protection to people who, but for such restrictions on stale claims, might be called upon to justify actions and conduct about which they could remember little. Documents may have been lost or destroyed and witnesses may have died or disappeared. Certainly, memories will have dimmed. In a case concerning delay in bringing a claim to trial, Lord Denning MR emphasised the risk of prejudice to defendants of having litigation hanging over their heads when he said:

> *The delay of justice is a denial of justice. Magna Carta will have none of it. '... To no-one will we deny or delay right or justice.' All through the years men have protested at the law's delays and counted it as a grievous wrong, hard to bear. Shakespeare ranks it among 'the whips and scorns of time' (Hamlet Act III, Scene 1). Dickens tells us how it 'exhausts finances, patience, courage, hope' (Bleak House).*

As with claims in contract, the statutory provisions are contained in the Limitation Act 1980, the latest in a long line of such statutes. Section 2 of the Act requires actions founded on tort to be brought within six years of the date on which the cause of action accrued.

The moment when the cause of action actually arises depends on the nature of the alleged tort. In the case of torts which are said to be actionable *per se* (such as trespass) the limitation period starts to run immediately. Where, on the other hand, the tort requires proof of damage, the period begins generally only when the damage is actually discovered or, at least, could have been discovered. So, if in the early hours of New Year's Day 2001 some inebriated driver crashed into your car you must issue proceedings by New Year's Eve 2007.

This does not mean, of course, that the judge must actually have heard the case by that date: it means only that the claimant must have issued the proceedings by that date. Once that is done the claimant may go on preparing his case even though, as with the thalidomide tragedy, the eventual award or a settlement of very complex litigation may still take some years. In contrast, where a claimant has taken no steps to get on with his claim within the relevant period, he will find that the courts refuse to hear the claim because it has become 'statute-barred'.

Where personal injury or even death has been caused, however, the limitation periods are shorter. In such cases the claim must be brought within a period of three years from either:

1. the date on which the cause of action accrued; or
2. the date of knowledge (if later) of the person injured.

This rule allowing such extension of the three-year rule is of fairly recent origin and was introduced in order to prevent injustice being caused to a claimant who did not realise that he had sustained injury, or, at least, did not realise how serious that injury was until more than three years had elapsed since the injury. Obviously, this is unlikely to be the case with a broken leg but, on the other hand, certain diseases can take a very long time to develop. In industrial medicine especially, claims based on bronchitis, emphysema, asbestosis and pneumoconiosis are not infrequently brought before the courts even though the origins of the illness may date back many years. For instance, over a lifetime's work in a factory a person may come into regular contact with asbestos. The fibres will have found their insidious way into his lungs and, although the claimant may cough and splutter from time to time, he may simply put it down to smoking too much. He may only realise the seriousness of his complaint, let alone its cause, as much as ten or more years after the first damage was done. If the standard three-year period were to be applied to such a case an obvious injustice would result. Today, therefore, such a claimant is allowed to bring his claim within three years of the date when he first had knowledge:

1. that the injury in question was significant; and
2. that the injury was attributable in whole or in part to the act or omission which is alleged to constitute negligence, nuisance or breach of duty; and
3. of the identity of the defendant.

Persons under the age of eighteen may not sue in their own names. Such people, minors in the eyes of the law, are said to be under a disability until they attain their majority. They may, however, bring their claim through someone such as a parent (now known as the claimant's **litigation friend**). Alternatively, they could wait until they are aged eighteen. The limitation period will start to run against this new adult on his eighteenth birthday. For example, a child injured at the moment of birth because of clinical negligence in the delivery room would be able to sue the hospital up to his 21st birthday which would, of course, also be the 21st anniversary of the negligence itself.

Limitation periods for negligence now have to be further considered against the background of the Latent Damage Act 1986. As the statute's title suggests, the legislation is concerned with the immensely difficult problems caused when the effects of negligence do not become manifest until many years have elapsed and, in any event, more than the six-year period which traditionally applies to actions in negligence. Say, for example, that Jerry is an architect who designs houses. One of the houses Jerry built was negligently designed but lasted ten years before Jerry's negligent design caused the roof to cave in. On a strict view of the traditional period of limitation, the negligence which caused the loss had occurred over six years earlier. Accordingly, the now homeless householder would have become statute-barred without even realising that he had any possible cause of action against Jerry. A similar problem had arisen in *Pirelli General Cable Works Ltd* v. *Oscar Faber & Partners* 1983 when the House of Lords had to consider a claim against consulting engineers who had been negligent in their design of a very tall chimney. Cracks were discovered only in 1977 although the evidence was that the cracks could not have occurred later than April 1970, the year after the engineers did their work. The House of Lords held that in those circumstances the plaintiffs were statute-barred. The court held that a cause of action in tort for negligence in the design or workmanship in a building accrued when physical damage actually occurred whether or not the plaintiff could actually have discovered that damage. In the House of Lords the judges readily accepted that such a law was both harsh and absurd and they looked forward to the prospect of reform as a result of the Law Commission's consideration of the problem. The Commission's recommendations found their way into the Latent Damage Act 1986.

The Latent Damage Act 1986 (which does not apply to personal injuries) provides for an extension to the usual six-year period so that a claimant is given three years in which to bring his claim starting from the date of actual discovery (or the date when a reasonable person would have discovered it). A longstop of protection for defendants (such as architects) is, nevertheless, provided by the inclusion (for the first time in English law) of an absolute overall period of fifteen years from the alleged act of negligence.

Cases like *Pirelli* will be very few and far between. Rather, the general principle remains and is intended to ensure some certainty and finality to the threat of litigation. The rule necessarily involves something of a compromise but takes account of views such as those of Lord Simon:

> As a means of resolution of civil contention, litigation is certainly preferable to personal violence. But it is not intrinsically a desirable activity ... Parliament has passed Acts ... limiting the time within which actions at law must be brought. Truth may thus be shut out, but society considers that truth may be bought at too high a price, that truth bought at such expense is the negation of justice.

6.10 Defamation

'Sticks and stones may break my bones but words will never hurt me.'

Not everyone is as fortunate. The result of the former may be evident when you visit the victim as he lies, swathed in best National Health Service bandages, in a hospital bed. A person attacked by words alone may not be as obviously deserving of sympathy or redress but may, in a sense, be as badly injured. For instance, would you open your mouth to a dentist who, you had heard, frequently pulled out the wrong tooth? Would you consult a solicitor rumoured to be dishonest or have your tonsils removed by a surgeon who, it was said, couldn't even carve the Sunday roast without making a mess of it? Obviously, if this sort of tale got around, the dentist, the solicitor and the surgeon wouldn't just be offended – they would be ridiculed and perhaps even impoverished for few people, if any, would still go to them. Of course, if the stories are true then they will have no redress; the public, after all, must be protected against incompetent service. On the other hand, if the rumours are unfounded then those people will have suffered unjustly. Our law, therefore, sets out to protect a person's good name from unfounded sullying.

Anyone maligned in this way may sue the rumour-monger or mudslinger for the tort of *defamation*.

Defamation is something more than a mere insult or derogatory comment but cannot safely be defined too narrowly or too precisely. How far a person is affected by unkind words will depend not just on the words used but also on the people who must then judge him. A suggestion that Auntie Flo had three whole glasses of sweet sherry last night may, in the view of the local Ladies' Temperance Society, reduce her to the ranks of fallen women. In contrast, to tell a conference of burglars, muggers and safe-blowers from the East End that it was Fingers who hurled that brick through the jeweller's window may only evoke the reaction that he was a fool to have left the best sparklers behind.

At first the solution adopted by the courts was for the judge to ask whether the statement was one which tended to bring the person 'into hatred, contempt or ridicule'.

... three whole glasses of sherry last night ...

A different criterion was adopted by the House of Lords in *Sim* v. *Stretch* 1936, where the court had to decide whether or not a suggestion that the plaintiff had been obliged to borrow money from his housemaid was defamatory. The plaintiff argued that this implied that he was not the sort of person to whom anyone ought to give credit. The defendant replied, in effect, that those words were just not reasonably capable of giving such a defamatory meaning. The House of Lords agreed with the defendant, and Lord Atkin put forward the test used today:

> *The conventional phrase exposing the plaintiff to hatred, ridicule and contempt is probably too narrow. The question is complicated by having to consider the person or class of persons whose reactions to the publication is the test of the wrongful character of the words used ... I propose in the present case the test: would the words tend to lower the plaintiff in the estimation of right-thinking members of society generally?*

Once again, the law imposes a necessarily objective test. Even so, what is defamatory will vary from one age and set of circumstances to another. So, in *Slazengers Ltd* v. *Gibbs & Co.* 1916, where it had been suggested during the course of the First World War that a company was German, the judge held that, given the circumstances in 1916, the statement had indeed been defamatory.

The present test has the merit that a person's reputation may still be affected even though not so badly as to evoke feelings of hatred, contempt or ridicule. For instance, a suggestion that a woman has been raped may well set tongues wagging – even though not with such sentiments as hatred. *Youssoupoff* v. *Metro-Goldwyn-Mayer Ltd* 1934 concerned the film *Rasputin, the mad monk*, which suggested that Princess Alexandrovna of Russia, the wife of Prince Youssoupoff, had been seduced by the clerical gentleman in question. The film company argued that, because of the necessary lack of consent on the part of the princess, it was not defamatory to say that a woman of the best character had been raped by a man of the worst. The argument did not succeed and the lady recovered £25,000 for the slur on her reputation.

In contrast, in *Byrne* v. *Deane* 1937 the court held that the words complained of were not defamatory. For some time a golf club had been running a neat line in 'one-armed bandit' gambling machines, known, not inappropriately perhaps, as 'diddlers'. The fun came to an end when the local constabulary, 'acting on information received', as they say, came to take the machines away. On the next day a bit of paper went up on the club noticeboard. It bore this poetic lament:

> For many years upon this spot
> You heard the sound of a merry bell
> Those who were rash and those who were not
> Lost and made a spot of cash
> But he who gave the game away
> May he byrnn in hell and rue the day
> *Diddleramus*

Mr Byrne argued that the peculiar mis-spelling of the word 'burn' suggested in effect that he had been telling tales out of school and, as his lawyers phrased it, had been guilty of 'underhand disloyalty' to other members of the club. The Court of Appeal held that to suggest that a citizen had reported unlawful activity to the police would not lower him in the estimation of right-thinking members of society generally, even if it had not done very much for his popularity with his fellow members.

If a newspaper publishes an article under the headline 'Beautiful Princess Raped by Mad Monk', its intended meaning is pellucidly clear. What, on the other hand, would be the position where the sub-editor accidentally gets two news items the wrong way round? The result might be that a photograph of Mr Green, whose giant marrow has won first prize at Kew Gardens, appears with the unfortunate caption: 'The police appealed yesterday for help from the public in tracing a sex offender known as *The Kew Groper*, whose photograph was also released by the police.' The mistake, though innocently made, is not very pleasant for Mr Green. Whether or not a person suffering from what lawyers called an **innuendo** has to prove knowledge of the blunder on the part of a publisher has been considered by the courts on a number of occasions.

One such case was *Hulton & Co.* v. *Jones* 1910. The *Sunday Chronicle* published a commentary on a motor-car festival in France. The article described the festive gaiety of the scene and, for a bit of local colour, added:

> ... Whist! There is Artemus Jones with a woman who is not his wife, who must be, you know – the other thing! ... Who would suppose by his goings on, that he was a churchwarden at Peckham?

At the time the newspaper published the article it thought its description only fictional. One reader, however, was not very happy about it. He was neither a churchwarden (in fact he was a barrister) nor did he live in London SE15, but his name was indeed Artemus Jones. The newspaper never intended to defame the real Mr Jones – indeed it did not even know of his existence – but Mr Jones called some of his friends to give evidence that they had thought that the article had referred to him. The plaintiff recovered damages of £1,750 for this defamation and, on appeal, the House of Lords held that it was no defence for the newspaper to say that it had not actually intended to defame Mr Jones if reasonable people could take the story as being defamatory of him. The House of Lords approved the judgment of Farrell LJ who, in the Court of Appeal, had put it this way:

> *If a man chooses to make statements of fact about persons whom he names, as in this case, I see no reason why he should not be liable to everyone whom he injures who can convince a jury that he is reasonably intended by the words used.*

Cassidy v. *Daily Mirror Newspapers Ltd* 1929 was a somewhat similar case. The defendant newspaper published a photograph of the plaintiff's husband together with a young lady, with a caption to the effect that the happy couple had announced their engagement. It was an innocent enough mistake on the part of the newspaper but, when the plaintiff called friends to say that they had been led to believe that the woman whom they knew as Mrs Cassidy was, in fact, a kept woman, it cost the newspaper £500 in damages.

Since 1952 newspapers have been able to take advantage of a special defence to cover this sort of slip-up – the 'offer of amends', discussed below.

Even more abstruse innuendoes have given rise to litigation. For example, in *Tolley* v. *Fry* 1931 a prominent amateur golfer, Cyril Tolley, sued the defendant chocolate manufacturers following the appearance of one of their advertisements in the *Daily Mail*. Under a caricature of the plaintiff, depicting him playing golf with a packet of a certain make of chocolate protruding from his pocket, was this verse:

> The caddie to Tolley, said 'Oh, Sir.
> Good shot Sir! That ball, see it go, Sir.
> My word how it flies.
> Like a cartet of Fry's.
> They're handy, they're good and priced low, Sir.'

Although on the face of it this was admittedly not expressly defamatory, the plaintiff contended that, by its innuendo, the advertisement suggested that he had accepted money for the caricature, so prostituting his status as an amateur golfer and that he had, therefore, been guilty of unworthy conduct. The House of Lords held that the advertisement and its verse were capable of giving that defamatory meaning by the innuendo.

More recently, in *Charleston* v. *News Group Newspapers Ltd* 1995, the *News of the World* avoided liability for publishing photographs of 'Neighbours' stars where the pictures had been doctored so as to impose the faces of two residents of Ramsay Street onto the barely clothed bodies of others then engaged in sexual activity. As the distinguished custodian of popular British public morality enquired of its faked picture in equally faked antipodean expression:

> *Strewth! What's Harold up to with our Madge?*

Neither Harold nor Madge (the latter part played by actress Anne Charleston) had known anything about the computerised manipulation of the photographs. She and her fellow actor Ian Smith brought proceedings for libel, arguing that the headlines were defamatory because their 'ordinary and natural meaning' was that these actors, well-known to millions of soap viewers in the civilised world and Australia, had posed for pornographic pictures. The judge had firstly to decide whether the photographs were indeed capable of bearing such an ordinary and natural meaning. In the smaller print of the newspaper report, the *News of the World* had made clear that 'the famous faces from the TV soap are the unwitting stars of a sordid computer game that is available to their child fans'. The newspaper underlined this point in other ways, doing so, as Lord Bridge caustically remarked, 'in a tone of self-righteous indignation which contrasts oddly with the prominence given to the main photograph'.

Journalistic ethics apart, could publication, admittedly not defamatory as a whole, still be libellous on the ground that some readers will have read only part of the published matter over their Sunday breakfast? Lord Nicholls (perhaps even pausing to consider the attention law students might give to his own speech) explained the issue:

> *Everybody reads selectively, scanning the headlines and turning the pages. One reader, whose interest has been quickened by an eye-caption headline or picture, will pause and read an article. Another reader, with different interests or less time, will read the headline and pass on, leaving the article unread. What if a headline, taken alone or with an attached picture, is defamatory, but the text of the article removes the defamatory invitation? That is the question of law raised by this appeal.*

In answering that question the House of Lords could not accept that the plaintiffs could bring an action for libel on the basis of a defamatory meaning conveyed only to that limited category of readers who read only the headlines.

Even the juxtaposition of wax models was held to be defamatory in *Monson* v. *Tussauds Ltd* 1894. The defendant waxworks had exhibited a wax model of the plaintiff near the Chamber of Horrors. The model held a gun in its hand. This was a little unfortunate because the plaintiff had recently been tried in Scotland for murder by shooting and had been discharged on that country's verdict of 'not proven'. The Court of Appeal held that this unhappy juxtaposition was defamatory.

Because the words, the caricature or even the waxworks must refer specifically to the claimant it is not possible to defame a whole class of people. As one judge put it:

> *If a man wrote that all lawyers were thieves, no particular lawyer could sue unless there was something to point to the particular individual.*

Nevertheless, even though the victim may not be named a description may be so detailed as to make it obvious who is being referred to. So it was in *J'Anson* v. *Stuart* 1787, when a newspaper referred to a man whose name was similar to an admiral, Anson, saying:

> *This diabolical character, like Polyphemus the man-eater, has but one eye, and is well known to all persons acquainted with the name of a certain noble circumnavigator.*

So, it would be defamatory to say that all grey-haired solicitors who drove old Sunbeam cars and practised in the little village of Barking-up-the-Wrongtree were dishonest; only one such gentleman is likely to be found there.

A factual and far more hurtful example of this principle was seen in *Hayward* v. *Thompson* 1981. In the spring of 1978 *The Sunday Telegraph* carried as front page news the heading: 'Two More in Scott Affair'. This was the continuing story of Norman Scott, a former male model whose dog, a Great Dane, had been shot by an airline pilot called Andrew Newton who was later sent to prison for this crime. There was a sensational outburst in court by Scott when he alleged that he had once had a homosexual relationship with the then leader of the Liberal party, Jeremy Thorpe. Regardless of the truth of the suggestion (which was denied) this titbit of scandal whetted the appetite of Fleet Street. There was added zest to the story when Newton later alleged that he had been paid £5,000 to shoot not the dog but Scott himself. Who had paid this money? The crime correspondent of *The Sunday Telegraph* came up with a suggestion that the names of two people connected with this incident had been given to the police. He wrote:

> *One is a wealthy benefactor of the Liberal party and the other is a businessman from the Channel Islands. Both men, police have been told, arranged for a leading Liberal supporter to be 'reimbursed' £5,000, the same amount Mr Andrew Newton alleges he was paid to murder Mr Scott.*

A week later the same crime correspondent wrote that the police wanted to interview Mr Jack Hayward, 'the Bahamas-based millionaire, who once gave the Liberal party £150,000 to help pay its overdraft and boost its election fighting fund'.

This was obviously an explicit reference to Jack Hayward, later described by Lord Denning MR as 'a man of the highest character and reputation'. Although no longer permanently resident in Britain he had remained intensely loyal to his native country. He had used his great wealth most generously to support many worthy causes, such as buying Lundy Island for the National Trust and bringing Brunel's ship the *SS Great Britain* back to its home at Bristol. His generosity also extended to the Liberal party to whose election funds he made very substantial contributions in the years 1970 to 1975. His own character was quite beyond doubt and this was belatedly recognised in 1986 by the grant of a knighthood.

In the first *Sunday Telegraph* article Mr Hayward had not been named but was the reference not clearly to him? Jack Hayward sued for libel. The court had regard to the old principle of *Hulton & Co. v. Jones* 1910. Lord Denning MR remarked on the newspaper's approach to the offending article:

> *If the defendant intended to refer to the plaintiff, he cannot escape liability simply by not giving his name. He may use asterisks or blanks. He may use initials or words with a hidden meaning. He may use any other device. But still, if he intended to refer to the plaintiff, he is liable. He is to be given credit for hitting the person whom he intended to hit. The law goes further. Even if he did not aim at the plaintiff or intend to refer to him, nevertheless if he names the plaintiff in such a way that other persons will read it as intended to refer to the plaintiff, then the defendant is liable.*

Applying this principle to the particular facts of the case it was quite clear that, when *The Sunday Telegraph*'s correspondent wrote in his first article of 'a wealthy benefactor of the Liberal party', he had intended to refer to Jack Hayward. Such a libel cost the paper £50,000 damages to Mr Hayward.

Finally, in order for a statement to be defamatory it must have been published. Apart from the risk of a bloody nose you are safe from actions for defamation if you simply tell a person precisely what you think of him. Anyway, mere vulgar abuse is not defamation. Your liability only arises if you tell someone else your thoughts or if another person overhears you. The principle extends to what is written; so if you are going to write poison-pen letters you would be well advised to use a good thick envelope, mark it *Private and Confidential* and stick it down well. Sending the same greetings on the back of a postcard would amount to publication because of the number of people who could read the message as it went on its way. Indeed, the law even presumes that someone, such as the postman, will in fact read it.

What a man tells his wife does not amount to publication, for in this context the law presumes man and wife to be one person but any further disclosures, such as to a neighbour, will do so. If that neighbour in turn has a newsy little chat with another neighbour and so on right down the street, then each of them could be liable because each repetition amounts to a separate publication.

The implication of such repetition could, of course, be calamitous in some instances, such as that of a bookshop selling hundreds of copies of a book which defamed someone. Such a situation arose in *Vizetelly* v. *Mudie's Select Library Ltd* 1900 when the proprietors of a library had circulated copies of a book which, unknown to them, was defamatory of Mr Vizetelly and so they were liable to pay him damages. The way round this potentially hard rule is for the defendant to show that the dissemination had been innocent, by proving that he did not know that the book was defamatory and that he had not been negligent in not finding out that it was in fact defamatory. In this case, however, the library was unable to rely on that defence because it had ignored a publisher's circular which had asked for all copies of the book to be returned.

The arrival of the Internet could easily allow grossly defamatory material to be sent around the world almost instantly. Fortunately for the Internet Service Providers (ISP) section 1 of the Defamation Act 1996 provides that mere provision of 'access to a communication system by means of which a statement is transmitted, or made available, by a person over whom he has no effective control' is insufficient for the ISP to be considered an author, editor or publisher. The avoidance of liability for defamation, however, also requires that the ISP took reasonable care in relation to the publication and neither knew nor had reason to believe that what he did caused or contributed to the publication of a defamatory statement.

The first such ISP to feel the effect of this rule was that in *Godfrey* v. *Demon Internet* 2000 when the defendant ISP paid damages of £15,000 to a physicist who had earlier asked Demon to remove certain postings sent anonymously to a news-group on the internet.

a) Libel and slander

Having decided whether or not a statement is defamatory, the court's next task is to determine whether it is libel or slander. English law retains a curious historical distinction between defamation which is in a permanent form and that which is only transient.

Libel is defamation in a permanent form such as writing, printing and painting; **slander**, on the other hand, is usually spoken. The distinction is not necessarily as simple as that and, even disregarding recondite discussion about, say, sky-writing or a ship's flag-signals, difficulties have in the past arisen over films, television and the theatre. Parliament has now resolved these uncertainties. The Defamation Act 1952 provides that defamatory statements on radio or television shall be libel. The Theatres Act 1968 further provides that defamation on stage shall also be libel.

The distinction is more than of purely academic or historical interest. While slander is only a tort, libel can also be a crime, even though today criminal prosecutions for libel are few and far between. Admirers of Oscar Wilde will know of his prosecution of the Marquess of Queensberry at the Old Bailey in 1895 for criminal libel when the noble pugilist had called at Wilde's club to leave a visiting-card with a defamatory message: 'To Oscar Wilde posing as a somdomite.' In fact, the aristocrat had meant to say 'sodomite' but spelt the word incorrectly. It was, of course, Queensberry's acquittal which led to Wilde, in his turn, being prosecuted and eventually going to prison in Reading Gaol for the maximum term then permitted.

A much-publicised private prosecution for criminal libel was brought against the editor and distributors of *Private Eye* by City financier Sir James Goldsmith, following an article about Goldsmith and Lord Lucan entitled 'All's Well that Ends Elwes'. The action was dropped only days before the Old Bailey trial was due to start. In turn, *Private Eye* apologised, withdrew its various allegations and agreed to contribute towards the cost of the proposed prosecution.

Libel is also actionable *per se* (that is, without proof of damage) while, in order to recover damages for slander, a claimant must normally prove that he has suffered actual loss. There are, however, a few exceptional kinds of slander which are actionable *per se*:

1. imputation of a criminal offence which is punishable with imprisonment;
2. imputation of a contagious or infectious disease of the sort that would stop others from associating with the claimant;
3. imputation of unchastity in a woman, an exception which is the result of the Slander of Women Act 1891;
4. imputation of unfitness or incompetence in the claimant's work. The old limitations on this exception have been removed by the Defamation Act 1952, section 2, which provides:

> In an action for slander in respect of words calculated to disparage the plaintiff in any office, profession, calling, trade or business held or carried on by him at the time of the publication, it shall not be necessary to allege or prove special damage, whether or not the words are spoken of the plaintiff in the way of his office, profession, calling, trade or business.

b) Defences to defamation

Justification

Certain special defences are applicable only to alleged libel or slander.

It is, of course, of the essence in defamation that the words complained of are untrue. So if the dentist does habitually pull the wrong tooth or the solicitor is dishonest then neither can make any complaint: he has only been revealed for what he is. Provided that a defendant to an action for defamation can show that what he said or wrote about the claimant was substantially true, he may rely on that justification. Put in the words of one nineteenth-century judgment:

> ...the law will not permit a man to recover damages in respect of an injury to a character which he either does not, or ought not to, possess.

For example, by calling evidence of Wilde's dubious relationships with a number of uncouth young men, Queensberry was able to show that his allegations about Wilde were substantially true and, therefore, justified.

Even so, not every word of the allegation has to be true. For example, if a newspaper reports that a burglar pleaded guilty to 99 thefts it will not be liable to the burglar for libel if it was only 98 separate offences: its report was still substantially true. Similarly, in *Alexander* v. *N.E. Railway* 1865 the defendants successfully pleaded justification following a report that the plaintiff had been fined for riding on the railway without a valid ticket and had been sentenced to three weeks' imprisonment if the fine were not paid. In fact, it was only two weeks' imprisonment which hung over the plaintiff's head but the court held that the report was still substantially true. This rule has been preserved and clarified by section 5 of the Defamation Act 1952 which provides:

> In an action for libel or slander in respect of words containing two or more distinct charges against the plaintiff, a defence of justification shall not fail by reason only that the truth of every charge is not proved if the words not proved to be true do not materially injure the plaintiff's reputation having regard to the truth of the remaining charges.

More recently, the magazine *Private Eye* made another contribution to the earnings of the legal profession and, incidentally, to the line of authorities on malice in publication. In *Herbage* v. *Pressdram Limited* 1984 a man described in the law reports as an 'investment adviser' (but from whom some clients experienced great difficulty in getting their money back) sought an injunction to prevent *Private Eye* from publishing further details of certain convictions which, under the provisions of the Rehabilitation of Offenders Act 1974, were deemed 'spent'. Herbage issued a writ for libel. *Private Eye* said that it would justify the articles and denied publishing the articles maliciously. If Lord Gnome's publication had, in fact, been prompted by malice – that is, prompted by some irrelevant, spiteful or improper motive – there could be no defence of qualified privilege. The Court of Appeal was not convinced that such malice was present and refused to grant the injunction sought, which would have prevented further mention of Herbage's background in *Private Eye*. Incidentally, at Easter 1986 Herbage was extradited from the United Kingdom to America to face serious fraud charges.

Fair comment In a democracy the citizen's criticism and comment on the country and his fellow-citizens are allowed and sometimes still even encouraged. This attitude is reflected in the defence of fair comment, which may be raised where the subject-matter is one of public interest. Lord Denning MR said:

> *It is the right of every man in Parliament or out of it, in the Press or over the broadcast, to make fair comment, even outspoken comment, on matters of public interest.*

More recently, in *Reynolds* v. *Times Newspapers Limited* 1999 Lord Nicholls reminded us of the role of what is traditionally called 'fair comment' when remarking:

> *At times people must be able to speak and write freely, uninhibited by the prospect of being sued for damages should they be mistaken or misinformed. In the wider public interest, protection of reputation must then give way to a higher priority.*

What then is of 'public interest'? Obviously the way in which our rulers walk the corridors of power, whether in Whitehall or in the local council offices, is the object of legitimate public interest as, it seems, also are the tax affairs of public figures. At the very least, the ordinary taxpayer has an interest in the apparent ability of others high in political connection or patronage ably to minimise the State's take of their own wealth and the council-tax payer has a similar legitimate interest to know whether his hard-earned cash is being squandered on beer and skittles for the boys in the Town Hall. On the other hand, is it necessarily a matter of public interest that the town clerk has taken a mistress, provided that she does not interfere with the discharge of his duties?

The scope of 'public interest' was examined by the Court of Appeal in *London Artists Ltd* v. *Littler* 1969. Emile Littler was an impresario who had published a letter in which he suggested that the plaintiffs were part of a conspiracy to kill off a successful play. When sued, he raised the defence of fair comment. But was the play's future a matter of public interest? The Court of Appeal thought it was, and Lord Denning MR favoured a wide view of the terms when he said:

> *I would not myself confine it within narrow limits. Whenever a matter is such as to affect people at large so that they may be legitimately interested in, or concerned at, what is going on; or what may happen to them or to others; then it is a matter of public interest on which everyone is entitled to make fair comment.*

At first sight the defences of justification and fair comment look very similar. Indeed, in practice, they are often raised together. One important distinction, however, is that justification deals with facts; fair comment deals with people's opinions.

The distinction between an expression of an opinion and a statement of fact may sometimes be difficult to draw. For someone to say that Tchaikovsky's '1812' Overture is the worst bit of music ever written is obviously an indication that, in his opinion, it is a less than euphonious composition. Others may disagree. In any event, no one can prove it either way: it is simply a matter of opinion.

A less obvious difficulty came before the House of Lords in *Dakhyl* v. *Labouchere* 1908. The plaintiff held a number of degrees from a foreign seat of learning. One of them was that of doctor of medicine and the plaintiff practised as an ear, nose and throat specialist. The defendant newspaper described him as a 'quack of the rankest species'. No one seriously suggested that the gentleman in question was related to some species of mallard. But were the words to be taken as meaning that the plaintiff was not even entitled to practise as a doctor (an offence), or only as an opinion that he was not reckoned as quite the best man to go to if you had a sore throat? The House of Lords held that this was a matter where it was open to the defendant to rely on fair comment.

Where this defence is raised, it is obviously necessary to show that the comment was, indeed, fair and not one prompted by spite or petty vindictiveness. What is and what is not fair was considered by the Court of Appeal in *Slim* v. *Daily Telegraph* 1968. Horace Slim was a solicitor who worked for a company called 'Vitamins'. The company wanted to be able to drive its vans down a narrow footpath in Hammersmith. It was indeed so narrow that the council had put up a notice prohibiting even bicycles from using it, and this NO CYCLING notice had been signed by the same Horace Slim at a time when he had been Town Clerk to Hammersmith. This apparent about-turn in Mr Slim's loyalties was picked up by a correspondent to the *Daily Telegraph*. The letters were certainly insulting to Mr Slim: they suggested that he was inconsistent in his loyalty (namely that he ran with the hare and hunted with the hounds) and also that he was dishonest (in that he went behind the scenes and used 'back-door' influence to persuade his old chums who still worked for the council to relax the restrictions on the use of the footpath). The defendant newspaper maintained that the articles were fair comment on a matter of public interest. The Court of Appeal agreed but also noted that Mr Slim had acted properly in discharging his duty to his new client. Lord Denning MR discussed the various meanings which the articles could have:

> They may strike some readers in one way and others in another way. One person may read into them imputations of dishonesty, insincerity and hypocrisy (as the judge did). Another person may only read into them imputations of inconsistency and want of candour (as I would). In considering a plea of fair comment, it is not correct to canvass all the various imputations which different readers may put upon the words. The important thing is to determine whether or not the writer was actuated by malice. If he was an honest man expressing his genuine opinion on a subject of public interest, then no matter that his words conveyed derogatory imputations: no matter that his opinion was wrong or exaggerated or prejudiced; and no matter that it was badly expressed so that other people read all sorts of innuendoes into it; nevertheless, he has a good defence of fair comment. His honesty is the cardinal test. He must honestly express his real view. So long as he does this, he has nothing to fear, even though other people may read more into it. I stress this because the right of fair comment is one of the essential elements which go to

make up our freedom of speech. We must ever maintain this
right intact. It must not be whittled down by legal refine-
ments.

Lord Nicholls went on in *Reynolds* v. *Times Newspapers Limited* 1999
to express his view that the word 'fair' had now become both meaningless and misleading. The true test today, he suggested, was whether the
opinion, however exaggerated, obstinate or prejudiced, was honestly
held by the person expressing it. In the same case, Lord Nicholls took
note of the residual limitations of this defence:

> *It is important to keep in mind that this defence is concerned*
> *with the protection of comment, not imputations of fact ...*
> *One constraint does exist upon this defence. The comment must*
> *represent the honest belief of its author. If the plaintiff proves he*
> *was actuated by malice, this ground of defence will fail.*

Privilege Some of society's needs are regarded as being so important that the possibility that harm may be done to an individual is considered a price
worth paying for the greater good of the country as a whole. Examples
are the need for free debate in Parliament and similarly unfettered scope
for the proper presentation of cases coming before the courts.

Our law, therefore, provides that in certain circumstances what was
said or written will be privileged and cannot be the subject of any subsequent actions for defamation. Some occasions are so very important
that they are said to be **absolutely privileged**, no matter what is said or
expressed. Other occasions merit only a **qualified privilege**: in this case
the privilege will be lost if the words were prompted by malice.

Absolute privilege will attach to the following occasions:

<u>Proceedings in Parliament</u> The Bill of Rights 1688 provided that:

> ...the freedom of speech and debates or proceedings in Par-
> liament ought not to be impeached or questioned in any court
> or place out of Parliament.

This, of course, needs now to be seen both in the light of the decision of
the House of Lords in *Pepper* v. *Hart* 1993 (see Unit 1.6) and in *Hamilton* v. *Al Fayed* 1999. Further, in the summer of 2000 the government
announced plans to remove such protection where its use could act as a
cloak for corrupt practices.

Parliament has long had its own internal procedure for dealing with
unparliamentary conduct but no one may sue a Member of Parliament
for what he has said within the walls of the Palace of Westminster. The
same politician campaigning at an election in the local church hall or
market-place must be more careful, however. Section 10 of the Defamation Act 1952 provides:

> A defamatory statement published by or on behalf of a candi-
> date in any election to a local government authority or to Par-
> liament shall not be deemed to be published on a privileged
> occasion on the ground that it is material to a question in
> issue in the election, whether or not the person by whom it is
> published is qualified to vote at an election.

Such privilege has been fully exploited by a couple of Members of Parliament in particular. In 1985 Brian Sedgemore, a Labour MP, called for a public inquiry into the collapse of Johnson Matthey Bankers. This bank had to be rescued by the Bank of England after the JMB collapse in the autumn of 1984 with spectacular debts of some £248 million. The Hon. Member for Hackney South and Shoreditch used his parliamentary privilege to make serious allegations of bribery and dishonesty involving the use of prostitutes and dubious currency dealings in Nigeria. In 1993, in a personal statement made to the House of Commons, after his resignation from the government, Michael Mates, a Conservative MP, was able to use such privilege roundly to condemn the conduct of the Serious Fraud Office which, he alleged, was itself seriously flawed in its treatment of Asil Nadir, the former chairman of Polly Peck plc.

In 1986, however, many people, both inside and outside the House of Commons, were critical of the use of parliamentary privilege by a Conservative back-bencher who claimed to be fighting a national crusade to protect little children. The Member for Littlebrough and Saddleworth used his privilege to give publicity to the name of an Essex doctor who had allegedly raped an eight-year-old girl. The Director of Public Prosecutions (see Unit 3.7) had already decided that this doctor should not be prosecuted. Nevertheless, even though he would neither be tried for this alleged offence nor given any sort of redress through the courts for these grievous allegations, the doctor's identity became widely known and, no doubt, great distress was caused both to him and to his family.

Other Members of Parliament strongly disapproved of such attempts at making unbridled use of this privilege. Parliament itself put a check on this conduct. The then Speaker (who presides over parliamentary debate and keeps order), impartial as between opposing political factions, warned against the wanton abuse of this ancient privilege:

> *Freedom of speech is essential to the work of Parliament. It is the responsibility of every MP to ensure that he uses his freedom in a way that does not needlessly damage those who do not enjoy privilege and in a way that does not damage the good name of this House.*

Further restraint upon parliamentary privilege (and restraint set against the real damage done to that same good name of the House brought about by certain politicians' 'cash for questions') was proposed in the summer of 2000. Following the report of the Law Commission (see Unit 1.9c)) two years earlier the Home Secretary announced proposals to sweep away the 'protective cloak' of seventeenth-century parliamentary privilege so as to amend the Bills of Rights 1689. If carried into legislation such moves would remove protection against allegations of corrupt dealings by Members in the House of Parliament.

Publication of parliamentary proceedings Verbatim reports of parliamentary debates are carried in the official record, Hansard. Under the Parliamentary Papers Act 1840 all reports and papers published by the House of Commons and the House of Lords are privileged.

Legal proceedings Where there are issues of credibility to be resolved at trial, lawyers acting for one party may well have to greet a witness called by the other side with the suggestion that he is a liar upon whose evidence no right-thinking person would place any reliance. Fortunately for lawyers, such suggestions are made on privileged occasions. This privilege extends to judges, lawyers, jury and witnesses.

The extent to which a witness's immunity might be limited was considered by the House of Lords in *Darker* v. *Chief Constable of the West Midlands Police* 2000 when the defendant sought to strike out claims against the police which, among others, alleged that West Midlands police officers had fabricated evidence. The House of Lords rejected the argument that witnesses should enjoy immunity from civil actions where it was being alleged that those witnesses had been guilty of deliberate fabrication of statements. Lord Hope was able nevertheless to confirm the general principles of immunity for witnesses and lawyers:

> *My Lords, when a police officer comes to court to give evidence he has the benefit of an absolute immunity. This immunity, which is regarded as necessary in the interests of the administration of justice and is granted to him as a matter of public policy, is shared by all witnesses in regard to the evidence which they give when they are in the witness box. It extends to anything said or done by them in the ordinary course of any proceedings in a court of justice. The same immunity is given to the parties, their advocates, jurors and judge.*

Reports of court proceedings are similarly privileged. Section 3 of the Law of Libel Amendment Act 1888 provides:

> A fair and accurate report in any newspaper of proceedings publicly heard before any court exercising judicial authority shall, if published contemporaneously with such proceedings be privileged: Provided that nothing in this section shall authorize the publication of any blasphemous or indecent matter.

Similarly, communications passing between a lawyer and his client are privileged, although there is some doubt about whether this privilege is absolute or only qualified. It is considered so vital for people to be able to talk freely and fearlessly to their legal advisers that the lawyer cannot be compelled to disclose what was said without the consent of his client. Of course, what was said to the lawyer must have been said to him in his professional capacity and not as mere tittle-tattle on the golf course.

Statements made by one officer of State to another in the course of his duty For instance, in *Chatterton* v. *Secretary of State for India* 1895 the defendant had written to say that the Commander-in-Chief in India had recommended the removal of the plaintiff's name to the half-pay list as his retention on the active list was undesirable. The Court of Appeal was clear that any such communication was a matter of State and, as such, absolutely privileged.

More recently in *Mahon* v. *Rahn* 2000 the Court of Appeal confirmed that absolute privilege attached to a document created during the course of an investigation by a financial regulator. Bankers had been asked by the Securities Association to provide information on a firm of stock-brokers. A copy of the letter was seen by the Serious Fraud Office and led to a prosecution which collapsed. The stockbrokers alleged that the letter had been libellous. Conscious that the flow of information to financial regulators might be seriously impeded if informants feared that they might be troubled by future libel proceedings, the Court of Appeal ruled that absolute privilege attached to such communications.

The most important example of qualified privilege is where the words complained of were written or spoken because of some legal or moral duty. This is an area of uncertain extent and it is not possible to lay down any exhaustive list of occasions to which the privilege attaches. Certain requirements, however, must be satisfied. These were considered by the Court of Appeal in *Watt* v. *Longsdon* 1930. The defendant was a company director who wrote to the chairman of the board about the plaintiff, describing Mr Watt in his letter as

> *a blackguard, a thief, a liar and to whom friendship was a totally unknown thing, and who lived and lives exclusively to satisfy his own passions and lust.*

The letter was seen by the chairman of the board and by the plaintiff's wife. The court held that the director was under a duty to communicate with the chairman and that the chairman was under a corresponding duty to receive the letter. It was, therefore, privileged. Doubtless Mrs Watt was not uninterested in her husband's supposed secret life, but because the director had no duty to her, either legal or moral, the second communication was not privileged. The court emphasised that the duty must be a reciprocal one and approved the judgment of Lord Atkinson who, in an earlier case, had said:

> *...a privileged occasion is, in reference to qualified privilege, an occasion where the person who makes a communication has an interest or a duty, legal, social or moral, to make it to the person to whom it is made, and the person to whom it is so made has a corresponding interest or duty to receive it. This reciprocity is essential.*

The application of qualified privilege was considered further in *Beach* v. *Freeson* 1971. The defendant, a Member of Parliament, received a complaint from one of his constituents about the plaintiffs, a firm of solicitors. He wrote to the Law Society and told them that he had received other complaints about the firm. The solicitors sued for libel but the court held that the communication enjoyed qualified privilege because, as a Member of Parliament, the defendant had an interest in passing on his constituent's complaint about the solicitors to the proper quarter.

In recent years, however, the once good name of the House had indeed become tarnished by allegations of corruption among Members of Parliament and, in particular, by their asking questions in return for sums of cash contained in brown envelopes. One customer of those ready to abuse their privileged position was to say that he had been advised to pay for this service as: 'You need to rent an MP just like you rent a London taxi.' One advantage of this device was that parliamentary privilege would protect those questions which could always be phrased not only in such a way as to promote the interests of that politician's customer but also to make disparaging comments about others, such as business rivals, now unable to sue for defamation. In *Hamilton* v. *Al Fayed* 1999 a former Member of Parliament who had lost his seat in the May 1997 general election sued Mohamed Al Fayed, in respect of allegations made by the owner of Harrods in a television interview some four months before the electorate in the once safe Tory seat of Tatton robustly dispensed with the politician's services in favour of the BBC correspondent, Martin Bell.

Firstly, the plaintiff waived his privilege under section 23 of the Defamation Act 1996 after a preliminary point had been raised by the *Guardian* newspaper, which had published allegations of planted questions in 1994, contending that the hearing of the libel action would itself contravene section 1 of the Bill of Rights 1688. In doing so, Neil Hamilton took advantage of a change brought about specifically in the 1996 statute to assist any claim by a Member of Parliament for defamation. Secondly, lawyers for the owner of the famous Knightsbridge emporium argued that the libel action of Mr Hamilton would also constitute an attack on Parliament's own investigation into Mr Hamilton's conduct as delivered to the Committee on Standards and Privileges by Sir Gordon Downey, whose report only appeared after the 1997 general election. The House of Lords rejected this preliminary argument holding that, while the Bill of Rights prohibited direct criticism by the courts of anything said or done in the course of parliamentary proceedings, it did not prevent criticism by other persons. Mr Hamilton's libel action did not, therefore, involve any imputation of criticism of the other investigations into his conduct.

A recent attempt by the gentlemen of the press to extend the defence of privilege to include a new and quite specific category of qualified privilege, 'political information', came before the House of Lords in *Reynolds* v. *Times Newspapers Limited* 1999. Albert Reynolds, former Taioseach (Prime Minister) of Ireland had resigned from his post in November 1994. Shortly afterwards, *The Sunday Times*, published in Britain, published a major report under the title 'Why a fib too far proved fatal for the political career of Ireland's peacemaker and Mr Fixit'. Albert Reynolds brought libel proceedings in respect of the article, contending that there was a sting in the article suggesting that he had deliberately and dishonestly misled the Da'il (the Irish Parliament) and his Cabinet colleagues. At trial, the jury rejected the newspaper's defence of justification but decided that the article had not been written or published maliciously. If, therefore, the judge were to rule that the occasion had been privileged, the newspaper would succeed in the defence of qualified privilege. On a number of occasions the law already recognised the concept of 'qualified privilege' as when a former employer is asked to provide a reference on someone seeking a new job. Here, however, the press wanted to create a specific new category of such privilege. In rejecting this argument the House of Lords expressed the view that such an extension of the common law would not provide adequate protection for people's reputations. It would not be right to develop 'political information' as a particular category attracting qualified privilege. Further, said Lord Nicholls, it would be unsound in principle to distinguish political discussion from discussion of other matters of serious public concern. Even so, this important decision confirmed that the courts would continue to recognise qualified privilege where the press had a duty to report even if the press made a mistake, provided as before that the allegation had not been made maliciously or recklessly. Freedom of the press still mattered for, as Lord Nicholls was to say less than a year before the implementation of the Human Rights Act 1998:

> My starting point is freedom of expression. The high importance of freedom to impart and receive information and ideas has been stated so often and so eloquently that this point needs no elaboration in this case. At a pragmatic level, freedom to disseminate and receive information on political matters is essential to the proper functioning of the system of parliamentary democracy cherished in this country.

Offer of amends   Where a slip had been made of the kind which led to cases such as *Hulton & Co.* v. *Jones* and *Cassidy* v. *Daily Mirror Newspapers Ltd*, publishers are now able to seek the protection of a statutory defence.

Such a defence was introduced by section 4 of the Defamation Act 1952 and is now set out in the later Defamation Act 1996 so that, under section 2, a person who has published a statement alleged to be defamatory of another may offer to make amends under that section. Such offer, which must be in writing, is an offer to make a suitable correction of the statement complained of and a sufficient apology to the aggrieved party. Such offer must also include an undertaking to publish the correction and apology and, perhaps, also to pay agreed compensation and costs.

The person who complains about the statement must then decide whether to accept such an offer. Acceptance will put an end to proceedings for defamation. If the offer is not accepted, the very fact that it was made can operate as a defence in some cases and as relevant in mitigation of damages in all cases.

c) Remedies

If a person's darkest secrets have been the subject of salacious comment at thousands of breakfast tables up and down the country as happy families tuck into their cornflakes and pass round the *Sunday Slur*, he will look to the law to protect him in two separate ways. Firstly, he will want to stop the newspaper in question from publishing any more defamatory statements in the next week's paper. Secondly, he will expect compensation for the libel he has already suffered.

He may be able to obtain an injunction from the court to stop further publication if he can show that he has what lawyers call a *prima facie* case of libel against the newspaper, that is, that there may be something in the claimant's claim. If the newspaper then adopts a 'publish and be damned' philosophy in the face of this injunction, it will be in contempt of court; it is possible that its particular form of damnation could even be the sequestration (confiscation) of its assets and perhaps even the imprisonment of its editor.

Secondly, the person defamed can ask the court to award him damages. As we have seen, the courts will presume that the claimant has suffered loss in a case of libel but in slander – subject to the four exceptions – his losses must be actually proved.

The range of awards for defamation has been very wide and this is often said to be, in part, the consequence of leaving the quantum (the amount of cash) of the award to a jury which may still sit in cases of alleged defamation.

In Unit 4.19, we saw that in cases of breach of contract the aim of an award of damages is to put the injured party in the position in which he would have been had the contract been properly carried out. In cases of tort the aim is different: the courts try to put the victim in the position in which he would have been had the defendant not injured him, so far as money alone can do so. It is notoriously difficult to assess how much a man's good name is worth and the position is further complicated by two special sorts of award that can be made – one unusually low and one unusually high.

It may be that the jury finds that, on all the evidence, the claimant has been defamed. They may, nevertheless, think so very little of him that they reflect their contempt of him in the size of the award. Such damages are accordingly known as **contemptuous damages**. For example, in *Dering* v. *Uris* 1964 the jury found that, in his book *Exodus*, Leon Uris had indeed libelled the plaintiff, a doctor who had conducted unsavoury operations on prisoners at a German concentration camp during the Second World War. Nevertheless, they evidently felt little sympathy for what the plaintiff had done and awarded him contemptuous damages of one halfpenny – the smallest coin in the realm at that time.

In another case, in October 1893, Express Newspapers had to pay a mere halfpenny to a legal executive (see Unit 2.5) called Barry Pamplin. This gentleman thought that he had found a sure-fire way to save money on parking fines. He had cleverly registered his car in the name of his young son (who, in law, was too young to commit an offence). The newspaper in question had taken exception to this little dodge and described Mr Pamplin as 'a slippery unscrupulous spiv'.

At the other end of the scale the jury may feel that the defendant has acted so appallingly that he ought to be made to pay very heavily indeed. Such damages are designed to make an example of the defendant and perhaps to punish him. These damages are known, therefore, as **exemplary** or **punitive damages**. A court's freedom to award such damages has been limited by two decisions of the House of Lords.

In *Rookes* v. *Barnard* 1964 Lord Devlin indicated his dislike for exemplary damages, because, he thought, there was a danger of confusing the civil and criminal functions of the law. Nevertheless, he approved their use on occasion – for example, where the defendant's conduct has been calculated by him to make a profit for himself which may well exceed the compensation payable to the plaintiff. This, of course, will often be the case where a newspaper has published an article about someone in public life and has led up to that publication with a barrage of publicity – for the publishers know that such are the foibles of human nature that the story will boost sales.

A similar problem came before the courts in *Cassell & Co. Ltd* v. *Broome* 1972. Cassells had published a book entitled *The Destruction of Convoy PQ17*, which had been written by David Irving. The book told the story of a British naval reverse in the Second World War, involving the sinking of a large number of merchant ships on their way to Russia and the killing of their crews by the enemy. The author suggested that much of the blame lay on Captain Broome who had commanded the convoy. The author had already experienced some lack of enthusiasm in getting the book published. This was scarcely surprising in view of its libellous content: indeed, the book was sold on the basis of its sensationalism. The jury found that the book was indeed defamatory and awarded Captain Broome £15,000 as compensation for his loss; they then went on to add on a further £25,000 by way of exemplary damages against both the author and the publishers.

A recent attempt to extend the award of exemplary damages beyond the parameters established in *Rookes* v. *Barnard* came before the Court of Appeal in *AB* v. *South West Water Services Limited* 1993. No fewer than 182 different plaintiffs claimed damages against South West Water Services Limited after suffering the effects of drinking contaminated water. A large quantity of aluminium sulphate had contaminated the water system at the treatment works in Cornwall. The water company was in due course prosecuted and admitted a breach of statutory duty in failing to supply wholesome water. In short, the defendants agreed that they had to pay damages to those who had suffered ill-effects. The plaintiffs, however, went further. They complained that the defendants had sent out misleading letters asserting that their water was safe to drink, that the defendants then withheld information and in other ways behaved in an arrogant and high-handed manner. Were these failings sufficient to justify an award in exemplary damages in addition to ordinary damages? A number of factors militated against the award of exemplary damages, said the Court of Appeal. Firstly, public nuisance was not one of the torts considered by the House of Lords in *Rookes* v. *Barnard*. Secondly, the sheer number of plaintiffs made the claim unsuitable. The court would be unable to assess the amount of exemplary damages to be awarded to any individual without knowing at the outset the total cost of the damages to the defendant. Finally, anger and indignation at the conduct of a litigant was not a proper subject for compensatory damages.

Recent high awards of damages against the police awarded to claimants by juries, clearly expressing their profound disapproval of the thuggish behaviour of certain police officers, came before the Court of Appeal in *Thompson* v. *Commissioner of Police for the Metropolis* 1997. The appeal against an award of no less than £51,500 in favour of Claudette Thompson was heard together with another appeal in a claim brought by Kenneth Shu which had led to a jury awarding him no less than £200,000 as exemplary damages after a number of police officers had assaulted and racially abused Mr Shu before arresting him. Mr Shu suffered post-traumatic stress disorder in addition to his physical injury. It was also implicit in the jury's verdict that the police had falsified their evidence. Some might see such high levels of damages also as a reflection of the frustration felt by a number of the public at the apparent inability or unwillingness of the police properly or at all to discipline, let alone dismiss, their dishonest or violent employees. The Court of Appeal went on, somewhat controversially, to give guidance as to the appropriate level of damages against the police so that any award would be dependent upon the rank of the officer who carried out the assault or had committed some other wrong. Juries are now to be told that it is open to them, in exceptional cases, to award damages to punish the defendant where there had been conduct (including oppressive or arbitrary behaviour) by police officers which deserved exceptional remedy. These damages are unlikely to be less than £5,000 but might be as much as £25,000 with an absolute maximum of £50,000 in cases where the officer concerned held at least the rank of Superintendent. Further guidance from the Court of Appeal as to the level of damages indicated that, in 1997 and in a straightforward case of wrongful arrest and imprisonment, the starting point was likely to be about £500 for the first hour during which the claimant has been deprived of his or her liberty. The hourly rate would then be substantially reduced so as to keep the damages proportionate to those in a personal injury case and the £500 was clearly intended to compensate also for the initial shock of being arrested. A figure of £3,000 might be thought to be broadly appropriate for a claimant who had been wrongly kept in custody for 24 hours. Cases of malicious prosecution would attract an award of around £2,000 and, where a full Crown Court trial had been involved with a prosecution continuing for as long as two years, an award of about £10,000 could be thought appropriate.

A long-standing criticism of allowing juries to measure the damages (seemingly in telephone numbers at times) was that there was so often an immense disparity between awards made by judges in respect of, say, broken limbs and awards made by juries for merely broken pride. Matters came to a head in *Sutcliffe* v. *Pressdram Limited* 1990 when the wife of the notorious murderer known as 'The Yorkshire Ripper' sued *Private Eye* for libel. The jury awarded Mrs Sonia Sutcliffe no less than £600,000, an award which led the *Eye*'s startled editor, Ian Hislop, to remark: 'If that's justice, then I'm a banana!'

Rather more profound criticism was levelled against the magnitude of this award by *Private Eye*'s lawyers and, in the Court of Appeal, the court pointed out that trial judges in libel actions ought to give guidance to the jury as to the financial implications of the sum they might award by pointing out, for example, what investment income such sum might produce.

Such assistance from the Court of Appeal was long overdue for the contrast between judges' awards for personal injury and juries' awards for defamation had grown too stark. Section 8 of the Courts and Legal Services Act 1990 empowered the Court of Appeal to substitute its own award where the damages awarded by the jury in the first place are thought excessive or inadequate. The traditional reluctance of the Court of Appeal to intervene in jury awards in defamation cases was put aside, for example, in *Rantzen* v. *Mirror Group Newspapers Limited* 1993 when damages of £250,000 earlier awarded to Esther Rantzen, presenter of the BBC programme *That's Life* and chairman of ChildLine were reduced to £110,000. Despite the wounding suggestion under the article

'Esther and the Sex Pervert Teacher' the judges took note that she had not suffered any financial loss or any social damage. She continued to be an extremely successful television presenter.

The contrast between judges' awards and the lottery stakes with jury awards could be seen all too clearly in two cases from the mid-1980s. In December 1985, in an unusual case which itself attracted considerable publicity, two women sued a man who had raped them. One woman, who had been 'trussed up like a chicken', repeatedly stabbed and then left to die, recovered £10,480 for this horrendous experience. Another woman, a mother of two, who had undergone a five-and-a-half hour degrading sexual ordeal recovered £7,080.

Some days later, actress Charlotte Cornwell complained to a High Court jury that she had been left 'sick and humiliated' after being labelled 'Wally of the Week' by a *Sunday People* television critic who had evidently been less than enraptured by the plaintiff's role in the television programme *No Excuses*. Of her talent as an actress, the paper had said, 'She can't sing, her bum is too big and she has the sort of presence that blocks lavatories.' The plaintiff actress alleged malice. The television critic in question and her newspaper claimed that the review was fair comment on a matter of public interest.

Of course the situation had been foreseen half a century earlier by Noel Coward in his advice to Mrs Worthington:

> *Don't put your daughter on the stage, Mrs Worthington,*
> *Don't put your daughter on the stage.*
> *She's a bit of an ugly duckling you must honestly confess,*
> *And the width of her seat would surely defeat her chances of*
> *   success.*

The television critic was found by the jury to have gone beyond the bounds of acceptable criticism and led to an award to the Shakespearean actress in the sum of £10,000, the sort of figure which at least offers some consolation for lamentations such as that of Iago in *Othello*:

> *Good name in man and woman, dear my lord,*
> *Is the immediate jewel of their souls:*
> *Who steals my purse steals trash; 't is something, nothing*
> *'T was mine, 't is his, and has been slave to thousands;*
> *But he that filches from me my good name*
> *Robs me of that which not enriches him,*
> *And makes me poor indeed*
> *Othello*, Act III, Scene 3

6.11 *Questions*

1. a) What must a claimant prove in order to succeed in an action for negligence against a defendant?
   b) Gordon constructs a reservoir on his land. One night a storm occurs and, as a result of heavy rainfall, the reservoir overflows on to the adjoining land of Michael, drowning several of Michael's sheep. Discuss what remedies, if any, Michael may have against Gordon.

2. a) Explain the term 'vicarious liability' in the context of the law of torts.
   b) Roberts was driving his employer's vehicle to transport goods to a supplier when he negligently struck Watson's car. Advise Watson as to whom he may sue. Would the advice alter if Roberts were driving the vehicle to attend a football match?

3. By reference to decided cases explain how the courts approach the issue of whether a defendant has broken a duty of care which exists in any given case, indicating whether any changes in the law in this area are desirable.

4. Carol owned and operated a café. One evening her employee Darren, against express instructions from Carol left the 'Super Quick Frier' turned on after the restaurant closed. The oil in the frier caught fire and considerable damage was done to the restaurant. The fires spread to an adjoining shop and to a flat above. Diane, the occupier of the flat, became trapped in a back room. She was so terrified by the fire that she was unable to climb out of the window and descend a ladder which had been put in place by the fire brigade. John, a fireman, entered the flat to rescue Diane and was injured by the flames. He succeeded in rescuing Diane who was taken to hospital in a state of shock. The fire spread further to a warehouse owned by Artistic Supplies Ltd. As the materials in the warehouse were destroyed Artistic Supplies Ltd was unable to fulfil orders. The company had no insurance cover for such losses. Advise each party suffering harm as a result of the fire as to any claims they may have for compensation.

5. Victoria and David are neighbours. David, to annoy Victoria, always has a bonfire on a Monday, which is Victoria's washday. One Monday, Victoria's washing is badly marked by smoke from David's bonfire since the wind was blowing strongly in the direction of her washing line. In order to prevent further damage she went round into David's garden and stamped out the fire.
   a) Explain whether Victoria may sue David for the tort of nuisance.
   b) Explain two defences which David may raise.
   c) Explain whether David may sue Victoria for trespass.
   d) What defences may Victoria raise?
   e) What remedies may David apply for?

6. Mr Barr, the owner of a two-star hotel, hired Sadler & Co., independent contractors, to repair the hotel's faulty lift. The day after repairs were completed, Mr Fell, a guest staying at the hotel, was badly injured when the lift broke down as he was using it. Mr Fell now seeks your advice as to whether or not he would succeed in an action against Mr Barr under the tort of occupier's liability.

7. A well-known newspaper had published an article in which it stated that Mr Pratt, a forty-year-old Wakefield man, had been convicted of serious drug offences. Another Mr Pratt, a forty-year-old restaurant owner, who also lives in Wakefield, now claims he is being shunned by friends and is losing custom because people believe he is the convicted man. The actual facts of the article were true of an architect called Mr Pratt, but the newspaper did not mention this – though that fact and the man's address were known to the editor. The restaurant owner is now intending to sue. Advise the newspaper.

8. A few months ago Charles purchased a pony called Pandy for his thirteen-year-old daughter, Cecilia. The following incidents have occurred:
    a) By leaning over the fence, Pandy has eaten all the fruit off the apple tree belonging to Ben, Charles' neighbour.
    b) Recently Pandy attempted to bite Cecilia but she thought that he was being playful. Pandy has now bitten Cecilia's friend, Abigail.
    c) After the above incident Pandy escaped through a gap in the fence on to the road. Simon, a motor-cyclist, suffered injury after swerving to avoid hitting Pandy.
    Advise Charles of his liabilities (if any) in tort.

9. Prince and Company were a firm of surveyors. They were asked by Rupert to consider a piece of land he was intending to buy and to advise him on its suitability for his purpose and the price he should pay. Rupert intended to use the land to build an amusement park. Prince and Company prepared their report and were paid by Rupert. Rupert bought the land but was then unable to finance development and sold the land to Simon, who intended to develop an amusement park on the land and relied on Prince and Company's report when deciding that the land was suitable for this purpose.

    Building work began and large quantities of gravel were delivered for use for various purposes. The gravel was stored in enormous heaps near the boundary with adjoining land belonging to Thomas, a farmer. A prolonged period of rain made the gravel heaps unstable and they began to slide into Thomas's land, destroying fences and making grazing land unusable for a complete season.

    When the park was completed, residents in two neighbouring villages complained about the noise, dust and increased traffic flow. Smells from the burger bar in the amusement park deterred local residents from using the local fish and chip shop: they said that the smell 'put them off' fried food of any kind.

    a) Consider whether Simon has a good cause of action against Prince and Company.
    b) Discuss the possible actions against Simon that might be brought by Thomas and by local people.
    c) To what extent do the torts of nuisance and *Rylands* v. *Fletcher* provide adequate protection for owners of land?

    (AQA)

Table of cases

Table of statutes

Index